MW01042085

INTERNATIONAL
LAW
FOR
SEAGOING OFFICERS

TITLES IN THE SERIES

The Bluejacket's Manual

Career Compass

The Chief Petty Officer's Guide

Command at Sea

Dictionary of Modern Strategy and Tactics

Dictionary of Naval Abbreviations

Dictionary of Naval Terms

Division Officer's Guide

Dutton's Nautical Navigation

Farwell's Rules of the Nautical Road

Naval Ceremonies, Customs, and Traditions

The Naval Institute Guide to Naval Writing

The Naval Officer's Guide

Naval Shiphandler's Guide

The Newly Commissioned Officer's Guide

Principles of Naval Weapon Systems

Principles of Naval Engineering

The Professional Naval Officer: A Course to Steer By

Reef Points

A Sailor's History of the U.S. Navy

Watch Officer's Guide

Operations Officer's Guide

Saltwater Leadership

THE U.S. NAVAL INSTITUTE
BLUE & GOLD PROFESSIONAL LIBRARY

For more than 100 years, U.S. Navy professionals have counted on specialized books published by the Naval Institute Press to prepare them for their responsibilities as they advance in their careers and to serve as ready references and refreshers when needed. From the days of coal-fired battleships to the era of unmanned aerial vehicles and laser weaponry, such perennials as *The Bluejacket's Manual* and the *Watch Officer's Guide* have guided generations of Sailors through the complex challenges of naval service. As these books are updated and new ones are added to the list, they will carry the distinctive mark of the Blue and Gold Professional Library series to remind and reassure their users that they have been prepared by naval professionals and meet the exacting standards that Sailors have long expected from the U.S. Naval Institute.

INTERNATIONAL
LAW
FOR
SEAGOING OFFICERS
6TH EDITION

CRAIG H. ALLEN

NAVAL INSTITUTE PRESS
ANNAPOLIS, MARYLAND

Naval Institute Press
291 Wood Road
Annapolis, MD 21402

© 2014 by the United States Naval Institute
All rights reserved. No part of this book may be reproduced or utilized in any form or by any means, electronic or mechanical, including photocopying and recording, or by any information storage and retrieval
system, without permission in writing from the publisher.

Library of Congress Cataloging-in-Publication Data
Allen, Craig H., 1951- author.
  International law for seagoing officers / Craig H. Allen. — 6th edition.
    pages cm
  Summary: "Allen, the author of Farwell's Rules of the Nautical Road, brings clarity and context to international law for the seagoing professional. This book is the only work that addresses the international law
of the sea from the perspective of the United States (which is one of the few nations that is not a party to
the comprehensive 1982 U.N. Convention on the Law of the Sea). Following an introduction to public
international law and a short history of the law of the sea, chapters describe the rules that apply in ports and
in the adjacent maritime zones, including the territorial sea, exclusive economic zone, archipelagic waters
and the high seas. Of greatest interest to the seagoing professional are chapters dealing with military and
intelligence activities in the maritime domain, maritime law enforcement activities and the use of force at
sea"— Provided by publisher.
  Includes bibliographical references and index.
  ISBN 978-1-61251-462-8 (hardback) — ISBN 978-1-61251-461-1 (xml) — ISBN 978-1-61251-461-1
(ebook) 1. Law of the sea. 2. Harbors—Law and legislation. 3. Contiguous zones (Law of the sea) 4.
Economic zones (Law of the sea) 5. Territorial waters. 6. Sea-power. 7. War, Maritime (International law)
8. United Nations Convention on the Law of the Sea (1982) I. Brittin, Burdick H. International law for
seagoing officers. II. Title.
  KZA1145.A45 2014
  341.4'5—dc23
                                                                                                2014003622

♾ Print editions meet the requirements of ANSI/NISO z39.48-1992 (Permanence of Paper).
Printed in the United States of America.

22 21 20 19 18 17 16 15 14   9 8 7 6 5 4 3 2 1
First printing

Contents

List of Figures and Tables   viii

List of Acronyms   ix

Preface to the Sixth Edition   xv

Acknowledgments   xvii

CHAPTER 1.   Introduction to International Law   1

CHAPTER 2.   Historical Development of the Law of the Sea   39

CHAPTER 3.   Baselines and Maritime Boundary Delimitation   64

CHAPTER 4.   Internal Waters, Canals, and Ports   80

CHAPTER 5.   The Territorial Sea, Contiguous Zone, International Straits,
             and Archipelagic Waters   101

CHAPTER 6.   The Exclusive Economic Zone   124

CHAPTER 7.   The Continental Shelf and International Seabed   139

CHAPTER 8.   The High Seas and Enclosed/Semi-enclosed Seas   151

CHAPTER 9.   Status of Vessels and Aircraft   174

CHAPTER 10. Marine Stewardship and International Law   202

CHAPTER 11. Maritime Law Enforcement   227

CHAPTER 12. Military Activities in the Maritime Domain   271

CHAPTER 13. Use of Force in the Maritime Domain   310

CHAPTER 14. State Responsibility, Remedies, and Countermeasures   335

CHAPTER 15. Dispute Resolution Forums and Procedures   348

             Conclusion   367

APPENDIX A. Glossary   369

APPENDIX B. Charter of the United Nations (1945)   387

APPENDIX C. United Nations Convention on the Law of the Sea (1982)   401

APPENDIX D. United States Senate Committe on Foreign Relations
             Draft Declarations, Understandings, and Conditions, 2007   465

             Index   471

Figures and Tables

FIGURES

FIGURE 1. Legal Boundaries of the Oceans and Airspace   49

FIGURE 2. A Juridical Bay   69

FIGURE 3. Straight Baseline across a Deeply Indented Coast   72

FIGURE 4. Straight Baseline across Fringing Islands   72

FIGURE 5. Archipelagic Baselines   76

FIGURE 6. Strait of Hormuz   113

FIGURE 7. Strait of Gibraltar   115

FIGURE 8. The Role of Maritime Security Operations   283

TABLES

TABLE 1. LOS Convention Restrictions on Surveys, Intelligence Collection, and Research Activities   133

TABLE 2. Coastal State Jurisdiction to Conduct Pollution Investigations   212

Acronyms

ADIZ	air defense identification zone
AIS	automatic identification system
APPS	Act to Prevent Pollution by Ships
ARG	amphibious ready group
ASL	archipelagic sea-lanes
ASW	antisubmarine warfare
ATS	Antarctic Treaty System
CBP	Customs and Border Protection
CCAMLR	Convention on the Conservation of Antarctic Marine Living Resources
CDS	compulsory dispute settlement
CERCLA	Comprehensive Response, Compensation and Liability Act
CGPCS	Contact Group on Piracy off the Coast of Somalia
CGUFP	U.S. Coast Guard Use of Force Policy
CIA	Central Intelligence Agency
CINCPACFLT	Commander-in-Chief, Pacific Fleet
CIO	competent international organization
CJCS	Chairman, Joint Chiefs of Staff
CLCS	Commission on the Limits of the Continental Shelf
CMF	Combined Maritime Forces
COFI	FAO Committee on Fisheries
COLREGS	International Regulations for Preventing Collisions at Sea
COTP	captain of the port
CSG	carrier strike group
CSR	Continuous Synopsis Record
CTF	combined task force
DHS	Department of Homeland Security
DMA	dangerous military activities
DOALOS	UN Division for Ocean Affairs and the Law of the Sea
DoD	Department of Defense
DOJ	Department of Justice
DPRK	Democratic People's Republic of Korea (North Korea)
DTVIA	Drug Trafficking Vessel Interdiction Act
ECDIS	electronic chart display and information system
ECS	extended continental shelf
EEZ	exclusive economic zone
EMIO	expanded maritime interception operations
ENMOD	Convention on the Prohibition of Military or Any Other Hostile Use of Environmental Modification Techniques
EU	European Union

FAO	Food and Agriculture Organization
FBI	Federal Bureau of Investigation
FCMA	Fishery Conservation and Management Act
FCN	friendship, commerce, and navigation
FIR	flight information region
FON	freedom of navigation
FP	force protection
FPSO	floating production, storage, and offloading
FSIA	Foreign Sovereign Immunities Act
FTCA	Federal Tort Claims Act
FSV	fully submersible vessel
GAIS	generally accepted international standards
GATT	General Agreement on Tariffs and Trade
GESAMP	Group of Experts on Scientific Aspects of Marine Environmental Protection
GHG	greenhouse gas
GIFA	Governing International Fishery Agreement
HA/DR	humanitarian assistance/disaster response
HITRON	Helicopter Interdiction Squadron
HNS	hazardous and noxious substances
HSFCA	High Seas Fishing Compliance Act
HYDROLANT	Hydro-Atlantic message
HYDROPAC	Hydro-Pacific message
IAEA	International Atomic Energy Agency
IC	intelligence community
ICAO	International Civil Aviation Organization
ICC	International Criminal Court
ICCPR	International Covenant on Civil and Political Rights
ICE	Immigration and Customs Enforcement
ICESCR	International Covenant on Economic, Social, and Cultural Rights
ICJ	International Court of Justice
ICNAF	International Commission for Northwest Atlantic Fisheries
ICP	UN Open-Ended Informal Consultative Process on Oceans and the Law of the Sea
ICTY	International Criminal Tribunal for the former Yugoslavia
IDF	Israeli Defense Forces
IED	improvised explosive device
IFF	identification, friend or foe
ILA	International Law Association
ILC	International Law Commission
IMB	International Maritime Bureau
IMCO	Intergovernmental Maritime Consultative Organization
IMO	International Maritime Organization
INA	Immigration and Nationality Act
IO	international organization
IOC	Intergovernmental Oceanographic Commission
ISA	International Seabed Authority

ISPS	International Ship and Port Facility Security
ISR	intelligence, surveillance, and reconnaissance
ITLOS	International Tribunal for the Law of the Sea
IUU	illegal, unregulated, and unreported
JIATF	Joint Interagency Task Force
LEDET	law enforcement detachment
LEO	law enforcement operations
LLGDS	landlocked and geographically disadvantaged states
LMR	living marine resources
LOAC	law of armed conflict
LOS	law of the sea
LOS Convention	U.N. Convetion on the Law of the Sea (1982)
LPR	lawful permanent resident
LRIT	long-range identification and tracking
MARAD	U.S. Maritime Administration
MARPOL	International Convention for the Prevention of Pollution of the Sea by Vessels
MCPI	maritime counterproliferation interdiction
MDLEA	Maritime Drug Law Enforcement Act
MEPC	Marine Environment Protection Committee
MFN	most favored nation
MIO	maritime interception operations
MLAT	mutual legal assistance treaty
MLE	maritime law enforcement
MLLW	mean lower-low-water
MODU	mobile offshore drilling unit
MOTR	Maritime Operational Threat Response
MOZ	maritime operational zone
MSC	Maritime Safety Committee
MSC	Military Sealift Command
MSO	maritime security operations
MSR	marine scientific research
MTSA	Maritime Transportation Security Act
NAFO	Northwest Atlantic Fisheries Organization
NATO	North Atlantic Treaty Organization
NCV	noncompliant vessel
NDP	Naval Doctrine Publication
NGO	nongovernmental organization
nm	nautical mile
NMIO	National Maritime Intelligence-Integration Office
NORDREGS	Northern Canada Vessel Traffic Services Zone Regulations
NOTAM	notice to airmen
NOTMAR	notice to mariners
NPT	Treaty on the Non-proliferation of Nuclear Weapons
NRT	National Response Team
NSS	National Security Strategy
NTR	normal trade relations

NTTP   naval tactics, techniques, and procedures
OCSLA   Outer Continental Shelf Lands Act of 1953
ODA   Ocean Dumping Act
ODS   ozone-depleting substances
OFAC   Office of Foreign Assets Control (U.S. Treasury)
ONDCP   U.S. Office of National Drug Control Policy
ONF   Operation New Frontier
OST   Open Skies Treaty
OTH   over the horizon
P-5   permanent five (members of U.N. Security Council)
PCA   Posse Comitatus Act
PCASP   privately contracted armed security personnel
PCIJ   Permanent Court of International Justice
PMSC   private maritime security company
PSC   port state control
PSI   Proliferation Security Initiative
PSSA   particularly sensitive sea area
PVA   Public Vessels Act
ReCAAP   Regional Co-operation Agreement on Combating Piracy
RFMO   regional fisheries management organization
ROE   rules of engagement
R2P   responsibility to protect
RUD   reservation, understanding, and declarations (to a treaty)
RUF   rules on the use of force
SALCON   International Convention on Salvage
SAR   search and rescue
SCA   Suez Canal Authority
SNO   statement of no objection
SOC   special operations capable
SOE   state-owned enterprise
SOF   special operations forces
SOFA   status of forces agreement
SOLAS   Safety of Life at Sea
SORM   International Convention on Standard Organization and Watchkeeping
            for Seafarers
SOSUS   Sound Surveillance System
SPLOS   states parties to the Law of the Sea Convention
SPSS   self-propelled semisubmersible vessel
SROE   standing rules of engagement
SSCS   Sea Shepherd Conservation Society
STCW   International Convention on Standards of Training, Certification and
            Watchstanding for Seafarers
SUA   Convention for the Suppression of Unlawful Acts against the Safety of
            Maritime Navigation
TEZ   total exclusion zone
TFG   Transitional Federal Government (Somalia)
TNC   transnational corporation

TOC	transnational organized crime
TTP	tactics, techniques, and procedures
TWIC	Transportation Worker Identification Credential
UAV	unmanned aerial vehicle
UCMJ	Uniform Code of Military Justice
UDHR	Universal Declaration of Human Rights
UMV	unmanned marine vehicle
UN	United Nations
UNCED	UN Conference on Environment and Development
UNCTAD	United Nations Conference on Trade and Development
UNEP	UN Environment Programme
UNESCO	United Nations Educational, Scientific, and Cultural Organization
UNFCC	UN Framework Convention on Climate Change
UNHCR	UN High Commissioner for Refugees
UNODC	UN Office on Drugs and Crime
USCIS	U.S. Citizenship and Immigration Services
USV	unmanned surface vehicle
UUV	unmanned underwater vehicle
VBSS	visit, board, search, and seizure
VCLT	Vienna Convention on the Law of Treaties
VMS	vessel monitoring system
VOC	volatile organic compound
WMD	weapons of mass destruction

Preface to the Sixth Edition

THIS BOOK WAS FIRST PUBLISHED IN 1956 TO BRING CLARITY AND CONTEXT TO INTERNATIONAL LAW for the seagoing professional. Whether an academy midshipman or cadet, a seasoned commanding officer or master mariner, or an attorney advising one, the authors' hope has been that the reader will find the book both accessible and useful.

The first edition was written by the late Burdick H. Brittin, a retired captain in the U.S. Navy who served as both a line officer and a judge advocate. Brittin distinguished himself as a naval officer early in his career—in fact, just one month after reporting to his first destroyer—when he and three other ensigns on board the USS *Aylwin* (DD-355), which was moored in Pearl Harbor on December 7, 1941, swiftly got the ship under way on that fateful Sunday morning with less than half the crew and began to engage enemy planes while still steaming out of the harbor. The destroyer's late-arriving CO and XO commandeered a whale boat and attempted to rejoin the ship after it cleared the harbor but were unable to board until the following day. Brittin would later see combat in the Coral Sea, Midway, Kwajalein, Saipan, Guam, Okinawa, the Battle of the Philippine Sea, and the Aleutian Islands. By the end of the war Brittin had collected thirteen battle stars and had been awarded the Purple Heart and Silver Star, the latter awarded for "conspicuous gallantry and intrepidity" as XO of the USS *Kidd* (DD-661) when, although seriously wounded during a kamikaze attack on the destroyer, he took command in the heat of battle after the CO was disabled. In a storied legal career that followed his early years as a line officer, Brittin was appointed the first director of the Navy Judge Advocate General's International Law Division (Code 10) and served on the U.S. delegation to the 1958 and 1982 law of the sea conferences, as an adviser to the International Law Commission, as vice chair of the Council on Ocean Law, and as a member of the senior advisory committee of the Woods Hole Oceanographic Institution and the Ocean Science Policy Committee of the National Academy of Sciences.

Captain Brittin authored five editions of this book. In the foreword to the fifth edition, published in 1986, Elliott Richardson, former ambassador-at-large and chief U.S. delegate to the Third UN Conference on the Law of the Sea, observed that "nonfiction books don't keep going into new editions if they aren't useful." He went on to describe this book as "a reliable source of guidance for those whose concerns with ocean space require a firm grasp of the rights and obligations that flow from the principles governing its use."

Much has changed in the quarter century since Ambassador Richardson penned his foreword. The Cold War came to an end, the Iron Curtain fell, and the Soviet Union dissolved. The Reagan-era six-hundred-ship Navy was allowed to shrink to fewer than three hundred, and that number is likely to fall still lower. While the former Soviet fleet temporarily disappeared, the last decade of the twentieth century and the first of the twenty-first witnessed a rapid buildup of the Chinese navy and paranaval fleet, the return of Russia, and the disquieting conjunction of unpredictable regimes and nuclear weapons programs in North Korea and Iran. In the wake of the September 11, 2001, attacks on the World Trade Center and the Pentagon, a multitude of new maritime security measures have been implemented, two new combatant commands were stood up (Northern Command and Africa Command), and the Department of Homeland

Security was established. Operation Noble Eagle was launched to protect the homeland, and Operation Enduring Freedom and Operation Iraqi Freedom vastly expanded the global reach and elevated the operations tempo of maritime security operations for more than a decade. Naval forces from NATO and even Japan, China, India, and Pakistan dispatched fleets to the African coast in response to a surge in piracy in the greater Indian Ocean. A variety of autonomous and semiautonomous unmanned vehicles (some armed) now ply the world's airspaces and waters. As many of the world's traditional fisheries collapsed, catcher fleets shifted to the furthest reaches of the Southern Ocean and began taking unexploited species. The emerging "green mandate" required vessels to comply with routing measures to protect the environment and marine mammals and imposed restrictions on sonar usage, waste emissions, and toxic and greenhouse gas emissions. Climate changes are progressively reducing the Arctic icecap, opening that hitherto "no-man's sea" to seasonal surface navigation and resource exploitation.

One thing has not changed in the intervening years since the fifth edition was published: the United States is still not a party to the 1982 UN Convention on the Law of the Sea. As a nonparty to the global treaty that more than 160 other states have formally acknowledged now prescribes the rule set governing the oceans and seas, the United States and its vessels and aircraft occupy a sometimes confusing and often awkward "outlier" position. The effect of the U.S. position as a nonparty to the convention is emphasized throughout this book. At the same time, the book offers a pragmatic and reasoned approach for addressing the complexities that outlier position adds for those who operate on, under, and over the sea.

Craig H. Allen
Judson Falknor Professor of Law and of Marine Affairs,
University of Washington, Seattle

Acknowledgments

SEVERAL EXPERTS GENEROUSLY AGREED TO REVIEW SOME OR ALL OF THE BOOK'S EARLIER DRAFTS. Although I take full responsibility for any remaining errors or omissions, I want to acknowledge the invaluable contribution of Capt. Joe Baggett, USN (JAGC, Ret., now serving as the deputy director of Code 10, the International and Operational Law Division of the Navy's Office of the Judge Advocate General). I also want to thank members of the Law Department of the U.S. Coast Guard Academy, including Capt. Glenn Sulmasy, Cdr. Russ Bowman, and Cdr. Chris Tribolet, for our frequent professional exchanges on maritime law enforcement issues during my year on the academy faculty. I further acknowledge my debt to the expert faculty in the International Law Department of the U.S. Naval War College, including Professors Dennis Mandsager, Jack Grunawalt, Michael Schmidt, and Wolff Heintschel von Heinegg.

The book would not have been possible without the faculty research support provided by the University of Washington and by Yale Law School and the U.S. Coast Guard Academy during my visits there or the assistance provided by the professional librarians of the Marian Gould Gallagher Law Library at the University of Washington School of Law and the Lillian Goldman Law Library at Yale Law School.

The sixth edition builds on its predecessor editions by Captain Brittin. In addition, I have updated some of my own writings and incorporated them into this book. Chapters 11, 12, and 14 are informed by *Maritime Counterproliferation Operations and the Rule of Law* (Praeger, 2007). Chapter 13 draws on my contribution to volume 81 of the Naval War College Bluebook.

Finally, I owe a lasting debt to William T. Burke, a teacher, scholar, and mentor, who as a founding pioneer in interdisciplinary law and marine affairs studies introduced me to the law of the sea and inspired my generation to promote the public order of the oceans.

Introduction to International Law

Seagoing officers have long understood the importance of international law in their profession. When asked more than two centuries ago to describe the most desirable qualifications in a naval officer, John Paul Jones included familiarity with the principles of international law "because such knowledge may often, when cruising at a distance from home, be necessary to protect his flag from insult or his crew from imposition or injury in foreign ports."[1] In *Command at Sea*, Adm. James Stavridis and Rear Adm. Robert Girrier highlight the importance of international law to commanding officers and stress their obligation to report any violation of international law by U.S. citizens and foreign governments or nationals to their fleet commander, the chief of naval operations, and the local ambassador or consul, via the defense or naval attaché.[2] Actual or even perceived disregard of the law can have consequences well beyond an insult to the flag. It should therefore come as no surprise that today's *Navy Regulations* require all persons in the Navy Department to conform to international law. In fact, some sixty articles in the *Navy Regulations* relate in some degree to international law.[3] Perhaps that is why, among the nation's war colleges, only the U.S. Naval War College—the first war college established in the world— has a dedicated international law department and includes international law in its required core curriculum. In fact, international law was among the first subjects taught at the college, whose instructors caution that "failure to comply with international law ordinarily involves greater political and economic costs than does observance."[4]

As Captain Brittin repeatedly emphasized in the prior editions of this book, this "is not a lawyer's law book." Although it is hoped that attorneys will find the book helpful, it is primarily intended for seagoing officers who will confront international law questions in their daily operations. Nor is the book intended to serve as a substitute for official service publications or advice by legal counsel. Happily, officers need no longer resolve the legal aspects of critical at-sea decisions alone. Since the time of Tocqueville,[5] lawyers have answered the call to help keep the Republic strong and true to its founding principles. Those principles include respect for the rule of law. Naval battle groups and Navy–Marine Corps expeditionary groups now have ready access to their group's deployed staff judge advocate. Additionally, the availability of instant global communications channels provides the commander or master at sea with ready access to expert legal counsel ashore. In applying that legal advice, however, it is important to bear in mind that international

---

1. John Paul Jones, quoted in H. C. Washburn, What It Means to Be an Officer in the United States Navy To-Day, 43 U.S. Naval Inst. Proc. 2897, 2907 (1917).
2. James Stavridis & Robert Girrier, Command at Sea 251 (6th ed. 2010).
3. See, e.g., U.S. Navy Regulations (1990) arts. 0705, 0914, & 1135. See also Marine Corps Order 3300.4 (Oct. 20, 2003); U.S. Coast Guard Regulations, COMDTINST M5000.3B (1992).
4. See, e.g., Commander's Handbook on the Law of Naval Operations [hereinafter "Commander's Handbook"], NWP 1-14M/MCWP 5-12.1/ COMDTPUB P5800.7A (July 2007), at 20.
5. Alexis de Tocqueville, Democracy in America, vol. I, bk. XVI (1835).

law merely sets the floor on prudent action. Just as policy and prudential considerations often dictate that rules of engagement limit the use of force to a greater extent than does international law, the wise seagoing officer will recognize that prudence and professionalism often dictate a course of conduct more exacting than the minimum that international law would require.

A. THE SCOPE OF INTERNATIONAL LAW

International law can be defined as the body of rules of conduct, enforceable by external sanctions, that confers rights and imposes obligations primarily, though not exclusively, on sovereign states.[6] This definition distinguishes rules or norms of behavior that are legally enforceable from those that are not, a distinction that is overlooked by some international relations texts, which lump together all norms or rules of behavior without regard to those that are legally enforceable.

The study of international law typically begins with an examination of the history, theories, and sources of international law and its relationship to the domestic law of the individual states. An examination of the concept of the nation, or "state," and the related concepts of territorial sovereignty and interstate relations usually follows. In the international context, sovereignty includes an internal dimension that defines the relationship of the state to the persons, objects, and activities within that state's territory, and an external dimension that governs its foreign relations.[7] An examination of sovereignty logically leads to a discussion of the nature and limits of the prescriptive and enforcement jurisdiction of states. International law depends for its validity both on the consent of states, as expressed in customs and treaties, and on the existence of an international community of states and individuals. An increasingly important element in any examination of international law is the principle of state responsibility for internationally wrongful acts.

Next for consideration in the study of international law is the status and role of nonstate actors, such as international organizations, corporations, and individuals, along with ships and aircraft, to the extent that international law defines the status, rights, or obligations of each. Finally, any study of international law must consider the means and methods for resolving disputes and the rules governing the threat or use of force.

Moving beyond the general overview of public international law, specialized fields of international law include human rights law; the law of the sea; the law of armed conflict (also known as the law of war or international humanitarian law); international criminal law; international environmental law; international trade law; international litigation and arbitration; and the international legal regimes for Antarctica, outer space, and cyberspace. This volume, written for seagoing officers, focuses on the law of the sea, although several of those other international law topics are necessarily included. For example, the chapter on maritime law enforcement raises questions on the jurisdiction of states, nationality, statelessness, international criminal law, the use of force, human rights, and state responsibility. Thus, while the book is tailored to the needs of the seagoing officer, those needs will often call for an examination of subjects beyond the law of the sea.

B. HISTORICAL BACKGROUND

International law came into being along with the emergence of separate communities, or proto-states, whose creation stemmed from a combination of geographic, economic, cultural,

---

6. Restatement (Third) of the Foreign Relations Law of the United States [hereinafter "Restatement FRLUS"] §
   101 (1987); Commander's Handbook, supra, at 20.
7. Internal and external sovereignty issues and their relationship to federalism in the United States are analyzed in
   U.S. v. Curtiss-Wright Export Corp., 299 U.S. 304 (1936); Medellín v. Texas, 552 U.S. 491 (2008); and Arizona v.
   U.S., 132 S. Ct. 2492 (2012).

linguistic, and religious factors. These early state-communities first developed rules for internal conduct based on the moral code prevailing at the time. The principles that grew out of such community moral codes were then "externalized" by the rulers as a guide in their conduct of relations with other state-communities. At first the rules were based on the rulers' personal interpretation of the codes, but they gradually became defined, gained public support, and acquired a "traditional" character as concrete rules of general conduct. Many of the rules in use today can be traced to those early usages.

The historical roots of international law run deep. As early as 1400 BCE the pharaohs of Egypt and rulers of nearby areas entered into agreements that dealt with the recognition of individual sovereignty. They also negotiated arrangements for the handling of refugees and immigrants. In 500 BCE the Indian Code of Manu addressed the conduct of warfare and attempted (admittedly without much success) to establish norms for the treatment of prisoners of war and the use of poison and other inhumane weapons. The city-states of Greece, including Athens and Sparta, were so geographically limited that in many ways they depended on each other both economically and for defense against Persian invaders. As a result, these sovereign communities developed a keen awareness of their shared interests. With this awareness came growth in the scope of the rules governing relations between states. Greek contributions to modern international law include elements of treaty law (methods of negotiation, interpretation, and conditions of termination), principles of international arbitration, the immunity of ambassadors, the right of asylum, and the rights and duties of aliens in foreign states.

Neither the era of Roman hegemony nor the period that followed the empire's decline beginning in the third century were conducive to the development of international law. While it is true that Roman law, particularly Rome's *jus gentium*—a theoretically "universal" law that was common to all, including non-Romans—would prove to have a significant influence on later international law theories, Roman hegemony left little room for a true system of international law based on the sovereign equality of states. The Holy Roman Empire and the system of feudalism that dominated Europe during the medieval period of the ninth to fifteenth centuries were likewise not favorable to international law. That changed during the age of exploration and the Renaissance. Scholars in France, Italy, Spain, Germany, and England made important contributions to international legal theory in the sixteenth and seventeenth centuries. One of the most noteworthy contributions was by a young Dutch lawyer, Hugo Grotius (de Groot). Many view his *De Jure Belli ac Pacis*, published in 1625, as the seminal treatise on the early law of nations (what Jeremy Bentham would later call "international law").[8] While the theoretical foundations provided by scholars of this era were certainly important milestones in the development of international law, modern international law is often traced to 1648 and the Peace of Westphalia,[9] which ended the bloody Thirty Years' War and marked the demise of the Holy Roman Empire and the rise of secular nation-states.

By the end of the nineteenth century, the law of nations had expanded even more. International efforts to compile uniform regulations for preventing collisions at sea date back to rules introduced in the 1860s by Great Britain, France, and the United States. Those early rules were

---

8. Jeremy Bentham, An Introduction to the Principles of Morals and Legislation (1781). Blackstone's definition of the "law of nations," as understood in eighteenth-century England, was broader than "international law." It included at the time such subjects as bills of lading and exchange and the maritime law of freight, demurrage, insurance, bottomry, and shipwrecks. William Blackstone, Commentaries on the Law of England bk. 4, ch. 5, at 67 (1765–69). The first three listed "private" law elements of the law of nations were later absorbed into U.S. domestic law, reducing the scope of the law of nations to those laws governing the relations among states.

9. The Peace of Westphalia was concluded by the Treaty of Münster and the Treaty of Osnabrük. See The Peace of Westphalia, 1648, 1 Consol. Treaty Series 198.

modified at a conference of maritime nations in Washington, D.C., in 1889 and were subsequently adopted by the nations concerned. The international agreement on October 13, 1884, to adopt the meridian passing through the Observatory of Greenwich as the global reference meridian for longitude and time calculations resolved the crucial issue of international timekeeping. Prior to the agreement there were thousands of time zones based on local solar observations. Now, marine charts show not only locations but also indicate the time zone of that location relative to Greenwich. Other accomplishments during this period include international treaties outlawing slavery and slave trading. Concerns over infectious diseases and health led to international sanitation measures. Administrative procedures and agencies were established to facilitate the transmission of mail and telegraph messages throughout the world. The seas of the world were free for all to use, and canals connecting the great oceans were opened for international trade. Individuals and their property could move about freely in many foreign lands, and foreign vessels could expect to enjoy most of the same navigation rights as domestically flagged vessels. Extradition agreements ensured that persons who fled a country after committing a crime were returned to face justice.

The scope of international law at the beginning of the twentieth century was indeed broad, and the subjects it covered were matters of mutual convenience. Agreements as to what the law should be in particular cases were relatively easy to reach—until two world wars and a devastating and persistent global depression in the first half of the twentieth century exposed the limits of international law in addressing the most consequential questions of international relations. The devastation and suffering of that period shook the confidence of many in the historical approach to international relations and law and persuaded progressive reformers to enhance international law and make it more effective through the creation of international organizations. Although the first attempt, the League of Nations, was unable to avert the Great Depression or World War II, the United Nations and the family of international economic organizations that came out of the 1944 Bretton Woods Conference owe a considerable debt to the League's path-breaking role as a global international organization. The UN's role in international relations and international law, including the law of the sea, is now pervasive.

C. THEORIES OF INTERNATIONAL RELATIONS AND INTERNATIONAL LAW

International law is best examined and understood through the lens of international relations theory. Few seagoing professionals would regard international law as an end in itself; nor would most legal theorists. Writing shortly after the founding of the United Nations, international jurist and law professor Philip Jessup characterized the relationship between international law and international relations in this way: "The function of international law is to provide a legal basis for the orderly management of international relations."[10]

International relations theory and international law theory have value in proportion to the degree to which they explain events and aid in modeling, shaping, and predicting future actions.[11] Such explanatory theories must be distinguished from normative prescriptions or personal preferences. The test for the explanatory international relations and international law theories described below is the extent to which the theory explains the actual practice of states—at least those states most relevant to the particular inquiry—and therefore aids in shaping and predicting

10. Philip C. Jessup, A Modern Law of Nations 20 (1948). Professor Jessup served as a judge on the International Court of Justice from 1961 to 1970.
11. See generally Kenneth N. Waltz, Theory of International Politics (2010); Hans J. Morgenthau & Kenneth W. Thompson, Politics among Nations ch. 1 (1993).

future behavior. Theories are formulated, revised, or discarded when they no longer accurately describe state practice. Thus, some theories that prevailed during the first half of the twentieth century did not survive the Cold War, the short-lived New World Order following the dissolution of the Soviet Union, or the more recent Global War on Terror period.[12]

1. International Relations Theories

International relations theorists typically characterize the global legal system as anarchic. In choosing that label they are not suggesting that it is necessarily chaotic, but rather that it is a horizontal system, in contrast to a hierarchical one. State sovereignty and equality are the central organizing principles of international relations.[13] There is no higher power to impose order on sovereign states. Judge Max Huber explained in the *Island of Palmas* arbitration decision that

> sovereignty in the relations between States signifies independence. Independence in regard to a portion of the globe is the right to exercise therein, to the exclusion of any other State, the functions of a State. Territorial sovereignty . . . involves the exclusive right to display the activities of a State. This right has as corollary a duty: the obligation to protect within the territory the rights of other States, in particular their right to integrity and inviolability in peace and in war, together with the rights which each State may claim for its nationals in foreign territory.[14]

States undeniably remain the principal actors in the international system. The Charter of the United Nations protects the sovereignty of each state by expressly prohibiting states from using or threatening force against another state's territorial integrity or political independence.[15] Together with the noninterference norm, which prohibits interference in a state's internal affairs, this nonaggression norm recognizes and requires respect for the state's internal sovereignty.[16]

Several international relations theories have competed for acceptance over the years. A common classification divides the theoretical approaches into liberalism, idealism, and realism.[17] Another approach to classifying international relations theories distinguishes between interest-based theories and norm-based theories.[18] While not completely dismissing the role of the state interests in their relations, the norm-based theories posit that international law significantly affects state behavior and that states do in fact adhere to international law most of the time. Adherents to norm-based theories tend to emphasize the influence of principled ideas, such as peace, prosperity, and the inherent rights of the individual. By contrast, interest-based theories

---

12. Because international law now extends to wholly intrastate activities, such as how a state treats its own nationals in their civil and political affairs, international law theory must address more than just its role in interstate relations. That dimension of international relations theory is beyond the scope of this book for seagoing officers.

13. Early sovereignty writers include Thomas Hobbes, John Locke, and Jean-Jacques Rousseau. Modern works include Jeremy A. Rabkin, Law without Nations? Why Constitutional Government Requires Sovereign States (2005).

14. Island of Palmas case (Netherlands v. U.S.), Rep. Int'l Arb. Awards, vol. II, at 829–71 (Apr. 4, 1928).

15. Charter of the United Nations, art. 2, June 26, 1945, 59 Stat. 1031, T.S. No. 933, as amended in 1963 (16 U.S.T. 1134), 1965 (19 U.S.T. 5450), and 1971 (24 U.S.T. 2225). Article 0916 of U.S. Navy Regulations requires that the territorial integrity of foreign nations be respected.

16. These norms are implemented in the United States in part by the Neutrality Act of 1794 (18 U.S.C. § 960).

17. Each is defined in the glossary in appendix A. See generally Jack Snyder, One World, Rival Theories, Foreign Policy (Nov.–Dec. 2004), at 53–62.

18. See Oona A. Hathaway, Between Power and Principle: An Integrated Theory of International Law, 72 Univ. Chi. L. Rev. 469 (2005).

generally posit that states can be viewed as unitary, rational actors that strive to further their own interests by employing the instruments of national power (diplomatic, information, military, and economic) to achieve their policy objectives.[19] Interest-based theories tend to emphasize the state's security and support the idea that its best guarantee is superior relative power,[20] both individually and through either an effective balance of power or collective defense approach. Adherents to interest-based theories discount, but do not dismiss, the effect of international law in international relations. A state pursuing security and its own economic and political interests might adopt the rhetoric of norms and values but will ultimately act in furtherance of its own interests. An interesting variation of the pure interest-based school holds that states do indeed act primarily in pursuit of their national interests, but do so consistently with their national identity, which is a reflection of values widely held within the state.[21] In the United States those values include convictions regarding a constitutionally limited government, universal suffrage, and individual rights. Most Americans include respect for the rule of law as a core tenet of their national creed. It is perhaps no accident, therefore, that the nation's oldest commissioned warship is named the USS *Constitution* and that newly commissioned officers swear to support and defend the Constitution of the United States against all enemies, foreign and domestic.

Grounded in a rational, utilitarian calculus, interest-based theories have long dominated the actual practice (if not the rhetoric) of international relations at the highest levels of government. Increasingly, however, even realists (and military planners) recognize that both force and legitimacy are essential elements of an effective national strategy. The "principles of joint operations" in U.S. joint doctrine lists the nine traditionally accepted principles of warfare but adds three more principles, including the principle of "legitimacy,"[22] tacitly recognizing that force without legitimacy engenders resentment and resistance, while legitimacy without the backing of a credible force is vulnerable to being overthrown.[23]

2. International Law Theories

Law school and graduate courses in international law and international relations typically devote considerable attention to the various theories of international law.[24] The three primary schools of thought in general jurisprudence are natural law, legal positivism, and legal realism.[25] International law jurisprudential theory adds international legal process (a specialized application of legal process theory). Another view with roots in the writings of Judge Philip Jessup posits the emergence of a "transnational legal process."[26] As more fully developed by Professor Harold Koh, the concept transcends the traditional international law concepts and in particular embraces a dynamic legal process model that rejects the central role of states in international law

---

19. Hans J. Morgenthau, Politics among Nations (5th ed. 1978). In the words of onetime British foreign minister Lord Palmerston, a state has no permanent friends or enemies; only its interests are eternal.
20. History, including U.S. history since the founding years, suggests that a state's interest in international law may be inversely related to its relative power, with the least powerful states being most concerned with the protections afforded by international law. The modern concern for legitimacy places greater emphasis on law and its institutions and processes.
21. Robert Cooper, The Breaking of Nations: Order and Chaos in the Twenty-First Century 74 & 127–38 (2003).
22. Chairman, Joint Chiefs of Staff, Joint Pub. 3-0, Joint Operations, at I-2 (2011).
23. Cooper, The Breaking of Nations, supra, at 88.
24. International Rules: Approaches from International Law and International Relations (Robert J. Beck et al. eds., 1996); The Methods of International Law (Steven R. Ratner & Anne-Marie Slaughter eds., 2004).
25. See appendix A.
26. Philip Jessup, Transnational Law 2 (1956) (defining transnational law as "all law which regulates actions or events that transcend national frontiers").

and the dichotomy between international law and domestic law (called municipal law by some writers) and between public law and private law.[27] A provocative wave of recent scholarship draws on rational choice theory, highlights the limits of international law, and subjects many of the assumptions commonly made about international law to rigorous scrutiny.[28]

Before examining the various theoretical aspects of international law it will be helpful to briefly consider why, from a practical point of view, states agree to rules of international law and then adhere to them, even when compliance might conflict with the state's short-term national interests. First, states adopt some international rules to promote uniformity. Uniformity is particularly important with regard to international shipping and aviation safety standards and international telecommunications protocols. Second, states may consent to international rules in order to obtain reciprocity; that is, they may agree to limit their sovereignty in exchange for the promise of similar treatment by the reciprocating states. Examples include reciprocal trade agreements; treaties of friendship, commerce, and navigation; regional port state control agreements; and status of forces agreements.[29] Finally, some international goals can be achieved only through concerted action based on enforceable international rules. Examples include protecting the ocean commons from pollution and overfishing and addressing transborder threats such as global warming, ocean acidification, and ozone depletion.

It is customary in any examination of the jurisprudence of international law to cite the works of early skeptics such as John Austin,[30] who questioned whether international law really is "law." The skeptic critique begins with the previously mentioned observation that the global legal system is anarchic in that all states enjoy sovereign equality. There is no global "sovereign"—no global legislature or global executive, and no international court that can compel a sovereign state to appear before it unless that state has consented to the court's jurisdiction.[31] Given those limiting attributes, international law necessarily operates very differently from the domestic law of a sovereign state.

The true effect of international law on states' behavior in their international relations remains in dispute. At one extreme, some international relations theorists suggest that international law is the summum bonum (highest good) of international relations, having a paramount stature and pervasive effect on state behavior. At the opposite end are those, particularly the realists, who dismiss or at least seriously discount the role of international law in the conduct of international relations. They believe that state interests can be most effectively achieved through the exercise of mature judgment backed by robust instruments of national power, without the constraint of international rules that might prove inimical to the state's interest in a given situation.[32] Realists assert that because one state can never be certain of another state's intentions, it would be culpable folly to rely on international law or the demonstrably flawed concept of collective security to

---

27. See Harold Hongju Koh & Oona A. Hathaway, Foundations of International Law and Politics 190–204 (2005).
28. See, e.g., Jack Goldsmith & Eric Posner, The Limits of International Law (2005); Eric Posner, The Perils of Global Legalism (2010) (highlighting the problems of global collective action).
29. See R. Chuck Mason, Status of Forces Agreement (SOFA): What Is It, and How Has It Been Utilized (Cong. Research Serv., Jan. 5, 2011).
30. John Austin, The Province of Jurisprudence Determined 208 (1832). For a more charitable view of international law by one of Austin's contemporaries, see Henry Wheaton, Elements of International Law with a Sketch of the History of the Science (1836).
31. Restatement FRLUS, introductory note to Part I. See also H. L. A. Hart, The Concept of Law ch. X (1961).
32. Writing in the early nineteenth century, Clausewitz dismissed international law thusly: "Attached to force are certain self-imposed, imperceptible limitations hardly worth mentioning, known as international law and custom, but they scarcely weaken it." Carl von Clausewitz, On War 75 (1832) (Michael Howard & Peter Paret eds. & transl., 1976). See also Colin S. Gray, War, Peace and International Relations: An Introduction to Strategic History ch. 2 (2007).

safeguard the state. Some go so far as to label international law epiphenomenal,[33] perhaps nothing more than an after-the-fact rationalization by states of their interest-based conduct. The critique of U.S. foreign policy during the post–World War I era by longtime diplomat George Kennan captures the realist school's skeptical view of international law: "I see the most serious fault of our past policy formulation to lie in something that I might call the legalistic-moralistic approach to international problems. . . . It is the belief that it should be possible to suppress the chaotic and dangerous aspirations of governments in the international field by the acceptance of some system of legal rules and restraints."[34]

Not surprisingly, most legal scholars, lawyers, and judges tend to put greater faith in international law's ability to influence behavior, whether of individuals or states.[35] Legal empiricists respond to the skeptics by pointing out that whatever the theoretical limitations of international law, as a practical matter most states follow most rules of international law most of the time.[36] And even when they depart from the rules of international law they often attempt to excuse their departure with international law explanations. For seagoing officers, the debate is largely academic. Whatever the relative merits of the various theories, no seagoing officer would deny the influence of international law. They feel no less compelled to respect international law rules on state sovereignty and access to ports than to give way to a vessel not under command. Echoing that pragmatic approach, the scholar Hedley Bull concluded that the most compelling reason to classify certain international rules as "law" is that those most concerned with international relations, both public and private, consider them to be law.[37]

Over the centuries, a recurring jurisprudential debate among legal scholars has focused on two possible theoretical bases for international law. The natural law theory (*lex naturalis*) was expounded in the first century BCE by the Roman Marcus Tullius Cicero, who argued, in sharp contrast to the Greek Sophists, that law does not, and cannot, begin with men (or states). Rather, "true law is right reason in agreement with nature." Although natural law was often derived from or associated with religious doctrine in its formative years, later proponents of natural law such as Samuel von Pufendorf and Emmerich de Vattel sought to ground it on secular principles.

According to natural law theory, law is universal and we obtain knowledge of it deductively. Because it is universal and eternal, Cicero wrote, "there will not be different laws at Rome and at Athens, or different laws now and in the future, but one eternal and unchangeable law will be valid for all nations and all times, and there will one master and ruler, that is, God, over us all, for he is the author of this law, its promulgator, and its enforcing judge."[38] Natural law theory underpins the heroine's defiance of the king in the Greek tragedy *Antigone* and is implicated in "just war" theories and some arguments for nullification and conscientious objector status. It is often associated with the so-called Wilsonian school of international relations.[39] Natural law

---

33. Anthony Clark Arend, Do Legal Rules Matter? International Law and International Politics, 38 Va. J. Int'l L. 107, 108 (1998).
34. George F. Kennan, American Diplomacy 96 (1957). The realist view is also evident in Henry Kissinger, A World Restored 1 (1954) ("Whenever peace—conceived as the avoidance of war—has been the primary objective of a power or a group of powers, the international system has been at the mercy of the most ruthless member of the international community").
35. Vattel's dictum captures this view: in international law, strength and weakness count for nothing; "[a] dwarf is as much a man as a giant; a small republic is no less a sovereign state than the most powerful kingdom." Emmerich de Vattel, Le Droit de Gens (The Law of Nations) bk. I, § 18 (Joseph Chitty & Edward D. Ingraham eds., 1883).
36. Louis Henkin, How Nations Behave 47 (1979).
37. Hedley Bull, The Anarchical Society 136 (1977).
38. Marcus Tullius Cicero, De Re Publica, bk. 3, ¶ 22 (ca. 54–51 BCE; Clinton Walker Keyes transl. 1928).
39. See Walter Russell Mead, Special Providence: American Foreign Policy and How It Changed the World (2002) (describing the Wilsonian school—named after President Woodrow Wilson—belief that the United States

is also evident in the Declaration of Independence, with its appeal to "the Laws of Nature and of Nature's God." To adherents of the natural law approach, the law is not a mere handmaiden of international relations, nor does it spontaneously grow out of those relations unhinged from morality or principle. Rather, international law has an existence and a force separate and apart from those relations.

The positivist legal theory, by contrast, argues that international law is made by sovereign states, not discovered by a process of deduction. To the positivist, history, in particular the innumerable religious wars, amply demonstrates the futility and perils of grounding international law on supposed universal moral principles. Positivists also point out that much of international law, including the law of the sea, has no obvious moral dimension. Consider, for example, the rules governing the negotiability of ocean bills of lading, passage through international straits, or internationally standardized fog signals for vessels. For positivists, the sovereignty of nation-states dictates that international law must be based on the consent of states rather than moral or religious belief.[40] States may give that consent expressly by ratifying a treaty, or implicitly through state practice, acquiescence in the practice of other states, or both. The positivist theory finds judicial support in the decision by the Permanent Court of International Justice (PCIJ) in the *S.S.* Lotus case, a dispute arising out of France's objection to Turkey's exercise of jurisdiction over a French merchant marine officer involved in a fatal collision with a Turkish vessel on the high seas. In that case, the PCIJ explained that "international law governs the relations between independent states. The rules of law binding upon states therefore emanate from their own free will as expressed in conventions or by usages generally accepted as expressing principles of law. . . . Restrictions upon the independence of states cannot therefore be presumed."[41] What might be characterized as the "freedom principle" follows from the court's decision. It posits that, as a corollary of sovereignty, states are presumed to be free under international law to exercise their governmental powers. The International Court of Justice (ICJ) reaffirmed the *S.S.* Lotus holding in its 2010 advisory opinion on Kosovo's declaration of independence from the Republic of Serbia.[42]

In the formative years of the American Republic, a debate of sorts over the two international law theories took place between two distinguished justices of the U.S. Supreme Court. The subject was slavery, and the jurists were Chief Justice John Marshall and Associate Justice Joseph Story. In an 1822 decision on the circuit court, Story relied on natural law theory to conclude that slavery violated the law of nations.[43] He was overruled three years later, however, in the Supreme Court's Antelope decision authored by Chief Justice Marshall. The *Antelope* was a Spanish-flag vessel transporting nearly three hundred African slaves that was seized by the U.S. Revenue Cutter Service cutter *Dallas* while on patrol off the coast of Africa. The question before the court was whether the slave trade violated international law (at that time called the law of nations), and therefore justified the boarding. In apparent agreement with Story's earlier decision,

---

supports both its moral obligation and its national interest by spreading democratic and social values throughout the world while creating a peaceful international community that accepts the rule of law).

40. In John Locke's view, the legitimacy of a nation-state rests on consent of the governed. The positivists raise that consensual basis to the international level. By contrast, in theocratic states or states that give religious canons or sectarian law priority over other laws, international law is more likely to be subordinated to religion.

41. The S.S. *Lotus* case (France v. Turkey), 1927 P.C.I.J. (ser. A) No. 9 (Sept. 7).

42. Accordance with International Law of the Unilateral Declaration of Independence in Respect of Kosovo, Advisory Opinion, 2010 I.C.J. 403 (July 22). In language that parallels the PCIJ's decision in the S.S. *Lotus* case, the court concluded that because "general international law contains no applicable prohibition of declarations of independence," Kosovo's declaration did not violate international law. Id. at 438–39.

43. La *Jeune Eugénie*, 26 Fed. Cas. 832 (C.C.D. Mass. 1822) (No. 15551).

Marshall acknowledged that it "will scarcely be denied" that slavery is contrary to the law of nature. He went on to hold, however, that "whatever might be the answer of a moralist to this question, a jurist must search for its legal solution in those principles of action which are sanctioned by the usages." After examining "usage" (i.e., state practice), Marshall ruled that, unlike piracy, slave trading did not violate the law of nations (that was later changed by treaty), and that the U.S. cutter therefore had no right to search and seize the Spanish-flag *Antelope*.[44]

Positivism, with its central proposition espousing the primacy of state consent, remains the dominant theory in international tribunals and U.S. courts. It derives from the sovereign equality of states. The Vienna Convention on the Law of Treaties, discussed below, recognizes that a treaty binds only those states that have consented to be bound. The "persistent objector" rule in customary international law (also discussed below) similarly recognizes the consensual basis of customary international law. Nevertheless, natural law theory (and transcendent sectarian law) occasionally creeps back in, particularly with arguments for new *jus cogens* norms, even though the Vienna Convention on Treaties makes it clear that peremptory norms are based on acceptance by the community of states as a whole. Additionally, some writers argue that the need to address some global issues is so pressing that action cannot rely on the requirement to gain individual states' consent.[45]

[handwritten margin note: jus cogens / what compels the law]

The role and influence of international courts differs in important respects from the role of their national counterparts, which are familiar to most readers (see chapter 15 on the role of international tribunals). The vast majority of disputes concerning law of the sea issues that do make it to a court end up in the courts of a nation-state, not an international tribunal. This is in part because only a minority of states have consented in advance to the jurisdiction of the ICJ (among the five permanent members of the UN Security Council, only the United Kingdom has consented) or the International Tribunal for the Law of the Sea (ITLOS).[46] International arbitration further reduces the number of cases that come before international courts. Finally, even when disputes are submitted to an international tribunal, the international legal system generally rejects the common law stare decisis approach, by which past judicial decisions serve as binding precedents, thus limiting the future effect of decisions by international courts.

D. SUBJECTS AND OBJECTS OF INTERNATIONAL LAW

International law has historically distinguished the *subjects* of international law from its *objects*. Subjects have rights and obligations directly under international law. They are said to have "international legal personality." States are the principal subjects of international law; indeed, states are the principal authors of international law and the only subjects with full international legal personality. Objects are distinguished from subjects in that international law applies to them only indirectly. They do not "make" international law; rather, international law acts on them. Although the distinction between international law subjects and objects continues to have some explanatory value in understanding the sources and effect of international law, the distinction has eroded in practice as entities and individuals formerly classified as objects have gained aspects of international legal personality.

---

44. The *Antelope*, 23 U.S. (10 Wheat.) 66 (1825).
45. Jonathan I. Charney, Universal International Law, 87 Am. J. Int'l L. 529 (1993).
46. As of February 15, 2013, 33 of the 165 states parties to the LOS Convention had designated ITLOS as their preferred forum for resolution of disputes, and 20 had designated the ICJ as their first choice.

1. States

States are the fundamental and indispensable elements of international relations and international law. Indeed, without states (also referred to as nations, nation-states, and countries) there would be no need for international law.[47] History has demonstrated that states can be transient. City-states and even nation-states merge, former colonies gain independence, republics such as the Soviet Union and Yugoslavia break up, and self-determination movements and power struggles tear states apart. The combined effect of these events has been a steady climb in the number of states. In fact, UN membership has grown from the original 51 member states in 1945 to more than 190 today.

The international law on states begins with the threshold question regarding the essential elements of statehood. What attributes does a state have? Is Taiwan, Monaco, or Vatican City a state?[48] How are new states created? Could entrepreneurs establish a new state on an offshore artificial island? What is the legal effect if existing states or international organizations (e.g., UNESCO or the UN General Assembly) "recognize" a claimant such as the Palestinian Territories or Kosovo as a state? A four-part test is commonly applied to assess whether a given entity is a state. To qualify as a state the entity must have a permanent population, a defined territory, a government, and the capacity to enter into relations with other states.[49] Some theorists would apply a more demanding standard of "effective control" to the "government" element. Others would add a requirement that the putative state must have a monopoly on the legitimate use of force within the state's territory, a requirement increasingly relevant in this age of failing and failed states and the proliferation of armed groups.

The international law test for statehood has been largely indifferent as to whether the putative state is secular or theocratic and whether it operates as a liberal democracy, an authoritarian monarchy, or an outright dictatorship. But other states and international organizations increasingly do care. As a result, even if a putative state meets the four-part legal test for statehood, other states might refuse to give it formal recognition or admit it to international organizations.[50] Similarly, following a change in an existing state's government the new government will not necessarily be recognized by other states, particularly if the new government came to power through extraconstitutional means, thus highlighting the distinction between recognition of a state and recognition of the government of a state.[51]

States have rights and obligations under international law.[52] They are sovereign within their territory and may extend their jurisdiction to their nationals and to some activities outside their borders. Sovereignty represents the consolidation and concentration of governmental power in a

---

47. Recent usage distinguishes the three terms. "Nation" places emphasis on a people and their ancestral ties, common language, customs, and religion. "State" stresses the authority or the government of a geographical entity. "Country" typically refers to a territory and its physical boundaries. International law was formerly known as the law of "nations," and that usage is still found in organizational titles such as the League of Nations and United Nations.

48. Restatement FRLUS § 201 n.8.

49. See Montevideo Convention on the Rights and Duties of States, art. 1, Dec. 26, 1933, 165 L.N.T.S. 20; Restatement FRLUS § 201.

50. Restatement FRLUS §§ 202–203.

51. Historically, a distinction has been drawn between de facto and de jure recognition. De jure recognition was historically extended to governments that came to power through legitimate constitutional processes, while de facto recognition referred to governments that had gained effective control, but might have done so by unconstitutional means, such as through a coup d'état. The more common distinction today is between formal recognition and tacit recognition, with some states abandoning the practice of formal recognition altogether.

52. Restatement FRLUS § 206. Those rights include the right to be free from the use or threat of use of force against the state's territorial integrity or political independence; the inherent right of individual and collective

single entity, especially the power to make and enforce laws to protect the state's borders and its people, always subject to the relevant geographical limits.[53] State sovereignty is protected by the nonintervention and nonaggression norms mentioned above.[54]

The obligations of states are too often overlooked or ignored. A state is, of course, accountable to its nationals and owes its primary obligation to them; but states also owe an obligation to other states. Some of those obligations are set out in the UN Charter. Others are prescribed by the treaties to which the state consents or in customary law, including the law of the sea. States that breach their obligations to other states bear international responsibility, may be required to make reparation, and are subject to sanctions.

2. International Organizations

Sovereign states acting individually might be able to achieve the desired level of domestic prosperity and order within their borders; however, threats to internal security often come from outside, and no single state can effectively protect the global trade, transportation, and communications systems. The international order needed for internal security and the global trade, transportation, and communications systems almost certainly requires international law and international organizations. To provide a ready forum for consultation and cooperation, states have established a number of international intergovernmental organizations.[55] From an international law perspective, international organizations (IOs), including global IOs such as the United Nations, must be distinguished from "world government."[56] World government abolishes individual state sovereignty and replaces it with a single legislative, executive, and judicial authority whose powers are paramount (a single "superstate"). With world government there is no need for international law.

Special-purpose IOs can be traced to the Universal Postal Union established in 1865 and the International Telegraph (now Telecommunications) Union in 1875. It is now well established that some IOs possess elements of international legal personality.[57] That development was recognized

---

self-defense; the right to be free from outside interference in its internal affairs; the right to engage in international relations on principles of sovereign equality of all states; the right to confer "nationality" on persons, aircraft, and ships; the right to exercise diplomatic protection; the legal capacity to bring and defend suits in international tribunals; the competency to "make" international law with other states; and the right to extend or deny recognition to other states, their governments, or both. Other "rights" might turn on recognition by other states and international organizations. See generally International Law Commission, Draft Declaration on Rights and Duties of States, 1949 Y.B. Int'l L. Comm'n 178, 287.

53. Restatement FRLUS § 206 cmt. b.

54. See Declaration on the Inadmissibility of Intervention and Interference in the Internal Affairs of States, G.A. Res. 36/103, U.N. Doc. A/RES/36/103 (1981); Declaration on Principles in International Law concerning Friendly Relations and Co-operation among States in Accordance with the Charter of the United Nations, G.A. Res. 2625 (XXV), U.N. GAOR 25th Sess., Supp. No. 18, Annex (Oct. 24, 1970), U.N. Doc. A/8028 (1971) (declaring that "no State or group of States has the right to intervene, directly or indirectly, for any reason whatever, in the internal or external affairs of any other State"). The General Assembly resolution was relied on by the International Court of Justice in the *Nicaragua* decision. Military and Paramilitary Activities (Nicaragua v. U.S.), 1986 I.C.J. 14, 101 (June 27).

55. Restatement FRLUS § 221.

56. A variant of world government is the "global governance" movement, which seeks to empower "educated professionals." Global governance was defined by two of its advocates as "the complex of formal and informal institutions, mechanisms, relationships, and processes between and among states, markets, citizens and organizations, both inter- and non-governmental, through which collective interests on the global plane are articulated, duties, obligations and privileges are established, and differences are mediated through educated professionals." Thomas G. Weiss & Ramesh Thakur, The UN and Global Governance: An Idea and Its Prospects (2006).

57. Restatement FRLUS § 223.

by the ICJ in the *Reparations for Injuries* case involving a claim by the United Nations following the 1948 assassination of one of its diplomats.[58] In concluding in its advisory opinion that the UN had standing to assert a claim in its own capacity as an international organization, even though the UN Charter itself conferred no such power, the ICJ explained that an entity such as the UN might be a "subject" of international law even though it lacks the full measure of legal personality enjoyed by states. The court concluded that "the subjects of law in any legal system are not necessarily identical in their nature or in the extent of their rights, and their nature depends upon the needs of the community. Throughout its history, the development of international law has been influenced by the requirements of international life, and the progressive increase in the collective activities of States has already given rise to action upon the international plane by certain entities which are not States."[59] Accordingly, IOs may assert claims under international law in their own name. Additionally, they may enter into treaties with states or other IOs and request advisory opinions from international tribunals. IOs and their member states' delegations and secretariat staffs are extended a measure of immunity equivalent to the diplomats of states.[60] IOs, like any organization, have their own rules that are binding on members. Those organizational norms, while not necessarily a source of international law, influence the behavior of states.

International organizations can be global or regional, and their competency can be general or specific (sometimes called functional). The UN is an example of an IO whose competency is global and general, while NATO and the Arctic Council are examples of regional organizations with specific, functional mandates. The distinction has more than theoretical importance. In their approach to IOs whose charge is global and general, some theorists and jurists have argued that a liberal interpretation should be applied in construing the constitutive treaty that established the organization. That is, rather than strictly limiting the IO to the powers expressly enumerated in the treaty that established the organization, that constitutive treaty should be read to include by implication those powers "necessary and proper" for carrying out the enumerated powers. In the ICJ's decision in the *Reparation for Injuries* advisory opinion, Judge Green Hackworth (of the United States) sharply criticized that argument, explaining that the UN is an organization of "delegated and enumerated powers . . . [and that] Powers not expressed cannot be freely implied."[61] Judge Hackworth's critique recognizes that, unlike the U.S. Constitution, the UN Charter does not include a "necessary and proper clause."[62]

The typical structure of an IO consists of an assembly comprising all member states, a smaller council elected by the members, one or more specialized committees, and perhaps a secretariat.[63] Later chapters will introduce the concept of the "competent international organization" (CIO)

---

58. Advisory Opinion on Reparations for Injuries in the Service of the United Nations, 1949 I.C.J. 174 (Apr. 11).
59. Id. See also Restatement FRLUS §§ 221–223.
60. Restatement FRLUS §§ 467–470.
61. Advisory Opinion on Reparations, 1949 I.C.J. at 198 (Dissenting Opinion of Judge Hackworth). Under that strict interpretation, the General Assembly's power to undertake peacekeeping operations in the absence of a Security Council decision might have been ruled *ultra vires*; however, a later ICJ advisory opinion upheld such operations. See Advisory Opinion on Certain Expenses of the United Nations, 1962 I.C.J. 151 (July 20). It is clear that the Security Council could order such measures; thus peacekeeping in itself is not *ultra vires* under the UN Charter. The court rejected the argument by France and the Soviet Union that the assembly had violated the principle of "separation of powers" by encroaching on the powers of the council.
62. In defining the legislative powers of Congress, Article I, section 8 of the U.S. Constitution provides that it includes the power to "make all Laws which shall be necessary and proper for carrying into Execution the foregoing [enumerated] Powers." That clause was given a broad interpretation by the U.S. Supreme Court in McCulloch v. Maryland, 17 U.S. 316 (1819).
63. This IO architecture is associated with President Wilson's design for the League of Nations, whose Covenant is part of the 1919 Treaty of Versailles. Wilson was likely influenced by Immanuel Kant's Perpetual Peace project. Immanuel Kant, Perpetual Peace (1795, C. J. Friedrich transl. & ed., 1948).

under international law. International maritime law is often developed under the auspices of a CIO, such as the International Maritime Organization (IMO). Chapter 2 describes CIOs that play such a role in law of the sea issues.

The United Nations was established in 1945 with its headquarters in New York overlooking the East River. Selected articles of the UN Charter are reproduced in appendix B. The organization comprises six principal organs: the General Assembly, Secretariat, Security Council, Economic and Social Council, Trusteeship Council (now largely inactive), and International Court of Justice (ICJ), the principal judicial organ of the United Nations located in The Hague.[64]

UN membership is open to all "peace-loving" states, subject to voting rules set out in the charter. The General Assembly, consisting of all member states, is divided into six main committees,[65] along with a number of other standing and ad hoc committees. The assembly meets every autumn at UN headquarters. All states have equal voting rights on assembly resolutions; however, funding responsibilities follow the "common but differentiated responsibility" rule. A simple majority vote is sufficient on most matters, giving a vote by the island state of Nauru with its population of nine thousand the same effect as a vote by China or India. "Important" matters must be approved by two-thirds of the assembly.[67]

The majority of governments that participated in the drafting of the UN Charter were opposed to conferring on the UN legislative power to enact binding rules of international law.[68] As a corollary, they also rejected proposals to confer on the General Assembly the power to impose certain general conventions on states by some form of majority vote. Rather, they conferred on the assembly the power to make recommendations on any questions or matters within the scope of the charter,[69] and to study and make recommendations for the purpose of "encouraging the progressive development of international law and its codification."[70]

The UN Security Council consists of five permanent members (China, France, Russia, the United Kingdom, and the United States) and ten rotating members who serve two-year terms.[71] Resolutions by the Security Council on issues other than "procedural matters" require the affirmative vote of at least nine members, including the "concurring vote" of the five permanent members—the so-called P-5.[72] This voting rule gives each of the P-5 members a virtual veto over any proposal other than procedural matters. As the Soviet Union learned in the run-up to the 1950–53 Korean conflict, merely abstaining from a vote or not being present when a vote is taken will not defeat a Security Council resolution if it is supported by at least nine other council members. In fact, abstentions by P-5 members are now common and will not prevent passage of a resolution. For example, the Security Council resolution authorizing the use of force to address the 2011 Libyan conflict passed despite abstentions by two of the P-5 (China and Russia)

---

64. UN Charter, supra, art. 7.

65. The First Committee (disarmament and international security issues), Second Committee (economic and financial issues), Third Committee (social, humanitarian, and cultural issues), Fourth Committee (special political and decolonization matters), Fifth Committee (administrative and budgetary matters), and Sixth Committee (international law issues).

66. UN Charter, supra, art. 18.

67. Id.

68. International Law Commission, Introduction to the International Law Commission, available at http://untreaty.un.org/ilc/ilcintro.htm (accessed Feb. 1, 2013).

69. UN Charter, supra, arts. 10–12.

70. Id. art. 13(1).

71. The Chinese seat was originally occupied by the Republic of China. It was transferred to the People's Republic of China in 1971. The seat originally assigned to the Soviet Union was transferred to Russia after the breakup of the Soviet Union in 1991.

72. UN Charter, supra, art. 27.

along with abstentions by Brazil, Germany, and India (three states that have long lobbied for a permanent seat on the council). In contrast to resolutions of the General Assembly, which are not binding, decisions of the Security Council bind all states. In construing and complying with Security Council resolutions, strict attention must be paid to the terms used. States are bound by the council's "decisions" (indicated in the resolution by the verb "decides"). By contrast, a resolution that merely "calls upon" states to take or refrain from taking action is generally considered precatory.

The UN and its collective security approach (examined in chapter 13) showed brief promise in the early 1990s following Iraq's invasion of Kuwait, leading some to opine that a "new world order" had emerged after the dissolution of the Soviet Union ended the Cold War. Although the Security Council did manage to pass a resolution authorizing the use of force to expel Iraq from Kuwait in 1991, the military action was not an exercise of "collective security" as envisioned by the architects of the UN Charter. Rather, a coalition of some thirty willing and able (and supporting) states acted in collective self-defense with Kuwait while most of the other UN members looked on. Moreover, cooperation among the P-5 on international peace and security issues proved to be short-lived, forcing NATO members to intervene in the former Yugoslavia without Security Council authorization and an even smaller coalition of states to intervene on behalf of Libyan insurgents fighting to overthrow Muammar Gaddafi in 2011.

In the final analysis, the United Nations will be no more or less effective than its member states require it to be. Calls for reform are common. Proposals to reconstitute the Security Council by adding more members or at least more veto-yielding permanent members have been discussed and debated but never brought to a vote. Such a change would require an amendment to the charter, and any of the existing permanent members of the council have the power to veto such an amendment.[73] In the meantime, despite its less than perfect performance in achieving the goals set out in the charter, the UN remains a powerful source of legitimacy in the international system.

3. Individuals

In the years since World War II, individuals have increasingly acquired elements of international legal personality. As with IOs, however, the legal personality of individuals differs in significant ways from the personality of states. Individuals cannot enter into treaties, make customary international law, or acquire territory in a sovereign capacity. With rare but important exceptions, individuals may not bring claims in international courts (though they are often permitted to bring suit in domestic courts for violations of international law). Only states have standing in most international courts, and it is for states to espouse claims on behalf of one their nationals injured in violation of international law by another state. Lastly, individuals cannot wage war, a principle that has been sorely tested by terrorist organizations and other armed groups over the last several decades.

Individuals do have "nationality," a concept defined by both international law and domestic law. Nationality refers to the relationship between a state and an individual. The citizen pledges loyalty to the state, and the state in turn protects the individual. Socrates is said to have boldly declared some 2,500 years ago that he was not a citizen of Athens or of Greece, but rather a citizen of the world. The reality today, however, is that a person without nationality is in a "condition deplored in the international community." In the United States, stripping a person of

---

73. Id. art. 108.

citizenship would constitute cruel and unusual punishment in violation of the Eighth Amendment to the Constitution.[74]

Individuals acquire nationality at birth, although they may later acquire a new nationality through the granting state's naturalization rules. Questions relating to a person's nationality are largely, though not entirely, left to the law of the granting state.[75] The relevant 1930 Convention declared that "it is for each State to determine under its own law who are its nationals. This law shall be recognized by other States in so far as it is consistent with international conventions, international custom, and the principles of law generally recognized with regard to nationality."[76] The "consistency" qualification in that convention was put to the test in *Nottebohm's* case, in which the ICJ ruled that a state is not required to give legal effect to another state's grant of citizenship through naturalization when that individual does not have a "genuine link" to the granting state.[77] The common bases for granting nationality at birth are found in the *jus soli* rule (nationality based on place of birth) and, in some states, the *jus sanguinis* rule (nationality at birth based on nationality of parents).[78] The Fourteenth Amendment to the U.S. Constitution adopts the former rule, while U.S. statutes also include the latter.[79] Questions concerning the *jus soli* rule are occasionally raised when a child is born on board a U.S. vessel or aircraft.[80]

Until World War II, there was little international law directly applicable to individuals, who were widely viewed as mere objects of international law. One prominent exception was the international law of piracy, under which individuals were subject to arrest and punishment for committing the international crime of piracy. The war crimes tribunals convened in Nuremburg and Tokyo following World War II heralded the emergence of a new international criminal law, under which individuals could be prosecuted for violating any one of several war-related crimes defined by international law.[81] At the same time, and partly in response to the genocide and crimes against humanity that occurred during the war, most prominently in the Holocaust, international law turned its attention to the human rights and fundamental freedoms of individuals.

Drawing on the UN Charter, the 1948 Universal Declaration of Human Rights (UDHR) inaugurated the modern era of international human rights.[82] The UDHR was followed by the International Covenant on Civil and Political Rights (ICCPR)[83] and the International Covenant on Economic, Social, and Cultural Rights (ICESCR).[84] Other rules of international law

---

74. Trop v. Dulles, 356 U.S. 86, 101–02 (1958) (holding that stripping a military deserter of his U.S. citizenship violated the Eighth Amendment prohibition on cruel and unusual punishment).
75. Restatement FRLUS § 211.
76. Convention on Certain Questions relating to the Conflict of Nationality Laws, art. 1, Apr. 13, 1930, 179 L.N.T.S. 89, No. 4137.
77. Nottebohm's case (Liechtenstein v. Guatemala), 1955 I.C.J. 4 (Apr. 6). See also Restatement FRLUS § 211.
78. In the United States, the term "national" includes resident aliens who owe allegiance to the United States. See 8 U.S.C. § 1101(a)(22) (the term "national of the United States" means [1] a citizen of the United States, or [2] a person who, though not a citizen of the United States, owes permanent allegiance to the United States). See also 50 U.S.C. § 1801(i) (defining "United States person" similarly).
79. See, e.g., 8 U.S.C. § 1401 (nationals and citizens of the United States at birth); Restatement FRLUS § 212.
80. See, e.g., Lam Mow v. Nagle, 24 F.2d 316 (9th Cir. 1928) (holding that a child born on board a U.S.-flag vessel while on the high seas does not meet the *jus soli* rule).
81. The London Charter of 1942 named three international crimes: crimes against the peace, crimes against humanity, and war crimes. The charter further provided that even a head of state was not immune from prosecution and that obedience to orders was not a complete defense.
82. Universal Declaration of Human Rights, Dec. 10, 1948, G.A. Res. 217 (III 1948).
83. International Covenant on Civil and Political Rights, Dec. 6, 1966, 999 U.N.T.S. 171, S. Treaty Doc. 95-20. The United States ratified the ICCPR in 1992.
84. International Covenant on Economic, Social, and Cultural Rights [hereinafter "ICESCR"], Dec. 16, 1966, 993 U.N.T.S. 3; S. Treaty Doc. No. 95-19. The United States is not a party.

addressed the obligations of states to aliens within their borders and the related doctrine of "diplomatic protection" by which the alien's state of nationality could intervene on behalf of a national injured by another state's violation of international law.

To varying degrees, identifiable groups of individuals are gaining international recognition. For example, ethnic, linguistic, and religious minorities and women and children are increasingly singled out for differential treatment under human rights and refugee laws. At the other end of the spectrum, certain terrorist groups have been the object of a broad variety of international sanctions and countermeasures, including the use of armed force in self-defense by states against such organizations and their members. Although international law embraces the principle of self-determination, it generally opposes the use of force, even by separatist groups who would employ violence in the exercise of their self-determination right. The affected state may therefore use reasonable force if necessary to quell any violent separatist acts.

4. Ships, Aircraft, and Spacecraft

According to prominent and authoritative treaties, ships and aircraft also have "nationality."[85] Indeed, under the "private" maritime law (i.e., admiralty law) of some states a ship may be arrested and sued in its own name in an in rem action to enforce a maritime lien. Some ships lack nationality. Such "statelessness" is a particularly sad condition for vessels. As is discussed more fully in later chapters, U.S. courts have labeled stateless vessels "international pariahs."[86] Vessels and aircraft may also be protected by international law. A number of antiterrorism conventions expressly prohibit terrorist acts against vessels, offshore installations, and aircraft. International law also addresses the status of satellites and other spacecraft and state responsibility for such craft.[87] Chapter 9 examines the status of ships and aircraft and rules regarding nationality.

5. Corporations

Corporations, sometimes referred to as "juridical" entities or individuals because they are created by the states under whose laws they are incorporated, also possess nationality.[88] Transnational corporations (TNCs), often consisting of a complex web of parent and subsidiary elements with uncertain lines of control, responsibility, and allegiance, have become a source of concern. Confusion arises over questions concerning jurisdiction based on nationality when applied to parent and subsidiary corporations incorporated or operating in more than one state.[89] Of particular relevance to the seagoing officer is the now common practice of allocating ship ownership, management, and operations among several corporate owners, charterers, and operating companies, each of which may be incorporated in a different state. Obtaining jurisdiction over all of the corporations implicated in a civil or criminal wrong involving a vessel can be challenging.

---

85. Restatement FRLUS § 501.
86. U.S. v. Marino-Garcia, 679 F.2d 1373, 1382 (11th Cir. 1992).
87. See, e.g., Treaty on Principles Governing the Activities of States in the Exploration and Use of Outer Space, Including the Moon and Other Celestial Bodies, art. VIII, Jan. 27, 1967, 18 U.S.T. 2410, 610 U.N.T.S. 205. See also Convention on the Registration of Objects Launched into Outer Space, Jan. 14, 1975, 28 U.S.T. 695, 1023 U.N.T.S. 15. A 1979 treaty on the moon has only thirteen parties, not including the United States.
88. Restatement FRLUS § 213.
89. Id. § 414. State-owned enterprises (SOEs) present a unique jurisdictional challenge. Because they are owned by the state, they may have, or at least claim, some measure of sovereign immunity. In addition, the SOE's property might be exempt from provisional or final remedies. See, e.g., Carnival Cruise Lines Inc. v. Oy Wartsila AB, 159 B.R. 984, 1002 (S.D. Fl. 1993) (holding that the defendant company Valmet Oy, owned 80 percent by a foreign government, was a "foreign state" under the Foreign Sovereign Immunities Act).

State-owned enterprises (SOEs), essentially corporate entities owned by a state—such as a state-owned airline or shipping line—pose some of the same problems as privately held TNCs, along with unique issues posed by potential claims to sovereign immunity.

6. Nongovernmental Organizations

Nongovernmental Organizations (NGOs) take a variety of forms. Most are composed of individuals, often of multiple nationalities; others draw their members from business and industry.[90] NGOs tend to focus on a single issue or a closely related cluster of issues, such as human rights or environmental protection. The growth in NGOs, both national and international, has been astronomical in recent years. Given their number and often overlapping areas of focus, NGOs frequently compete with each other for public attention and to garner supporting funds. NGOs further their program objectives by informing, persuading, lobbying, shaming, if necessary litigating, and even by engaging in direct action targeting those engaged in activities the NGO opposes.

Most NGOs lack the attributes of international legal personality. A prominent exception is the International Committee for the Red Cross, which exercises protective powers under the Geneva Conventions on the law of armed conflict.[91] Despite their lack of legal personality, NGOs are undeniably influential. The days when NGOs sat silently in the "back of the room" while representatives of nation-states carried out the business of IOs and diplomatic conferences are passing. Increasingly, NGOs are demanding a seat at the table and are being given one, particularly in European Union (EU) functions.

Questions have been raised about NGOs' lack of transparency, particularly in regard to their membership and sources of funding. The tactics of some NGOs have also been called into question. For example, direct-action measures at sea by NGOs that endanger the safety of navigation were condemned by the International Maritime Organization. Greenpeace was also temporarily stripped of its NGO observer status at the IMO in response to some of its practices that endangered ships and their crews.[92] Violent tactics by antiwhaling protesters were recently condemned by a U.S. court as piracy.[93]

E. SOURCES OF INTERNATIONAL LAW

Before examining how international law is made and where it may be found, it will be useful to distinguish the term "law" from the broader term "norms." Norms that guide behavior may rely on a variety of political, diplomatic, economic, cultural, religious, and practical motivations for their efficacy. The distinguishing feature of international law is that it consists of norms that are legally enforceable. Theoretically, that would suggest that international law enjoys greater relative normativity (i.e., it is more compelling) than do nonlegal norms. A category of nonlegal norms confusingly referred to as "soft law" generally refers to norms that are not legally enforceable (and are therefore not "law") but nevertheless have an influence on behavior and might one

---

90. Maritime examples include the International Chamber of Shipping, the World Shipping Council, and the World Ocean Council.
91. Commander's Handbook, supra, ¶¶ 3.11 & 6.2.2.
92. See U.S. Department of State, Digest of United States Practice in International Law 1989–1990, at 456–59 (documenting protests the United States filed with the governments of the Netherlands, Finland, and Sweden regarding dangerous at-sea tactics by Greenpeace protest vessels endangering U.S. submarine activities).
93. Institute of Cetacean Research v. Sea Shepherd Conserv. Soc'y, 708 F.3d 1099 (9th Cir. 2013). The decision is examined in the piracy materials in chapter 12.

day lead to legally enforceable norms. Soft law instruments applicable in marine environmental protection matters are examined in chapter 10.

The international legal "system" consists of sources of law, processes for making and enforcing that law, and their related institutions. The sources of law define its substance (rights and obligations), processes, and available remedies. In the U.S. domestic legal system, the "sources" commonly relied on are the federal and state constitutions; statutes; regulations promulgated by administrative agencies; and court decisions, including those that establish or modify common law rules. Those sources may be augmented or clarified by research and analysis reports that provide "evidence" of or commentaries on the law, such as restatements of the law, treatises, and law review articles.

Knowledge of the sources of international law is critical for the naval officer. Article 0914 of *Navy Regulations*, for example, directs that "on occasions when injury to the United States or to citizens thereof is committed or threatened in violation of the principles of international law or in violation of rights under a treaty or other international agreement, the senior officer present shall consult with the diplomatic or consular representatives of the United States, if possible, and . . . *shall take such action as is demanded by the gravity of the situation.*"

A common starting point for identifying the sources of international law is Article 38 of the ICJ Statute,[94] which provides that international law is principally made and found in three "sources."[95] The first and increasingly dominant source is the treaties or conventions expressly consented to by states. The other two sources are customary international law, impliedly consented to by the states, and certain general principles of law. In addition, "evidence" of international law may be found in the decisions of international and national tribunals and the works of respected publicists (legal scholars).[96] In approaching the materials that follow, it is important to bear in mind that the "boundaries" between conventional international law (treaties) and customary international law are not rigid. Several examples will demonstrate their complementary relationship. A treaty might be drafted to "codify" existing customary international law practices, and some or all of a treaty's provisions may later "ripen" into rules of customary law that are binding even on states not party to the treaty. Similarly, the "ordinary meaning" on which treaty interpretation rests is often distilled from state practice. Subsequent state practice may also be relied on in interpreting a treaty.

1. Customary International Law

Notwithstanding the proliferation of treaties in the twentieth century, customary international law (once known as the "law of nations") still serves an indispensable role in the international regime. The ICJ Statute refers to customary international law as a "general practice accepted as law."[97] That means a putative rule of customary law must meet two definitional requirements:

---

94. Statute of the International Court of Justice, art. 38, June 26, 1945, 59 Stat. 1055, 3 Bevans 1197. Article 38 provides that in deciding cases in accordance with international law, the court will apply: (1) international conventions, whether general or particular, recognized by the contesting parties; (2) international custom, as evidence of a general practice accepted as law; (3) general principles of law recognized by nations; and (4) judicial decisions and the teachings of the most highly qualified publicists as subsidiary means for the determination of rules of law.

95. As used here, the term "sources" refers both to the origins of international law and to where that law can be found.

96. Restatement FRLUS §§ 102–103.

97. ICJ Statute, supra, art. 38. See also Right of Passage over Indian Territory (Portugal v. India), 1960 I.C.J. 6 (Apr. 12) (holding that Portugal's claimed "right" of passage to resupply its colony, Goa, was based on mere courtesy or comity).

it must be evident in a general and consistent practice of states, and it must be followed out of a sense of legal right or obligation.[98] The "practice" element is an objective one and is established empirically by examining what states actually do. The practice need not be ancient or universally followed. The ICJ has concluded that "passage of only a short period of time is not necessarily, or of itself, a bar to the formation of a new rule of customary law."[99] The second element, often referred to as *opinio juris* (short for *opinio juris sive necessitatus*) or more simply "a sense of legal right or obligation," is a subjective one and may be proven by declarations of the states or inferred from state practice.[100] In the *Libya/Malta Continental Shelf* case, the court reaffirmed that "it is of course axiomatic that the material of customary international law is to be looked for primarily in the actual practice and *opinio juris* of States."[101]

In the earlier-cited *S.S.* Lotus case the PCIJ ruled that a party asserting that a rule of customary law constrains or compels state action bears the burden of proving the existence of the rule.[102] Evidence of state practice may be found in a variety of sources, including yearbooks and international law digests prepared by states and the states' diplomatic correspondence. Within the United States, the most widely relied on source of state practice has been the various digests of U.S. practice in international law prepared by or on behalf of the Office of the Legal Adviser of the U.S. Department of State (and occasionally by nonofficial reporters). On the international level, the annual *Report on Oceans and the Law of the Sea* prepared by the UN secretary-general each year since 1994, as part of the UN Open-Ended Informal Consultative Process on Oceans and the Law of the Sea (discussed in chapter 2), often includes similar reports on major maritime activities and legal positions taken by states and international organizations.

To lead to a rule of customary law, state practice need only be "general and consistent," not universal and invariable. When the practice is not universal, however, the practice by "specially affected" states will be given greater weight in determining the existence of a rule of customary law. For example, on the question involving the transit passage rights of warships, those states with large navies or merchant fleets and states bordering international straits would be "specially affected" by the putative rule. In examining state practice it is also important to bear in mind that a state that persistently objects to an inchoate, emerging norm is not bound by the resulting rule of customary law.[103]

Not all general and consistent state practice ripens into rules of customary law. The *opinio juris* component distinguishes legally enforceable rules of customary law from practices grounded on principles of comity or courtesy, neither of which is legally enforceable.[104] A state might adhere to a general practice out of comity, courtesy, or simply because the practice coincides with its interests. It is customary, for example, to accord certain honors to a visiting head of state, but the honors are rendered as a courtesy, not out of a sense of legal obligation. Similarly, as a courtesy a warship might return a dip of the national flag by a passing merchant vessel or fly the flag of a host nation during a port visit, but it is not compelled by international law to do so. By contrast, it has been a long-standing custom to extend immunity to foreign diplomats and

---

98. Restatement FRLUS § 102 cmts. b & c.

99. North Sea Continental Shelf cases (Fed. Rep. Germany v. Denmark/Fed. Rep. Germany v. Netherlands), 1969 I.C.J. 3, 43 (Feb. 20).

100. Id. at 44. See also Arrest Warrant case (Dem. Rep. Congo v. Belgium), 2002 I.C.J. 3 (Feb. 14).

101. Continental Shelf case (Libya v. Malta) ¶ 27, 1985 I.C.J. 13 (June 3).

102. The S.S. *Lotus* case (France v. Turkey), 1927 P.C.I.J. (ser. A) No. 9 (Sept. 7).

103. See Anglo-Norwegian Fisheries case (U.K. v. Norway), 1951 I.C.J. 116 (Dec. 18).

104. "Comity" refers to the effect one state gives to the legislative, executive, and judicial acts of another state. Comity has been described as something more than mere courtesy yet less than a legal obligation. See Hilton v. Guyot, 159 U.S. 113 (1895); Restatement FRLUS § 101 cmt. e.

warships. States do so not merely as a matter of courtesy or comity but rather because they feel a legal obligation to do so. In the *North Sea Continental Shelf* cases the ICJ explained the *opinio juris* element in customary law:

> In order to achieve this result, two conditions must be fulfilled. Not only must the acts concerned amount to a settled practice, but they must also be such, or be carried out in such a way, as to be evidence of a belief that this practice is rendered obligatory by the existence of a rule of law requiring it. The need for such a belief, i.e., the existence of a subjective element, is implicit in the very notion of the *opinio juris sive necessitatis*. The States concerned must therefore feel that they are conforming to what amounts to a legal obligation. The frequency, or even habitual character of the acts is not in itself enough. There are many international acts, e.g., in the field of ceremonial and protocol, which are performed almost invariably, but which are motivated only by considerations of courtesy, convenience or tradition, and not by any sense of legal duty.[105]

International law recognizes two unique nontreaty norms. Peremptory norms (as they are called in the Vienna Convention on the Law of Treaties [VCLT]), or *jus cogens* norms (as they are more commonly called), are those rules of international law "accepted and recognized by the international community of States as a whole as a norm from which no derogation is permitted and which can be modified only by a subsequent norm of general international law having the same character."[106] Peremptory norms include the international law rule prohibiting slavery.[107] Although in most cases customary law and treaties are coequal sources of international law, a treaty provision that conflicts with a peremptory norm is void.[108] A second unique class of legal norms, *erga omnes* obligations, implicates what the law refers to as the "standing" or "admissibility" issue in disputes between states under international law. The general rule is that only a state that has suffered actual harm from another state's violation of international law has "standing" to assert a claim for the violation. *Erga omnes* norms (i.e., obligations owed to the international community as a whole) are an exception to the general rule. Any state may initiate an action to enforce an *erga omnes* norm. That said, few rules of international law are *erga omnes*.[109] Some commentators also distinguish between high-level "principles" of international law and more specific rules. The International Law Association, for example, characterizes the freedom of the

---

105. North Sea Continental Shelf cases (Fed. Rep. Germany v. Denmark/Fed. Rep. Germany v. Netherlands), ¶ 77, 1969 I.C.J. 3 (Feb. 20).

106. Convention on the Law of Treaties [hereinafter "Vienna Convention on Treaties"], art. 53, May 23, 1969, 1155 U.N.T.S. 336, 8 I.L.M. 679 (1969). The United States signed the VCLT on April 24, 1970, but has not ratified it. See also Congressional Research Service, Treaties and Other International Agreements: The Role of the United States Senate, S. Rpt. 106-71, 106th Cong., 2d Sess. (2001).

107. Restatement FRLUS § 102 cmt. k. In preparing the proposed text for the Vienna Convention on Treaties, the International Law Commission (ILC) declined to identify any peremptory norms, while suggesting that such norms are few in number. See ILC Commentary on the Vienna Convention on the Law of Treaties, 1966 Y.B. Int'l L. Comm'n, vol. II, at 187, 247–48 (commentary on draft art. 50).

108. See Ian Sinclair, The Vienna Convention on the Law of Treaties 18 (2d ed. 1984). See also The Oxford Guide to Treaties (Duncan B. Hollis ed., 2012).

109. Restatement FRLUS § 902 n.1. Barcelona Traction, Light, and Power Co. Ltd. (Belgium v. Spain), ¶¶ 33–34, 1970 I.C.J. 3 (Feb. 5) (*obiter dictum* listing as *erga omnes* proscriptions against interstate aggression, genocide, slavery, and racial discrimination). See also East Timor (Portugal v. Australia) 1995 I.C.J. 90 (June 30) (dissenting opinion of Judge Weeramantry, arguing that rights of self-determination and permanent sovereignty over natural resources are rights *erga omnes*).

seas as a "high level principle," while the requirement for submarines in innocent passage to surface and show their flag is a "rule."[110]

2. Conventional International Law (Treaties)

In theory, all international law could be based on customary law sources; however, the advantages of treaty-based rules outweigh the flexibility of customary law in some applications. Much of the doubt and indeterminacy inherent in customary law can be overcome by negotiating a treaty. Indeed, treaty negotiation might expose the weakness of assertions regarding an existing customary law rule. Some treaties also include measures for resolving disputes involving the treaty's meaning or application. Additionally, some domestic legal systems give greater effect to treaties than to customary law.

In contrast to customary international law rules, which are based on the implied consent of states, conventional international law is based on the express consent of the states parties to be bound by the agreement. Parties to a treaty have a duty to perform their treaty obligations in good faith, a principle commonly expressed as the *pacta sunt servanda* rule.[111] Given their basis in express consent of the parties, it follows that treaties do not create rights or obligations for nonparties.[112] A narrow exception concerns the rare treaty that creates an "objective regime," such as the UN Charter.[113]

The Vienna Convention on the Law of Treaties defines a treaty as a written agreement between states that is governed by international law.[114] While that definition limits the scope of treaties controlled by the VCLT, international tribunals have also recognized the validity of unwritten treaties,[115] and treaties with or by international organizations are not uncommon.[116] In each case, however, the entities involved have treaty-making capacity and the instrument is intended to create rights and obligations, or to establish relationships, that will be governed by international law. In international practice, the international agreement's title is not critical. An international agreement might be denominated a treaty, charter, convention, pact, covenant, or protocol.[117] A given treaty may simply codify existing rules of customary law (much as a statute in the United States might codify existing common law) to provide greater certainty and predictability. Alternatively, or in addition, it might extend or modify existing law by "progressive development" or override an undesirable rule of customary law.

---

110. International Law Association, Statement of the Principles Applicable to the Formation of General Customary International Law 10–11 (2000).
111. Restatement FRLUS § 321.
112. Restatement FRLUS § 324. See also U.S. v. Cardena, 585 F.2d 1252, 1261 (5th Cir. 1978) (holding that a crewmember on a Colombian vessel could not assert a defense under the 1958 Convention on the High Seas because Colombia was not a party to the convention).
113. The ICJ relied on this rationale in the 1949 *Reparation for Injuries Suffered* case involving Israel before it gained state status, in which the court declared the UN possessed "objective international personality."
114. Vienna Convention on Treaties, supra, art. 2(a).
115. Restatement FRLUS § 331 cmt. b & n.4 (citing as authority The Legal Status of Eastern Greenland [Denmark v. Norway], 1933 P.C.I.J. Ser. A/B No. 53 [Sept. 5]).
116. The restatement adopts the term "international agreement" to include both treaties in the Article II sense and executive international agreements not submitted to the Senate for advice and consent under Article II. See Restatement FRLUS § 301.
117. The U.S. Constitution distinguishes between treaties and compacts and agreements with foreign governments, but does not define these terms. U.S. Const. art. I, § 10, cl. 1 & 3.

a. Treaty Formation and Termination

States generally choose to enter into treaties when the gains of doing so outweigh the costs (i.e., on the basis of a relative gains analysis). Treaties may be bilateral, such as a reciprocal treaty of friendship, commerce, and navigation between two states (examined in chapter 4), or multilateral. Multilateral treaties, often called conventions, are typically drafted by state delegates at diplomatic conferences convened for that purpose. Such conferences may be conducted under the auspices of a specialized international organization, such as the IMO. On occasion, the International Law Commission (a commission of international law experts established by the UN General Assembly) may prepare a draft text for the conferees. At the conclusion of the conference, state representatives may "sign" the final text of the convention. Generally, such signatures simply attest that the signed version is authentic; they do not express the signing state's consent to be bound by the convention, thus highlighting the difference between being a treaty "signatory" and a treaty "party."

A state generally expresses its consent to be bound to a treaty by a later act of ratification or accession. A state's ratification might include *reservations* (excluding or modifying parts of the convention with respect to the reserving state),[118] if the convention permits them, or the state's *understandings* regarding the meaning of the convention and *declarations* regarding its application to the state. The U.S. Senate often includes all three (colloquially referred to as "RUDs") as conditions to its advice and consent.[119] Multilateral conventions typically provide that the convention will not enter into force until a certain minimum number of states have ratified or acceded to the instrument. In response to concerns raised by "secret" treaties, the UN Charter now requires that all treaties be registered with the UN Secretariat.[120]

Parties to a treaty are permitted to suspend or derogate from some or all of its terms if the treaty so provides.[121] For example, in limited circumstances, the 1982 Law of the Sea Convention permits a coastal state to suspend temporarily the right of innocent passage in selected locations. Parties may also completely terminate their obligations under the treaty by denouncing it if the treaty so provides.[122] Where the treaty is silent on the issue, international law recognizes only a few bases for suspension or termination. For example, a party might be justified in suspending or terminating with respect to another party who has materially breached the treaty[123]

---

118. Restatement FRLUS § 313; Vienna Convention on Treaties, supra, arts. 19–23; International Law Commission Report on the Work of Its Sixty-second Session (Reservations to Treaties), U.N. Doc. A/65/10 (2010), at 10–269. The traditional rule with respect to multilateral treaties was that all states parties had to accept a state's reservation for it to be valid. The ICJ's advisory opinion on reservations to the Genocide Convention took a more liberal view, which is now largely incorporated into Article 19 of the VCLT. The Reservations to the Convention on the Prevention and Punishment of the Crime of Genocide, 1951 I.C.J. 15 (Advisory Opinion of May 28). See also Armed Activities on the Territory of the Congo (Dem. Rep. Congo v. Rwanda), 2006 I.C.J. 6 (holding that Rwanda's reservation to the Genocide Convention was not incompatible with the convention's object and purpose).
119. Restatement FRLUS § 314. A common "understanding" attached by the Senate to various treaties is that some or all of the treaty is not self-executing in the United States. The provision of a treaty made under the authority of the United States that is not self-executing is still "law of the land" under Article VI of the Constitution, but it is not judicially enforceable; rather, implementation and enforcement are left to the political branches. Curtis A. Bradley, International Law in the U.S. Legal System 41–42 (2013).
120. UN Charter, supra, art. 102.
121. Restatement FRLUS § 333.
122. Id. § 332.
123. Vienna Convention on Treaties, supra, art. 60; Restatement FRLUS § 335. When the government of New Zealand banned port calls by nuclear-powered ships or ships carrying nuclear weapons, the United States suspended the mutual defense agreement with that state. See generally Michael C. Pugh, The ANZUS Crisis: Nuclear Visiting and Deterrence (1989).

or where there has been a fundamental change of circumstances (referred to as the *rebus sic stantibus* rule).[124]

b. Treaty Interpretation

Like all written instruments, treaties may contain ambiguities or otherwise give rise to conflicting interpretations by the parties.[125] The VCLT codifies the accepted approach to treaty interpretation.[126] It provides that a treaty shall be interpreted in good faith in accordance with the ordinary meaning to be given to its terms in their context and in light of the treaty's object and purpose.[127] Subsequent practice in the application of the treaty that establishes the agreement of the parties regarding its interpretation will also be taken into account in interpreting a treaty.[128] The VCLT further provides that recourse may be had to external, supplementary means of interpretation, including the preparatory work of the treaty (commonly referred to as the *travaux préparatoires*) and the circumstances of its conclusion, but only when necessary to confirm the meaning obtained by the above means of interpretation, or to determine the meaning if the interpretation by that method leaves the meaning ambiguous or obscure or would lead to a result that is manifestly absurd or unreasonable.[129] U.S. lawyers, accustomed to liberal use of "legislative history" in interpreting domestic statutes, might find the VCLT's approach to the use of *travaux préparatoires* unduly restrictive. And, in fact, courts in the United States (which is not a party to the VCLT) are generally more liberal in their use of the *travaux* than the VCLT would sanction.[130] U.S. courts also generally give deference to the executive branch's interpretation of a treaty,[131] particularly interpretations made by an agency charged with implementing the treaty.[132]

Well-drafted treaties often include provisions for resolving disputes when more than one treaty applies to a given dispute and they provide conflicting rules. For example, Article 103 of the UN Charter provides that any conflict between a state's obligations under the charter and any other treaty will be resolved in favor of the charter obligation. Similarly, Article 293 of the 1982 UN Convention on the Law of the Sea (LOS Convention) provides that only "rules of international law not incompatible with [the] Convention" will be applied in cases falling within the convention's dispute settlement procedures. Two interpretive canons of construction are

---

124. Vienna Convention on Treaties, supra, art. 62; Restatement FRLUS § 336.
125. Treaty interpretation and the search for "ordinary meaning" must recognize that treaties inevitably have gaps in their coverage. The gap may exist because the treaty negotiators considered but could not reach agreement on the issue, or because the issue never occurred to them. Treaties also commonly include vague or ambiguous terms. The ambiguity may be attributable to the negotiators' considered decision to use general terms, in order to secure broad agreement, or because general terms were believed to be better suited to achieving the treaty's remedial purposes.
126. Vienna Convention on Treaties, supra, arts. 31–32; Restatement FRLUS § 325.
127. Vienna Convention on Treaties, supra, art. 31. Given the fact that most laws have more than one object and purpose, particularly those that balance competing state interests, Article 31 should acknowledge that the treaty's text should be interpreted in light of its objects and purposes.
128. Id. art. 31(3)(b). Although subsequent state practice may be used as in interpretive aid, the VCLT conferees rejected the ILC's draft Article 41, which would have asserted that subsequent state practice can modify the terms of a treaty.
129. Id. art. 32.
130. Zicherman v. Korean Air Lines Ltd., 516 U.S. 217 (1996) (explaining that because treaties are not just law of the land here but are also an agreement between states, the negotiating and drafting history as well as the postratification understandings of the parties are relevant); Air France v. Saks, 470 U.S. 392, 396 (1985). See also Restatement FRLUS § 325 cmts. e & g.
131. Restatement FRLUS § 112 cmt. c.
132. Sumitomo Shoji Am. Inc. v. Avagliano, 457 U.S. 176, 184–85 (1982) (holding that "the meaning attributed to treaty provisions by the Government agencies charged with their negotiation and enforcement is entitled to great weight").

commonly employed in international law to resolve conflicts. In situations involving a conflict between two applicable rules of international law, the *lex specialis derogat generali* canon calls for application of the specialized rule over the general rule if the two cannot be harmonized.[133] The *lex posterior derogat priori*, or "last in time," canon provides that in cases of irreconcilable conflict between two applicable rules, the more recent rule prevails over the earlier rule.

c. Relationship between Treaties and Customary International Law

Understanding the relationship between treaties and customary law is critical to those called on to determine the relevant law of the sea rules with respect to states that are not parties to the 1982 LOS Convention. Chapter 2 includes a fuller discussion on that relationship.

Treaties and customary law are coequal sources of international law. One is not necessarily superior to the other.[134] As mentioned earlier, a treaty might codify customary international law. States that ratify the treaty are bound by it (the treaty applies to them *ex proprio vigore*, or by its own force). States that choose not to ratify the treaty remain bound by the applicable rules of customary law.[135] Assuming the treaty accurately codified those rules, the treaty's articles, while not applicable *ex proprio vigore*, may be relied on as evidence of the customary law applicable to nonparties.

Some or all of a treaty might also later "ripen" or "pass" into customary international law rules.[136] Put another way, a customary law rule may "crystallize," by state practice, around the treaty article. To make that determination it would be necessary to apply the test for determining if a rule of customary law exists (i.e., state practice followed out of a sense of legal right or obligation). Even if the test reveals that a customary law rule exists, however, the customary rule might not be identical with the analogous treaty provision. For example, it is clear that a customary law right-of-transit passage through international straits now exists; however, the customary law rule might differ from the detailed articles on that subject in the 1982 LOS Convention. Again, resort to state practice and *opinio juris* would be necessary to determine the content of the customary law rule.

d. International Agreements in the United States

"Treaty" is a term of art in the United States. Article II of the U.S. Constitution authorizes the president to negotiate treaties, but the Senate must, by a two-thirds vote, give their advice and consent before the president can ratify such an instrument.[137] Not all international agreements

---

133. The canon, while applicable in the law of the sea context, does not suggest that the "general" rule is necessarily rendered irrelevant anytime a "special" rule applies. See Southern Bluefin Tuna case (Australia & New Zealand v. Japan), Arbitral Tribunal Award of Aug. 4, 2000, ¶ 52, 39 I.LM. 1359 (2000). Moreover, where the general rule is deemed to be fundamental, it may prevail over a specialized rule of lesser stature.

134. See Restatement FRLUS § 102 cmt. j. For the United States, which is still a party to the 1958 Geneva conventions on the law of the sea, but not to the 1982 LOS Convention, the relationship between treaties and customary law is an important one; see chapter 2.

135. Vienna Convention on Treaties, supra, art. 38.

136. See Restatement FRLUS § 102 cmt. i. The ICJ has cautioned that "it is not lightly to be presumed that a State which has not [ratified a treaty] though at all times fully able and entitled to do so, has nevertheless somehow become bound in another way." North Sea Continental Shelf cases (Fed. Rep. Germany v. Denmark/Fed. Rep. Germany v. Netherlands), 1969 I.C.J. 4, 26 (Feb. 20).

137. See Restatement FRLUS § 303. One issue not yet directly answered by the U.S. Supreme Court concerns whether the president has the power to terminate or denounce a treaty previously consented to by the Senate without first returning to the Senate for advice and consent. See Restatement FRLUS § 339; Goldwater v. Carter, 444 U.S. 996 (1979) (vacating the lower court's decision without a majority decision on whether the president may unilaterally denounce a treaty). A lower court later relied on the plurality opinion in *Goldwater v. Carter* to dismiss a challenge to the president's unilateral termination of the ABM Treaty on the ground that it presented a nonjusticiable political question. See Kucinich v. Bush, 236 F. Supp.2d 1 (D.D.C. 2002).

by the United States take the form of a treaty within the meaning of and subject to the procedures in Article II. In U.S. practice, it is therefore customary to use the term "international agreement" to refer collectively to both treaties (which are subject to Article II of the Constitution) and executive international agreements (which are not). Those executive international agreements—which are fully binding on the United States as a matter of international law—take one of three forms: sole executive agreements entered into on the president's sole authority; congressional-executive agreements, which are negotiated by the president and approved by a majority vote in both houses of Congress; and executive agreements contemplated by a prior Article II treaty.[138] Lest the reader believe that the role of those executive international agreements must be insignificant because they are not mentioned in the Constitution, a 2009 survey noted that the United States had entered into roughly 1,900 Article II treaties and more than 17,000 international agreements. A U.S. Department of State treaty expert reports that over the past two decades the United States averaged approximately 20 treaties per year, compared with some 300 executive agreements.[139]

3. General Principles of Law

General principles of law widely recognized by domestic legal systems occasionally serve as a third source of international law, though rarely in law of the sea matters.[140] To qualify under Article 38 of the ICJ Statute, a general principle must be "recognized by civilized nations." That phrase is commonly understood today to mean that the principle must be accepted by virtually every mature legal system in the world. The role of general principles of law is often described as interstitial—a "gap filler" that is applied only when there is no conventional or customary law rule on point (i.e., to fill a lacuna in the law). International courts have, for example, drawn on general principles to justify reliance on circumstantial evidence to prove a fact in dispute, for rules or principles of estoppel and *res judicata*, and for questions on evidentiary privileges. Some progressive commentators argue that general principles empower international courts to exercise broad equitable powers.[141] Others see general principles of law as a largely untapped means of constraining state action while avoiding the burden of proving that a particular state consented to a rule of international law. A subset of that group argues that the law is sufficiently broad and complete that judges can and should answer every question or conflict that arises by merely interpreting existing law rather than admitting a *non liquet* gap in the law.[142] They favor liberal interpretations of existing law and generous resort to soft law sources to constrain the discretion of government officials to exercise policy discretion.

---

138. See U.S. Dep't of State, 11 Foreign Affairs Manual ch. 700. Executive international agreements must be reported to Congress, in accordance with the 1972 Case-Zablocki Act, 1 U.S.C. § 112b.

139. Robert E. Dalton, National Treaty Law and Practice: United States, annex I, in National Treaty Law and Practice 820 (Duncan B. Hollis et al. eds., 2005).

140. Restatement FRLUS § 102 cmt. l.

141. See, e.g., Restatement FRLUS § 102 cmt. m. See, e.g., North Sea Continental Shelf cases (Fed. Rep. Germany v. Denmark/Fed. Rep. Germany v. Netherlands), 1969 I.C.J. 3, 53 (Feb. 20), in which the court drew on equitable principles when existing international law did not provide a rule of decision.

142. For examples of such "perfect law" thinking, see Harry P. Monaghan, Our Perfect Constitution, 56 N.Y.U. L. Rev. 353 (1981); Mark Tushnet, Our Perfect Constitution Revisited, in Terrorism, the Laws of War, and the Constitution (Peter Berkowitz ed., 2005); Cass Sunstein, A Constitution of Many Minds 22–25 (2009). Some international law commentators have concluded that the *non liquet* concept is obsolete. Others point to the ICJ's 1996 Advisory Opinion on the Legality of the Threat or Use of Nuclear Weapons as a modern decision that effectively declared a *non liquet*. 1996 I.C.J. 226 (July 8).

4. Decisions of International and National Courts and Arbitral Tribunals

Decisions by international courts, such as the International Court of Justice and the International Tribunal for the Law of the Sea, serve as a subsidiary source for determining the rules of international law. Decisions by international arbitral bodies (consisting of arbitrators rather than judges) serve a similar role, particularly with respect to law of the sea issues, because the 1982 LOS Convention expressly provides for arbitration of disputes under the convention. Finally, decisions by the various domestic courts, including admiralty, prize, and consular courts, on questions of international law also serve an evidentiary role. Because they are national courts, however, their decisions are more likely to reflect that nation's particular view on international law. Thus, outside the jurisdiction issuing the decision, national court opinions may not be considered to be as authoritative as the judgments of international tribunals. In the United States, by virtue of the stare decisis principle discussed below, prior decisions by U.S. courts will be binding as a matter of domestic law unless overruled.

It is often remarked that international courts do not "make" international law; only states have that power. The alert reader will immediately detect the differing effect given to judicial decisions under U.S. law and international law. The Anglo-American common law legal system adheres to the doctrine of stare decisis, under which prior decisions by a controlling court are binding on the courts in future cases. Those domestic court systems are also hierarchical. Lower federal courts are bound to follow controlling decisions by the U.S. Supreme Court. Thus, if the U.S. Supreme Court previously ruled that international law either permits or prohibits certain conduct, the Court's decision will be binding in future cases brought in federal and state courts in the United States.

International law does not formally adhere to the stare decisis doctrine,[143] a point the ICJ Statute confirms. Article 38 of the statute provides that in resolving disputes, the court shall apply, "subject to the provisions of Article 59, judicial decisions . . . as subsidiary means for the determination of the rules of law." Article 59 of the statute in turn makes it clear that the court's decisions have no binding force except between the parties and in respect of that particular case (a corollary of the consensual basis of international law). Despite the subsidiary role played by judicial decisions in international law, it would be unwise to conclude that prior decisions by international courts are irrelevant. On the contrary, although they may not constitute controlling precedent, prior decisions on law of the sea issues, particularly well-reasoned decisions coming out of the ICJ or ITLOS and subscribed to by all or most of the judges, are quite likely to serve as "persuasive" authority of the law in future disputes.[144]

The horizontal architecture of the international judicial system and the propensity of its component courts and tribunals to reach conflicting decisions on the content of the international law of the sea is frequently a source of concern. Notwithstanding occasional assertions to the contrary by some ICJ judges,[145] there is no established hierarchy among international tribunals.

---

143. ICJ Statute, supra, art. 59.
144. The approach accords with the principle of *jurisprudence constante* followed in civil law jurisdictions, by which judges strive for sequential consistency within the court's decisions. Arguably, by freely and frequently citing its preceding decisions without reexamining the underlying legal bases, the ICJ has established a de facto rule of stare decisis. See Territorial and Maritime Dispute (Nicaragua v. Colombia), ¶ 100, 2012 I.C.J. (Nov. 19) (referring to the tribunal's "constant jurisprudence" on the evidentiary value of maps).
145. Rosalyn Higgins, a former judge and president of the ICJ, has suggested that the ICJ is superior to other international courts. At the January 2005 conference on International Law in the United States Legal System: Observance, Application, and Enforcement, at Santa Clara University, she referred to the ICJ as the "highest international court in the world." See also Rosalyn Higgins, A Babel of Judicial Voices? Ruminations from the Bench, 55 Int'l & Comp. L. Q. 791 (2006).

For example, the International Criminal Tribunal for the former Yugoslavia (ICTY) expressly rejected the "effective control" rule fashioned in another case by the ICJ, noting that "this Tribunal is an autonomous international judicial body, and although the ICJ is the 'principal judicial organ' within the United Nations system to which [this] Tribunal belongs, there is no hierarchical relationship between the two courts. Although [this tribunal] will necessarily take into consideration other decisions of international courts, it may, after careful consideration, come to a different conclusion."[146]

5. Teachings of the Most Highly Qualified Publicists

A second subsidiary means for determining the rules of international law consists of the "teachings of the most highly qualified publicists." Such "teachings" by legal scholars are subsidiary in that, like judicial decisions and opinions, they are not a source of law in themselves, but rather may serve as evidence of what the law is. Scholars and lawyers interested in the field of international law have, through the centuries, put down in writing the rules and customs in force in their day. Publicists perform a valuable service because they help to crystallize international law concepts and practices. Perhaps the most famous publicist, particularly among law of the sea scholars, was Hugo Grotius, whose treatise *De Jure Belli ac Pacis* (*The Law of War and Peace*), published in 1625, earned for him the title "Father of International Law." A later publicist, Emmerich de Vattel, published his treatise *Le Droit des Gens* (*The Law of Nations*) in 1758. The fact that national courts cited the treatise in making decisions, diplomats quoted it in negotiations, and foreign offices used it as a primary reference book is evidence of its excellence. Lassa Oppenheim's *International Law*, termed by one commentator "the most influential English textbook of international law," is now in its ninth edition.[147] In the United States, distinguished international law commentators such as Henry Wheaton, whose *Elements of International Law* was first published in 1836; John Bassett Moore; and Philip Jessup have been particularly influential.[148]

The International Law Commission, established by the UN General Assembly in 1947, is a source of influential scholarship. Article 13 of the UN Charter charged the General Assembly to initiate studies and make recommendations for the purpose of encouraging the progressive development of international law and its codification. In this respect the ILC, which does much of the codifying, is strengthening the law in the same manner as did the earlier publicists cited above. For example, the ILC's draft articles and commentary on the law of the sea, published in 1956, formed the basis for the conventions on the law of the sea negotiated at the 1958 Geneva conference. In the United States, jurists often resort to the *Restatement of Foreign Relations Law of the United States*, now in its third series. While influential, however, the *Restatement* is not without its critics, both academic and judicial.[149] Moreover, the most recent edition was completed in 1987 and, despite periodic updates, is showing its age.[150]

A few writers went beyond describing the existing law and included in their treatises comments or suggestions on what they felt the law should be. The U.S. Supreme Court famously

---

146. Prosecutor v. Delalić (Čelebići case), ¶ 24, 40 I.L.M. 630 (ICTY App. Chamber 2001).

147. Oppenheim's International Law (Robert Jennings and Arthur Watts eds., 9th ed. 1992).

148. John Bassett Moore, A Digest of International Law (8 vols., 1906); Philip C. Jessup, A Modern Law of Nations (1948); Frances Wharton, A Digest of International Law of the United States (3 vols., 1886); Green H. Hackworth, Digest of International Law (8 vols., 1940–44); and Marjorie M. Whiteman, Digest of International Law (15 vols., 1963–73).

149. See William T. Burke, Customary Law of the Sea: Advocacy or Disinterested Scholarship? 14 Yale J. Int'l L. 508 (1989); U.S. v. Yousef, 327 F.3d 56, 99–100 (2d Cir. 2003).

150. In late 2012 the American Law Institute announced that work was about to begin on the fourth series of the *Restatement of Foreign Relations Law of the United States*.

warned in the seminal *Paquete* Habana decision that the writings of publicists "are resorted to by judicial tribunals, not for the speculations of their authors concerning what the law ought to be, but for trustworthy evidence of what the law really is."[151] While courts welcome well-researched and reasoned analyses on what the law is (*lex lata*), they are generally less interested in academic opinions about what the law should be (*lex ferenda*). A century after the *Paquete* Habana decision, the U.S. Court of Appeals for the Second Circuit lamented the growing trend toward advocacy at the expense of scholarship in academic publications. In *United States v. Yousef*, a criminal trial of a principal in the first World Trade Center bombing, the court commented on contemporary academic legal writing, including one article by a law professor who asserted that international law is not made by states but rather by law professors and other authors. In response, the court explained: "Some contemporary international law scholars assert that they themselves are an authentic source of customary international law, perhaps even more relevant than the practices and acts of States. . . . This notion—that professors of international law enjoy a special competence to prescribe the nature of customary international law wholly unmoored from legitimating territorial or national responsibilities, the interests and practices of States, or (in countries such as ours) the processes of democratic consent—may not be unique, but it is certainly without merit."[152] The court went on to comment on the accuracy of *Restatement* as evidence of international law: "The Restatement (Third), a kind of treatise or commentary, is not a primary source of authority upon which, standing alone, courts may rely for propositions of customary international law. Such works at most provide evidence of the practice of States, and then only insofar as they rest on factual and accurate descriptions of the past practices of states, not on projections of future trends or the advocacy of the 'better rule.'"[153]

6. Other Evidence of International Law

Although not mentioned in Article 38 of the ICJ Statute, several other instruments or documents are sometimes cited or relied on as evidence of international law. Each year, the growing family of international organizations promulgates hundreds if not thousands of organizational resolutions. The most consequential are those issued by the UN Security Council. Under the UN Charter, decisions by the Security Council bind all states.[154] No similar binding effect is accorded to resolutions of the General Assembly.[155] In fact, the possibility of assigning the assembly such a lawmaking function, essentially creating a world parliament that could enact legislation by majority vote, was discussed when the charter was being negotiated, but the proposal was rejected. Nevertheless, some General Assembly resolutions, particularly those widely approved by especially affected states, can be evidence of state practice and, depending on the language used in the text, a declaration by the member states concerning their views on existing customary law.[156] Those resolutions might also serve as the basis for future development of customary law.

---

151. The Paquete *Habana*, 175 U.S. 677, 700 (1900).
152. U.S. v. Yousef, 327 F.3d at 101–02.
153. Id. at 99–100.
154. UN Charter, supra, art. 25. Security Council resolutions are examined in chapter 12.
155. Id. art. 10. The ICJ has at times relied on General Assembly resolutions as evidence of customary law. See, e.g., Advisory Opinion on Legal Consequences of the Construction of a Wall in the Occupied Palestinian Territory, 2004 I.C.J. 136 (July 9).
156. Restatement FRLUS § 103 cmt. c & n.2. One relevant example is the General Assembly resolution calling for a ban on the use of large-scale drift nets on the high seas. UN, General Assembly, G.A. Res. 46/215, U.N. Doc. A/RES/46/215 (Dec. 20, 1991) (Large-Scale Pelagic Driftnet Fishing and Its Impact on the Living Marine Resources of the World's Oceans and Seas).

It should also be noted that some IOs, such as the International Civil Aviation Organization, are authorized by their organic charters to issue resolutions that are binding on their members.[157] Finally, as is more fully discussed in chapters 9 and 10, resolutions of certain "specialized agencies" and "competent international organizations," such as the International Maritime Organization and the Food and Agriculture Organization,[158] may constitute "generally accepted international standards," which are given legal effect under various articles of the 1982 LOS Convention. Military manuals, such as the *Commander's Handbook on the Law of Naval Operations* and the Department of Defense's *Law of War Manual*, and diplomatic correspondence may also serve as evidence of the issuing state's position on international law issues.[159] "Diplomatic correspondence" refers to letters or documents declaratory of the issuing state's position in regard to a particular issue. Many such documents are published by states. The Department of State's *Foreign Relations of the United States*, consisting of some 350 volumes dating from 1861, as well as various white books and white papers, are examples. Such documents afford a valuable source of information regarding the views of states on unsettled questions.

F. JURISDICTION

"Jurisdiction" refers to the legal competency of a state to exercise governmental powers.[160] A state has jurisdiction over the persons, things, and activities within the territory over which it is sovereign. Even within its sovereign territory, however, certain persons (diplomats), places (embassies), vessels (warships), and aircraft (state aircraft) enjoy some measure of immunity from the territorial state's exercise of jurisdiction. Those immunities are discussed in section H below and in subsequent chapters.

International law draws a distinction between the state's jurisdiction to prescribe laws (legislative jurisdiction), its jurisdiction to enforce those laws (enforcement jurisdiction), and the jurisdiction of the state's courts to adjudicate disputes.[161] Prescriptive jurisdiction deals with the state's power to make its law applicable to the activities, relations, or status of persons, whether by legislation, executive act, administrative rule, or determination by a court. Enforcement jurisdiction is concerned with the state's power to compel compliance with its law through its courts and executive, administrative, police, or other nonjudicial action.[162] For example, the United States has jurisdiction to prescribe laws prohibiting crimes committed on board a U.S.-flag merchant vessel, but representatives of the United States could not board the vessel while it is in a foreign port to enforce those laws without that state's consent.[163] Doing so would violate the other state's sovereignty. This example demonstrates that jurisdiction to prescribe is a necessary precondition

---

157. Restatement FRLUS § 102 cmt. g.
158. See, e.g., FAO, Committee on Fisheries, Code of Conduct for Responsible Fisheries, Oct. 31, 1995, FAO Doc. 95/20/REV/1; U.N. Sales No. E98.V.11 (Oct. 31, 1995).
159. Classified manuals and other government publications, access to which is restricted to "official use only," such as the *U.S. Coast Guard Maritime Law Enforcement Manual*, do not serve a similar purpose.
160. A number of treaties impose obligations on states to regulate persons, vessels, or activities under their "jurisdiction and control." Too often, however, no distinction is drawn between the concepts of jurisdiction and control. See, e.g., Restatement FRLUS § 601 cmt. c (the phrase "activities within its jurisdiction and control" includes activities in a state's territory and on the coastal waters that are under its jurisdiction, as well as activities on ships flying its flag or on installations on the high seas operating under its authority). See also id. § 502(1)(b) cmt. c & § 521 cmt. c.
161. Restatement FRLUS §§ 401 & 522; Commander's Handbook, supra, ¶ 3.11.
162. Civil cases are enforced primarily through the courts. By contrast, criminal cases typically include a host of nonjudicial enforcement measures by the executive.
163. Restatement FRLUS §§ 432(2) & 433.

to taking an enforcement action, but it is not always sufficient.[164] Enforcement might have to await the ship's return to the United States or necessitate the defendant's extradition from the foreign state. Jurisdiction to adjudicate cases involving alleged violations of the state's prescriptions is limited by the doctrines of personal jurisdiction and sovereign or official immunity.[165]

It is important to note that some legal regimes do not merely authorize a state to assert its jurisdiction; rather, they impose an affirmative duty on states to exercise their jurisdiction. For example, states have an obligation under international law to exercise effective jurisdiction and control over vessels flying their flag.[166] Any assessment of the effectiveness of international law to achieve global goals must consider both the adequacy of its prescriptions and the level of compliance. Legal prescriptions in themselves are of little utility unless they are substantially complied with. Substantial compliance nearly always requires effective enforcement measures. Expanding prescriptive jurisdiction while limiting enforcement jurisdiction to flag states is not necessarily a formula for success in promoting global order.

1. The Bases for Jurisdiction under International Law

Among the most frequently cited decisions by an international court on state jurisdiction is the PCIJ's judgment in the 1927 case involving the SS Lotus. In it the PCIJ first announced the principle that limits on a state's jurisdiction will not be presumed.[167] The burden is therefore on the party asserting that international law limits another state's jurisdiction to prove it to the court. At the same time, the court recognized that international law does prohibit one state from enforcing its laws in the territory of another state, at least in the absence of that other state's consent.

Over the years, customary international law has recognized six bases of jurisdiction to prescribe laws: territory, effects, nationality, protective, passive personality, and universal.[168] It bears repeating here that these are bases for *prescriptive* jurisdiction even though courts have on occasion incorrectly relied on them to uphold *enforcement* jurisdiction. The first and most widely accepted basis of prescriptive jurisdiction—territorial jurisdiction— refers to a state's competency to prescribe and enforce laws throughout its territory. A variation of strict territorial jurisdiction is what is alternately referred to as "objective territoriality" or "effects-based" jurisdiction, which refers to a state's jurisdictional competency over acts that occur outside its territory but have a substantial and foreseeable effect within its territory.[169] The LOS Convention article

---

164. Id. § 431(1). International law is generally more permissive in its approach to state prescriptive jurisdiction than with respect to enforcement jurisdiction. Concurrent prescriptive jurisdiction is also more common than concurrent enforcement jurisdiction.

165. It should be noted that even when sovereign or official immunity precludes an exercise of enforcement or adjudication jurisdiction, the responsible state still bears international responsibility for violations by vessels, aircraft, or officials that are attributable to the state.

166. Restatement FRLUS § 502; Rivard v. U.S., 375 F.2d 882 (5th Cir. 1957).

167. The S.S. *Lotus* case (France v. Turkey), 1927 P.C.I.J. (ser. A) No. 9 (Sept. 7).

168. The jurisdictional bases can be traced back to the Draft Convention on Research in International Law of the Harvard Law School, Jurisdiction with Respect to Crime, 29 Am. J. Int'l L. 435, 467 (Supp. 1935). See also Restatement FRLUS §§ 402 & 404. The *Restatement* includes an article on "limitations on jurisdiction to prescribe" (Restatement FRLUS § 403), but it is not clear whether it is an accurate statement of the legal or comity rule. See Hartford Fire Ins. Co. v. California, 509 U.S. 764 (1994); Phillip R. Trimble, The Supreme Court and International Law: The Demise of Restatement Section 403, 89 Am. J. Int'l L. 53 (1995).

169. Courts may or may not require that the effect be foreseeable or substantial. Weltover Inc. v. Rep. of Argentina, 941 F.2d 145 (2d Cir. 1991), aff'd 504 U.S. 607 (1992) (interpreting the Foreign Sovereign Immunities Act). Objective territoriality or effects-based jurisdiction has been cited as a possible basis for jurisdiction over "hovering vessels" and the "constructive presence" doctrine examined in chapter 11. It is important to note, however, that objective territoriality supports *prescriptive* jurisdiction, not *enforcement* jurisdiction.

on unauthorized high-seas broadcasting, which authorizes "any state where the transmission can be received" to prosecute the broadcasters, provides an example.[170] Assertions of effects-based jurisdiction, particularly those involving antitrust laws, have been somewhat controversial. "Nationality jurisdiction" extends to the individuals, corporations, and other juridical entities of the state and to ships and aircraft registered in the state. "Protective jurisdiction" refers to the state's power to reach activities outside its territory that threaten the state's security or other vital interests or interfere with the state's governmental functions. It has been relied on to prohibit counterfeiting the state's currency and making false statements to obtain visas or other travel documents,[171] as well as terrorist acts intended to influence the nation's foreign policy.[172] A state exercises "passive personality jurisdiction" (sometimes called "passive nationality" jurisdiction) when it prohibits extraterritorial acts that target nationals of the state. The United States has relied on that basis to criminalize terrorist acts against U.S. nationals and assaults on U.S. law enforcement officers and on U.S. passengers on foreign cruise ships.[173] The sixth basis is "universal jurisdiction," which extends to a narrow class of offenses that are universally condemned.[174] Any state may exercise jurisdiction over universal crimes. The fact that the universality principle is limited to crimes that are universally condemned eliminates the danger that an individual might be prosecuted for an act that was legal where it was committed. Piracy is the best-known crime of universal jurisdiction.

2. Effect of Treaties on Jurisdiction

The customary international law of jurisdiction described above can be modified or limited by treaties.[175] For example, a treaty may confer on its parties jurisdiction to prescribe and enforce laws consistent with the terms of the treaty. Examples may be found in the family of treaties on terrorism, which impose an obligation to prescribe laws implementing the treaties' prohibitions and to prosecute individuals who violate those laws or to extradite them to another state for prosecution. The 1982 LOS Convention both allocates and limits the jurisdiction of flag states, coastal states, and port states. The LOS Convention's jurisdictional provisions may be further modified by the family of maritime safety, security, environmental protection, and fisheries conservation treaties negotiated under the auspices of the IMO or FAO. As the following chapters will demonstrate, the LOS Convention's jurisdictional articles take a number of forms. They may assign or limit the states' prescriptive jurisdiction or make such jurisdiction exclusive, concurrent, or universal. Even when a state may lawfully prescribe civil or criminal laws, the LOS Convention may limit the states' enforcement jurisdiction. Finally, the convention's articles may

---

170. UN Convention on the Law of the Sea [hereinafter "LOSC"], art. 109(3), Dec. 10, 1982, S. Treaty Doc. 103-39 (1994); 1833 U.N.T.S. 3.

171. U.S. v. Pizzarusso, 388 F.2d 8 (2d Cir. 1968). The court limited the application of protective jurisdiction to offenses in which "the conduct is generally recognized as a crime under the laws of states that have reasonably developed legal systems." Id. at 10.

172. U.S. v. Yousef, 327 F.3d 56 (2d Cir. 2003). Historically, the United States resisted claims to jurisdiction based on the passive personality principle, at least in cases in which the acts occurred in a state that was both willing and able to prosecute the individual. See Restatement FRLUS § 402 cmt. g & n.3.

173. U.S. v. Yunis, 681 F. Supp. 898, 899–903 (D.D.C. 1988). United States v. Benitez, 741 F.2d 1312, 1316 (11th Cir. 1984) (passive personality principle invoked to approve prosecution of Colombian citizen convicted of shooting U.S. drug agents in Colombia). See also, e.g., 18 U.S.C. § 7(8).

174. Restatement FRLUS § 404. The list of universal jurisdiction crimes in the *Restatement* has been criticized as over-inclusive.

175. For a discussion of the relationship between the six customary law bases for jurisdiction and jurisdiction based on a treaty, see U.S. v. Yousef, 327 F.3d 56 (2d Cir. 2003).

limit the means that may be used in carrying out enforcement activities and the punishment that can be imposed or may provide detained vessels and their crews with access to international tribunals to obtain their "prompt release" on the posting of reasonable security to pay any fines that may later be assessed. Each of these issues is examined in the chapters that follow.

3. Jurisdictional Analysis

The determination of which state or states have jurisdiction over a matter requires examination of the nationality of the person who committed the relevant act (jurisdiction *ratione personae*), the place (jurisdiction *ratione loci*), and the nature of the activity (jurisdiction *ratione materiae*). Jurisdiction may be exclusively vested in one state or concurrent among two or more states. In light of the multiple customary law bases for jurisdiction described above, it is not surprising that maritime incidents can give rise to concurrent jurisdiction. The 2002 incident involving the tank ship *Prestige* demonstrates the complexity of jurisdictional inquiries today. After the vessel suffered an onboard casualty, the captain sought temporary refuge in a Spanish port to make emergency repairs. Spanish authorities denied the request and directed him to steer the *Prestige* away from the coast. The tanker later broke in two and foundered, releasing 70,000 tons of oil that damaged coastal ecosystems and fouled the beaches of Spain and France. The vessel was under the command of a Greek master, owned by a Liberian company, operated by a Greek company, and registered in the Bahamas. The incident occurred in Spain's exclusive economic zone. This incident raised questions regarding which state or states had jurisdiction over any criminal action against the vessel's master for possible negligence or civil actions against the vessel's owner and operator. Issues of prescriptive and enforcement jurisdiction in the maritime domain are examined in chapter 11.

G. RELATIONSHIP OF INTERNATIONAL LAW AND DOMESTIC LAW

International law has traditionally concerned itself with relations among states. The growing body of international law governing human rights and international trade and environmental protection is challenging that historical assumption as well as the nonintervention norm. Unfortunately, international law and domestic law are often depicted as conflicting rather than complementary. The truth is, both serve important, even indispensable roles. Some matters are governed exclusively by international law, some exclusively by domestic law, and some by elements of both. Domestic law shapes and informs international law, and vice versa. Domestic law may also provide the rule of decision in an international tribunal if it rises to the level of a general principle of law. In construing and applying U.S. law, including the U.S. Constitution, courts on occasion turn to international or comparative law sources.[176] It bears repeating, however, that despite the growing synergies between international law and domestic law and the availability of international tribunals, most issues continue to be controlled by the domestic law of the states, and most litigation over international law issues is carried out in the domestic courts.

1. Domestic Law in International Courts

The relationship between international law and the domestic law of states entails two broad inquiries. The first inquiry concerns the effect of domestic law in the international system. It has been shown that a widely adopted rule of domestic law might constitute a general principle of law

---

176. See, e.g., Roper v. Simmons, 543 U.S. 551 (2005); Lawrence v. Texas, 539 U.S. 558 (2003).

directly applicable under Article 38 of the ICJ Statute. International tribunals may also be called on to apply the domestic law of a given state in adjudicating a case arising under international law. For example, an international court might have to construe and apply a state's vessel registration law to determine if that state does indeed have standing to assert a claim as the vessel's flag state. At the same time, international law places a clear limit on the effect of domestic law: a rule of domestic law will not excuse what would otherwise be a violation of international law. The rule is best stated in the Vienna Convention on the Law of Treaties: "A party may not invoke the provisions of its internal law as justification for its failure to perform a treaty."[177]

The second inquiry concerns the effect of international law within a given state.[178] The effect of international law in a state's domestic legal system is determined by that state's domestic law (subject, of course, to the principle that domestic law will not excuse an international law violation).[179] International law is not, like constitutional law, necessarily "superior" to a sovereign state's domestic law, although a state might choose to give it that effect. How this principle is applied is what distinguishes monist and dualist states.[180] As the term suggests, monist states adopt the concept of a single legal system and do not draw a distinction between international law and domestic law. A monist state's domestic law incorporates and enforces international law applicable to the state. By contrast, a dualist state does not automatically incorporate and enforce international law as part of its domestic law. In dualist states, international law is separate from domestic law unless and until the state incorporates it into domestic law. In the United Kingdom, for example, no treaty is enforceable under the state's domestic law (i.e., it is not self-executing) unless it is enacted by Parliament.[181] Few states are unequivocally monist or dualist. A state might be monist with respect to treaties but not customary law, or with respect to customary law but not treaties. The United States is a dualist state, but unlike the United Kingdom it does recognize that some treaties or, more commonly, some parts of some treaties, can be self-executing.

The relationship between international law and domestic law can be demonstrated by the commonly used "which forum are you in?" exercise for law students. An agent (advocate) pleading before the ICJ at The Hague would not argue that a state should be excused from a violation of international law because the international rule conflicts with the state's domestic constitution. That same advocate standing before the U.S. Supreme Court in Washington, D.C., would not likewise argue that the government should be excused from a violation of the U.S. Constitution because the relevant constitutional rule conflicts with an international law rule.[182]

---

177. Vienna Convention on Treaties, supra, art. 27; Greco-Bulgarian "Communities," 1930 P.C.I.J. (ser. B) No. 17 (July 31), at 32. In federally organized states, the national government bears international responsibility for violations of international law by its constituent state and local governments.

178. In the United States, "foreign relations law" refers to international law as it applies to the United States and to domestic law that has substantial significance for the foreign relations of the United States or has other substantial consequences. See Restatement FRLUS § 1.

179. The Supreme Court has held that Congress may legislate to implement a treaty even when, in the absence of the treaty, the subject matter would not be within Congress' legislative authority. See Missouri v. Holland, 252 U.S. 416 (1920). In early 2013 the U.S. Supreme Court granted a writ of certiorari in a case that is likely to reconsider parts of its earlier decision in Missouri v. Holland. See Bond v. U.S., 681 F.3d 149 (3d Cir. 2012), cert. granted, 81 U.S.L.W. 3092 (2013).

180. Curtis A. Bradley, Breard, Our Dualist Constitution, and the Internationalist Conception, 51 Stan. L. Rev. 529 (1999) (suggesting that the U.S. interest in international legal compliance is structurally subordinated to its commitment to federalism and its dualist legal system).

181. By treaty and implementing legislation, the United Kingdom has agreed that the decisions of the European Court of Human Rights have direct application in the state.

182. See Restatement FRLUS § 302(2); Reid v. Covert, 354 U.S. 1 (1957); Boos v. Barry, 485 U.S. 312 (1988). Similarly, the advocate would not argue to the U.S. Supreme Court that the Court is bound by an international tribunal's interpretation of international law, absent evidence that the tribunal's judgments were self-executing.

2. International Law in the United States

The role and effect of international law in the federal and state courts in the United States are actually a bit more complex than the simple "which forum?" exercise would suggest.[183] The United States is a dualist state; however, in applying that label a distinction must be drawn between the role and effect of customary law and treaties, and of self-executing treaties and treaties that are not self-executing.[184] The following brief introduction to the issues is supplemented by a context-specific application to the law of the sea in chapter 2.

Article II of the Constitution allocates the responsibility for making treaties in the United States to the president and the Senate. Article VI—the Supremacy Clause—then goes on to describe their status and position relative to other sources as follows: "This Constitution, and the Laws of the United States which shall be made in Pursuance thereof; and all Treaties made, or which shall be made, under the Authority of the United States, shall be the supreme Law of the Land; and the Judges in every State shall be bound thereby, any Thing in the Constitution or Laws of any State to the Contrary notwithstanding."[185]

Article VI fails to make clear the relationship of the Constitution, laws of the United States made in pursuance of the Constitution, and treaties (although all three preempt conflicting state laws). On its face, Article VI does not establish a priority between treaties and statutes or distinguish between self-executing and non-self-executing treaties.[186] Nor does it mention customary international law (then part of the law of nations).[187] It is now well established that the U.S. Constitution is the supreme law of the land and that any treaty or statute that conflicts with the Constitution is not enforceable in federal or state courts in the United States.[188] Beyond that well-established principle, however, the relationship between domestic and international law in the United States is complex. In 1900 the U.S. Supreme Court declared in the *Paquete* Habana case that "international law is part of our law." That brief but vague pronouncement has been the subject of more than a century of debate and analysis. Was the Court referring to *all* sources of international law, both conventional and customary? What does it mean to be "part of our law"? Does "our law" refer to federal law or state law? The Court went on to explain that "where there is no treaty, and no controlling executive or legislative act or judicial decision, resort must be had to the customs and usages of civilized nations."[189] Thus, the Court effectively subordinated customary international law (customs and usages of nations) to controlling executive and legislative acts and judicial decisions. The Court also subordinated customary international law to treaties,

---

Such decisions are, however, entitled to respect as a matter of comity. See Sanchez-Llamas v. Oregon, 548 U.S. 331 (2006).

183. See Restatement FRLUS §§ 1, 111–115.
184. See Bradley, International Law in the United States, supra, chs. 2 & 5.
185. U.S. Constitution art. VI.
186. In its 2008 decision in Medellín v. Texas, 552 U.S. 491 (2008), the U.S. Supreme Court held that even though a treaty might constitute an international commitment, it is not binding as a matter of domestic law in the United States unless the treaty is self-executing or Congress has enacted an implementing statute. The Court went on to explain that a "non-self-executing treaty, by definition, is one that was ratified with the understanding that it is not to have domestic effect of its own force." Id. at 527.
187. In the United States, the courts take judicial notice of customary international law. See The Paquete *Habana*, 175 U.S. 677, 708 (1900) (courts administering the law of nations are bound to take judicial notice of customary law, and to give effect to it, in the absence of any treaty or other public act of their own government in relation to the matter). However, the law of another state (foreign law) must be proven by the proponent. See Fed. R. Civ. P. 44.1.
188. See, e.g., Reid v. Covert, 354 U.S. 1 (1957).
189. *The Paquete* Habana, 175 U.S. at 700.

as a matter of U.S. domestic law, even though it is generally accepted that neither is necessarily superior to the other as a matter of international law.

In evaluating the Court's decision in the *Paquete* Habana case as it relates to public international law cases and the Court's admonition that "international law is part of our law," it is important to keep in mind that the Court was "sitting as the highest *prize court* of the United States,"[190] a subject that fell within the federal courts' admiralty and maritime jurisdiction.[191] The Court explained that the rule of international law at issue in the case "is one which prize courts administering the law of nations are bound to take judicial notice of, and to give effect to, in the absence of any treaty or other public act of their own government in relation to the matter."[192] Moreover, the majority opinion in *Paquete* Habana by Justice Gray bolstered its admonition regarding the role of international law as "part of our law" first by citing Justice Gray's earlier opinion in *Hilton v. Guyot*, a case involving a private international law question regarding the choice of law applicable in a dispute between individuals,[193] and by citing two presidential proclamations issued in the early days of the Spanish-American War that, in the Court's estimation, "clearly manifest[ed] the general policy of the Government to conduct the war in accordance with the principles of international law sanctioned by the recent practice of nations."[194] Accordingly, application of international law in the Supreme Court's seminal "international law is part of our law" case was dictated both by the basis for the Court's jurisdiction (prize) and by the presidential proclamation. Finally, any application of customary international law in U.S. federal courts must further be reconciled with the Federal Rules of Decisions Act, which directs federal courts to apply *state* law in civil cases to all questions not governed by the U.S. Constitution, a treaty, or a federal statute.[195] Customary international law is not mentioned.[196] Because federal criminal prosecutions must be based on a federal statute,[197] customary law will apply in a federal criminal case only when incorporated by the statute.[198]

---

190. Id. at 714 (emphasis added).

191. In its *Paquete* Habana decision the Court also cited its seminal admiralty decision on high-seas collisions in The *Scotia*, 81 U.S. (14 Wall.) 170, 187 (1871) (explaining that the "question still remains, what was the law of the place where the collision occurred . . . it was not the law of the United States, nor that of Great Britain . . . but that it was the law of the sea"). See also The *Nereide*, 13 U.S. (9 Cranch) 388, 423 (1815), which was also a prize case within the Court's admiralty and maritime jurisdiction and was therefore necessarily governed by the law of nations rules on prize.

192. Id. at 708.

193. Hilton v. Guyot, 159 U.S. 113, 163 (1895) (international law "is part of our law, and must be ascertained and administered by the courts of justice as often as such questions are presented in litigation between man and man, duly submitted to their determination").

194. Id. at 712.

195. See 28 U.S.C. § 1652 ("The laws of the several states, except where the Constitution or treaties of the United States or Acts of Congress otherwise require or provide, shall be regarded as rules of decision in civil actions in the courts of the United States, in cases where they apply"). Claims brought under a federal court's admiralty and maritime or prize jurisdiction (28 U.S.C. § 1333(1) & (2)), like *The Paquete* Habana, are not "civil actions," and are not governed by the Rules of Decision Act.

196. Congress may by statute expressly call for application of customary law. In *Sosa v. Alvarez-Machain*, the U.S. Supreme Court repeated its earlier declaration that "international law is part of our law" (542 U.S. at 729–30); however, in that civil case, customary law was expressly made applicable by Congress when it enacted the Alien Tort Statute, 28 U.S.C. § 1350. Similarly, the Supreme Court has held that the Uniform Code of Military Justice incorporates by reference the rules and precepts of "the law of nations." See Hamdan v. Rumsfeld, 548 U.S. 557, 613 (2006).

197. U.S. v. Hudson & Goodwin, 11 U.S. (7 Cranch) 32, 32–34 (1812).

198. See, e.g., *U.S. v. Smith*, in which the Supreme Court applied the law of nations in a prosecution for piracy because Congress incorporated the law of nations definition of piracy into the statute. U.S. v. Smith, 18 U.S. (5 Wheat.) 153, 160–61 (1820). See also U.S. v. Dire, 680 F.3d 446, 455 (4th Cir. 2012) (same).

Two other doctrines of U.S. law and the international law limits on state jurisdiction should be noted. First, the U.S. Supreme Court has established a presumption that U.S. laws do not apply extraterritorially unless courts have found evidence of that intent in the statute.[199] Second, an otherwise constitutional statute enacted by Congress in excess of international law limits is not for that reason alone invalid.[200] Congress has the power to enact statutes that might violate international law,[201] though the courts will go to some lengths to avoid such a construction, often by invoking the canon of construction announced by the Supreme Court in *Murray v. The Schooner* Charming Betsy.[202] Although enforcement of such a statute would constitute a violation of international law for which the United States would be responsible, the statute would be enforceable in U.S. domestic courts. Finally, it bears repeating here that statutes or agency regulations, such as the *U.S. Navy Regulations* and *Coast Guard Regulations*, may impose an independent duty to adhere to international law. The offices of the judge advocate general for the services, particularly the Navy's International and Operational Law Division (Code 10) and the Coast Guard's Office of Maritime and International Law (CG-0941), stand ready to provide advice on reconciling service obligations with international law duties.

3. Conflict of Laws

When more than one state has jurisdiction, both choose to exercise that jurisdiction, and the laws they enact conflict with each other, it must be determined which state's law will be applied. That is the focus of the field of conflict of laws. Globalization and the accompanying rapid growth in international trade, transport, travel, and communications is testing the limits of traditional conflict-of-laws doctrines (called private international law in some states). For example, what laws control the criminal responsibility of the above-mentioned Greek master of a Bahamian-flag tanker whose alleged negligence results in an oil spill that subsequently pollutes the waters and coastlines of Spain and France? Which state's law applies to a high-seas collision between a French steamship and a Turkish vessel in which eight individuals on the Turkish vessel are killed (the *S.S.* Lotus case)? Or a hit-and-run collision between a U.S.-flag fishing vessel and a Cypriot-flag vessel with Russian officers in the U.S. exclusive economic zone in which all but one of the fishing vessel crew perish (the 2001 collision between F/V *Starbound* and tank ship *Virgo*)?

Two or more states, each invoking a different basis of prescriptive jurisdiction, may come into conflict if they both or all attempt to enforce those laws. The conflict of laws that arise in

199. See Kiobel v. Royal Dutch Petroleum Co., 133 S. Ct. 1659 (2013); Morrison v. Nat'l Australian Bank, 130 S. Ct. 2869 (2010); EEOC v. Arabian Am. Oil Co., 499 U.S. 244, 248 (1991). The Court has recognized an exception to the general rule for statutes that depend for their effectiveness on extraterritorial application. U.S. v. Bowman, 260 U.S. 94 (1922). See U.S. v. Mitchell, 553 F.2d 1996, 1002 (5th Cir. 1977) (reversing a U.S. citizen's conviction for violating the U.S. Marine Mammal Protection Act while in Bahamian waters).

200. Such a conflict is posed by the Shanghai Communiqué of 1972, in which the president vowed that the United States would not challenge the PRC's claim that Taiwan is part of China; and the 1979 Taiwan Relations Act, 22 U.S.C. §§ 3301–3316, which provides that the United States will treat Taiwan the same as other "foreign countries, nations, states, governments and similar entities." See Joint Communiqué of the USA and the People's Republic of China, U.S.-China, Feb. 27, 1972, 66 Dep't St. Bull. 435, 437–38 (1972).

201. See, e.g., The *Nereide*, 13 U.S. (9 Cranch) 388, 423 (1815) (Marshall, C.J.) (holding that, while courts are bound by the law of nations, Congress may manifest its will to apply a different rule by passing an act for that purpose); McCulloch v. Sociedad Nacional de Marineros de Honduras, 372 U.S. 10, 21–22 (1963) (holding that Congress may enact laws superseding the law of nations if the affirmative intention of Congress is clearly expressed).

202. Murray v. The Schooner *Charming Betsy*, 6 U.S. (2 Cranch) 64, 118 (1804) ("An act of Congress ought never to be construed to violate the law of nations if any other possible construction remains"). But see Sampson v. Fed. Rep. of Germany, 250 F.3d 1145, 1152–53 & n.4 (7th Cir. 2001) (limiting application of the canon). One author argues that because the canon is designed to guard against an inadvertent breach by Congress of international

such cases might be between international law and the domestic law of a state. When the issue is governed by domestic law, questions often arise as to which state's law should apply. In some circumstances, admittedly rare, international law will provide a rule to resolve conflict-of-laws questions,[203] but often the choice is made on the principle of comity or a rule of reasonableness, not legal obligation. Over the years, a number of choice-of-law rules have been propounded to guide the courts.[204] They include *lex fori* (apply the law of the forum hearing the case), *lex loci delicti* (law of the place of the wrong), *lex loci contractus* (law of the place where a contract was made), *lex electra* (the law preselected by the parties, usually in a contract), and *lex patriae* (the law of nationality or, in the case of vessels, the law of the flag). In the United States, the law of the flag is given great weight. For example, in *Lauritzen v. Larson* the U.S. Supreme Court explained that it is settled doctrine in the United States that the law of the flag governs all matters of discipline on a ship and all things done on board that affect only the ship and those belonging to it, and that do not involve the peace and dignity of the country or the tranquility of the port.[205] Chapter 4 examines the application of port state laws to vessels.

H. STATE RESPONSIBILITY AND SOVEREIGN IMMUNITY

Throughout much of history, sovereign immunity shielded governments from liability to others injured by government activities. The days when the law peremptorily proclaimed that "the king can do no wrong" have largely passed in most of the world. It is now generally accepted under international law that a state bears responsibility for any harm caused by an act in violation of international law that was committed by or is otherwise attributable to the state. For example, the LOS Convention requires states to make reparation for certain unjustified enforcement actions and for harms caused by the state's warships.

The doctrine of state responsibility (examined more fully in chapter 14) has been likened to the domestic law of "torts," which assigns liability for certain wrongs that injure another. The law of state responsibility must be distinguished from the related concepts of state liability and sovereign immunity under domestic law. For example, following a collision between a U.S. Army Corps of Engineers dredge and a privately owned commercial vessel in which the dredge committed statutory fault by violating the applicable rules of the road, the U.S. government will likely be liable to the owner of the commercial vessel. To bring such a claim in a domestic court, however, the vessel owner must demonstrate that the U.S. government has waived its sovereign immunity for such claims.[206] Although such "private" maritime law (admiralty) tort claims are beyond the scope of this book,[207] the closely related issue of sovereign immunity of warships and state aircraft is more fully examined in chapter 9.

---

law, the canon should apply even to treaty provisions that are not self-executing. Bradley, International Law in the U.S., supra, at 54. However, it only applies when the statute is ambiguous. See also Restatement FRLUS § 114; Trans World Airlines v. Franklin Mint Corp., 466 U.S. 243 (1984) (declaring a "firm and obviously sound canon of construction against finding implicit repeal of a treaty in ambiguous congressional action").

203. See Barcelona Traction, Light, & Power Co. (Belgium v. Spain), 1970 I.C.J. 3, 105 (Feb. 5).

204. Choice of law is less of a problem with respect to criminal laws. The U.S. Supreme Court long ago held that no nation enforces the penal laws of another state. The *Antelope*, 10 Wheat. 66, 123 (1825). However, when a crime is committed on a vessel while in a foreign port, both the flag state and the port state have jurisdiction. Compare U.S. v. Flores, 289 U.S. 137, 154–55 (1933) (holding that the flag state's law governs all crimes committed on board) with Mali v. Keeper of the Common Jail (Wildenhus' case), 120 U.S. 1, 12 (1887) (U.S. law applied to a murder committed on board a foreign ship while moored in a U.S. port).

205. Lauritzen v. Larsen, 345 U.S. 571, 584–86 (1953).

206. Restatement FRLUS §§ 451–452.

207. See Thomas J. Schoenbaum, Admiralty and Maritime Law, vol. 2, ch. 20 (5th ed. 2011).

Historical Development of the Law of the Sea

The law of the sea examined in this book is a branch of public international law. It is distinguished from private maritime law, which forms the substantive and procedural core of admiralty law practice in the United States.[1] The peacetime law of the sea is also distinguished from the law of naval warfare; that is, the law applicable to armed conflicts at sea, including relevant rules from the Hague and Geneva conventions and the related customary international law. The law of naval warfare, particularly the law of neutrality, blockade, and the belligerent right of visit and search, is examined in chapter 12 and in other, more specialized treatises.[2]

Just as the UN Charter is the fundamental text for international relations, the 1982 UN Convention on the Law of the Sea (LOS Convention) is the fundamental text for ocean space, and as such is the focus of this book. While far-reaching in its coverage, however, the LOS Convention also serves as the framework for a complicated web of other international and regional agreements on a range of closely related subjects, which include vessel safety and security, pollution prevention, and the conservation and management of marine resources. A cautionary note: not all states are parties to the convention. The United States is perhaps the most conspicuous nonparty; yet, since 1983 the United States has adhered to nearly all of the convention as a matter of customary law and has expected other states to do the same. Section E below examines some of the challenges a seagoing officer will face in applying the LOS Convention's rules to issues involving the United States and other states that have not ratified or acceded to the convention, together with suggested approaches to resolving those issues.

A. IMPORTANCE OF THE INTERNATIONAL LAW OF THE SEA

The law of the sea provides the legal regime applicable to two-thirds of the planet. Its geographic and oceanographic reach in itself signals its immense importance. It is sometimes said to support three pillars of the state's national interests: defense, commerce, and access to living and nonliving resources. The law of the sea and international trade law reinforce each other: the law of the sea enables international trade by sea, and international trade agreements promote maritime commerce. Mariners, fishermen, and even oceanographers need not be persuaded of the importance of the international law of the sea. All those to whom the sea is important must understand the law of the sea. A stable, predictable law of the sea regime that balances navigation, conservation, and marine environmental protection interests with national and homeland

---

1. See Restatement FRLUS, introductory note to Part V.
2. See, e.g., Commander's Handbook on the Law of Naval Operations, NWP 1-14M/MCWP 5-12.1/ COMDT-PUB P5800.7A (July 2007); Louise Doswald-Beck, San Remo Manual on International Law Applicable to Armed Conflicts at Sea [hereinafter "San Remo Manual"] (1994).

security needs is vital to the United States. Throughout its history the Republic has enjoyed the protection of two close and constant allies: the Atlantic and the Pacific, vast oceanic buffers that provided security and made it easy for the nation to isolate itself when it chose to. At the same time, the United States has long been a trading nation whose economy depended on access to the seas. In an analysis written in 1890 naval strategist Capt. Alfred Thayer Mahan highlighted the importance of naval mobility on the seas.[3] Many consider Mahan, who later served as president of the U.S. Naval War College, to be the founding architect of the modern U.S. bluewater navy. Mahan did not champion U.S. sea power for its own sake, however; he understood the importance of maritime commerce and knew that commerce craves security.

Describing the sea as a "great highway," Mahan's analysis demonstrated the "profound influence of sea commerce upon the wealth and strength of countries." History has certainly borne that out. Since 1950 ocean trade has increased sixteenfold, double the growth rate of the combined world gross domestic product. Today some 100,000 cargo vessels transport more than 8 billion tons of cargo each year—roughly 90 percent (by weight) of all internationally traded goods. The 2004 Commission on Ocean Policy report predicted that seaborne trade volume would double by 2024. Cruise ship capacity has grown ninefold since 1980. Although the global economic crisis that began in 2007 hit global shipping markets particularly hard, they appear to be recovering as of 2013. With the rebound of maritime trade, shipping companies are evaluating the feasibility of navigating the increasingly ice-free Arctic routes and the impact of an expanded Panama Canal. As traffic volumes and vessel speeds rise, the seas will bear little resemblance to the wide-open commons envisioned by Grotius back when a ship might go weeks or even months without sighting another sail. Concomitantly with this growth, the risk of accidents involving vessels transporting oil, flammable gases, or noxious cargoes—or carrying thousands of passengers—will grow.

Risks to and posed by the marine transportation sector extend beyond human inadvertence or neglect. Piracy, once thought to have passed, like smallpox, into the pages of history, is once again a serious threat to maritime security in some seas. Ransom piracy in particular has again proven to be both profitable for the pirates and difficult for the world's navies and coast guards to eradicate. The terrorist attacks on the USS *Cole* and the tankers *Limburg* and *M. Star* demonstrate that neither warships nor supertankers are safe from armed assaults. The marine transportation system is especially vulnerable to illegal and terrorist activities because its scale, its complexity, and the pace of its activity often overwhelm national enforcement capabilities and private-sector protective measures. Increased regional and international cooperation to disrupt illegal activity before contraband is loaded onto vessels has become a key component in a layered maritime security approach that stretches from the point of loading to discharge and encompasses the transportation legs in between.

Offshore oil and natural gas, methane hydrate deposits, and polymetallic nodule fields offer tremendous economic benefits for the states that can bring them to market. At the same time, the exploration, extraction, and production processes necessary to bring them to market pose significant environmental challenges. The discovery of unique hydrothermal vent communities lying miles deep and beyond the reach of the light necessary for photosynthesis captivated marine biologists and the biotechnology industry. Mining companies, on the other hand, view the vent sites as a potential source for commercially valuable sulfide crusts, the extraction of which would destroy the surrounding biological community. Offshore wind farms and hydrokinetic installations will create new navigation challenges for the mariner. Finally, sea-based communities may

3. Alfred Thayer Mahan, The Influence of Sea Power upon History, 1660–1782, at 25 (1890).

yet become a reality. Visionaries such as Jacques Cousteau first built oceanaut habitats on the seabed more than half a century ago.[4] More commercially minded entrepreneurs envision new sovereign states on offshore reefs or abandoned offshore platforms.[5] A well-financed group of libertarians has begun to explore the feasibility of creating independent "seasteads" that would provide relief from such inconveniences as taxation and other regulations.[6]

Protection of the marine environment and conservation of its living marine resources are matters of urgent international concern. The sea is home to more than a million discovered species and probably a million more that have yet to be discovered. Roughly 90 million metric tons of fish are harvested from the sea by capture fisheries each year, and aquaculture and mariculture operators produce another 60 million tons.[7] For a variety of reasons, those harvest levels are almost certainly not sustainable. Marine living resources and their habitats are suffering the cumulative and possibly irreversible effects of overfishing, ocean acidification, thermal disruption, habitat destruction, and pollution. A disturbingly large proportion of the world's fish stocks are in decline. Some species are already extinct or in imminent danger of becoming extinct, threatening to further impoverish the ocean's biodiversity. The planet's coral reefs have become the equivalent of the miner's canary, their demise signaling a lethal deterioration of the marine biosphere.

The oceans have long been used as receptacles for humans' wastes, either intentionally through dumping, ocean outfalls, and vessel waste discharges, or unintentionally through the vast soup of sediments, nutrients and pesticides, and other toxic substances carried to sea by rivers or washed down from the atmosphere. Nutrient discharges (nitrogen and phosphorus) have been implicated in vast offshore hypoxic "dead zones." Vessel ballast water practices have resulted in a massive transfer of nonindigenous species into ecosystems ill prepared to deal with them.

Natural hazards have always been a feature of the ocean and coastal zone. The devastating Boxing Day tsunami that struck in the western Pacific in late 2004, the Japanese Tōhoku earthquake and tsunami of 2011, and the massive storm surge that accompanied Hurricane Katrina in 2005 and Hurricane Sandy in 2012 bear witness to threats posed by an angry sea. Those disasters came at a time when humankind is attempting to understand, control, and ameliorate the effects of weather pattern phenomena such as the El Niño Southern Oscillation (ENSO) and longer-term climate change, caused in part by increasing levels of atmospheric greenhouse gases. Oceanic phytoplankton plays a vital role in converting carbon dioxide into oxygen, a critical ecosystem service that mitigates global warming and ocean acidification. This had led some to advocate "ocean fertilization," to stimulate phytoplankton production, thereby increasing their uptake of carbon dioxide.

Despite the implementation of increasingly stringent environmental protections laws beginning in the early 1970s, the situation confronting the United States remains deeply troubling. The nation has more than 95,000 miles of coastline and an exclusive economic zone covering

4. Jacques Cousteau established *Conshelf I* in 1962. A successor, *Conshelf III*, established in 1965 off the coast of Nice, France, in one hundred meters of water, supported six oceanauts for three weeks. The U.S. Navy established three Sealab underwater habitats (*Sealabs I, II,* and *III*) between 1964 and 1969.

5. See U.S. v. Ray, 423 F.2d 16 (5th Cir. 1970) (examining the legality of a proposal to establish "Atlantis, City of Gold" on reefs off the coast of Florida). In re Duchy of Sealand, 80 Int'l L. Rep. 683 (Ad. Ct. of Cologne, 1978) (proposal to establish the "Duchy of Sealand" on an abandoned antiaircraft platform eight nautical miles off the U.K. coast).

6. See Seasteading Institute, available at http://www.seasteading.org/ (accessed Feb. 1, 2013). A similar proposal tentatively labeled "Blueseed" would involve a permanently moored cruise ship located off northern California, just beyond the U.S. territorial sea.

7. FAO, Committee on Fisheries, Fishery and Aquaculture Statistics for 2010 (2012).

more than 3.3 million square miles. It obtains roughly 30 percent of its oil and 25 percent of its natural gas from offshore wells. Surveys of the Arctic continental shelf pinpointing previously unknown deposits suggest those numbers might rise significantly. U.S. coastal waters support diverse ecosystems, provide essential habitat for numerous marine protected species, serve as a vital highway for waterborne trade, produce much-needed food and energy, and provide unparalleled recreational opportunities. In fact, revenues from coastal tourism in the United States doubled between 1990 and 2000 and continue to grow. Increasingly, however, the diverse ecosystems found in U.S. coastal and ocean zones are coming under increasing stress from growing coastal population densities, conflicting uses of waterways, habitat alterations, overfishing, pollution, and thermal and chemical disruptions. A concerted push to shift to renewable energy sources now has offshore renewable energy installations competing with navigation, fishing, and recreational uses of the coastal seas.

While deeply committed to stewardship of the marine environment, the United States has long recognized and defended the traditional freedoms of navigation and overflight on and over the world's oceans for military and commercial purposes. Internationally agreed-upon freedoms of navigation—a key to the nation's ability to import raw materials and export finished products to global markets—are essential to economic security. Freedom of navigation and overflight is also essential for national security because it enables the worldwide movement of U.S. military forces and the sealift and airlift needed for their support. Balancing freedom of navigation against marine stewardship goals will undoubtedly challenge future generations.

The United States has consistently and aggressively enforced laws concerning drug and illegal migrant smuggling, customs regulations, conservation and management of living marine resources in its exclusive economic zone, and marine safety and environmental protection. International maritime criminal activities pose a clear and present threat to our borders, economy, environment, and national security, one that demands an extensive offshore law enforcement capability and presence. Newly emerging threats include terrorism, arms trafficking, evasion of international trade sanctions, and piracy, each with potential maritime components. To meet those threats, the United States increasingly relies on a "layered" maritime security framework that includes at-sea operations that are enabled by enhanced maritime domain awareness capabilities.

B. FROM CUSTOMARY LAW ROOTS TO THE 1982 LOS CONVENTION

The coastal state's sovereignty over a narrow belt of adjacent seas and freedom of navigation and its corollary, flag state jurisdiction and control, are the central organizing principles for the oceans and seas. In the littorals, where the seas adjoin the land territory of states, the coastal state's sovereignty and the principles of freedom of navigation often come into conflict. The history of the international law of the sea is largely one of a dialectic process of claims and responses over oftentimes conflicting uses of the sea, shaped in large measure by the influences of geography, politics, economics, technology, and information distribution. Competing flag and coastal state claims have been the fulcrum of the law's evolution. State claims on adjacent seas have variously been called sovereignty, sovereign rights, title, possession, jurisdiction, and control.[8] In addition, states have claimed a variety of usufructuary (use) rights in the sea. Those uses may be consumptive (resource extraction) or nonconsumptive (navigation), and may be exclusive of other states or inclusive with other states. Nevertheless, the overarching organizing principle of the law of the

---

8. In U.S. v. California, Justice Frankfurter distinguished between the sovereign's *dominion* (proprietary interests in a space) and *imperium* (political sovereignty over a space). 332 U.S. 19, 43–44 (1947) (Frankfurter, J. dissenting).

sea remains what it was in the seventeenth century: coastal state control over a narrow band of adjacent seas, freedom of navigation beyond that belt, and the primacy of flag state jurisdiction.

1. Customary International Law of the Sea

The history of private and public maritime law stretches over nearly four millennia. Elements of maritime law can be found in the Code of Hammurabi, written in the eighteenth century BCE. Rome's Lex Antonian (ca. 44 BCE) espoused freedom of navigation. Roman trade also relied on elements of the seventh-century Rhodian maritime code. The customary starting point for the international law of the sea, however, is AD 1493, when Pope Alexander VI issued a papal bull following Columbus' voyage of discovery. The pope purported to divide the world's oceans and unclaimed lands between Spain and Portugal. The bull, enforceable under pain of excommunication, was modified and confirmed in the 1494 Treaty of Tordesillas, under which Spain claimed the lands and waters west of a line 370 marine leagues west of the Cape Verde Islands (running through modern Brazil), and Portugal claimed the lands and waters east of that line. Such grandiose claims based on a bilateral treaty appear risible today. Indeed, Portugal's efforts to enforce its claim in the East Indies in the early seventeenth century led to a celebrated debate over the legal status of the oceans.[9] That debate pitted the Dutchman Hugo Grotius as the advocate of freedom of the seas (*Mare Liberum*, 1609) against England's John Selden, who championed the Stuart monarchy's position that the seas are subject to national control and jurisdiction (*Mare Clausum*, 1635). Grotius' position, first published as a legal brief for his employer, the Dutch East India Company,[10] eventually prevailed.

Although the commonly accepted narrative declares that Grotius' vision of free seas "won" the "battle of the books" and established the freedom of navigation and fishing, that is an overstatement. Some coastal states, mostly motivated by security concerns or the need to protect local fisheries, continued to assert claims to bands of waters off their shores. Cornelius van Bynkershoek, an eighteenth-century Dutch legal publicist, provided one of the early rationales offered to justify such territorial sea claims. In *De Dominio Maris* (1702) Bynkershoek argued that state territorial sea claims, like terrestrial claims, could be perfected by an exercise of effective occupation and control. By that logic, coastal states were justified in extending national claims seaward as far as their weapons could control.[11] The "cannon shot" rule of thumb for such control justified claims up to one marine league, or three nautical miles, seaward.

One of the earliest law of the sea claims made by the United States was lodged by Thomas Jefferson, who, as President Washington's secretary of state, asserted in correspondence to Great Britain and France in 1793 that the United States claimed a three-mile territorial sea. Many other states made similar territorial sea claims, some even exceeding the cannon shot rule and claiming the seas as far as the eye could see—up to twenty miles.[12]

---

9. The case, litigated in Amsterdam, concerned the Dutch East India Company's capture of the Portuguese vessel *Santa Catarina* off Singapore. Grotius' brief in the follow-on prize case proved successful and formed the basis for his later enlarged essay *Mare Liberum*.

10. Beginning in the latter half of the sixteenth century, Dutch traders sent ships to territories claimed by Spain and Portugal in the East Indies. At the time, Protestant Holland was at war with Catholic Spain and Portugal. The Dutch-Portuguese War in the East Indies was largely an extension of the Eighty Years' War for Dutch independence (1568–1648), which provided the legal grounds for Dutch warships and privateers to take prizes such as the *Santa Catarina*.

11. Although the legal rationale of effective occupation and control would seem to put the emphasis on the range of the coastal state's weapons, the coastal state's security concerns likely placed greater emphasis on keeping foreign warships beyond the range of the warships' cannons.

12. John Bassett Moore, A Digest of International Law, vol. 1, at 702 (1906). Jefferson did acknowledge that some state claims extended to "the extent of human sight, estimated at upwards of twenty miles." Id.

As maritime activities expanded, states sought, through such accommodations as the right of innocent passage, to strike an appropriate balance between the common interest in preserving freedom of navigation and the needs of coastal states to maintain adequate control over activities in their adjacent littorals. Chief Justice John Marshall described the process and considerations in the formation of such customary approaches in a case involving a so-called hovering vessel when he observed that if "coastal state claims unnecessarily vex and harass foreign lawful commerce, foreign nations will resist their exercise. If they are reasonable and necessary to secure their laws from violation, they will be submitted to."[13]

Freedom of the seas began to erode in the latter half of the twentieth century. The modern "ocean enclosure movement" began with two proclamations issued by President Harry Truman in 1945. The first Truman proclamation asserted a claim of jurisdiction and control over natural resources of the seabed and subsoil of the continental shelf contiguous to the United States.[14] The second proclamation asserted a right to establish a high-seas "conservation zone," within which fishing by any nations would be "subject to the regulation and control of the United States."[15] Although there was no basis in international law for either proclamation at the time they were made, a number of coastal states responded with similar claims, particularly with respect to the continental shelf.

During the period leading up to the first Geneva conference on the law of the sea in 1958, when the law of the sea was almost entirely a matter of customary international law, the so-called World Court (referring to both the ICJ and its predecessor, the PCIJ) decided three cases that were to influence the future direction of the law of the sea. The first was the *S.S. Lotus case*, decided by the PCIJ in 1927. In that case, the court addressed the state's jurisdiction over vessel collisions on the high seas. The second important decision, and the first case decided by the new ICJ, was the 1949 *Corfu Channel* case, which concerned the right of innocent passage by warships through international straits. The third decision was the *Anglo-Norwegian Fisheries* case, decided by the ICJ in 1951, which remains an important reference on questions concerning territorial sea baselines. The chapters that follow refer to all three decisions.

The customary international law process of claim and counterclaim proved a less than satisfactory means to develop a clear, predicable, and widely adhered to law of the sea. Efforts to codify and further develop the customary international law through multilateral treaties enjoyed varying degrees of success. The League of Nations convened its Committee of Experts for the Progressive Codification of International Law, whose work led to the 1930 Hague Conference for the Codification of International Law. Their efforts, though ultimately unsuccessful in codifying the international law of state responsibility or of the territorial sea, were augmented by the work of the private International Law Association, the Institute of International Law, and Harvard Law School. In 1949 the International Law Commission began preparing draft texts for a new law of the sea convention. The ILC's work, which relied extensively on the research and draft articles prepared for the 1930 conference, served as the basis for the 1958 Conference on the Law of the Sea held at Geneva. Coincidentally, as the ILC was preparing the convention drafts for the 1958 conference on the law of the sea, state representatives gathered in Geneva to

---

13. Church v. Hubbard, 6 U.S. (2 Cranch) 187, 235 (1804).

14. Proclamation No. 2667, Policy of the United States with Respect to the Natural Resources of the Subsoil and Sea Bed of the Continental Shelf, Sept. 28, 1945, 3 C.F.R. 67 (1943–48).

15. Proclamation No. 2668, Policy of the United States with Respect to Coastal Fisheries in Certain Areas of the High Seas, Sept. 28, 1945, 3 C.F.R. 68 (1943–48). The United States did not enact laws with respect to this second Truman proclamation until the Bartlett Act was passed in 1966, after the 1958 Convention on Fishing and Conservation of the Living Resources of the High Seas entered into force.

draft the four conventions on the law of armed conflict. Those four "1949 Geneva conventions" built in part on earlier codification efforts at the 1899 and 1907 Hague Peace Conferences, which continue to serve as the core for much of the contemporary law of naval warfare. Selected elements of the law of naval warfare are examined in chapters 12 and 13.

2. UNCLOS I and the Four 1958 Geneva Conventions

The first successful attempt at committing the international law of the sea to treaties, now referred to as UNCLOS I (the first UN-sponsored diplomatic conference on the law of the sea), took place in Geneva over a nine-week period in 1958 and involved eighty-six states.[16] That conference, working with the drafts and commentaries prepared by the ILC,[17] produced four conventions: the Convention on the Territorial Sea and Contiguous Zone, the Convention on the High Seas, the Convention on the Continental Shelf, and the Convention on Fishing and Conservation of the Living Resources of the High Seas.[18] Of the four, only the High Seas Convention declared that it was a codification of customary law.[19] In truth, parts of all four conventions constituted progressive development of the law (some more than others). The Convention on the Continental Shelf, for example, adopted the term "sovereign rights" to describe the coastal state's interest in the shelf's natural resources, rather than the "jurisdiction and control" language used in the Truman proclamation. Although all four conventions eventually attracted sufficient ratifications to enter into force, including ratifications by the United States, states were free to pick and choose which of the four to ratify.

3. UNCLOS II: The Failed 1960 Conference

When the Convention on the Territorial Sea and Contiguous Zone was being drafted in 1958, the UNCLOS I conferees were unable to agree on the maximum breadth of the territorial sea. State claims of three, four, six, and twelve—and even two hundred—miles negated any possibility that there was a "general and consistent" state practice on the matter.[20] Logic would dictate that because the contiguous zone was defined by the 1958 convention as an area seaward of the territorial sea, and the contiguous zone was limited by the convention to twelve nautical miles, any territorial sea claim of more than twelve nautical miles would be inconsistent with that convention. Such arguments based on logic failed, however, to halt or reverse the seaward march of territorial seas. To provide greater uniformity and promote wider acceptance of the conventions, the UN General Assembly called for a second diplomatic conference, which convened in 1960. The second conference (UNCLOS II) was charged with resolving two contested issues: the lim-

---

16. See Arthur H. Dean, The Geneva Conference on the Law of the Sea: What Was Accomplished? 52 Am. J. Int'l L. 607 (1958) (Dean chaired the U.S. delegation to UNCLOS I). See also Philip C. Jessup, The Geneva Conferences on the Law of the Sea: A Study in International Law-Making, 52 Am. J. Int'l L. 730 (1958).

17. International Law Commission, Articles concerning the Law of the Sea with Commentaries, 1956 Y.B. Int'l Law Comm'n, vol. II, at 265–301. See also Comments by Governments on the Draft Articles concerning the Law of the Sea Adopted by the International Law Commission at its Eighth Session, 1958 U.N. Official Records, vol. 1, at 75.

18. The conventions and documents of the 1958 Geneva UNCLOS I conference are available at http://untreaty .un.org/cod/avl/ha/gclos/gclos.html (accessed Feb. 1, 2013).

19. Convention on the High Seas [hereinafter "1958 Convention on the High Seas"], Preamble, Apr. 29, 1958, 13 U.S.T. 2312, 450 U.N.T.S. 82.

20. In the 1956 Santiago Declaration by Chile, Ecuador, and Peru the states asserted sole jurisdiction and sovereignty over a territorial sea extending seaward two hundred nautical miles. See Laws and Regulations on the Regime of the Territorial Sea, U.N. Doc. ST/LEG/SER.B/6, at 723 (1956). See also Montevideo Declaration on the Law of the Sea, May 8, 1970, U.N. Doc. A/A.C.138/34 (1971).

its of the territorial sea and fisheries beyond the territorial sea. The United States and Canada proposed a compromise rule that would permit coastal states to extend their territorial seas to six nautical miles and add a fishery zone extending six nautical miles beyond the territorial sea. The "six-plus-six rule" failed by a single vote to reach the two-thirds majority necessary for adoption (even if the conference had agreed, it is doubtful that the amendment would have been widely ratified).[21] When the delegates were unable to reach an agreement, the conference adjourned. In the ensuing years, territorial sea claims continued to range from three to two hundred nautical miles. The situation was further complicated by the fact that the nature of the interests claimed by coastal states in the adjacent sea varied, with some asserting complete sovereignty over the waters while others asserted only jurisdiction and control over the natural resources in the zone.

The 1958 Convention on the Continental Shelf presented a similar indeterminacy problem. It defined the continental shelf as the seabed and subsoil of the submarine area adjacent to the coast "to a depth of 200 meters or, beyond that limit, to where the depth of the superjacent waters admits of the exploitation of the natural resources of the said areas."[22] The outer limit was thus more a function of evolving technology than physical factors. In addition to valuable oil and gas resources on the adjacent shelf, strategic minerals in manganese nodules on the deep seabed began to attract the attention of exploration and investment companies from developed states and also from the developing states, which were concerned that they would be denied the benefits of what their champion, Maltese ambassador Arvid Pardo, declared in 1967 was the "common heritage of mankind." Many states, including the group that came to be known as "landlocked and geographically disadvantaged states" (LLGDS), lobbied for clearer limits on coastal state continental shelf claims and a regime for the deep seabed beyond those coastal state continental shelf zones that would avert a tragedy of the commons and a first-come-first-served grab by the industrially developed states.

4. Pressure Builds to Revisit the 1958 Conventions

The shortcomings of the 1958 Geneva conventions became more apparent with each passing year. Because the "law of the sea" was divided among four conventions, and states were left free to choose which to ratify and which to ignore, the regime fell well short of providing a universal and comprehensive regime for the oceans. Few states—and none of the distant-water-fishing states—ratified the High Seas Fishing Convention. Most of the flag-of-convenience states rejected the Convention on the High Seas and its "genuine link" requirement, while states in the "two-hundred-mile territorial sea club" rejected the Convention on the Territorial Seas and Contiguous Zone. The Optional Protocol, which would have provided a means for resolving disputes arising under the conventions, was rejected by most states, including the United States. Geopolitical history partly explains the reluctance of some states to accede to the 1958 regime. Many of the states that gained their independence following World War II were not among the eighty-six that attended UNCLOS I, and might therefore not have felt any allegiance to its conventions. Further, the states that came to be known as the Group of 77 actively worked for a new global regime (the New International Economic Order) that would distribute a larger portion of the world's economic benefits to developing states.[23]

21. See Arthur H. Dean, The Second Geneva Conference on the Law of the Sea: The Fight for Freedom of the Seas, 54 Am. J. Int'l L. 751 (1960).
22. Convention on the Continental Shelf [hereinafter "1958 Convention on the Continental Shelf"], art. 1, Apr. 29, 1958, 15 U.S.T. 471, 499 U.N.T.S. 311.
23. See, e.g., Declaration on the Establishment of a New International Economic Order, G.A. Res. 3201 (S-VI), U.N. Doc. A/RES/3201 (May 1, 1974).

No less important, the use of the oceans continued to evolve. In fact, technological developments had begun to challenge the law of the sea even before the 1958 conference adjourned. The steady growth in carrier-based aviation and submarine capability, the advent of nuclear power, the supertanker, the distant-water factory trawler, and, more recently, unmanned aerial and marine vehicles have challenged lawmakers to keep pace with technology. Coastal states looking to the heavens now find that the stars have been joined by thousands of artificial satellites, many of which are collecting images and data on the state's terrestrial and maritime features and activities. Avaricious criminal organizations have also been quick to adopt new technologies, including semisubmersible vehicles for transporting narcotics and unmanned aerial vehicles to facilitate their transit.

By the middle of the twentieth century it was no secret that many high-seas fisheries were in serious danger. Under pressure from distant-water fleets employing ruthlessly efficient fish location, catching, processing, and freezing technologies, a number of key fish stocks collapsed. Early attempts to control high-seas fisheries through multilateral fisheries commissions, such as the International Commission for Northwest Atlantic Fisheries (ICNAF), largely failed.[24] Coastal states responded with a variety of unilateral measures. In 1966 the United States enacted the Bartlett Act, extending its fisheries jurisdiction to a distance of twelve nautical miles from the baseline.[25] In 1972 Iceland, whose local fishermen were increasingly being forced to compete with distant-water fishing fleets from the United Kingdom and West Germany, extended its fisheries zone to fifty miles.

Uncertain and expanding coastal state jurisdictional claims were a serious concern for states that depended on freedom of navigation. Throughout much of the Cold War, nuclear-powered submarines carrying nuclear-capable ballistic missiles formed a key leg in the U.S.-NATO and Soviet "nuclear triads." The effectiveness of those submarines as a deterrent depended on their ability to navigate the oceans while remaining undetected. Expanding the coastal state territorial seas from three to twelve miles would potentially enclose more than one hundred navigational straits and would subject submarines to an "innocent passage" rule that would require them to surface and show their flag. Moreover, the right of innocent passage over a state's territorial sea does not extend to aircraft. Additionally, a few states took the position that warships were not entitled to innocent passage. Finally, under some circumstances coastal states have a limited power to suspend innocent passage. As states whose national defense depended on mobility, the United States and the Soviet Union shared a concern over such expanded coastal state claims.

5. UNCLOS III: 1973–1982

The Third UN Conference on the Law of the Sea (UNCLOS III) was formally convened by the UN General Assembly in 1973 (note that UNCLOS III refers not to the present *convention* but to the *conference* of delegates who drafted the convention).[26] The conference's achievements, coming after a decade of meetings involving the participation of more than 150 states, are one of

---

24. ICNAF operated from 1949 to 1978. In 1979 it was replaced by the Northwest Atlantic Fisheries Organization (NAFO). See Article V of the Convention on Cooperation in the Northwest Atlantic Fisheries, Oct. 24, 1978.
25. Bartlett Act, Pub. L. No. 89-658, 80 Stat. 908 (1966). In 1976 Congress repealed the Bartlett Act and replaced it with the more comprehensive Fisheries Conservation and Management Act (now known as the Magnuson-Stevens Act), which asserted U.S. control over fisheries out to two hundred miles from the baseline.
26. UN, General Assembly, G.A. Res. 3067 (XXVIII), Nov. 16, 1973. UNCLOS III built on work by the UN Committee on Peaceful Uses of the Seabed and the Ocean Floor beyond the Limits of National Jurisdiction dating back to 1967.

the signal successes of international lawmaking.[27] Operating this time without a draft convention prepared by the ILC,[28] the UNCLOS III conferees carried out the task of drafting the convention in three principal committees. The First Committee focused on the deep seabed provisions; the Second Committee's charge included the articles addressing the jurisdictional zones other than the deep seabed, maritime boundaries, and the rights and obligations of states; the Third Committee addressed marine scientific research and protection of the marine environment. The task of refining and harmonizing the texts developed by the substantive committees and ensuring the accuracy of translations into the convention's six authentic language texts fell to the Drafting Committee.[29]

The negotiating texts of the LOS Convention were developed through a complex consensus procedure. The rules of procedure for the conference included an agreement that established four principles for guiding negotiations: first, recognition that the problems of the seabed are interrelated and need to be considered as a whole; second, the belief that to be effective, the treaty must be broadly accepted; third, agreement that every effort should be made to reach agreement on substantive matters through consensus; and, fourth, there would be no vote on such substantive matters until all efforts at consensus had been exhausted.[30] In the end, the United States voiced strong reservations against some of the convention provisions, particularly the Part XI deep seabed articles, and called for a vote on adoption. The final vote for adoption of the text was 130 states in favor, 4 against, and 17 abstentions.

The final UNCLOS III product, the 1982 LOS Convention, is described in the convention's Preamble. The Preamble opens with an acknowledgment that a number of developments occurring since the 1958 and 1960 conferences "have accentuated the need for a new and generally acceptable Convention on the law of the sea."[31] Next, it repeats the theme heard throughout the conference that "the problems of ocean space are closely interrelated and need to be considered as a whole." In contrast to the 1958 conventions on the law of the sea, which permitted states to ratify some, all, or none of its four conventions, the 1982 LOS Convention is a package deal; it does not permit reservations.[32] The Preamble makes it clear that some parts of the convention are a codification of existing international law while others constitute progressive developments of the law. The final paragraph of the preamble confirms the drafters' intent that, even though the convention is intended to address the problems of ocean space comprehensively, it does not do so completely. Articles 311 and 237 of the convention go on to explain the relationship between the LOS Convention and other sources of international law, including other maritime conventions and customary law.

---

27. The UNCLOS III proceedings were reported by John R. Stevenson and Bernard H. Oxman in a series of articles in the *American Journal of International Law* from 1974 to 1982. See 68 Am. J. Int'l L. 1 (1974), 69 Am. J. Int'l L. 1 (1975), 69 Am. J. Int'l L. 763 (1975), 71 Am. J. Int'l L. 247 (1977), 72 Am. J. Int'l L. 57 (1978), 73 Am. J. Int'l L. 1 (1979), 74 Am. J. Int'l L. 1 (1980), 75 Am. J. Int'l L. 211 (1981), and 76 Am. J. Int'l L. 1 (1982). See also William Wertenbaker, The Law of the Sea, New Yorker (Aug. 1, 1983, & Aug. 8, 1983).
28. Some observers attribute that direct approach to drafting the convention to developing states' distrust of the ILC.
29. See United Nations Convention on the Law of the Sea, 1982: A Commentary, vol. I, at 135 (Myron Nordquist ed., 1985). The goal of the drafting committee was "to improve linguistic concordance, to the extent possible, and to achieve juridical concordance in all cases" (Report of the Chairman of the Drafting Committee, Mar. 2, 1981, A/CONF.62/L.67/Rev.1, in Third United Nations Conference on the Law of the Sea, Official Records, vol. XV, at 145).
30. Rules of Procedure for the Third Conference on the Law of the Sea, U.N. Doc. A/CONF.62/30/Rev. 3.
31. LOSC, Preamble.
32. LOSC art. 309.

6. 1982 UN Convention on the Law of the Sea

The 1982 UN Convention on the Law of the Sea, which is reproduced in part in appendix C, spans 320 articles (arranged in 17 "parts") and 9 annexes. When the convention was opened for signature in Jamaica in December 10, 1982, the president of UNCLOS III, Tommy Koh of Singapore, characterized it as a "constitution for the oceans."[33] Many of the 117 states that signed it viewed the convention as the most comprehensive international law project ever completed (and a feat unlikely to be repeated). The convention provided that the regime would enter into force one year after sixty states had ratified it. Guyana provided the key ratification in 1993, and the convention entered into force on November 16, 1994. By January 30, 2014, 166 states had become a party to the convention.

For the most part, the 1982 LOS Convention takes a "zonal" approach to the oceans, under which states' rights, jurisdiction, and obligations vary according to the location of the activity.[34] Each of the zones, which are depicted in Figure 1, are reckoned from the "baseline" (discussed in chapter 3). All waters landward of the baseline constitute the "internal" (not "inland") waters of the state. Moving seaward from the baseline, the offshore waters are divided into the territorial sea, the contiguous zone, the exclusive economic zone (EEZ), and the high seas. In addition, the LOS Convention creates, for the first time, a new regime for "archipelagic waters." The coastal state's submerged lands extend from the baseline to the outer edge of the territorial sea and are followed by the continental shelf (perhaps to include an "extended" continental shelf for states with wide continental margins) and the deep seabed, which is beyond national jurisdiction (also called "the Area").

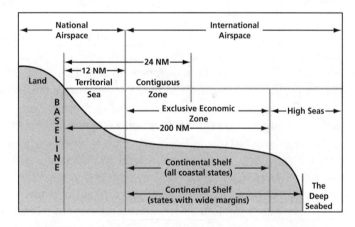

FIGURE 1. **Legal Boundaries of the Oceans and Airspace**

The extent of the coastal state's interests in the adjacent waters and subjacent seabed are variously expressed in terms of sovereignty, sovereign rights, jurisdiction and control, and various rights and freedoms, with "sovereignty" indicating the widest measure of rights and jurisdiction. As a general rule, the extent of the coastal state's rights and jurisdiction is inversely related to the distance seaward from the baseline. The convention makes it clear that all states that are party to it (the states parties) have a duty to exercise their rights, jurisdiction, and freedoms in a manner that does not constitute an abuse of rights and to fulfill in good faith their obligations under the convention.[35]

Despite the breadth of the LOS Convention, it is not and was not intended to be a complete or final codification of law governing maritime affairs; numerous other treaties and a surviving

---

33. See also Tommy T. B. Koh, A Constitution for the Oceans: The Law of the Sea in the United Nations Convention on the Law of the Sea xxxiv (1983).
34. Parts of the convention, such as Part XII on protection of the marine environment and Part XIII on marine scientific research, address issues that transcend a single zone.
35. See LOSC art. 299.

and evolving body of customary law supplement it. Most of the law applicable to vessels, their crews, and maritime activities is still found in the domestic law of the cognizant coastal and flag states. Finally, some at-sea activities are not governed by law at all, but rather by principles of comity, courtesy, and the sound judgment of seagoing officers.

7. Post–UNCLOS III Developments

The 1982 LOS Convention lays down a comprehensive regime for the world's oceans and seas. Although it did not enter into force until 1994, much of the world adhered to the convention between 1982 and 1994, creating a substantial body of customary law during that period.[36] Several other important developments occurred in the twelve years between the final session of UNCLOS III in 1982 and 1994, when the convention entered into force. In 1990, faced with the likelihood that the convention would enter into force without the participation of most of the developed states, Secretary-General Javier Pérez de Cuéllar brokered what would become the Agreement relating to the Implementation of Part XI of the United Nations Convention on the Law of the Sea of 10 December 1982. Working from a draft colloquially known as the "boat paper" (a reference to the illustration on its cover page), delegates developed and presented to the UN General Assembly a proposed substantial revision of the convention's deep seabed mining provisions. The Part XI Implementation Agreement was adopted by the General Assembly in 1995 and entered into force July 28, 1996.[37] The United States signed the Part XI Implementation Agreement in 1994, thereby qualifying for provisional membership in the International Seabed Authority (ISA). That membership ended in 1998, however, because the United States did not timely accede to the 1982 LOS Convention or ratify the Part XI agreement.

While the peacetime law of the sea was under development within the United Nations and other international organizations, an important project to clarify and modernize the law of naval warfare was launched by a group of international lawyers and naval experts, participating in their personal capacities, under the auspices of the International Institute of Humanitarian Law in San Remo, Italy, in 1988. In 1994 the institute adopted the *San Remo Manual on International Law Applicable to Armed Conflicts at Sea*. Among its many other important contributions, the manual provides a carefully reasoned reconciliation of the existing law of naval warfare with the new maritime zones set out in the 1982 LOS Convention, including the twelve-nautical-mile territorial sea, archipelagic waters, and EEZs, together with the rights of transit and archipelagic sea-lanes passage.

The future direction of the international law of the sea was shaped in part by four products that emerged from the 1992 UN Conference on Environment and Development (UNCED), known as the "Rio Earth Summit." UNCED produced the Rio Declaration on Environment and Development (the "Declaration of Principles"), Agenda 21 (an "action plan" for achieving sustainable development), the Convention on Biological Diversity, and the UN Framework Convention on Climate Change. Neither the Declaration of Principles nor Agenda 21 is a treaty, yet even as "soft law" they have had an important influence on the interpretation and implemen-

---

36. The relevant state practice was documented by the United Nations. See UN Division of Ocean Affairs and Law of the Sea, Practice of States at the Time of Entry into Force of the United Nations Convention on the Law of the Sea, U.N. Sales No. E.94.V.13 (1994).
37. Agreement relating to the Implementation of Part XI of the United Nations Convention on the Law of the Sea of 10 December 1982 [hereinafter "Part XI Implementation Agreement"], July 28, 1994, S. Treaty Doc. 103-39, 1836 U.N.T.S. 3, 33 I.L.M. 1309 (1994). The United States signed but has not ratified the agreement. See Bernard H. Oxman, The 1994 Agreement and the Convention, in Law of the Sea Forum: The 1994 Agreement on Implementation of the Seabed Provisions of the Convention on the Law of the Sea, 88 Am. J. Int'l L. 687 (1994).

tation of the LOS Convention. For example, prompted by a recommendation in Agenda 21, the UN General Assembly convened a diplomatic conference in 1995 to develop an agreement to promote effective implementation of the LOS Convention on certain fish stocks. The result, a second implementation agreement on conservation and management of straddling and highly migratory fish stocks, entered into force in 2001.[38]

The 1982 LOS Convention has aptly been described as a framework treaty that will serve as the centerpiece for a web of related international agreements and customary law on such subjects as fisheries conservation and management, environmental protection, and vessel safety and security. In its *M/V* Saiga decision, the first case filed in the International Tribunal for the Law of the Sea, the tribunal confirmed the continuing role of customary law in the international law of the sea. In that case the tribunal turned to customary law to assess whether a coastal state's enforcement officers had used excessive force in stopping and boarding a foreign-flag vessel, a subject not addressed by the LOS Convention.[39]

Not all developments in the law of the sea since 1982 have been the product of formal international lawmaking processes, and some developments are the subject of growing concern, particularly those characterized as "creeping jurisdiction."[40] Examples include idiosyncratic interpretations or applications of the rules on drawing baselines and assertions of substantive rights or jurisdiction that exceed those permitted by the LOS Convention (both are discussed in later chapters). One of the more notorious and potentially threatening coastal state assertions is China's U-Shaped "Nine-Dash-Line" claim to sovereignty over virtually all of the South China Sea.[41] Iran's recurring threat to retaliate against international sanctions by blocking passage through the Strait of Hormuz is also a cause of grave international concern. The growing number of at-sea encounters between competing claimants and the reluctance of some states to submit such claims to arbitration or adjudication has created serious regional security situations. A few writers have suggested convening an "UNCLOS IV" to address perceived weaknesses in the 1982 LOS Convention, but most consider the probability that such a conference would succeed remote.

Nevertheless, change is to be expected. No one suggests that the law of the sea has reached an "end of history." Indeed, the history so far reflects an ongoing effort to accommodate the interests of coastal and maritime states while also adapting to meet the challenges posed by new technologies and ocean usages. It would be shortsighted to fear or resist adaptation in the law to those new technologies and usages. International law, including the LOS Convention, provides legitimate mechanisms and processes for adapting the law to new challenges and opportunities. That process is increasingly facilitated and institutionalized by international organizations.

C. INTERNATIONAL ORGANIZATIONS AND THE LAW OF THE SEA

International law creates international organizations (IOs) and defines their mission. Some of those IOs in turn help to create, interpret, implement, and amend the international legal regime

38. UN Agreement for the Implementation of the Provisions of the United Nations Convention on the Law of the Sea of 10 December 1982 relating to the Conservation and Management of Straddling Fish Stocks and Highly Migratory Fish Stocks [hereinafter "Straddling Fish Stocks Agreement"], Aug. 4, 1995, S. Treaty Doc. No. 104-24, 2167 U.N.T.S. 88, 34 I.L.M. 1542 (1995). The United States is a party.
39. M/V *Saiga* (St. Vincent & the Grenadines v. Guinea), ITLOS Case No. 2, Judgment of July 1, 1999, 38 I.L.M. 1323 (1999). The tribunal explained that in the absence of LOS Convention provisions on the use of force in the arrest of ships, the court will turn to customary international law, which is applicable in ITLOS proceedings by virtue of Article 293 of the LOSC.
40. Bernard H. Oxman, The Territorial Temptation: A Siren Song at Sea, 100 Am. J. Int'l L. 830, 837–49 (2006).
41. Masahiro Miyoshi, China's "U-Shaped Line" Claim in the South China Sea: Any Validity under International Law? 43 Ocean Dev. & Int'l L. 1 (2012).

and monitor compliance, while also providing technical, scientific, and financial resources to states in need of assistance in developing the necessary means to effectively carry out their obligations. International organizations may be global or regional, and their missions may be general or specialized. Many of the IOs described below contribute to the UN secretary-general's annual reports on ocean affairs and the law of the sea.

1. The UN and the Law of the Sea

In contrast to several other global conventions, the 1982 LOS Convention did not establish a new implementing international organization or secretariat or call for regular meetings by a conference of the parties.[42] The UNCLOS III conferees chose instead to assign a number of the organizational duties to the secretary-general of the UN. Those duties include receiving and maintaining the instruments of ratification or accession and the charts and coordinates deposited by states showing the maritime limits of their offshore zones. The UN also directly supports the work of the Commission on the Limits of the Continental Shelf. The LOS Convention calls on the secretary-general to convene meetings of states parties, at which the parties elect the members of the International Tribunal for the Law of the Sea and adopt its budget. Meetings of states parties (referred to by the acronym SPLOS, for "states parties to the Law of the Sea Convention") may also be convened for review conferences dealing, for example, with the provisions on deep seabed mining or for amending the convention.

Recognizing the need for an ongoing periodic review of law of the sea issues, in 1999 the UN General Assembly established the UN Open-Ended Informal Consultative Process on Oceans and the Law of the Sea (ICP).[43] The UN Division for Ocean Affairs and the Law of the Sea (DOALOS) plays a key facilitation role in the annual ICP process.[44] DOALOS bears the laboring oar in preparing the secretary-general's annual report on ocean affairs and the law of the sea and assists and advises states in the integration of the marine sector in their development planning. DOALOS also coordinates with the secretariats of related conventions, such as the Convention on Biological Diversity and the UN Commission on Sustainable Development, which monitors progress on the Agenda 21 plan of action. The ICJ, the principal judicial arm of the UN, has long played a role in the development of the law of the sea. Its role is examined in chapter 15, and many of its decisions are cited in other chapters.

2. International Organizations Established by the 1982 LOS Convention

The 1982 LOS Convention called for the establishment of three specialized entities: the International Seabed Authority (ISA), the International Tribunal for the Law of the Sea (ITLOS), and the Commission on the Limits of the Continental Shelf (CLCS). The final act of UNCLOS III directed the UN secretary-general to convene a preparatory commission (Prepcom) after fifty states had signed or acceded to the convention. The Prepcom was charged with making the necessary preparations to establish the ISA and ITLOS. In 1994 the ISA was established in Kingston, Jamaica. ITLOS was established in Hamburg, Germany, that same year and began its work in 1996. The twenty-one-member CLCS was established in 1997 and presently operates

---

42. Article 319 of the LOS Convention does make provision for the UN secretary-general to "convene necessary meetings of States Parties in accordance with this Convention." Since 1994, the UN has hosted annual meetings of states parties to the Law of the Sea Convention.

43. See generally Serguei Tarassenko & Ilaria Tani, The Function and Role of the United Nations Secretariat in Ocean Affairs and the Law of the Sea, 27 Int'l J. Marine & Coastal L. 683 (2012).

44. See Secretary-General's Bulletin ST/SGB/1997/8 (Organization of the Office of Legal Affairs) ¶ 7.2.

out of the UN headquarters in New York. It adopted its rules of procedure in 1997 and its scientific and technical guidelines in 1999. The CLCS received its first extended continental shelf
submission (from Russia) in 2001 and issued its first recommendation in 2002. The organization
and function of these three IOs are more fully described in the chapters that follow.

3. The International Maritime Organization

The International Maritime Organization (IMO), originally established as the Inter-governmental Maritime Consultative Organization (IMCO) by a 1948 convention, is the first global institution established to focus on marine affairs and marine environmental protection.[45] The IMO
formally began operations in 1959 and has the status of a "specialized agency" of the United
Nations in accordance with Article 57 of the UN Charter. Its mission is to facilitate cooperation
among states on technical matters affecting international shipping in order to achieve the highest
practicable standards of maritime safety and efficiency in navigation. The central importance of
the organization's role is made apparent by the frequent references in the 1982 LOS Convention
to standards established through the "competent international organization," in most cases a
reference to the IMO.[46]

The IMO follows the organizational design common among international organizations,
consisting of an assembly and council, a secretariat headed by a secretary-general, and specialized committees. Perhaps its best-known committee, the Maritime Safety Committee (MSC), is
responsible for the safety of navigation, radio communication, life-saving arrangements, search
and rescue, ship design and equipment, fire protection, standards of training and watch-keeping,
containers and cargoes, and the carriage of dangerous goods. The Marine Environment Protection Committee (MEPC) is charged with administering and coordinating the activities concerning the prevention and control of marine pollution. The Legal Committee is responsible for all
legal matters within the mandate of the IMO and also prepares draft legal instruments for the
IMO Council. The Technical Cooperation Committee plays a key role in promoting sustainable
development in the marine sector. It has responsibility for the establishment of directives and
guidelines for the execution and review of the program of assistance to developing countries in
maritime transport. The IMO also sponsors the World Maritime University in Malmö, Sweden;
the International Maritime Law Institute in Msida, Malta; and the International Maritime Academy in Trieste, Italy.

4. The Food and Agriculture Organization

The Food and Agriculture Organization (FAO) was established as a specialized agency of the
UN in 1945. Its mission is to raise the level of nutrition and standards of living; improve the
production, processing, marketing, and distribution of food, agricultural products, and fisheries;
and to eliminate hunger. It carries out its mandate through four activities: putting needed information within reach, sharing policy expertise, providing a meeting place for nations, and
applying knowledge in the field.

The FAO also roughly follows the organizational design common among international
organizations. A conference of all member states meets biennially and elects the council and

---

45. Convention on the Inter-governmental Consultative Organization [hereinafter "IMO Convention"], Mar. 6,
    1948, 9 U.S.T. 621, 289 U.N.T.S. 48. IMCO was renamed International Maritime Organization in 1982.
46. See IMO, Implications of the United Nations Convention on the Law of the Sea for the International Maritime
    Organization, IMO Doc. LEG/MISC.6, Sept. 10, 2008. For a discussion of the phrase, see Definitions for the Law
    of the Sea: Terms Not Defined by the 1982 Law of the Sea Convention 137–49 (George K. Walker ed., 2012).

the director-general, who heads the FAO Secretariat. One of the five major committees within the FAO, the Committee on Fisheries (COFI), reviews the FAO's work in the field of fisheries, conducts periodic general reviews of international fishery problems, examines other specific matters relating to fisheries, and makes recommendations for their resolution. Much of the FAO's fishery activity is carried out through its regional commissions or in cooperation with regional fishery bodies.

5. Regional Seas Programmes

Since 1974, groups of states have entered into cooperative "regional seas" arrangements to improve the marine environment in their region. By early 2013 eighteen such agreements establishing Regional Seas Programmes had been concluded. Regional Seas Programmes are now in place in the northeast and northwest Pacific, the Baltic and Mediterranean Seas, the Persian Gulf, the Caribbean, and a dozen other regions, including the Arctic and Antarctic. The UN Environment Programme (UNEP) facilitates the Regional Seas Programme. The programs are examined more closely in chapter 10.

6. Other International Organizations with Cognizance over Law of the Sea Issues

Several other organizations have made notable contributions on law of the sea issues. The UN Educational, Scientific, and Cultural Organization (UNESCO) developed a treaty on the protection of underwater cultural heritage.[47] UNESCO's Intergovernmental Oceanographic Commission (IOC) plays an important role in the promotion of marine scientific research. The UN Conference on Trade and Development (UNCTAD) has addressed the transfer of marine technology and such shipping questions as treatment of vessels in ports and flags of convenience. The International Atomic Energy Agency, International Labor Organization, World Health Organization, and World Meteorological Organization also serve important roles, as do the Arctic Council, the International Whaling Commission, and other regional fisheries management organizations (RFMOs). The International Institute for Humanitarian Law in San Remo, Italy, produces manuals and training materials on the law of naval warfare. Informal organizations such as the North Pacific and the North Atlantic Coast Guard forums serve important coordination functions. Finally, mention must be made of the World Trade Organization. Although its competency is limited to international trade in goods and services and cross-border investments, the WTO's General Agreement on Tariffs and Trade (GATT) has been featured in several high-profile disputes over U.S. efforts to protect dolphin and turtle stocks by imposing import restrictions on tuna and shrimp respectively.[48] In addition, Article V of the GATT provides for the freedom of "traffic in transit," which extends to vessels and other means of transport.

---

47. Convention on the Protection of the Underwater Cultural Heritage, Nov. 6, 2001, 2562 U.N.T.S. 1, 41 I.L.M. 40 (2002). The United States did not sign the convention and is not expected to ratify or accede to it. See generally Jean Allain, Maritime Wrecks: Where the Lex Ferenda of Underwater Cultural Heritage Collides with the Lex Lata of the Law of the Sea Convention, 38 Va. J. Int'l L. 747 (1998).
48. See generally Marrakesh Agreement Establishing the World Trade Organization, Annex 1A, The Legal Texts: The Results of the Uruguay Round of Multilateral Trade Negotiations (1999), 1867 U.N.T.S. 14, 33 I.L.M. 1143 (1994).

D. THE UNITED STATES AND THE LAW OF THE SEA CONVENTIONS

The United States ratified all four of the 1958 Geneva conventions and is still formally a party to them. The fact that most other states parties to the 1958 conventions have denounced them in favor of the 1982 LOS Convention, however, limits the relevance of the 1958 conventions as a matter of international law.[49] As a matter of domestic law, the fact that the United States is a party to the 1958 conventions is important because treaties are the "law of the land" under Article VI of the U.S. Constitution. Moreover, Congress has given express recognition to the continuing relevance of the 1958 conventions by incorporating some of their terms into federal statutes. For example, the Drug Trafficking Vessel Interdiction Act, enacted by Congress in 2008, refers to Article 5 of the 1958 Convention on the High Seas in addressing vessel documentation requirements.[50] Similarly, the Maritime Drug Law Enforcement Act refers to the same 1958 convention in defining a vessel without nationality.[51]

The United States declined to sign the 1982 LOS Convention, citing objections to its deep seabed mining regime. Since 1983, however, the United States has taken the position that most of the 1982 LOS Convention articles other than the deep seabed provisions represent customary international law. In the 1983 U.S. Oceans Policy Statement, President Ronald Reagan declared, with respect to the convention, that "the United States is prepared to accept and act in accordance with the balance of interests relating to traditional uses of the oceans—such as navigation and overflight. In this respect, the United States will recognize the rights of other States in the waters off their coasts, as reflected in the Convention, so long as the rights and freedoms of the United States and others under international law are recognized by such coastal States."[52]

In 1983 President Reagan also proclaimed a two-hundred-nautical-mile exclusive economic zone.[53] At more than 3.3 million square nautical miles, the U.S. EEZ is the largest and arguably the richest in the world. Five years later, the president issued a second proclamation,[54] extending the U.S. territorial sea from three nautical miles to twelve nautical miles, but only for international law purposes. It is important to note that some U.S. statutes still define the U.S. territorial sea, for purposes of that particular statute, as extending seaward only three nautical miles. As a result, those U.S. laws will not apply to activities beyond three nautical miles unless and until Congress amends the statutes. Finally, in 1999, President Bill Clinton exercised the presidential proclamation power to extend the U.S. contiguous zone seaward from the outer edge of the twelve-nautical-mile territorial sea to a distance of twenty-four nautical miles from the baseline.[55] The contiguous zone proclamation raised international law questions for some, who pointed out that as a party to the 1958 Convention on the Territorial Sea and Contiguous Zone, the United States was bound by the twelve-nautical-mile seaward limit on contiguous zones under Article 24 of that convention.

In 1994, after the UN General Assembly adopted the Part XI Implementation Agreement amending the 1982 LOS Convention's seabed mining provisions, President Clinton presented

---

49. Article 311(1) leaves open possible application of the 1958 conventions between a state that ratified or acceded to the 1982 LOS Convention but did not denounce the 1958 convention and another state that is a party to the 1958 convention but has not ratified or acceded to the 1982 LOS Convention (e.g., the United States).
50. 46 U.S.C. § 70508(c)(2)(A).
51. See, e.g., 46 U.S.C. § 70502(b)(2)(A), (c)(1)(B), & (e)(2).
52. Statement by the President [hereinafter "Ocean Policy Statement"], 19 Weekly Comp. Pres. Doc. 383 (Mar. 10, 1983); U.S. Oceans Policy, 83 Dep't State Bull., June 1983, at 70, 22 I.L.M. 464 (1983).
53. Proclamation 5030, Exclusive Economic Zone of the U.S., Mar. 10, 1983, 3 C.F.R. § 22 (1984).
54. Proclamation 5928, Territorial Sea of the U.S., Dec. 27, 1988, 3 C.F.R. § 546 (1989).
55. Proclamation 7219, Contiguous Zone of the U.S., Sept. 2, 1999, 3 C.F.R. § 7219 (1999).

the LOS Convention and Part XI Implementation Agreement to the Senate for its advice and consent.[56] Under Article II of the U.S. Constitution, approval by a two-thirds majority of the Senate is required for U.S. accession. So far, that advice and consent has been withheld.

The decision to become a party to the 1982 LOS Convention, as modified by the Part XI Implementation Agreement, remains surprisingly controversial. The first recommendation to come out of the blue ribbon U.S. Commission on Ocean Policy, chaired by former chief of naval operations and secretary of energy James Watkins, was a recommendation that the United States accede to the 1982 Convention.[57] On February 25, 2004, the Senate Committee on Foreign Relations, with the support of the administration of President George W. Bush, unanimously recommended to the full Senate that the United States accede to the 1982 LOS Convention and the Agreement relating to the Implementation of Part XI.[58] The committee's recommendation was subject to four "declarations" and twenty-two "understandings." Most of the committee's recommended declarations and understandings were adopted from the Clinton administration's 1994 letter transmitting the convention to the Senate for its advice and consent and the attached ninety-seven-page commentary on the convention's articles prepared by the Department of State.[59] The Clinton administration understandings were in turn largely consistent with the position of the U.S. delegation during the UNCLOS III negotiations and with President Reagan's 1983 Ocean Policy Statement, but also reflected the changes made by the 1994 Part XI Implementation Agreement.[60]

Because the full Senate did not vote on the committee's 2004 recommendation before the end of the 108th Congress, the matter was returned to the committee. In 2007 the committee again held hearings and favorably reported out the convention, yet the recommendation again failed to reach the full Senate for a vote. The 2007 committee recommendation was, like the 2004 recommendation, subject to proposed declarations and understandings.[61] Although the full Senate has not yet acted, the committee's proposed declarations and understandings are an important interpretive aid for U.S. practitioners. They are reproduced in appendix D and are frequently referred to in later chapters because the seagoing officer should be aware of the position the United States has taken and will defend through such measures as the freedom of navigation program.[62] At the same, time, because the United States is not a party to the LOS

---

56. President's Message to Congress Transmitting United Nations Convention on the Law of the Sea, with Annexes, Dec. 10, 1982, S. Treaty Doc. 103-39 (1994), reprinted in Annotated Supplement to the Commander's Handbook on the Law of Naval Operations [hereinafter "Annotated Supplement to Commander's Handbook"], annex A1-2, NWP 1-14M (1997). Paragraph numbering in the 1997 Annotated Supplement does not always coincide with the numbering in the current (2007) edition of the nonannotated *Handbook*.

57. See U.S. Commission on Ocean Policy, An Ocean Blueprint for the 21st Century 444–45 (2004).

58. Senate Committee on Foreign Relations, Report on the United Nations Convention on the Law of the Sea, S. Exec. Rpt. 110-09 (Dec. 18, 2007). See also William L. Schachte Jr., The Unvarnished Truth: The Debate on the Law of the Sea Convention, 61 Naval War College Rev. 119 (2008).

59. "Understandings" attached to treaties are binding under domestic law. See Auguste v. Ridge, 395 F.3d 123, 142 (3d Cir. 2005); Avero Belgium Ins. v. American Airlines Inc., 423 F.3d 73, 79 (2d Cir. 2005) (en banc) (a treaty acceded to by the United States with a statement of understanding becomes effective only subject to that understanding).

60. See, e.g., Third United Nations Conference on the Law of the Sea, Montego Bay, Jamaica, Note by the Secretariat, at 243–44, U.N. Doc. A/CONF.62/WS/37 (Dec. 10, 1982).

61. Senate Committee on Foreign Relations, Report on the United Nations Convention on the Law of the Sea, S. Exec. Rpt. No. 110-9 (the committee's proposed declarations, understandings, and conditions are reproduced in appendix D). A tabular side-by-side comparison of the committee's 2004 and 2007 proposed understandings is available in J. Ashley Roach & Robert W. Smith, Excessive Maritime Claims, appendix 9, at 775–814 (3d ed. 2012).

62. To the extent the Senate understandings and those recommended by the Clinton administration in presenting the LOS Convention to the Senate reflect the U.S. position throughout UNCLOS III, they are evidence of the "ordinary meaning" of the convention's terms.

Convention, the understandings—read in conjunction with the 1983 Ocean Policy Statement—also represent the U.S. position on the analogous customary international law rules.

In 2012 the Senate Committee on Foreign Relations convened a third round of hearings on the convention.[63] Convention proponents and opponents again exchanged views on the convention's merits, the relationship between conventional and customary international law, revenue sharing with respect to resources extracted from the extended continental shelf, the role of international organizations, and the merits of a compulsory process for adjusting disputes between and among states.[64] A recurring point of contention concerned the effect of accession to the convention on U.S. sovereignty (particularly the requirements for compulsory dispute settlement) and security (potential restrictions on "military activities"). Despite letters and testimony in support of accession from the Departments of Defense, State, and Homeland Security; the chairman of the joint chiefs of staff; the chief of naval operations; and the commandant of the Coast Guard, the 2012 initiative failed to even reach a vote within the committee before the 112th congressional term expired in January 2013.

Given the uncertain fate of the LOS Convention in the U.S. Senate, the following discussion approaches the law of the sea through two frameworks. It draws primarily on the 1982 LOS Convention, which is a treaty binding on more than 160 states, but at the same time it examines the extent to which the LOS Convention articles accurately reflect customary international law. Whether any given rule of the international law of the sea is based on a treaty or customary law has important ramifications in domestic courts of the United States. Under Article VI of the U.S. Constitution treaties are "law of the land" (see chapter 1), and if a provision of the treaty is self-executing, it will preempt conflicting state law. The relationship between treaties and the other sources of federal law is somewhat more complicated. In U.S. domestic courts the federal Constitution is superior to treaties or statutes, but treaties and statutes are equal in legal stature.[65] In cases in which both a treaty and a statute are on point, the court will endeavor to give effect to both if fairly possible. Moreover, even though Congress has the power to supersede a treaty by statute, courts generally will find that a later statute has superseded a treaty only if Congress' intent to do so is clear.[66] If such an intent is clear, the last-in-time rule controls.[67] Should application of the last-in-time rule in the domestic system result in a violation of the treaty, however, the United States would be in breach of its international obligation.

Chapter 1 briefly introduced the concept of self-executing treaties. In the early days of the Republic, Chief Justice John Marshall determined that not all treaties have direct application in U.S. courts. In *Foster and Elam v. Neilson*, the Court explained that

> a treaty is in its nature a contract between two nations, not a Legislative Act. It does not generally effect, in itself, the object to be accomplished [i.e., it is

---

63. For a collection of essays on the merits of accession to the convention by military, government, and academic experts, see The Law of the Sea Convention: US Accession and Globalization (Myron H. Nordquist et al. eds., 2012).

64. For a chronology of actions taken in the U.S. Senate, see U.S. Library of Congress "Thomas" entries for S. Treaty Doc. 103-39, at http://thomas.loc.gov/cgi-bin/ntquery/z?trtys:103TD00039 (accessed Feb. 1, 2013).

65. The Cherokee Tobacco, 78 U.S. (11 Wall.) 616 (1870).

66. The Head Money Cases, 112 U.S. 580 (1884).

67. Whitney v. Robinson, 124 U.S. 190 (1888) (holding that a later-in-time statute prevails over a treaty); Cook v. U.S., 288 U.S. 102 (1933) (holding that a later-in-time treaty prevails over a statute). See also U.S. v. Ray, 423 F.2d 16 (5th Cir. 1970) (explaining that, to the extent that any of the terms of the 1953 Outer Continental Shelf Lands Act are inconsistent with the later-ratified 1958 Geneva Convention on the Continental Shelf, "they should be considered superseded"). The court in *U.S. v. Ray* failed to distinguish between self-executing and non-self-executing provisions of the convention.

not self-executing], especially so far as its operation is infra-territorial; but is carried into execution by the sovereign power of the respective parties to the instrument.

In the United States, a different principle is established. Our Constitution declares a treaty to be the law of the land. It is, consequently, to be regarded in courts of justice as equivalent to an Act of the Legislature, whenever it operates of itself without the aid of any legislative provision. But when the terms of the stipulation import a contract, when either of the parties engages to perform a particular act, the treaty addresses itself to the political, not the judicial department; and the legislature must execute the contract before it can become a rule for the Court.[68]

In the years since that 1829 decision, U.S. courts have been called on numerous times to distinguish those treaties (or, more accurately, those individual provisions of treaties) that are self-executing from those that are not.[69] Nevertheless, the self-execution question remains "perhaps one of the most confounding in treaty law."[70]

Of particular relevance to the seagoing officer is the principle that should the Senate give its advice and consent and the president accede to the 1982 LOS Convention, the effect of any given provision of the convention in the courts of the United States will turn on whether that provision is self-executing.[71] In examining the predecessor 1958 Convention on the High Seas, the U.S. Court of Appeals for the Fifth Circuit held that Article 6 of that convention, which confers exclusive jurisdiction over vessels on the high seas on the vessel's flag state, was not self-executing.[72] The Senate's proposed declarations and understandings expressly address which sections of the 1982 LOS Convention it has determined would be self-executing if the United States accedes to the convention.[73] Additionally, Congress may limit a criminal defendant's right to invoke international law defenses, as it has in the Maritime Drug Law Enforcement Act.[74]

The effect of a rule of customary international law in U.S. courts is more tenuous. The role of customary law and its relationship to domestic law in the United States was famously articulated by Justice Gray in the *Paquete* Habana decision:

International law is part of our law, and must be ascertained and administered by the courts of justice of appropriate jurisdiction as often as questions of right

---

68. Foster and Elam v. Neilson, 27 U.S. (2 Pet.) 253, 314 (1829); Cornejo v. County of San Diego, 504 F.3d 853, 856 (9th Cir. 2007) (holding that for "any treaty to be susceptible to judicial enforcement it must both confer individual rights and be self-executing"); Restatement FRLUS § 111(4); Louis Henkin, Foreign Affairs and the Constitution 198–204 (2d ed. 1996).

69. The Court recently examined the self-executing treaty doctrine in Medellín v. Texas, 522 U.S. 491 (2008). Federal courts have made it clear that the question whether a treaty provision is self-executing is distinct from the question whether the provision creates a private right of action. The Supreme Court has also held that private rights of action to enforce federal law must be created by Congress. Alexander v. Sandoval, 532 U.S. 275, 286 (2001).

70. U.S. v. Postal, 589 F.2d 862, 876 (5th Cir. 1979).

71. At least some parts of the UN Charter are not self-executing. Sei Fujii, v. California, 242 P.2d 617 (Cal. 1952) (holding that Articles 55 and 56 are not self-executing); Medellín v. Texas, 522 U.S. at 508–09 (Article 94 is not self-executing). See also Flores v. S. Peru Copper Corp., 414 F.3d 233, 250, n.24 (2d Cir. 2003); Frolova v. USSR, 761 F.2d 370, 373–74 (7th Cir. 1985).

72. U.S. v. Postal, 589 F.2d at 884.

73. See S. Exec. Rpt. No. 110-9, understanding 24 (reprinted in appendix D). In addition to those listed in the committee's draft understandings, Articles 290(6) and 292(4) might be deemed self-executing.

74. 46 U.S.C. § 70505.

depending upon it are duly presented for their determination. For this purpose, where there is no treaty and no controlling executive or legislative act or judicial decision, resort must be had to the customs and usages of civilized nations, and, as evidence of these, to the works of jurists and commentators who by years of labor, research, and experience have made themselves peculiarly well acquainted with the subjects of which they treat. Such works are resorted to by judicial tribunals, not for the speculations of their authors concerning what the law ought to be, but for trustworthy evidence of what the law really is.[75]

Two aspects of the decision stand out. First, although customary international law is part of "our" law, the Court has made it clear that—as a matter of U.S. law—customary law can be overridden by a "treaty on point," or a "controlling executive or legislative act or judicial decision." As chapter 1 explains, Congress can (and sometimes does) legislate in excess of international law limits. Accordingly, even with respect to customary law, the United States is a dualist state in which domestic legislation can displace customary law. The second point—a question of greatest concern to lawyers and judges, not mariners—is that the Court, in characterizing customary law as "our" law, failed to specify whether it was referring to our federal law or our general common law, a question best explored in other sources.[76] There is a marked tendency to read too much into the Court's finding that international law applied in the *Paquete* Habana case. The case concerned application of prize law during an armed conflict with Spain, which the Court acknowledged was necessarily governed by international law. In addition, a key presidential proclamation had directed that the United States was to conduct itself during the conflict in accordance with international law.

Whether or not the U.S. Supreme Court's decision in *Paquete* Habana is understood to suggest that customary international law is self-executing even beyond prize cases, and can be applied by the courts without congressional implementation (as Congress has done in the Alien Tort Statute and the statute criminalizing piracy), courts may still be reluctant to base their decisions solely on customary law, especially if the executive branch argues against such an application.[77] Nevertheless, customary law serves an important interpretive role in the United States. In a well-known interpretative canon announced in *Murray v. The Schooner* Charming Betsy, the Supreme Court held that an "act of Congress ought never to be construed to violate the law of nations if any other possible construction remains."[78] Adherence to this canon of construction reduces the chances that the United States will violate an international obligation.

E. THE 1982 LOS CONVENTION AS CUSTOMARY INTERNATIONAL LAW

Several nations, particularly in the early years following completion of the 1982 LOS Convention, argued that the convention was an "all or nothing" package deal, and that a state could not

---

75. The Paquete *Habana* 175 U.S. 677, 700 (1900).
76. See, e.g., Curtis A. Bradley, International Law in the U.S. Legal System ch. 5 (2013) (concluding that it is unlikely that customary international law has the status of "federal law" under Article III or Article VI of the Constitution); Sampson v. Fed. Rep. of Germany, 250 F.3d 1145, 1152–53 & n.4 (7th Cir. 2001).
77. Phillip R. Trimble, A Revisionist View of Customary International Law, 33 UCLA L. Rev. 665 (1983). See Agora: May the President Violate Customary International Law? 80 Am. J. Int'l L. 913 (1986) (commenting on Garcia-Mir v. Meese, 788 F.2d 1146 [11th Cir. 1986]); Michael D. Ramsey, The Constitution's Text in Foreign Affairs 342–61 (2007).
78. Murray v. The Schooner *Charming Betsy*, 6 U.S. (2 Cranch) 64, 118 (1804).

take advantage of the convention's favorable articles unless it was a party.[79] Nevertheless, many of those same states claimed rights set out in the convention during the twelve-year period before the convention entered into force. For example, a number of states claimed two-hundred-nautical-mile EEZs well before the 1982 LOS Convention entered into force—some even before the convention was opened for signature in 1982. The only legal basis for doing so would have been that the rights set out in the convention already reflected customary international law.

It is a well-established principle of international law that treaties generally bind only states that manifest their consent to be bound; they do not create rights or obligations for nonparties.[80] It is equally well established, however, that one or more of the terms of a given treaty may codify customary international law when written, or may later ripen into a rule of customary law.[81] Under such circumstances, even states that have not ratified the treaty are bound by the rule of customary international law it incorporates; at least if the state has not persistently objected to the rule as it developed.[82] In the 1969 *North Sea Continental Shelf* cases, the ICJ acknowledged that there is "no doubt that this process is a perfectly possible one and does from time to time occur: it constitutes indeed one of the recognized methods by which new rules of customary international law may be formed."[83] The court cautioned, however, that "this result is not lightly to be regarded as having been attained."

The *Restatement (Third) of Foreign Relations Law of the United States*, published in 1987, takes the position that many of the LOS Convention articles represent customary law.[84] That position was controversial at the time the *Restatement* was published, but the position that most of the convention reflects customary law has gained general acceptance in the intervening decades. For example, in 1985, almost a decade before the 1982 LOS Convention entered into force, the ICJ concluded in the *Libya-Malta Continental Self* case that it is "incontestable" that the convention's EEZ regime has become part of customary international law.[85] In a 2012 maritime dispute between Nicaragua and Colombia, the ICJ determined that a number of LOS Convention articles reflect customary international law and were therefore binding on Colombia, a nonparty to the convention.[86]

The U.S. decision not to accede to the LOS Convention and to rely instead on customary international law to protect its interests poses a number of diplomatic and operational risks. To meet the burden of proof on international law rules announced in the *S.S.* Lotus case, a state that is a party to the LOS Convention and wishes to invoke it against another state party faces a comparatively easy task: the existence of a rule and its content are established by reference to the convention. By contrast, a state forced to rely on customary international law in its claim against another state must prove both that a rule of customary law exists and the terms of that

79. The introduction to the official version of the convention emphasizes that it is "the conceptual underpinnings of the Convention as a 'package' which is its most significant quality. . . . It became the leitmotiv of the Conference and in fact permeates the law of the sea as it exists today."

80. Vienna Convention on Treaties, supra, art. 34.

81. Id. art. 38.

82. The 1982 LOS Convention recognizes this effect in Article 317(3), which cautions that even after a state renounces the 1982 Convention as a treaty, some of its terms may nevertheless be binding (as customary law).

83. North Sea Continental Shelf cases (Fed. Rep. Germany v. Denmark/Fed. Rep. Germany v. Netherlands), ¶ 71, 1969 I.C.J. 3 (Feb. 20).

84. Restatement FRLUS, introduction to Pt. V. See also William T. Burke, Customary Law of the Sea: Advocacy or Disinterested Scholarship? 14 Yale J. Int'l L. 508 (1989).

85. Continental Shelf case (Libya v. Malta) 1985 I.C.J. 13 (June 3).

86. See Territorial and Maritime Dispute (Nicaragua v. Colombia), 2012 I.C.J. (Nov. 19) (concluding that the twelve-nautical-mile territorial sea and LOSC articles 13, 76(1), and 121 are customary law).

rule. The latter requirement should not be taken lightly.[87] There is little doubt that customary law recognizes the rights of innocent, transit, and archipelagic sea-lanes passage; however, it will be no easy task to establish that the customary law rule is identical with the detailed articles in the LOS Convention. Establishing state practice as evidence of custom when the vast majority of the states today are acting in accordance with their rights and obligations as a party to the 1982 Convention may also prove difficult.

F. RECOMMENDED APPROACH TO INTERNATIONAL LAW OF THE SEA QUESTIONS

International law operates over all five domains of human activity: land, sea, airspace, outer space, and cyberspace. The current legal regime for the oceans has been under development for more than four hundred years. Nevertheless, determining and applying international law to maritime affairs continues to be challenging, even for attorneys who have practiced in the field for decades. The existence of a rule may be contested, its terms might be obscure, and it might come into conflict with another rule. The seagoing officer can therefore be forgiven for feeling challenged by poorly or incompletely understood legal rules.

A staff judge advocate or other legal adviser soon learns that the questions commonly posed by clients generally fall into one of three categories. First, there are questions concerning issues in which the law applies and its terms are sufficiently clear that the legal adviser can provide the commander or operator with a reliable legal opinion. The second category consists of questions concerning issues for which there is some law on point, but the law is not entirely clear. The answer might therefore more closely resemble a navigator's estimated position than a pinpoint fix. A third category of questions consists of those on which there might be some relevant law, but none is directly on point, and the choice on a course of action lies largely in the domain of policy and operational judgment. Regardless of the category, the best lawyers are careful to distinguish legal advice from policy recommendations and to warn the client of any uncertainties in the state of the law.

In approaching international law questions, the reader is encouraged to first clarify the source of the law or laws that control. Chapter 1 identifies the accepted sources of international law, including treaties, customary law, and general principles, together with secondary evidence of the law such as international and national judicial decisions and the works of publicists. Although treaties certainly dominate international maritime law, the temptation to turn reflexively and exclusively to treaties must be resisted. Treaties apply only between states that have ratified them. In the absence of a treaty between the parties, resort must be to customary international law. Further, states commonly enter reservations when they ratify multilateral conventions. Assuming the reservation is valid, the treaty must be applied to the reserving state consistent with its reservation. Finally, treaties may also be amended from time to time. It is therefore important to ensure that whatever treaty text is relied on is up to date and that the parties involved have both ratified the amendments.

Treaty interpretation always begins with the text.[88] In most cases, it also ends there—but not always. One sea-minded legal academic likens legal terms to nautical terminology: some terms are pinpoint clear (e.g., "noon" and "midnight") while other terms suggest not a point but rather

---

87. See ILA, Committee on Formation of Customary (General) International Law: Final Report of the Committee (2000). Part IV addresses the interplay between treaties and customary law rules.

88. A useful reference for interpreting terms used but not defined in the LOS Convention is Professor George Walker's Definitions for the Law of the Sea (2011). The U.S. Supreme Court has consistently emphasized that treaty interpretation begins with the text. For a recent example of the Court's approach to treaty interpretation,

a range (e.g., "dusk" and "twilight"). The LOS Convention's definition of a low-tide elevation in Article 13 would seem to fall into the first category, while the Article 121(3) definition of a mere "rock" might leave the mariner feeling a bit "dusky." Established interpretation methods require that the treaty's terms be given their ordinary meeting unless a specialized meaning was intended. Account must be taken of the treaty's object and purpose. On occasion, subsequent practice of the states in applying the treaty may also be relevant.[89] However, state practice must be approached with caution. The Vienna Convention on the Law of Treaties limits "subsequent practice in the application of the treaty" to that "which establishes the agreement of the parties regarding its interpretation."[90] More important, the common understanding of two or more parties to a treaty on the meaning to be given to the treaty's terms does not necessarily affect the meaning ascribed to the term by states not participating in the practice or to an analogous customary international law rule.

When resorting to the works of publicists, one should bear in mind that not all treatises are given equal weight as "evidence" of international law. Three have stood the test of time in the law of the sea field. They include Colombos' *The International Law of the Sea*, O'Connell's two-volume *The International Law of the Sea*, and McDougal and Burke's *Public Order of the Oceans*.[91] As those venerable treatises began to show some age, *The Law of the Sea* by Robin Churchill and Vaughan Lowe emerged as one of the most respected English-language treatises.[92] *The International Law of the Sea* by the Australian team of Donald Rothwell and Tim Stephens is also excellent.[93] In addition, a thorough and meticulous examination of the 1982 LOS Convention and its negotiating history is available in the multivolume *United Nations Convention on the Law of the Sea, 1982: A Commentary* prepared by Myron Nordquist and others under the auspices of the University of Virginia Center for Oceans Law and Policy (sometimes called the "Virginia Commentaries"). The seven-volume commentaries, published between 1985 and 2011, provide a detailed article-by-article analysis of the LOS Convention. In its first decision, ITLOS hailed Professor Nordquist's commentaries as the "most authoritative" source on the 1982 convention.[94]

The writings of scholars who participated actively and extensively in UNCLOS III, such as Professor Bernard Oxman, are given great weight. Other valuable resources include the blue books on international law studies published periodically by the U.S. Naval War College's inter-

---

see Abbott v. Abbott, 130 S. Ct. 1983, 1990 (2010). The Court noted in that case that it gives great weight to the executive branch's interpretation of the treaty. Id. at 1993. But see Hamdan v. Rumsfeld, 548 U.S. 557, 629–31 (2006) (giving no deference to the executive branch's interpretation of the Geneva conventions on the law of armed conflict).

89. One law of the sea expert suggests that "over time the practice is what determines the purport of the treaty." William T. Burke, State Practice, New Ocean Uses, and Ocean Governance under UNCLOS, in Ocean Governance: Strategies and Approaches for the 21st Century 222 (Thomas A. Mensah ed., 1996).

90. Vienna Convention on Treaties, supra, art. 31(3)(b). Recognizing the dual nature of a treaty as an international agreement and domestic law, U.S. courts will endeavor to construe an ambiguous treaty provision in a manner "consistent with the shared expectations of the contracting parties." Olympic Airways v. Husain, 540 U.S. 644, 650 (2004). In doing so, the courts may look to the post-ratification understandings of the parties as reflected in part in foreign judicial decisions. See, e.g., Eastern Airlines Inc. v. Floyd, 499 U.S. 530 (1991); Zicherman v. Korean Air Lines Co. 516 U.S. 217 (1996).

91. C. John Colombos, The International Law of the Sea (6th ed. 1967); D. P. [Daniel Patrick] O'Connell, The International Law of the Sea vols. 1 & 2 (Ivan Shearer ed., 1982); Myres S. McDougal and William T. Burke, Public Order of the Oceans (1987).

92. RR. Churchill & A.V. Lowe, The Law of the Sea (3d ed. 1999).

93. Donald Rothwell & Tim Stephens, The International Law of the Sea (2010).

94. The M/V *Saiga* (St. Vincent & the Grenadines v. Guinea), ITLOS Case No. 2, Judgment of July 1, 1999, 38 I.L.M. 1323 (1999).

national law department since 1901, the annual *Yearbook of the International Tribunal for the Law of the Sea*, the *Law of the Sea Bulletins* and other monographs on law of the sea issues published by the UN Division for Ocean Affairs and the Law of the Sea, the proceedings of periodic conferences by the Law of the Sea Institute (presently hosted by the University of California at Berkeley), and the University of Virginia Center for Ocean Law and Policy. Finally, the *Commander's Handbook on the Law of Naval Operations* plays a unique role in that it is, like the treatises cited above, evidence of international law, but it is also an assertion by the United States and may therefore serve as evidence of *opinio juris*.[95] The *Commander's Handbook* is frequently referred to throughout this book, in large part in recognition that it is jointly promulgated by the U.S. Navy, U.S. Marine Corps, and U.S. Coast Guard, and therefore reflects the common understanding of all three maritime services. The U.S. Naval War College's international law department also prepares an *Annotated Supplement to the Commander's Handbook* that is extensively relied on by judge advocates in the offices of the Judge Advocate General of the Navy and Coast Guard, the Marine Corps' Staff Judge Advocate to the Commandant, and in the fleet and field.

---

95. See W. Michael Reisman & William K. Lietzau, Moving International Law from Theory to Practice: The Role of Military Manuals in Effectuating the Law of Armed Conflict, 64 U.S. Nav. War Coll. Int'l L. Studies 1 (Horace B. Robertson Jr. ed., 1991).

3

Baselines and Maritime Boundary Delimitation

L aw of the sea issues typically involve a combination of spatial and functional approaches. The spatial approach examines the respective rights and duties of states in the various maritime zones, including the states' internal waters, territorial seas, contiguous zones, exclusive economic zones, and continental shelves, and on the high seas. The functional approach examines selected activities that take place in the various zones, such as navigation and overflight, resource extraction, scientific research, maritime law enforcement, military activities, and measures to protect the marine environment (see chapters 4–8). Navigation and overflight, protection of the marine environment, maritime law enforcement, and military activities and the use of force are examined in greater detail in chapters 9–13.

The spatial or zonal approach adopted by the 1982 LOS Convention requires consideration of three geographical issues. The first issue, which is examined in this chapter, concerns the methods for determining the "baseline" and "base points" from which the various zones are measured. The second issue, addressed in chapters 5–7, concerns the horizontal and vertical dimensions of each zone. The final issue concerns the method for resolving potential "overlaps" of the maritime zones if opposite and adjacent states each attempt to claim the full geographic measure the 1982 LOS Convention would permit, but their proximity precludes it. For example, if two opposite states are less than twenty-four nautical miles apart, both cannot obtain a full twelve-nautical-mile territorial sea. Accordingly, a method must be available for delimiting the boundary between the two states' territorial seas. These maritime boundary delimitation questions are covered near the end of this chapter.

Disputed maritime claims are among the most highly charged law of the sea issues, implicating as they do sovereignty and resource access stakes. Resolution of the three threshold questions identified above typically requires examination of both international and domestic law sources. Coastal states commonly make claims under their internal domestic law regarding baselines, boundaries, zones of state interest, and jurisdiction. Those claims, some of which are accompanied by notifications to the UN secretary-general, can trigger protests by other states that believe the claims are inconsistent with international law. Despite their origin in domestic actions by the claiming states, resolution of interstate disputes will ultimately turn on application of international law. As the ICJ made clear in the *Anglo-Norwegian Fisheries* case in 1951, the delimitation of sea areas always has "an international aspect; it cannot be dependent merely on the will of the coastal State as expressed in its municipal law. Although it is true that the act of delimitation is necessarily a unilateral act, because only the coastal State is competent to undertake it, the validity of the delimitation with regards to other States depends upon international law."[1] The sections that follow address those international law rules.

---

1. Anglo-Norwegian Fisheries case (U.K. v. Norway), 1951 I.C.J. 116, 132 (Dec. 18).

A. THE SOURCES OF BASELINE CONTROVERSIES

Three issues concerning coastal state baseline claims have proven contentious: first, the legality of decisions by some states to claim straight baselines; second, claims involving bays; and third, the status and effect of islands and similar maritime features (see sections B.1.e and B.2 below). Claims to bays take one of two forms. "Juridical" bays are coastal state waters that meet the 1982 LOS Convention definition of a bay. "Historic" bays are bays that meet the test under customary international law for a claim based not on the bay's physical configuration, but rather on the nature and duration of its usage, the adjacent state's control over those waters, and the responses of other states to the adjacent state's assertion of control.[2] A number of U.S. Supreme Court cases involve disputes between the federal government and one or more U.S. states in which the state government asserted a juridical or historic bay claim (in order to extend the state's boundaries) that was disputed by the federal government. In those cases, the U.S. Supreme Court generally applied the relevant rules of international law while often deferring to the federal government's interpretation of that body of law.[3]

Territory is an indispensable element in the four-part test for an entity to qualify as a state (see chapter 1). States are sovereign within their territory. Sovereignty carries with it the rights to be free from outside interference in the state's internal affairs and to be free from the use of force or the threat to use force against the state's territorial integrity or political independence. *U.S. Navy Regulations* requires that the territorial integrity of foreign states be respected.[4] The state's territory is the starting point for determining the state's rights and jurisdiction in adjacent sea areas. Historically, states have acquired territory by cession (e.g., the Louisiana and Alaska territories), annexation (e.g., Texas), occupation, prescription, and accretion. At one time forcible acquisition by conquest was recognized as a basis for acquiring sovereignty over territory; however, the 1932 Stimson Doctrine, by which the United States announced that it would deny recognition to international territorial changes obtained by force, and the 1945 UN Charter have discredited such forcible acquisitions.[5]

Islands and similar maritime features present a number of contested issues. The first, which is not governed by the LOS Convention, concerns disputes between or among states over which state has sovereignty over "insular" features in the maritime domain such as rocks and islands. Prominent examples include the Falkland Islands in the South Atlantic and the Senkaku, Spratly, and Paracel Islands in the western Pacific.[6] Other issues that *are* governed by the LOS Convention concern the distinction between artificial and naturally formed islands, and between true islands and mere rocks incapable of sustaining human habitation (sometimes called "juridical rocks") and low-tide elevations. The importance of a feature's classification can be seen in the

---

2. See UN Secretariat, Historic Bays: Memorandum by the Secretariat of the United Nations, U.N. Doc. A/CONF.13/1 (Sept. 30, 1957) (submitted to UNCLOS I). Although the four conventions that came out of UNCLOS I sidestepped the legal test for historic bays or waters, one of the conference resolutions addressed the issue. See UN Secretariat, Juridical Regime of Historic Waters, Including Historic Bays, U.N. Doc. A/CN.4/143 (Mar. 9, 1962).

3. See generally Gerald J. Mangone, Marine Boundaries: States and the United States, 21 Int'l J. Marine & Coastal L. 121 (2006).

4. U.S. Navy Regulations, supra, art. 0916.

5. Secretary of State Henry Stimson announced the doctrine carrying his name in diplomatic notes to China and Japan in 1932. More recently, Article 2(4) of the UN Charter prohibits the use of force against the territorial integrity of another state. It follows that territorial acquisitions obtained in violation of Article 2(4) are illegal.

6. See J. Ashley Roach, Base Points and Baselines in Maritime Boundary Delimitation, in Maritime Border Diplomacy 269, 285–300 (Myron Nordquist & John N. Moore eds., 2012); Sovereignty over Palau Ligitan and Palau Sipadan (Indonesia v. Malaysia), 2002 I.C.J. 625 (Dec. 17).

fact that juridical rocks generate only a territorial sea while true islands also generate an EEZ and continental shelf. The drawing of baselines, which concerns whether a group of islands qualifies as a "fringe" for purposes of drawing straight baselines, or an archipelago for purposes of drawing archipelagic baselines that enclose the state's archipelagic waters, has been another contentious issue. Shifting baselines due to subsidence of the landmass or rising sea levels is a growing concern, particularly for small-island developing states and states with unstable deltas.

High-resolution aerial and satellite imagery and sophisticated computer graphics applications have added much-needed accuracy to the determination and display of coastlines and their nearshore and offshore features. Indeed, widely accessible tools such as Google Earth make detailed information on the world's coastlines and many of the offshore insular and hydrographic features available to anyone with access to the Internet. These developments hold out great promise for developing the factual bases for determining sovereignty and jurisdictional claims over disputed maritime features. Whether more accurate and available information will promote peaceful settlement of disputed maritime claims remains to be seen.

B. LEGAL TESTS FOR ESTABLISHING THE TERRITORIAL SEA BASELINE

All maritime zones are measured from the baseline (sometimes called the "territorial sea baseline") and the base points that form the line. As a result, any calculation of the lateral extent of the coastal state's control over the adjacent seas and seabed areas begins with a determination of the proper baseline. Some states have been demonstrably aggressive in their baseline claims, leading to diplomatic protests and even to operational challenges by other states.[7] The U.S. freedom of navigation program, discussed at the end of this chapter, is a well-known example of one state's response to excessive maritime claims.

Disputes over baseline determinations reportedly date back at least four centuries.[8] The 1951 *Anglo-Norwegian Fisheries* case remains an important benchmark in the modern era of baseline disputes. The 1958 Convention on the Territorial Sea and Contiguous Zone addressed baseline determinations in articles that were largely viewed at the time as a codification of customary law.[9] The convention adopted the position that the location of the baseline is primarily a question of the physical characteristics of the coastline. Acknowledging the tremendous variety in the physical geography of coastlines, the 1982 LOS Convention sets out two approaches to establishing the juridical baseline: the "normal" baseline method and the "straight" baseline method.[10] Assuming that some portions of the state's coastline meet the conditions for straight baselines, the coastal state is permitted to determine baselines by any combination of methods provided for in the relevant articles, in order to suit the differing physical conditions.[11] Thus, a state might adopt the normal baseline in some areas and straight baselines in others—assuming the latter areas meet the legal tests for straight baselines.

---

7. Then-existing national legislation on baselines is compiled in UN Division for Ocean Affairs and the Law of the Sea, The Law of the Sea: Baselines: National Legislation with Illustrative Maps, U.N. Sales No. E.89V.10 (1989).

8. See Lewis M. Alexander, Baseline Delimitations and Maritime Boundaries, 23 Va. J. Int'l L. 503 (1983).

9. Convention on the Territorial Sea and Contiguous Zone [hereinafter "1958 Convention on TTS and CZ"], arts. 3–13, Apr. 29, 1958, 15 U.S.T. 1606, 516 U.N.T.S. 207.

10. Commander's Handbook, supra, ¶ 1.4.

11. LOSC art. 14. The baseline provisions are in Part II of the Convention (Articles 5–16). See generally UN Division for Ocean Affairs and the Law of the Sea, The Law of the Sea: Baselines: An Examination of the Relevant Provisions of the UN Convention on the Law of the Sea, U.N. Sales No. E.88V.5 (1989).

1. The Normal Baseline

The law of the "sea" applies to oceans, bays, gulfs, and seas. If coastal physical geography was simple and uniform throughout the world, the rule for establishing the baseline could be similarly simple and uniform, calling for nothing more than a choice among the various tidal plane intersections with the shore. But coastal geography is neither simple nor uniform. Some coastlines are deeply indented; others are riddled with bays, rivers, deltas, reefs, rocks, and islands; or supplemented or altered by groins, jetties, and harbor works. Still others may be undergoing changes brought on by natural erosion or accretion processes or rising sea levels.[12] Nation-states' (and U.S. coastal states') desire to push their baseline seaward to enclose as much of the adjacent sea areas as possible further complicates the situation. Other nations (and the federal government within the United States) may denounce such claims as excessive and challenge them.

Article 5 of the LOS Convention prescribes that the "normal" baseline is, except where specialized rules apply, the low-water line along the coast.[13] The convention does not define "low-water line."[14] The tidal range varies according to the periodic solar and lunar cycles and coastal geography. Areas that experience "mixed" tides have two low tides in a given tidal day, one of which is lower than the other. Thus, in some areas there are three possible "low-water" lines: the mean of all low tides (mean low water), the mean of the higher low-water lines, and the mean of the lower low-water lines. As a matter of international law, nations are generally free to adopt any of the low-water lines so long as they meet the convention's requirement to provide notice to other states by publishing their claims on officially recognized large-scale charts (note, however, that the choice might affect the classification of certain land features such as low-tide elevations).[15] The United States, which is subject to mixed tides in a number of locations, has adopted the mean lower low-water (MLLW) line for its baseline.[16] By contrast, the majority of states do not differentiate between the three measures, referring instead simply to the "low-water" mark.

The 1958 Convention on the Territorial Sea and Contiguous Zone made no special provisions for baselines around reefs or atolls. However, the 1982 Convention provides that in the cases of islands situated on atolls and islands having fringing reefs, the baseline for measuring the breadth of the territorial sea is the seaward low-water line of the reef, as shown by the appropriate symbol on charts officially recognized by the coastal state.[17]

---

12. David D. Caron, When Law Makes Climate Change Worse: Rethinking the Law of Baselines in Light of a Rising Sea Level, 17 Ecology L. Q. 621 (1990).

13. LOSC art. 5. See also 33 C.F.R. § 2.05–10 (defining the baseline under U.S. law); Restatement FRLUS § 511 cmt. h. The ICJ adopted the low-water line as reflective of customary law in its 1951 Anglo-Norwegian Fisheries case (U.K. v. Norway), 1951 I.C.J. 116, 128 (Dec. 18).

14. Several references are available to guide the reader in understanding terms used in the LOS Convention when the convention does not itself provide a definition. One source is the LOS Glossary, prepared by the International Hydrographic Bureau, which defines the "low-water line" as "the intersection of the plane of low water with the shore or the line along a coast, or beach, to which the sea recedes at low water." See International Hydrographic Bureau, Consolidated Glossary of Technical Terms Used in the United Nations Convention on the Law of the Sea, IHB Special Pub. No. 41, reprinted in Annotated Supplement to the Commander's Handbook, supra, annex A1-5.

15. See generally LOSC arts. 5 & 16. "Large-scale" charts cover smaller areas, but with greater detail than small-scale charts. Article 4(6) of the 1958 Convention on the Territorial Sea and Contiguous Zone required only publication of straight baselines. The 1982 LOS Convention requirements are more extensive.

16. U.S. v. California, 381 U.S. 139, 175–76 (1965) (adopting the definition of the baseline in the 1958 Convention on the Territorial Sea and Contiguous Zone for use in defining the "coastline" under the U.S. Submerged Lands Act, 43 U.S.C. § 1301(c), and construing it to refer to mean lower low water). See also Marjorie M. Whiteman, 4 Digest of International Law 137–94 (1965).

17. LOSC art. 6. See also Baselines: An Examination, supra, at 5–12; Ian Kawaley, Delimitation of Islands Fringed with Reefs: Article 6 of the 1982 Law of the Sea Convention, 41 Int'l & Comp. L. Q. 152 (1992).

a. Mouths of Rivers

Fixing the baseline in areas where a river discharges into the sea turns on how the river meets the sea. If the river flows directly into the sea, the baseline is a straight line across the mouth of the river between points on the low-water line of its banks.[18] If the river flows into an estuary that empties into the sea, the rules for bays should be applied to the estuary.[19] In contrast to the rule for juridical bays (discussed below), the LOS Convention puts no limit on the length of straight closing lines for rivers that flow directly into the sea. Some have argued that the maximum closing line for river mouths should not be wider than the limit for bays (twenty-four nautical miles), but that position has not been generally accepted.

b. Juridical Bays

Perhaps no other LOS Convention article concerning maritime jurisdictional baselines has generated more written commentary than Article 10 dealing with juridical bays.[20] Under the 1982 LOS Convention a juridical bay (in contrast to a historic bay, discussed below) is defined as a well-marked indentation whose landward penetration is in such proportion to the width of the bay's mouth that the water area constitutes more than a "mere curvature of the coast." The semicircle test is applied to determine if an indentation is more than a "mere curvature" and therefore qualifies as a juridical bay.[21] The coastal indentation qualifies as a juridical bay only if its water area is as large as, or larger than, that of the semicircle whose diameter is a line drawn across the mouth of that indentation.[22] If the enclosed water area is less than the area of the semicircle, the waters do not qualify as a bay and cannot be closed by a straight baseline across the entrance. It should be added that the rule on juridical bays applies only to bays whose coasts belong to a single state.[23]

Assuming the indentation qualifies as a bay under the Article 10 rule above, the bay's closing line must still be established. If the bay entrance does not exceed twenty-four nautical miles, the closing line may be drawn between the low-water marks at the ends of the bay entrance. The enclosed waters are considered internal waters and the offshore zones are calculated from the closing line. If, however, the entrance of the bay is more than twenty-four nautical miles wide, a straight baseline of twenty-four nautical miles is "walked inland" in such a manner that the line encloses the maximum area of water possible.

The rules on juridical bays are illustrated in figure 2. To determine whether the waters in the illustration qualify as a bay under Article 10 rather than as a mere curvature of the coast, a semicircle is drawn with a diameter equal to the thirty-six-nautical-mile-wide line defining the entrance. It can readily be seen that because the waters extend well inland, the area of water inside that thirty-six-nautical-mile closing line is roughly twice as large as the area of a thirty-six-nautical-mile-diameter semicircle. Thus, the waters qualify as a juridical bay. Because the entrance is greater than twenty-four nautical miles, however, the closing line must be walked

---

18. LOSC art. 9; Commander's Handbook, supra, ¶ 1.4.4.

19. See International Law Commission, Articles concerning the Law of the Sea with Commentaries, 1956 Y.B. Int'l L. Comm'n, vol. II, at 271–72; Whiteman, 4 Digest of International Law, supra, at 339–43.

20. Baselines: An Examination, supra, at 28. See also Philip C. Jessup, The Law of Territorial Waters and Maritime Jurisdiction ch. VIII (1927).

21. In applying the rule, the U.S. Supreme Court observed that the test is what mariners see, not what lawyers invent. See Alaska v. U.S., 545 U.S. 75, 94 (2005).

22. LOSC art. 10; Restatement FRLUS § 511 cmt. f; Commander's Handbook, supra, ¶ 1.4.3.

23. So, for example, a body such as the Strait of Juan de Fuca leading from the Pacific Ocean to Puget Sound, and which is bordered by the United States and Canada, could not qualify as a juridical bay. It might, however, qualify as internal waters if the waters meet the legal test for historic title.

inland in such a way that a closing line twenty-four nautical miles in length encloses the largest possible water area. The twenty-four-nautical-mile-long closing line is the baseline for the bay. The waters inside the twenty-four-nautical-mile baseline are internal waters.

Applying its interpretation of international law, the U.S. Supreme Court held in 1985 that Long Island Sound qualifies as a juridical bay, even though the western end of the sound narrows into a river separating Long Island from the mainland.[24] Earlier, in *United States v. California*, the Supreme Court concluded that the waters of Monterey Bay also meet the legal test for a juridical bay.[25]

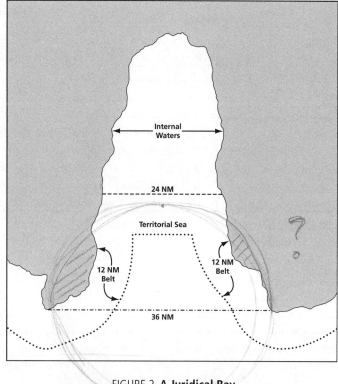

FIGURE 2. **A Juridical Bay**

c. Ports and Roadsteads

The 1982 LOS Convention includes baseline accommodations for ports, roadsteads, and harbor works that might otherwise fall outside the coastal state's internal waters. Article 11 of the convention provides that in drawing the baseline, the outermost permanent harbor works that form an integral part of the harbor system are regarded as forming part of the coast.[26] The definition of harbor works extends to structures such as jetties and breakwaters erected along the coast to protect against erosion, but not to piers or dikes.[27] The structures need not be connected to the shoreline to qualify as permanent harbor works. Offshore installations and artificial islands do not qualify,[28] but the coastal state may establish safety zones around such structures.[29]

Roadsteads are areas near the shore where vessels may anchor in a position of safety. Under Article 12 of the 1982 LOS Convention, roadsteads that are normally used for the loading, unloading, and anchoring of ships, and which would otherwise be situated wholly or partly out-

---

24. U.S. v. Maine (Rhode Island and New York Boundary case), 469 U.S. 504 (1985). The Court assimilated Long Island to a peninsula. The closing eastern line was established from Montauk Point on Long Island to Watch Hill Point, R.I.
25. U.S. v. California, 381 U.S. 139 (1965).
26. See also Commander's Handbook, supra, ¶ 1.4.6.
27. See Maritime Delimitation of the Black Sea (Romania v. Ukraine), ¶ 130, 2009 I.C.J. 61 (Feb. 3).
28. LOSC art. 11. See also U.S. v. California, 447 U.S. 1, 4 n.3, & 8 (1980); U.S. v. California, 432 U.S. 40, 41–42 (1977); U.S. v. Louisiana, 394 U.S. 11, 36–38 (1969). A compilation of the then-existing historic waters claims is available in Whiteman, 4 Digest of International Law, supra, at 233–39.
29. LOSC art. 60.

side the outer limit of the territorial sea, are nevertheless included in the territorial sea.[30] This rule was carried forward from the 1958 Convention on the Territorial Sea and Contiguous Zone, during an era when most states limited their territorial sea claims to three nautical miles. With the extension of the territorial sea to twelve nautical miles under the 1982 Convention, the roadstead rule has lost most of its practical significance.

d. Low-Tide Elevations

Article 13 of the LOS Convention, which the ICJ has determined reflects customary international law,[31] defines a low-tide elevation (sometimes called a "covering rock") as a naturally formed area of land that is surrounded by and above water at low tide but submerged at high tide. Where such a low-tide elevation is situated wholly or partly within twelve nautical miles from the mainland or an island (the lawful breadth of the territorial sea), the low-water line on that elevation may be used as the baseline.[32] If the low-tide elevation is situated more than twelve nautical miles from the mainland or an island, it does not affect the baseline.

e. Islands

Islands are defined in Article 121 of the 1982 LOS Convention as naturally formed areas of land,[33] surrounded by water, that are above water at high tide.[34] Islands are thus distinguished from low-tide elevations, which are submerged at high tide.[35] Article 121, which the ICJ has determined also reflects customary international law,[36] distinguishes between two categories of islands: true islands and "mere" rocks. They are distinguished under Article 121(3) by the fact that true islands are capable of sustaining human habitation or economic life of their own, and rocks are not.[37] The consequences of a feature's classification are literally far-reaching. The territorial sea, contiguous zone, EEZ, and continental shelf of a true juridical island are determined by the same provisions applicable to other land territory.[38] Thus, a true island can support a claim for an EEZ and continental shelf. In contrast to true islands, mere rocks generate a territorial sea but do not support a claim to an EEZ or continental shelf.[39] The LOS Convention does not define the relevant classification terms, and their application has proven both controversial and consequential.[40] The distinction between islands and rocks was raised but not answered by Judge Vuka in the ITLOS decision involving a prompt release action brought against Australia

30. LOSC art. 12. Restatement FRLUS § 511 n.2.
31. See Territorial and Maritime Dispute (Nicaragua v. Colombia), ¶ 182, 2012 I.C.J. (Nov. 19).
32. LOSC art. 13. See also U.S. v. Louisiana, 394 U.S. at 40–47; Commander's Handbook, supra, ¶ 1.5.3.
33. An opinion that considered, but did not decide, the possibility of a "floating island" comprised of 99 percent ice, arose out of a homicide on an "ice island" variously called T-3 and Fletcher Ice Island. T-3, first sighted in 1947, was seven miles long, four miles wide, and one hundred feet thick. See U.S. v. Escamilla, 467 F.2d 341, 344 (4th Cir. 1972).
34. LOSC art. 121; UN Division for Ocean Affairs and the Law of the Sea, The Law of the Sea: Regime of Islands, U.N. Sales No. E.87.V.11 (1987). See also Restatement FRLUS § 511 cmt. g; U.S. v. Alaska, 521 U.S. 1 (1997) (rejecting Alaska's claim that Dinkum Sands qualifies as an island for purposes of determining maritime boundaries in the Beaufort Sea).
35. See Commander's Handbook, supra, ¶ 1.5.3.
36. See Territorial and Maritime Dispute (Nicaragua v. Colombia), supra, ¶ 139.
37. For a compilation of claims involving small, uninhabited, insular features, see J. Ashley Roach, Maritime Boundary Delimitation: United States Practice, 44 Ocean Dev. & Int'l L. 1, table 1 (2013).
38. Using the relevant formula, Area = πr^2, a radius of 200 miles yields an EEZ of 125,664 square miles.
39. See Jonathan I. Charney, Rocks That Cannot Sustain Human Habitation, 93 Am. J. Int'l L. 863 (1999).
40. For the United States, the island-versus-rock question has been raised regarding the status of Navassa Island, a two-square-mile island in the Caribbean between Jamaica and Haiti and claimed by the United States and Haiti.

on behalf of the fishing vessel *Volga*.[41] Judge Vuka questioned Australia's reliance on Heard and MacDonald Islands in drawing the EEZ boundaries for the reason that, in the judge's opinion, their capability to sustain human habitation was doubtful. The issue is squarely and divisively presented in the western Pacific, where coastal state claims over some insular features and the related offshore zones implicate, in part, the juridical distinction between low-tide elevations, rocks, and islands, driving some states to construct the LOS Convention equivalent of Potemkin villages on stilts to bolster the feature's claim to human habitability.[42] The requirement that islands be "naturally formed" has also raised questions in cases involving artificial measures taken in response to subsidence or rising sea levels. Existing law provides no clear distinction between naturally formed but artificially preserved or enhanced islands and true artificial islands, some of which are constructed on submerged rocks.[43] Given that the LOS Convention expressly allows for continuity of baselines in certain highly unstable areas, such as deltas, it would seem reasonable to accord similar treatment to islands that require stabilization to maintain their existing status and functionality. Alternatively, the concept of indelible navigability might be applied by analogy to these artificially "fortified" islands.[44] Neither theory would support claims based on enhancements to "upgrade" low-tide elevations to rocks or rocks to true islands, or to extend the seaward extent of existing islands.

2. Straight Baselines

In approaching the subject of straight baselines it is important to distinguish "normal" baselines—some of which may be straight—from the special rules for nonnormal straight baselines and archipelagic baselines. For example, a state following the rules for normal baselines is permitted to draw a straight line across certain juridical bays and river mouths. Similarly, an archipelagic state is permitted to draw straight archipelagic baselines between adjacent islands. The rules for drawing baselines across juridical bays and rivers are addressed above, and archipelagic baselines are examined later in this chapter. This section focuses on the specialized rules for nonnormal straight baselines constructed in accordance with Article 7 of the LOS Convention.

Although the ICJ recognized the legality of straight baselines under customary law in 1951,[45] and later sanctioned straight baselines in the 1958 Convention on the Territorial Sea and Contiguous Zone, the 1982 LOS Convention further develops and clarifies the regime for straight baselines.[46] Article 7 of the 1982 Convention provides that in localities where the coastline is

---

The U.S. Maritime Claims Reference Manual suggests that Navassa Island is a true Article 121(1) island; however, the "limits of the exclusive economic zone around Navassa Island remain to be determined." DoD, Under Secretary of Defense for Policy, Maritime Claims Reference Manual, DoD 2005.1-M, 633 (June 23, 2005). See also Jones v. U.S., 137 U.S. 202 (1890) (prosecution for murder committed on Navassa Island).

41. The *Volga* case (Russia v. Australia), Prompt Release, ITLOS Case No. 11, Judgment of Dec. 23, 2002, 42 I.L.M. 159, 179–80 (2003) (Vuka, J.); The *Monte Confurco* case (Seychelles v. France), Prompt Release, ITLOS Case No. 6, Judgment of Dec. 18, 2000, 125 Int'l L. Rep. 293, 205.

42. The fact that some of the involved states also assert jurisdiction over military vessels and activities in their EEZs increases the stakes.

43. The status of Okinotori Island (Okinotorishima), which Japan artificially fortified with transplanted coral to support an EEZ claim, engendered protests from China.

44. The rule of indelible navigability in the United States provides that once a body of water meets the legal test for navigability, subsequent changes do not strip it of its navigable status. See U.S. v. Appalachian Elec. Power Co., 311 U.S. 377, 408 (1940).

45. Anglo-Norwegian Fisheries case (U.K. v. Norway), 1951 I.C.J. 116 (Dec. 18).

46. J. Ashley Roach & Robert W. Smith, Straight Baselines: The Need for a Universally Applied Norm, 31 Ocean Dev. & Int'l L. 47 (2000); W. Michael Reisman & Gayle S. Westerman, Straight Baselines in International Boundary Delimitation (1992).

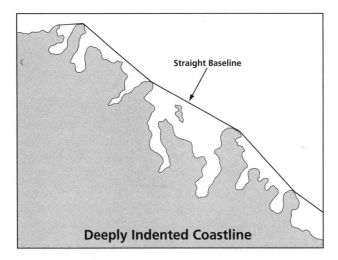

FIGURE 3. **Straight Baseline across a Deeply Indented Coast**

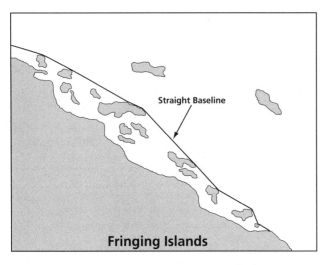

FIGURE 4. **Straight Baseline across Fringing Islands**

"deeply indented and cut into," or where there is a "fringe of islands along the coast in its immediate vicinity," the method of straight baselines joining appropriate points may be employed.[47] Nevertheless, the ICJ has cautioned that the method of straight baselines is to be "applied restrictively."[48]

Figure 3 illustrates a section of a coastline that is deeply indented and cut into and would therefore qualify for straight baselines under Article 7. The figure depicts two qualifying features taken from the rules on straight baselines: the indentations are in close proximity to each other; and the depth of their penetration, as measured from the closing straight baseline, is greater than half the length of the closing straight baseline segment.

Article 7 also permits straight baselines to be drawn where there is a fringe of islands along the coast in its immediate vicinity. The term "immediate vicinity" is not defined in the convention. The relevant distance for calculating the island's proximity to the coastline, however, is generally measured from the nearshore edge of the island fringe to the low-water line on the adjacent coastline.[49] The proximity of the islands' inner edge to the coastline must be "immediate." UN technical experts on baselines have taken the position that such fringing islands must be within twenty-four nautical miles of the mainland to be used in constructing straight baselines.[50] A third element in the test requires that the fringe of islands as a whole masks at least half of the main coastline in the area where the straight baseline is drawn.

Figure 4 illustrates a section of the coastline with a fringe of islands in the immediate vicinity of the adjacent coastline. The most landward point of each of the fourteen islands composing the

47. LOSC art. 7; Anglo-Norwegian Fisheries case (U.K. v. Norway), 1951 I.C.J. Rep. 116 (Dec. 18) (confirming the right of Norway to adopt straight baselines); Restatement FRLUS § 511cmt. h.
48. Maritime Delimitation and Territorial Questions (Qatar v. Bahrain), ¶¶ 212–14, 2001 I.C.J. 40 (Mar. 16).
49. Baselines: An Examination, supra, at 22.
50. Id.

fringe is no more than twenty-four nautical miles from the coastline, and each of those islands is no more than twenty-four nautical miles from the adjacent island to which the straight baseline is drawn. The proximity rule excludes the two islands located well offshore (a straight baseline to those islands would also violate the rule that the baseline must not depart from the general direction of the coastline); thus, a normal baseline would be drawn around those outer islands.

Where the presence of a delta and other natural conditions renders the coastline "highly unstable," the baseline may be constructed across selected points along the furthest seaward extent of the low-water line.[51] Under the delta rule, subsequent regression of the low-water line will not in itself require a change to the baseline. The existing baseline remains effective until changed by the coastal state in accordance with the convention.[52] To qualify under the rule for deltas, the area must first meet the legal test for straight baselines (i.e., it must be deeply indented or include fringing islands) and must be highly unstable.[53]

Article 7 does not permit straight baselines to be drawn to and from low-tide elevations unless a lighthouse or similar installation that is permanently above sea level has been built on them, or when the drawing of baselines to such elevations has received general international recognition.[54]

When drawing straight baselines the coastal state must not depart to any appreciable extent from the "general direction" of the coast (the straight baselines depicted in figures 3 and 4 conform to that rule). Additionally, the sea areas lying within the baselines must be sufficiently "closely linked to the land domain" to be subject to the regime of internal waters.[55] This latter requirement gives additional meaning to the rule that fringing islands must be in the "immediate vicinity" of the coastline. When the establishment of a straight baseline under Article 7 has the effect of enclosing as internal waters areas that were not formerly classified as such, the LOS Convention recognizes the importance of preserving navigation freedoms and therefore confers a right of innocent passage through the newly enclosed waters.[56]

The U.S. Supreme Court has held that straight baselines can be applied in the United States only with the federal government's approval (not on the claim by a U.S. state).[57] Although several coastal areas of the United States would likely qualify under Article 7 for straight baselines, the federal government has declared that its policy is not to use straight baselines.[58] This reluctance is attributable to the historically strong national interest in preserving freedom of navigation.

3. Historic Bays (Historic Waters)

The LOS Convention recognizes,[59] but does not define, the concept of "historic waters" and "historic bays"; that is, waters that are accorded the status of internal waters not because they meet the juridical test for bays established by Article 10 of the LOS Convention, but rather because the coastal state has consistently claimed the waters as internal waters and other states

51. LOSC art. 7(2).
52. Id. art. 7; U.S. Department of State, Digest of United States Practice in International Law 1978, at 942–43.
53. Baselines: An Examination, supra, at 24.
54. Id. art. 7(4).
55. The requirement that the claimed waters must be "closely linked" to the land domain resonated with the archipelagic states, which argued at UNCLOS III that they enjoyed a similar relationship with what they called their "archipelagic waters."
56. LOSC art. 8.
57. U.S. v. California, 381 U.S. 139, 167–69 (1965).
58. U.S. Department of State, Cumulative Digest of U.S. Practice in International Law 1981–1988, vol. II, at 1779.
59. See LOSC art. 10(6).

have acquiesced in those claims.[60] The concept is roughly similar to prescriptive title theories of adverse possession and easement by prescription in the common law of property. When claims to historic waters or bays are contested, it should be noted that Article 298 of the LOS Convention permits a state to declare that it does not accept any of the procedures for compulsory settlement of disputes involving historic bays or titles.[61]

The legal test for historic title claims is complex. In the 1951 *Anglo-Norwegian Fisheries* case, the ICJ recognized that waters that would ordinarily not qualify as internal waters under the governing law for baselines might nevertheless qualify for such status on the basis of the state's "historic title."[62] The court set out three requirements to support a historic title claim: (1) the state must exercise sovereign authority over the area; (2) such authority must have been exercised regularly for a considerable period of time; and (3) other states must have acquiesced in the claiming state's exercise of authority.[63] Despite the apparent simplicity of that test, subsequent ICJ cases on questions of historic titles have cast serious doubt on the notion that a "single regime" exists for determining historic waters or historic bays. Rather, it now seems clear that the court has adopted a context-specific, case-by-case approach to those determinations, which the court has characterized as a "particular regime for each of the concrete recognized cases."[64]

In a series of domestic coastal boundary cases, the U.S. Supreme Court set out the test for historic bay or waters status in disputes between states in the United States or between a state and the federal government. That test considers three factors, which generally mirror the international law rule: the state's exercise of authority over the area claimed, the continuity of that exercise of authority, and the response by other states to the claiming state's assertion of authority.[65] Under the Supreme Court's test, mere absence of protests by foreign states does not constitute proof of acquiescence, absent a showing that foreign states knew or reasonably should have known of the claim.[66] By contrast, the ICJ has held that mere toleration is sufficient to establish this element.[67]

In *United States v. Alaska*, a case concerning a claim by the state of Alaska that the waters of Cook Inlet qualified as a historic bay, the Supreme Court applied its earlier test and rejected Alaska's claim.[68] As with a number of earlier cases involving similar claims by state governments against the United States, the federal government in that case opposed the extension of internal waters under the historic waters theory.[69] The federal government's restrictive view was also

60. Commander's Handbook, supra, ¶ 1.4.3. The handbook describes a five-part legal test for historic title: the coastal state's exercise of authority over the waters must be open, effective, long term, and continuous, and other states must have acquiesced in the coastal state's exercise of authority over the waters. The handbook adds that the United States takes the position that acquiescence must be affirmatively demonstrated and that a mere absence of protest does not establish acquiescence. See also Clive Ralph Symmons, Historic Waters in the Law of the Sea: A Modern Re-appraisal (2008); Whiteman, 4 Digest of International Law, supra, at 233–42 (compilation of historic bays).

61. LOSC art. 298(1)(a)(i). These exclusions from what would otherwise be compulsory dispute settlement procedures under Part XV of the LOSC are examined in chapter 15.

62. Anglo-Norwegian Fisheries case (U.K. v. Norway) 1951 I.C.J. 116, 130 (Dec. 18).

63. Id.

64. Continental Shelf case (Tunisia v. Libya), 1982 I.C.J. 18, 74 (Feb. 24). See also Land, Island and Maritime Frontier Dispute (El Salvador v. Honduras), 1992 I.C.J. 351 (Sept. 11).

65. See, e.g., U.S. v. Louisiana (The Louisiana Boundary Case), 394 U.S. 11, 23 (1969).

66. U.S. v. Alaska, 422 U.S. 184, 200 (1975).

67. Anglo-Norwegian Fisheries case (U.K. v. Norway) 1951 I.C.J. 116, 138–39 (Dec. 18).

68. U.S. v. Alaska, 422 U.S. 184, 203–04 (1975).

69. The U.S. Supreme Court has concluded that two water bodies meet the test for historic waters: Mississippi Sound and Block Island Sound. See U.S. v. Louisiana (Alabama and Mississippi Boundary Case), 470 U.S. 93, 103 (1985); U.S. v. Maine (Rhode Island and New York Boundary Case), 469 U.S. 504, 526 (1985). It rejected claims by

evident when it opposed the former Soviet Union's historic bay claim to Peter the Great Bay and Canada's claim of historic title to Hudson Bay.[70] One of the most notorious historic bay claims concerns Libya's assertion that the 273-nautical-mile-wide Gulf of Sidra qualifies as a historic bay, and is therefore internal waters of Libya. The United States persistently objected to Libya's claims. The objections took the form of both diplomatic protests and freedom of navigation operational challenges, some of which provoked violent confrontations.

4. Charts and Lists of Geographical Coordinates

The 1982 LOS Convention gives coastal states two options for publicizing their baseline-related claims.[71] They may display on charts of an appropriate scale either the baselines from which the territorial sea is measured or the outer limits of the territorial sea. Lines of delimitation drawn for roadsteads and for delimiting the territorial sea of opposite or adjacent states must also be displayed.[72] Alternatively, a list of geographical coordinates may be substituted.[73] The coastal state is required to give due publicity to such charts or lists of geographical coordinates and to deposit a copy with the UN secretary-general. Despite the mandate imposed by the 1982 Convention, the UN reports that only about one-third of the states have complied.[74]

C. ARCHIPELAGIC BASELINES

A legal regime for archipelagic states was first formally recognized with the 1982 Convention.[75] An "archipelagic state" is a state whose territory is wholly composed of one or more archipelagos and other islands.[76] An "archipelago" is further defined as a "group of islands, including parts of islands, interconnecting waters and other natural features, which are so closely interrelated that such islands, waters and other natural features form an intrinsic geographical, economic and political entity, or which historically have been regarded as such."[77] The definition excludes states that are partly mainland or continental and partly insular, such as the United States and Greece, even if the state includes one or more archipelagos.

   The rules for archipelagic baselines are similar to those for straight baselines (see LOS Convention, Article 47, in appendix C). Archipelagic states are entitled, but not required, to "draw straight archipelagic baselines joining the outermost points of the outermost islands and drying reefs," subject to a number of restrictions set out in the LOS Convention.[78] Figure 5 illustrates the application of the LOS Convention articles on archipelagic baselines.

---

adjacent states that Cook Inlet, Santa Monica Bay, San Pedro Bay, Florida Bay, Nantucket Sound, and numerous bays along the coast of Louisiana qualify. See J. Ashley Roach & Robert W. Smith, Excessive Maritime Claims 35–36 (3d ed. 2012). Although Delaware Bay (ten miles wide at the entrance) and Chesapeake Bay (twelve miles wide at the entrance) are sometimes mentioned as historic waters, those bays qualify as juridical bays under the 1982 LOS Convention. Id. at 54–55. The same is true of Monterey Bay (nineteen miles wide).

70. Whiteman, 4 Digest of International Law, supra, at 233–42.
71. See Clive R. Simmons & Michael W. Reed, Publicity and Charting Requirements: An Overlooked Issue in the UN Convention on the Law of the Sea, 41 Ocean Dev. & Int'l L. 77 (2010).
72. Charts reflecting U.S. Coast Guard decisions regarding the location of the territorial sea baseline for the purposes of Coast Guard jurisdiction are maintained in each Coast Guard district office. See 33 C.F.R. § 2.10-1.
73. LOSC art. 16.
74. UN Division for Ocean Affairs and Law of the Sea, Law of the Sea Information Circular No. 34 (Oct. 2011), at 6 (reporting that only 55 of the 162 states parties have met the requirement).
75. Indonesia and the Philippines argued for recognition of their unique archipelagic geography in UNCLOS I, but the 1958 conventions did not recognize a distinct regime for such states.
76. LOSC art. 46(1); Commander's Handbook, supra, ¶ 1.5.4.
77. LOSC art. 46(2).
78. Id. art. 47(1).

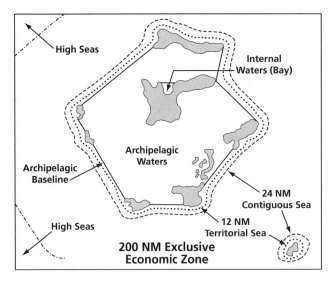

FIGURE 5. **Archipelagic Baselines**

The first restriction is that the main islands of the archipelagic states must lie within the archipelagic baseline, and the area inside the baseline must be such that the ratio of the water area to the land and atoll area is between 1:1 and 9:1.[79] Second, any given archipelagic baseline must not exceed 100 nm (except that up to 3 percent can extend up to 125 nm).[80] Third, archipelagic baselines must be drawn in a way that does not depart to any appreciable extent from the general configuration of the archipelago. Moreover, they may not be drawn to and from low-tide elevations, unless lighthouses or similar installations that are permanently above sea level have been built on them or a low-tide elevation is situated wholly or partly at a distance not exceeding the breadth of the territorial sea from the nearest island. Finally, archipelagic baselines may not be drawn in such a manner as to cut off from the high seas or the EEZ the territorial sea of another state. As with the rule on territorial sea baseline claims, the archipelagic state is required to give due publicity to its archipelagic waters charts or geographical coordinates and to deposit a copy with the UN secretary-general.

Within its archipelagic waters, the archipelagic state may draw closing lines for the delimitation of internal waters in accordance with the LOS Convention's rules for rivers, bays, and ports.[81] The adjacent maritime zones (territorial sea, contiguous zone, EEZ, and continental shelf) are then measured from the archipelagic baseline.[82]

The archipelagic state is sovereign in the waters enclosed by the baseline, along with the superjacent airspace and the seabed,[83] subject to the LOS Convention provisions on innocent passage[84] and archipelagic sea-lanes passage.[85] The nature of the states' rights and responsibilities over archipelagic waters and the right of archipelagic sea-lanes passage regime are further examined in chapter 5.

D. MARITIME BOUNDARY DELIMITATION

Maritime boundary disputes take a variety of forms.[86] In some cases the dispute concerns disagreement over historical and factual issues. In others the dispute arises over the interpretation and application of the governing legal standards to those facts. This section briefly examines the latter category of disputes. The LOS Convention separately prescribes the methods for delim-

79. Id. art. 47(1).
80. Id. art. 47(2).
81. Id. art. 50.
82. Id. art. 48.
83. Id. arts. 49(1) & (2).
84. Id. art. 52.
85. Id. art. 53.
86. See generally International Maritime Boundaries, vol. 6 (David A. Colson & Robert W. Smith eds., 2011).

iting the territorial sea, EEZ, and continental shelf boundaries between states with opposite or adjacent coasts. At the outset, however, it should be noted that the LOS Convention and the courts have injected equitable considerations into some delimitation rules, thereby rendering application of the rule judicially malleable and the outcomes less predictable. Further, the rules apply only to delimitation cases. Although the principles of restraint and equitable considerations incorporated into the rules on delimitations prescribe a wise and prudent approach, they are not legally compelled outside the boundary delimitation context.

1. Delimitation of the Territorial Sea

Where the coasts of two states are opposite (i.e., separated by water) or adjacent (i.e., the states share a land border), the 1982 LOS Convention provides that neither state is entitled to extend its territorial sea beyond the median line between their respective baselines. This restriction does not apply in certain cases involving historic waters or other special circumstances.[87]

2. Delimitation of the EEZ and Continental Shelf

The rules regarding delimitation of the EEZ and continental shelf between opposite or adjacent states depart from the presumptive "median line" rules in Article 15 applicable to the territorial sea. Articles 74 (delimitation of the EEZ) and 83 (delimitation of the continental shelf) both begin by declaring that delimitation is to be effected by agreement.[88] Additionally, the decision is to be made on the basis of international law, but in a way that achieves an equitable solution.[89] The LOS Convention further provides that if no agreement is reached within a reasonable time, the states are to follow the dispute settlement procedures in Part XV of the convention (see chapter 15). Until such an agreement is reached, the states must make every effort to enter into provisional arrangements and to avoid actions that might jeopardize the objective of reaching a final agreement. In a rare maritime delimitation case submitted to ITLOS (most are brought in the ICJ), in 2012, the tribunal resolved a dispute between Bangladesh and Burma (Myanmar) over delimitation of the two states' territorial seas, EEZs, and continental shelves in the Bay of Bengal.[90] The ITLOS judgment was widely praised as an exemplar of procedural and substantive fairness.

3. U.S. Maritime Boundaries

The United States has settled some, but not all, of its maritime boundary delimitation disputes with opposite and adjacent states.[91] For example, continental shelf and EEZ boundary disputes with Mexico were resolved by a pair of treaties.[92] In a dispute referred to a chamber of the ICJ by

---

87. LOSC art. 15.
88. The ICJ concluded that Articles 74 and 83 reflect customary international law. Territorial and Maritime Dispute (Nicaragua v. Colombia), supra, ¶ 139.
89. LOSC art. 74. See, e.g., North Sea Continental Shelf cases (Fed. Rep. Germany v. Denmark/ Fed. Rep. Germany v. Netherlands), ¶ 71, 1969 I.C.J. 3 (Feb. 20).
90. Dispute concerning Delimitation of the Maritime Boundary between Bangladesh and Myanmar in the Bay of Bengal (Bangladesh v. Myanmar), ITLOS Case No. 16, Judgment of Mar. 14, 2012, 51 I.L.M. 844–915 (2012).
91. See NOAA, Office of General Counsel, Maritime Zones and Boundaries, available at http://www.gc.noaa.gov/gcil_maritime.html (accessed Feb. 1, 2013).
92. See, e.g., Treaty on Maritime Boundaries between the United Mexican States and the United States of America (Caribbean Sea and Pacific Ocean), May 4, 1978, 1997, S. Exec. Doc. No. F, 96-1 (1979); Treaty between the Government of the United States and the Government of the United Mexican States on the Delimitation of the Continental Shelf in the Western Gulf of Mexico beyond 200 Nautical Miles, June 9, 2000, S. Treaty Doc. No. 106-39 (2000).

the United States and Canada, the court opted to select a common boundary for the EEZ and continental shelf in the Gulf of Maine.[93] Maritime boundaries with Canada in the Beaufort Sea, Dixon Entrance, and Strait of Juan de Fuca have yet to be resolved. A boundary treaty with Cuba was successfully negotiated but stalled in the Senate in 1980. It has, however, been provisionally extended.[94] A boundary delimitation agreement for the Bering Strait between the former Soviet Union and the United States was concluded in 1990 and approved by the U.S. Senate the following year; however, the Duma for the Russian Federation, successor to the Soviet Union, has not yet approved the treaty.

Over the past sixty years, the most contentious maritime boundary disputes have not been between the United States and adjacent nation-states, but rather between the federal government and individual states seeking to expand their jurisdiction at the expense of federal waters. Some of those disputes were adverted to above in the discussion of baseline determination, but a complete discussion of those cases is beyond the scope of this book.[95]

E. EXCESSIVE MARITIME CLAIMS AND THE FREEDOM OF NAVIGATION PROGRAM

The term "excessive maritime claims" refers to maritime claims by coastal states that exceed the parameters prescribed in relevant international laws, either spatially or in terms of the coastal state's assertions of rights and jurisdiction within the zone.[96] The related phrase "creeping jurisdiction" refers to coastal state extensions in quantity or quality. For example, the phrase equally includes a claim to extend the territorial sea beyond the twelve-nautical-mile limit and qualitative changes in the nature of the coastal state's asserted control over resources and activities in that zone, such as a requirement to provide advance notice to the coastal state or obtain its consent before transiting the waters. Excessive maritime claims may be protested or challenged by other states in a variety of ways, including diplomatic protests and operational assertions by vessels and aircraft.

Commonly relied on sources for identifying coastal state claims, both legal and excessive, are the DoD's *Maritime Claims Reference Manual* and the privately prepared and highly regarded treatise *Excessive Maritime Claims.*[97] The online *CIA World Factbook* also provides relevant maritime information on states. The stated "principal purpose" of the *Maritime Claims Reference Manual* is to facilitate the DoD's freedom of navigation (FON) program.[98] The FON program was formally launched in 1978 and reaffirmed in President Reagan's 1983 Ocean Policy Statement, which announced that "the United States will exercise and assert its navigation and overflight rights and freedoms on a worldwide basis in a manner that is consistent with the balance of interests reflected in the [1982 LOS] Convention. The United States will not, however, acquiesce in unilateral acts of other States designed to restrict the rights and freedoms of the international community in navigation and overflight and other related high seas uses."[99]

93. Delimitation of the Maritime Boundary in the Gulf of Maine Area (Canada/U.S.), 1984 I.C.J. 246 (Oct. 12).
94. Maritime Boundary Agreement between the United States of America and the Republic of Cuba, Dec. 16, 1977, Sen. Treaty Doc. No. 96-8; see also U.S. Department of State, Limits in the Seas, Pub. No. 110: Maritime Boundary: Cuba/U.S. (1980).
95. See generally Aaron L. Shalowitz, Shore and Sea Boundaries, vols. 1 & 2 (1962).
96. See Roach & Smith, Excessive Maritime Claims, supra, at 17–18.
97. Department of Defense, Under Secretary of Defense for Policy, Maritime Claims Reference Manual, DoD 2005.1-M (June 23, 2005); Roach & Smith, Excessive Maritime Claims, supra.
98. Maritime Claims Reference Manual, supra, Foreword.
99. Noteworthy operational challenges predating the FON program's formal launch in 1978 include the Royal Navy's challenge to Albania in the Corfu Channel in 1946 and the United States' challenge to Indonesia's archipelagic waters claims in the Lombok Strait and Malacca Straits in 1957.

The FON program includes both diplomatic measures and operational assertions. It targets excessive straight baseline claims; restrictions on innocent passage, transit passage, or archipelagic sea-lanes passage; notification or consent requirements; and restrictions on military and intelligence activities in the EEZ.[100] Although there is a preference for challenging excessive claims through diplomatic means, operational assertions are considered necessary to preserve the United States' status as a persistent objector to excessive maritime claims. Operational assertions are carried out by the geographical combatant commanders in accordance with presidential and DoD directives.[101] As a matter of policy, the United States does not give the coastal state notice before an operational assertion is carried out (even when carried out against "friendly" states). Indeed, the coastal state might not learn of the operation until the annual report on FON activities is published. Although the vast majority of assertions against excessive maritime claims, particularly those involving transits of international straits, are conducted without further review, selected operational assertions undergo high-level interagency review. Since the FON program was launched, the United States has lodged more than 100 diplomatic protests and carried out more than 350 operational assertions.[102]

---

100. See generally Commander's Handbook, supra, ¶ 2.8.

101. See National Security Presidential Directive 49 (1990); Presidential Decision Directive 32 (Freedom of Navigation) (1995); Department of Defense Instruction C-2005.1 (U.S. Program for the Exercise of Navigation and Overflight Rights at Sea), June 21, 1983; CJCS Inst. 2420.10B (United States Freedom of Navigation Program).

102. Freedom of Navigation Operational Assertions are tabulated by the DoD at http://policy.defense.gov/ OUSDPOffices/ASDforGlobalStrategicAffairs/CounteringWeaponsofMassDestruction/FON.aspx (accessed Feb. 1, 2013).

4

Internal Waters, Canals, and Ports

Ports and internal waters have long been treated differently under international law than the oceans, to which the law of the sea generally applies. In fact, most of the international legal regime regarding the status of ports and access to ports and internal waters is found not in the LOS Convention but rather in other bilateral and multilateral treaties and customary international law.[1] One should not, however, overestimate the role of international law in defining the regime for ports and internal waters, where the port state's domestic law still clearly dominates. In the United States that includes a large body of federal, state, and local laws.

A. INTERNAL WATERS

For states other than archipelagic states,[2] all waters lying landward of the state's baseline form part of the state's internal waters.[3] That classification generally holds true even if the state validly claims straight baselines or historic waters. Article 2 of the 1982 LOS Convention makes it clear that the state has more than mere "jurisdiction" over its internal waters. The convention holds, as did the 1958 Convention on the Territorial Sea and the Contiguous Zone before it, that the state is sovereign in its internal waters.[4] In the *Corfu Channel* case, the ICJ defined sovereignty as the whole body of rights and attributes that a state possesses in its territory, to the exclusion of all other states.[5] Sovereignty extends to all persons, property, and activities within the state's territory, but may be subject to recognized exceptions, such as the rules on sovereign and diplomatic immunity. The state also has an international obligation to warn transiting vessels of dangers in its waters and, more generally, to protect nonnationals within the state's territory from harm.[6]

Foreign vessels enter a state's internal waters for a variety of reasons, including cargo and passenger loading and discharge, to obtain fuel or provisions, and to seek shelter or make repairs. Some merely pass through one state's internal waters while en route to or from another state.

---

1. The LOS Convention does impose some limits on the port state's enforcement jurisdiction over vessels voluntarily in its ports. See, e.g., LOSC arts. 218 & 219.
2. The waters landward of the archipelagic state's baseline may be a combination of archipelagic waters and internal waters. This chapter is applicable to those parts that constitute internal waters. Archipelagic waters are discussed in chapter 5. Although this chapter distinguishes internal waters from ports for purposes of analysis, it is important to recognize that no clear line of demarcation separates one from the other.
3. LOSC art. 8(1). The U.S. definition of internal waters is set out in 33 C.F.R. §§ 2.05–20 & 2.24. See also Restatement FRLUS § 511cmt. e; Vladimir D. Degan, Internal Waters, 17 Neth. Y.B. Int'l L. 3, 44 (1986); Vasilios Tasikas, The Regime of Maritime Port Access: A Relook at Contemporary International and United States Law, 5 Loyola Mar. L. J. 1 (2007).
4. 1958 Convention on TTS and CZ, supra, art. 1.
5. The Corfu Channel case (U.K. v. Albania) 1949 I.C.J. 1 (Apr. 9). A more comprehensive description of sovereignty is provided by Judge Max Huber in the Island of Palmas arbitration discussed in chapter 1.
6. Restatement FRLUS § 511cmt. e & § 512 cmt. c. International human rights law protections extend even to the state's own nationals.

Three legal issues are commonly presented by a foreign vessel's entry into a state's internal waters or a foreign aircraft's flight over such waters. The first is whether foreign vessels or aircraft have navigation or overflight rights in or over a state's internal waters. The second concerns the extent to which a foreign vessel or aircraft that voluntarily enters a state's internal waters or the superjacent airspace is subject to the laws and regulations of that state. Third, assuming foreign vessels and aircraft do not otherwise enjoy navigation or overflight rights in another state's internal waters, is whether an exception is made when the ship or aircraft is in distress or validly claims force majeure.

1. Navigation and Overflight in Internal Waters

The general rule regarding foreign vessels is that, in the absence of a right conferred by a treaty, such vessels have no navigation rights in a foreign state's internal waters.[7] As section C of this chapter explains, that rule also applies to ports. There are two exceptions to the rule for internal waters enclosed by certain straight baselines. The first occurs in those cases in which the coastal state has established a straight baseline that has the effect of enclosing as internal waters areas that had not previously been considered as such. In such cases, vessels have a right of innocent passage through those waters.[8] Second, where the straight baseline encloses waters that would otherwise fall within the regime for international straits, a right of transit passage applies.[9] A third exception for vessel entry in cases of distress or force majeure is discussed in section A.3 below.

The airspace above the state's internal waters is "national airspace," as is the airspace above its land territory and territorial sea.[10] In general, foreign military and commercial aircraft have no right to enter or overfly national airspace without consent, except pursuant to treaty (such as the Chicago Convention on Civil Aviation discussed in chapter 9) or where a right of transit passage applies.[11] The exception for aircraft entry in cases of distress or force majeure is discussed in section A.3 below.

2. Application of Coastal State Laws in Internal Waters

Because internal waters are sovereign waters, the coastal state has prescriptive and enforcement jurisdiction over all vessels entering (or overflying) those waters as well as the persons on board, subject always to sovereign immunity rules.[12] The port state's enforcement jurisdiction within its territory is exclusive. Absent consent, the flag state cannot exercise enforcement jurisdiction

---

7. See Military and Paramilitary Activities (Nicaragua v. USA), ¶¶ 212–13, 1986 I.C.J. 14, 111 (June 27) (concluding that there is no right to enter the internal waters of another state); Anglo-Norwegian Fisheries case (U.K. v. Norway), 1951 I.C.J. 116, 125 (Dec. 18) (concluding that there is no right of access to internal waters, even those previously used by foreign vessels for navigation). See also Khedivial Line S.A.E. v. Seafarers' Int'l Union, 278 F.2d 49, 52 (2d Cir. 1960) (finding no U.S. precedents that held that the law of nations accords an unrestricted right of access).

8. LOSC art. 8(2).

9. Id. art. 35(a).

10. Convention on Civil Aviation [hereinafter "Chicago Convention on Civil Aviation"], arts. 1 & 2, Dec. 7, 1944, 61 Stat. 1180, T.I.A.S. No. 1591, 15 U.N.T.S. 295. See also Int'l Civil Aviation Organization, Doc. 7300/9 (9th ed. 2006). As the full title suggests, the Chicago Convention applies to civil aircraft. Military and other "state" aircraft neither benefit from nor are bound by the convention; however, they fly with "due regard" for its operating prescriptions.

11. Marjorie M. Whiteman, 9 Digest of International Law 309–22 (1968).

12. Additionally, vessels transiting the state's internal waters (and territorial seas) en route to one of the state's ports must comply with any applicable conditions of port entry (discussed in section C below).

(or deploy a shore patrol) in the foreign state's territory.[13] The general rule was announced by the U.S. Supreme Court in 1812 in *The Schooner Exchange v. McFaddon* case. In a decision that ultimately examined the question of sovereign immunity, the Court began by stating the general proposition: with respect to foreign vessels "the jurisdiction of a nation within its own territory is necessarily exclusive and absolute."[14] The Court went on to explain that a foreign vessel's entry into a U.S. port is based not on a right of entry, but rather on express or implied consent. That general rule on jurisdiction may be, and often is, modified by treaty, such as the many bilateral treaties of friendship, commerce, and navigation (FCN) or status-of-forces agreements (SOFAs).[15]

The legal regime for internal waters within the United States is complex, largely as a result of the nation's federated structure. Within internal waters, the federal and state governments share regulatory authority. How that authority is allocated turns in part on whether the waters are "navigable." Under U.S. law, internal waters are subject to the jurisdiction of the individual states in which they lie. Internal waters that meet the federal test for "navigable waters of the United States" are also subject to federal jurisdiction. In exercising that jurisdiction the federal government may choose to preempt state regulatory authority.[16] It is important to bear in mind, however, that the legal tests for "navigability" vary according to the subject matter being regulated. For example, the test for jurisdiction over vessel safety matters differs from the test for applicability of federal criminal laws, and both of those tests differ from the test for the admiralty and maritime jurisdiction of the federal courts. Those U.S. law tests are beyond the scope of this book.[17]

3. Entry by Vessels or Aircraft under Claim of Distress or Force Majeure

Customary international law has long recognized a right of access for vessels in cases of distress or force majeure.[18] While that history may be long, it has not necessarily been consistent in defining or distinguishing the concepts of distress, force majeure, and "safe harbor," or in its application of those concepts.[19] Although the terms "distress" and "force majeure" are often used interchangeably (and sometimes disjunctively without any attempt to distinguish them), that practice masks an important distinction.

One of the earliest known formal recognitions of the right of a foreign ship in distress to seek refuge (or "safe harbor") in another state's ports or internal waters was issued by Queen Elizabeth I in 1602 when she instructed her ambassadors that they were to declare that use of the ports and

---

13. U.S. Navy Regulations Article 0922(2) addresses the requirement to obtain foreign state consent before deploying a shore patrol.

14. The Schooner *Exchange* v. McFaddon, 11 U.S. (7 Cranch) 116, 136 (1812). See also Restatement FRLUS § 511cmt. b.

15. Selected FCN treaties are posted by the U.S. government's Trade Compliance Center at http://tcc.export.gov/Trade_Agreements/All_Trade_Agreements/index.asp (accessed Feb. 1, 2013).

16. See U.S. v. Locke, 529 U.S. 89, 112–17 (2000) (holding that federal law preempted various state of Washington tanker regulations).

17. See generally Thomas Schoenbaum, Admiralty and Maritime Law ch. 1, § 1-3 (5th ed. 2011).

18. See Restatement FRLUS § 512 n.5. See also "Force Majeure" and "Fortuitous Event" as Circumstances Precluding Wrongfulness: Survey of State Practice, International Judicial Decisions and Doctrine—Study Prepared by the Secretariat, 1978 Y.B. Int'l L. Comm'n, vol. II, at 66–76, U.N. Doc. No. A/CN.4/315.

19. See Kate A. Hoff Claim (U.S. v. Mexico), (1929) 4 Rep. Int'l Arb. Awards 444 (1951); The *Creole* (1853), in John Bassett Moore, International Arbitrations 824 (1896). But see Cushin and Lewis v. the King, [1935] Can. Exch. 103 (1933–34) Ann, Dig. 207 ("putting into port under constraint does not carry any legal right to exemption from local law or local jurisdiction"); Statement by Secretary of State Daniel Webster, Aug. 1, 1842, quoted in John Bassett Moore, A Digest of International Law, vol. 2, at 353, 354 (1906).

coasts of England was free for traffic by vessels of states in amity and those avoiding the dangers from tempests.[20] Both the 1958 Convention on the Territorial Sea and Contiguous Zone and the 1982 LOS Convention expressly refer to force majeure and distress as grounds for stopping or anchoring while in innocent passage;[21] however, neither convention defines those terms or addresses the further entry into a state's internal waters or ports.[22] "Distress" is generally understood by mariners to refer to a high-level threat to the ship or its crew that may be caused by an internal condition such as fire or flooding, or an external condition such as severe weather.[23] "Force majeure" refers to a superior force that threatens the ship and is generally, but not necessarily, external to the ship, such as an approaching hurricane.[24] A ship in distress requires assistance. By contrast, a ship faced with a force majeure may require nothing more than temporary shelter in a safe harbor. The terms are employed in two distinct applications. In the first usage, the question is whether a vessel that would otherwise have no right to enter a state's internal waters or port will be allowed to do so in order to relieve its distress. In the second application, the question is whether the distress or force majeure will excuse the vessel from certain liabilities or regulatory obligations that are otherwise incumbent on foreign vessels that enter the port.[25]

a. Maritime Distress

Chapter 8 discusses the long-standing duty of mariners and coastal states to assist vessels in distress. Chapter 5 addresses the circumstances under which a right of "passage" through a foreign state's territorial sea might include a right to stop or anchor when necessary as a result of distress (or force majeure), as well as a right of a vessel to enter a foreign state's territorial sea to render assistance to another vessel, aircraft, or person in distress (the right of distress entry). This section examines the right of a vessel to enter a foreign state's internal waters or port when in distress.

The term "distress" seems to have no single authoritative definition under international law. An early U.S. Supreme Court case defined distress as an "urgent necessity based upon a well-grounded apprehension of the loss of the vessel, its cargo, passengers or crew."[26] Four qualifications to that early definition should be noted. First, some nations limit distress to cases involving

---

20. Thomas Wemyss Fulton, The Sovereignty of the Sea: An Historical Account of the Claims of England to the Dominion of the British Seas, and of the Evolution of the Territorial Waters, with Special Reference to the Rights of Fishing and the Naval Salute 110–11 (1911).
21. 1958 Convention on TTS and CZ, supra, art. 14(3); LOSC art. 17(2).
22. For a discussion of the phrase "generally accepted," see Walker, Definitions for the Law of the Sea, supra, at 169–75, 197–205.
23. Lawyers of the International Law Commission who compiled the Draft Articles on State Responsibility adopted a narrow view of the terms "distress" and "force majeure," limiting those terms to situations involving strict necessity. The ILC definitions, which are examined in chapter 14 of this book, are ill suited for maritime operations because they would undermine the safety of navigation by discouraging mariners from seeking shelter in those cases where they are uncertain whether their vessel's condition constitutes distress or force majeure under international law, thus exposing their vessels, crew, and cargo to greater danger. Happily, Article 55 of the Draft Articles recognizes the supervening role of *lex specialis* rules, such as the distinctly maritime concepts of distress and force majeure.
24. In its extensive examination of the primary and secondary rules of force majeure, the ILC concluded, among other things, that the term "force majeure" includes situations with roots in human causes. 1978 Y.B. Int'l L. Comm'n, vol. II, at 66–69.
25. For example, vessels arriving in the United States under claim of force majeure are exempt from the requirement to file an advance notice of arrival (unless carrying dangerous cargo). 33 C.F.R. § 160.203(b)(3). Exemptions may also extend to tonnage taxes on the vessel and duties on its cargo.
26. The *New York*, 16 U.S. (3 Wheat.) 59 (1818) (examining defense of distress or *vis major* to what would otherwise be a customs violation).

danger to life and exclude situations involving only danger to property.[27] Second, the threshold for a distress determination is likely lower in cases involving the right of assistance entry, which permits rescue vessels to enter a foreign state's territorial sea to render assistance to a vessel in distress,[28] than it would be for the vessel in distress to enter the foreign state's internal waters or port. Third, the right of distress entry is not absolute. Any request for distress entry is evaluated in light of the risk posed to the coastal state's marine environment and the danger that the vessel might become an obstruction to navigation or otherwise threaten the coastal state's interests. Fourth, not all states fully extend the right to aircraft.

Friendship, commerce, and navigation treaties typically include a right of distress entry. For example, the 1956 FCN treaty between the United States and Nicaragua provides that "vessels of either Party that are in distress shall be permitted to take refuge in the nearest port or haven of the other Party, and shall receive friendly treatment and assistance."[29] An analogous treaty with Colombia is arguably more expansive, providing that

> whenever the citizens of either of the contracting parties shall be forced to seek refuge or asylum, in the rivers, bays, ports or dominions of the other with their vessels, whether merchant or of war, public or private, through stress of weather, pursuit of pirates or enemies, or want of provisions or water, they shall be received and treated with humanity, giving to them all favor and protection for repairing their ships, procuring provisions, and placing themselves in a situation to continue their voyage, without obstacle or hindrance of any kind or the payment of port fees or any charges other than pilotage, except such vessels continue in port longer than forty eight hours counting from the time they cast anchor in port.[30]

In the Supreme Court's decision in *The Schooner* Exchange case cited earlier, the Court noted the effect of such treaties: "In almost every instance, the treaties between civilized nations contain a stipulation to this effect in favor of vessels driven in by stress of weather or other urgent necessity. In such cases, the sovereign is bound by compact to authorize foreign vessels to enter his ports. The treaty binds him to allow vessels in distress to find refuge and asylum in his ports, and this is a license which he is not at liberty to retract." The fact that the right is occasionally written into treaties has suggested to some scholars the absence of such a right under customary law, but that argument is not well founded. As always, the test for a rule of customary international law is a combination of state practice and *opinio juris*.

Most states extend the right to enter national airspace over internal waters in cases of distress to military and other state aircraft. The right has been expressly extended to civil aircraft. The Chicago Convention on Civil Aviation provides the following:

---

27. See, e.g., ACT Shipping (Pte) Ltd. v. Minister for the Marine and Others [The MV *Toledo*], [1995] 2 Irish L. Rep. Monthly 30, 48–49 (Irish High Ct Admiralty). The 1979 Convention on Search and Rescue (SAR), which divides search-and-rescue operations into three phases (uncertainty, alert, and distress), defines the distress phase of a SAR incident as a "situation wherein there is a reasonable certainty that a vessel or a person is threatened by grave and imminent danger and requires immediate assistance." International Convention on Maritime Search and Rescue [hereinafter "SAR Convention"], Apr. 27, 1979, T.I.A.S. No. 11,093, 1403 U.N.T.S., Annex, ch. 1, ¶ 1.11.

28. This right of assistance entry is briefly adverted to in the innocent passage article of the 1982 LOS Convention. See LOSC art. 18(2). That right is examined in chapter 5.

29. Treaty of Friendship, Commerce and Navigation (U.S.-Nicaragua), art. XIX(5), Jan. 21, 1956, 9 U.S.T. 449, T.I.A.S. No. 4024.

30. Colombia Peace, Amity, Navigation and Commerce Treaty (U.S.-Colombia), art. 9, Dec. 12, 1846, 9 Stat. 881, Treaty Series 544.

ARTICLE 25. Aircraft in Distress

Each contracting State undertakes to provide such measures of assistance to aircraft in distress in its territory as it may find practicable, and to permit, subject to control by its own authorities, the owners of the aircraft or authorities of the State in which the aircraft is registered to provide such measures of assistance as may be necessitated by the circumstances. Each contracting State, when undertaking search for missing aircraft, will collaborate in coordinated measures which may be recommended from time to time pursuant to this Convention.[31]

Going beyond the requirement with respect to civil aircraft, the United States has permitted state aircraft, including military aircraft, in distress to land in the United States on many occasions, even at the height of the Cold War. The 1989 "dangerous military activities" (DMA) agreement between the United States and the former Soviet Union addressed unintentional or distress entry into the respective state territories.[32] When an aircraft enters and lands due to distress, the crew is to be treated humanely and must be permitted to make immediate contact with the flag state's diplomatic or consular officials. The sovereign immunity of military and other state aircraft is to be respected, and the aircraft must be permitted to depart once repairs are complete.

Not all states recognize a right of distress entry for state aircraft. For example, following the 2001 midair collision between a U.S. Navy EP-3E (Aries II) electronic reconnaissance plane and a Chinese F-8 interceptor jet seventy miles southeast of Hainan Island, the stricken EP-3E declared itself in distress and made an emergency landing on Hainan Island, within China. China disputed the lawfulness of the EP-3E's entrance and landing without China's prior consent.[33] The crew was held in "protective custody" and the aircraft was boarded, searched, and partially disassembled by the Chinese under the pretext of investigating the collision.

b. Maritime Force Majeure

The French phrase "force majeure" (in Latin, *vis major*) is roughly translated as "superior force." The international law doctrine of force majeure confers limited legal immunity on vessels that are forced to seek refuge or repairs within the jurisdiction of another state as a result of uncontrollable forces or conditions.[34] This limited immunity, which shares characteristics of the necessity and act of God defenses, prohibits coastal state enforcement of laws breached as a result of the vessel's entry under force majeure. Treaty definitions may differ, but under customary international law, force majeure is generally supported only by the existence of overwhelming conditions or forces (e.g., severe storm, fire, disablement, mutiny) of such magnitude that they threaten loss of the vessel, crew, or cargo unless immediate corrective action is taken. Vessels

31. Chicago Convention on Civil Aviation, supra, art. 25.
32. Agreement on the Prevention of Dangerous Military Activities (U.S.-USSR) [hereinafter "DMA Agreement"], June 12, 1989, No. 27309; Commander's Handbook, supra, ¶ 2.10.2.
33. See Sean D. Murphy, Contemporary Practice of the United States relating to International Law, 95 Am. J. Int'l L. 626, 630–32 (2000).
34. U.S. Coast Guard, Maritime Law Enforcement Manual, COMDTINST M16247.1 (series) [hereinafter "Coast Guard MLE Manual"], at ¶ B-4.a. Article 2 of the 1910 Brussels Collision Convention effectively precludes a finding of fault when the collision was caused by force majeure. International Convention for the Unification of Certain Rules of Law with respect to Collision between Vessels, art. 2, Sep. 23, 1910, U.N. Regulation No. 134(a). The Brussels Collision Convention does not define force majeure; however, it appears to apply to both external and internal conditions.

entering a state's internal waters under claim of force majeure are subject to boarding to validate their claim and may be directed to a specific location (not necessarily the port or anchorage of their choice). A vessel's claim of force majeure will be denied if the vessel was in the vicinity of the territorial waters with the intent to violate that state's law or the vessel violates the state's law after it enters the territorial seas.[35]

In the 1815 *Brig* Concord decision, the U.S. Supreme Court explained the application of force majeure to a claim by the U.S. government for duties on imported goods. Writing for the Court, Justice Joseph Story explained that "where goods are brought by superior force, or by inevitable necessity, into the United States, they are not deemed to be so imported, in the sense of the law, as necessarily to attach the right to duties."[36]

In the United States, the Coast Guard captain of the port (COTP) has statutory authority to deny entry to vessels; however, that authority is expressly subject to "recognized principles of international law."[37] The Coast Guard has referred to the doctrine of force majeure as a "right" under international law similar to the right of innocent passage,[38] and has defined force majeure as "a doctrine of international law which confers limited legal immunity upon foreign vessels that are forced to seek refuge or repairs within the jurisdiction of another State due to uncontrollable external forces or conditions."[39] The Coast Guard COTP has authority to verify and accept or reject claims of force majeure for the purpose of enforcing applicable laws. In processing claims for force majeure entry, the cognizant Coast Guard sector commander, acting in his or her capacity as the COTP, generally follows the guidance in an internal Coast Guard directive on places of refuge, using procedures set out in the Maritime Operational Threat Response Plan. In addition, the National Response Team has produced a guidance document for use in force majeure decision making.[40]

c. Places of Refuge

As the foregoing sections explain, a claim of distress may give rise to a qualified right to enter internal waters (and raises the question of the duty of rescue),[41] while the claim of force majeure is best viewed as a defense to application of the coastal or port state's laws. A vessel might invoke force majeure even though not presently in distress when, for example, an oncoming hurricane would endanger the vessel if it remained at sea. If that distinction is sound, the threshold for a right of distress entry would logically be higher than the threshold for an exemption or qualified immunity from coastal state law due to a force majeure. To some extent, the emerging "places of refuge" framework combines attributes of both concepts.

---

35. U.S. Coast Guard, Model Maritime Operations Guide, at 2–13 (Apr. 21, 2003, as amended), available at http://www.uscg.mil/international/affairs/MMOG/English/ (accessed Feb. 1, 2013).
36. The Brig *Concord*, 13 U.S. (9 Cranch) 387, 387 (1815).
37. 33 U.S.C. § 1232(e); 33 C.F.R. § 160.107.
38. See, e.g., 33 C.F.R. § 165.1122(c). See also 33 U.S.C. § 1228(b). The Supreme Court's 1812 decision in The Schooner *Exchange* v. McFaddon suggested such a right existed.
39. U.S. Coast Guard, Places of Refuge Policy, Commandant Instruction 16451.9 (July 17, 2007). Volume 6 of the U.S. Coast Guard Marine Safety Manual also discusses the Coast Guard's policy on force majeure.
40. National Response Team (NRT), Guidelines for Places of Refuge Decision-Making, July 26, 2007, available on the NRT website: http://www.nrt.org.
41. In cases of distress involving merchant vessels, the master typically files a "protest of distress." A protest is a solemn declaration made on oath by a ship's master that circumstances beyond his control have, or may have, given rise to loss or damage to his ship, its cargo, or to other property such as a pier or dock, or have caused him to take action (such as leaving an unsafe port) that might render the vessel owner liable to legal action by another party. The protest should be made as soon as possible after arriving in port, and not later than twenty-four hours after such arrival.

In response to several high-profile incidents involving stricken vessels whose masters requested and were denied permission to enter a foreign state's waters to make critical emergency repairs, including most prominently the vessels *Erika* (1999), *Castor* (2000), and *Prestige* (2002), the IMO facilitated international efforts to develop a consistent and predictable place of refuge regime.[42] The rules on distress or force majeure entry were largely developed in the Age of Sail. As sail gave way to steam (powered by coal and then oil), however, coastal sailing packets carrying cotton and grain yielded the seas to supertankers and LNG and LPG carriers with cargoes of crude oil and noxious chemicals, significantly altering the risk calculus applicable to a state's decision to permit a foreign vessel to enter its ports.[43] Add to that the risk of the vessel sinking in a heavily used navigation channel, effectively blockading the port, and the port authority's dilemma when faced with a distress entry request becomes clear.[44] In 2003, shortly after the *Prestige* incident, the IMO issued guidelines for states in designating places of refuge for ships in need of assistance.[45] The U.S. Coast Guard issued a directive setting out the U.S. places of refuge policy in 2007.[46] The Coast Guard decision process under that policy directive was successfully put to the test during the January 2007 force majeure entry into Honolulu, Hawaii, by the Chinese cargo ship *Tong Cheng* after the vessel suffered a serious hull fracture at sea.

B. CANALS, STRAITS, AND RIVERS SUBJECT TO INTERNATIONAL AGREEMENTS

The LOS Convention preserves the legal effect of existing treaties governing certain international straits, such as the Montreux Convention governing the Turkish Straits.[47] When the waters are governed by such a treaty, the LOS Convention articles on straits do not apply.[48] Similar agreements exist with respect to certain critical canals such as the Kiel,[49] Panama, and Suez.[50]

---

42. See Places of Refuge for Ships: Emerging Environmental Concerns of a Maritime Custom (Aldo Chircop ed., 2005). The IMO has served as a forum for examining the respective state responsibilities for the safe recovery and disposition of migrants, refugees, and other persons rescued at sea. The IMO-led initiative, which followed the August 2001 incident involving the M/V *Tampa*'s recovery of more than four hundred Afghan refugees off the coast of Australia, was coordinated with the UN High Commissioner for Refugees (UNHCR). See Review of Safety Measures and Procedures for the Treatment of Persons Rescued at Sea, IMO Res. A.920(22) (2001). It led to amendments to the SOLAS and SAR Conventions in 2006. See also IMO, Guidelines on the Treatment of Persons Rescued at Sea, IMO Res. MSC.167(78) (2004); IMO/UNHCR, Rescue at Sea: A Guide to the Principles and Practice as Applied to Migrants and Refugees (2006).

43. Pollution concerns prompted some EU states to announce that they would condition any such entry on an acceptable financial responsibility guarantee.

44. The Nairobi Wreck Convention is intended to address part of this concern. International Convention on the Removal of Wrecks, May 18, 2007, 46 I.L.M. 697 (2007) (not in force).

45. IMO, Guidelines on Places of Refuge for Ships in Need of Assistance, Res. A.949(23) (Dec. 5, 2003).

46. U.S. Coast Guard, Places of Refuge Policy, Commandant Instruction 16451.9 (July 17, 2007).

47. Montreux Convention regarding the Régime of the Turkish Straits, Nov. 9, 1936, 173 L.N.T.S. 214. See generally Christos L. Rozakis & Petros N. Stagos, The Turkish Straits (1987).

48. LOSC art. 35(c) (exempting from Part III "straits in which passage is regulated in whole or in part by long-standing international conventions in force specially relating to such straits").

49. The Kiel Canal in northern Germany was given the status of an international waterway by the 1919 Treaty of Versailles.

50. The Suez Canal is owned and maintained by the Suez Canal Authority (SCA) of Egypt. Under Article 1 of the Constantinople Convention respecting the Free Navigation of the Suez Maritime Canal, March 2, 1888, the canal may be used "in time of war as in time of peace, by every vessel of commerce or of war, without distinction of flag." The Suez Canal was closed from 1967 to 1975 as a result of the hostilities between Egypt and Israel. The Torrijos-Carter Treaties of Sep. 1, 1977 (officially, the Treaty concerning the Permanent Neutrality and Operation of the Panama Canal and The Panama Canal Treaty) ensure similar access to the Panama Canal, while reserving to the United States permanent authority to defend the canal if it is ever placed under threat as a neutral water passage). See also Panama Canal Act of 1979, 93 Stat. 452; 22 U.S.C. § 3618 (defense of canal).

Similarly, the Barcelona Convention and the Statute on the Régime of Navigable Waterways of International Concern address ports, rivers, and artificial canals with international significance.[51]

Rivers that lie entirely within one nation-state are considered part of that state's territory and are called national rivers. By contrast, rivers that form a boundary between two or more states are deemed international rivers. Most international rivers are open to navigation by vessels of all states. The same rule is being increasingly applied to rivers that lie in the territory of one state, but which serve as lines of communication for an interior state. Under those circumstances, the state in which a river lies may not exercise its sovereignty in a manner that would impede the free flow of traffic to and from the interior state.

If an international river is not navigable, as in the case of the Rio Grande,[52] the territorial boundary between the states bordering the river lies at the river's geographical center. If the river is navigable, as in the case of the Saint Lawrence River between the United States and Canada, the center of the deepest channel (the "thalweg") marks the boundary line. The rationale for using the thalweg rather than the geographical center was explained by the U.S. Supreme Court in 1934: "If the dividing line were to be placed in the centre of the stream rather than in the centre of the channel, the whole track of navigation might be thrown within the territory of one state to the exclusion of the other."[53] In the absence of an agreement with the affected states, a state whose boundary is determined by an international river may not, by construction or otherwise, change the river's natural course or alter the thalweg; nor may it divert or lower the waters of the river, thereby impeding navigation. If gradual natural action changes the course of an international river and thereby creates a new thalweg, the boundary shifts to the new thalweg to ensure continued navigation access.

C. PORTS

The concept of the "port state" (as distinguished from the related concepts of "coastal state" and "flag state") begins with the principle that a state's territorial sovereignty extends to its ports.[54] The term "port" is not defined in the LOS Convention. Under U.S. law it is defined as "any place to which ships may resort for shelter or to load or unload passengers or goods, or to obtain fuel, water, or supplies."[55] Vessels may seek access to seaports for a variety of reasons, the primary one being commercial opportunity. In a globalized economy in which more than 90 percent of the goods traded among nations are transported by vessel, a merchant vessel's access to seaports is vital.

1. Access of Foreign Vessels to Ports

Surprisingly, neither the LOS Convention nor any other generally applicable treaty confers a right of access to foreign ports (though the LOS Convention makes some allowance for landlocked states). Nor is there a general customary right of access to foreign ports, except in cases of distress.[56] Commercial ports are presumed to be accessible to vessels of all states

---

51. Convention and Statute on the Régime of Navigable Waterways of International Concern, Apr. 20, 1921, 7 L.N.T.S. 7 & 36. Whiteman, 9 Digest of International Law, supra, at 1133–34.
52. U.S. v. Rio Grande Irrigation Co., 174 U.S. 690, 699 (1899).
53. New Jersey v. Delaware, 291 U.S. 361, 380 (1934).
54. LOSC arts. 2(1), 11, & 12.
55. 47 U.S.C. § 153(19).
56. See Louise de La Fayette, Access to Ports in International Law, 11 Int'l J. Marine & Coastal L. 1, 2 (1996).

willing to comply with the applicable conditions on entry,[57] however, and access may be further ensured through treaties and nondiscrimination and most-favored-nation (MFN) treatment obligations.[58]

The general presumption in favor of port access does not extend to warships and fishing vessels.[59] Warships are typically required to follow formal diplomatic clearance or informal naval visits agreement procedures for foreign port visits.[60] Some states also restrict or prohibit access to strategically important ports by nuclear-powered ships or ships carrying (or which refuse to confirm whether they are carrying) nuclear weapons or material.[61] The coastal state may temporarily suspend access in exceptional cases for imperative reasons, such as the security of the state or public health. The state may also condition entry of a foreign ship into its internal waters or ports on compliance with its laws and regulations.

Even when there exists a right or presumption of port access, that right does not carry with it immunity from port state regulation. In principle, a state may exercise jurisdiction with respect to a ship in its port and over activities on board such ship, but in practice, port states usually have only limited interest in exercising jurisdiction over the vessel's internal activities, except when the peace of the port is disturbed. The peace-of-the-port rule is examined below. The coastal state may also exercise jurisdiction to enforce international standards with respect to some activities that occurred prior to entry into its ports or internal waters (e.g., the illegal discharge of pollutants).[62]

a. A Customary International Law Right of Port Access?

The *Restatement* takes the position that as a general rule, maritime ports are open to foreign ships on condition of reciprocity.[63] While that might be true as a matter of comity, however, it is not true as a matter of customary law, with the exception discussed above for vessels in distress. The most common source of confusion is a 1958 arbitration decision involving Saudi Arabia in which the arbitrators announced that, "according to the great principle of public international law, the ports of every state must be open to foreign vessels and can only be closed when the vital interests of the state so require."[64] The arbitrator's dictum has been widely criticized as an

---

57. The highly regarded treatise of Professors McDougal and Burke summarizes the thinking. See McDougal & Burke, supra, at 99–117. While it is desirable to provide access to ports, not every wise policy choice is codified into a rule of law. Indeed, reciprocity seems to be a prime consideration of states in opening their ports to foreign vessels.

58. The protections historically provided by most-favored-nation treaty clauses (now called normal trade relations, or NTR) and national treatment clauses has eroded as more and more states have entered into bilateral and multilateral free trade agreements and customs zones. GATT Article 24 authorizes member states to enter into such preferential trade agreements, which now number approximately three hundred. See General Agreement on Tariffs and Trade 1994 [hereinafter "GATT 1994"], art. 24, Apr. 15, 1994, Marrakesh Agreement Establishing the World Trade Organization, Annex 1A, The Legal Texts: The Results of the Uruguay Round of Multilateral Trade Negotiations (1999), 1867 U.N.T.S. 187 (1994).

59. McDougal & Burke, supra, at 109–10 & n.59. Article 13 of the 1923 Statute on the Régime for Ports excludes warships from its right of port access.

60. See Chief of Naval Operations, Port Visits by U.S. Navy Ships to Foreign Countries, OPNAVINST C3128.3U (Nov. 10, 2008) (classified). Naval visit agreements generally permit informal notifications through naval rather than diplomatic channels.

61. See Canadian Transp. Co. v. U.S., 663 F.2d 1081 (D.C. Cir. 1980) (denying plaintiff's challenge to Coast Guard's denial of entry to the port of Norfolk, Va. [a strategically vital Navy port], to vessel under the "special interest vessel" program).

62. LOSC art. 218; Lauritzen v. Larsen, 345 U.S. 571, 577 (1953).

63. Restatement FRLUS § 512 n.3.

64. Saudi Arabia v. Arabian American Oil Company (Aramco), Award of Aug. 23, 1958, 27 Int'l L. Rep. 167, 212 (1958).

inaccurate statement of the law at the time it was made,[65] and it is no truer as a matter of law today.[66]

b. Treaty-Based Right of Port Access

Several other legal sources address access to foreign ports and internal waters. The first is the 1923 Statute on the International Régime of Maritime Ports.[67] The 1923 statute grew out of the Covenant of the League of Nations, Article 23 of which charged the members to "maintain freedom of communication and of transit and equitable treatment for the commerce of all members of the League."[68] Article 1 of the 1923 statute in turn provided that "subject to the principle of reciprocity . . . every Contracting State undertakes to grant the vessels of every other Contracting State equality of treatment with its own vessels, or those of any other State whatsoever, in the maritime ports situated under its sovereignty or authority, as regards freedom of access to the port, the use of the port, and the full enjoyment of the benefits as regards navigation and commercial operations which it affords to vessels, their cargoes and passengers."[69]

Although it provides a broad, treaty-based right of port access, the 1923 Maritime Ports Statute has not been widely ratified (the United States is not a party). The second treaty provision, Article V of the General Agreement on Tariffs and Trade (GATT), is more widely ratified; however, it is also more limited in its reach. Paragraph 2 of GATT Article V provides that "there shall be freedom of transit through the territory of each contracting party, via the routes most convenient for international transit, for traffic in transit to or from the territory of other contracting parties. No distinction shall be made which is based on the flag of vessels, the place of origin, departure, entry, exit or destination, or on any circumstances relating to the ownership of goods, of vessels or of other means of transport."[70]

The Article V "freedom of transit" provision protects a limited right of transit through other states that are party to the GATT, but it does not confer a right to enter a port to load or offload cargo.[71] It should also be noted that the rights set out in paragraph 2 of Article V are subject to more stringent port, vessel, and cargo security measures in the wake of the September 11, 2001, attacks. The EU relied in part on Article V in its challenge to Chile's restrictions on transshipping fish products;[72] however, the dispute was settled before the issue was adjudicated on the merits.[73]

---

65. Cf. A. Vaughan Lowe, The Right of Entry into Maritime Ports in Customary Law, 14 San Diego L. Rev. 597 (1986).
66. Military and Paramilitary Activities in and against Nicaragua (Nicaragua v. U.S.), ¶¶ 212–14, 1986 I.C.J. 14 (June 27) (concluding that states enjoy sovereign right to control access to ports).
67. Statute on the International Régime of Maritime Ports, art. 3, annexed to the Convention on the International Régime of Maritime Ports, Dec. 9, 1923, 28 L.N.T.S. 115. Fewer than fifty states have ratified the convention. The United States is not party to either the statute or the convention.
68. League of Nations Covenant, art. 23, June 28, 1919, 225 Consol. Treaty Series 188. Article 23 was also the catalyst for the 1921 Barcelona conference that produced the Convention and Statute on the Régime of Navigable Waterways of International Concern discussed above.
69. Id. art. 1.
70. GATT 1994, supra, art. V(2).
71. See GATT 1994, supra, art. V(1). See generally Nora Neufeld, Article V of the GATT 1994—Scope and Application, Doc. G/C/W/408 (2004), available at http://r0.unctad.org/ttl/ppt-2004-11-24/wto.pdf (accessed Feb. 1, 2013).
72. European Commission, Report to the Trade Barriers Regulation Committee (1999), TBR proceedings concerning Chilean practices affecting transit of swordfish in Chilean ports, at 46–50, available at http://trade.ec.europa .eu/doclib/docs/2004/october/tradoc_112193.pdf (accessed Feb. 1, 2013). See also Case on Conservation of Swordfish Stocks between Chile and the European Community in the South-Eastern Pacific Ocean before Special Chamber of the Tribunal (EU v. Chile) ITLOS Case No. 7 (dismissed).
73. See Neufeld, Article V of GATT, supra, at 8.

The third possible source of a right of port access lies in the many bilateral treaties of friendship, commerce, and navigation (FCN treaties) entered into between states, many of which address port access and extend "national treatment," "most favored nation treatment," or both to the contracting parties on a reciprocal basis. A typical FCN treaty port access clause provides that

> vessels of either High Contracting Party shall have liberty, on equal terms with vessels of the other High Contracting Party and on equal terms with vessels of any third country, to come with their cargoes to all ports, places and waters of such other High Contracting Party open to foreign commerce and navigation. Such vessels and cargoes shall in all respects be accorded national treatment and most favored nation treatment within the ports, places and waters of such other High Contracting Party; but each High Contracting Party may reserve exclusive rights and privileges to its own vessels with respect to the coasting trade, inland navigation and national fisheries.[74]

FCN treaties commonly limit access to those ports "open to foreign commerce and navigation," and exempt fishing vessels and warships from the port access provisions.[75] Such vessels may, however, be included in port access provisions for vessels in distress. The FCN treaty between the United States and Italy, for example, provides that "if a vessel of either High Contracting Party shall be forced by stress of weather or by reason of any other distress to take refuge in any of the ports, places or waters of the other High Contracting Party not open to foreign commerce and navigation, it shall receive friendly treatment and assistance and such repairs, as well as supplies and materials for repair, as may be necessary and available. *This paragraph shall apply to vessels of war and fishing vessels*, as well as to vessels as defined in paragraph 2 of Article XIX."[76] The treaty reserves to the parties the right to restrict access when "necessary for the protection of the essential interests . . . in time of national emergency."[77]

Some status-of-forces agreements address conditions for access by military vessels and aircraft. Among other things, SOFAs may specify whether visiting warships are exempt from compulsory pilotage requirements or other conditions on entry.[78] For example, Article V of the SOFA between the United States and Japan[79] provides:

> 1. United States and foreign vessels and aircraft operated by, for, or under the control of the United States for official purposes shall be accorded access to any port or airport of Japan free from toll or landing charges. When cargo or passengers not accorded the exemptions of this Agreement are carried on such vessels and aircraft, notification shall be given to the appropriate Japanese authorities, and their entry into and departure from Japan shall be according to the laws and regulations of Japan. . . .

---

74. Treaty of Amity, Economic Relations, and Consular Rights (U.S.-Iran), art. X.3, Aug. 15, 1955, 8 U.S.T. 899.
75. See, e.g., Treaty of Friendship, Commerce and Navigation (U.S.-Japan), art. XIX(7), Apr. 2, 1953, T.I.A.S. 2863.
76. Treaty of Friendship, Commerce and Navigation (U.S.-Italy), art. XX(4), Feb. 2, 1948, 12 U.S.T. 131 (emphasis added).
77. Id. art. XXI.
78. Guidance on the relationship between a ship and its embarked navigational pilot is set out in Article 0856 of the U.S. Navy Regulations and Article 4-2-3 of U.S. Coast Guard Regulations.
79. Agreement under Article VI of the Treaty of Mutual Cooperation and Security between Japan and the United States of America, regarding Facilities and Areas and the Status of United States Armed Forces in Japan, Jan. 19, 1960, 11 U.S.T. 1652.

3. When the vessels mentioned in paragraph 1 enter Japanese ports, appropriate notification shall, under normal conditions, be made to the proper Japanese authorities. Such vessels shall have freedom from compulsory pilotage, but if a pilot is taken pilotage shall be paid for at appropriate rates.[80]

c. LOS Convention Accommodations for Landlocked States

The 1982 LOS Convention recognizes the serious disadvantage of states that have no seacoast ("landlocked" states),[81] and seeks to accommodate their trade and transportation needs through access and freedom-of-transit provisions.[82] Part X of the LOS Convention provides landlocked states with a right of access to and from the sea, to enable them to exercise their high-seas freedoms and other rights under the convention.[83] The right of access provides landlocked states with a qualified freedom of transit through the territory of transit states by all means of transport.[84] The terms for exercising the freedom of transit are to be worked out by agreement between the landlocked state and the transit state; however, the traffic in transit is not subject to customs duties, taxes, or other charges except charges levied for specific services rendered in connection with such traffic.[85] Ships flying the flag of landlocked states are also entitled to treatment equal to that accorded to other foreign ships in maritime ports.[86] The accommodations in Part X constitute an exception to the transit state's obligations under MFN clauses in trade agreements.[87]

2. Status of Foreign Ships in Ports

The right of port access does not preclude application of entry conditions, port state regulations, or port state enforcement (often called "port state control") of international safety and security regimes, such as those imposed by the Safety of Life at Sea (SOLAS) Convention to promote port and vessel safety and security.[88] Vessels and cargoes passing through a state's internal waters and ports could pose actual or perceived risks to the safety or security of other vessels in the port, port facilities, surrounding infrastructure, and populations, as well as to the waterways themselves. Port states can and do prescribe and enforce laws designed to manage those risks, subject to the established rules of immunity for public vessels and diplomats. Such measures may include port access restrictions, entry conditions, and port state control screening and inspection requirements.[89]

---

80. Id. art. V. Article XI of the SOFA exempts U.S. vessels and aircraft from Japanese customs examinations, and Article XVII addresses jurisdiction of the respective states over members of the U.S. military in Japan.

81. LOSC art. 124. See also United Nations Convention on the Law of the Sea 1982: A Commentary, vol. III, at 371–457 (Satya Nandan et al. eds., 1995); Whiteman, 9 Digest of International Law, supra, at 10143–63.

82. UN Division of Ocean Affairs and the Law of the Sea, Rights of Access of Land-Locked States to and from the Sea and Freedom of Transit, Sales No. E.87.V.5 (1987).

83. See also the discussion above of GATT Article V.

84. "Transit states" and "means of transport" are defined in LOSC arts. 124 & 125 respectively.

85. LOSC arts. 124 & 127.

86. Id. art. 131.

87. Id. art. 126.

88. International Convention for the Safety of Life at Sea [hereinafter "SOLAS Convention"], Nov. 1, 1974, 32 U.S.T. 47, 1184 U.N.T.S. 2. See generally Rosalie Balkin, The International Maritime Organization and Maritime Security, 30 Tulane Mar. L. J. 1 (2006).

89. The U.S. statutory scheme includes port and vessel security measures prescribed by the Magnuson Act and its implementing regulations (50 U.S.C. §§ 191–195; 33 C.F.R. pt. 6 and Exec. Order 13,273), the Ports and Waterways Safety Act (33 U.S.C. § 1226), and regulations issued under the Maritime Transportation Security Act (33 C.F.R. pts. 101–06).

Additional security measures apply to the vessel's crew and passengers,[90] and the port state may have specially adapted rules on the vessel's responsibility for stowaways.[91]

Warships and other public vessels enjoy sovereign immunity whether on the high seas or in the internal waters and ports of a foreign state (see chapter 9). The U.S. Supreme Court recognized a warship's immunity while in a foreign port in its 1812 decision in *The Schooner* Exchange *v. McFaddon* cited earlier. In that case, the Court identified a principle of public law that "national ships of war entering the port of a friendly power open for their reception are to be considered as exempted by the consent of that power from its jurisdiction."[92] Although in the absence of a treaty such ships have no right of entry into a foreign state's internal waters or ports, if admitted they are immune from the port state's jurisdiction.[93] Accordingly, the port state jurisdiction provisions discussed in the following sections have only limited application to warships and other public vessels.

Commanding officers of warships may be confronted with a number of demands by foreign port authorities that conflict with the warship's sovereign immunity. Those demands may include assessment of port taxes or fees; a requirement to fly the national flag of the port state;[94] requests by port state officials to board and inspect the vessel; and requests to produce crew lists, crew health–related information, liberty lists, or information on weapons or stores.[95] Because the appropriate response to such demands depends on both the law of sovereign immunity and

90. Professional mariners must now comply with requirements for personal identification (which often includes biometric identifiers) and restrictions on their movement in foreign ports. In the United States, the requirement to obtain the Transportation Worker Identification Credential (TWIC) has been controversial.

91. Stowing away on a vessel or aircraft is a felony under U.S. law. See 18 U.S.C. § 2199. In many states, including the United States, shipowners are held financially responsible for repatriating stowaways brought into the state and for their maintenance pending return. See, e.g., Dia Nav. Co. Ltd. v. Immigration & Naturalization Service, 1994 A.M.C. 2921 (3d Cir. 1994) (reviewing U.S. policy making ship owners responsible for the costs of and the actual detention of asylum-seeking stowaways). See also IMO, Guidelines on the Allocation of Responsibilities to Seek the Successful Resolution of Stowaway Cases, IMO Res. A.871(20) (1997).

92. The Schooner *Exchange* v. McFaddon, 11 U.S. (7 Cranch) 116, 145–46 (1812). See also id. at 147 ("a public armed ship, in the service of a foreign sovereign, . . . should be exempt from the jurisdiction of the country").

93. The dominant view on the principle of sovereign immunity of warships while in the internal waters of a foreign state (in contrast with immunity while in the foreign state's territorial sea or on the high seas) has been that the source of that immunity is found in customary international law, not the LOS Convention. A 1926 convention that would have codified the immunity of warships and other government vessels while denying immunity to such ships engaged in commercial activities attracted relatively few ratifications. See International Convention for the Unification of Certain Rules regarding the Immunity of State Owned Vessels, art. 3, Apr. 10, 1926, 26 Am. J. Int'l L. Supp. 566 (1932). Some elements of the 1926 Convention can now be found in Article 26 of the draft UN Convention on Jurisdictional Immunities of States and Their Property, Annex to UNGA Res. 59/38 (Dec. 2, 2004) (not in force). A 2012 order by ITLOS directing Ghana to release the Argentine naval training tall ship ARA *Libertad* accredited Argentina's argument that Article 32 of the LOS Convention on the sovereign immunity of warships might apply not just in the foreign state's territorial sea, but also in its internal waters. See The ARA *Libertad* case (Argentina v. Ghana), ITLOS Case No. 20, Provisional Measures, Order of 15 December 2012. By contrast, the joint separate opinion in that case by Judges Wolfrum and Cot (¶¶ 38–46) rejected the view that Article 32 of the convention applied in a state's internal waters. They explained in paragraph 26 of the opinion: "Our analysis that internal waters in principle are not covered by the Convention, but by customary international law, is largely confirmed by the travaux préparatoires of the Convention. It is telling that during the long years of the Third Conference on the law of the Sea, not a word was said about including provisions on the legal regime of ports and internal waters in the Convention. No delegation at any moment suggested otherwise."

94. A warship cannot be compelled to fly the flag of a foreign state, although it might choose to fly the national flag of the host nation (always from a position inferior to that of the warship's own national ensign) as a courtesy during a port visit or when rendering honors. See U.S. Navy Regulations, supra, arts. 1258 & 1277; U.S. Coast Guard Regulations, supra, arts. 14-8-1(B) & 14-8-20 & 21.

95. A list of concerns compiled by U.S. Pacific Command included port state demands that visiting warships provide the port state with crew lists (India), pay port fees/taxes (Malaysia), or permit boarding (Australia).

national policies (and failure to agree to the demands might result in the warship being ordered by the port state to depart the port),[96] guidance on responding to such demands and on personal identification and travel document requirements for crewmembers going ashore or leaving or joining the vessel while in port should be sought from national, fleet, or theater commanders or their staff judge advocates.[97]

Warships and other public vessels in foreign ports might also find themselves confronted with a request for temporary refuge or asylum by a foreign national or for protection of a U.S. national in the foreign state.[98] Such matters demand scrupulous attention to the law, policy, and procedures prescribed by higher authority and close interagency coordination.[99] Because they overlap in some respects with the immigration regime examined in chapter 11, temporary refuge, asylum, and the *non-refoulement* rule in refugee law are addressed in that chapter.

Foreign port public health quarantines present a unique case.[100] The practice of ordering arriving vessels and travelers into quarantine as a precaution against the spread of infectious diseases formally dates to the fourteenth century, when England implemented the practice to stem the Black Death, which had claimed 30 percent of Europe's population. Vessels that had called on ports of concern were placed into quarantine for thirty to forty days. Over the centuries, the practice has been invoked to combat cholera, plague, smallpox, and pandemic flu strains.

The requirements of states imposing quarantine conditions vary, but they typically deem vessels arriving from foreign ports to be in quarantine until given pratique—clearance from the port's health authority to enter the port, disembark persons, and commence operations. *U.S. Navy Regulations* and *U.S. Coast Guard Regulations* direct commanding officers and aircraft commanders to comply with applicable quarantine regulations and restrictions.[101] At the same time, they are encouraged to request pratique in accordance with the port state regulations. The arriving vessel proceeds to a designated quarantine anchorage and hoists the Quebec flag or otherwise communicates its request to port authorities for free pratique. The vessel then awaits boarding by the state's designated quarantine inspector. The inspector examines the vessel's

96. A 1990 episode in which a Brazilian court ordered the USS *Greenling* (SSN-614) to depart Brazilian waters, apparently in contravention of the views of the state's executive branch, demonstrates that a state's courts and its elected branches do not always agree on accommodating foreign warship visits. An environmental group had challenged the legality of permitting the nuclear-powered warship in a Brazilian port. See Department of State, Digest of U.S. Practice in International Law 1989–1990, at 476–77. See also Congressional Research Service, Navy Nuclear-Powered Surface Ships: Background Issues and Options for Congress (2008); J. C. Woodliffe, Port Visits by Nuclear Armed Naval Vessels: Recent State Practice, 35 Int'l & Comp. L. Q. 730 (1986).
97. See Commander's Handbook, supra, ¶ 2.1 (status of warships); U.S. Coast Guard, Foreign Affairs Policy Manual, COMDTINST M5710.5 (Jan. 2012), appendix C.
98. Refugee/asylum questions are analyzed differently when the ship or aircraft to which the request is made is in a foreign port. First, the potential asylee does not have the status of a refugee unless and until "outside" the territory of his or her state of nationality. See Convention relating to the Status of Refugees, art. 1(2), Jul. 28, 1951, 189 U.N.T.S. 150, as modified by Protocol relating to the Status of Refugees, adopted, Nov. 18, 1966, 606 U.N.T.S. 267. Second, merchant vessels are not immune from the territorial sovereignty of the foreign state in which the port is located, so asylum is not available on such vessels. Accordingly, port state law enforcement officials may board foreign nonpublic vessels and remove fugitives. See Whiteman, 9 Digest of International Law, supra, at 135–36. See also Asylum case (Colombia v. Peru), 1950 I.C.J. 266 (Nov. 20).
99. Commander's Handbook, supra, ¶ 3.3 (asylum and temporary refuge) (highlighting critical difference between Department of Navy policy and U.S. Coast Guard policy). See also Coast Guard MLE Manual, supra, appendix L; U.S. Navy Regulations, supra, art. 0914; Commander's Handbook, supra, ¶ 3.3.4 (defense of U.S. nationals).
100. Commander's Handbook, supra, ¶ 3.2.3.
101. U.S. Navy Regulations, supra, art. 0859; U.S. Coast Guard Regulations, art. 4-1-28; Commander's Handbook, supra, ¶ 3.2.3. Information on port quarantine measures and procedures may be found in the relevant fleet guides and sailing directions.

documents, certificates, and logs and conducts the necessary vessel and crew inspection to determine whether to grant pratique (free or provisional), order the vessel into quarantine, or direct the vessel to depart the port. Some states extend expedited "radio pratique" procedures to warships.

3. Port State Conditions on Entry

The 1982 LOS Convention carefully allocates jurisdiction by zones extending seaward from the baseline. The coastal state's jurisdiction varies across the four zones, beginning with the territorial sea and extending to the contiguous zone, EEZ, and high seas. Generally, the LOS Convention does not permit a coastal state to "supplement" its zonal jurisdiction over foreign vessels by claiming that their activities outside the relevant zone have an "effect" within the state's territory. The coastal state may, however, impose conditions for entry into its ports.[102] It is important to distinguish a state's power to prescribe conditions of port entry, which extend to the vessel before it enters the port, from prescriptions that apply to the vessel after it enters the port state's waters. Measures in the latter category are addressed in section C.4 below.

More than a century ago, the U.S. Supreme Court explained in *Patterson v. The Bark* Eudora that "the implied consent to permit [a foreign vessel] to enter our harbors may be withdrawn, and if this implied consent may be wholly withdrawn, it may be extended upon such terms and conditions as the government sees fit to impose."[103] The 1982 LOS Convention confirms in passing the continued validity of that rule in what has come to be known as "conditions of port entry." The convention briefly adverts to port entry conditions in two articles. Article 25, which addresses the "rights of protection" of the coastal state with respect to foreign vessels in innocent passage through its territorial sea, provides that "in the case of ships proceeding to internal waters or a call at a port facility outside internal waters, the coastal State also has the right to take the necessary steps to prevent any breach of the conditions to which admission of those ships to internal waters or such a call is subject."[104]

Similarly, Article 211, which addresses the prevention and control of pollution from vessels, refers to requirements by port states "for the prevention, reduction and control of pollution of the marine environment as a condition for the entry of foreign vessels into their ports or internal waters, or for a call at their off-shore terminals." The Senate Committee on Foreign Relations' proposed "understanding" of the 1982 LOS Convention (see appendix D, understanding 13) announces its understanding that "the Convention recognizes and does not constrain the long-standing sovereign right of a State to impose and enforce conditions for the entry of foreign vessels into its ports, rivers, harbors, or offshore terminals, such as a requirement that ships exchange ballast water beyond 200 nautical miles from shore or a requirement that tank vessels carrying oil be constructed with double hulls."

---

102. Restatement FRLUS § 512 n.3 (the coastal state may condition the entry of foreign ships into its ports on compliance with its laws and regulations); 33 U.S.C. § 1228 (conditions for entry into U.S. ports); 33 C.F.R. § 160.107 (Coast Guard's authority to deny entry).

103. Patterson v. The Bark *Eudora*, 190 U.S. 169, 178 (1903). The Court quoted: "Mr. Justice Blackburn in *Queen v. Anderson*, L.R. 1 Crown Cases Reserved 161, 'A ship which bears a nation's flag is to be treated as a part of the territory of that nation. A ship is a kind of floating island.' Yet when a foreign merchant vessel comes into our ports, like a foreign citizen coming into our territory, it subjects itself to the jurisdiction of this country."

104. LOSC arts. 25(2), 211(3), & 255. Examples of commonly imposed entry conditions include advance transmission of cargo manifests and crew and passenger lists and compliance with advance notice of arrival requirements.

How far does the power to attach conditions of entry go? One expert commentator reads the authority quite broadly, concluding that the LOS Convention contains "no restriction" on the right of a state to establish port entry requirements, "including those regarding the construction, manning, equipment, or design of ships."[105] Although that is true of the LOS Convention (subject to prohibitions on discriminatory treatment), other treaties, including several developed through the IMO, do in fact set limits on port state prescriptive and enforcement jurisdiction. FCN treaties and trade agreements extending MFN or national treatment status to selected nations might also be relevant. It should also be noted that nothing in the historical understandings of a nation's power to impose conditions for port entry, the above-mentioned treaties, or the federal statute delegating that power to the U.S. Coast Guard suggests that the fifty states within the United States are permitted to rely on the conditions of entry rationale applicable to nation-states to extend their regulatory reach beyond the territorial limits prescribed by Congress in the Submerged Lands Act or to impose regulations different from or in addition to those imposed by the federal government.[106]

Aggressive application of the conditions for port entry rationale can prove controversial. Australia's 2006 regulation establishing a compulsory pilotage requirement for vessels transiting the Torres Strait, an environmentally vulnerable and navigationally challenging strait used for international navigation, is perhaps the best-known example.[107] The 2006 regulation provoked a number of protests from other nations, including the United States, which argued that the measure overstepped the limits prescribed by the LOS Convention on Australia's regulatory power over vessels in transit through an international strait. Australia subsequently issued a second marine notice that preserves the compulsory pilotage requirement but states that Australia will not "suspend, deny, hamper or impair transit passage and will not stop, arrest or board ships that do not take on a pilot."[108] The notice goes on to warn, however, that "the owner, master and/or operator of the ship may be prosecuted on the *next entry* into an Australian port, for both ships on voyages to Australian ports *and ships transiting the Torres Strait en route to other destinations*" (emphasis added). In effect, Australia turned the compulsory pilotage requirement into a condition for port entry. The second marine notice raised two questions. The first was whether the LOS Convention's strict limits on a coastal state's jurisdiction to regulate vessels in transit passage through an international strait can in fact be circumvented by recasting the regulation as a condition for entry into the state's internal waters or ports. If the answer to that first question is yes, how far can the port state go? Could the owner or master of a vessel that

---

105. Bernard H. Oxman, The Territorial Temptation: A Siren Song at Sea, 100 Am. J. Int'l L. 830, 844 (2006). The United States exercises such control over the overwhelming majority of vessels operating off its coast. Id.

106. See U.S. v. Locke, 529 U.S. 89, 116 (2000) (explaining that a "state's jurisdiction and authority are most in doubt" when the state attempts to extend them to "a vessel operator's out-of-state obligations and conduct"). More generally, the U.S. Supreme Court established early in the nation's history that the state's police powers with respect to the channels and instrumentalities of interstate and foreign maritime commerce are limited to the state's territory and may be further restricted by preemptive federal legislation. Gibbons v. Ogden, 22 U.S. (9 Wheat.) 1 (1824); New York v. Miln, 36 U.S. (11 Pet.) 102 (1837). Congress may, however, authorize the states to prescribe such requirements, as it has done with pilotage for certain classes of vessels. See Cooley v. Bd. of Wardens of the Port of Philadelphia, 53 U.S. (12 How.) 299 (1851).

107. See Australian Maritime Safety Authority, Marine Notice 8/2006 (2006). See generally Sam Bateman & Michael White, Compulsory Pilotage in the Torres Strait: Overcoming Unacceptable Risks to a Sensitive Marine Environment, 40 Ocean Dev. & Int'l L. 184 (2009); Robert Beckman, PSSAs and Transit Passage—Australia's Pilotage System in the Torres Strait Challenges the IMO and UNCLOS, 38 Ocean Dev. & Int'l L. 325 (2007); Julian Roberts, Compulsory Pilotage in International Straits: The Torres Strait PSSA Proposal, 37 Ocean Dev. & Int'l L. 93, 94–104 (2006).

108. Australian Maritime Safety Authority, Marine Notice 16/2006 (2006).

transited the strait without taking a pilot during a 2010 voyage that did not include an entry into an Australian port be prosecuted for its 2010 "violation" on arrival in an Australian port in 2015 after a voyage that did not include a pilotless transit through the strait? If in 2010 the vessel did not enter an Australian port, how could it be in violation of a condition of port entry? And if in 2015, while en route to an Australian port, it did not transit Torres Strait without a pilot, what port entry condition did it violate?

4. Port State Regulation of Vessels Voluntarily in the Port

Under customary international law and the 1982 LOS Convention, a state's jurisdiction over its internal waters is functionally equivalent to its jurisdiction over the state's land territory. Neither customary international law nor the 1982 LOS Convention significantly restricts a port state's authority to inspect vessels, other than sovereign immune vessels, voluntarily in its ports or internal waters.[109] Accordingly, states have broad jurisdiction to prescribe and enforce regulations on foreign, nonpublic vessels within their internal waters and ports.[110]

That general rule may be modified by treaty, however. For example, in *Wildenhus' Case* (1887), involving an intracrew homicide on board a Belgian-flag steamship while berthed in a New Jersey port, the Supreme Court explained that it is "part of the law of civilized nations that, when a merchant vessel of one country enters the ports of another for the purposes of trade, it subjects itself to the law of the place to which it goes *unless, by treaty or otherwise*, the two countries have come to some different understanding or agreement."[111] Thus, FCN treaties or consular relations treaties might provide a treaty-based right of port entry, limit the port state's jurisdiction over vessels flying the flag of the other treaty party, or both.[112] For example, a typical treaty on consular relations provides:

> Without prejudice to the right of the administrative and judicial authorities of the territory to take cognizance of crimes or offenses committed on board the vessel when she is in the ports or in the territorial waters of the territory and which are cognizable under the local law or to enforce local laws applicable to vessels in ports and territorial waters or persons and property thereon, it is the common intention of the High Contracting Parties that the administrative and police authorities of the territory should not, except at the request or with the consent of the consular officer, (a) concern themselves with any matter taking place on board the vessel unless for the preservation of peace and order or in the interests of public health or safety, or (b) institute prosecutions in respect of crimes of offenses committed on board the vessel unless they are of a serious

---

109. The "voluntariness" qualifier acknowledges the exceptions for vessels entering as the result of force majeure or distress.

110. Bens v. Compania Naviera Hidalgo, S.A., 353 U.S. 138, 142 (1957) (holding that it is "beyond question that a ship voluntarily entering the territorial limits of another country subjects itself to the laws and jurisdiction of that country"). See also Jurisdiction over Vessels, in U.S. Department of State, Cumulative Digest of United States Practice in International Law 1981–1988, vol. 2, at 1374–82 (1994); Whiteman, 9 Digest of International Law, supra, at 107–55 (arrival or departure of vessel at foreign port).

111. See Mali v. Keeper of the Common Jail ("Wildenhus' Case"), 120 U.S. 1, 12 (1887) (emphasis added).

112. Foreign consuls provide a number of services to visiting nationals, vessels, and aircraft, particularly commercial vessels and aircraft and merchant mariners. See Vienna Convention on Consular Relations, art. 5(k) & (l), Apr. 24, 1963, 21 U.S.T. 77, 596 U.N.T.S. 261. Naval and Coast Guard attachés or liaison officers attached to the embassy staffs may perform supporting duties.

character or involve the tranquility of the port or unless they are committed by
or against persons other than the crew.[113]

The Supreme Court's decision in *Wildenhus' Case* also recognized that even in the absence of
a binding treaty, the port state will typically decline to exercise its enforcement jurisdiction under
principles of comity, unless the violation disturbs the peace of the port.[114] The continuing validity
of the holdings in *Wildenhus' Case* was confirmed by the U.S. Department of State during a 1985
incident involving a crewmember from a Soviet-flag freighter in New Orleans.[115]

5. The Port State Control Regime

Port states enjoy broad jurisdiction over nonpublic foreign vessels voluntarily in their ports,
subject to any limits imposed by relevant treaties. In addition, the port state may impose entry
conditions applicable to the vessel while transiting the territorial sea and enforce relevant port,
vessel, and cargo security measures. There is also a growing trend to confer jurisdiction on states
to prescribe and enforce laws applicable to foreign vessels voluntarily in their ports even when
the vessel was not in waters where the port state would have zonal jurisdiction at the time it
committed the violation. Such jurisdiction may be found in Part XII of the LOS Convention, the
Straddling Fish Stocks Implementation Agreement,[116] several IMO-sponsored conventions (e.g.,
MARPOL),[117] and even UN Security Council resolutions.[118] In approaching such measures, it
is important to distinguish the jurisdiction of the port state over foreign vessel activities while
in its waters from the jurisdiction of a port state to prescribe and enforce on foreign vessels in
its ports laws applicable to the vessel's conduct before entering the port state's waters. In light of
the close relationship between the port state control regime and other measures to protect and
preserve the marine environment, this chapter will defer a detailed examination of the regime to
chapter 10.

---

113. Convention between the United States and United Kingdom relating to Consular Officers, 165 U.N.T.S. 122
(1953). At one time, the United States maintained consular courts in China, Siam, Turkey, Morocco, Muscat,
Abyssinia, Persia, and territories formerly part of the Ottoman Empire, including Egypt. See 22 U.S.C. §§
141–143 (repealed in 1956).
114. See Wildenhus' Case, 120 U.S. at 12–14 (acknowledging jurisdiction over foreign nonpublic vessels voluntarily in
port, but abstaining from interference with internal discipline on such vessels unless conduct disturbs peace of the
port); Cunard S.S. Co. v. Mellon, 262 U.S. 100, 123–24 (1923). See also Spector v. Norwegian Cruise Line Ltd.
545 U.S. 119 (2005) (holding that a clear statement of congressional intent is necessary before a general statutory
requirement can interfere with matters that concern a foreign-flag vessel's internal affairs and operations, as contrasted with statutory requirements that concern the security and well-being of U.S. citizens or territory); Coast
Guard MLE Manual, supra, at ¶ B-4.c.
115. The incident concerned Miroslav Medvid, a seaman on the Soviet cargo ship *Marshal Konev*. Medvid jumped
overboard and swam to shore in Louisiana on October 24, 1985. After questioning him, the U.S. Immigration and
Naturalization Service determined that he was not seeking political asylum and returned him to his ship, setting
off a public protest by those who believed he was being coerced to return. Several interviews and medical exams
later, Medvid repeatedly confirmed that he wished to return to the Soviet Union and was allowed to rejoin his
ship. See Marian Nash Leich, Contemporary Practice of the United States relating to International Law, 80 Am.
J. Int'l L. 612, 622–27 (1986); Report by the U.S. Senate, Committee on the Judiciary, Subcommittee on Immigration and Refugee Policy, Hearings on Political Asylum Procedures for Alien Crewmen and How They Were
Applied to a Soviet Seaman Miroslav Medvid, Nov. 5–7, 1985, S. Hrg. 99-541.
116. Straddling Fish Stocks Agreement, supra, art. 23.
117. International Convention for the Prevention of Pollution of the Sea by Vessels [hereinafter "MARPOL Convention"], Nov. 2, 1973, T.I.A.S. No. 10561, 1340 U.N.T.S. 184, as amended by 1978 Tanker Safety and Pollution
Prevention Protocol, June 1, 1978, 1340 U.N.T.S. 61.
118. For example, S.C. Res. 1973, ¶ 13 (Mar. 17, 2011), called on port states to take action to enforce an arms embargo
on Libya during that state's 2011 civil war.

By its terms, the LOS Convention imposes few limits on the authority of port states to inspect foreign vessels voluntarily in port. The port state's jurisdiction may, however, be limited by other treaties, such as an applicable bilateral FCN or one of the many IMO-sponsored conventions. On the other hand, the port state's role respecting safety of foreign vessels is not entirely permissive. The LOS Convention imposes a "duty to detain" on port states that, on request or on their own initiative, have ascertained that a foreign vessel within one of their ports is "in violation of applicable international rules and standards relating to seaworthiness of vessels and thereby threatens damage to the marine environment."[119] Under such circumstances the port state must take administrative measures to prevent the vessel from sailing.[120] Parties to the SOLAS Convention have a similar duty to intervene and/or detain foreign vessels to prevent a vessel from sailing until unseaworthy conditions are corrected.[121]

Over the past two decades, port state control measures have significantly enhanced maritime safety and pollution prevention.[122] At least eight IMO-sponsored conventions contain express provisions for port state enforcement. These conventions vary in the extent of control they grant to port states. Generally, each requires that port states accept valid certificates as evidence of compliance with the convention unless there are grounds for believing the actual condition of the ship or its equipment does not correspond substantially with the conditions reflected in the certificates.[123] The SOLAS Convention requires that any inspections or surveys be carried out by officers of the flag state or its designated surveyor, and confines port state remedial measures to nonpunitive interventions or detentions.[124] By contrast, the MARPOL Convention permits the port state not only to inspect foreign vessels but also to take enforcement action against foreign vessels found to be in violation.[125] Both conventions require port states to avoid unduly delaying a ship and call for compensation by the port state for any loss or damage suffered as a result of an undue delay or detention.[126]

In response to a number of terrorist attacks on vessels and port facilities, and out of concern over the demonstrated risk posed by vessels and their crews and cargo to the security of port states, the IMO member states adopted a number of important maritime security measures, including the International Ship and Port Facility Security (ISPS) Code amendments to the SOLAS Convention. The ISPS Code, which entered into force in 2004, prescribes a variety of security measures for ships, ports, and government agencies. In anticipation of the new IMO security measures, Congress enacted the Maritime Transportation Security Act (MTSA) in 2002.[127] Among other things, the MTSA extended the legal definition of the U.S. territorial sea to twelve nautical miles for security matters.

Although port states have broad powers to promulgate bona fide safety and security regulations, the LOS Convention bans discriminatory treatment of foreign vessels (as does GATT Article V).[128] Despite that general ban, virtually all port state control regimes more closely

---

119. LOSC art. 219.
120. Id. The state may permit the vessel to proceed to the nearest repair yard. On removal of the causes of the violation, it must permit the vessel to proceed. Id.
121. SOLAS Convention, supra, ch. I, reg. 19(c).
122. The U.S. Coast Guard launched its Port State Control Initiative on May 1, 1994. The program is designed to identify substandard vessels and vessel-operating companies and force them to either comply with applicable vessel safety and pollution prevention standards or remain outside U.S. waters.
123. See, e.g., MARPOL Convention, supra, art. 5(2); SOLAS Convention, supra, ch. I, reg. 19(b).
124. SOLAS Convention, supra, ch. I, reg. 19.
125. MARPOL Convention, supra, art. 6.
126. Id. art. 7.
127. Maritime Transportation Security Act, Pub. L. No. 107-295, 116 Stat. 2064 (2002); 33 C.F.R. pts. 101–107.
128. See, e.g., LOSC arts. 24(1)(b), 25, 26, 42(2), 52(2), & 227.

scrutinize vessels registered in states that have been found to be lax in exercising jurisdiction and control over their vessels. Nothing in the LOS Convention bans consideration of a vessel's flag state and the degree of diligence historically exercised by that flag state in controlling its vessels. Limited resources, practical necessities, and concern for vessel and cargo mobility in fact compel port state control authorities to employ risk management measures that focus enforcement actions on the known or most probable violators. Port state control regimes that "blacklist" or "graylist" certain flag states (and vessel owners and operators and vessel classification societies) on the basis of their past records have long recognized this. A vessel that scores high on the combined safety or security risk assessment matrix will almost certainly be boarded once it arrives, and if the risk assessment warrants, may even be boarded offshore before arrival.[129]

The LOS Convention provides a number of safeguards for foreign-flag vessels subject to enforcement measures by coastal or port states, to guard against abusive investigative practices, unreasonable detentions, and hearing procedures that are fundamentally unfair.[130] Port states that violate the convention's safeguards may be liable for any resulting damage or losses suffered by the vessel.[131] Legal actions against port states for failing to promptly release vessels and crews on the payment of reasonable security for any assessed penalties may be subject to the convention's provisions for compulsory dispute settlement if both the port state and flag state are parties to the convention.[132]

---

129. The United States may also impose conditions on entry for vessels coming from a foreign port that in its determination has failed to maintain adequate security measures. See 46 U.S.C. § 70110.
130. LOSC arts. 223–31.
131. Id. art. 232.
132. Id. art. 292.

5

The Territorial Sea, Contiguous Zone, International Straits, and Archipelagic Waters

The 1982 LOS Convention divides the waters seaward of the baseline into four juridical zones: the territorial sea, contiguous zone, exclusive economic zone, and high seas (see figure 1). The rights and obligations of the coastal state and the various flag states and other potential user states vary from one zone to another. Freedom of navigation and overflight, for example, span a continuum ranging from the high seas, where states enjoy the greatest degree of freedom, to the foreign state's internal waters, where consent is required for entry, absent imperative conditions such as distress or force majeure. Falling between those two extremes are, in order, the regimes for the territorial sea, contiguous zone, and EEZ, together with the specialized regime for archipelagic waters. This chapter examines the regimes applicable in a state's territorial sea, contiguous zone, and archipelagic waters, with particular attention to the regimes of innocent passage, transit passage, and archipelagic sea-lanes passage. Chapters 6 and 8 examine the EEZ and high seas regimes respectively, and chapter 7 focuses on the continental shelf and deep seabed beyond national jurisdiction.

A. THE TERRITORIAL SEA

Coastal states are sovereign in their adjacent territorial sea,[1] which may now extend up to twelve nautical miles seaward from the baseline.[2] The ICJ has determined that the twelve-nautical-mile limit on the territorial sea in Article 3 of the LOS Convention is also a rule of customary international law.[3] Although that conclusion was not arrived at in accordance with the court's own test for a customary law rule,[4] it is likely accurate as to the breadth of the territorial sea. A more significant problem with the court's statement, and one that invites caution before reading too much into it, is the fact that the breadth of the sea cannot be considered in isolation from the nature of the state's claims respecting those waters. Since 1983 the United States has consistently taken the position that it will recognize a state's twelve-nautical-mile territorial sea claim only

---

1. LOSC art. 2; Restatement FRLUS § 512. The term "territorial waters" is sometimes used to collectively refer to the state's territorial sea and its internal waters. As a matter of domestic law, neither the title (territorial sea) nor the attribution of sovereignty means that the territorial sea is in fact "territory" of the state for all purposes, an important distinction when determining whether a migrant has reached the "territory" of the destination state.
2. LOSC arts. 3 & 4. Seven states claim territorial seas in excess of twelve nautical miles: Benin, Congo, Ecuador, Liberia, Peru, Somalia, and Togo. See DoD, Under Secretary of Defense for Policy, Maritime Claims Reference Manual, DoD 2005.1-M (June 23, 2005); J. Ashley Roach & Robert W. Smith, Excessive Maritime Claims 148, table 6 (3d ed. 2012).
3. See Territorial and Maritime Dispute (Nicaragua v. Colombia), ¶ 177, 2012 I.C.J. (Nov. 19).
4. The two-part test, examined in chapter 1, was set out in North Sea Continental Shelf cases (Fed. Rep. Germany v. Denmark/Fed. Rep. Germany v. Netherlands), ¶ 77, 1969 I.C.J. 3 (Feb. 20).

"so long as the rights and freedoms of the United States and others under international law are recognized by such coastal States."[5]

As a consequence of the coastal state's sovereignty over the territorial sea, foreign vessels have no right to navigate those waters (absent distress or force majeure) unless they fall within the innocent or transit passage "servitudes" in the law of the sea described below, or they are the beneficiaries of some other treaty-based right. If such vessels are nevertheless permitted by the coastal state to navigate in its territorial sea, they are subject to any conditions attached to the coastal state's consent and to the attendant regulatory power of the coastal state on terms consistent with the LOS Convention.

The state's sovereignty extends to the superjacent airspace over the territorial sea as well as the subjacent seabed and subsoil. The sovereignty of coastal states in their territorial sea must be exercised in accordance with the applicable provisions of the LOS Convention and "other rules of international law."[6] In particular, the coastal state's sovereignty is subject to two servitudes in favor of foreign vessels: a right of innocent passage and a right of transit passage through any portion of the territorial sea that constitutes an international strait.[7] These servitudes, which seek to balance the common interest in freedom of navigation with the coastal state's interest in peace, good order, and security in the immediately adjacent seas, are discussed below. In addition to the duty to accommodate the passage rights of foreign ships, a coastal state is also subject to limits on its exercise of jurisdiction over criminal matters and civil matters respecting vessels transiting its territorial sea.

1. The Right of Innocent Passage

The right of innocent passage emerged in customary international law long before the 1958 or 1982 conventions on the law of the sea.[8] The 1958 Convention on the Territorial Sea and Contiguous Zone largely codified the existing customary law rule of innocent passage in Article 14.[9] The 1982 LOS Convention fleshes out the 1958 convention regime by adding a list of activities in Article 19 that render a vessel's passage noninnocent. It must be emphasized that innocent passage is a right recognized by both conventional and customary international law, not a mere privilege, license, or act of comity, courtesy, or grace that can be granted or withheld at the coastal state's discretion. As a right, it cannot be subject to prior coastal state consent, nor can the right be conditioned on prior notice to the coastal state (as if it were a condition on port entry). Moreover, failure to give prior notification does not render the vessel's passage noninnocent under Article 19.[10] It is also important to recognize that the United States conditions its recognition of the twelve-nautical-mile territorial sea claims of other states on the claiming state's recognition of the right of innocent (and transit) passage. Thus, it has been the consistent U.S. position since 1983 that, as a nonparty to the 1982 LOS Convention, "the United States will recognize the rights of other States in the waters off their coasts, as reflected in the [1982 LOS] Convention, so long as the rights and freedoms of the United States and others under international law are

5. Statement by the President [hereinafter "Ocean Policy Statement"], para. 6, 19 Weekly Comp. Pres. Doc. 383 (Mar. 10, 1983); U.S. Oceans Policy, 83 Dep't State Bull., June 1983, at 70, 22 I.L.M. 464 (1983).
6. LOSC art. 2(3). The "other rules of international law" referred to include the law of naval warfare.
7. Id. arts. 17 & 38; Restatement FRLUS §§ 512–513.
8. Restatement FRLUS § 513 n.1.
9. 1958 Convention on TTS and CZ, supra, art. 14.
10. See Whiteman, 4 Digest of International Law, supra, at 404–17 (summarizing U.S. protests).

*look this up again.

recognized by such coastal States."[10a] The ongoing U.S. freedom of navigation program demonstrates the nation's commitment to that 1983 policy.

The right of innocent passage through waters of the territorial sea extends to the ships of all states, whether coastal or landlocked.[11] In construing and applying the innocent passage article, careful attention must be given to the structure of the LOS Convention. The right of innocent passage in Article 17 is set out in subsection 3.A of Part II of the convention, and as the caption to subsection 3.A makes clear, it is therefore applicable to "all ships," a class that includes warships and other public vessels as well as nuclear-powered vessels and vessels transporting nuclear or other inherently dangerous or noxious substances.[12] It is also important to recall that the ICJ's seminal 1949 decision in the *Corfu Channel* case upheld the *innocent* passage of British warships.[13] Given the clear distinction between the passage rights of warships and other vessels in the 1936 Montreux Convention regarding the Régime of the Turkish Straits, which was drafted little more than a decade earlier, the ICJ was certainly aware of the possibility that warship passage rights might be narrower than passage rights of merchant vessels.

The right of innocent passage is not unlimited. The detailed innocent passage regime set out in the 1982 LOS Convention has several restrictions not found in the transit passage regime through international straits. The first important limitation is that aircraft have no right of innocent passage.[14] Second, to qualify for innocent passage, the LOS Convention requires submarines and other underwater vehicles to navigate on the surface and show their flag.[15] Nuclear-powered ships and ships carrying nuclear or other inherently dangerous or noxious substances are required to carry documents and observe special precautionary measures established for such ships by international agreements.[16] During time of armed conflict, belligerent vessels may exercise the right of innocent passage through the territorial sea of neutral states, subject to the restrictions in Articles 19 and 21 of the LOS Convention.[17]

Determining whether a vessel is in innocent passage under the 1982 LOS Convention requires a two-step analysis. First, Article 18 is applied to determine if the vessel is in "passage." Next, Article 19 is applied to the manner of the vessel's passage to determine if the passage is innocent.

ARTICLE 18. Meaning of passage

1. Passage means navigation through the territorial sea for the purpose of:
   (a) traversing that sea without entering internal waters or calling at a roadstead or port facility outside internal waters; or
   (b) proceeding to or from internal waters or a call at such roadstead or port facility.
2. Passage shall be continuous and expeditious. However, passage includes stopping and anchoring, but only in so far as the same are incidental to ordinary navigation or are rendered necessary by *force majeure* or distress or for the purpose of rendering assistance to persons, ships or aircraft in danger or distress.[18]

10a. See Ocean Policy Statement, supra, p. 1.
11. LOSC art. 17; Restatement FRLUS § 513.
12. Restatement FRLUS § 513 cmt. h & n.2. On the validity of nuclear-free zones, see Commander's Handbook, supra, ¶ 2.6.6.
13. The Corfu Channel case (U.K. v. Albania.) 1949 I.C.J. 1 (Apr. 9).
14. Restatement FRLUS § 513 cmt. i.
15. LOSC art. 20.
16. Id. art. 23.
17. San Remo Manual, supra, ¶ 31.
18. LOSC art. 18.

Interpretations of paragraph 2 regarding what constitutes "ordinary navigation" circumstances that would necessitate stopping and anchoring vary. Few would dispute that it includes a right to stop and anchor for brief periods while awaiting favorable conditions for entering port. Ordinary navigation would not, however, include a long-term layup (such stops would also violate the "continuous and expeditious" requirement).[19] Assuming the vessel is in "passage," Article 19 then provides a definition of "innocence" that focuses on the vessel's activity while it is in the territorial sea and the effect of that activity on the coastal state. The requirement that any "passage" be continuous and expeditious and the list of activities in Article 19, quoted below, that will render a foreign vessel's passage noninnocent, together with the coastal state's right to take steps to prevent noninnocent passage, provide ample protection for the coastal state's security interests.

ARTICLE 19. Meaning of innocent passage

1. Passage is innocent so long as it is not prejudicial to the peace, good order or security of the coastal State. Such passage shall take place in conformity with this Convention and with other rules of international law.
2. Passage of a foreign ship shall be considered to be prejudicial to the peace, good order or security of the coastal State if in the territorial sea it engages in any of the following activities:
    (a) any threat or use of force against the sovereignty, territorial integrity or political independence of the coastal State, or in any other manner in violation of the principles of international law embodied in the Charter of the United Nations;
    (b) any exercise or practice with weapons of any kind;
    (c) any act aimed at collecting information to the prejudice of the defense or security of the coastal State;
    (d) any act of propaganda aimed at affecting the defense or security of the coastal State;
    (e) the launching, landing or taking on board of any aircraft;
    (f) the launching, landing or taking on board of any military device;
    (g) the loading or unloading of any commodity, currency or person contrary to the customs, fiscal, immigration or sanitary laws and regulations of the coastal State;
    (h) any act of wilful and serious pollution contrary to this Convention;
    (i) any fishing activities;
    (j) the carrying out of research or survey activities;
    (k) any act aimed at interfering with any systems of communication or any other facilities or installations of the coastal State;
    (l) any other activity not having a direct bearing on passage.[20]

The chapeau in paragraph 2 of Article 19 uses the present tense of the verb ("engages in") when referring to activities by the vessel while it is in the territorial sea, thereby excluding from

---

19. The requirement that passage be continuous and expeditious was intended in part to address concerns over "hovering" vessels. International Law Commission, Articles concerning the Law of the Sea with Commentaries, 1956 Y.B. Int'l L. Comm'n, vol. II, at 265–301.
20. LOSC art. 19. See generally Whiteman, 4 Digest of International Law, supra, at 343–417.

consideration past activities by the vessel before it entered the territorial sea.[21] The reference to "peace, good order or security" in paragraph 1 has much in common with the "peace of the port" doctrine applicable in internal waters that distinguishes among activities based on whether they have consequences that extend beyond the vessel.

Close inspection of Article 19 reveals that the question of "innocence" does not turn on a violation of the laws of the coastal state. Such a violation is neither necessary nor sufficient to render a vessel's passage noninnocent. A vessel might be guilty of a minor oil discharge in violation of the coastal state's pollution laws, yet that minor spill would not render its passage noninnocent. Similarly, the coastal state's laws might not prohibit research or survey activities in its territorial sea, yet those activities would nevertheless render the vessel's passage noninnocent. It is also important to bear in mind that a foreign vessel whose passage is noninnocent is not by that fact alone violating international law. For example, a submarine that transits a foreign state's territorial sea submerged is not entitled to the rights of a vessel in innocent passage (in contrast to transit passage), and the coastal state may prohibit its submerged navigation and take steps to prevent it. However, submerged navigation through another state's territorial sea does not in itself constitute a violation of the LOS Convention.[22]

Opinions differ on whether Article 19 is to be strictly or expansively construed, and whether the list of activities in paragraph 2 is exhaustive or merely suggestive. The list of noninnocent activities now in Article 19 was not included in the 1958 Convention on the Territorial Sea and Contiguous Zone. The United States and the former Soviet Union formally took the position in the 1989 "Jackson Hole Agreement" that the list of activities in Article 19 that render passage noninnocent is exhaustive.[23] That conclusion is buttressed by textual and contextual evidence. For example, Article 19 lacks the telltale "inter alia" qualifier inserted by the treaty drafters in other LOS Convention articles (e.g., before the list of high-seas freedoms in Article 87) to indicate the list that follows is merely suggestive rather than exhaustive.

The last activity listed in Article 19, "any other activity not having a direct bearing on passage," has been called a "catchall" clause by some, but that characterization fails to recognize that Article 18 provides essential context for determining the meaning of "passage." An objective determination of whether the vessel is engaged in an activity "not having a direct bearing on passage" must refer back to the meaning of "passage" in Article 18. An activity that has a direct bearing on any of the activities described in Article 18 would not be disqualified from the innocent passage rights by Article 19(l).

Notwithstanding the absence of any textual support for a prior notice or consent requirement for foreign vessels to engage in innocent passage, some coastal states have sought to impose

---

21. In international law, the term "chapeau" (French for "hat" or "cap") refers to an unnumbered introductory clause or paragraph that "covers" several subsequent provisions. Treaty provisions that incorporate a chapeau require a two-tiered analysis that examines both the chapeau and the individual provisions that follow. Important LOSC chapeaux can be found in Articles 19(2), 87(1), and 110(1). The critical role of the chapeau in determining the meaning and effect of the provisions that follow is emphasized in The WTO Appellate Body Report on U.S. Import Prohibitions on Certain Shrimp and Shrimp Products, WT/D558/AB/R, ¶ 118 (Oct. 12, 1998), 38 I.L.M. 118 (1999). The structural point here is that everything that follows the chapeau must be construed and applied consistently with that chapeau.
22. The U.S. position is set out in Commander's Handbook, supra, ¶ 2.5.2.1.
23. 1989 USA-USSR: Joint Statement with Attached Uniform Interpretation of Rules of International Law Governing Innocent Passage, Jackson Hole, WY, Sept. 23, 1989, 14 Law of the Sea Bulletin 12–13 (1989), 28 I.L.M. 1444 (1989); Annotated Supplement to the Commander's Handbook, annex A2-2. Paragraph 3 provides that "Article 19 of the Convention of 1982 sets out in paragraph 2 an exhaustive list of activities that would render passage noninnocent. A ship passing through the territorial sea that does not engage in any of those activities is in innocent passage." While it is true that the U.S.-USSR interpretation is not binding on other states, it has been labeled "very influential" in light of the position of the two parties. Churchill & Lowe, supra, at 86.

such a requirement.[24] The issue was debated during the run-up to UNCLOS I in 1958. Under pressure from some coastal states, the ILC had included a prior notice requirement in its draft of what would become the Convention on the Territorial Sea and Contiguous Zone.[25] The provision was deleted at the conference, however, and was not included in the 1958 convention. It now seems clear that a "right" cannot be conditioned on obtaining prior permission to engage in the activity. Even a requirement for prior "notice" may be deemed to "impair" or "hamper" the right, in violation of Article 24, particularly when a failure to give prior notice leads to a denial of the right or other interference with the vessel's passage. Nevertheless, more than thirty states purport to require either prior authorization or notification before a foreign vessel may exercise its right of innocent passage in their waters. Some of those states apply the requirement only to foreign warships or to nuclear-powered ships or ships carrying nuclear weapons.[26]

When the U.S. Senate Committee on Foreign Relations reported out the 1982 LOS Convention for advice and consent, it recommended that the president include the following understanding on innocent passage: "Any determination of non-innocence of passage by a ship must be made on the basis of acts it commits while in the territorial sea, and not on the basis of . . . cargo, armament, means of propulsion, flag, origin, destination, or purpose."[27] The position set out in the committee's proposed understanding, largely taken from the 1989 Jackson Hole Agreement with the USSR, is consistent with the ICJ's decision in the *Corfu Channel* case, in which the court held that the inquiry into whether a transiting warship's passage is "innocent" turns on the manner of passage, not the vessel's motive.[28]

2. Right of Assistance Entry

The entry of an assisting vessel into the territorial seas of a foreign state to render assistance to another vessel or aircraft (the right-of-assistance entry) must be distinguished from the right of a vessel in distress to enter another state's territorial sea or internal waters to ameliorate its peril.[29]

---

24. For example, when China ratified the LOS Convention in 1996 it stated: "The People's Republic of China reaffirms that the provisions of the United Nations Convention on the Law of the Sea concerning innocent passage through the territorial sea shall not prejudice the right of a coastal state to request, in advance, in accordance with its laws and regulations, a foreign state to obtain advance approval from or give prior notification to the coastal state for the passage of its warships through the territorial sea of the coastal state." UN, Oceans and the Law of the Sea, Declarations and Statements: China, available at http://www.un.org/Depts/los/convention_agreements/convention_declarations.htm#China%20Upon%20ratification (accessed Feb. 1, 2013). The statement amounts to a reservation within the meaning of Article 2(d) of the Vienna Convention on the Law of Treaties and therefore violates Article 309 of the LOS Convention. See also Article 6 of China's Law on the Territorial Sea and the Contiguous Zone, Feb. 25, 1992 ("To enter the territorial sea of the People's Republic of China, foreign military ships must obtain permission from the Government of the PRC").
25. See ILC, Articles concerning the Law of the Sea with Commentaries, supra, at 265–301.
26. Individual state claims are collected in DoD, Under Secretary of Defense for Policy, Maritime Claims Reference Manual, DoD 2005.1-M (June 23, 2005), DoD Maritime Claims Reference Manual, available at http:// www.dtic.mil/whs/directives/corres/html/20051m.htm (accessed Feb. 1, 2013). See also U.S. Department of State, Pub. No. 36, Limits in the Seas: National Claims to Maritime Jurisdictions (Robert W. Smith ed., 6th ed. 2000).
27. Senate Committee on Foreign Relations, Report on the United Nations Convention on the Law of the Sea, S. Exec. Rpt. No. 110-09, understanding 2(c) (reprinted in appendix D). The United States has long taken the position that because the listed activities must take place in the territorial sea (see Article 19(2)), the vessel's cargo, its destination, or the purpose of its voyage cannot be used as a criterion for determining whether its passage is innocent.
28. See Whiteman, 4 Digest of International Law, supra, § 19.
29. Assistance entry for vessels in distress must also be distinguished from entry into the territory or territorial sea of another state to defend U.S. nationals and the internationally recognized countermeasure of rescue. See Commander's Handbook, supra, ¶ 3.10.1.1; Coast Guard MLE Manual, supra, ¶ B-4.e. Moreover, the legality of entering a foreign state's territorial sea must be distinguished from the legality of the activities conducted in those waters after entry, especially when those activities might include the use of force or the exercise of enforcement jurisdiction.

Both rights are based on humanitarian considerations, and both turn on the existence of some level of distress, but they otherwise diverge. All ship and aircraft commanders have an obligation to assist those in danger of being lost at sea. The obligation is codified in the 1982 LOS Convention,[30] the SOLAS Convention,[31] and in *U.S. Navy Regulations* and *U.S. Coast Guard Regulations*.[32] On occasion, the distressed vessel or aircraft will be located in a foreign state's territorial sea. In such cases, the long-recognized duty of mariners to come to the aid of those in distress permits assistance entry into the territorial sea by ships or, under certain circumstances, aircraft without permission of the coastal nation in order to engage in legitimate efforts to render immediate rescue assistance to those in danger or distress at sea.[33] The situation of those imperiled must rise to the level of "a clearly apparent risk of death, disabling injury, loss, or significant damage."[34] The right of assistance entry applies only to rescues in which the location of the persons or property in danger or distress is reasonably well known. It does not extend to conducting area searches for persons or property in danger or distress when their location is not yet reasonably well known.[35]

Article 18(2) of the LOS Convention only indirectly addresses the right of assistance entry. It recognizes that a vessel engaged in providing such assistance does not thereby lose its "passage" status, while apparently relegating the legal basis for the right of assistance entry to customary law. The customary law on the right of assistance entry is more fully developed for vessels than for aircraft. In this regard it should be noted that while the right of innocent passage exists for vessels through territorial seas, no such right exists for aircraft in the airspace above the territorial seas. Nevertheless, for states that are party to the SAR Convention, Article 3.1.2 of the annex to that convention encourages a state to grant assistance entry "into *or over* its territorial sea or territory," without distinguishing between ships and aircraft. The United States has bilateral agreements with Canada and Mexico to facilitate assistance entry between the bordering states in such cases,[36] and some bilateral agreements on migrant operations provide for assistance entry.[37] A nonbinding 1998 agreement between the United States and China also provides a forum for consultation on a variety of issues, including SAR activities.[38]

---

30. LOSC art. 98.
31. SOLAS Convention, supra, ch. V, reg. 33(1).
32. See, e.g., U.S. Navy Regulations, supra, art. 0925; U.S. Coast Guard Regulations, supra, arts. 4-1-7 & 4-2-5; Commander's Handbook, supra, ¶ 3.2.1.2.
33. For states that are party to the SAR Convention, it provides that "unless otherwise agreed between the States concerned, a Party should authorize, subject to applicable national laws, rules and regulations, immediate entry into or over its territorial sea or territory of rescue units of other Parties solely for the purpose of searching for the position of maritime casualties and rescuing the survivors of such casualties." SAR Convention, supra, annex, art. 3.1.2.
34. See Commander's Handbook, supra, ¶ 2.5.2.6; Commander, Joint Chiefs of Staff, CJCSI 2410.01D, Guidance for the Exercise of the Right-of-Assistance Entry (May 1, 2010); Annotated Commander's Handbook, supra, annex A2-4.
35. See Statement of Policy by the Department of State, the Department of Defense, and the United States Coast Guard concerning Exercise of the Right of Assistance Entry, Aug. 8, 1986. U.S. forces will conduct *area searches* within U.S.- recognized foreign territorial seas or archipelagic waters only with the permission of the coastal state (emphasis added).
36. See Treaty to Facilitate Assistance to and Salvage of Vessels in Territorial Waters (U.S.-Mexico), June 13, 1935, T.I.A.S. No. 905, 49 Stat. 3359; MOU between U.S. Coast Guard, U.S. Air Force, the Canadian Forces and the Canadian Coast Guard on Search and Rescue, Mar. 24, 1995.
37. See, e.g., Agreement concerning Cooperation in Maritime Migration Enforcement (U.S.–Dominican Republic), art. 10, May 20, 2003.
38. Military Maritime Consultative Agreement (U.S.–People's Rep. China), Jan. 19, 1998; see also Commander's Handbook, supra, ¶ 2.10.3.

3. Sea-lanes and Traffic Separation Schemes in the Territorial Sea

To facilitate and enhance safety of navigation in the territorial sea, the coastal state may establish sea-lanes and traffic separation schemes.[39] The regulatory regime for such safety-of-navigation measures draws on the LOS Convention, the COLREGS Convention,[40] and the SOLAS Convention.[41] The IMO serves as the competent international organization for such matters and is closely involved in the process. In designating sea-lanes or traffic separation schemes, the coastal state is required to take into account IMO recommendations,[42] any channels customarily used for international navigation, any special characteristics of particular ships and channels, and the density of traffic.[43] Sea-lanes and traffic separation schemes must be marked on duly published charts.[44] They are also published in the IMO's publication *Ships' Routeing*.[45] Nonpublic vessels exercising the right of innocent passage may be required to use such sea-lanes and traffic separation schemes. In particular, tankers, nuclear-powered ships, and ships carrying nuclear or other inherently dangerous or noxious substances or materials may be required to confine their passage to such sea-lanes.[46] Warships, auxiliaries, and government ships operated on exclusively government service are not legally required to comply with traffic separation schemes and other vessel-routing measures while in innocent passage.[47] They must, however, operate with due regard for the safety of navigation. Sea-lanes and other vessel routing measures are examined further in chapter 10.

4. Duties of the Coastal State

In the *Corfu Channel* case, the ICJ concluded that a coastal state has a duty to warn foreign ships passing through its territorial sea of known dangers.[48] The LOS Convention largely codifies that rule, requiring that the coastal state give appropriate publicity to any danger to navigation within its territorial sea of which it has knowledge.[49] Additional coastal duties may be prescribed by other treaties, such as the Convention on Search and Rescue, which is examined in chapter 8.

5. Rights of the Coastal State to Take Protective Measures

The LOS Convention permits the coastal state to take "necessary steps" in its territorial sea to prevent passage that is not innocent.[50] At the very least, those steps would include the full range

39. LOSC art. 22; Restatement FRLUS § 513 cmt. d.
40. Convention on the International Regulations for Preventing Collisions at Sea [hereinafter "COLREGS Convention"], Oct. 20, 1972, 28 U.S.T. 3459, 1050 U.N.T.S. 16. COLREGS Rule 10 prescribes the rules for navigating in a traffic separation scheme.
41. SOLAS Chapter V addresses such safety of navigation measures.
42. See IMO, IMO Res. A.572(14), General Provisions on Ships' Routeing, Nov. 20, 1985.
43. LOSC art. 22(3).
44. Id. art. 22(4).
45. IMO, Ships' Routeing, IMO Pub. 927 (10th ed. 2010). The publication includes navigation information on IMO-approved traffic separation schemes, deep-water routes, areas to be avoided, mandatory ship reporting systems, mandatory routing systems, mandatory no anchoring areas, archipelagic sea-lanes, and other routing measures, such as recommended tracks, two-way routes, and recommended directions of traffic flow, together with the rules and recommendations on navigation that are associated with particular traffic areas and straits.
46. LOSC art. 22(2).
47. See SOLAS Convention, supra, ch. V, reg. 8(c); Commander's Handbook, supra, ¶ 2.5.3.1.
48. The Corfu Channel case (U.K. v. Albania) 1949 I.C.J. 1 (Apr. 9). In holding that the coastal state has a duty to provide, for the benefit of shipping in general, notice of the existence of a hazard in its territorial waters and to warn an approaching ship of the imminent danger, the court invoked "certain general and well-recognized principles, namely: elementary considerations of humanity, even more exacting in peace than in war; the principle of the

of measures available to a state exercising a right of approach and visit on the high seas.[51] In the case of ships proceeding to internal waters or a call at a port facility outside internal waters, the coastal state also has the right to take the necessary steps in the territorial sea to prevent any breach of the conditions to which admission of those ships is subject.[52]

The coastal state may, without discrimination in form or in fact among foreign ships, suspend innocent passage temporarily in specified areas, but only when such suspension is "essential" to the protection of the coastal state's security, including weapons exercises.[53] Such suspension may take effect only after having been duly published. In practice, such suspensions are reported to the UN for publication.[54]

No charge may be levied on foreign ships by reason only of their passage through the territorial sea.[55] However, nondiscriminatory charges may be levied on a foreign ship passing through the territorial sea as payment for specific services rendered to the ship.

6. Prescriptive Jurisdiction over Vessels in Innocent Passage

The coastal state may prescribe laws and regulations applicable to foreign vessels in innocent passage through its territorial sea; however, it may not "hamper" the innocent passage of a foreign vessel, except "in accordance with" the LOS Convention.[56] That qualification means that it may not impose requirements on foreign vessels that have the practical effect of denying or impairing the right of innocent passage; nor can it discriminate in form or fact against the vessels of any state or vessels carrying cargo to, from, or on behalf of any state.[57]

Vessels in a state's territorial sea not engaged in innocent passage are subject to the full sovereignty of the coastal state, as qualified by the rules of sovereign immunity and any other applicable rights and protections under international law. Vessels entitled to transit the territorial sea in innocent passage under the two-step test set out above are subject to a more limited class of coastal state laws and regulations and safety measures.[58] All such coastal state laws must be in conformity with other rules of international law, including other relevant provisions of the LOS Convention.

Article 21 enumerates eight (and only eight)[59] subjects over which the coastal state is competent to legislate with respect to foreign vessels in innocent passage.[60] Those eight subjects are

---

freedom of maritime communication; and every State's obligation not to allow knowingly its territory to be used for acts contrary to the rights of other States." Id. at 22.

49. LOSC art. 24(2).
50. LOSC art. 25(1); Commander's Handbook, supra, ¶ 2.5.2.4. See also United Nations Convention on the Law of the Sea 1982: A Commentary, vol. II, at 229 (Satya N. Nandan & Shabtai Rosenne eds., 1993).
51. Restatement FRLUS § 513. See generally Ivan A. Shearer, The Development of International Law with Respect to the Law Enforcement Role of Navies and Coast Guards in Peacetime, 71 U.S. Nav. War Coll. Int'l L. Studies 429, 433 (1998) (concluding that the "necessary steps" likely encompass the "standard procedures of approach, stopping, boarding, investigation and possibly arrest").
52. LOSC art. 25(2).
53. LOSC art. 25. See also Commander's Handbook, supra, ¶ 2.5.2.3.
54. See UN, Suspension of Innocent Passage, available at http://www.un.org/Depts/los/convention_agreements/innocent_passages_suspension.htm (accessed Feb. 1, 2013).
55. LOSC art. 26.
56. LOSC art. 24(1); Restatement FRLUS § 513(2)(a); Commander's Handbook, supra, ¶ 2.5.2.2.
57. LOSC art. 24(1).
58. Id. arts. 21–25; Restatement FRLUS § 513(2)(b) cmt. c & n.3.
59. Article 21 lacks the "inter alia" qualifier, which would indicate the list is not exhaustive.
60. The subjects are: (1) safety of navigation and the regulation of maritime traffic; (2) protection of navigational aids and facilities and other facilities or installations; (3) protection of cables and pipelines; (4) conservation of the

extended for foreign nuclear-powered ships and ships carrying nuclear or other inherently dangerous or noxious substances by Articles 22 and 23. It is noteworthy that Article 23 recognizes that nuclear-powered ships and ships carrying nuclear or other dangerous or noxious cargoes are eligible to exercise the right of innocent passage; however, that provision does not in itself mean that navigation by such vessels constitutes "passage" under Article 18 or that it is "innocent" under Article 19. It also bears repeating that Article 24 forbids discrimination in form or in fact against vessels of any particular state or ships carrying cargoes to, from, or on behalf of any state. Coastal state laws may not apply to the design, construction, manning, or equipment of foreign ships in innocent passage unless they are giving effect to generally accepted international rules or standards. Foreign ships, including foreign warships,[61] exercising the right of innocent passage through the territorial sea are required to comply with those laws and the rules on the prevention of collisions at sea.

7. Enforcement Jurisdiction in Relation to Foreign Ships in Passage

Any exercise of enforcement jurisdiction against a foreign vessel while in passage disrupts the vessel's navigation. Accordingly, the LOS Convention imposes both precatory and mandatory limits on such enforcement actions. They are set out in Article 27, which addresses the exercise of criminal jurisdiction, and Article 28, which deals with civil jurisdiction.[62] Those limits may, of course, be modified by other treaties or negated by flag state consent. Foreign nonpublic vessels not in innocent (or transit) passage are subject to the full sovereignty of the coastal state.

Article 27 of the LOS Convention sets out two distinct rules applicable to the coastal state's exercise of criminal enforcement jurisdiction. The first is a precatory restraint (as evidenced by the qualifier "should not") on the coastal state's enforcement jurisdiction over vessels in passage when the crime was committed during the passage,[63] and the second is a mandatory rule (evidenced by the qualifier "may not") that applies when the crime was committed before the vessel entered the territorial sea and the ship is only passing through the territorial sea without entering the state's internal waters.[64] Exceptions to these restrictions are included in the article.[65] Article 28 adopts the same two-part approach to the coastal state's civil enforcement jurisdiction. It provides that the coastal state "should not" stop or divert a foreign ship passing through the territorial sea for the purpose of exercising civil jurisdiction in relation to a person on board the

---

living resources of the sea; (5) prevention of infringement of the fisheries laws and regulations of the coastal state; (6) preservation of the environment of the coastal state and the prevention, reduction, and control of pollution thereof; (7) marine scientific research and hydrographic surveys; and (8) prevention of infringement of the customs, fiscal, immigration, or sanitary laws and regulations of the coastal state.

61. Warships are not exempt from compliance; however, they are immune from any enforcement action by the coastal state. See LOSC arts. 30–32.
62. See generally Restatement FRLUS § 513 cmt. e.
63. LOSC art. 27(1). This provision is best characterized as a codification of the existing rule of comity, by which coastal states generally refrain from exercising their jurisdiction, even though not legally required to do so.
64. Id. art. 27(5).
65. Exceptions to the rule are recognized when (1) the consequences of the crime extend to the coastal state, (2) the crime is of a kind to disturb the peace of the country or the good order of the territorial sea, (3) the assistance of the local authorities has been requested by the master of the ship or by a diplomatic agent or consular officer of the flag state, or (4) such measures are necessary for the suppression of illicit traffic in narcotic drugs or psychotropic substances. For states that are party to the Brussels Convention on Penal Jurisdiction in Matters of Collision, May 10, 1952, 439 U.N.T.S. 233, a coastal state's criminal jurisdiction is further limited in collision matters. Exceptions to the mandatory rule in Article 27(5) of the LOSC for crimes committed before the vessel entered the territorial sea include those set out in Part XII of the convention on protection of the marine environment and rules with respect to laws and regulations adopted in accordance with Part V on the exclusive economic zone.

ship.[66] It next provides that the coastal state "may not" levy execution against or arrest the ship for the purpose of any civil proceedings, save only in respect of obligations or liabilities assumed or incurred by the ship in the course, or for the purpose, of its voyage through the waters of the coastal state. The coastal state may, however, levy execution against or arrest a foreign ship lying in the territorial sea, or passing through the territorial sea after leaving internal waters pursuant to civil proceedings.

8. The U.S. Territorial Sea Regime

The territorial sea regime in the United States is a complex mix of international and domestic law.[67] In 1988 President Reagan issued a proclamation extending the U.S. territorial sea from three to twelve nautical miles, but only for international purposes.[68] The presidential proclamation constitutes an assertion under customary law and is fully consistent with the 1983 U.S. Ocean Policy Statement and the 1982 LOS Convention. The 1988 proclamation made it clear that it did not alter existing legislation or federal-state boundaries and jurisdiction, all of which were then based on a three-nautical-mile territorial sea. The qualification was not surprising: the president may not, by simple executive proclamation, amend federal statutes.[69] Such amendments require legislative action by Congress, and Congress has not yet taken a comprehensive approach in its statutory definitions concerning the breadth of the territorial sea. As a result, U.S. domestic laws (and the implementing agency regulations) enacted before 1988 will not apply territorially to activities beyond three nautical miles until they are amended by Congress.

A bill titled the Territorial Sea and Contiguous Zone Extension and Enforcement Act of 1992 was introduced in the 102nd Congress, but it was never enacted.[70] Nevertheless, the House Committee on Merchant Marine and Fisheries report on the bill continues to provide a helpful commentary on territorial sea and contiguous zone issues under U.S. domestic law.[71] An annually updated Coast Guard regulation summarizes the U.S. regulatory approach to the territorial sea.[72] As of 2013, it provides that federal statutory references to the term "territorial sea" mean a twelve-nautical-mile territorial sea in certain specified sections of the Ports and Waterways Safety Act and the Vessel Bridge-to-Bridge Radiotelephone Act, for criminal jurisdiction under Title 18 of U.S. Code,[73] and in interpreting international law. For all other purposes, federal statutory references to the "territorial sea" mean a three-nautical-mile territorial sea.

---

66. LOSC art. 28. See also International Convention on the Arrest of Ships, Mar. 12, 1999, U.N. Doc. A/CONF.188.6 (the arrest of a ship is distinguished from the arrest of a person on board the ship); Restatement FRLUS § 513 cmt. e.

67. Part of that complexity results from congressional neglect and part from the nation's federated structure and the role and concurrent jurisdiction of the states of the United States in the territorial sea.

68. Proclamation 5928, Territorial Sea of the United States, Dec. 27, 1988, 3 C.F.R. § 546 (1989). See generally Symposium: Extension of the U.S. Territorial Sea to Twelve Miles: Legal and Policy Issues 2 Terr. Sea J. (1992).

69. One court of appeals thought otherwise, but the court's reasoning ignores the plain language of the proclamation, which precludes any effect on domestic legislation. See In re Air Crash off Long Island, 209 F.3d 200, 213 (2d Cir. 2000) (concluding that the presidential proclamation had the effect of redefining the territorial applicability of the Death on the High Seas Act).

70. H.R. 102-3842 (not enacted). A similar bill was introduced in 1988 following President Reagan's twelve-nautical-mile territorial sea proclamation.

71. See H.R. Rep. 102-843(I), Aug. 12, 1992.

72. 33 C.F.R. § 2.22.

73. See Antiterrorism and Effective Death Penalty Act of 1996, Pub. L. No. 132, § 901, 110 Stat. 1214, 1317 (expansion of the territorial sea). See also U.S. v. One Big Six Wheel, 166 F.3d 498 (2d Cir. 1999) (analyzing the effect of the 1996 act on federal criminal jurisdiction).

B. NAVIGATION IN INTERNATIONAL STRAITS

Expanded jurisdictional claims by nations over waters adjoining their coasts that were formerly part of the "high seas" erode historically protected navigational freedoms. They also significantly expand the reach of potential neutral territory during time of armed conflict, thus limiting the operational reach of belligerent vessels. The UNCLOS III conferees recognized that if all coastal nations expanded their territorial sea claims from three to twelve nautical miles, more than one hundred straits around the world that were subject to high-seas freedom of navigation under the traditional law of the sea regime would be absorbed into the expanded territorial seas.[74] The newly absorbed straits would include vital strategic passages such as the Strait of Hormuz, the only passage to the oil-exporting terminals in the Arabian/Persian Gulf (see figure 6), the Strait of Gibraltar (see figure 7), the Strait of Dover (nineteen nautical miles wide), the Strait of Malacca (twenty nautical miles wide and the main sea route between the Pacific and Indian Oceans),[75] and Bab el Mandeb (fourteen nautical miles wide and connecting the Indian Ocean with the Red Sea and Suez Canal).[76] Because those straits would fall within waters claimed as territorial seas, under the preexisting law of the sea ships could transit them only in compliance with the restrictive "right of innocent passage" regime, a right that can be suspended by the bordering state under some circumstances. Moreover, aircraft have no innocent passage right to overfly another nation's territorial sea, and submarines are compelled to navigate overtly in order to qualify for innocent passage.

UNCLOS III strikes a different balance for straits used for international navigation than for other waters of a state's territorial sea, where only a right of innocent passage applies.[77] The right of transit passage differs from innocent passage in several important respects.[78] First, the right of transit passage extends to aircraft (civil and military) as well as vessels. Second, vessels have a right to transit international straits in their "normal mode," meaning, among other things, that submarines need not surface and display their national flag, as they must do while in innocent passage. Unlike innocent passage, the right of transit passage may not be suspended. Additionally, the coastal state is more limited in the range of laws and regulations it may apply to foreign vessels in transit passage than to those in innocent passage. In comparing the two transit regimes it is also noteworthy that the transit passage regime does not include a provision similar to Article 23 in the innocent passage regime applicable to foreign nuclear-powered ships and ships carrying nuclear or other inherently dangerous or obnoxious materials.

1. Straits Used for International Navigation

The right of transit passage applies to straits used for international navigation. A strait is a narrow passage of water between two landmasses or between a landmass and an island or a group

---

74. By one count, 153 straits transect waters between 6 and 24 nautical miles of a coastal state baseline and would therefore fall within a coastal state's territorial sea if those seas were all extended from 3 to 12 nautical miles.

75. See Safety of Navigation in the Straits of Malacca and Singapore, Singapore J. Int'l & Comp. L. 486–96 (1998).

76. Some straits are more strategic than others. For example, there are alternatives to the Strait of Malacca (although most alternative routes run through Indonesian archipelagic waters). In fact, with a limiting draft of sixty-two feet, Malacca is too shallow for some fully laden tankers or for submerged transit by submarine. By contrast, there is no alternative to the Strait of Hormuz for ships bound for the Arabian/Persian Gulf.

77. Commander's Handbook, supra, ¶ 2.5.3.1; Louis M. Alexander, International Straits, 64 U.S. Nav. War Coll. Int'l L. Studies 91 (1991).

78. Although both regimes share the term "passage," the definition in Article 18 on innocent passage does not control in questions of transit passage. The right-of-transit "passage," which extends to aircraft, is conducted in the vessel's or aircraft's "normal mode," which may differ in important respects from the Article 18 definition of "passage."

of islands connecting two larger sea areas.[79] Straits are variously denominated as straits, channels, sounds, and passes. However, the term does not include artificial canals. Only straits that are used for international navigation between one part of the high seas or an EEZ and another part of the high seas or an EEZ are subject to the legal regime of transit passage.[80] The LOS Convention transit passage regime does not apply to a strait used for international navigation if there exists through the strait a route through the high seas or through an EEZ of similar convenience with respect to navigational and hydrographical characteristics.[81]

Figure 6 illustrates the Strait of Hormuz, a heavily traveled strait between Iran and Oman used for international navigation. The strait connects the Gulf of Oman and the Arabian/Persian Gulf. As shown by the dotted lines, both of the gulfs connected by the strait include areas beyond twelve nautical miles of any state, and are therefore high seas or EEZs, depending on the claims by the coastal states.

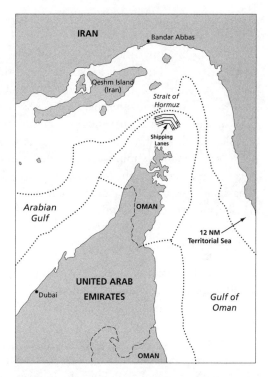

FIGURE 6. **Strait of Hormuz**

The strait therefore meets the Article 37 definition. Because the strait narrows to less than twenty-four nautical miles along the boundary between Iran's and Oman's territorial seas, there is no high-seas or EEZ route through the strait; thus it is not excluded by Article 36. Accordingly, all ships and aircraft enjoy a right of nonsuspendable transit passage through the strait.

One point of disagreement over the application of Article 37 concerns the question of whether a strait must currently be used for international navigation or need only be susceptible of being so used. The United States takes the position that the definition set out in the LOS Convention does not depend on present use.[82] This issue is particularly important in the Arctic

79. See International Hydrographic Bureau, Consolidated Glossary of Technical Terms Used in the United Nations Convention on the Law of the Sea, IHB Special Pub. No. 41, reprinted in Annotated Supplement to the Commander's Handbook, supra, annex A1-5.

80. LOSC art. 37. The U.S. Senate understanding stipulates that "the words 'strait' and 'straits' are not limited by geographic names or categories and include all waters not subject to Part IV that separate one part of the high seas or exclusive economic zone from another part of the high seas or exclusive economic zone or other areas referred to in Article 45." See Senate Committee on Foreign Relations, Report on the United Nations Convention on the Law of the Sea, S. Exec. Rpt. 110-09 (Dec. 18, 2007), understanding 3(C) (reprinted in appendix D).

81. LOSC art. 36. Japan apparently sought to avoid exposing certain of its island channels less than twenty-four nautical miles wide to a right of transit passage by claiming less than twelve-nautical-mile territorial seas in the area (and therefore leaving open a corridor outside the territorial seas) in the vicinity of Tsushima, Osumi, Soya (La Perouse), and Tsugaru Straits. See U.S. Department of State, Bureau of Oceans and International Environmental and Scientific Affairs, Limits in the Seas No. 120, Straight Baselines and Territorial Sea Claims Japan, April 30, 1998. That strategy will not be effective unless the open corridor is "of similar convenience with respect to navigational and hydrographical characteristics." LOSC art. 36; Commander's Handbook, supra, ¶ 2.5.3.2.

82. The U.S. Senate understanding stipulates that "the term 'used for international navigation' includes all straits *capable* of being used for international navigation." S. Exec. Rpt. No. 110-09, understanding 3(D) (emphasis

Northwest Passage, where seasonal ice recession now permits navigation by a variety of commercial and even recreational vessels.[83]

The LOS Convention sets out three variations on the general transit passage scheme described above. The first is for straits connecting one part of the high seas or EEZ and another part of the high seas or EEZ, where the strait is formed by an island of a state bordering the strait and its mainland, and there exists seaward of the island a route through the high seas or EEZ of similar navigational and hydrographical characteristics.[84] The second exception is for the so-called dead-end straits, which connect an area of the high seas or EEZ with a state's territorial sea.[85] Straits falling within these exceptions to the transit passage regime are, however, subject to a nonsuspendable right of innocent passage.[86] The last exception is for straits regulated by a long-standing international convention, such as the Turkish Straits connecting the Black Sea and Mediterranean Sea, the Danish Straits, and the Strait of Magellan.[87]

2. Right of Transit Passage

Freedom of navigation is vital to maritime commerce and naval mobility. Under international law, the ships and aircraft of all nations, including warships, auxiliary vessels, and military aircraft, enjoy the right of unimpeded transit passage through international straits and their approaches.[88] During times of armed conflict, the right of transit passage through a neutral state's territorial sea is preserved to belligerent warships and auxiliary vessels and military and auxiliary aircraft, and their passage does not affect the coastal state's neutrality.[89]

"Transit passage" is defined as the exercise of the freedoms of navigation and overflight solely for the purpose of continuous and expeditious transit in the normal modes of operation utilized by ships and aircraft for such passage. While exercising the right of transit, passage ships and aircraft are required to proceed without delay through or over the strait; refrain from any threat or use of force against the sovereignty, territorial integrity, or political independence of states bordering the strait; and refrain from any activities other than those incident to their normal modes of continuous and expeditious transit, unless rendered necessary by force majeure or by distress.[90]

---

added) (reprinted in appendix D). See Donald R. Rothwell, The Canadian-U.S. Northwest Passage Dispute: A Reassessment, 26 Cornell Int'l L. J. 331 (1993).

83. Support for that interpretation is found in the ICJ judgment in the Corfu Channel case, in which the court did not qualify the requirement for usage with temporal or quantitative conditions such as "customary" use or "substantial" use. See generally McDougal & Burke, supra, at 207. See also Donald R. Rothwell, International Straits and Trans-Arctic Navigation, 43 Ocean Dev. & Int'l L. 267 (2012).

84. LOSC art. 38(1).

85. Id. art 45(1)(b). There may be no suspension of innocent passage through such straits. The Gulf of Aqaba and the Strait of Tiran at its entrance, which provide Israel and Jordan with access to the Red Sea, was designated an international waterway subject to a nonsuspendable right of innocent passage by Article V of the 1979 Treaty of Peace between Egypt and Israel. See Jonathan E. Fink, The Gulf of Aqaba and the Strait of Tiran: The Practice of "Freedom of Navigation" after the Egyptian-Israeli Peace Treaty, 42 Nav. L. Rev. 121 (1995).

86. LOSC art. 45(2).

87. Id. art. 35(c). To avoid restrictions on "capital ships" that may transit the Turkish Straits under the Montreux Convention, the former Soviet Union classified the aircraft carrier Kiev an "antisubmarine warfare cruiser."

88. The Senate understanding stipulates that "all ships and aircraft, including warships and military aircraft, regardless of, for example, cargo, armament, means of propulsion, flag, origin, destination, or purpose, are entitled to transit passage and archipelagic sea-lanes passage in their 'normal mode.'" S. Exec. Rpt. No. 110-09, understanding 3 (reprinted in appendix D). The understanding is largely copied from paragraph 2 of the 1989 USA-USSR: Joint Statement Governing Innocent Passage, supra.

89. San Remo Manual, supra, at ¶¶ 23, 24, & 27–30; Commander's Handbook, supra, ¶ 7.3.6.

90. Restatement FRLUS § 513(3) cmt. j & n.3.

Transit passage exists throughout the entire strait and the approaches to the strait.[91] Thus, if under the prevailing conditions the preferred deep-water route is located just one mile off the coastline, vessels engaged in transit passage would be permitted to follow that route (while remaining seaward of the baseline) rather than confine their passage to the center of the strait. The rule is illustrated in figure 7 depicting the Strait of Gibraltar. Vessels and air-

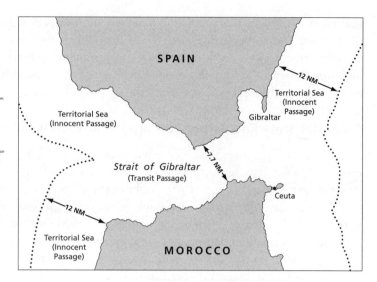

FIGURE 7. **Strait of Gibraltar**

craft navigating the strait in transit passage are not required to chart a course through the center of the strait, a matter of particular importance for submerged submarines or vessels launching and recovering aircraft. While transiting craft must remain outside either coastal state's internal waters, they are generally free to choose any navigationally sound course through the strait, so long as they comply with any applicable traffic schemes and collision avoidance rules and with the requirement that the transit be continuous and expeditious.

3. Normal Mode of Operations

Vessels exercising the right of transit passage have the right to unimpeded transit, in their normal mode of transit.[92] The LOS Convention does not define "normal mode" of transit.[93] The negotiating history makes it clear that the term includes submerged transit by submarines, because that is their "normal mode." The United States takes the position that "normal mode" for warships includes operations consistent with sound navigation practices and security of the force, and therefore includes the use of their electronic detection and navigational devices such as radar, sonar, and depth-sounding devices; formation steaming; launching and recovering of aircraft

---

91. The right is sometimes said to apply "shoreline to shoreline." See Commander's Handbook, supra, ¶ 2.5.3.1. Because that might include a coastal state's internal waters (where the coastal state enjoys full sovereignty), it would be more accurate to say that it extends baseline to baseline, subject, of course, to the requirement that such waters are part of the "strait." See LOSC art. 35(a).

92. LOSC art. 38. See also William L. Schachte Jr. & J. Peter A. Bernhardt, International Straits and Navigational Freedoms, 33 Va. J. Int'l L. 527 (1993); W. Michael Reisman, The Regime of Straits and National Security: An Appraisal of International Lawmaking, 74 Am. J. Int'l L. 48 (1980); UN Division for Ocean Affairs and the Law of the Sea, The Law of the Sea: Straits Used for International Navigation—Legislative History of Part III of the United Nations Convention on the Law of the Sea, U.N. Sales Nos. E.91.V.14 (1991) Vol. I & E.92.V.14 Vol. II (1992).

93. The U.S. Senate understanding stipulates that "normal mode" includes, inter alia, (1) submerged transit of sub-marines; (2) overflight by military aircraft, including in military formation; (3) activities necessary for the security of surface warships, such as formation steaming and other force protection measures; (4) underway replenishment; and (5) the launching and recovery of aircraft. See S. Exec. Rpt. No. 110-09, understanding 3 (reprinted in appendix D).

(including unmanned aerial vehicles); mine countermeasures activities (including employment of mine-hunting aircraft and vessels); use of air and surface search radars; and active and passive antisubmarine warfare (ASW) measures.[94] At the same time, however, the convention expressly prohibits foreign ships from engaging in marine scientific research or survey activities while in transit passage, absent coastal state consent.

4. Coastal State Regulatory Authority over Vessels in Transit Passage

Coastal state control over vessels engaged in transit passage through a strait used for international navigation is more restricted than over vessels merely in innocent passage.[95] The coastal state may not suspend or hamper the right of transit.[96] As with innocent passage, the right of transit passage is subject to other applicable rules of international law,[97] including the law of naval warfare, the UN Charter, and binding resolutions of the UN Security Council. The coastal state may also adopt a limited class of laws and regulations relating to vessels in transit passage; however, those laws and regulations are limited to generally accepted international standards with respect to pollution prevention regulations.[98] The coastal state may not impose construction, design, equipment, or manning requirements on vessels in transit passage.[99] Coastal state laws may not discriminate in form or fact among foreign vessels and must not have the practical effect of denying, hampering, or impairing the right of transit passage.[100] Coastal nations bordering international straits may designate sea-lanes and prescribe traffic separation schemes to promote navigational safety (see figure 6).[101] However, such sea-lanes and separation schemes must be approved by the IMO in accordance with generally accepted international standards. Merchant ships and government-operated ships operated for commercial purposes must respect properly designated sea-lanes and traffic separation schemes.[102] Warships, auxiliaries, and government ships operated on exclusively government service are not legally required to comply with traffic separation schemes and other routing measures.[103] They must, however, operate with due regard for the safety of navigation. States bordering international straits and user states are encouraged to cooperate in the establishment and maintenance of navigation and safety aids and for the prevention and control of pollution.[104]

Part III of the LOS Convention establishing the regime for international straits does not address limitations on the coastal state's civil or criminal enforcement jurisdiction, as does Part II on the innocent passage regime in Articles 27 and 28. Given the coastal state's more limited

---

94. S. Exec. Rpt. No. 110-09, understanding 3 (reprinted in appendix D).

95. LOSC art. 37.

96. Id. art. 44. See also The Corfu Channel case (U.K. v. Albania) 1949 I.C.J. 1 (Apr. 9).

97. LOSC art. 39(1)(b).

98. Id. art. 42(1).

99. This limitation actually appears in the innocent passage regime, but the limitation should apply a fortiori to the transit passage regime. Id. art. 21(2).

100. Id. art. 42(2).

101. Id. art. 41.

102. Id. art. 41(7).

103. See SOLAS Convention, supra, ch. V, reg. 8(c); Commander's Handbook, supra, ¶ 2.5.3.1.

104. LOSC art. 43. For an example of such a cooperative agreement and an aids-to-navigation fund, see International Maritime Organization, Singapore Statement on the Meeting of the Straits of Malacca and Singapore: Enhancing Safety, Security and Environmental Protection, IMO/SGP 1/4, Sep 6, 2007. See also Hiroshi Terashima, Transit Passage and Users' Contributions to the Safety of Straits of Malacca and Singapore, in Freedom of Seas, Passage Rights and the 1982 Law of the Sea Convention (Myron H. Nordquist et al. eds., 2009).

competency with respect to foreign vessels in transit passage through international straits, it seems clear that the coastal state does not have greater enforcement powers with respect to vessels in transit passage than those in innocent passage. Whether its enforcement jurisdiction is more limited with respect to vessels in transit passage is not clear. A textual argument can be made that Articles 27 and 28, which limit the coastal state's enforcement jurisdiction over nonpublic vessels "passing through the territorial sea," apply equally to vessels in both innocent and transit passages. That construction is bolstered by Article 34(1), which saves the coastal state's sovereignty and jurisdiction in international straits. The contrary structural interpretation hinges on the fact that Articles 27 and 28 appear in Section 3 of Part II, which is titled "Innocent Passage in the Territorial Sea." Whichever interpretation proves to be more persuasive, it is clear that with respect to enforcement of marine pollution regulations against foreign ships in international straits, Article 233 of the convention controls. It permits the coastal state to take "appropriate enforcement measures" only in cases in which the violation causes major damage.

5. Transit Passage in the United States

Unimak Pass through Alaska's Aleutian Island chain is the most heavily traveled international strait in U.S. waters. Located on the great circle route between ports in northern Asia and North America, the ten-nautical-mile-wide strait accommodates more than seven thousand merchant vessel transits annually.[105] Consistent with the LOS Convention's limits on coastal state jurisdiction over vessels in transit passage, federal statutes include important exemptions for foreign vessels in transit passage through such straits.[106] Increased shipping activity in the Arctic has heightened concerns for navigation safety and environmental protection in Unimak Pass and its approaches, as well as in the nearby Bering Strait. Any measures adopted to address those concerns must be consistent with the international straits regime.

Occasionally, questions arise regarding the possible application of the international straits regime to the Florida Strait lying between the southern tip of that state and the northern coast of Cuba roughly ninety nautical miles to the south. Assuming that the waters do in fact constitute a "strait," it is clear that they are used for international navigation between one part of the high seas or an EEZ and another part of the high seas or an EEZ. Questions arise, however, regarding application of Article 36, which denies a right of transit passage in territorial waters of a strait used for international navigation if there exists through the strait a route through the high seas or through an EEZ of similar convenience with respect to navigational and hydrographical characteristics.[107] There are, in fact, multiple routes through the Florida Strait that lie in one of the two adjacent states' EEZs and outside their territorial seas; however, an argument could be made that the presence of strong currents and shoals, banks, and cays, as well as future oil exploration and production operations, may render the EEZ routes less convenient (and more dangerous) than the territorial sea routes "with respect to navigational and hydrographical characteristics."[108]

---

105. Transportation Research Board, Risk of Vessel Accidents and Spills in the Aleutian Islands: Designing a Comprehensive Risk Assessment—Special Report 293 (2009). The grounding and breakup of the M/V *Selendang Ayu*, a large bulk grain carrier, in 2004 resulted in six fatalities and spilled 336,000 gallons of heavy fuel oil near the Aleutian Islands.

106. See, e.g., 46 U.S.C. § 3702(e), 33 U.S.C. § 1223(d)(2), and 33 C.F.R. §§ 104.105, 160.103, 164.02.

107. LOSC art. 36.

108. Id. See Churchill & Lowe, supra, at 90, which cites the Florida Strait as an example that falls within the Article 36 exclusion; however, the authors do not address the navigational or hydrographical convenience qualification.

C. NAVIGATION IN ARCHIPELAGIC WATERS

Only nations that qualify as archipelagic states under the 1982 LOS Convention may claim archipelagic baselines (see chapter 3 regarding the rules for constructing archipelagic baselines).[109] States that are geographically continental nations but that also have some island archipelagos do not qualify.[110] For example, the United States is a continental state and therefore could not legally claim archipelagic baselines around the Hawaiian Islands archipelago.

Waters inside archipelagic baselines are deemed archipelagic waters (see figure 5). The archipelagic state is sovereign within its archipelagic waters.[111] However, those waters are subject to the convention rules on innocent passage and, in selected areas, archipelagic sea-lanes passage. The innocent passage regime for archipelagic waters mirrors the regime for innocent passage through the territorial sea.[112] By contrast, the archipelagic sea-lanes passage regime is nearly identical with the right of transit passage through straits used for international navigation, and in fact incorporates by reference several of the transit passage regime rules.[113]

The similarities between transit passage and archipelagic sea-lanes passage should not come as a surprise. Like the legitimization of twelve-nautical-mile territorial seas under the LOS Convention, the adoption of archipelagic waters has the effect of enclosing waters that were historically straits used for international navigation, such as Indonesia's Sunda Strait and Lomboc Strait. For maritime states, the innocent passage regime did not adequately serve navigation rights in such straits. As a result, they were willing to agree to the new archipelagic waters regime only if it accommodated their navigation and overflight concerns.

The archipelagic state is permitted but not required to designate archipelagic sea-lanes (ASL) and air routes within its archipelagic waters and the adjacent territorial sea, where the right of archipelagic sea-lanes passage will apply.[114] If designated, such ASL and air routes must comply with the parameters established by the convention and must first be submitted to the IMO.[115] If the archipelagic state fails to designate ASL or its designated lanes are incomplete, archipelagic sea-lanes passage rights apply in all routes normally used for international navigation and overflight.[116] In all other archipelagic waters (other than internal waters) the regime of innocent passage applies.[117]

Archipelagic sea-lanes passage is defined under international law as the exercise of the freedom of navigation and overflight for the sole purpose of continuous, expeditious, and unobstructed transit through archipelagic waters in the normal modes of operations.[118] All ships and aircraft enjoy the right of archipelagic sea-lanes passage while transiting ASL and air routes.[119] Additionally, vessels and aircraft retain the right to use all normal routes for transits through

109. LOSC art. 46(a); Annotated Supplement to Commander's Handbook, supra, table A1-7 (listing nineteen states that claimed archipelagic waters by 1997); UN Division for Ocean Affairs and the Law of the Sea, The Law of the Sea: Archipelagic States—Legislative History of Part IV of the United Nations Convention on the Law of the Sea, U.N. Sales No. E.90.V.2 (1990); UN Division for Ocean Affairs and the Law of the Sea, The Law of the Sea: Practice of Archipelagic States, U.N. Sales No. E.92.V.3 (1992).
110. See Restatement FRLUS § 511 cmt. i & n.6.
111. LOSC arts. 2(1) & 49.
112. LOSC art. 52; Restatement FRLUS § 513(4) cmt. k; Commander's Handbook, supra, ¶ 2.5.4.1.
113. LOSC arts. 53 & 54. Article 54 incorporates the transit passage rules in Articles 39, 40, 42, and 44.
114. Id. art. 53(1).
115. Id. art. 53(9). See also IMO, Ships' Routeing, supra, part H.
116. Id. art. 53(12). See also S. Exec. Rpt. No. 110-09, understanding 3(E) (reprinted in appendix D).
117. Id. art. 52.
118. Id. art. 53(3).
119. Id. art. 53(2).

areas of archipelagic waters where there are no designated sea-lanes.[120] During times of armed conflict, the right of archipelagic sea-lanes passage through a neutral state's archipelagic waters is preserved to belligerent warships and auxiliary vessels and military and auxiliary aircraft, and their passage does not affect the archipelagic state's neutrality.[121] The right of archipelagic sea-lanes passage through designated sea-lanes, as well as through all normal routes, cannot be hampered or suspended by the archipelagic nation for any purpose.[122] In contrast to the innocent passage regime, the archipelagic sea-lanes passage regime is not limited by the list of noninnocent activities in Article 19. Ships and aircraft engaged in archipelagic sea-lanes passage are subject to the same duties applicable to vessels engaged in transit passage.[123] The IMO issued guidance for ships transiting archipelagic waters in 1999.[124]

D. THE CONTIGUOUS ZONE

The modern contiguous zone regime has its roots in coastal state efforts to take protective measures against "hovering" vessels that operated in conjunction with small boats while remaining just beyond the coastal state's territorial sea in order to circumvent enforcement of the customs laws by the coastal state.[125] As such, it shares aspects of the constructive presence doctrine examined in the context of the right of hot pursuit in chapter 11. The contiguous zone is closely associated with the territorial sea regime.[126] It was no coincidence that, among the four possible 1958 Geneva conventions, the contiguous zone regime was codified with the territorial sea articles in the Convention on the Territorial Sea and Contiguous Zone,[127] or that the present article on the contiguous zone (Article 33) is in Part II of the 1982 LOS Convention, with the territorial sea articles. Article 33 provides that a coastal state may establish a contiguous zone extending from the outer limit of the territorial sea to a distance of not more than twenty-four miles seaward of the baseline.[128] The contiguous zone will therefore lie entirely within the state's EEZ if both are claimed.

1. Coastal State Regulation in the Contiguous Zone

Within its contiguous zone a coastal state may exercise the control necessary to prevent infringement of its customs, fiscal, immigration, or sanitary laws and regulations within its territorial seas or to punish such infringements when the violation is committed within its territory or territorial

---

120. S. Exec. Rpt. No. 110-09, understanding 3(E) (reprinted in appendix D).
121. San Remo Manual, supra, ¶¶ 23, 25, & 27–30; Commander's Handbook, supra, ¶ 7.3.7.
122. LOSC art. 54, incorporating by reference Article 44.
123. Id. art. 54, incorporating by reference Article 39.
124. IMO, Safety of Navigation Circular SN/Cir. 206, Jan. 8, 1999.
125. See, e.g., Church v. Hubbard, 6 U.S. (2 Cranch) 187, 235 (1804).
126. The ILC's commentaries on the draft articles it prepared for the 1958 UNCLOS I conferees remains an important reference on development of the contiguous zone regime. See ILC, Articles concerning the Law of the Sea with Commentaries, supra, art. 66, at 265–301.
127. At the same time, Article 1 of the Convention on the High Seas defined the "high seas" as all waters not included in any state's territorial sea or internal waters; thus the state's contiguous zone was part of the high seas.
128. LOSC art. 33; Restatement FRLUS § 513 cmt. f. Article 121 does not expressly address whether "rocks incapable of sustaining human habitation" generate a contiguous zone. Logic would suggest, however, that if such rocks generate a territorial sea, the coastal state could establish a contiguous zone, to prevent or punish violations of its customs, fiscal, immigration, or sanitary laws in its territory or territorial sea.

sea.[129] The coastal state's subject matter competence within the contiguous zone is limited to the four listed areas: customs, fiscal, immigration, and sanitary matters.[130] The contiguous zone regime does not extend to security interests;[131] however, the competency to enforce "customs" laws may extend to cargo import and export controls grounded on security concerns.[132] The United States has rejected as unlawful any peacetime coastal state security zones seaward of the state's territorial sea.[133]

Close reading of Article 33 reveals that it nowhere uses the term "jurisdiction." The state's competency is limited to "control" measures to prevent and punish violations within the territorial sea or territory of the coastal state.[134] The contiguous zone regime is thus not an independent basis for the coastal state to exercise prescriptive jurisdiction.[135] The "prevent and punish" authorization suggests that the contiguous zone regime is akin to the conditions on port entry regime examined in chapter 4. Both authorize measures to *prevent* violations. Customs laws seek to prohibit importation of contraband and smuggled goods. "Preventing" violations (the verb used in both Article 33 on the contiguous zone and Article 25(2) on conditions of port entry) suggests measures that may be taken before a violation has occurred and would find their principal application to vessels inbound to the coastal state's territorial sea or internal waters. Such measures might include actions to prevent the vessel from entering the territorial sea (or the port with respect to conditions for entry), but not to arrest or seizure (because no violation has yet occurred). By contrast, "punishing" violations that have already occurred in the state's territory or territorial sea would most likely be invoked against vessels outbound from the territorial sea or internal waters after having violated the coastal state's law in its territory or territorial sea.[136]

---

129. LOSC art. 33; Whiteman, 4 Digest of International Law, supra, at § 20; Restatement FRLUS § 513 cmt. f; A. Vaughan Lowe, The Development and Concept of the Contiguous Zone, 1981 Brit. Y.B. Int'l L. 109 (1982). The term "sanitary" comes from the French *sanitaire*, which is limited to health and quarantines measures. The U.S. Senate understanding declares that "the United States understands that, with respect to article 33, the term 'sanitary laws and regulations' includes laws and regulations to protect human health from, inter alia, pathogens being introduced into the territorial sea." S. Exec. Rpt. No. 110-09, understanding 19 (reprinted in appendix D).

130. See United Nations Convention on the Law of the Sea 1982: A Commentary, vol. II, at 266–75 (ed. Satya N. Nandan and Shabtai Rosenne, 1995).

131. U.S. Department of State, Cumulative Digest of United States Practice in International Law 1981–1988, vol. 2, at 1860–61 (1994). Nevertheless, at least three states (Cambodia, Sudan, and Syria) claim security jurisdiction in their twenty-four-nautical-mile contiguous zone. See DoD Maritime Claims Reference Manual, supra (entries for the three states). See also UN Division for Ocean Affairs and the Law of the Sea, The Law of the Sea: National Legislation on Territorial Sea, the Right of Innocent Passage and the Contiguous Zone U.N. Sales No. E.95.V.7 (1995).

132. Restatement FRLUS § 511cmt. k.

133. Commander's Handbook, supra, ¶ 1.6.4; Roach & Smith, Excessive Maritime Claims, supra, at 157. See also George V. Galdorisi & Kevin R. Vienna, Beyond the Law of the Sea 147 (1997) (describing U.S. concerns over claims by sixteen states to national security measures in the contiguous zone). The Maritime Transportation Security Act of 2002 extended the definition of the U.S. territorial sea for purposes of security measures to twelve nautical miles. The implementing regulations can be found in 33 C.F.R. pts. 101–107.

134. Coast Guard MLE Manual, supra, at ¶ B-4.g.

135. Shigeru Oda, The Concept of the Contiguous Zone, 11 Int'l & Comp. L. Q. (1962). But see A. V. Lowe, The Commander's Handbook on the Law of Naval Operations and the Contemporary Law of the Sea, 64 U.S. Nav. War Coll. Int'l L. Studies 109 (1991), observing that "many State claims to contiguous zones assert the right to punish not only infringements committed within the territory or territorial sea of the State, but also infringements committed within the contiguous zone itself; in short, *they claim both jurisdiction to enforce and jurisdiction to prescribe*." Id. at 112 (emphasis added). Because the contiguous zone generally lies entirely within the coastal state's EEZ (if one is claimed), the coastal state may exercise its prescriptive jurisdiction under Article 56 of the convention over those waters.

136. See U.S. v. Best, 172 F. Supp.2d 656 (D.V.I. 2001) (dismissing alien-smuggling charges involving boat interdicted sixteen nautical miles off the U.S. coast after holding that the presidential proclamation extending the U.S.

Enforcement action could be taken against a foreign vessel while it is in the contiguous zone even if the circumstances did not meet the conditions for the exercise of hot pursuit.

States also have the duty to protect objects of an archaeological and historical nature found at sea.[137] In order to control traffic in such objects, the coastal state may, in applying Article 33, presume that their removal from the seabed in the contiguous zone without its approval would result in an infringement within its territory or territorial sea of the laws and regulations referred to in Article 33. However, nothing in Articles 33 or 303 (on archaeological and historical objects found at sea) affects the rights of identifiable owners, the law of salvage or other rules of admiralty, or laws and practices with respect to cultural exchanges.

2. The U.S. Contiguous Zone Regime

In 1999 President Clinton issued a proclamation extending the U.S. contiguous zone seaward from the outer edge of the twelve-nautical-mile territorial sea (proclaimed by President Reagan in 1988) to a distance of twenty-four nautical miles from the baseline.[138] The proclamation did not affect existing statutory definitions of the zone, and Congress has not provided all of the necessary conforming amendments.[139] Accordingly, for the purposes of the Federal Water Pollution Control Act (also known as the Clean Water Act), the contiguous zone extends from three nautical miles to twelve nautical miles seaward from the baseline. For all other statutes, the contiguous zone means all waters from twelve nautical miles to twenty-four nautical miles seaward of the baseline, but in no case extending into the territorial sea of another nation.[140] In the Maritime Drug Law Enforcement Act, Congress extended U.S. jurisdiction over drug-trafficking offenses by foreign vessels located in the contiguous zone to three situations: the vessel is in the contiguous zone and (1) is entering the United States, (2) has departed the United States, or (3) is a hovering vessel.[141] The first and third situations should, of course, be applied consistently with the applicable "prevent and punish" language of the LOS Convention's contiguous zone regime, the constructive presence doctrine, or both.

E. AIR NAVIGATION OVER COASTAL WATERS

Air navigation rights vary by location. Partly in recognition of the higher risks and reduced identification and reaction times posed by aircraft, navigation in national airspace is restricted. "National airspace" includes the skies over the state's territory, internal waters, archipelagic

contiguous zone to twenty-four nautical miles authorizes the government to "punish only the 'infringement of [those] laws and regulations *committed within its territory and territorial sea*'" [emphasis in original]), rev'd on other grounds, 304 F.3d 308 (3d Cir. 2002).

137. LOSC art. 303.

138. Proclamation 7219, Contiguous Zone of U.S., Sept. 2, 1999, 3 C.F.R. § 7219 (1999); James Carlson, Presidential Proclamation 7219: Extending the United States' Contiguous Zone—Didn't Someone Say This Had Something to Do with Pollution? 55 U. Miami L. Rev. 487 (2001).

139. See, e.g., 19 U.S.C. § 1401(j), extending "customs waters" seaward four marine leagues (twelve nautical miles). The United States at one time also promulgated "customs enforcement areas" (19 U.S.C. § 1701), but they were discontinued in 1946.

140. 33 C.F.R. § 2.28.

141. 46 U.S.C. § 70502(c)(1)(F). The term "hovering vessel" is defined in 19 U.S.C. § 1401(k) as (1) any vessel that is found or kept off the coast of the United States within or without the customs waters, if, from the history, conduct, character, or location of the vessel, it is reasonable to believe that such vessel is being used or may be used to introduce or promote or facilitate the introduction or attempted introduction of merchandise into the United States in violation of the laws of the United States; and (2) any vessel that has visited a vessel described in paragraph 1.

waters, and territorial sea (see figure 1) and extends upward to the lower limit of "outer space."[142] States are sovereign within their national airspace. In the absence of a treaty, there is no right to enter another state's national airspace.[143] Nor do aircraft have a right of innocent passage in the airspace over a foreign state's territorial sea. Accordingly, consent of the coastal state is required to enter national airspace, except during the exercise of transit passage or archipelagic sea-lanes passage, or for assistance entry. Overflight rights and responsibilities of civil aircraft are pre-scribed by the widely ratified 1944 Convention on Civil Aviation (commonly known as the "Chi-cago Convention"). Those overflight rights do not extend to military or other "state" aircraft.[144] Nonetheless, as is discussed in chapter 4, international law recognizes a right of entry for foreign aircraft, state or civil, when such entry is due to distress.[145] A peacetime right for military aircraft in distress to enter national airspace without express coastal state consent, when the security of the coastal state is not threatened, is consistent with established international practice.

The airspace beyond any nation's territorial sea is "international airspace." All aircraft, including military aircraft, enjoy freedom of overflight in international airspace, subject to appli-cable air navigation rules and regulations.[146] Nevertheless, coastal states may exercise some level of control over aircraft in the adjacent international airspace. Those measures take the form of air defense identification zones and flight information regions.

1. Air Defense Identification Zones

An air defense identification zone (ADIZ) is a unilaterally established zone encompassing interna-tional airspace adjacent to a nation's coastline that is designed to enhance national security during peacetime by requiring aircraft that enter the zone to identify themselves and state their inten-tions.[147] Rapid identification is facilitated by the aircraft transmitting ("squawking") an assigned "identification, friend or foe" (IFF) code, which can be received by ground stations and other aircraft. States are permitted to establish an identification requirement for aircraft on entry into an ADIZ only as a precondition for granting permission to enter that nation's national airspace. States may not require aircraft that are transiting through an ADIZ but are not entering national airspace to comply. An ADIZ thus operates in a manner similar to conditions on port entry for vessels. Some U.S. ADIZs extend up to two hundred nautical miles beyond the baseline.[148]

---

142. There is no agreed-upon definition of the upper limit of national or international airspace, where "outer space" begins. The commonly held conclusion is that outer space begins at the lowest altitude at which artificial satellites can be placed in orbit without free-falling to earth. It is widely recognized today that all nations have freedom of access to outer space and no nation may appropriate it to its national airspace. See Commander's Handbook, supra, ¶ 2.11.1.

143. Id. ¶ 2.7.1.

144. Article 3(c) of the Chicago Convention on Civil Aviation provides that "no state aircraft of a contracting State shall fly over the territory of another State or land thereon without authorization by special agreement or other-wise, and in accordance with the terms thereof."

145. Commander's Handbook, supra, ¶ 2.7.1.

146. Id. ¶ 2.9.3.

147. Id. ¶ 2.7.2.3; Restatement FRLUS § 521 n.2; Peter A. Dutton, Caelum Liberum: Air Defense Identification Zones outside Sovereign Airspace, 103 Am. J. Int'l L. 691 (2009). See also 14 C.F.R. § 99.1.

148. China's East China Sea Air Defense Identification Zone, established in late 2013, drew immediate protests from Japan and the United States because the ADIZ extended over the unoccupied Senkaku Islands claimed by Japan and it was not clear whether China was claiming that, contrary to international law, the ADIZ regulations would be extended to aircraft transiting through the zone without entering China's national airspace.

2. Flight Information Regions

In accordance with the Chicago Convention,[149] the International Civil Aviation Organization (ICAO) establishes flight information regions (FIRs), which encompass both national and international airspace.[150] The purpose of FIRs is to promote safety of flight operations by requiring aircraft to file flight plans and by providing flight information services, weather, routing, and alert services to aircraft. ICAO assigns responsibility for managing each FIR. Civil aircraft are required to comply with applicable FIR requirements. Although the Chicago Convention is not applicable to state aircraft,[151] it is U.S. policy for its state aircraft to follow ICAO flight procedures, including the filing of flight plans, and to utilize FIR services on routine point-to-point flights. Military aircraft, however, generally do not follow ICAO flight procedures when engaged in military contingency operations, politically sensitive missions, and routine aircraft carrier operations. When not following ICAO procedures, military aircraft fly with "due regard" for aviation safety. It should also be noted that, despite some suggestions to the contrary, diplomatic clearance is not required for military or auxiliary aircraft to fly through a FIR without entering the foreign state's national airspace.

3. Open Skies Treaties

Arms limitation and reduction treaties may call for verification visits and inspections or other confidence-building measures. One such confidence-building initiative was the 1992 Open Skies Treaty (OST) between the NATO and Warsaw Pact states.[152] The OST requires the thirty-four states parties to permit other parties to conduct a certain number of compliance verification overflights of their territory. Overflights are conducted by unarmed aircraft equipped with the sensors appropriate to their verification mission. The entire territory of the state is subject to OST overflights, including the airspace over military installations. The U.S. Department of State reports that approximately one hundred observation flights are conducted each year. The United States typically receives six to eight observation flights by Russian aircraft each year and conducts fourteen to sixteen flights over Russia.[153]

149. Chicago Convention on Civil Aviation, supra, arts. 1 & 2.
150. Commander's Handbook, supra, ¶ 2.7.2.2.
151. Chicago Convention on Civil Aviation, supra, art. 3a.
152. Treaty on Open Skies (with twelve annexes), Mar. 24, 1992 S. Treaty Doc. 102-37. See also Commander's Handbook, supra, ¶ 2.7.3.
153. U.S. Department of State, Open Skies Treaty Fact Sheet (Mar. 23, 2012), available at http://www.state.gov/r/pa/prs/ps/2012/03/186738.htm (accessed Feb. 1, 2013).

6

The Exclusive Economic Zone

Oceans and seas cover 70 percent of the planet. Some 36 percent of that ocean area lies within 200 nautical miles of one of 152 coastal and island states' baselines and may therefore be subject to some measure of control by those states under the 1982 LOS Convention. The exclusive economic zone (EEZ; illustrated in figure 1) is a zone within which the adjacent coastal state has certain enumerated rights and obligations and may exercise limited jurisdiction.[1]

A. HISTORICAL DEVELOPMENT OF THE EEZ

With the exception of a narrow band of seas variously extending from three to twelve nautical miles from shore and denominated the territorial sea, the oceans were historically open to all states and subject to no state's sovereignty. Near the middle of the twentieth century that practice began to change, first with the 1945 Truman proclamation on the continental shelf (examined in chapter 7) and later with more expansive coastal state claims over the water column. The coastal state enclosure claims were motivated in part by the goal of ensuring that the coastal state would have sole or at least priority access to the natural resources in the zone. Concerns over the growing threat of pollution from vessels and ocean dumping also led to a demand for greater coastal state jurisdiction over potentially harmful activities beyond the traditional three-nautical-mile territorial sea. Expansive claims were particularly common among Latin American states.

In 1946 Argentina claimed jurisdiction over the adjacent continental shelf. In contrast to the Truman proclamation, Argentina's claim extended to the seas above the shelf. In 1947 Chile announced two-hundred-nautical-mile territorial waters claim. Chile's claim, which extended to the natural resources in the water column (not just the continental shelf), was triggered in part by a desire to expel the Japanese whaling fleet, which was returning to the offshore waters of Chile following the World War II hiatus. Peru soon followed Chile's lead. In 1952 Ecuador joined Peru and Chile in the Santiago Declaration, which asserted rights over a two-hundred-nautical-mile offshore zone.[2] At roughly the same time Egypt, Ethiopia, Saudi Arabia, Libya, and Venezuela claimed twelve-nautical-mile territorial seas, and Indonesia and the Philippines asserted rights in the waters within their respective archipelagos. The "cod wars" between the United Kingdom

---

1. United Nations Convention on the Law of the Sea 1982: A Commentary, vol. II, at 491–821 (Satya Nandan et al. eds., 1993); UN Division for Ocean Affairs and the Law of the Sea, The Law of the Sea: Exclusive Economic Zone—Legislative History of Articles 56, 58, and 59 (of Part V) of the UN Convention on the Law of the Sea, U.N. Sales No. E.92.V.8 (1992).

2. See Laws and Regulations on the Regime of the Territorial Sea, U.N. Doc. ST/LEG/SER.B/6, at 723 (1956). The Santiago Declaration of 1952 was reaffirmed by the Montevideo and Lima Declarations.

and Iceland arose after Iceland laid claim to an exclusive fishing zone of fifty nautical miles in 1972 and then extended it to two hundred nautical miles in 1975.[3]

In 1958 UNCLOS I confronted a multitude of coastal state claims that varied in both geographic reach and substantive dimensions. The four Geneva conventions (see chapter 2) failed to resolve the breadth of the territorial sea and included only a vaguely limited continental shelf regime. In fact, the only fixed limit established by the 1958 conventions was on the contiguous zone, which could extend up to twelve nautical miles from the baseline. Although none of the 1958 conventions included what could be called an "economic zone" concept, the Convention on Fishing and Conservation of the Living Resources of the High Seas did recognize coastal states' particular interest in the conservation and management of fisheries in waters adjacent to their territorial sea.[4] The convention allowed coastal states to take unilateral measures for fisheries conservation on the high seas adjacent to their territorial waters, but it was not widely accepted or implemented.

As UNCLOS III got under way in the early 1970s, only twenty-five states adhered to the traditional three-nautical-mile territorial sea. Sixty-six states claimed a twelve-nautical-mile territorial sea, fifteen claimed seas of between four and ten nautical miles, and eight claimed two-hundred-nautical-mile seas. Striking a balance that would satisfy the states claiming extended territorial seas without extinguishing all of the traditional high-seas freedoms proved to be a challenge. The LOS Convention's transit passage regime for international straits, described in chapter 5, protects many traditional freedoms. The challenge of accommodating coastal states' demands for greater control over adjacent marine natural resources and environmental protection measures, however, would require a new paradigm. The EEZ concept provided the needed framework.[5]

The EEZ is one of the most progressive features of the 1982 LOS Convention. It legitimated coastal state claims over the natural resources in up to 38 percent of oceans. Archipelagic states and states with long coastlines reaped the largest benefits from the EEZ regime. The United States, France, Australia, and Russia are among its major beneficiaries. The new regime was quickly embraced. In 1985, almost a decade before the LOS Convention entered into force, the ICJ held that the "institution of the EEZ" had become part of customary law.[6] The UN's most recent tabulation reports that well over one hundred states have claimed two-hundred-nautical-mile offshore zones of some kind.[7] The economic benefits of the EEZ regime are manifest. The claimed waters include the world's most productive fishing grounds. As a result, almost 99 percent of the world's capture fisheries now fall within some nation's sovereign rights.

B. NATURE AND BREADTH OF THE EEZ

The 1982 LOS Convention permits a coastal state to claim an EEZ extending up to 200 nautical miles from the baseline.[8] The coastal state has sovereign rights in the natural resources within

---

3. See Fisheries Jurisdiction case (U.K. v. Iceland), 1974 I.C.J. 175 (July 25); Regulations concerning the Fishery Limits off Iceland, July 15, 1975, 14 I.L.M. 1282 (1975).
4. Convention on Fishing and Conservation of the Living Resources of the High Seas, Apr. 29, 1958, 17 U.S.T. 138, 559 U.N.T.S. 285.
5. See Ann L. Hollick, Origins of the 200 Mile Offshore Zones, 71 Am. J. Int'l L. 404 (1977).
6. Continental Shelf case (Libya v. Malta) 1985 I.C.J. 13, 33–34 (June 3). See also Restatement FRLUS § 514 cmt. a.
7. UN Table of Claims to Maritime Jurisdiction (July 15, 2011). This figure does not include continental shelf claims. Some were only fisheries zones. Benin, Congo, Ecuador, Liberia, Peru, and Somalia continue to claim two-hundred-nautical-mile territorial seas. See also UN Division for Ocean Affairs and the Law of the Sea, The Law of the Sea: National Legislation on the Exclusive Economic Zone, U.N. Sales No. E.93.V.10 (1993).
8. LOSC art. 57. See also Restatement FRLUS § 514; David J. Attard, The Exclusive Economic Zone in International Law (1987).

its EEZ and has jurisdiction over a limited range of activities.[9] Beyond the EEZ (if claimed) lie the high seas, which are not subject to the sovereignty of any state.[10] Because most states claim a 12-nautical-mile territorial sea, the EEZ is typically 188 nautical miles wide, measured from the outer limit of the territorial sea to the 200-nautical-mile line (see figure 1).[11]

C. ALLOCATION OF RIGHTS, DUTIES, AND JURISDICTION IN THE EEZ

Part V of the 1982 LOS Convention is divided into three groupings: the rights, duties, and jurisdiction allocated to the coastal state; the rights reserved to states other than coastal states; and a third group of "unallocated" rights. An overview of each of the three groups will be followed by a more focused examination of the EEZ regime on living marine resources, marine environmental protection, platforms and installations, marine scientific research, and military activities. As is more fully described in chapter 15, several important issues relating to the EEZ regime are exempt from the compulsory dispute settlement requirements of the LOS Convention.

1. Rights, Duties, and Jurisdiction of the Coastal State in the EEZ

Within its adjacent EEZ the coastal state enjoys the exclusive right to control, conserve, and manage all living and nonliving natural resources in the water column and the underlying seabed and subsoil.[12] The coastal state's sovereign rights also extend to the production of energy from the water, currents, and wind. In addition to its sovereign rights in resources, the coastal state has jurisdiction over marine scientific research and the establishment and use of artificial islands, installations, and structures in the EEZ. The coastal state also has jurisdiction to prescribe measures for the protection and preservation of the marine environment. In fact, Part XII of the Convention imposes affirmative obligations on the coastal state to protect the marine environment that extends throughout the EEZ. In exercising its rights and performing its duties the coastal state is required to exercise due regard for the rights and duties of other states and must respect the sovereign immunity of public vessels.[13] The coastal state may also prescribe laws in accordance with the convention and "other rules of international law," but only insofar as those "other laws" are not incompatible with the LOS Convention's EEZ articles. ITLOS confirmed that compatibility limitation in the *M/V Saiga* case decision examined in section C.3 below.

If both zones are claimed by the coastal state, the state's EEZ overlaps with the contiguous zone. Additionally, the EEZ may overlap with the continental shelf out to a distance of two hundred nautical miles. Where the coastal state's EEZ rights overlap with rights under the continental shelf regime in Part VI, the more specific continental shelf provisions in Part VI control.[14] In contrast to the territorial sea innocent passage regime, the coastal state does not have the power to restrict or prevent passage through its EEZ.

Although the EEZ regime was designed to ensure that the coastal state would be able to conserve, manage, and protect natural resources in the zone, a few states have expansively interpreted the EEZ articles in an attempt to reach activities not contemplated by the drafters. In doing so they may encroach on rights and freedoms reserved to other states. A prominent law of the sea expert has noted, for example, that the modern ocean enclosure movement has shifted

---

9. LOSC art. 56; Restatement FRLUS § 511 cmt. b.
10. LOSC art. 89.
11. The EEZ charting requirements are set out in LOSC art. 75.
12. LOSC art. 56.
13. Id. art. 236.
14. Id. art. 55; Restatement FRLUS § 515 cmt. a.

from arguments about geographic limits of offshore zones to arguments about the substantive limits of the coastal state's rights and interests in those zones.[15]

2. Rights and Duties of Other States in the EEZ

Article 58 of the LOS Convention allocates the rights of states other than the coastal state in two parts. Article 58(1) provides that in the EEZ all states, whether coastal or landlocked, enjoy the high-seas freedoms referred to in Article 87 of navigation and overflight and of the laying of submarine cables and pipelines, and other internationally lawful uses of the sea related to those freedoms, such as those associated with the operation of ships, aircraft, and submarine cables and pipelines.[16] In exercising such rights, states must give due regard to the interests of other states in their exercise of the freedom of the high seas.[17]

Article 58(2) adds to the aforementioned freedoms by stipulating that the high-seas provisions in Articles 88–115 of the convention apply, along with other pertinent rules of international law, in the EEZ insofar as they are not incompatible with the EEZ regime.[18] That means, for example, that a warship can conduct a right-of-visit boarding (Article 110), continue a hot pursuit (Article 111), or take action against a pirate ship (Articles 105 and 107) in a foreign state's EEZ. It also means that the immunity of warships and other public vessels recognized in Articles 95 and 96 apply within the EEZ. The "other pertinent rules of international law" includes, among other things, the law of naval warfare.[19] In exercising their rights and performing their duties in the EEZ, states must exercise due regard for the rights and duties of the coastal state and comply with the laws and regulations adopted by the coastal state in accordance with the LOS Convention. Additionally, the exercise of such rights is limited by Article 300, which requires that all rights be exercised in a manner that does not constitute an abuse of rights.

3. Unattributed Rights and Jurisdiction in the EEZ

EEZs are carved out of waters that were formerly high seas, where the high-seas freedoms applied. Part V sets out what is clearly more than a two-hundred-nautical-mile exclusive fisheries zone but also considerably less than a two-hundred-nautical-mile-wide territorial sea.[20] Article 59 was drafted to provide a mechanism for resolving questions regarding rights and jurisdictional competencies that are not expressly allocated to either the coastal state or other "user" states

---

15. Bernard H. Oxman, The Territorial Temptation: A Siren Song at Sea, 100 Am. J. Int'l L. 830, 839 (2006).

16. LOSC art. 58. Attempts to define these freedoms as a narrow right to transit the EEZ ignore the clear textual recognition that it includes "other internationally lawful uses of the sea related to those freedoms, such as those associated with the operation of ships" and aircraft.

17. LOSC art. 87.

18. Some writers mistakenly reverse the sense of that qualification, asserting that the activities covered in Articles 88–115 must be "compatible with" the EEZ regime rather than "not incompatible with" the EEZ regime. The difference might seem subtle, but it arguably puts the burden of proof on the coastal state to prove incompatibility rather than on the navigating state to prove compatibility.

19. See, e.g., San Remo Manual, supra, ¶ 10(c) (areas of naval warfare), 34, & 35 (EEZ and continental shelf); Commander's Handbook, supra, ¶ 7.3.8.

20. Commentators have debated whether, in cases of doubt, the EEZ should be viewed as having a residual high-seas character or a residual territorial-seas character. Article 59 seems to suggest that the answer is probably "neither." Article 59 does not prescribe a beginning presumption of either high-seas freedoms or coastal state control. However, the importation of high-seas articles by Article 58 must not be overlooked. See Instrument of Ratification by the Kingdom of the Netherlands, ¶ 4 ("The coastal state does not enjoy residual rights in the EEZ. The rights of the coastal state in its EEZ are listed in article 56 of the Convention, and can not be extended unilaterally"), available at http://www.un.org/Depts/los/convention_agreements/convention_declarations .htm#Netherlands%2013%20February%202009 (accessed Feb. 1, 2013).

by the other articles in the convention.[21] Accordingly, Article 59 is consulted and applied only *after* it has been determined that the right or jurisdiction in question has not been allocated by another article, and any analysis must therefore begin with the articles that attribute rights and jurisdiction, not with Article 59.[22]

Article 59 provides that in cases in which the convention does not attribute rights or jurisdiction to the coastal state or to other states within the EEZ, and a conflict arises between the interests of the coastal state and any other state or states, the conflict should be resolved on the basis of equity and in the light of all the relevant circumstances, taking into account the respective importance of the interests involved to the parties as well as to the international community as a whole.[23] Notwithstanding attempts to seize on or even manufacture ambiguities in the allocation articles of the convention, Article 59 does not apply to the freedoms of navigation and overflight referred to in Article 87, the laying of submarine cables and pipelines, or any other internationally lawful uses of the sea related to those freedoms, such as those associated with the operation of ships, aircraft, and submarine cables and pipelines, and compatible with the other provisions of the convention. Those rights are expressly attributed by Article 58.[24] It is also important to recall that freedom of navigation is considered to be one of the general principles of international law, and any doubtful case involving a possible conflict between freedom of navigation and a lesser principle should be resolved in favor of freedom of navigation.[25]

In evaluating the rights and obligations of other "user" states in another state's EEZ, the distinction between paragraphs 1 and 2 of Article 58 must not be overlooked. Application of Articles 88–115 in the EEZ under Article 58(2) must not be incompatible with the EEZ regime. No such qualification is attached to the incorporation of Article 87 high-seas freedoms under Article 58(1). Both paragraphs are, however, subject to the obligation in paragraph 3 of Article 58 for user states to "have due regard to the rights and duties of the coastal State" and "comply with the laws and regulations adopted by the coastal State in accordance with" the LOS Convention and other rules of international law, insofar as they are not incompatible with Part V of the convention.

The allocation of rights in the EEZ between the coastal state and other states was among the issues presented in the first case decided by ITLOS.[26] In the *M/V* Saiga case between Saint Vincent and Guinea, one issue before the tribunal was whether a Vincentian-flag tanker could lawfully deliver fuel to ("bunker") a fishing vessel located in Guinea's EEZ. Saint Vincent argued that the coastal state's competency was limited by Article 56 (and, to a lesser extent, Article 58(3)), which does not include bunkering, and that bunkering instead fell within the freedom of navigation

21. The right or jurisdiction in question might also be addressed by the contiguous zone or continental shelf articles.
22. One treatise suggests that "given the nature of the EEZ as a coastal state economic zone, Article 59 could conceivably be interpreted so that unattributed *economic* rights would usually fall to coastal states, while unattributed rights of a *non-economic* nature would fall to other states." Donald R. Rothwell & Tim Stephens, The International Law of the Sea 87 (2010) (emphasis added). That approach, while arguably consistent with the ITLOS decision in the *M/V Saiga* case, which suggests that an activity such as bunkering fishing vessels might be an economic activity within the coastal state's competency, would likely not satisfy states that take an expansive interpretation of the EEZ articles on marine scientific research and protection of the marine environment.
23. LOSC art. 59; Restatement FRLUS § 514 cmt. b & n.2.
24. LOSC art. 58. The EEZ regime is in derogation of high-seas freedoms formerly available in those waters. If a right or freedom is preserved to all states by the high-seas articles of the 1982 LOS Convention, and not expressly negated by the EEZ articles, the burden should be on the coastal state to show that it does not fall within the scope of protected rights under Article 58.
25. Churchill & Lowe, supra, at 12.
26. M/V Saiga (St. Vincent & the Grenadines v. Guinea), Case No. 2, Judgment of July 1, 1999, ¶¶ 150–52, 120 Int'l L. Rep. 143, 38 I.L.M. 1323 (1999).

or "other internationally lawful uses" allocated to user states by Article 58(1).[27] The tribunal first acknowledged that the issue posed questions under both Guinean domestic law and international law. However, consistent with the principle discussed in the *North Sea Continental Shelf* case and *Nottebohm's* case (described in chapter 1), the tribunal also pointed out that "even if it is conceded that the laws of Guinea which the *Saiga* is alleged to have violated are applicable in the manner that is claimed by Guinea, the question remains whether these laws, as interpreted and applied by Guinea, are compatible with the Convention."[28]

Guinea characterized the bunkering operation as an "economic" activity and asserted that its prohibition was consistent with the convention's EEZ articles. In support of that claim it reasoned that the EEZ is not part of the territorial sea or high seas, but rather "a zone with its own legal status (a *sui generis* zone)."[29] From that proposition, Guinea argued that rights and jurisdiction in the EEZ that the convention does not expressly attribute to the coastal state do not automatically fall under the freedom of the high seas reserved to other states. After observing that the LOS Convention does not expressly attribute the right to engage in or regulate bunkering in the EEZ, the tribunal proclaimed that "it does not follow automatically that rights not expressly attributed to the coastal State belong to other States or, alternatively, that rights not specifically attributed to other States belong as of right to the coastal State."[30] The tribunal then rejected requests from both states to adjudge and declare that the contested right to bunker vessels was allocated to either the coastal state or other states and disposed of the case instead on the basis that, without regard to the attribution of rights question, the enforcement actions taken by Guinea were not consistent with applicable provisions of the LOS Convention.[31] Accordingly, there was no need for the tribunal to resort to Article 59 in its decision.[32]

D. LIVING MARINE RESOURCES OF THE EEZ

The international law on conservation and management of living marine resources in the EEZ is complex.[33] This section provides a synopsis of that law. Readers seeking a more detailed treatment of the law are encouraged to consult one of the many excellent treatises on international fisheries law cited in chapter 10.

1. Conservation of EEZ Living Resources

Part V of the LOS Convention embraces a sustainable use approach to living marine resources (LMR) of the EEZ. That approach is reflected in the balance struck between Article 61 on conservation of LMR (the sustainability prong) and Article 62 on utilization of those resources (the use prong). The Part V regime then goes on to single out several unique fisheries for individ-

---

27. Id. at ¶ 123. See also id. ¶ 127 (concluding that the convention does not empower a coastal state to apply its customs laws in the EEZ, other than with respect to offshore structures and to the contiguous zone to the extent that it lies within the EEZ).
28. Id. at ¶ 122.
29. Id. at ¶ 125.
30. Id. at ¶ 137.
31. Id. at ¶¶ 137–38.
32. The court concluded, for example, that Guinea's exercise of hot pursuit did not conform to Article 111 of the convention. In separate opinions, Judges Vukas and Laing did address the Article 59 issue.
33. See UN Division for Ocean Affairs and the Law of the Sea, The Law of the Sea: Conservation and Utilization of the Living Resources of the Exclusive Economic Zone—Legislative History of Articles 61 and 62 of the United Nations Convention on the Law of the Sea, U.N. Sales No. E.95.V.21 (1995).

ual treatment, including anadromous[34] and catadromous[35] fish stocks, marine mammals,[36] trans-boundary (i.e., shared and straddling) fish stocks,[37] and highly migratory species.[38] The latter two categories are the subject of the 1995 Agreement on Straddling Fish Stocks and Highly Migratory Fish Stocks.[39] A final category, sedentary species inhabiting the seabed, is relegated to the continental shelf regime discussed in chapter 7.[40]

Article 61 requires the coastal state to determine the allowable catch for LMR within its EEZ.[41] In doing so, the state must take into account the best scientific evidence available to it. While a number of factors enter into the calculation of any given fishery's maximum sustainable yield,[42] the coastal state must ensure that fish stocks are not endangered by overexploitation.[43] More specific guidance is available in the nonbinding FAO Code of Conduct for Responsible Fisheries, which is examined in chapter 10.

2. Utilization of EEZ Living Resources

The LOS Convention requires the coastal state to promote the objective of optimum utilization of the LMR in its EEZ.[44] No such requirement is imposed with respect to LMR in the territorial sea or sedentary species of the continental shelf. It is important to note that the coastal state's optimum utilization duty is subject to the conservation obligations imposed by Article 61 (i.e., utilization must be sustainable). If the coastal state does not have the capacity to harvest the entire allowable catch, it is required to give other states access to the surplus, having particular regard for landlocked and geographically disadvantaged states in the region.[45] In granting foreign vessels access to its EEZ, the coastal state may impose a wide array of conservation measures and other terms and conditions.[46]

3. Management and Enforcement

Article 73 sets out the measures a coastal state may take in the exercise of its enforcement jurisdiction over LMR in the EEZ. They include boarding, inspection, arrest, and judicial proceedings.[47] Article 73 also includes a requirement for the coastal state to promptly release foreign ves-

---

34. LOSC art. 66.
35. Id. art. 67.
36. Id. art. 65. The legal regime for marine mammals is confused somewhat by the inclusion of seven families of cetaceans in the list of "highly migratory species" in annex I of the LOS Convention.
37. LOSC art. 63.
38. Id. art. 64.
39. Agreement for the Implementation of the Provisions of the United Nations Convention on the Law of the Sea of 10 December 1982 Relating to the Conservation and Management of Straddling Fish Stocks and Highly Migratory Fish Stocks, Aug. 4, 1995, 2167 U.N.T.S. 88, 34 I.L.M. 1542 (1995). The Straddling Stocks Agreement introduces a number of progressive measures, particularly in the areas of environmental and resource protection. For example, it adopts a precautionary approach to fisheries exploitation and allocates expanded powers to port states to enforce conservation and management measures.
40. LOSC art. 68.
41. Id. art. 61(1).
42. Id. art. 61(3) & (4).
43. Id. art. 61(2).
44. Id. art. 62(1).
45. Id. art. 62(2), and arts. 69 & 70.
46. Id. art. 62(4). The United States used Governing International Fishery Agreements (GIFAs) for this purpose. See 16 U.S.C. § 1822.
47. LOSC art. 73(1). The term "measures" was given a broad construction by the ICJ in the Fisheries Jurisdiction case (Spain v. Canada), ¶¶ 62–73 & 84, 1998 I.C.J. 432 (Dec. 4).

sels and their crews on the posting of reasonable security,[48] and forbids imposition of a sentence of imprisonment for violations of fisheries laws in the EEZ, absent an agreement to the contrary among the states concerned.[49]

E. MARINE ENVIRONMENTAL PROTECTION MEASURES IN THE EEZ

The 1982 LOS Convention allocates to the coastal state jurisdiction over "the protection and preservation of the marine environment."[50] The nature and limits of the coastal state's prescriptive and enforcement jurisdiction are fleshed out in Part XII of the convention and in several related marine environmental protections conventions, including MARPOL and the London Dumping Convention. The Part XII regime fully preserves the sovereign immunity of warships and other public vessels.[51] While the LOS Convention goes to some lengths to specify the enforcement measures a coastal state may take with respect to foreign vessels fishing in its EEZ, the coastal state's enforcement measures with respect to pollution in the EEZ are much less developed.

Commentators have observed that some coastal states invoke their jurisdiction over marine environmental protection matters to reach a broad array of navigation and other activities preserved to user states under Article 58, sometimes without adhering to the established international framework.[52] As is further discussed in chapter 10, Article 211(6) of the LOS Convention and the SOLAS and MARPOL Conventions provide a legitimate framework for extending heightened protection to environmentally sensitive areas in the EEZ. In addition, Article 234 authorizes additional protections for certain ice-covered areas within a state's EEZ. Nevertheless, the jurisdictional assertions sometimes exceed the substantive limits on coastal state jurisdiction under the applicable conventions.[53] A few coastal states have, for example, asserted that they have jurisdiction to restrict or prohibit the transport of radioactive materials through their EEZ. Most of the disputes on that question arose over the periodic transport of spent fuels from Japanese power-generation reactors to reprocessing facilities in the United Kingdom and France.[54] A unique dispute arose in 2003–4 when the United States was evaluating plans to transport a decommissioned nuclear reactor from the San Onofre generating station in southern California to a disposal site on the U.S. East Coast by sea, via Cape Horn. On learning of the plans, Chile asserted a right to impose a number of conditions on any transit through its EEZ, including prior notice and minimum safety standards. Not to be outdone, Argentina claimed it would ban the shipment from its EEZ altogether.

F. MARINE SCIENTIFIC RESEARCH IN THE EEZ

Scientists are currently engaged in a variety of research efforts to find ways to help control, mitigate, or at least model and predict the problems posed by marine pollutants, the recurring El Niño phenomenon, and global warming and its effect on sea levels. It is widely recognized

---

48. LOSC art. 73(2). See also LOSC art. 292. Prompt release actions are examined in chapter 15.

49. Id. art. 73(3).

50. Id. art. 56(1)(b)(iii).

51. Id. art. 236.

52. See, e.g., Rothwell & Stephens, supra, at 94–95; Oxman, The Territorial Temptation, supra, at 843–49.

53. The coastal state's prescriptive and enforcement jurisdiction over vessel-source pollution is set out in Articles 211 and 220. The Safety of Life at Sea Convention and the International Code for the Safe Carriage of Packaged Irradiated Nuclear Fuel, Plutonium and High Level Radioactive Wastes on Board Ships (INF Code) prescribe requirements for the maritime transport of nuclear materials. Liability for maritime transporters is governed by the Convention relating to Civil Liability in the Field of Maritime Carriage of Nuclear Material.

54. See Jon M. Van Dyke, Sea Shipment of Japanese Plutonium under International Law, 24 Ocean Dev. & Int'l L. 399 (1993).

that oceanographic research is essential if we are to develop the understanding necessary for responsible development and management of the living and nonliving resources in the oceans. Recognizing the need to promote better understanding of the oceans and their processes, Part XIII of the LOS Convention prescribes a detailed regime for the conduct of marine scientific research (MSR).[55]

To appreciate the balance struck by the convention's MSR regime, it is important to bear in mind that not all nations engage in MSR or consider MSR activities to be universally beneficial. Some developing nations view MSR as a luxury enjoyed by only a handful of developed nations, and one that is too often conducted solely for the benefit of the sponsoring nations.[56] Accordingly, the LOS Convention articles on MSR represent a compromise that nominally encourages MSR while at the same time conditioning access to engage in MSR activities in coastal state waters or on their continental shelves on actual or tacit coastal state consent. The consequences for oceanographers and for progress in marine science are far from ideal.

1. Distinguishing Marine Scientific Research from Surveys and Intelligence Collection

The freedom to engage in marine scientific research on the high seas is expressly preserved, while similar activities in a foreign state's continental shelf and EEZ are subject to that state's consent. The LOS Convention does not directly define "marine scientific research" with respect to either the high-seas right or the coastal state consent regime. The absence of a definition has opened the door for some states to classify military and hydrographic surveys in the EEZ or on the continental shelf as "marine scientific research" requiring coastal state consent. Those familiar with the negotiating history of the MSR regime from UNCLOS I through UNCLOS III understand why no MSR definition was included: states simply have not been able to agree on a legal definition.[57] The 1982 LOS Convention sidesteps the definition issue but does identify the defining principles of all marine scientific research.[58] Collectively, those principles provide a rough working definition of MSR activities. The first principle is that MSR is conducted exclusively for peaceful purposes. Second, it is conducted with appropriate scientific methods and means that are compatible with the convention. Third, except for certain economically important information,[59] states are directed to publish or otherwise disseminate "knowledge resulting from marine scientific research,"[60] a requirement that distinguishes MSR from military surveys and intelligence activities.[61] Hydrographic and military surveys are carried out to facilitate noneconomic uses of the seas and do not implicate the coastal state's sovereign rights in natural

---

55. See LOSC pt. XIII. See generally Florian H. Th. Wegelein, Marine Scientific Research (2005); Alfred A. H. Soons, Marine Scientific Research and the Law of the Sea (1982).

56. See Churchill & Lowe, supra, at 403–04. See generally UN Division for Ocean Affairs and the Law of the Sea, The Law of the Sea: Marine Scientific Research: Legislative History of Article 246 of the United Nations Convention on the Law of the Sea [hereinafter "MSR Legislative History"], 82–83, U.N. Sales No. E.94.V.9 (1994) (quoting remarks by a Chinese delegate, asserting that "it was a well-known fact that the super-Powers, relying on their superiority in marine technology, were stealthily gathering marine intelligence on a large scale in order willfully to plunder marine resources under the screen of scientific research. To justify themselves, the super-Powers had resorted to the fallacy of so-called 'pure science'").

57. See generally MSR Legislative History, supra, at 1–3, 6–7, & 11–15 (documenting early attempts to define scientific research); Walker, Definitions for the Law of the Sea, supra, at 241–44.

58. LOSC art. 240. See also Commander's Handbook, supra, ¶ 2.6.2.1.

59. LOSC art. 249(2).

60. Id. art. 244.

61. See generally Sam Bateman, Hydrographic Surveying and Marine Scientific Research in Exclusive Economic Zones, in Freedom of Seas, Passage Rights and the 1982 Law of the Sea Convention (Myron H. Nordquist et al. eds., 2009).

resources or jurisdiction over marine pollution prevention or scientific research.[62] Such surveys are increasingly important for the safe navigation of manned and unmanned submersible craft that employ sonar navigation methods, which require precise bottom contour charts.[63]

In addressing questions of access to the continental shelf or EEZ of a foreign state for MSR, the convention divides all such MSR into two categories: (1) research carried out exclusively for peaceful purposes and in order to increase scientific knowledge of the marine environment for the benefit of all humankind ("pure research"), and (2) research having a direct significance for the exploration and exploitation of natural resources ("applied research").[64] The *Marine Scientific Research Implementation Guide* prepared by the UN Office for Ocean Affairs and the Law of the Sea in 1991, since revised, provided important additional guidance on the application of the LOS Convention Part XIII MSR regime. For example, the 1991 *Guide* acknowledged that the convention distinguishes between MSR and hydrographic surveys and concluded that because survey activities (and prospecting and exploration activities) are governed elsewhere in the convention (see table 1), "this could indicate that these activities do not fall under the regime of Part XIII."[65] The "revised" *Guide* prepared in 2010 simply notes that "survey activities" are dealt with elsewhere than in Part XIII.[66]

The 1991 *Guide*'s conclusion was based on the fact that hydrographic surveys and intelligence collection activities are addressed in the territorial sea and international straits articles,[67] along with research activities, but only marine scientific research is included in the EEZ articles (see table 1).[68] Additionally, Article 40 draws a distinction between hydrographic survey ships and marine scientific research ships. The logical conclusion is that the convention articles on MSR do not apply to surveys and intelligence collection activities.[69] The draft U.S. Senate understanding

TABLE 1. **LOS Convention Restrictions on Surveys, Intelligence Collection, and Research Activities**

Activity	Territorial Seas: Innocent Passage	Straits: Transit Passage	EEZ
Hydrographic Surveys	Art. 19(2)(j)	Art. 40	No restriction
Intelligence Collection	Art. 19(2)(c)	No restriction	No restriction
Marine Scientific Research	Arts. 19(2)(j), 245	Arts. 40, 245	Art. 246

62. Wegelein, Marine Scientific Research, supra, at 80 & 81.
63. The January 17, 2013, grounding of the USS *Guardian* (MCM-5) on Tubbataha Reef in the Philippine Sulu Sea highlights the importance of accurate, multisource hydrographic and charting data to safe navigation. After the grounding, the National Geospatial-Intelligence Agency determined that the digital nautical chart display of the reef was off by eight nautical miles, partly because of the NGA's reliance on LANDSAT-based commercial satellite imagery of the area.
64. LOSC art. 246.
65. UN Office for Ocean Affairs and the Law of the Sea, Marine Scientific Research: A Guide to Implementation of the United Nations Convention on the Law of the Sea, 1991 [hereinafter "MSR Implementation Guide"], at 1, ¶ 2 (a copy of this earlier edition is on file with the author). See also LOSC arts. 19(2)(j), 21(1)(g), & 40.
66. UN Division for Ocean Affairs and the Law of the Sea, Marine Scientific Research: A Revised Guide to Implementation of the United Nations Convention on the Law of the Sea, 2010 [hereinafter "Revised MSR Implementation Guide"], U.N. Sales No. E.10.V.12, at 6. The Guide drafters offered no explanation for revising their 1991 understanding of the distinction between MSR and survey activities.
67. The actual language used in Article 19(2)(c) is "any act aimed at collecting information to the prejudice of the defense or security of the coastal State."
68. See LOSC art. 56(1)(b)(ii).
69. See Commander's Handbook, supra, ¶ 2.6.2.2.

affirms the U.S. position that the phrase marine scientific research in Part XIII does not include prospecting for and exploration of natural resources; hydrographic surveys; military activities, including military surveys; environmental monitoring and assessment; or activities related to submerged wrecks or objects of an archaeological and historical nature.[70]

2. Marine Scientific Research Rights and Obligations

Under the LOS Convention all states have a duty to facilitate marine scientific research and to promote international cooperation in such activities.[71] As with other uses of the oceans and sea-bed, the LOS Convention's provisions for MSR generally adopt a zonal approach, under which respective state rights and obligations vary according to the location of the activity. All such MSR activities are, however, subject to Part XII of the convention, which establishes the obligation for all states to protect and preserve the marine environment. Coastal state consent is required for any MSR within its EEZ or on its continental shelf.[72] The consent regime favors "pure" research over "applied" research, as those terms are defined above.[73] Generally, coastal states are obliged to grant consent for pure scientific research in their EEZ, but they may withhold consent for "applied" research projects of direct significance for the exploration and exploitation of natural resources.[74] MSR activities within another state's waters must be carried out in a manner that avoids unjustifiably interfering with the coastal state's exercise of its sovereign rights in the zone,[75] and in accordance with the obligations imposed by the LOS Convention and the coastal state.[76] The coastal state may require, for example, that it be allowed to participate in the research, that it be provided with copies of the research reports, that it be given access to all data and samples and an assessment of those samples or data, that any installations or equipment installed for the project be removed on completion of the research, and that the research results be made available internationally as soon as practicable.[77] At the same time, the convention recognizes the right of the coastal state to condition access for MSR in its EEZ on an agreement by the researchers to withhold publication of any research results of a project of direct significance for the exploration and exploitation of natural resources.[78]

The LOS Convention articles prescribing the MSR regime must be read in conjunction with Part XIV, which prescribes a framework for transferring technology for the benefit of developing nations. States are required by the convention to cooperate in promoting the development and transfer of marine science and technology on fair and reasonable terms and conditions.[79] Toward that end, states are to promote the establishment of guidelines, criteria, and standards for marine technology transfer.[80] Measures to promote technology transfer may include technical coopera-

---

70. S. Exec. Rpt. No. 110-09, understanding 5 (reprinted in appendix D); see also Commander's Handbook, supra, ¶ 2.6.2.1. By contrast, China apparently relies on its MSR jurisdiction to require its prior consent for military intelligence activities and hydrographic or military surveying in its EEZ.
71. LOSC arts. 239 & 242.
72. Id. art. 56. See also Restatement FRLUS § 514 cmt. h (MSR within EEZ).
73. LOSC art. 246(5). The convention does not use the terms "pure research" or "applied research." It does, however, distinguish between research carried out "exclusively for peaceful purposes and in order to increase scientific knowledge of the marine environment for the benefit of all mankind," id. art. 246(3); and MSR activities that are of "direct significance for the exploration and exploitation of natural resources," id. art. 246(5)(a).
74. LOSC art. 246(5). The coastal state may withhold its consent on other grounds as well. See id. art. 246(5)(b)–(d).
75. Id. art. 246(8).
76. Id. arts. 240 & 248–50.
77. Id. art. 249(1).
78. Id. art. 249(2).
79. Id. art. 266.
80. Id. art. 271.

tion programs, exchanges of scientists and technologists, public conferences, and establishment of marine science and technological research centers.[81]

While the LOS Convention professes to promote and facilitate marine scientific research, the actual record is disappointing. Marine scientists have documented the adverse consequences of a regime that forces them to obtain consent from coastal states before they may conduct research in the nation's EEZ or on its continental shelf. One empirical study covering a six-year period found that some nations denied U.S. scientists permission to conduct research more than 25 percent of the time. Reports by the U.S. Department of State, which facilitates the international MSR application process for U.S. researchers, document similar problems. The department found that several nations routinely delayed decisions on granting access or revoked permission at the last minute. Some states prohibited the scientists involved from publishing their research results, a restriction widely condemned by the scientific community. The LOS Convention purports to prohibit coastal states from delaying or denying consent unreasonably; however, it lacks an effective means for enforcing the prohibition. Moreover, the convention's compulsory dispute settlement provisions carve out an exception that generally exempts decisions by coastal states to deny or restrict access for MSR from the settlement process. It therefore remains to be seen whether the convention will ever live up to its promise to promote and facilitate marine scientific research.

G. ARTIFICIAL ISLANDS, INSTALLATIONS, AND STRUCTURES IN THE EEZ

Mariners confront an ever-growing number and variety of offshore structures. Oil and gas exploration and production platforms have been joined by "fields" of offshore renewable energy facilities. Entrepreneurs are even studying the feasibility of "seastead" communities offshore. The safety of those offshore structures and of vessels that must navigate among and around them are matters of serious concern. Those concerns are addressed to a limited degree in the LOS Convention. For those states that are party to the Convention on Suppression of Unlawful Acts against the Safety of Maritime Navigation (SUA Convention) and its protocols,[82] the security of offshore installations on the continental shelf is significantly enhanced by that regime.[83]

Artificial islands, installations, and structures do not possess the status of islands.[84] As a result, they have no territorial sea of their own, and their presence does not affect the delimitation of the territorial sea, EEZ, or continental shelf. In the EEZ, the coastal state has the exclusive right to construct and to authorize and regulate the construction, operation, and use of (1) artificial islands, (2) installations and structures for the purposes provided for in Article 56 and other economic purposes, and (3) installations and structures that may interfere with the exercise of the rights of the coastal state in the zone.[85] The coastal state has exclusive jurisdiction over all

---

81. Id. arts. 269 & 275–77.

82. Convention for the Suppression of Unlawful Acts against the Safety of Maritime Navigation [hereinafter "1988 SUA Convention"], Mar. 10, 1988, S. Treaty Doc. No. 101-1, 1678 U.N.T.S. 201. See also Protocols of 2005 to the Convention concerning Safety of Maritime Navigation and to the Protocol concerning Safety of Fixed Platforms on the Continental Shelf [hereinafter "2005 SUA Protocol"], Oct. 14, 2005, S. Treaty Doc. No. 110-8.

83. Protocol for the Suppression of Unlawful Acts against the Safety of Fixed Platforms Located on the Continental Shelf [hereinafter "1988 SUA Platforms Protocol"], March 10, 1988, S. Treaty Doc. No. 101-1, 1678 U.N.T.S. 304. The protocol is limited to "fixed platforms" that are permanently attached to the seabed and used for resource exploration or exploitation or other economic purposes. Id. art. 1(3).

84. LOSC art. 60(8). Deepwater ports are commonly included in the class of artificial islands. See Deepwater Port Act, 33 U.S.C. §§ 1501–1529.

85. LOSC art. 60(1). Close reading reveals that the article draws a distinction between artificial islands (in Article 60(1)(a)) and installations and structures (in Article 60(1)(b)). The latter are restricted to installations and struc-

three categories of offshore structures in its EEZ. That jurisdiction extends to customs, fiscal, health, safety, and immigration laws and regulations.[86] The coastal state is required to give notice when such structures are established and to provide for their removal when no longer used.[87] To ensure the safety of navigation and offshore structures, the coastal state may establish safety zones around the structures.[88] Such zones must take into account relevant IMO standards and, with few exceptions, cannot exceed five hundred meters.[89] All ships must respect these safety zones and comply with generally accepted international standards regarding navigation in the vicinity of artificial islands, installations, structures, and safety zones. <u>Artificial islands, installations, and structures and the safety zones around them may not be established where they might interfere with the use of recognized sea-lanes essential to international navigation.</u>[90]

H. MILITARY ACTIVITIES IN THE EEZ

Attempts to turn exclusive *economic* zones into maritime *security* zones are not only inimical to the peace, they are also illegal.[91] If all coastal states claimed two-hundred-nautical-mile EEZs, those zones would collectively cover 38 percent of the oceans, including the littoral zones critical to the naval mobility on which international peace and security depend. Although provision is made for *safety* zones around artificial islands and platforms, those zones are limited in most cases to five hundred meters.[92] <u>Nowhere in Part V is it suggested that the EEZ regime can also be used to restrict or prohibit military activities that are consistent with the high-seas freedoms applicable within the zone.</u> Nevertheless, some coastal states have attempted to expand the EEZ and contiguous zone regimes to include security interests.[93]

In contrast to the territorial sea regime—where the innocent passage articles expressly recognize and protect the coastal state's security interests—neither the contiguous zone regime nor the EEZ regime confers on the coastal state competency to implement measures to protect the coastal state's peace, good order, or security.[94] Outside the territorial sea, those state interests are protected by the universal provisions of Article 2 of the UN Charter, not the law of the sea. The U.S. Senate's proposed understandings reaffirm the position of the United States, as proclaimed by President Reagan's 1983 Ocean Policy Statement. The Senate understanding makes clear that, with respect to the EEZ, the United States understands that

---

tures "for the purposes provided for in article 56 and other economic purposes"; coastal state rights over artificial islands are not similarly restricted.

86. LOSC art. 60(2).

87. Id. art. 60(3).

88. Id.; Commander's Handbook, supra, ¶ 1.8.

89. Exceptions to the five-hundred-meter limit must be authorized by generally accepted international standards or recommended by the IMO.

90. LOSC art. 60(7).

91. Restatement FRLUS §§ 401, 522; Commander's Handbook supra, ¶¶ 1.6.4 & 2.6.4.

92. See also 33 C.F.R. part 106 (OCS facility security requirements).

93. States that restrict military activities in the EEZ include Bangladesh, Brazil, Burma, Cape Verde, China, India, Indonesia, Iran, Kenya, Malaysia, Maldives, Mauritius, North Korea, Pakistan, the Philippines, Portugal, and Uruguay. See DoD Maritime Claims Reference Manual, available at www.dtic.mil/whs/directives/corres/htm-l/20051m.htm (accessed Jan. 1, 2012). See also U.S. Naval War College, China Maritime Studies Institute, Military Activities in the EEZ: A U.S.- China Dialogue on Security and International Law in the Maritime Commons (Peter Dutton ed., 2011).

94. See Brian Wilson, An Avoidable Maritime Conflict: Disputes regarding Military Activities in the Exclusive Economic Zone, 41 J. Mar. L. & Com. 421 (2010); George V. Galdorisi & Alan G. Kaufman, Military Activities in the Exclusive Economic Zone: Preventing Uncertainty and Defusing Conflict, 32 Cal. W. Int'l L. J. 253 (2002).

(A) all States enjoy high seas freedoms of navigation and overflight and all other internationally lawful uses of the sea related to these freedoms, including, inter alia, military activities, such as anchoring, launching and landing of aircraft and other military devices, launching and recovering water-borne craft, operating military devices, intelligence collection, surveillance and reconnaissance activities, exercises, operations, and conducting military surveys; and

(B) coastal State actions pertaining to these freedoms and uses must be in accordance with the Convention.[95]

The Senate understanding on activities in the EEZ should be read in conjunction with its understanding on the scope of the marine scientific research regime examined above, which does not include military activities, including military surveys.

I. THE U.S. EEZ

The United States claimed a two-hundred-nautical-mile exclusive fishery conservation zone in 1976, several years before the 1982 LOS Convention established the concept's legitimacy. The 1976 Fishery Conservation and Management Act (FCMA),[96] which extended to all marine life except birds, marine mammals, and highly migratory species, was controversial when passed. In fact, the Senate Committee on Foreign Relations and most executive branch agencies, including the Departments of Defense and State, opposed the act as being inconsistent with existing international law.[97] In 1983, shortly after the 1982 LOS Convention was completed, President Reagan issued a proclamation establishing a two-hundred-nautical-mile EEZ.[98] The U.S. "fishery conservation zone" was later redesignated the "exclusive economic zone,"[99] and in 1996 the FCMA was renamed Magnuson-Stevens Fishery Conservation and Management Act.[100] The Magnuson-Stevens Act applies throughout the EEZ, as do some U.S. pollution prevention and response laws.

At more than 3.3 million square nautical miles—larger than the U.S. landmass—the U.S. EEZ is the largest and arguably the richest in the world.[101] The U.S. EEZ overlaps with the U.S. contiguous zone in the waters between twelve and twenty-four nautical miles seaward of the baseline and with the continental shelf out to two hundred nautical miles. In contrast with the U.S. continental shelf, which was statutorily implemented through the Outer Continental

---

95. S. Exec. Rpt. No. 110-09, understanding 4 (reprinted in appendix D).

96. Fishery Conservation and Management Act, April 13, 1976, Pub. L. No. 94-265, 90 Stat. 331. The original act has been amended numerous times and was renamed the Magnuson-Stevens Act in honor of its principal architects.

97. U.S. Senate, Committee on Foreign Relations, S. Rpt. No. 94-459 (1975). Some of the objections are set out in President Gerald Ford's signing statement. See Statement by the President upon Signing H.R. 200 into Law, 94th Cong., 1st Sess. (1976); 12 Weekly Comp. Pres. Docs, No. 16 (Apr. 13, 1976).

98. Proclamation 5030, Exclusive Economic Zone of the United States, Mar. 10, 1983, reprinted in 3 C.F.R. § 22 (1984). See also U.S. Department of State, Exclusive Economic Zone and Maritime Boundaries; Notice of Limits, 60 Fed. Reg. 43825 (1995) (official publication of the geographic limits of the U.S. EEZ); James E. Bailey III, Comment, The Exclusive Economic Zone: Its Development and Future in International and Domestic Law, 45 La. L. Rev. 1269 (1985).

99. See 16 U.S.C. § 1802(11).

100. Pub. L. 104-208, Div. A, Title I, § 101(a), [Title II, § 211], Sept. 30, 1996, 110 Stat. 3009-41.

101. If Australia's EEZ claims in Antarctica and around Heard and McDonald Islands were recognized as lawful, its total EEZ area might exceed that of the United States.

Shelf Lands Act,[102] Congress has not yet enacted comprehensive legislation implementing the U.S. EEZ.[103]

On most matters, the U.S. EEZ regime closely follows the LOS Convention. For example, the U.S. Senate understandings regarding military activities in the EEZ reflect long-standing U.S. practice toward other states. One prominent area of departure is marine scientific research, which the United States has long championed. Accordingly, in proclaiming its EEZ in 1983, the United States declined to assert jurisdiction over marine scientific research activities within the EEZ. President Reagan explained in the Ocean Policy Statement accompanying the 1983 EEZ proclamation that "while international law provides for a right of jurisdiction over marine scientific research within such a zone, the Proclamation does not assert this right. I have elected not to do so because of the United States interest in encouraging marine scientific research and avoiding any unnecessary burdens. The United States will nevertheless recognize the right of other coastal States to exercise jurisdiction over marine scientific research within 200 nautical miles of their coasts, if that jurisdiction is exercised reasonably in a manner consistent with international law."[104] Regrettably, few nations have followed the U.S. example.[105]

---

102. See, e.g., Outer Continental Shelf Lands Act, Aug. 7, 1953, Pub. L. No. 212, ch. 345, 67 Stat. 462, codified as amended at 43 U.S.C. §§ 1331–1356.

103. See 33 C.F.R. § 2.30, which relies solely on the 1983 presidential proclamation.

104. Prior authorization is always required for MSR in the U.S. territorial sea. Prior authorization is also required by the United States for five categories of research activities in the EEZ, including research in a national marine sanctuary or marine protected area or research that involves marine mammals or other protected marine species. See U.S. Department of State, Bureau of Oceans and International Environmental and Scientific Affairs, Marine Scientific Research Authorizations, available at http://www.state.gov/e/oes/ocns/opa/rvc/index.htm (accessed Feb. 1, 2013).

105. See Judith Fenwick, International Profiles on Marine Scientific Research 182, 184 (1992) (finding that of 116 nations that assert jurisdiction over MSR activities in their coastal waters, only 9 limit such jurisdiction to 12 nautical miles).

The Continental Shelf and International Seabed

arine geologists and cartographers approach the seabed as a physical feature of the planet to be explored, sounded, mapped, probed, drilled, sampled, and studied. For government officials and law specialists, however, the seabed is as much a legal construct as a physical domain. Proof of that claim may be found in the fact that there are numerous areas of the ocean where the physical continental margin indisputably extends no more than fifty nautical miles seaward from the baseline, and yet under the law of the sea the legal, or "juridical," continental shelf will extend seaward four times that distance. Moreover, the law somewhat artificially divides the seabed among three legal regimes: the seabed beneath the territorial sea; the continental shelf; and the international seabed, or as it is formally known, "the Area" (see figure 1). The legal regimes for the continental shelf and international deep seabed are complex, and only the elements essential for seagoing officers are covered in this book. To that end, section A briefly addresses the legal status of the seabed beneath the territorial sea; section B then examines the continental shelf regime, including its provisions for claims to an extended continental shelf; and section C provides an overview of the legal regime for the deep seabed beyond national jurisdiction (the Area).[1]

A. SEABED BENEATH THE TERRITORIAL SEA

Article 2 of the 1982 LOS Convention affirms the principle, first codified in the 1958 Convention on the Territorial Sea and the Contiguous Zone, that the sovereignty of a coastal state over its adjacent territorial sea extends to the seabed and subsoil beneath those waters. Thus, in the twelve-nautical-mile territorial sea claimed by most coastal states, the state has more than mere jurisdiction over, or sovereign rights in, the seabed and subsoil and their resources; it is sovereign. Article 2 requires, however, that the coastal state exercise its sovereignty in accordance with other applicable provisions of the LOS Convention and other rules of international law. This would include, for example, Article 208 of the LOS Convention regarding the prevention of pollution from seabed activities in national jurisdiction. Because the coastal state is sovereign in the seabed beneath the territorial sea, other states have no right of access to its natural resources or to conduct marine scientific research or lay submarine cables or pipelines there.

---

1. The terms "deep seabed" and "deep ocean floor" refer to the seabed beyond the physical continental margin, some of which falls within the coastal state's two-hundred-nautical-mile juridical continental shelf. The terms "international seabed" and "the Area," refer to the seabed beyond national jurisdiction. See figure 1.

B. THE CONTINENTAL SHELF

The legal, or "juridical," continental shelf begins at the outer boundary of the territorial sea. How far seaward the shelf extends and the rights and obligations of various states in the seabed and subsoil of the shelf have been the subject of keen international attention since 1945. In considering those seaward limits, one must bear in mind that the Area begins where the continental shelf ends, and the resources of the Area are the common heritage of humankind. All states share in that common heritage, even those with minimal continental shelves (the geographically disadvantaged states) or no shelf at all (the landlocked states). Coastal states' extended-continental-shelf claims (for states with continental margins extending more than two hundred nautical miles seaward) therefore come in part at the expense of landlocked and geographically disadvantaged states and their right to share in common heritage resources.

1. Early Developments in the Continental Shelf Regime

Coastal state claims to continental shelf resources beyond the territorial sea began with occasional claims to an exclusive right to certain pearl and sponge fisheries on the seabed. Most commentators, however, date the true beginning of the modern continental shelf regime to the 1945 proclamation by President Truman that asserted U.S. "jurisdiction and control" over the natural resources of the adjacent continental shelf.[2] Many think that the modern ocean enclosure movement itself began with that proclamation. The natural resources President Truman had in mind were the huge offshore oil and gas deposits that would fuel the nation's postwar industrialization.

2. 1958 Convention on the Continental Shelf

Other states were quick to follow Truman's 1945 continental shelf claim, prompting one respected publicist to declare in 1950 that the continental shelf regime had become "instant" customary international law.[3] In the mid-1950s the ILC made a number of attempts to define the "continental shelf" and coastal state jurisdiction over its resources. The commission's work formed the basis for what would become the 1958 Convention on the Continental Shelf. The seaward extent of the continental shelf under the 1958 convention and the coastal state's right in the shelf are examined below. By 1969 the ICJ had concluded that the concept of the continental shelf, as set out in Articles 1–3 of the 1958 convention, had crystallized into a rule of customary international law, binding even on those states that were not a party to the convention.[4] The court concluded that under customary law, coastal states had the sovereign right to explore and exploit the natural resources of the shelf. The court's conclusion was largely based on its understanding that a state's continental shelf is the "natural prolongation of the land territory" of the state.[5] That characterization was later incorporated into Article 76 of the 1982 LOS Convention and helps explain why a state need not affirmatively claim its continental shelf, as it must an EEZ.

---

2. Proclamation No. 2667, Policy of the United States with Respect to the Natural Resources of the Subsoil and Seabed of the Continental Shelf [hereinafter "1945 Continental Shelf Proclamation"], Sept. 28, 1945, 10 Fed. Reg. 12,303 (1945), 3 C.F.R. 67 (1943–48 Comp.), 59 Stat. 884 3 C.F.R.; see also Marjorie M. Whiteman, 4 Digest of International Law 752–64 (1965). See generally Ann L. Hollick, U.S. Oceans Policy: The Truman Proclamations, 17 Va. J. Int'l L. 23 (1976).

3. Hersch Lauterpacht, Sovereignty over Submarine Areas, 27 British Y.B. Int'l L. 376, 431 (1950).

4. North Sea Continental Shelf cases (Fed. Rep. Germany v. Denmark/Fed. Rep. Germany v. Netherlands) 1969 I.C.J. 3, 23 (Feb. 20).

5. Id.

3. 1982 Law of the Sea Convention

The 1982 UN Convention on the Law of the Sea,[6] which superseded the four 1958 Geneva conventions on the law of the sea (including the Convention on the Continental Shelf) for all states that are party to the 1982 Convention,[7] differs in several important respects from its 1958 predecessor. Two differences stand out: the 1982 LOS Convention's provisions for determining the seaward extent of the shelf are remarkably different; and the 1982 convention supplemented the continental shelf rules with a new EEZ regime, which in many ways now overlaps the continental shelf regime in waters out to two hundred nautical miles. That overlap is examined below.

a. Geographic Extent of the Continental Shelf

The 1945 Truman proclamation did not specify the outer limit of the newly claimed continental shelf. However, a statement that accompanied the proclamation asserted that the shelf extended seaward to the point where the superjacent waters were no more than one hundred fathoms (six hundred feet).[8] The proclamation made it clear that the claim in no way infringed on navigation rights in the superjacent waters.[9]

In the 1958 Convention on the Continental Shelf the conferees adopted the shelf definition developed by the ILC, which defined the continental shelf to include "the seabed and subsoil of the submarine areas adjacent to the coast but outside the area of the territorial sea, to a depth of 200 meters, or, beyond that limit, to where the depth of the superjacent waters admits of the exploitation of the natural resources of the said areas."[10] For most states, the two-hundred-meter isobath (very close to the one-hundred-fathom isobath announced earlier by the United States) was located roughly forty to fifty nautical miles offshore. For states with more extensive continental margins, however, the two-hundred-meter isobath was up to several hundred miles offshore. The 1958 definition, dependent on a rapidly evolving exploitation "technology," failed to provide a satisfactory basis for determining the outer limit of the continental shelf. Some observers foresaw a day when depth would no longer be a limiting factor on exploitation, permitting those states in possession of the necessary technology to lay claim to the entire seabed, to the disadvantage of the less-developed states, which lacked the needed technology.

As UNCLOS III got under way, coastal states generally favored a legal regime for the continental shelf that extended coastal state control over the seabed and subsoil out to at least two hundred nautical miles, regardless of the actual physical features of that seabed. The outer limit of the shelf would then coincide with that of the EEZ. At the same time, however, roughly thirty states with a continental margin that physically extended more than two hundred nautical miles (the so-called wide-margin states) argued for a regime that would give legal recognition to their shelf claims beyond the EEZ.[11] The convention essentially meets both demands. First, it establishes the two-hundred-nautical-mile EEZ limit as the minimum boundary of the continental

---

6. The continental shelf provisions are in Part VI of the LOS Convention (Articles 76–85). See also Restatement FRLUS § 515.

7. See LOSC art. 311(1).

8. Statement Accompanying Continental Shelf Proclamation, reprinted in 13 U.S. Dep't of State Bull. 484 (1945). See generally Whiteman, 4 Digest of International Law, supra, at 752–64.

9. The ILC characterized the high-seas freedom as a "paramount principle." See ILC, Articles concerning the Law of the Sea with Commentaries, art. 66, 1956 Y.B. Int'l L. Comm'n, vol. I, at 296.

10. 1958 Convention on the Continental Shelf, supra, art. 1. An isobath is an imaginary line connecting points of equal water depth.

11. The states included Argentina, Australia, Canada, India, Madagascar, Mexico, Sri Lanka, and France with respect to its overseas possessions. The United States and the former Soviet Union also have shelves that physically extend more than two hundred nautical miles in some areas.

shelf for seabed and subsoil exploitation, satisfying the geologically disadvantaged. It satisfies the states possessed of a broader physical continental margin by providing a formula and process for establishing an extended continental shelf (ECS) boundary beyond two hundred nautical miles. To bring some order and finality to the process for evaluating coastal state ECS claims, it also established the Commission on the Limits of the Continental Shelf, which comprises experts in geology, geophysics, and hydrography. The commission's mission is to evaluate the data submitted by coastal states making ECS claims and provide recommendations on their consistency with the convention.[12] Coastal state ECS claims that are consistent with the CLCS recommendations are final and binding.[13] The LOS Convention originally required all states making ECS claims to submit their claims and the supporting data to the CLCS not later than ten years after the convention entered into force for that state. However, the original deadline proved unworkable for many states and was later extended.[14]

As defined by the 1982 LOS Convention (and customary law),[15] a nation's juridical continental shelf now begins at the outer limit of the territorial sea[16] and extends seaward for a distance of at least two hundred nautical miles from the baseline.[17] If a state's physical continental margin[18] extends more than two hundred nautical miles from the baseline, as does the U.S. margin in several areas, the convention provides a procedure for the state to perfect its ECS claim beyond the presumptive two-hundred-nautical-mile limit.[19]

The convention prescribes two limiting measures on coastal state ECS claims. First, it provides that a state's ECS cannot extend more than 100 nautical miles beyond the 2,500-meter isobath or 350 nautical miles from the baseline.[20] The outer limit lines of the state's continental shelf and the lines of delimitation must be shown on charts of a scale adequate for ascertaining their position.[21] Where appropriate, lists of geographical coordinates of points may be substituted for such lines. The coastal state must give due publicity to such charts or lists of geographical coordinates and deposit a copy of each such chart or list with the secretary-general of the UN.

Second, to equitably offset continental shelf extensions that would encroach into the Area—humankind's common heritage—the convention requires coastal states to contribute to a system for sharing the revenue or contributions in kind derived from the exploitation of mineral

---

12. Information on the limits of the continental shelf beyond two hundred nautical miles from the baseline must be submitted by the coastal state to the CLCS.

13. LOSC art. 76(8).

14. For current information, see UN, Oceans and Law of the Sea, Issues with respect to Article 4 of annex II to the convention (ten-year time limit for submissions), available at http://www.un.org/Depts/los/clcs_new/issues_ten_years.htm (accessed Apr. 1, 2013).

15. See Continental Shelf case (Libya v. Malta), 1985 I.C.J. 13, 29–36 (June 3) (recognizing, as a matter of customary law, the coastal state's sovereign rights in the natural resources of a juridical continental shelf out to a minimum of two hundred nautical miles, regardless of the geologic extent).

16. The coastal state is sovereign over the submerged lands beneath the state's territorial sea. See LOSC art. 2. Accordingly, such submerged lands are not included within the juridical continental shelf. See id. art. 76(1).

17. LOSC art. 76(1).

18. The continental margin includes the continental shelf, continental slope, and continental rise. See LOSC art. 76(3).

19. Id. art. 76(2)–(10). See also Final Act of the Third United Nations Conference on the Law of the Sea, Annex II (Statement of Understanding concerning a Specific Method to Be Used in Establishing the Outer Edge of the Continental Shelf).

20. LOSC art. 76(2)–76(10). To preempt possible claims out to, for example, the Mid-Atlantic Ridge and similar ridges in other oceans, the convention provides that the coastal state must observe the 350-nautical-mile limit with submarine ridges (even if the alternative 2,500-meter/100-nautical-mile limit would extend the shelf farther offshore). LOSC art. 76(6); Restatement FRLUS § 511 n.8. See generally Bernard Oxman, The Third United Nations Conference on the Law of the Sea: Eighth Session, 74 Am. J. Int'l L. 1, 19–22 (1979).

21. LOSC art. 84.

resources beyond two hundred nautical miles.[22] Those payments or contributions are then equitably distributed among states parties to the convention through the International Seabed Authority. A developing state that is a net importer of a mineral resource produced from its continental shelf is exempt from the revenue-sharing requirement.

b. Rights of the Coastal State over the Continental Shelf

The 1945 Truman proclamation asserted only "exclusive [U.S.] jurisdiction and control" over the natural resources of the continental shelf. The 1958 convention made a qualitative change to the coastal state's claim, substituting the phrase "sovereign rights" for "exclusive jurisdiction and control."[23] While not defined in the convention, the broader phrase "sovereign rights" certainly includes the exclusive right to explore and exploit the shelf's natural resources, together with the jurisdiction necessary to ensure that those rights are effectively enforced. The 1982 LOS Convention carries forward the sovereign rights language. Article 77 of that convention now provides that "the coastal State exercises over the continental shelf sovereign rights for the purposes of exploring it and exploiting its natural resources."[24] "Natural resources" includes both living and nonliving natural resources, but it does not include shipwrecks on or embedded in the shelf.[25] The resources contemplated by the LOS Convention shelf regime include mineral and other nonliving resources of the seabed and subsoil, along with sedentary species of living resources.[26]

The coastal state's rights over the continental shelf do not depend on occupation or (in contrast to EEZ rights) on express proclamation.[27] In contrast to the EEZ regime, the coastal state's rights in the continental shelf are exclusive, in that if it does not explore the shelf or exploit its resources no other state may do so without the coastal state's consent.[28] It follows that if such activities are authorized by the coastal state, they are subject to any relevant laws governing continental shelf activities enacted by the consenting state.[29] Coastal states have concomitant obligations regarding protection of the marine environment of the continental shelf. Those are discussed in chapter 10.

The coastal state has the exclusive right to regulate seafloor drilling anywhere on its continental shelf.[30] Coastal state consent is also required for any marine scientific research on its

22. LOSC art. 82; Restatement FRLUS § 515 cmt. a.
23. 1958 Convention on the Continental Shelf art. 2(1). The coastal state also has jurisdiction over installations on the shelf. Id. art. 5.
24. LOSC art. 77(1).
25. Treasure Salvors Inc. v. Unidentified Wrecked and Abandoned Sailing Vessel (the *Atocha*), 569 F.2d 330 (5th Cir. 1978) (holding that the U.S. government did not have jurisdiction and control over a wreck on the seabed by virtue of the Outer Continental Shelf Lands Act because the act is limited to "natural resources"). The UNESCO-sponsored UCH Convention purports to extend the coastal state's authority to marine archaeological objects on the continental shelf and in the EEZ; however, the United States rejected the convention. See Convention on the Protection of Underwater Cultural Heritage, arts. 9 & 10, Nov. 2, 2001, 41 I.L.M. 40 (2002).
26. Id. art. 77(4).
27. LOSC art. 77(3); see also North Sea Continental Shelf cases (Fed. Rep. Germany v. Denmark/Fed. Rep. Germany v. Netherlands), 1969 I.C.J. 3, 23 (Feb. 20).
28. LOSC art. 77(2); Restatement FRLUS § 515 cmt. b; cf. U.S. v. Ray, 423 F.2d 16, 21–22 (5th Cir. 1970) (applying the 1958 Convention on the Continental Shelf and holding that consent of the United States is required to construct an artificial island on coral reefs located on the U.S. continental shelf).
29. Within the United States, the relevant laws include, for example, the Outer Continental Shelf Lands Act, 43 U.S.C. §§ 1331–1356, and, with respect to applicable living marine resources, the Magnuson-Stevens Fishery Conservation and Management Act, 16 U.S.C. §§ 1801–1883.
30. LOSC art. 81; Restatement FRLUS § 515 cmt. d.

continental shelf.[31] However, a coastal state with an extended shelf may not withhold its consent to marine scientific research on the shelf beyond two hundred nautical miles on the ground that the project is of direct significance for the exploration and exploitation of natural resources, unless it has already begun exploration or exploitation in the area or will begin within a reasonable time.[32] The coastal state has the exclusive right to construct and to authorize and regulate the construction, operation, and use of artificial islands and certain installations and structures on the shelf,[33] as well as exclusive jurisdiction over those structures.[34] Such artificial islands, installations, and structures do not possess the status of islands.[35] As a result, they have no territorial sea of their own, and their presence does not affect the delimitation of the territorial sea, the EEZ, or the continental shelf.

Coastal states must give notice of the construction of artificial islands, installations, or structures and provide for a permanent means of giving warning of the structure's presence. Such structures may not be established where they would interfere with the use of recognized sea-lanes essential to international navigation. Any installations or structures that are abandoned or disused must be removed to ensure safety of navigation, and in a manner that gives due regard to fishing, protection of the marine environment, and the rights and duties of other states.[36] The coastal state must publicize the depth, position, and dimensions of any installations or structures not entirely removed.

Where necessary, reasonable safety zones may be established around artificial islands, installations, and structures to ensure the safety of navigation and of the artificial islands, installations, and structures.[37] Appropriate notice of the safety zone is required. The breadth of the safety zones is determined by the coastal state, taking into account applicable international standards; however, they cannot extend more than five hundred meters from the structure, except as authorized by generally accepted international standards or as recommended by the International Maritime Organization. Ships (and environmental protesters)[38] are required to respect safety zones and comply with generally accepted international standards regarding navigation in the vicinity of artificial islands, installations, structures, and safety zones.

---

31. LOSC art. 56 (coastal state jurisdiction over marine scientific research in the EEZ); id. art. 246(1) (same for the continental shelf); see also Restatement FRLUS § 514 cmt. h (marine scientific research within the EEZ) & § 515 cmt. d & n.2 (marine scientific research on the continental shelf). Marine scientific research in the EEZ is examined in chapter 6.

32. LOSC art. 246(6).

33. Id. art. 80, provides that Article 60, applicable in the EEZ, applies mutatis mutandis to artificial islands, installations, and structures on the continental shelf. Paragraphs 1 and 2 of Article 60 set out an important distinction between artificial islands and the other classes of offshore structures.

34. LOSC art. 80 (incorporating by reference Article 60(2)). This includes jurisdiction with regard to customs, fiscal, health, safety, and immigration matters. The United States exercises its jurisdiction over offshore artificial islands, installations, and structures through a combination of federal and state law. The federal scheme addresses safety, security, and environmental protection measures and certain claims for personal injury or wrongful death. The scheme incorporates the relevant state criminal law. See Outer Continental Shelf Lands Act of 1953, 43 U.S.C. §§ 1333, 1356, 33 C.F.R. parts 140–47; Deepwater Port Act of 1974 33 U.S.C. § 1518, 33 C.F.R. parts 148–50; 18 U.S.C. § 2281.

35. LOSC art. 80 (incorporating by reference Article 60(8)).

36. Id. (incorporating by reference Article 60(3)). See also LOSC art. 1(5)(a)(i) (defining "dumping" to include disposal of platforms or other artificial structures); IMO, IMO Res. A.672(16), Oct. 19, 1989 (Guidelines and Standards for the Removal of Offshore Installations and Structures on the Continental Shelf and Exclusive Economic Zone); 30 C.F.R. parts 250 & 256.

37. LOSC art. 80 (incorporating by reference Article 60(4) & (5)). See also Stuart Kaye, International Measures to Protect Oil Platforms, Pipelines, and Submarine Cables from Attack, 31 Tul. Mar. L. J. 377 (2007).

38. Safety zone violations by environmental protest groups have become an area of concern. Violations of safety zone regulations promulgated under authority of the U.S. Outer Continental Shelf Lands Act are punishable by civil

c. Rights and Obligations of Other States in the Continental Shelf

States other than the coastal state enjoy important rights in the shelf and superjacent waters. The coastal state must exercise its rights over the continental shelf in a way that does not infringe on or unjustifiably interfere with the navigation and other rights and freedoms of other states.[39] Consistent with customary international law and the 1958 Continental Shelf Convention, the 1982 LOS Convention provides that the rights of the coastal state over the continental shelf do not affect the legal status of the superjacent waters or of the airspace above those waters.[40] At the same time, the 1982 Convention permits states to claim an EEZ extending up to two hundred nautical miles seaward, and the coastal state will enjoy certain rights and jurisdiction with respect to those waters under the EEZ articles (see chapter 6).[41] On extended continental shelves, any activities in the superjacent waters beyond two hundred nautical miles are governed by the convention's high-seas articles.[42]

The LOS Convention preserves the right of all states to lay submarine cables and pipelines on the continental shelf.[43] Whether the right to lay cables extends to cabled seabed acoustic device arrays such as the U.S. Sound Surveillance System (SOSUS) has not been authoritatively determined.[44] With respect to pipelines (but not cables), the coastal state's consent is required for delineation of the pipeline's location and course.[45] When laying pipelines or cables, states must have due regard to any cables or pipelines already in position.[46] Additionally, the coastal state over whose continental shelf the cables are laid may require that any cable and pipeline projects comply with reasonable measures to facilitate exploration of the shelf and exploitation of the coastal state's resources and to protect the marine environment.[47] The coastal state may not impede the laying or maintenance of the cables or pipelines.[48]

4. Relationship between Continental Shelf and EEZ Legal Regimes

In addition to any rights obtained under the convention's continental shelf articles, coastal states possess the sovereign right to explore and exploit the natural resources of the seabed, subsoil, and superjacent waters within an EEZ (if they claim one) up to two hundred nautical miles seaward of the baseline.[49] Thus, the continental shelf and EEZ regimes potentially overlap in their cov-

---

penalties and/or fines of up to $100,000 and imprisonment for up to 10 years (33 C.F.R. § 140.35). Depending on the nature of the acts and the extent to which they endanger a vessel's or platform's safety, 18 U.S.C. §§ 2280–2281—the U.S. laws that implement the 1988 SUA Convention and its protocol protecting fixed platforms—provide a possible second basis for prosecution and imprisonment.

39. LOSC art. 78(2).
40. Id. art. 78(1).
41. Id. art. 56.
42. Id. art. 78(1).
43. Id. art. 79(1).
44. See generally Tullio Treves, Military Installations, Structures and Devices on the Seabed, 74 Am. J. Int'l L. 808 (1980). The United States installed the top-secret SOSUS network of underwater acoustic devices cabled to naval ocean processing facilities in Whidbey Island, Wash., and Norfolk, Va., beginning in 1952 to detect Soviet submarines. The system was declassified in 1991, and access to SOSUS data has been selectively extended to scientific researchers.
45. LOSC art. 79(3).
46. Id. art. 79(5).
47. Id. art. 79(2).
48. Id. art. 79(2).
49. Id. art. 56; Restatement FRLUS § 514.

erage of natural resources of the seabed or subsoil out to the two-hundred-nautical-mile limit.[50] This led some UNCLOS III negotiators to argue that the continental shelf regime was largely redundant for states with an EEZ and that the shelf regime should therefore be abolished. They failed to persuade the other conferees, however, and as a result, where a coastal state asserts claims to both an EEZ and a continental shelf, the two regimes overlap out to a distance of two hundred nautical miles.[51] Because both regimes prescribe rights and obligations regarding marine resources, the LOS Convention includes provisions for resolving conflicts between the two. One such adjustment concerns the "sedentary species" of the shelf, as defined in Article 77.[52] The LOS Convention stipulates that sedentary species are governed by the rules for the continental shelf set out in Part VI, not the rules for living resources of the EEZ in Part V.[53] The exceptional treatment of sedentary species highlights an important distinction between the continental shelf and EEZ regimes. The coastal state has resource conservation, management, and allocation responsibilities under the EEZ regime; however, no such obligations were included in the continental shelf articles. Congress' statutory approach to the two domains also differs in the United States.[54]

5. The U.S. Continental Shelf

The United States first claimed differential rights in the adjacent continental shelf in 1945. The 1953 Submerged Lands Act confirms that the adjacent states have title to offshore waters and submerged lands out to three nautical miles, except for Texas and the Gulf coast of Florida, where the states' title extends to three marine leagues (nine nautical miles).[55] The U.S. seabed areas seaward of those "submerged lands" of the states are referred to as the "outer continental shelf" and are governed by the Outer Continental Shelf Lands Act of 1953 (OCSLA).[56]

The OCSLA does not specify the outer limit of the continental shelf of the United States (which is determined by international law). Arguably, the United States is bound by the limits imposed by the 1958 Convention on the Continental Shelf, to which it is still a party, except to the extent those limits have been superseded by customary international law. The ICJ has held that, as a matter of customary law, coastal states have sovereign rights in the natural resources of their continental shelf out to a minimum of two hundred nautical miles, regardless of the geologic extent of the continental margin.[57] While as a matter of conventional law Article 76 of the LOS Convention permits a state to assert a claim to a continental shelf beyond two hundred nautical miles, it is doubtful that the convention's ECS provisions have ripened into a rule of customary law.[58]

---

50. See Restatement FRLUS § 511 cmts. c & j, & § 515 cmt. a; Churchill & Lowe, supra, at 123 & 128–30.

51. See Churchill & Lowe, supra, at 145.

52. Sedentary species are defined as "organisms which, at the harvestable stage, either are immobile on or under the seabed or are unable to move except in constant physical contact with the seabed or the subsoil." LOSC art. 77(4). The U.S. Magnuson-Stevens Fishery Conservation and Management Act employs the very different term "continental shelf fishery resources." See 16 U.S.C. § 1802(7). See Whiteman, 4 Digest of International Law, supra, at 864–65 (documenting Japanese protests to inclusion of Alaska king crab in the definition).

53. LOSC art. 68.

54. The Outer Continental Shelf Lands Act implements the shelf regime for the United States. By contrast, although the president proclaimed, as a matter of international law, an EEZ extending two hundred nautical miles seaward in 1983, Congress has yet to enact comprehensive implementing legislation.

55. See Submerged Lands Act of 1953, 43 U.S.C. §§ 1301, 1311.

56. Outer Continental Shelf Lands Act of 1953, 43 U.S.C. §§ 1302, 1331–1338, & 1340–1356.

57. Continental Shelf case (Libya v. Malta), 1985 I.C.J. 13, 33 (June 03).

58. It seems clear that paragraphs 1–3 of Article 76 reflect customary law. Whether that is true of the ECS paragraphs has not yet been authoritatively answered. See Territorial and Maritime Dispute (Nicaragua v. Colombia), ¶ 118,

The U.S. continental margin likely extends more than two hundred nautical miles from the baseline in areas off the Arctic coast of Alaska, two areas in the Gulf of Mexico, and in the southeast region of the Blake Plateau (off the southern Atlantic coast).[59] In its 2007 review of the 1982 LOS Convention's continental shelf articles, the U.S. Senate Committee on Foreign Relations concluded that the convention would potentially give the United States one of the largest continental shelves in the world; in the Arctic, for example, the U.S. continental shelf could extend as far as six hundred nautical miles from the Alaska coast.[60] As a nonparty to the LOS Convention, however, the United States cannot avail itself of the procedures to perfect such a claim before the Commission on the Limits of the Continental Shelf and thus render such a claim final and binding under Article 76(8).[61]

C. THE SEABED BEYOND NATIONAL JURISDICTION

Four salient facts characterize the regime for the deep seabed beyond national jurisdiction (the Area). The first, of course, is that the regime applies to those areas of the seabed beyond national jurisdiction. Second, like the oceans generally, the international seabed is reserved for peaceful purposes.[62] Third, the deep seabed regime regulates access to the "resources" of the Area, a term limited to mineral resources (and which therefore excludes living and genetic resources of the seabed, such as those found at hydrothermal vent sites). Fourth, the Area and those mineral resources have been deemed to be the common heritage of humankind. A fifth practical consideration in approaching these materials is that no one is currently exploiting the Area's mineral resources, and commercial exploitation is not likely to begin in the immediate future.

1. Historical Development of the International Seabed Regime

Until recently, deep-seabed mining interest focused on the deposits of polymetallic nodules, which were first discovered by the HMS *Challenger* expedition in 1873.[63] Polymetallic nodules (also called manganese nodules) are found in abyssal areas of the seabed at depths of 12,000 to 18,000 feet. Although the origin of the nodules is not fully understood, it is believed they precipitated from seawater over a period of millions of years.[64] Mineral components and concentrations of those nodules vary, but generally they include economically valuable manganese, cobalt,

---

2012 I.C.J. (Nov. 19) (declining to determine whether paragraphs 2–10 of Article 76 reflect customary law). The most persuasive argument can be found in the "natural prolongation" language in the ICJ's North Sea Continental Shelf decision and in Article 76(1). See J. Ashley Roach & Robert W. Smith, Excessive Maritime Claims 201–03 (3d ed. 2012) (quoting "United States Policy Governing the Continental Shelf of the United States of America"). But see Ted L. McDorman, The Entry into Force of the 1982 LOSC and the Article 76 Outer Continental Shelf Regime, 10 Int'l Marine & Coastal L. J. 165, 165 & n.10 (1995) (concluding that "it is difficult to accept that either the technical criteria of Article 76 or the formal processes of the provision have emerged as customary international law").

59. See U.S. Extended Continental Shelf Task Force, Extended Continental Shelf Project, available at http://continentalshelf.gov/ (accessed Feb. 1, 2013) (listing six areas where the United States "likely" has an ECS and nine areas where it "may" have a valid ECS claim).

60. S. Exec. Rpt. No. 110-09, supra, at 5.

61. LOSC art. 76(8); id. annex II.

62. LOSC art. 141. See also Treaty on the Prohibition of the Emplacement of Nuclear Weapons and Other Weapons of Mass Destruction on the Sea-bed and the Ocean Floor and in the Subsoil Thereof, Feb. 11, 1971, 23 U.S.T. 701, 955 U.N.T.S. 114. The reservation for peaceful purposes has not precluded use of the seabed for defensive purposes, including the laying of the SOSUS network to detect potentially hostile submarines.

63. On March 13, 1874, somewhere between Hawaii and Tahiti, the crew of HMS *Challenger* hauled in a trawl containing the first known deposits of manganese nodules from a depth of 15,600 feet.

64. See Department of Commerce, National Oceanic and Atmospheric Administration, Deep Seabed Mining: Report to Congress (Dec. 1993).

nickel, and copper. It was not until the 1950s that the potential of these potato-sized mineral deposits as sources of strategically important minerals was generally appreciated. Beginning in the late 1950s, several companies began prospecting the nodule fields to estimate their economic potential. By 1974 they determined that a 1.35-million-square-mile area of sea floor just north of the equator and between Mexico and Hawaii (the Clarion Clipperton Zone) held vast deposits of the nodules.

The 1958 Geneva conventions only briefly addressed the seabed beyond the continental shelf and its resources. The 1958 High Seas Convention included a list of high-seas freedoms, which included the right to lay submarine cables and pipelines on or under the seabed.[65] Exploitation of the natural resources of the seabed beneath the high seas was not among the listed high-seas freedoms, but the list was intentionally nonexhaustive.[66] The 1958 convention also recognized the right of states to take measures to prevent pollution resulting from "exploitation and explora- tion of the seabed and its subsoil."[67] Given that the parallel 1958 Convention on the Continental Shelf defined the shelf in a way that extended it to the limits of exploitability, it is perhaps not surprising that the Convention on the High Seas did not further define the rights and obligations of states with respect to exploiting the natural resources of the seabed beneath the high seas.

Serious international attention on a legal regime for access to the deep seabed began with Maltese ambassador Arvid Pardo's 1967 speech at the United Nations, during which he charac- terized the seabed and its resources as the "common heritage of mankind." In 1970 the members of the UN General Assembly agreed with Pardo, declaring by nonbinding resolution that the seabed beyond the limits of national jurisdiction and its resources are the common heritage of humankind, a concept that struck a welcome chord with proponents of the New Interna- tional Legal Order.[68] An earlier General Assembly resolution had called for a moratorium on the exploitation of seabed resources until a satisfactory legal regime was developed; however, it enjoyed less support than the later common heritage resolution.[69]

A formal legal regime for the seabed beyond national jurisdiction was completed in 1982, as Part XI of the 1982 LOS Convention.[70] The original Part XI was decidedly unsatisfactory to the United States and a number of other industrialized states, which declined to sign the conven- tion.[71] For more than a decade, disagreements over the seabed regime cast doubt on whether the LOS Convention would achieve broad acceptance. At the initiative of Secretary-General Pérez de Cuéllar, a series of informal consultations and meetings between 1990 and 1994 produced a modified approach to the seabed, which was codified in the 1994 Part XI Implementation Agree- ment.[72] The agreement addressed the concerns of most states that were reluctant to ratify the convention with its original Part XI provisions.[73] The United States signed the Implementation

---

65. 1958 Convention on the High Seas, supra, arts. 2 & 26.

66. The Article 2 list of freedoms was made nonexhaustive by inclusion of the critical "inter alia" qualifier.

67. 1958 Convention on the High Seas, supra, art. 24.

68. Declaration of the Principles Governing the Sea-bed and the Ocean Floor, and the Subsoil Thereof, Beyond the Limits of National Jurisdiction, G.A. Res. 2749(XXV), U.N. GAOR, 25th Sess., Supp. No. 28, U.N. Doc. A/8028 (1970).

69. Question of the Reservation Exclusively for Peaceful Purposes of the Sea-bed and the Ocean Floor, and the Sub- soil Thereof, Underlying the High Seas beyond the Limits of Present National Jurisdiction, and the Use of Their Resources in the Interests of Mankind. G.A. Res. 2574D(XXV), U.N. GAOR 24th Sess., Supp. No. 30, U.N. Doc. A/2834 (1969).

70. In 1980 Congress enacted the Deep Seabed Hard Mineral Resources Act, 30 U.S.C. §§ 1401–1473.

71. Twenty-one states either voted against the final convention text or abstained.

72. The Part XI Implementation Agreement and its history are reproduced in U.N. Publication Sales No. E.97.V.10.

73. See generally Bernard H. Oxman, Law of the Sea Forum: The 1994 Agreement on Implementation of the Seabed Provisions of the Convention on the Law of the Sea: The 1994 Agreement and the Convention, 88 Am. J. Int'l L. 687 (1994).

Agreement in 1994, and President Clinton presented the agreement and the original 1982 LOS Convention to the Senate for advice and consent on October 7, 1994.[74]

The 1994 Implementation Agreement is binding on all states that ratified or acceded to the LOS Convention after the 1994 Agreement was adopted and on all states that had ratified or acceded to the LOS Convention before the agreement was adopted but that later ratified the agreement. A handful of states that ratified or acceded to the LOS Convention before the agreement was adopted and that have not yet ratified the agreement are technically not bound by it. However, because any activities in the Area conducted under the auspices of the International Seabed Authority must be carried out under the terms of the agreement, even those states that have not yet ratified it will be effectively required to conduct any activities in the Area consistently with the agreement rather than the original version of Part XI.[75]

The examination that follows takes as its departure point the applicable article of the 1994 Part XI Implementation Agreement, which gives the agreement primacy over any conflicting provisions of the original Part XI regime in the LOS Convention. It provides that "the provisions of this Agreement and Part XI shall be interpreted and applied together as a single instrument. However, in the event of any inconsistency between this Agreement and Part XI, *the provisions of this agreement shall prevail.*"[76]

2. Definition of the Deep Seabed and Its Resources

"The Area" is defined by the LOS Convention as "the seabed and subsoil thereof, beyond the limits of national jurisdiction."[77] Accordingly, the boundaries of the Area cannot be definitively determined until all coastal state claims for an extended continental shelf are resolved. Consistent with the 1970 UN General Assembly resolution, the LOS Convention provides that the Area and its resources are the common heritage of humankind.[78] That means that no state may claim or exercise sovereignty or sovereign rights over any part of the Area or its resources; nor may any state or private entity appropriate any part of the Area or its resources, except as provided by the convention (as modified by the 1994 Implementation Agreement).[79] "Resources" of the Area are defined as "all solid, liquid or gaseous mineral resources in situ in the Area at or beneath the seabed, including polymetallic nodules."[80] Other minerals of interest include cobalt crusts found along some seamounts in the Pacific basin and polymetallic sulfide crust deposits formed by hydrothermal vents. The definition of "resources" plainly excludes living resources and nonnatural resources, such as shipwrecks on or embedded in the seabed.[81] Nevertheless—and perhaps because the economic benefits of mineral mining in the Area have so far failed to materialize—several proposals have been put forward to expand the Part XI regime and its common heritage approach to include living and/or genetic resources beyond national jurisdiction.

---

74. See William J. Clinton, Letter of Transmittal of Oct. 7, 1994, S. Treaty Doc. No. 103-39, at iii–iv, reprinted in Annotated Supplement to the Commander's Handbook, supra, annex A1-2.

75. See Churchill & Lowe, supra at 21 (concluding that the option of states not party to the 1994 agreement to operate under the original Part XI rules is "illusory").

76. Part XI Implementation Agreement art. 2(1) (emphasis added). A consolidated text that incorporates the revisions to Part XI made by the 1994 Implementation Agreement is available in International Seabed Authority, The Law of the Sea: Compendium of Basic Documents (2001), and is reproduced in documentary annex II of United Nations Convention on the Law of the Sea 1982: A Commentary, vol. VI, at 877–921 (Myron H. Nordquist et al. eds., 2002).

77. LOSC art. 1(1).

78. Id. art. 136.

79. Id. art. 137(1) & (3).

80. Id. art. 133(a).

81. Id. art. 303.

3. The International Seabed Authority

To administer mining activities in the Area, the 1982 LOS Convention established the International Seabed Authority (ISA) in Kingston, Jamaica.[82] The ISA comprises three principal organs: an Assembly, made up of all members of the ISA, with the power to set general policy; a Council of thirty-six elected members with the power to make executive decisions; and a Secretariat headed by the ISA secretary-general. "Activities in the Area" that are within the ISA's jurisdiction include "all activities for exploration for, and exploitation of, the resources of the Area."[83] Such activities must be carried out for the common benefit of all humankind and exclusively for peaceful purposes.[84] Although the function of the ISA is to regulate seabed mining in the Area, the ISA is also required to take measures to ensure that the marine environment is effectively protected from any harmful effects that may arise during those mining activities.[85] Pursuant to that authority, the ISA has developed an elaborate mining code, and it recently petitioned the Seabed Disputes Chamber of ITLOS for an advisory opinion on state responsibility for activities in the Area. The Seabed Disputes Chamber issued its opinion in 2011.[86]

4. U.S. Position on the Deep Seabed and Its Resources

The present position of the United States with respect to the international seabed provisions in Part XI of the 1982 LOS Convention and the 1994 Implementation Agreement is not entirely clear. The United States has never asserted that Part XI of the LOS Convention represents customary international law. On the contrary, in rejecting the convention in 1982, the United States was particularly critical of the Part XI seabed-mining regime. A decade later, however, the United States took an active role in efforts to reform Part XI and ultimately signed the 1994 Implementation Agreement, thus qualifying it for provisional membership in the ISA until 1998. As a signatory to the 1994 Implementation Agreement that has yet to ratify or expressly reject it, the United States is under a legal obligation not to defeat the object and purpose of the agreement unless or until such time as it makes its intention "clear" that it will not become a party to the agreement.[87] Evidence of such intent is plainly lacking. In fact, in its 2007 review of the LOS Convention, the U.S. Senate Committee on Foreign Relations reported that, "as modified, Part XI meets the objections raised by the United States and other industrialized countries concerning the original Convention. It is expected to provide a stable and internationally recognized framework in which mining can proceed in response to demand in the future for deep seabed minerals."[88] That said, as a nonparty to the LOS Convention, the United States has no rights under the convention or the 1994 agreement, except to the extent that some of the convention's articles might have codified existing customary international law when drafted or later crystallized into customary international law.

---

82. The ISA came into existence on November 16, 1994, on the entry into force of the 1982 Convention. The first secretary-general of the ISA was elected in March 1996, and the ISA became fully operational as an autonomous international organization in June 1996.

83. LOSC art. 1(3).

84. Id. arts. 140, 141.

85. Id. art. 145.

86. Responsibilities and Obligations of States Sponsoring Persons and Entities with Respect to Activities in the Area, Request for Advisory Opinion Submitted to the ITLOS Seabed Disputes Chamber, ITLOS Case No. 17, Advisory Opinion of Feb. 1, 2011, 50 I.L.M. 458 (2011).

87. Vienna Convention on Treaties, supra, art. 18. Any attempt to enforce the U.S. Deep Seabed Hard Mineral Resources Act of 1980 after 1994 would arguably put the United States in violation of its obligations as a signatory to the Part XI Agreement.

88. S. Exec. Rpt. No. 110-09, supra, at 5.

The High Seas and
Enclosed/Semi-enclosed Seas

The high seas—constituting roughly 60 percent of the world's oceans—are widely viewed as the last great global commons.[1] As such, the high seas pose a theoretical and practical challenge: how to fashion an acceptable and effective set of ordering principles for a vast region where the familiar rules of governance have been banished. Five principles have been incorporated into the law that governs the high seas. First, the high seas are reserved exclusively for peaceful purposes. Second, no state may subject any part of the high seas to its sovereignty.[2] Third, all states enjoy certain freedoms on the high seas. Fourth, those high-seas freedoms must be exercised with due regard for other states and their use of the seas. Fifth, vessels are, as a general rule, subject to the exclusive jurisdiction and control of their flag state while on the high seas.

This chapter examines those five principles, but the materials it presents must be approached in conjunction with several other chapters. Measures to protect the marine environment and to conserve and manage living marine resources of the high seas are addressed in chapter 10. Maritime law enforcement, much of which is conducted on the high seas, is examined in chapter 11. Military activities on the high seas and in other waters are covered in chapters 6 and 12. Cross-cutting issues concerning the use of force in the maritime domain and countermeasures in response to another state's violation of international law are addressed in chapters 13 and 14 respectively.

A. DEFINITION OF THE HIGH SEAS

Article 1 of the 1958 Convention on the High Seas defined the high seas as "all parts of the sea that are not included in the territorial sea or internal waters of a State."[3] That definition placed the contiguous zone within the high seas. By contrast, the 1982 LOS Convention does not define "high seas." Instead, it provides that the high-seas articles in Part VII of the LOS Convention (Articles 86–120) apply to "all parts of the sea that are not included in the exclusive economic zone, in the territorial sea or in the internal waters of a State, or in the archipelagic waters of an archipelagic State" (see figure 1).[4] It is important to note what Article 86 does not say. It does not say that none of the high-seas articles in Part VII applies in those other waters. In fact, it is well accepted that some of the Part VII articles do apply in the territorial seas and internal waters.

---

1. Other areas treated in some respects as a "commons" include the international seabed and outer space.
2. Rome, and later Venice, once claimed dominion over the entire Mediterranean Sea, as did Great Britain over the North Sea. The division of the world's oceans between Spain and Portugal by papal bull and the Treaty of Tordesillas in the fifteenth century is discussed in chapter 2.
3. 1958 Convention on the High Seas, supra, art. 1.
4. LOSC art. 86.

For example, Article 92 on the nationality of ships and Article 94 on the flag state's obligations respecting its vessels apply regardless of the vessel's location. Article 58(1) of the convention makes it clear that certain high-seas freedoms referred to in Article 87, including the freedoms of navigation and overflight, also apply in the EEZ (see chapter 6). Additionally, Article 58(2) provides that the high-seas provisions in Articles 88–115 apply in the EEZ, insofar as they are not incompatible with the EEZ articles. As a result of those saving provisions in Article 58, much of the convention's high-seas regime will apply in the various states' EEZs (and their contiguous zones, to the extent one is claimed and lies within the EEZ). Article 86 itself also expressly provides that it "does not entail any abridgement of the freedoms enjoyed by all States in the exclusive economic zone in accordance with article 58." Accordingly, much of the discussion that follows will be relevant in the EEZ as well.

B. GENERAL PRINCIPLES APPLICABLE TO THE HIGH SEAS

The five principles of the laws governing the high seas have a distinguished pedigree that spans more than four centuries. That history has been dominated by the need to accommodate the respective interests of flag states and coastal states, and to strike an appropriate balance when those interests come into conflict. The coastal state's sovereign interest in its territorial integrity and political independence is protected by the UN Charter.[5] The LOS convention emphasizes the principle of freedom of navigation, which facilitates the maritime commerce and naval mobility that is necessary for the security and prosperity of maritime states and is jealously safeguarded by them. Indeed, the mare liberum (freedom of the seas) doctrine espoused by Hugo Grotius in 1609 was principally motivated by Dutch maritime trading interests.[6]

The high seas accommodate a number of widely shared state interests. In an era in which global trade has become vital to states' economic well-being and supply chains are linked by just-in-time deliveries, maritime mobility plays an increasingly important role. Any interference with freedom of navigation impinges on the economic interests of all involved states. All states also share an interest in healthy and productive marine ecosystems. Finally, all states share an interest in a level of public order in the oceans sufficient to ensure the safety and security on which their territorial integrity, freedom of navigation, and the marine ecosystems depend. Threats to the public order come from an array of state and nonstate actors, including those engaged in or supporting piracy, armed attacks on vessels, organized crime, and transnational terrorism. Trafficking in weapons significantly adds to the lethal potential of those groups.

1. The High Seas Are Reserved for Peaceful Purposes

Article 301 of the 1982 LOS Convention (titled "peaceful uses of the seas") essentially restates Article 2(4) of the UN Charter by prohibiting the use of or threat to use force and requiring all states parties to the LOS Convention to comply with their charter obligation in the exercise of their rights and performance of their duties under the LOS Convention.[7] As such, Article 301

5. UN Charter, supra, arts. 2 & 33.
6. Hugo Grotius, The Freedom of the Seas; or the Right Which Belongs to the Dutch to Take Part in the East Indian Trade (James Brown Scott ed., 1916) (1608). The essay was also published in chapter 12 of Hugo Grotius, De Jure Praedae.
7. In an overlap with the general provision in Article 301, Article 88 of the LOS Convention provides that "the high seas shall be reserved for peaceful purposes." Similar "peaceful purposes" limitations are prescribed for the Area (LOSC art. 141) and marine scientific research (LOSC art. 240). There is no evidence to suggest that the drafters intended that the meaning of "peaceful uses" in Article 301 and "peaceful purposes" in the other articles would differ.

adds nothing to the state's existing obligations under the UN Charter; nor does it silently abolish the law of naval warfare. Attempts to designate some areas of the high seas as a "zone of peace" have been viewed as largely symbolic,[8] the prominent exception being the areas governed by the Antarctic Treaty System.[9]

Given the almost verbatim adoption of the UN Charter's language in Article 301, the "peaceful purposes" principle in the LOS Convention is widely, if not universally, understood to mean that the convention prohibits the use of force or the threat to use force on the high seas in violation of the UN Charter.[10] That the convention does not ban peacetime maritime security operations by warships, naval submarines, and military aircraft is apparent in its definition of "warships," its many provisions that address the rights and obligations of those military craft, and an option to exclude "military activities" from the convention's compulsory dispute settlement procedures. An "understanding" attached by the U.S. Senate Committee on Foreign Relations in its review of the 1982 LOS Convention affirms that "the United States understands that nothing in the Convention, including any provisions referring to 'peaceful uses' or 'peaceful purposes,' impairs the inherent right of individual or collective self-defense or rights during armed conflict."[11] The committee further explained that "this understanding, which is a statement of fact, underscores the importance the United States attaches to its right under international law to take appropriate actions in self-defense or in times of armed conflict, including, where necessary, the use of force."[12]

2. Activities on the High Seas Must Be Carried Out with Due Regard for Other States

As a global commons, the high seas are open to all states. No state may validly purport to subject any part of the high seas to its sovereignty.[13] Additionally, all states enjoy certain operational freedoms on the high seas. The high-seas freedoms must, like most internationally recognized rights and freedoms, be exercised with due regard for the interests of other states in their exercise of the freedom of the high seas,[14] and with respect to activities in the Area.[15] Those "other state"

---

8. See, e.g., UN General Assembly, Resolution 2832 (Dec. 16, 1971), G.A. Res. 2832 (XXVI) (designating the Indian Ocean as a "zone of peace").

9. The Antarctic Treaty provides that "(1) Antarctica shall be used for peaceful purposes only. There shall be prohibited, inter alia, any measure of a military nature, such as the establishment of military bases and fortifications, the carrying out of military maneuvers, as well as the testing of any type of weapon; (2) the present Treaty shall not prevent the use of military personnel or equipment for scientific research or for any other peaceful purpose." Antarctic Treaty, art. I, Dec. 1, 1959, 12 U.S.T. 794, 402 U.N.T.S. 71. See generally U.S. Department of State, Handbook of the Antarctic Treaty System (9th ed. 2002), available at http://www.state.gov/e/oes/rls/rpts/ant/ (accessed Feb. 1, 2013). Similarly, the Rush-Bagot Treaty of 1817 has largely demilitarized the Great Lakes and Lake Champlain. See also Commander's Handbook, supra, ¶ 2.6.5.2.

10. LOSC art. 88.

11. S. Exec. Rpt. No. 110-09, understanding 1 (reprinted in appendix D).

12. Id.

13. LOSC art. 89. This article confirms half of the Grotian argument that the seas are *res communis*. Article 87 confirms the second half of the Grotian argument, which concerns freedom of navigation and fishing.

14. Id. art. 87(2). Article 87(2) of the 1982 LOS Convention substitutes the phrase "due regard" for the "reasonable regard" standard in Article 2 of the 1958 Convention on the High Seas. See United Nations Convention on the Law of the Sea 1982: A Commentary, vol. III, ¶ 87 (Myron H. Nordquist et al. eds., 1995). The phrase "due regard" is also used in Articles 79, 27(4), 39(3)(a), 56(3), 58(3), 60(3), 66(3)(a), 142(1), 148, 161(4), 162(2)(d), 163(2), 167(2), 234, & 267, and in the annexes to the LOS Convention. See Walker, Definitions for the Law of the Sea, supra, at 179–88.

15. The "due regard" obligation was invoked by states challenging the closing of large areas of the high seas by states conducting nuclear weapons testing in the 1940s and 1950s. See generally Nuclear Test cases (New Zealand v. France/Australia v. France), 1974 I.C.J. 253 (Dec. 20); Myres S. McDougal, The Hydrogen Bomb Tests and the

interests include shared interests such as maritime safety, security, and stewardship. States must also exercise their high-seas freedoms in a manner that does not constitute an abuse of rights.[16]

3. Principle of Exclusive Flag State Jurisdiction

Every state, whether coastal or landlocked, has the right to sail ships flying its flag on the high seas.[17] The general rule is that a vessel on the high seas is subject to the exclusive jurisdiction of its flag state.[18] The general rule is nearly absolute for warships and other vessels owned or operated by the government and used exclusively on noncommercial government service.[19] While on the high seas they enjoy sovereign immunity under customary international law and the LOS Convention.[20] The convention recognizes certain exceptions to the general rule for nonpublic vessels. The exceptions are such that it might be more accurate to say that in a number of situations the flag state has "primary" jurisdiction rather than exclusive jurisdiction over such vessels.

4. Freedoms of the High Seas

All states enjoy certain freedoms on the high seas, subject to the principles described above and other applicable rules of international law. Those freedoms listed in Article 87 include, inter alia (meaning they include but are not limited to): (1) freedom of navigation, (2) freedom of overflight, (3) freedom to lay submarine cables and pipelines, (4) freedom to construct artificial islands and other installations permitted under international law, (5) freedom to fish, and (6) freedom to conduct scientific research.[21]

Historically, freedom of navigation has been an early casualty of interstate tensions and hostilities. In the early years of the American Republic, French and British interference with U.S. commercial shipping in order to enforce neutrality laws led to the Quasi-War with France and the War of 1812 with Great Britain. During the Cuban Missile Crisis of November 1962, the United States imposed what it styled a "quarantine" and others called a de facto (and illegal) blockade that restricted freedom of navigation on the high seas near Cuba.[22] During the conflict between the United Kingdom and Argentina over the Falkland Islands, the two belligerents subjected neutral shipping to a variety of measures, including maritime exclusionary zones. Similar warning or exclusion zones were employed by the U.S. Navy during the Iran-Iraq War of 1980–88.[23] More recently, Israel has interdicted several foreign vessels transporting weapons in regional waters under the laws of blockade, neutrality, and UN Security Council resolution enforcement.[24] Those control measures are examined in the law of naval warfare section of chapter 12.

International Law of the Sea, 49 Am. J. Int'l L. 356 (1955). The tests were hotly debated at the 1958 Geneva conference on the law of the sea, which later referred it to the UN General Assembly for appropriate action. See UNCLOS I, Resolution of Apr. 27, 1958.

16. LOSC art. 300.
17. Id. art. 90.
18. Id. art. 92(1).
19. A possible exception is a warship or other government ship or aircraft whose crew has mutinied and taken control of the ship or aircraft. See id. arts. 102–04. However, such a vessel would no longer meet the convention's definition of a "warship."
20. Id. arts. 95, 96. See also International Convention for the Unification of Certain Rules relating to the Immunity of State-Owned Vessels, art. 3, Apr. 10, 1926, 176 L.N.T.S. 199.
21. LOSC art. 87(1). Some of those freedoms are limited by provisions in Parts VI, VII.2, and XIII of the convention.
22. See Commander's Handbook, supra, ¶ 4.4.8 (suggesting three differences between quarantine and blockade).
23. See U.S. Naval War College, International Law Department, Maritime Operational Zones (Richard Jacques ed., 2006).
24. Some of the Israeli measures are discussed in chapter 11.

Environmental groups, including Greenpeace and the Sea Shepherd Conservation Society (SSCS), have employed a variety of confrontational protest measures on the high seas that were directed against vessels engaged in fishing, whaling, and oil and gas activities. One encounter in the Southern Ocean resulted in the destruction of a SSCS protest vessel and prompted the IMO to issue a resolution condemning "any action that intentionally imperils human life, the marine environment or property during demonstrations, protests or confrontations on the high seas."[25] Fixing civil liability for the harms caused by such direct action attacks can prove difficult.[26] On the other hand, at least one court has convicted environmental protesters of piracy following their attack on a vessel.[27]

C. FLAG STATE OBLIGATIONS

In what might be called the "Thames Formula" (a reference to the location of the International Maritime Organization in London), the law of the sea and the principal safety, security, and pollution prevention conventions that have developed under the auspices of the IMO over the past six decades assign the primary responsibility for ensuring that vessels comply with those conventions to the vessel's flag state.[28] The Thames Formula has its roots in customary law and the 1958 Convention on the High Seas. In preparing the 1958 convention, the ILC explained the rationale for flag state jurisdiction on the high seas: "This rule, which is generally recognized in international law, is one of the essential adjuncts of the principle of the freedom of the seas. The absence of any authority over ships sailing the high seas would lead to chaos."[29] Although the ILC's rationale certainly explains the need for flag state jurisdiction, it does not necessarily justify making the flag state's jurisdiction exclusive of other states.

The Thames Formula has not always worked well in practice, particularly in protecting the marine environment and living marine resources. In fact, some observers believe that making the flag state's jurisdiction exclusive, rather than concurrent, actually increases the risk of disorder on the high seas. The poor flag state performance record is explained by the fact that some states (the "unable" ones) lack the competence or capacity to meet their obligation to effectively police vessels flying their flag. Others (the "unwilling" ones) lack the will or commitment to do so, or even view their record of lax enforcement as an incentive for vessel owners to register ships with them, giving them a competitive advantage over responsible flag states.

1. The Registration Obligation

It bears repeating that any state—even a wholly landlocked state with no access to the sea—can be a flag state if it chooses. Should it choose to become a flag state, its obligations begin with

---

25. In January 2010, the Sea Shepherd Conservation Society vessel *Ady Gill* collided with a Japanese whaling vessel on the high seas, shearing off a section of the *Ady Gill*'s hull. Other SSCS vessels have also been involved in collisions and near-collisions with whaling vessels. IMO, Assuring Safety during Demonstrations, Protests or Confrontations on the High Seas, IMO Res. MSC.303(87) (May 17, 2010).

26. See, e.g., Fish & Fish Ltd. v. Sea Shepherd UK and Others (The *Steve Irwin*), [2012] Lloyd's L. Rep. Vol. 2, 409–15 (Adm. 2012) (holding that neither Sea Shepherd Conservation Society USA nor Paul Watson was legally responsible for attacks by the *Steven Irwin* on plaintiff's mariculture activities in the Mediterranean during SSCS's "Operation Blue Rage").

27. As discussed in the chapter 12 materials on piracy, U.S. and Dutch courts have ruled that some environmental protest activities constitute piracy under international law.

28. John Mansell, Flag State Responsibility: Historical Development and Contemporary Issues (2009).

29. ILC, 1955 Commentary to Draft Convention on the High Seas Article 4, reprinted in UN Division for Ocean Affairs and the Law of the Sea, Navigation on the High Seas: Legislative History of Part VII, Section 1 (Articles 87, 89, 90–94, & 96–98) of the UN Convention on the Law of the Sea, at 12, U.N. Sales No. E.89.V2 (1989).

vessel registration. Nonpublic vessels are, with some exceptions, required to be registered,[30] and flag states are required to issue those ships documents attesting to registration.[31] The flag state is also required to maintain a register of ships containing their names and particulars.[32]

It is for each state to fix the conditions for the grant of nationality to ships, for the registration of ships, and for the right to fly its flag (see chapter 9).[33] Although the LOS Convention requires a "genuine link" between the flag state and ships that are entitled to fly its flag,[34] it provides no criteria for evaluating whether a genuine link exists;[35] nor is there any mechanism for enforcing the genuine link requirement other than to report the matter to the flag state for action.[36] For that reason, much of the international focus has shifted from the genuine link requirement for registration to the requirement that each flag state exercise effective jurisdiction and control over its vessels.[37]

Ships (and aircraft) are given a form of legal personality not ascribed to ordinary chattels. They are said to have the "nationality" of the state whose flag they are entitled to fly.[38] The LOS Convention requires, however, that ships sail under the flag of only one state and that a ship may not change its flag during a voyage or while in a port of call, save in the case of a real transfer of ownership or change of registry.[39] A ship that is not validly registered in any state is termed "stateless." No state would have standing to assert diplomatic protection on behalf of a truly stateless vessel. In the opinion of one U.S. federal circuit court of appeals:

> Vessels without nationality are international pariahs. They have no internationally recognized right to navigate freely on the high seas. Moreover, flagless vessels are frequently not subject to the laws of a flag state. As such, they represent "floating sanctuaries from authority" and constitute a potential threat to the order and stability of navigation on the high seas. The absence of any right to navigate freely on the high seas coupled with the potential threat to order on

30. The 1986 Convention on Registration exempts vessels less than 500 tons, noncommercial vessels, and vessels not engaged in international voyages. UN Convention on Conditions for Registration of Ships, art. 2, Feb. 7, 1986. Additionally, registration and documentation requirements do not apply to public vessels.

31. LOSC art. 92(2). The United States has "firmly and successfully maintained that the regularity and validity of a registration can be questioned only by the registering state." Lauritzen v. Larsen, 345 U.S. 571, 584 (1952); Whiteman, 9 Digest of International Law, supra, at 7–11, 13–16. The international cases on this issue are discussed in chapter 9.

32. LOSC art. 94(2)(a).

33. Id. art. 91(1). This rule dates back to the Permanent Court of Arbitration's decision in the Muscat Dhows case. Muscat Dhows case (France v. Great Britain), 1916 Hague Ct. Rep. 93–109 (Perm. Ct. Arb. Aug. 8, 1905). See generally Boleslaw Boczek, Flags of Convenience: An International Legal Study (1962); Whiteman, 9 Digest of International Law, supra, § 1.

34. LOSC art. 91(1). This requirement was inspired by the ICJ's 1955 decision in Nottebohm's case, in which the court ruled that Guatemala was not required to give effect to Liechtenstein's grant of citizenship to an individual if he had no genuine link to the granting state. Nottebohm's case (Liechtenstein v. Guatemala), 1955 I.C.J. 4 (Apr. 6).

35. Relevant criteria may be found in the Convention on Conditions for Registration of Ships, Feb. 7, 1986, U.N. Doc. TD/RS/CONF/23 (1986), 26 I.L.M. 1236 (1987) (not in force); and 46 U.S.C. § 12102 (prescribing the "link" conditions necessary for registration in the United States). See generally Whiteman, 9 Digest of International Law, supra, at 7–11, 13–16.

36. See LOSC art. 94(6).

37. A state that has clear grounds to believe that proper jurisdiction and control with respect to a ship has not been exercised may report the facts to the flag state. On receiving such a report, the flag state is required to investigate the matter and, if appropriate, take any action necessary to remedy the situation. LOSC art. 94(6).

38. LOSC art. 91. The vessel's legal personality is manifested in private maritime law as well. For example, a vessel can be arrested and sued in rem (in its own name) to enforce a maritime lien on the vessel. See Alex T. Howard Jr., Personification of the Vessel: Fact or Fiction? 21 J. Mar. L. & Com. 319 (1990).

39. LOSC art. 92(1).

international waterways has led various courts to conclude that international law places no restrictions upon a nation's right to subject stateless vessels to its jurisdiction.[40]

A ship that sails under two or more flags may not claim either of the nationalities and may be "assimilated" to a ship without a nationality.[41] The convention does not prescribe rules or procedures for making such "assimilations"; nor does it define the effect of one state's assimilation on another state, including the vessel's flag state. Chapter 9 examines those issues.

Properly registered vessels sailing on the high seas are said to be subject to the exclusive jurisdiction of their flag state, save under exceptions provided by international treaty or the LOS Convention. The rule predates the 1982 LOS Convention. The PCIJ explained in the *S.S.* Lotus *LOTUS* dispute between France and Turkey in 1927 that "it is certainly true that—apart from certain special cases which are defined by international law—vessels on the high seas are subject to no authority except that of the State whose flag they fly."[42] That customary law principle was later codified in the 1958 Convention on the High Seas and the 1982 LOS Convention, although the relevant articles in those conventions speak in terms of "jurisdiction" over the vessel rather than "authority." Article 92(1) of the LOS Convention provides that "ships shall sail under the flag of one State and, save only in exceptional cases expressly provided for in international treaties or in this Convention, shall be subject to its exclusive jurisdiction on the high seas."[43]

In recognizing exclusive flag state jurisdiction over its vessels located on the high seas, neither the 1958 Convention on the High Seas nor the 1982 LOS Convention specifies which, if any, of the six customary international law bases of jurisdiction applies (i.e., territoriality or nationality). While it is true that, like certain aircraft, a vessel is said to have the nationality of the state whose flag it flies, if nationality were the only basis for jurisdiction, the flag state would not have jurisdiction over nonnationals on board the vessels. To overcome such conceptual difficulties, the courts have sometimes referred to a vessel as a "floating territory" of its flag state.[44] Because exclusive jurisdiction is lost when the vessel enters another state's waters, however, the basis cannot be strictly said to be territorial. The better view is that much of the flag state's jurisdiction is sui generis: grounded in customary law and treaties, including but not limited to the LOS Convention, rather than on one of the six bases of jurisdiction under customary international law.[45] With respect to matters beyond those expressly assigned to flag state jurisdiction

---

40. U.S. v. Marino-Garcia, 679 F.2d 1373, 1382 (11th Cir. 1982).

41. LOSC art. 92(2).

42. The S.S. *Lotus* (France v. Turkey), [1927] P.C.I.J. (ser. A) No. 10, at p. 25, ¶ 64 (Sept. 7).

43. See LOSC art. 92. See also Restatement FRLUS § 522; Robert C. F. Reuland, Note, Interference with Non-national Ships on the High Seas: Peacetime Exceptions to the Exclusivity of Flag-State Jurisdiction, 22 Vand. J. Transnat'l L. 1161 (1989). The predecessor article in the 1958 Convention on the High Seas was held not to be self-executing. Accordingly, an individual could not assert a violation of the article as a defense to prosecution. U.S. v. Postal, 589 F.2d 862, 873 (5th Cir. 1979).

44. Lauritzen v. Larson, 358 U.S. 571, 585 (1953). Earlier, in a case involving statutory interpretation, the Supreme Court referred to the "floating territory" concept as "a figure of speech, a metaphor," and concluded that flag-state jurisdiction "partakes more of the characteristics of personal than of territorial sovereignty." Cunard S.S. v. Mellon, 262 U.S. 100, 123 (1923). In the *S.S. Lotus* case, the PCIJ reasoned that a vessel is "assimilated" to the territory of its flag state. S.S. *Lotus*, supra, ¶ 64. If ships truly were "floating territory" of their flag states, nonpublic vessels could serve as platforms for asylum while in another state's internal waters or provide a basis for citizenship under the jus soli principle, but that is not the case. Cf. Lam Mow v. Nagle, 24 F.2d 316 (9th Cir. 1928) (holding that a person born on a U.S.-flag ship was not born in U.S. territory and was therefore not entitled to U.S. citizenship); Jee v. Weedin, 24 F.2d 962 (9th Cir. 1928) (Chinese immigrant did not "enter" the United States by embarking on a U.S.-flag vessel). See generally Whiteman, 9 Digest of International Law, supra, at 22–23, 37, & 39.

45. Treaty-based jurisdiction is binding only on other parties to the treaty and is therefore not truly universal.

by the LOS Convention or another applicable treaty, the flag state's jurisdiction might be most accurately characterized as "quasi territorial."[46] This quasi-territorial characterization was reinforced by ITLOS when it ruled that the flag state has standing to assert claims on behalf of the vessel's crew, even though they might not be nationals of the flag state. The tribunal explained that "the ship, everything on it, and every person involved or interested in its operations are treated as an entity linked to the flag state. The nationalities of the persons are not relevant."[47]

Returning to the *S.S. Lotus* case, in which the PCIJ declared that "it is certainly true that—apart from certain special cases which are defined by international law—vessels on the high seas are subject to no authority except that of the State whose flag they fly," it might not be immediately clear whether the court was referring to jurisdiction to prescribe, enforce, or adjudicate, or all three. The court answered that question in part by its hypothetical example involving a foreign warship on scene at the time of a high-seas collision. The court explained that if the warship were to send an officer to board the foreign vessel to conduct an investigation or take evidence, such an act (i.e., an exercise of enforcement jurisdiction) "would undoubtedly be contrary to international law."[48] On the other hand, the court's decision upheld Turkey's prosecution (i.e., jurisdiction to adjudicate a criminal case) of the French vessel's officer once he arrived in Turkey and its application of Turkish law to the French officer's case (jurisdiction to prescribe). Thus, in the court's opinion, the rule of exclusive flag state jurisdiction over vessels on the high seas was one of enforcement jurisdiction only. With respect to the issue of jurisdiction to prescribe and apply laws, the court explained that "by virtue of the principle of the freedom of the seas, a ship is placed in the same position as national territory," and "what occurs on board a vessel on the high seas must be regarded as if it occurred on the territory of the State whose flag it flies."[49] If, therefore, Turkey would have a basis for exercising its jurisdiction over persons who committed similar acts in France—based, for example, on the principle of an extraterritorial act having an effect in Turkey—then jurisdiction may similarly be extended to a French vessel on the high seas. Of course, states are free to reject such a permissive rule, as they later did for high-seas collision cases in the 1958 Convention on the High Seas and the 1982 LOS Convention.

Whether based on nationality or quasi territoriality, the flag state's jurisdiction over its nonpublic vessels must not be confused with the state's sovereignty with respect to its warships and other public vessels. The flag state's relationship to its commercial and recreational vessels is one of jurisdiction and control, not sovereignty. Accordingly, an impermissible interference with a foreign nonpublic vessel's navigation on the high seas would violate the rule of exclusive flag state jurisdiction, but it would not constitute a violation of the flag state's sovereignty.[50]

2. The Effective Jurisdiction and Control Obligation

The LOS Convention articles on flag state responsibility make it clear that the flag state's exercise of jurisdiction over its vessels is neither permissive nor discretionary. Flag states have an inter-

---

46. See John Bassett Moore, A Digest of International Law, vol. 1, § 174 (1906) (adopting the "quasi territorial" label). One corollary of the quasi-territorial nature of vessels is that an act by another vessel that has an "effect" on a state's vessel (colliding with the vessel and injuring someone on board) might give rise to effects-based jurisdiction. That theory was accepted by the PCIJ in the *S.S. Lotus* case.

47. The M/V *Saiga* No. 2, supra, ¶ 106. The breadth of the tribunal's statement sweeps in matters not contemplated by Article 94, and must therefore be grounded in nontreaty sources of law.

48. The S.S. *Lotus*, supra, ¶ 64.

49. Id. ¶ 65.

50. See Cunard S.S. Co. v. Mellon, 262 U.S. 100, 123 (1923) (holding that flag-state jurisdiction partakes more of personal jurisdiction than of territorial sovereignty). Contra U.S. v. Flores, 289 U.S. 137, 158–59 (1933) (merchant vessel is deemed to be part of the territory of the United States).

national duty to exercise jurisdiction and control over vessels registered in the state (examined in chapter 9).[51] A flag state's breach of its obligations under the LOS Convention might justify another state in taking proportionate countermeasures or initiating a legal action in an appropriate forum (see chapter 14). The flag state must exercise its jurisdiction and control in a manner that both is effective and does not constitute an abuse of rights.[52] The UN General Assembly has repeatedly drawn attention to the failure of some flag states to effectively fulfill their obligations to exercise effective jurisdiction and control over vessels flying their flag. In language analogous to the complementarity articles of the Rome Statute on the International Criminal Court,[53] some flag states are unable to do so, some are unwilling, and some are both. The assembly has gone on to urge the unable or unwilling flag states to get out of the business, by admonishing that flag states "without an effective maritime administration and appropriate legal frameworks to establish or enhance the necessary infrastructure, legislative and enforcement capabilities to ensure effective compliance with, and implementation and enforcement of, their responsibilities under international law," should "consider declining the granting of the right to fly their flag to new vessels, suspending their registry or not opening a registry."[54]

Although not suggested by the General Assembly, flag states that are unable to discharge their obligations on their own could choose, as some states already have, to enlist the assistance of other states through bilateral boarding agreements (discussed below)[55] or other interstate cooperative measures. Indeed, the port state control regime introduced in chapter 4 may effectively force such states to "outsource" some of their responsibilities, because vessels flying the flag of a state with a poor safety record are assigned a high-risk rating by port states, leading to heightened scrutiny and delay or even denial of port entry.[56]

3. Flag State Obligations for Warships and Other Sovereign Immune Vessels

Warships on the high seas have complete immunity from the jurisdiction of any state other than the flag state.[57] Naval auxiliaries and other ships owned or operated by a state and used only on government noncommercial service also have complete immunity from the jurisdiction of any state other than the flag state.[58] Although warships and other public vessels on the high seas are immune from enforcement actions by states other than their flag state, the flag state has the same "control" obligations with respect to its public vessels and bears international responsibility for the vessels' violations.

---

51. LOSC art. 94(1).
52. LOSC art. 300.
53. Under the complementarity rule in Article 17 of the Rome Statute, the ICC will defer investigation and prosecution of crimes to the nation-state with jurisdiction "unless the State is unwilling or unable genuinely to carry out the investigation or prosecution." Rome Statute of the International Criminal Court [hereinafter "Rome Statute of the ICC"], art. 17, July 17, 1998, 2187 U.N.T.S. 90.
54. G.A. Res. 66/231, ¶ 128 (2011); U.N. Doc. A/RES/66/231 (2011).
55. Granting consent in such cases actually enhances the flag state's control over its vessels. See Bernard H. Oxman, The Territorial Temptation: A Siren Song at Sea, 100 Am. J. Int'l L. 830, 844 (2006).
56. The UN General Assembly recently recognized that responsibility now extends beyond the flag state. In its 2011 resolution on the law of the sea, the assembly reaffirmed that "flag, port and coastal States all bear responsibility for ensuring the effective implementation and enforcement of international instruments relating to maritime security and safety, in accordance with international law, in particular the Convention, and that flag States have primary responsibility that requires further strengthening, including through increased transparency of ownership of vessels." G.A. Res. 66/231, supra, ¶ 127.
57. LOSC arts. 95, 29–32, & 236.
58. Id. art. 96.

D. ENFORCEMENT ON THE HIGH SEAS

Flag states have a positive obligation to exercise effective jurisdiction and control over their vessels. The obligation embraces both prescriptive and enforcement jurisdiction. A flag state's prescriptive jurisdiction over its vessels exists regardless of the vessel's location and extends to the vessel, its crew and passengers, and the cargo. When such vessels enter the EEZ, contiguous zone, territorial sea, archipelagic waters, or internal waters of another state, however, they are subject to the coastal state's sovereignty, sovereign rights, jurisdiction, or control, depending on the vessel's location and status. Jurisdiction in such cases may be shared concurrently between the coastal state and the flag state.

On the high seas the flag state's jurisdiction is said to be exclusive. Even for lawfully registered vessels, however, the general assertion that the flag state's jurisdiction or authority over its vessels while on the high seas is always exclusive is not quite true.[59] The LOS Convention includes several exceptions that permit non–flag states to "interfere" with vessels on the high seas or to exercise jurisdiction over such vessels, and other treaties may extend the enforcement powers of non–flag states even further.[60] Given the singular importance of the laws on enforcement jurisdiction to maritime law-enforcement operations, a more detailed examination of those issues is included in chapter 11.

1. Stateless Vessels

Customary law and the LOS Convention recognize that vessels without a nationality and vessels that have been "assimilated" to a vessel without a nationality do not, or potentially do not, enjoy the protection of exclusive flag state control.[61] Some modern commentators argue—contrary to the position adopted by U.S. courts—that a stateless vessel is not, by virtue of its stateless condition alone, subject to the jurisdiction of every state.[62] They argue instead for an examination of the recognized bases for jurisdiction under international law, including the territoriality, nationality, protective, and passive personality principles. At the same time, they point out (and U.S. courts generally agree) that any state exercising jurisdiction over the vessel must have first enacted laws applicable to that vessel and its activities in that particular location (see chapter 9 on legal issues raised by stateless vessels).

2. Vessels Engaged in Universal Crimes

Of the six recognized bases for jurisdiction under international law, universality is probably the most misunderstood. In the maritime domain, only one crime of universal jurisdiction is likely to be encountered: the crime of piracy, as defined by international law (definitions under domestic laws may differ). Other maritime crimes, such as slave transport and trading, are sometimes

59. For excerpts of the Department of State memorandum on maritime interdiction and law enforcement, including the exceptions to exclusive flag state jurisdiction on the high seas, see U.S. Department of State, Digest of United States Practice in International Law 1989–1990, at 448–52.
60. Professor Colombos took the position that non–flag state interference with vessels on the high seas is presumed to be illegitimate and that the burden is on the state asserting an exception. Colombos, supra, at 311. It is not clear whether the suggestion was based on his interpretation of the then-existing law, comity, or his policy preferences.
61. In holding that a stateless vessel (or, more accurately, the crew of a stateless vessel) has no rights under the law of the sea, the court in U.S. v. Cortes, 588 F.2d 106 (5th Cir. 1979), explained that "to secure the protection afforded merchant vessels on the high seas, a vessel must accept the duties imposed by registration. This the [defendant's vessel] failed to do; her crew cannot complain of the results." Id. at 110. See also U.S. v. Rosero, 42 F.3d 166, 171 (3d Cir. 1994).
62. Churchill & Lowe, supra, at 214.

incorrectly referred to as crimes of universal jurisdiction or confusingly referred to as "quasi-universal" crimes.[63]

The 1982 LOS Convention calls on all states, including flag states, to cooperate in suppressing a variety of activities deemed inimical to the public order. For example, since at least the nineteenth century all states have had an obligation to cooperate in the suppression of piracy and slave trading. In the twentieth century a requirement for all states to cooperate in suppressing illicit traffic in narcotic drugs and psychotropic substances was added. Similarly, states now have a duty to suppress unauthorized broadcasting from the high seas and trafficking in weapons and even humans. Finally, the LOS Convention requires states to cooperate to conserve and manage living marine resources on the high seas and to protect and preserve the marine environment. In all but one case (piracy), the obligation to suppress these activities does not confer universal jurisdiction.

3. The Right of Hot Pursuit

The right of hot pursuit is one of two "jurisdiction extenders" available to the coastal state (the other being the customary law doctrine of constructive presence) and a further exception to exclusive flag state jurisdiction on the high seas. It permits the coastal state, in strictly limited circumstances, to pursue a foreign vessel beyond areas over which the coastal state has some measure of territorial jurisdiction. Article 111 of the 1982 LOS Convention carries forward, with some additions, the hot pursuit doctrine set out in the 1958 Convention on the High Seas.[64] It provides that "the hot pursuit of a foreign ship may be undertaken when the competent authorities of the coastal State have good reason to believe that the ship has violated the laws and regulations of that State. Such pursuit must be commenced when the foreign ship or one of its boats is within the internal waters, the archipelagic waters, the territorial sea or the contiguous zone of the pursuing State, and may only be continued outside the territorial sea or the contiguous zone if the pursuit has not been interrupted."[65] The LOS Convention extends the right to violations in the EEZ.[66]

Close inspection of Article 111 reveals that it imposes a number of conditions and prerequisites for the exercise of hot pursuit. ITLOS ruled that all must be met for a hot pursuit to be lawful.[67] The hot pursuit rule and the related constructive presence doctrine are examined in chapter 11.

4. The Peacetime Right of Visit

The modern right of visit, as codified in Article 110 of the 1982 LOS Convention, represents an attempt to reconcile the principles of freedom of navigation and exclusive flag state control, on the one hand, and the common interest in ensuring effective enforcement of laws, on the other. It confers on warships and other duly authorized ships or aircraft the right to approach,

---

63. Article 99 of the LOS Convention requires all states to take effective measures to prevent and punish the transport of slaves in ships authorized to fly their flag (see chapter 11). Although the convention does not confer universal jurisdiction over such vessels, it does provide for a right of visit in situations in which a foreign warship has reasonable grounds for believing that a vessel is engaged in the slave trade. LOS Convention, art. 110.

64. 1958 Convention on the High Seas, supra, art. 23. See also Nicholas M. Poulantzas, The Right of Hot Pursuit in International Law (2d ed. 2002).

65. LOSC art. 111(1).

66. Id. art. 111(2).

67. The M/V Saiga No. 2, supra, ¶ 146.

board, and possibly search a foreign vessel located on the high seas under circumstances set out in the convention.[68] The right of visit is a valuable and sometimes essential tool in maritime law enforcement. Its exercise over the years has raised two recurring issues. The first concerns the relatively narrow grounds for exercising the right, and whether that list of grounds is likely to expand.[69] The second issue concerns the distinction between peacetime right-of-visit boardings and the similar right of belligerents to conduct visit, board, and search operations under the law of naval warfare.

The right of visit is sometime compared by lawyers in the United States to a "Terry stop" under U.S. constitutional law. In *Terry v. Ohio*, the U.S. Supreme Court held that law enforcement officers may, consistent with the Fourth Amendment prohibition on unreasonable searches and seizures, briefly stop an individual when they have a "reasonable suspicion" that the person has committed, is committing, or is about to commit a crime, and a "reasonable belief" that the person "may be armed and presently dangerous."[70] The reasonable suspicion standard for a Terry stop is lower than the probable cause standard that must generally be met before a more invasive search will be constitutionally permissible. Like a right-of-visit boarding, which requires a finding of "reasonable grounds for suspecting" a vessel is engaged in certain activities, the *Terry* doctrine essentially recognizes a limited power of law enforcement to "interfere" with an individual when justified by reasonable suspicion and belief.

a. The Customary International Law Right of Approach   *Approach ≠ visit*

Article 110 has its roots in two centuries of state practice and Article 22 of the 1958 Geneva Convention on the High Seas. Legal commentators and early court decisions distinguished between the "approach" on a vessel and a "visit," or boarding, of the vessel.[71] The right of approach, which predates what is now referred to as the right of visit, refers to the right to intercept the vessel; inspect it from a safe distance to determine its name, flag, and home port; and (modernly) to hail it on the radio and request information. The right to approach a vessel on the high seas to determine the vessel's identity and flag has been a common feature of the law of the sea for centuries.[72] For the latter half of the eighteenth century and much of the nineteenth century, naval vessels relied on the right of approach (sometimes called "reconnaissance" or *enquête ou vérification du pavilion*) in their efforts to interdict the twin scourges of piracy and slave trading and transport. The right of approach was examined in a seminal 1826 decision by the U.S. Supreme Court. Writing for the Court in *The* Marianna Flora case, Justice Joseph Story first distinguished between a belligerent's right of visitation and search in time of war and the peacetime right of approach. In describing the latter right, he explained that "in respect to ships of war sailing, as in the present case, under the authority of their government, to arrest pirates, and other public offenders, there is no reason why they may not approach any vessels descried at sea, for the

---

68. Marjorie M. Whiteman, 4 Digest of International Law § 7 (1965).
69. In particular, it is sometimes asked whether the listed grounds for a right of visit are likely to expand to meet the demand for high-seas enforcement of laws prohibiting trafficking in drugs, humans, and weapons, including weapons of mass destruction.
70. Terry v. Ohio, 392 U.S. 1, 30 (1968) (holding that the Fourth Amendment does not preclude a "stop and frisk").
71. Ian Brownlie, Principles of Public International Law 306–7 (James Crawford ed., 8th ed. 2012) (a right of "approach" is recognized by customary international law, even though not mentioned in the LOS Convention). See also Reuland, Interference with Non-national Ships, supra, at 1169–70; Whiteman, 4 Digest of International Law, supra, at 670. The comprehensive classical treatise is Joseph Lohengrin Frascona, Visit, Search, and Seizure on the High Seas (1938).
72. Colombos, supra, §§ 334–336, at 311–14; O'Connell, supra, vol. II, at 801–08; McDougal & Burke, supra, at 885–93, 909–14. See also Coast Guard MLE Manual, supra, ¶ 5.D.5.a.

purpose of ascertaining their real characters. Such a right seems indispensable for the fair and discreet exercise of their authority."[73]

One of the issues presented in the 1826 Marianna Flora case concerned whether the vessel being approached was justified in firing on the approaching vessel out of concern that it was in fact a pirate ship or otherwise harbored hostile intent. Justice Story explained the obligation of the vessel being approached: "No ship is, under such circumstances, bound to lie by, or wait the approach of any other ship. She is at full liberty to pursue her voyage in her own way, and to use all necessary precaution to avoid a suspected sinister enterprise or hostile attack."[74] With respect to the approached vessel's use of force, Justice Story added that "she is not at liberty to inflict injuries upon other innocent parties, simply because of conjectural dangers."[75]

As Justice Story's opinion demonstrates, the traditional right of the warship to approach during peacetime did not imply a duty by the approached vessel to respond or to slow or otherwise maneuver to accommodate the approach. Nor did the peacetime right of approach include at that time a right to board, or "visit," the vessel (*droit de visite*) if the approach failed to satisfy the warship of the vessel's innocence or the validity of its nationality. In the nineteenth-century "visitation crisis" between the United States and Great Britain, the United States denied that Great Britain had the right to visit (board) vessels on the high seas flying the U.S. flag and suspected of being engaged in the slave trade to determine if they were in fact U.S. vessels. Britain eventually agreed there was no such right in 1858.[76] Later, during the Prohibition period in the United States, the two states would again find themselves on opposite sides of the issue of boarding foreign vessels on the high seas, with the United States now asserting expanded boarding powers.[77]

When the ILC commenced its work on codifying the law of the sea in 1950, it began with the understanding that while the right of approach had long been a common practice in time of peace,[78] the right of visit presented a more difficult question. The historical position was that visit and search were strictly belligerent rights, and to exercise them in the absence of war was to offend against the freedom of the high seas.[79] The commission initially adhered to the traditional view and remained resistant to proposals that expanded the peacetime right of approach to include a follow-on right of visit and search.[80] Eventually, however, the ILC relented and

---

73. The *Marianna Flora*, 4 U.S. (11 Wheat.) 1, 43–44 (1826).

74. Id. at 44.

75. Id.

76. See Francis Wharton, Digest of International Law, vol. 3 at 122–71 (2d ed. 1887); Moore, Digest of International Law, supra, vol. 2 at 914–51.

77. Many of the mother ships operating off the U.S. Atlantic and Gulf of Mexico coasts during the Prohibition era flew the British flag and hailed from Canada or one of the British insular territories. See generally Harold Waters, Smugglers of Spirits: Prohibition and the Coast Guard Patrol (2007); Malcolm F. Willoughby, Rum War at Sea (2001).

78. See Summary Records of the 2nd Session, 1950 Y.B. Int'l L. Comm'n, vol. I, at 197, ¶ 134, U.N. Doc. A/CN.4/SER.A/1950 (concluding that "in the case of doubt as to the nationality of a ship, any State had the right to approach").

79. Id. at 197, ¶ 135 ("The right to approach does exist, but not the right of investigation"). The United States argued that "the right to visit and search a foreign vessel on the high seas is regarded as pertaining to a belligerent as such, and hence is a privilege which no State may exercise in time of peace." Summary Records of the 2nd Session, 1950 Y.B. Int'l L. Comm'n, vol. II, at 61–62, U.N. Doc. A/CN.4/SER.A/1950/Add.1. Indeed, in the initial year of its work on the Convention on the High Seas, all of the commission's members were in apparent agreement that it "was undesirable to allow it to be understood that a warship had the right to examine papers." 1950 Y.B. Int'l L. Comm'n, vol. I, at 198, ¶ 17. See also Colombos, supra, at 311.

80. See McDougal & Burke, supra, at 889 (noting that "from the beginning . . . [the ILC] adopted an explicit attitude . . . [that was] rigidly uncompromising in prohibition of interference").

included a qualified "noninterference" rule in its draft for the 1958 Geneva diplomatic conference. The commission was careful, however, to affirm its position that any right of visit is exceptional and vests only in the special situations described in the article. This was demonstrated in
its refusal to adopt a proposal that would have recognized a general right to verify a vessel's flag
regardless of whether the vessel was suspicious.[81]

b. Article 22 of the 1958 Convention on the High Seas

The UNCLOS I delegates who met in Geneva in 1958 incorporated an expanded right of visit
on the high seas. Article 22 of the 1958 Convention on the High Seas provides:

> 1. Except where acts of interference derive from powers conferred by treaty,
>   a warship which encounters a foreign merchant ship on the high seas is not
>   justified in boarding her unless there is reasonable ground for suspecting:
>
>   (a) That the ship is engaged in piracy; or
>   (b) That the ship is engaged in the slave trade; or
>   (c) That though flying a foreign flag or refusing to show its flag, the ship is,
>   in reality, of the same nationality as the warship.
>
> 2. In the cases provided for in sub-paragraphs (a), (b) and (c) above, the warship
>   may proceed to verify the ship's right to fly its flag. To this end, it may send
>   a boat under the command of an officer to the suspected ship. If suspicion
>   remains after the documents have been checked, it may proceed to a further
>   examination on board the ship, which must be carried out with all possible
>   consideration.
>
> 3. If the suspicions prove to be unfounded, and provided that the ship boarded
>   has not committed any act justifying them, it shall be compensated for any
>   loss or damage that may have been sustained.

In contrast to Article 110 of the 1982 LOS Convention, Article 22 of the 1958 Convention
on the High Seas lacked a title or caption and in fact did not use the terms "approach" or "visit."
The first paragraph also appears to equate "interference" with boarding. Despite the fact that
Article 22 authorized boarding and, in some cases, a "further examination," which clearly go
beyond the customary law right of approach, U.S. courts and commentators commonly continued to refer to the two rights simply as the right of approach.[82] The usage may reflect the fact
that, throughout much of its history, the United States opposed attempts to analogize between
the peacetime right of approach and the belligerent's right of visit and search.[83]

c. Peacetime Right of Visit under the 1982 LOS Convention

UNCLOS III delegates largely carried forward the right of visit codified under the 1958 Convention on the High Seas and added two new grounds for exercising the right. The right of visit
is now set out in Article 110 of the LOS Convention.

---

81. 1955 Y.B. Int'l L. Comm'n, supra, vol. I, at 33, ¶ 25.
82. See, e.g., U.S. v. Ricardo, 619 F.2d 1124, 1130 (5th Cir. 1980).
83. See Louis Sohn, Peacetime Use of Force on the High Seas, Comment, 64 U.S. Nav. War Coll. Int'l L. Studies 38,
    38 (1991).

ARTICLE 110. Right of visit

1. Except where acts of interference derive from powers conferred by treaty, a warship which encounters on the high seas a foreign ship, other than a ship entitled to complete immunity in accordance with articles 95 and 96, is not justified in boarding it unless there is reasonable ground for suspecting that:

   (a) the ship is engaged in piracy;

   (b) the ship is engaged in the slave trade;

   (c) the ship is engaged in unauthorized broadcasting and the flag State of the warship has jurisdiction under article 109;

   (d) the ship is without nationality; or

   (e) though flying a foreign flag or refusing to show its flag, the ship is, in reality, of the same nationality as the warship.

2. In the cases provided for in paragraph 1, the warship may proceed to verify the ship's right to fly its flag. To this end, it may send a boat under the command of an officer to the suspected ship. If suspicion remains after the documents have been checked, it may proceed to a further examination on board the ship, which must be carried out with all possible consideration.

3. If the suspicions prove to be unfounded, and provided that the ship boarded has not committed any act justifying them, it shall be compensated for any loss or damage that may have been sustained.

4. These provisions apply *mutatis mutandis* to military aircraft.

5. These provisions also apply to any other duly authorized ships or aircraft clearly marked and identifiable as being on government service.[84]

Like Article 22 of the 1958 Convention on the High Seas, Article 110 addresses the grounds for a warship to "interfere" with a foreign vessel on the high seas and the limited right of a warship to "board" the vessel. Close reading of Article 110 reveals that the right of visit comprises up to three distinct phases: the boarding phase; the document examination phase; and, in some cases, the search phase.[85] Thus, Article 110 explains that the warship may send over a boarding team to check the suspect vessel's documents and, if suspicion remains after inspecting the documents, the team may further examine the vessel.[86]

In exercising a right-of-visit boarding, the enforcing vessel is no longer limited to sending boarding teams over by small boat. In contrast to Article 22 of the 1958 Convention on the High Seas, which spoke only of sending a boarding team by boat, Article 110 of the 1982 LOS Convention expressly extends the right of visit to military aircraft and any other duly authorized ships or aircraft clearly marked and identifiable as being on government service. That change facilitates the now common practice for warships to send boarding teams by helicopter, particularly with respect to noncompliant vessels.

---

84. See LOSC art. 110. See also Restatement FRLUS § 522; Churchill & Lowe, supra, at 210–13; Commander's Handbook, supra, ¶ 3.4. By its terms, Article 110 applies only to vessels on the high seas; however, Articles 88–115 also apply within a coastal state's EEZ insofar as such an application would not be incompatible with the EEZ regime. LOSC art. 58(2).

85. LOSC art. 110(2).

86. Id. art. 110(2). See generally Whiteman, 4 Digest of International Law, supra, at 515–22; Anna van Zwanenberg, Interference with Ships on the High Seas, 10 Int'l & Comp. L. Q. 785 (1961).

Strictly speaking, the right of visit is only an exception to the noninterference duty, not a basis for exercising jurisdiction over foreign vessels on the high seas.[87] However, an approach and boarding initiated under the right of visit might reveal a basis for the boarding state to exercise jurisdiction (or to seek the flag state's consent to exercise jurisdiction). On the other hand, if the suspicions that prompted the visit prove to be unfounded, and the boarded vessel did not commit any act that justified the boarding, the vessel's owner must be compensated for any loss or damage sustained.[88]

As suggested earlier, the peacetime right of visit under the 1982 LOS Convention must be distinguished from the belligerents' right of visit and search to enforce the law of neutrality under the law of naval warfare or to enforce a blockade. Under the law of naval warfare, a belligerent warship may ensure the neutral character of merchant ships outside neutral territory—that is, it may confirm that a merchant vessel of a neutral state is not carrying contraband in support of the enemy (see chapter 12).[89]

d. Grounds for Exercising the Modern Right of Visit

The 1958 Convention on the High Seas provides three grounds for exercising a right of visit: suspicion that the vessel was engaged in (1) piracy or (2) the slave trade or (3) was of the same flag as the approaching warship. The 1982 LOS Convention added two new grounds for exercising the right: (4) suspicion that the vessel is without nationality (i.e., stateless) and (5) suspicion that it is engaged in unauthorized broadcasting. While both grounds are available to states that are party to the LOS Convention, the paucity of state practice casts doubt on whether customary international law recognizes a right of visit in cases of unauthorized broadcasting.[90] By contrast, substantial state practice without apparent protest confirms that the right can be exercised with respect to vessels suspected of being stateless.

Chapter 11 examines the common maritime law-enforcement applications of the right of visit. It should be noted here, however, that the right of visit is not necessarily triggered by suspicions relating to all of the activities that states have an obligation to suppress and/or prohibit. For example, all states have an obligation to suppress illicit traffic in narcotic drugs and psychotropic substances; however, there is no right of visit against vessels suspected of engaging in such trafficking. Similarly, several UN Security Council resolutions call on states to prevent trafficking in weapons of mass destruction and supplying of arms to designated terrorist groups, yet neither the LOS Convention nor the resolutions authorize right-of-visit boardings of ships suspected of violating the terms of the resolution. The *Restatement (Third) of Foreign Relations Law of the United States* "suggests" that the right to inspect foreign ships on the high seas can be extended to "ships carrying stolen nuclear materials or escaping terrorists."[91] It admits, however, that "the present international law on the subject is unclear,"[92] and is less than clear about whether its bold suggestion is based on legal competence to take such enforcement action or the customary law

---

87. See Restatement FRLUS § 522.
88. LOSC art. 110(3). The apparent rationale for strict liability for unfounded boardings is to deter abuses. See Brownlie, supra, at 308. While that goal certainly justifies liability, it does not necessarily justify strict liability rather than liability based on fault.
89. See San Remo Manual, supra, ¶ 118 (in exercising their legal rights in an armed conflict at sea, belligerent warships and military aircraft have a right to visit and search merchant vessels outside neutral waters when there are reasonable grounds for suspecting they are subject to capture).
90. Indeed, the unauthorized high-seas broadcasting problem had largely disappeared before the LOS Convention was completed in 1982.
91. Restatement FRLUS § 522 n.6.
92. Id. The reporters cite no legal authority for the "suggestion."

of countermeasures. Such arguments for an expansive reading of grounds for exercising the right of approach run up against several obstacles. Most notably, the paragraph 1 chapeau to Article 110 does not include an "inter alia" qualifier, the absence of which indicates that the five listed grounds for exercising the right are exhaustive.

5. Powers Conferred by Treaty

The 1982 LOS Convention recognizes that it may be supplemented by other treaties.[93] More particularly, the chapeau to Article 110, which prohibits states other than the flag state from interfering with a vessel's navigation, recognizes that acts of interference may be based on "power conferred by treaty." Important examples are the bilateral boarding agreements between the United States and flag states to conduct boardings to intercept the illicit transport of weapons of mass destruction or missile delivery systems,[94] and those tailored to the suppression of drug trafficking and migrant smuggling.[95] Although some commentators have argued that the term "treaty" should be limited to written agreements between states, there is no reason to conclude that Article 110 was meant to exclude oral, ad hoc, agreements. Oral international agreements, while not common, can be valid and binding "treaties," and significant state practice supports the validity of ad hoc oral agreements as a valid basis for boardings. The United States has long recognized the validity of ad hoc oral ship-boarding agreements with flag states (see chapter 11).

6. Powers Conferred by the UN Security Council

On occasion the UN Security Council has invoked its enforcement powers under Chapter VII of the UN Charter to restrict or prohibit trade to a state or area of conflict when necessary to preserve or restore international peace and security. All states are obligated to comply with Chapter VII enforcement measures,[96] and the state's obligations under the UN Charter take precedence over other treaty obligations,[97] including those under the LOS Convention. Accordingly, a Security Council decision authorizing or requiring foreign vessel interdictions on the high seas has the effect of overriding the flag state's exclusive jurisdiction. Such resolutions are rare (see chapter 12 on maritime security operations).

7. Consent to Enforcement Measures

A warship or other duly authorized vessel that encounters a foreign vessel that would otherwise be immune from interference with its navigation might nevertheless intercept, board, and even search the vessel pursuant to consent. Consent must be given by a party competent to do so, such as the flag state, the coastal state in whose waters the vessel is located, or the master of the

---

93. See LOSC art. 311(2) ("This Convention shall not alter the rights and obligations of States Parties which arise from other agreements compatible with this Convention and which do not affect the enjoyment by other States Parties of their rights or the performance of their obligations under this Convention").

94. The boarding agreements are posted at U.S. Department of State, Proliferation Security Agreement, Ship Boarding Agreements, available at http://www.state.gov/t/isn/c27733.htm (accessed Feb. 1, 2013).

95. As chapter 11 explains, the bilateral counternarcotics agreements operate within the framework established by Article 108 of the 1982 UN Convention on the Law of the Sea and Article 17 of the 1988 UN Convention against Illicit Traffic in Narcotic Drugs and Psychotropic Substances.

96. UN Charter art. 49 ("The Members of the United Nations shall join in affording mutual assistance in carrying out the measures decided upon by the Security Council").

97. Id. art. 103.

vessel.[98] In fact, the best way to honor the principle of flag state primacy and the sovereignty and paramount interest of coastal states in their adjacent waters, while at the same time conforming to relevant duties to "cooperate" in maintaining the public order, is for patrolling states to request consent to enforcement actions that infringe on the rights and interests of other states, and for the requested state to agree.[99] It is crucial in all cases in which actions are being carried out pursuant to consent that any limits placed on that consent be observed. If the consent is withdrawn and there is no other basis for exercising jurisdiction or control, the actions must be terminated. Flag states commonly authorize limited enforcement measures, such as a right to board but not to search or seize or otherwise exercise jurisdiction. The consenting state might also limit the use of force by the boarding state (see chapter 11 for more on consensual boardings).

E. COLLISIONS, NAVIGATION INCIDENTS, DISTRESS, AND RESCUE

States are directed by the LOS Convention to require the masters of ships flying their flag to render assistance to any person found at sea in danger of being lost, insofar as the master can do so without serious danger to his or her ship, the crew, or the passengers.[100] The master is further directed to proceed with all possible speed to the rescue of persons in distress. Additional obligations are imposed on vessels involved in a collision. Under those circumstances the masters of the involved vessels have an obligation to render assistance to the other ship, its crew, and passengers and, when possible, to inform the other ship of the name of the ship, its port of registry, and the nearest port at which it will call.[101] In the United States these obligations are set out in what is commonly referred to as the Standby Act[102] and in service regulations.[103] Breach of this humanitarian obligation in 1989 led to a dereliction-of-duty conviction of the commanding officer of the amphibious transport ship USS *Dubuque* (LPD-8).[104]

One of the U.S. Coast Guard's eleven missions is to "render aid to distressed persons, vessels, and aircraft on and under the high seas and on and under the waters over which the United States has jurisdiction."[105] The statute also authorizes the Coast Guard to "destroy or tow into port sunken or floating dangers to navigation,"[106] an authority that may be invoked in response

---

98. Consent as a fact precluding a finding of wrongfulness is examined in Article 20 of the ILC's Draft Articles on State Responsibility, which are addressed in chapter 14. The Commentary to Article 20 addresses the effect of consent by private parties.
99. See generally U.S. Department of State, Cumulative Digest of United States Practice in International Law 1981–1988, vol. 2, at 1386–99 (1994).
100. LOSC art. 98(1); see also 46 U.S.C. § 2304. The SOLAS Convention and the Salvage Convention impose a similar obligation. See SOLAS Convention, supra, ch. V, reg. 33(a); International Convention on Salvage [hereinafter "SALCON"], art. 10, Apr. 28, 1989, S. Treaty Doc. No. 102-12, 37 Stat. 1658, 1953 U.N.T.S. 193. One commentator has concluded that the SALCON is self-executing. Martin Davies, Whatever Happened to the Salvage Convention of 1989?, 39 J. Mar. L. & Com. 463, 463 (2008).
101. LOSC art. 98(1). Surprisingly, the convention does not directly address the obligations of the master regarding his vessel's crew or passengers, an issue that was hotly debated following the grounding of the *Costa Concordia* in Italian waters in 2012 that resulted in more than thirty deaths.
102. 46 U.S.C. § 2303. The statute includes a Good Samaritan immunity provision. See 46 U.S.C. § 2303(c). See also Warshauer v. Lloyd Sabaudo, S.A., 71 F.2d 146 (2d Cir. 1934) (affirming dismissal of complaint for damages arising from failure to rescue).
103. See, e.g., U.S. Navy Regulations, supra, art. 0925; U.S. Coast Guard Regulations, supra, art. 4-1-7.
104. See Jane Fritch, Balian Guilty in Viet Boat Case, to Get Reprimand, L.A. Times, Feb. 24, 1989, available at http://articles.latimes.com/1989-02-24/news/mn-266_1_refugee (accessed Feb. 1, 2013). The warship encountered a boat full of refugees fleeing Vietnam in the South China Sea and failed to do anything more than provide them with food and water. Only 52 of the 110 refugees who originally boarded the boat survived.
105. 14 U.S.C. § 88(a).
106. 14 U.S.C. § 88(a)(4).

to derelict vessels at sea. Some have suggested that the duty to render assistance to a vessel in distress can also provide a basis for exercising limited control or jurisdiction over a foreign-flag vessel on the high seas, notwithstanding the flag state's exclusive jurisdiction over the vessel. The question arises in two very different situations. In the first, on the approach of a law enforcement vessel, the crew of a vessel transporting illegal drugs scuttles the vessel in order to destroy the evidence needed for their prosecution. The now-sinking vessel's crew refuses assistance and shrewdly remains on board until the last possible minute to guard against the patrol vessel salvaging the "abandoned" vessel and its illicit cargo before it sinks. In the second application, sometimes called "collateral interdiction," a patrol vessel on the high seas comes on an overloaded or otherwise unseaworthy foreign vessel carrying irregular migrants and, by way of rendering assistance to the distressed vessel, removes the migrants and repatriates them to their state of origin (an action the patrol vessel could not take while the migrants remained on board the foreign-flag vessel, absent consent of the flag state).[107] This latter practice finds some support in the Migrant Smuggling Protocol to the Convention on Transnational Organized Crime, which opens the door to actions deemed necessary to relieve imminent danger to human life.[108]

Suggested rationales in support of involuntary assistance in situations involving intentionally scuttled vessels include constructive abandonment and implied owner or flag state consent. If the master and/or crew remain on the sinking vessel and refuse assistance (not uncommon with drug-trafficking vessels), a true abandonment rationale is unavailable. Under such circumstances, however, it can be argued that the master has violated his fiduciary obligation to the vessel owner and flag state, and that his refusal to accept assistance is therefore invalid, giving rise to a constructive abandonment. The alternative rationale—implied consent—is based on the argument that no responsible owner and flag state of a vessel being intentionally scuttled would object to assistance being provided, even over the master's refusal. Although one U.S. circuit court decision lends some support to the argument that assistance can, in some circumstances, be imposed notwithstanding the master's refusal,[109] that case involved assistance being rendered by the vessel's own flag state (the United States) and the case did not involve an assertion of law enforcement authority. It should also be noted that neither the constructive abandonment nor the implied consent rationales for a nonconsensual basis for boarding (and exercising jurisdiction over) distressed foreign vessels on the high seas has attracted wide support (or significant objections).

The LOS Convention calls on coastal states to promote the establishment of search-and-rescue (SAR) services and mutual SAR arrangements with neighboring states.[110] Those agreements

---

107. A vessel transporting irregular migrants or the migrants themselves might create a distress condition on the vessel in order to claim a right of distress entry into the destination state's internal waters or port, or to force the patrol vessel to remove the migrants and take them into the desired port, where they can apply for asylum.

108. Protocol against the Smuggling of Migrants by Land, Sea and Air, supplementing the UN Convention against Transnational Organized Crime, art. 8(5), adopted Nov. 15, 2000, 2241 U.N.T.S. (No. 39574), 40 I.L.M. 335, 385–94 (2001).

109. Thames Shipyard & Repair Co. v. U.S., 350 F.3d 247, 259 (1st Cir. 2003) (holding that in a life-threatening situation, the Coast Guard has authority to forcibly remove the master and crew from a vessel in distress; however, the decision to do so is discretionary). The court's decision rested on 14 U.S.C. § 88, which provides in relevant part: "(a) In order to render aid to distressed persons, vessels, and aircraft on and under the high seas and on and under the waters over which the United States has jurisdiction and in order to render aid to persons and property imperiled by flood, the Coast Guard may: (1) *perform any and all acts necessary* to rescue and aid persons and protect and save property" (emphasis added). The court went on, however, to make clear that it did not "accept that the phrase 'any and all' gives the Coast Guard carte blanche authority to engage in forcible evacuations in *less* than life-threatening emergencies." Id. at 259 (emphasis in original).

110. LOSC art. 98(2).

are facilitated in part by the IMO-sponsored International Convention on Maritime Search and Rescue.[111] Agreements between the United States and Canada and the United States and Mexico are described in chapter 5, section A.2. The member states of the Arctic Council recently concluded an agreement addressing SAR in that region.[112]

Following the Norwegian container ship *Tampa*'s rescue of 433 migrants from a sinking Indonesian ferry in the waters between Australia and Indonesia in 2001, and the widely reported difficulties the rescue vessel's master faced in gaining access to a port to offload the rescued migrants, the IMO and the UN high commissioner for refugees launched a sweeping review of the relevant international law. One result was amendments to the SOLAS and SAR Conventions, which now require the state responsible for the SAR region in which the assistance is rendered to exercise primary responsibility for ensuring the coordination and cooperation necessary to permit the rescuing vessel to disembark the rescuees with minimum delay to the ship's intended voyage.[113]

The 1982 LOS Convention imposes a duty on flag states to investigate high-seas marine casualties or navigation incidents involving ships flying their flag when the collision or navigation incident results in loss of life or serious injury to nationals of another state or causes serious damage to ships or installations of another state or to the marine environment.[114] The convention further requires flag states and the other involved states to cooperate in carrying out those inquiries and prohibits the arrest or detention of the ship, even as a measure of investigation, by any authorities other than those of the flag state.[115] The IMO has taken the lead in developing guidance for marine casualty investigations.[116] Although those LOS Convention provisions plainly impose a duty on flag states to investigate serious marine casualties on the high seas involving their vessels, they do not by themselves address whether the flag state's jurisdiction is exclusive in high-seas marine casualties.[117] The answer to that question begins with the *S.S.* Lotus case decided by the PCIJ. In that case, Turkey and France contested jurisdiction over a 1926 collision involving the Turkish steamer *Boz-Kourt* and the French steamship *Lotus* on the high seas, which resulted in the death of eight Turkish nationals who were on the *Boz-Kourt*. Following the collision, the *Lotus* voluntarily entered a Turkish port, where the *Lotus*' watch officer, one Lieutenant Demons, was arrested by Turkish authorities.[118] France argued that it alone had jurisdiction over a French officer on board a French vessel on the high seas. The case was submitted to the PCIJ

111. International Convention on Maritime Search and Rescue, Apr. 27, 1979, T.I.A.S. 11,093, 1403 U.N.T.S. The 1979 SAR Convention was substantially amended in 1998. See also International Aeronautical and Maritime Search and Rescue Manual [IAMSAR] (2010); United States National Search and Rescue Supplement (2000); Chairman, Joint Chiefs of Staff, Joint Pub. 3-50, National Search and Rescue Manual (1994).

112. Agreement on Cooperation in Aeronautical and Maritime Search and Rescue in the Arctic, May 12, 2011, 50 I.L.M. 1119 (2011).

113. See Frederick J. Kenney Jr. & Vasilios Tasikas, Australia's *Tampa* Incident: The Convergence of International and Domestic Refugee and Maritime Law in the Pacific Rim, 12 Pac. Rim L. & Pol'y J. 143 (2003); SOLAS Convention, supra, ch. V, reg. 33(1). See also IMO and UNHCR, Rescue at Sea: A Guide to Principles and Practices as Applied to Migrants and Refugees (2006).

114. LOSC art. 94(7). SOLAS Convention, supra, ch. I, reg. 21; MARPOL Convention, supra, arts. 8 & 12; and the International Labor Organization (ILO) No. 147, supra, art. 2(g) all impose similar duties to investigate.

115. LOSC art. 97(3).

116. See IMO, Code of International Standards and Recommended Practices for a Safety Investigation into a Marine Casualty or Marine Incident, IMO Res. A.849(20), as amended by IMO Res. A.884(21).

117. Article 58 provides that certain of the high-seas articles also apply within the EEZ. The duty to investigate marine casualties in Article 94 is among those listed for inclusion. Article 94(7) therefore applies in the EEZ insofar as it is not incompatible with the other rules in Part V on the EEZ.

118. Turkey asserted two bases for jurisdiction: effects (Demons' acts while on the French ship *Lotus* had an "effect" on the Turkish ship *Boz-Kourt*) and passive personality (the victims were Turkish).

for a decision.[119] Applying customary international law and the principles of legal positivism discussed in chapter 1, the PCIJ ruled that France had the burden of proving that a rule of international law prohibited Turkey from asserting jurisdiction. Because France failed to do so, the court upheld Turkey's position. The PCIJ decision came as a surprise to many maritime states, which had understood that the vessel's flag state had exclusive jurisdiction in such cases. In 1952 the PCIJ decision was effectively reversed in the Brussels Penal Jurisdiction in Matters of Collisions Convention, at least for states that ratified the convention.[120] The Brussels Convention rule of exclusivity was later incorporated into the 1958 Convention on the High Seas and carried forward into the 1982 LOS Convention.[121]

The 1982 LOS Convention assigns primacy over high-seas collision investigations to the respective vessel flag states.[122] It also provides that when a collision or any other navigation incident on the high seas involves the penal or disciplinary responsibility of the master or of any other person in the service of the ship, such proceedings can be brought only before the authorities of the flag state or of the state of which the person being disciplined is a national.[123] Moreover, in "remedial" actions against the vessel's master or crew, only the state that issued the mariner's license or certificate of competency may take action to revoke or suspend that license or certificate, even if the holder is not a national of the state that issued it.[124]

F. SUBMARINE CABLES AND PIPELINES ON THE HIGH SEAS

Much of the public and far too many mariners fail to appreciate the importance of submarine pipelines and cables, particularly the increasingly ubiquitous fiber-optic cable networks on which the vast majority of the world's high-speed communications depend. Only when a cable or pipeline is broken by a carelessly placed anchor or indiscriminate fishing practices do mariners and the public realize how much we now depend on this critical marine infrastructure.

Under the LOS Convention all states have the right to lay cables and pipelines on the bed of the high seas.[125] States are required to adopt laws prohibiting the willful or negligent breaking or injury of a submarine cable or pipeline by ships flying their flag or persons subject to their jurisdiction.[126] Damage to cables or pipelines during operations to save lives or ships is excused if the actor took the necessary precautions to avoid the damage. States are also required to adopt laws imposing liability for repair costs on any cable or pipeline owner subject to their jurisdiction that, in laying or repairing its own cable or pipeline, damages another cable or pipeline.[127] Finally, to provide vessel operators with an additional incentive to protect pipelines or cables, states are required to adopt laws to ensure that owners of vessels who can prove that, having taken all

---

119. The S.S. *Lotus* case (France v. Turkey), 1927 P.C.I.J. (ser. A) No. 9 (Sept. 7).
120. International Convention for the Unification of Certain Rules relating to Penal Jurisdiction in Matters of Collisions or Other Incidents of Navigation, May 10, 1952, 439 U.N.T.S. 233. The United States is not a party.
121. 1958 Convention on the High Seas, supra, art.11.
122. LOSC art. 94(7) & 97. See also NTSB v. Carnival Cruise Lines Inc., 723 F. Supp. 1488, 1490 (S.D. Fl. 1989) (holding that the NTSB had no jurisdiction to investigate an accident on the high seas involving only foreign-flag vessels).
123. LOSC art. 97(1).
124. LOSC art. 97(2).
125. Submarine cables include telegraph, telephone, and electrical cables as well as fiber-optic cables. LOSC art. 112. The rules regarding pipelines and cables on the continental shelf are examined in chapter 7.
126. LOSC art. 113. See, e.g., AT&T Co. v. M/V *Cape Fear,* 763 F. Supp. 97, 101 (D.N.J. 1991) (action for damages by cable owner against vessel under the Submarine Cable Act, 47 U.S.C. §§ 21–39).
127. LOSC art.114.

reasonable precautions to avoid entanglement, they sacrificed an anchor, a net, or any other fishing gear to avoid injuring a cable or pipeline, are indemnified by the owner of the cable or pipeline.[128]

G. CONSERVATION AND MANAGEMENT OF LIVING RESOURCES OF THE HIGH SEAS

The LOS Convention preserves the right of all states to engage in fishing on the high seas. However, that right is subject to any applicable treaty obligations, to the rights and duties of coastal states in certain transboundary fish stocks, and to the conservation and management provisions of the convention.[129] At the same time, all states have a duty to cooperate with other states in taking the measures necessary for the conservation of the living resources of the high seas.[130] More specifically, states whose nationals exploit identical living resources, or different living resources in the same area, are required to enter into negotiations with a view to taking the measures necessary for the conservation of the living resources concerned. To that end they are encouraged to establish regional fisheries management organizations.[131] The LOS Convention only briefly addresses the substantive and procedural measures for ensuring that high-seas fishing is conducted according to principles of sustainable use. It provides that allowable catch levels and other conservation measures must be based on the best scientific evidence available and that they are set at a level that will maintain or restore populations of harvested species at levels that can produce the maximum sustainable yield, as qualified by relevant environmental and economic factors. Conservation and allocation measures must also take account of the special requirements of developing states, historical fishing patterns, the interdependence of stocks, and any generally recommended international minimum standards. Finally, those measures must take into consideration the effects on species associated with or dependent on harvested species with a view to maintaining or restoring populations of such associated or dependent species above levels at which their reproduction might become seriously threatened.[132] The LOS Convention high-seas fishing articles are supplemented by several related agreements, including the High Seas Fishing Compliance Agreement.[133] Measures to promote stewardship of living marine resources are more fully examined in chapter 10.

H. ENCLOSED AND SEMI-ENCLOSED SEAS

Part IX of the LOS Convention addresses the status of enclosed and semi-enclosed seas.[134] The convention defines an "enclosed or semi-enclosed sea" as a gulf, basin, or sea surrounded by two or more states and connected to another sea or the ocean by a narrow outlet or consisting entirely or primarily of the territorial seas and EEZs of two or more coastal states.[135] Under that definition such seas may include portions of the high seas. Seas commonly mentioned as argu-

---

128. LOSC art. 115.
129. Id. art. 116.
130. Id. art. 117.
131. Id. art. 118.
132. Id. art. 119.
133. FAO, Agreement to Promote Compliance with International Conservation and Management Measures by Fishing Vessels on the High Seas [hereinafter "FAO High Seas Fishing Compliance Agreement"], Nov. 24, 1993, S. Treaty Doc. 103-24, 2221 U.N.T.S. 91, 33 I.L.M. 968 (1994).
134. United Nations Convention on the Law of the Sea 1982: A Commentary, vol. III, at 343–68 (Satya Nandan et al. eds., 1995).
135. LOSC art. 122.

ably falling within the definition include the Black Sea, Red Sea, Yellow Sea, Baltic Sea, Gulf of Thailand, and Arabian (Persian) Gulf. One author argues that the Mediterranean Sea should be included.[136] Others have made similar assertions regarding the Arctic Ocean and the Caribbean and South China Seas.[137]

States bordering an enclosed or semi-enclosed sea have an obligation to cooperate with each other in the exercise of their rights and in the performance of their duties under the LOS Convention.[138] The relevant subjects of cooperation include conservation and management of living resources, protection of the marine environment, and marine scientific research. The bordering states are encouraged to invite other interested states or international organizations to participate. A forum for such cooperation is provided by the UNEP Regional Seas Programme discussed in chapter 10. Some tout the LOS Convention provisions on enclosed and semi-enclosed seas as a progressive development in the law of the sea that will encourage cooperation. Others worry that the enclosed seas rules could provide a rationale for states to launch a new ocean enclosure movement that will further restrict freedom of navigation. In assessing the respective arguments it is important to keep in mind that the duty of cooperation under the enclosed seas articles does not in itself add to the coastal states' rights or jurisdiction in those seas; nor does it abridge the navigation rights enjoyed by other states in those waters.[139]

---

136. Budislav Vukas, The Mediterranean: An Enclosed or Semi-enclosed Sea? in The Law of the Sea: Selected Writings, vol. 45, ch. 15 (2004).

137. Nien-Tsu Alfred Hu, Semi-enclosed Troubled Waters: A New Thinking on the Application of the 1982 UNCLOS Article 123 to the South China Sea, 41 Ocean Dev. & Int'l L. 281 (2010).

138. LOSC art. 123.

139. Oxman, The Territorial Temptation, supra, at 843.

Status of Vessels and Aircraft

Many of the rights and obligations under the peacetime law of the sea and the law of naval warfare turn on whether the craft is a "vessel" or "ship" and if so, whether it is a warship or a government ship operated for noncommercial purposes. This chapter examines the peacetime law of the sea articles defining those terms before turning to two issues of particular salience today: stateless vessels, which are commonly engaged in illegal activities, and unmanned vehicles, which have begun occupying a more prominent role in naval and maritime law enforcement operations. It then closes with a brief survey of the status of aircraft and their navigation rights and obligations.

A. DEFINITION OF "VESSEL"

Whether or not a craft or object is a "vessel" or "ship" is of critical importance in any application of the LOS Convention. Unless stateless, a vessel has a flag state, which is assigned specific responsibilities by the LOS Convention and generally has exclusive jurisdiction over the craft while on the high seas. A vessel has a master (or person in charge), who is assigned responsibilities by the convention. A vessel enjoys certain navigation rights and duties under the convention. Vessels must adhere to the applicable rules on collision avoidance. If a vessel is seized by another state for certain fisheries or pollution violations, the convention provides a mechanism for its flag state to obtain the prompt release of the vessel and its crew.

Although the vast majority of watercraft presents no serious classification problems, new technologies and marine applications continue to introduce taxonomic challenges. Historically, uncertainty has surrounded the classification of a variety of inshore craft, including non-self-propelled barges and dredges, personal watercraft, permanently moored "riverboat" casinos, and floating homes and worker dormitories.[1] Vessel classification disputes have been common in the offshore oil and gas industry for decades. Although classifying drill ships was relatively easy, mobile offshore drilling units (MODUs); semisubmersible platforms; tension leg platforms; jack-up rigs; spar platforms; concrete island drilling systems; floating production, storage, and offloading (FPSO) craft; and floating renewable energy production platforms are less easily classified.

Two examples demonstrate the persistence and relevance of the classification challenge. When Denmark announced its plans to construct the Great Belt Bridge with a vertical clearance of 65 meters, Finland brought suit in the ICJ on the grounds that the bridge would interfere with the safe navigation of drill ships and oil rigs (some of which had an air draft of up to 175 meters) through the strait connecting Finland with the North Sea. Denmark replied that although merchant vessels enjoy a right of passage through the strait, the oil rigs in question were not vessels,

---

1. In U.S. admiralty law, the "vessel" classification also has a temporal element that generally excludes craft under construction before they are launched and craft that have been permanently withdrawn from navigation.

and therefore the navigation rights did not extend to them. The case was settled before the ICJ reached the issue.[2] More recently, the nature of the craft used by some migrants in attempts to cross the Florida Strait from Cuba to the United States, which have included everything from rubber inner tubes to makeshift rafts and converted automobiles, have raised questions regarding their possible status as "vessels" enjoying navigation rights and whether they are subject to exclusive flag state jurisdiction.[3]

More than two hundred years of experience, litigation, and commentary have failed to provide a final and satisfactory transsubstantive definition for the term "vessel" under U.S. law.[4] Perhaps it is unrealistic to expect that it would. The term has a number of applications, and the interpretations given to it are naturally influenced by the purpose and object of the statute or rule. Thus, the term might justifiably be interpreted differently when the purpose is to provide a remedy for an injured maritime worker[5] than when a creditor seeks to arrest a floating structure to enforce a debt for moorage fees in an admiralty in rem action.[6]

Following the practice in the 1958 Geneva conventions on the law of the sea, the English-language version of the 1982 LOS Convention alternately uses the terms "ship" and "vessel" without defining either.[7] By contrast, the Spanish, Russian, and French versions, which are equally authentic under the terms of the convention,[8] use only one word. The difference between the two approaches is largely academic, however: the negotiating history of the convention confirms that the English words "ship" and "vessel" are not to be interpreted to refer to different legal categories of watercraft.[9]

The English version of the LOS Convention uses the terms "ship" and "vessel" in both an unrestricted sense and a restricted sense. The unrestricted use of the term must be broad enough to include all of the vessel-related articles in the convention, which address subjects ranging from surface and subsurface navigation to fishing, oceanographic research, and ocean mining. The LOS Convention also serves as the framework under which other international agreements on maritime issues are given effect. Those other conventions often include their own "vessel" definitions that were tailored to the particular convention's purpose. Thus, a vessel might be defined differently for purposes of collision avoidance (the COLREGS Convention) than for ocean dumping restrictions (London Dumping Convention), vessel-source pollution (MARPOL Convention), or limitation of a "ship" owner's liability. It should therefore not be surprising that the LOS Convention does not include a single transsubstantive or universal definition.

---

2. Passage through the Great Belt (Finland v. Denmark), 1991 I.C.J. 12. See also Martti Koskenniemi, Case concerning Passage through the Great Belt, 27 Ocean Dev. & Int'l L. 255 (1996).

3. See Douglas Guilfoyle, Shipping Interdiction and the Law of the Sea 195 & n.114 (2009).

4. A transsubstantive definition is one that would transcend all substantive applications.

5. Stewart v. Dutra Const. Co., 543 U.S. 481 (2005).

6. Lozman v. City of Riviera Beach, 133 S. Ct. 735 (2013). The majority's decision appears at times to confuse the test for whether a watercraft is a vessel with the test for whether the vessel is "in navigation," a necessary predicate for workers on board the craft to benefit from seaman status.

7. See Warren Christopher, Letter of Submittal of Sept. 23, 1994, S. Treaty Doc. No. 103-39, at 93. Historical usage suggests that "ship" refers to large vessels and "boat" refers to smaller vessels. A ship often carries its own boats. The term "fishing vessel" is common, but one never hears of a "fishing ship," even though some exceed three hundred feet in length.

8. LOSC art. 320.

9. UN Division for Ocean Affairs and the Law of the Sea, Navigation on the High Seas: Legislative History of Part VII, Section 1 (Articles 87, 89, 90–94, 96–98) of the UN Convention on the Law of the Sea, at 80, U.N. Sales No. E.89.V2 (1989). See also Restatement FRLUS § 501 n.1 (reporting that the UNCLOS III drafting committee concluded that the words "ship" and "vessel" should be interpreted as equivalent). The position is of long standing; see Erastus C. Benedict, The American Admiralty §§ 215 & 218 (1850) (concluding that "ship" and "vessel" are equivalent terms).

In the absence of a definition for "vessel" in the LOS Convention, resort must be made to the established rules of treaty interpretation set out in the Vienna Convention on the Law of Treaties (that approach is applied in the context of unmanned marine vehicles in section F below). Logically, a broad, unrestricted meaning must be presumed to control application of a treaty article unless it is modified either by accompanying terms or qualifiers or by its position in the convention and the surrounding context. Thus, in codifying the freedom of navigation on the high seas, Article 90 uses the term "ship" in the unrestricted sense. Similarly, the caption accompanying Part II, Subsection 3.A on innocent passage rights indicates that the articles in that section (Articles 17–26) apply to "all ships" (unrestricted), while Section 3B is restricted to merchant ships, and Section 3C to warships and other public vessels respectively.

The U.S. Supreme Court took a similar restricted/unrestricted approach to defining "vessel" under U.S. law.[10] In a 2005 decision the Court confirmed that, unless otherwise indicated, the general definition of "vessel" codified by Congress in the Rules of Construction Act, 1 U.S.C. § 3, controls in all U.S. statutes enacted after 1871. That statute defines the term "vessel" broadly, to include "every description of watercraft or other artificial contrivance used, or capable of being used, as a means of transportation on water." The Court treated that definition as the unrestricted meaning of "vessel" in U.S. maritime law when it held that it "continues to supply the *default* definition of 'vessel' throughout the U.S. Code, 'unless the context indicates otherwise.'"[11] When the "context indicates otherwise," a restricted definition will be applied. In its 2013 decision in *Lozman v. City of Riviera Beach*, the Court adopted a "reasonable observer" test for determining whether a craft meets the 1 U.S.C. § 3 "capable of being used . . . as a means of transportation on water" requirement. Under that test, the Court will ask whether a reasonable observer, looking to the craft's physical characteristics and activities, would consider it designed to a practical degree for carrying people or things over water.[12] If so, the watercraft satisfies the transportation element of the definition.

Congress' early statutory definition of the term "vessel" has proven to be robust for nearly 150 years, even though the drafters could not have foreseen the myriad craft operating on, under, and skimming just above the waters today (e.g., nuclear submarines; air-cushion vehicles; LASH barges; wing-in-ground craft; and personal watercraft, or "jet skis"). Nevertheless, two years after the Supreme Court's decision in *Dutra*, holding that a non-self-propelled dredge was a vessel, Congress added an even more inclusive definition when it defined a "vessel" in a section of the criminal code as "any watercraft or other contrivance used or designed for transportation or navigation on, under, or immediately above, water."[13] Whether this broader definition, which is arguably better adapted to emerging watercraft technologies and applications, will someday occupy the "default" position held by the current version of 1 U.S.C. § 3 has yet to be determined.[14]

B. WARSHIPS AND OTHER PUBLIC VESSELS

Warships and other government vessels operated for noncommercial purposes raise several issues under the peacetime law of the sea and the law of naval warfare. The first peacetime law of the sea issue of interest is that certain enforcement actions can be carried out only by warships or other

---

10. Stewart v. Dutra Const. Co., 543 U.S. at 489–90.
11. Id. at 490 (emphasis added).
12. Lozman v. City of Riviera Beach, 133 S. Ct. at 741.
13. Pub. L. No. 109-177, § 307(b)(1), codified at 18 U.S.C. § 2311.
14. Only Congress has the power to amend the statutes to designate a new "default" vessel definition.

duly authorized ships.[15] Similarly, under the law of naval warfare only warships are entitled to exercise belligerent rights. Second, under most treaties, warships and other public vessels do not necessarily have the same port access rights as commercial vessels. As a rule, warships and naval auxiliaries require advance approval, obtained through diplomatic clearance procedures, before they may lawfully enter another state's port or internal waters.[16] Some states also purport to deny certain navigation rights to warships and military survey ships. Third, under the international law of state responsibility the conduct of warships and other government-owned or government-controlled vessels is directly attributable to the state.[17] Finally, the LOS Convention and customary law exempt warships and other public vessels from some of the requirements applicable to other vessels. For example, the LOS Convention registration requirements for nonpublic vessels examined in section C below do not apply to warships.[18] Additionally, although warships and similar public vessels have a duty to comply with coastal or port state regulations enacted in accordance with the LOS Convention, and their flag state bears international responsibility for harms those vessels cause, warships enjoy sovereign immunity from enforcement actions by the coastal state.[19]

1. Definition of "Warship"

To qualify as a warship a craft must, of course, be a ship. Accordingly, the earlier discussion on the definition of a ship is relevant here. Fortunately, the more specific definition of a warship eliminates most of the doubtful "vessel" cases. Article 29 of the LOS Convention defines a warship as "a ship belonging to the armed forces of a State bearing the external marks distinguishing such ships of its nationality, under the command of an officer duly commissioned by the government of the State and whose name appears in the appropriate service list or its equivalent, and manned by a crew which is under regular armed forces discipline."[20]

U.S. Coast Guard cutters under the command of a commissioned officer are thus warships.[21] A ship that otherwise meets the Article 29 definition of a warship but also carries some civilian

---

15. See, e.g., LOSC arts. 107, 110, & 111. The practice of embarking foreign "ship-riders" on U.S. warships or law enforcement vessels, who then conduct boardings of vessels flying the flag of the ship-riders' state, apparently does not violate the rules.

16. Commander's Handbook, supra, ¶ 2.5.1. Foreign port clearance issues are examined in chapter 4.

17. Attribution of conduct to the state will be an issue in the coming years for states that employ fishing vessels or other commercial vessels as surrogates for warships and other public vessels.

18. A U.S. Department of State authority explains: "Warships and other government operated noncommercial ships may probably be said to acquire nationality by virtue of their government operation, and no documentation in evidence thereof is called for because they are obviously government operated ships." Marjorie M. Whiteman, 9 Digest of International Law § 1, at 5 (1968).

19. While on the warship, the officers and crew benefit from the vessel's sovereign immunity; however, the warship's immunity does not follow them ashore. While ashore in a foreign country, they are fully subject to that country's jurisdiction, absent a status of forces or visiting forces agreement.

20. LOSC art. 29. See also Commander's Handbook, supra, para 2.2.1; 46 U.S.C. § 2101(47) (U.S. definition of "vessel of war").

21. Restatement FRLUS § 522 n.1. See also U.S. Coast Guard Regulations, supra, ¶ 10-2-1. Naval and Coast Guard vessels commanded by an enlisted officer-in-charge (rather than a commissioned officer) are classified as naval auxiliaries. See Commander's Handbook, supra, art. 2.3.1. But see United Nations Convention on the Law of the Sea 1982: A Commentary, vol. II, at ¶ 29.8(b) (Myron H. Nordquist ed., 1993) (more broadly construing "warship"). While the distinction between warships and authorized law enforcement vessels is not particularly important under the peacetime law of the sea, because both classes of vessels may exercise enforcement powers and both have sovereign immunity, it is important to note that under the law of naval warfare only warships may exercise belligerent rights.

crew or workers does not thereby lose its status as a warship.[22] Naval auxiliaries do not qualify as warships, but they do enjoy sovereign immunity as "other government ships operated for non-commercial purposes" described below. Classification of other "maritime agency" vessels, such as those employed by the People's Republic of China,[23] as either warships or "other government ships operated for noncommercial purposes" will turn on the definitions above. The fact that some Chinese paranavy vessels are armed (and have, in the past, fired on unarmed foreign vessels fishing in disputed waters) supports their classification as warships.[24] It should be noted, however, that the presence or absence of weapons on the vessel is not determinative.

U.S. policy declares that a warship does not lose its sovereign immunity or its status as property of the sovereign even if wrecked or sunk, unless the sovereign affirmatively abandons its interests in the vessel.[25] Such vessels cannot be salvaged without the consent of the flag state. As a matter of policy, the United States does not grant permission to salvage sunken U.S. warships that contain explosives or the remains of deceased service personnel.

2. Other Government Vessels Operated for Noncommercial Purposes

In broadly similar language, Article 32 of the LOS Convention identifies a class of "other government ships operated for non-commercial purposes," and Article 96 on sovereign immunity refers to "ships owned or operated by a State and used only on government non-commercial service." Either description of that class of vessels would satisfy the definition of a "public vessel" under U.S. law.[26] Coast Guard cutters and small craft that do not qualify as warships and vessels owned or operated by the Military Sealift Command (MSC) (whether under demise, time, or voyage charter),[27] the U.S. Army Corps of Engineers, National Oceanic and Atmospheric Administration, federal and state merchant marine academies, and federal maritime law enforcement agencies other than the Coast Guard, including Immigration and Customs Enforcement (ICE) and Customs and Border Protection (CBP), as well as state and local law enforcement and firefighting agencies, should present no difficulty in satisfying the definition.

---

22. Commander's Handbook, supra, ¶ 2.2.1; see also Jane G. Dalton, Future Navies, Present Issues, 59 Nav. War Coll. Rev. 17, 17–22 (winter 2006) (examining issues raised by the increasing use of civilian mariners on naval ships).

23. In addition to vessels of its Peoples' Liberation Army (Navy) vessels, China deploys "paranavy" vessels through five maritime agencies. They include the Maritime Police, General Administration of Customs, Fisheries Law Enforcement Command, and Marine Surveillance Branch, all of which were placed under the supervision of the State Oceanic Administration in early 2013. Those agencies carry out law enforcement activities and press China's claims to regional islands and waters under the operational direction of the Ministry of Public Security. The fifth agency, the Maritime Safety Administration, remained within the Chinese Ministry of Transport after the 2013 reorganization. In March 2013 China announced it was creating a unified Coast Guard commanded by the State Oceanic Administration.

24. For example, on March 20, 2013, a Chinese paranavy vessel fired into an unarmed Vietnamese vessel fishing in waters off the Hoang Sa/Paracel Islands, setting the fishing vessel's cabin on fire. The islands are claimed by Vietnam, China, and Taiwan.

25. Commander's Handbook, supra, ¶ 2.1.2. See also Sunken Military Craft Act, Pub. L. No. 108-375, 118 Stat. 1811 (2004), codified at 10 U.S.C. § 113 Note; David J. Bederman, Congress Enacts Increased Protections for Sunken Military Craft, 100 Am. J. Int'l L. 649 (2006).

26. 46 U.S.C. § 2101(24) defines a foreign "public vessel" as one that is owned or demise chartered and operated by the government of a foreign country and is not engaged in commercial service. Liability of foreign governments and their instrumentalities for certain torts and claims arising out of commercial activities is addressed in the Foreign Sovereign Immunities Act. See 28 U.S.C. §§ 1605 & 1610.

27. The sovereign immunity of such ships operated by the government under time or voyage charters was confirmed by the 1934 Additional Protocol to the 1926 Brussels Convention for the Unification of Certain Rules concerning the Immunity of State-Owned Vessels, 179 L.N.T.S. 199. See also Commander's Handbook supra, ¶ 2.3.2. Contrary to the 2007 Commander's Handbook, the United States does claim full sovereign immunity of MSC time-chartered vessels (but not voyage-chartered vessels) flying the U.S. flag.

3. State Responsibility for Its Public Vessels

Chapter 14 examines the principles of state responsibility for violations of international law that harm another state or its nationals, together with their relationship to sovereign immunity issues. The two concepts are distinguishable. If a warship's or other public vessel's violation harms another state, its flag state will bear international responsibility even though the vessel itself enjoys sovereign immunity with respect to any state other than its flag state. The LOS Convention expressly addresses several issues of state responsibility related to warships and other public vessels. For example, Article 30 of the convention addresses noncompliance by warships with the laws and regulations of the coastal state. It provides that "if any warship does not comply with the laws and regulations of the coastal state concerning passage through the territorial sea and disregards any request for compliance therewith which is made to it, the coastal State may require it to leave the territorial sea immediately."

Article 31 then goes on to address the responsibility of the flag state for damage caused by a warship or other government ship operated for noncommercial purposes. It states that "the flag State shall bear international responsibility for any loss or damage to the coastal State resulting from the non-compliance by a warship or other government ship operated for non-commercial purposes with the laws and regulations of the coastal State concerning passage through the territorial sea or with the provisions of this Convention or other rules of international law." A similar provision is included in the transit passage articles.[28]

4. Sovereign Immunity of Public Vessels

Article 95 provides that warships have complete immunity from the jurisdiction of any state other than the flag state. Article 96 extends that immunity to ships owned or operated by a state and used only on government noncommercial service,[29] but not to state-owned or state-operated vessels engaged in commercial service.[30] Thus, military and law enforcement vessels that do not qualify as warships may nevertheless be entitled to sovereign immunity under this article. By their terms, Articles 95 and 96 apply only to vessels on the high seas; however, by operation of Article 58(2) they apply as well in the EEZ of a state, to the extent that the immunity would not be incompatible with the EEZ regime.[31] Customary international law extends that immunity even further. Article 32 recognizes the customary law rule on sovereign immunity by making it clear that, with limited exceptions (set out in Articles 30 and 31), nothing in the LOS Convention affects the immunities of warships and other government ships operated for noncommercial purposes.[32] Sovereign immunity extends to small craft operating from warships.[33] *U.S. Navy*

28. LOSC art. 42(5).
29. As a matter of policy, the United States may choose to limit the scope of its sovereign immunity claims with respect to MSC vessels. Commander's Handbook, supra, ¶ 2.3.2.
30. The widely followed "restrictive" approach to sovereign immunity seeks to level the playing field for privately owned commercial vessels and state-owned and state-operated vessels engaged in commercial activities.
31. See LOSC art. 58(2) (extending Articles 88–115 to the EEZ).
32. Restatement FRLUS § 522 cmt. a. See also UN Convention on Jurisdictional Immunities of States, annex to UNGA Res. 59/38 (Dec. 2, 2004) (not in force). Article 16 preserves the immunity of warships and other public vessels. ITLOS suggested in an order on provisional measures that the sovereign immunity of warships while in foreign internal waters or ports might be grounded not only in customary law but also in Article 32 of the LOS Convention. The ARA *Libertad* case (Argentina v. Ghana), ITLOS Case No. 20, Provisional Measures, Order of 15 December 2012.
33. Violations of this immunity were evident in Iran's seizure of fifteen British sailors and marines who were conducting boardings near the Iraq-Iran maritime border from HMS *Cornwall*'s small boats in March 2007 and a similar seizure in 2004 of eight British sailors and marines from three British patrol boats that were operating independently.

Regulations provides, for example, that "boats shall be regarded in all matters concerning the rights, privileges and comity of nations as part of the ship or aircraft to which they belong."[34] The regulations further charge the parent ship's commanding officer to see that steps are taken to make their nationality evident at all times, reinforcing the view that such boats have "nationality."

By virtue of their sovereign immunity, warships and other public vessels have exclusive control over the persons or activities on board the vessel. They are immune from search or arrest regardless of location. The immunity further exempts them from foreign taxation and any requirement to identify personnel on board or to provide information on the nature of the vessel's weapons, stores, or property.[35]

C. VESSEL NATIONALITY, REGISTRATION, AND THE GENUINE LINK REQUIREMENT

Settled international law provides that the legal effect of a domestic act on the international plane requires a two-step inquiry that necessarily includes an international law component. For example, in adjudicating a state's maritime baseline claim, the ICJ explained that "it cannot be dependent merely on the will of the coastal State as expressed in its municipal law. Although it is true that the act of delimitation is necessarily a unilateral act . . . the validity of the delimitation with regards to other States depends upon international law."[36] A similar rule was applied to a dispute over an individual's nationality in the ICJ's decision in *Nottebohm's* case,[37] in which the court held that Guatemala was not required to recognize Liechtenstein's alleged right to assert diplomatic protection on behalf of one Friedrich Nottebohm, formerly a German citizen who later became a naturalized Liechtenstein citizen (under questionable circumstances), when evidence of a genuine link between Nottebohm and Liechtenstein was lacking. The effect of Liechtenstein's domestic act of naturalization on other states was ultimately determined by international law.

The ICJ appeared to retreat from its "genuine link" position five years later in its advisory opinion in the Constitution of the Maritime Safety Committee of the Inter-governmental Maritime Consultative Organization (IMCO).[38] In that case, the ICJ declined to examine whether there existed a genuine link between two flag-of-convenience states and the vessels registered in those states to calculate the states' aggregate tonnage for purposes of IMCO (now International Maritime Organization) committee membership. Although the advisory opinion rests on unique facts, one might ask why a flag state's decision with respect to vessel registration is given greater deference and less scrutiny than state decisions on territorial sea baselines or citizenship. Perhaps the answer lies in a perceived need to protect settled expectations in commercial maritime ventures, which could affect the interests of mortgagees, other lien holders, charterers, cargo shippers, and crewmembers. A vessel nationality scheme riddled with doubt would not well serve those expectations. A possible second explanation might be that a *Nottebohm* rule in vessel nationality cases would be unmanageable in a global inventory of commercial vessels that now exceeds 100,000 and with vessel control distributed among owners, charterers, and operators.[39] Regardless of the rationale, it now seems clear that despite the fact that the term "nationality"

---

34. U.S. Navy Regulations, supra, art. 0855; Commander's Handbook, supra, ¶ 2.3.3.
35. Commander's Handbook, supra, ¶ 2.1.1.
36. Anglo-Norwegian Fisheries case (U.K. v. Norway), 1951 I.C.J. 116, 132 (Dec. 18).
37. Nottebohm's case (Liechtenstein v. Guatemala), 1955 I.C.J. 1 (Apr. 6).
38. Advisory Opinion on the Constitution of the Maritime Safety Committee of the Inter-governmental Maritime Consultative Organization (IMCO), 1960 I.C.J. 150 (Mar. 25).
39. As of January 2012 the world fleet had reached 104,305 seagoing commercial ships. UN Conference on Trade and Development, Transport Newsletter No. 54 (2d Quarter 2012), at 16.

is used in referring to a state's relationship to individuals and to vessels and aircraft, that term is given a different meaning in the two applications.[40]

1. Qualifying as a Flag State

All states, whether coastal or landlocked, have the right to serve as flag states and sail ships flying their flag on the high seas.[41] With three exceptions for international organizations set out in the LOS Convention, only entities qualifying as states may confer nationality on a vessel.[42] A state need not have a coastline or ports to accommodate its vessels in order to serve as a flag state.[43] The fact that there is no requirement for a vessel to ever be physically present in its flag state is one of the many reasons for the growing concern over what some refer to as states that serve as "flags of convenience"[44] and others more charitably call "open registries."[45]

2. Vessel Nationality and Registration

Article 91 of the LOS Convention imposes four distinct obligations on the flag state.[46] First, the flag state must fix the conditions for the grant of its nationality. Second, it must prescribe the conditions for registering ships in its territory. Third, it must establish the conditions for the right to fly its flag. A ships is said to have the nationality of the state whose flag it flies, assuming it meets the conditions imposed by that state. The distinction between the conditions for registration and for the right to fly the flag is important because a ship might be exempt from state registration (or, as some states refer to it, "documentation") requirements, perhaps because of its sovereign immunity status or small size, yet it might still be entitled to fly the flag of a state. For example, the definition of a "vessel of the United States" extends to vessels numbered or titled under state law, in contrast to those registered under federal documentation laws.[47] The fourth obligation imposed by the convention on flag states is critical. All ships authorized to fly a state's flag must be issued documents to that effect, even if they are not otherwise required to be registered.[48] Absence of such a document may give rise to a presumption that the vessel is not

---

40. The ILC recognized the potential problem in using the term "nationality" to describe the relationship between a vessel and its flag state. See 1951 Y.B. Int'l L. Comm'n, vol. I, at 328–29, U.N. Doc. A/CN.4/42 (1951).

41. LOSC art. 90; Restatement FRLUS § 501 n.2. This principle is a corollary to the sovereign equality of states. See generally UN Office for Ocean Affairs and the Law of the Sea, Navigation on the High Seas: Legislative History of Part VII, Section 1 (Articles 87, 89, 90–94, & 96–98) of the UN Convention on the Law of the Sea, U.N. Pub. No. E.89.V.2 (1989).

42. LOSC art. 93 reserves the right of the UN, its specialized agencies, and the International Atomic Energy Agency to authorize vessels to fly their flags.

43. A state with no ports or maritime patrol capability can exercise effective jurisdiction and control over its vessels only by delegating some or all of its flag state responsibilities to others.

44. Boleslaw A. Boczek, Flags of Convenience: An International Law Study (1962). The U.S. Commission on Ocean Policy complained that "these flag states become havens for owners of substandard vessels seeking to avoid meaningful oversight." U.S. Commission on Ocean Policy Final Report: An Ocean Blueprint for the 21st Century 239 (2004).

45. The Rochdale Committee identified six features commonly found in open registry states: (1) the country allows noncitizens to own and control vessels, (2) access to and transfer from the register is easy, (3) taxes on shipping income are low or nonexistent, (4) the country of registration does not need the shipping tonnage for its own purposes but is keen to earn the tonnage fees, (5) manning by nonnationals is freely permitted, and (6) the country lacks the power (or the willingness) to impose national or international regulations on its ship owners. See Committee of Enquiry into Shipping, Report No. 51, HMSO 1970, Command 4337 (1970).

46. See generally H. Meyers, The Nationality of Ships (1967); Nigel P. Ready, Ship Registration (1999); Richard Coles & Edward Watt, Ship Registration: Law and Practice (2009).

47. 46 U.S.C. § 116.

48. See U.S. v. Ross, 439 F.2d 1355 (9th Cir. 1971) (surveying the possible methods of proving nationality).

entitled to fly any state's flag (i.e., that it is stateless). Article 94 adds a fifth requirement to the flag state's obligations. It requires flag states to maintain a register of vessels entitled to fly their flag.[49] To increase transparency in vessel ownership and control, the SOLAS Convention was recently amended to require vessels covered by SOLAS to carry a Continuous Synopsis Record (CSR) documenting key identification and ownership information on the vessel.[50]

In addition to the genuine link requirement, the LOS Convention imposes a second positive limitation on the state's registration competency: a state may not grant registration to a vessel that is already registered in another state, except as part of a real transfer of ownership or change of registry.[51] As a further measure to deter "flag-hopping" by fishing vessel owners who reregister their vessel in a less demanding state, in an attempt to circumvent the loss of fishing privileges granted by their original flag state because the vessel violated international conservation and management measures, the FAO member states developed the High Seas Fishing Compliance Agreement. The United States implemented the FAO agreement in 1995, with the High Seas Fishing Compliance Act (HSFCA).[52] The HSFCA, and similar laws enacted by other flag states, creates a potential conflict between two possible flag states. The potential for a conflict is evident in the HSFCA's definition of the term "vessel of the United States," which includes, inter alia, "a vessel that was once documented under the laws of the United States and, in violation of the laws of the United States, was either sold to a person not a citizen of the United States or *placed under foreign registry or a foreign flag, whether or not the vessel has been granted the nationality of a foreign nation.*"[53] The act thus potentially continues to treat a vessel registered in another state as a vessel of the United States.[54]

Customary international law gives the vessel's flag state broad discretion in determining what conditions a vessel must meet before it can be registered in the state and entitled to fly that state's flag. The *Muscat Dhows* case concerned a dispute between Great Britain and France over the validity of vessel registration. In its 1916 decision the arbitral tribunal announced the customary law rule that "generally speaking it belongs to every sovereign to decide to whom he will accord the right to fly his flag and to prescribe the rules governing such grants."[55] The tribunal then went on to uphold France's decision to authorize vessels belonging to the sultan of Muscat to fly the French flag. A nearly identical rule was adopted by Justice Robert Jackson, writing for the U.S. Supreme Court in *Lauritzen v. Larsen*, five years before the 1958 Geneva conventions on the law of the sea were completed:

> Perhaps the most venerable and universal rule of maritime law relevant to our
> problem is that which gives cardinal importance to the law of the flag. Each

---

49. LOSC art. 94(2)(a). The register need not include those "which are excluded from generally accepted international regulations on account of their small size." See also 46 U.S.C. § 12138 (U.S. list of documented vessels).

50. SOLAS Convention, supra, ch. XI-1, reg. 5; IMO Resolution A.959(23), Mar. 4, 2003. The CSR must include, inter alia, a "history" of the vessel's name, identification number, flag state, port of registry, registered owner, and bareboat charterer.

51. LOSC art. 92(1). The practice of "bareboat registration" does not violate the rule. See also Anti-reflagging Act, Pub. L. No. 100-239 § 4(a)(4); H.R. Rep. No. 100-423, reprinted in 1987 U.S.C.C.A.N. 3245.

52. Pub. L. 104-43, title I, §102, Nov. 3, 1995, 109 Stat. 367, codified at 16 U.S.C. ch. 75.

53. 16 U.S.C. § 5502(9)(C) (emphasis added). See also FAO High Seas Fishing Compliance Agreement, supra, art. III(5)(a) ("No Party shall authorize any fishing vessel previously registered in the territory of another Party that has undermined the effectiveness of international conservation and management measures to be used for fishing on the high seas unless . . .").

54. U.S. law also raises the possibility of concurrent jurisdiction over some crimes when the vessel is owned in whole or in part by a U.S. citizen or corporation, even if the vessel is registered in another state. See 18 U.S.C. § 7(1); U.S. v. Keller, 451 F. Supp. 631, 636–37 (D.P.R. 1978).

55. Muscat Dhows case (France v. Great Britain), 1916 Hague Ct. Rep. 93-109 (Perm. Ct. Arb. Aug. 8, 1905).

state under international law may determine for itself the conditions on which it will grant its nationality to a merchant ship, thereby accepting responsibility for it and acquiring authority over it. Nationality is evidenced to the world by the ship's papers and its flag. The United States has firmly and successfully maintained that the regularity and validity of a registration can be questioned only by the registering state.[56]

The 1958 Convention on the High Seas joins in a single article the genuine link requirement to the flag state's obligation to exercise jurisdiction and control over vessels flying its flag.[57] Article 5 of the 1958 Convention provides that:

1. Each State shall fix the conditions for the grant of its nationality to ships, for the registration of ships in its territory, and for the right to fly its flag. Ships have the nationality of the State whose flag they are entitled to fly. *There must exist a genuine link between the State and the ship; in particular, the State must effectively exercise its jurisdiction and control in administrative, technical and social matters over ships flying its flag.*

2. Each State shall issue to ships to which it has granted the right to fly its flag documents to that effect.[58]

The 1958 Convention's genuine link requirement was not popular with the flag-of-convenience states, most of which declined to ratify the convention. UNCLOS III settled on a different approach. In drafting Article 91 on the nationality of ships, the conferees removed the language regarding the duty to exercise effective jurisdiction and control from the vessel nationality article and relocated it to Article 94, which sets out the flag state's duties. Article 91 of the 1982 LOS Convention now provides that:

1. Every State shall fix the conditions for the grant of its nationality to ships, for the registration of ships in its territory, and for the right to fly its flag. Ships have the nationality of the State whose flag they are entitled to fly. There must exist a genuine link between the ship and the State.

2. Every State shall issue to ships to which it has granted the right to fly its flag documents to that effect.[59]

The 1982 Convention thus decoupled the genuine link requirement from the jurisdiction and control requirement. Article 91 fails to provide any criteria for assessing whether a genuine link exists,[60] and omits any recourse or remedy for other states that might question whether there is in

---

56. Lauritzen v. Larsen, 345 U.S. 571, 584 (1953) (relying in part on the nineteenth-century incident involving the vessel *Virginius*). The *Virginius* incident is described in John Bassett Moore, A Digest of International Law, vol. II, § 309 (1906). See also Restatement FRLUS § 501.

57. Restatement FRLUS § 501 cmt. b & nn.7–8.

58. 1958 Convention on the High Seas, supra, art. 5 (emphasis added).

59. LOSC art. 91; *M/V Saiga* (St. Vincent & the Grenadines v. Guinea), ITLOS Case No. 2, Judgment of July 1, 1999, ¶¶ 64–65, 38 I.L.M. 1323 (1999).

60. See Walker, Definitions for the Law of the Sea, supra, at 69–78. For examples of "genuine link" requirements, see the UN International Law Commission's 1955 draft of the Convention on the High Seas (the provisions were dropped from the actual 1958 convention), the Convention on Conditions for Registration of Ships, Feb. 7, 1986 (not in force), and 46 U.S.C. § 12103 (prescribing "link" conditions necessary for registration in the United States).

fact a genuine link between the vessel and its flag state.[61] In doing so, the 1982 LOS Convention has apparently given flag states unreviewable discretion in applying the genuine link requirement, at least in the view of ITLOS.[62] For that reason, much of the international focus has shifted from the genuine link requirement to the requirement that each flag state exercise jurisdiction and control over its vessels.

D. THE FLAG STATE'S OBLIGATION TO EXERCISE EFFECTIVE JURISDICTION AND CONTROL

The LOS Convention reaffirms the long-established principle that the primary responsibility for regulating vessels is assigned to the flag state.[63] Flag state obligations regarding vessel safety and environmental protection are examined in the context of port state control in chapter 4 and are further developed in chapter 10 on marine stewardship. This chapter focuses on the meaning of effective jurisdiction and control. At the outset it should be noted that while the LOS Convention requires flag states to exercise effective jurisdiction and control over its vessels, it does not distinguish between the concepts of "jurisdiction" and "control." Indeed, the two concepts are often conflated.[64]

"Jurisdiction" is generally understood to refer to a government's capacity to exercise legal authority over territory, persons, property, or activities.[65] Only governments exercise jurisdiction. By contrast, control is the power to direct and to take the measures necessary to compel compliance with those directions.[66] Private entities can and do exercise various forms of control over vessels, as do states. Control over a vessel could include, for example, vessel traffic control measures or directing a vessel to enter a particular port or anchorage or not to depart the port until certain repairs are completed. It is now clear that the flag state's duty to control vessels flying its flag extends beyond the physical ship itself.[67]

---

61. That is not to say that flag states are free to ignore the genuine link requirement in the LOS Convention or that other states may not take proportionate self-help countermeasures when a flag state does so. ITLOS decisions do, however, preclude the possibility of denying legal effect to a vessel registration on the ground there is no genuine link.

62. See The M/V *Saiga* No. 2, supra, ¶¶ 75–88. But see The M/V *Virginia G* case (Panama v. Guinea-Bissau), ITLOS Case No. 19, Order of Aug. 18, 2011 (finding admissible Guinea-Bissau's counterclaim that Panama violated LOSC Article 91 by granting its flag to a vessel that had no genuine link to the state).

63. LOSC arts. 92(1), 94; Restatement FRLUS §§ 502 & 520. Tension over the role of the flag state and the state in which the vessel owners and crew are nationals was evident in the 1990 interception of the MV *Hermann* on its voyage from Cuba to Mexico. The 250-foot freighter was owned by a Cuban shipping company and manned by Cubans, but was registered in Panama. As the flag state, Panama consented to a boarding by the U.S. Coast Guard to determine if the vessel was carrying contraband. However, the Cuban Foreign Ministry notified the United States that Cuba was ordering the vessel not to allow the boarding. Cuban television reported that the *Hermann*'s eleven-member Cuban crew stood ready with machetes, knives, and axes to repel any U.S. boarding. The Coast Guard cutter attempted to stop the vessel with disabling fire, but it escaped into Mexican waters, where it was met by the Mexican navy. Cuba protested the U.S. use of force. See U.S. Department of State, Digest of United States Practice in International Law 1989–1990, at 452–56.

64. The jurisdiction and control obligation extends to administrative, technical, and social matters. LOSC art. 94(1). See Restatement FRLUS § 502 cmt. g (concluding that a failure to exercise effective jurisdiction and control "may be a factor in determining a lack of a 'genuine link' between the flag state and the vessel").

65. In contrast to sovereignty and sovereign rights, which are generally understood to apply to territory and natural resources, "jurisdiction" generally extends to nonstate entities such as individuals, corporations, offshore facilities, and nonpublic vessels and aircraft. Jurisdiction over states implicates the doctrine of sovereign immunity. See Restatement FRLUS § 522 cmt. a.

66. The term "control" is also used in Article 33 on the contiguous zone and in the "port state control" context.

67. See, e.g., LOSC arts. 94(4) & 98.

Under the LOS Convention, the flag state's duty of control extends at a minimum to the master, officers, and crew. ITLOS suggested an arguably broader flag state role in the *M/V Saiga* case. The tribunal first confirmed that the vessel's flag state had standing to assert claims on behalf of the vessel's crew, even though they were not nationals of the flag state, and then explained that "the ship, everything on it, and every person involved or interested in its operations are treated as an entity linked to the Flag State. The nationalities of the persons are not relevant."[68] The potential reach of that sweeping dictum has not yet been tested.

Under the LOS Convention, control expressly extends to measures necessary to ensure safety at sea with regard to the construction, equipment, and seaworthiness of ships; their manning and crew training and labor conditions; the use of signals; and the prevention of collisions.[69] The flag state must also ensure that its vessels are periodically surveyed (i.e., inspected by qualified marine inspectors) and have on board such charts, nautical publications, and navigational equipment as needed for the safe navigation of the ship. The control responsibility requires the flag state to ensure that its ships are in the charge of a master and officers who possess appropriate qualifications,[70] and that the number and qualifications of the crew are appropriate for the type, size, machinery, and equipment of the ship. The master, officers, and crew must be conversant with the applicable international regulations concerning the safety of life at sea; the prevention of collisions; prevention, reduction, and control of marine pollution; and radio communications requirements.

The LOS Convention requires flag states, in their exercise of jurisdiction and control, to ensure that vessels flying their flag conform to generally accepted international regulations, standards, procedures, and practices for safety and protection of the marine environment.[71] The phrase "generally accepted international regulations, procedures, and practices" is not defined in the convention; however, it is widely understood to refer to international rules that are adopted under the auspices of a competent international organization, such as the IMO, and are widely ratified by the relevant states. The generally accepted international standards (GAIS) for maritime safety and pollution prevention (e.g., SOLAS, MARPOL, and STCW) are examined in chapter 10.[72] Recent amendments to those international standards in response to security concerns have imposed international requirements for certain vessels to have in place a ship security plan and to carry and use vessel-tracking technologies, including automatic identification system (AIS) transponders and long-range identification and tracking (LRIT) equipment and procedures.[73]

---

68. The *M/V Saiga* No. 2, supra, ¶ 106. See also Lauritzen v. Larsen, 345 U.S. 571, 586 (1953) (citing In Re Ross, 140 U.S. 453, 472 (1891), in holding that the nationality of the vessel is attributed to the vessel's crew). ITLOS did not likely intend to suggest that the actual state of nationality of any persons on the vessel lacked concurrent capacity to exercise diplomatic or consular protection on behalf of their nationals. See Report of the ILC on Work of its 58th Session, U.N. Doc. A/61/10 (2006) (draft art. 18); Churchill & Lowe, supra, at 209 ("A state retains jurisdiction over its nationals wherever they might be, whether on a foreign ship or anywhere else"). See also Cruz v. Zapata Ocean Resources, Inc., 695 F.2d 428, 433 (9th Cir. 1982); U.S. v. Arra, 630 F.2d 836 (1st Cir. 1980); Restatement FRLUS § 502 cmt. h & § 902(2).

69. LOSC art. 94(3).

70. The international standards for qualification are established by the Convention on Standards of Training, Certification and Watchstanding of Seafarers [hereinafter "STCW Convention"], Dec. 1, 1978, 1361 U.N.T.S. 190, as amended in 1995, S. Exec. Doc. EE 96-1, C.T.I.A. No. 7624.

71. LOSC art. 94(5).

72. The 2006 Maritime Labor Convention, a fourth generally accepted international agreement, entered into force on August 20, 2013. The United States is not a party.

73. International AIS and LRIT carriage requirements are prescribed by SOLAS Convention, ch. V. The U.S. requirements are prescribed in 46 U.S.C. §§ 70114 & 70115. See also International Maritime Organization Resolution MSC Res. 202(81).

The LOS Convention sets a high evidentiary bar ("clear grounds") on complaints against flag states and then provides only limited recourse when one state believes that a given vessel's flag state is not exercising effective jurisdiction and control over the vessel. Specifically, Article 94(6) provides that "a State which has clear grounds to believe that proper jurisdiction and control with respect to a ship have not been exercised may report the facts to the flag State. Upon receiving such a report, the flag State shall investigate the matter and, if appropriate, take any action necessary to remedy the situation." Notwithstanding that demonstrably toothless provision, one example will suffice to demonstrate that the "complain and wait" rule in the LOS Convention is not the concerned state's only option in the face of ineffective flag state control. In the current era of muscular port state control the concerned state may also deny foreign vessels flying selected flags access to its ports or internal waters or subject them to heightened scrutiny on arrival and may detain a vessel if it is found to be unseaworthy. The practice thus addresses substandard vessels and ineffective flag states.

E. STATELESS VESSELS AND VESSELS ASSIMILATED TO STATELESSNESS

The commonly cited principle of exclusive flag state jurisdiction over vessels on the high seas (and in the contiguous and exclusive economic zones on matter not falling within the coastal state's competence) turns on two preliminary requirements. First, the craft must be a "vessel." Second, the vessel must be entitled to fly the flag of a state. For merchant and fishing vessels, the right to fly a state's flag is normally established by registration. For recreational and other small craft, the state might grant nationality by some method other than registration, such as the numbering and state registration schemes used in the United States.

Under international law, the nationality of a ship is treated as a question of fact to be decided by the tribunal if contested.[74] Nationality is typically proven by documents issued by the flag state. In the United States, a certificate of documentation issued by the U.S. Coast Guard is conclusive evidence of nationality for international law purposes, but not in a proceeding conducted under the laws of the United States.[75] Other evidence of nationality includes the flag flown from the vessel (if any),[76] the home port displayed on the stern, and claims by the master or person in charge.[77] The vessel's displayed name and IMO identification number also permit enforcement vessels or aircraft on patrol to determine the vessel's nationality from available government and commercial databases and to contact the claimed flag state to request confirmation of the vessel's nationality.

Customary law,[78] the 1958 Convention on the High Seas,[79] and the 1982 LOS Convention all recognize two classes of vessels that may not invoke the principle of exclusive flag state jurisdiction against the enforcement vessels of another state: vessels that are without a nationality and

---

74. See The M/V *Saiga* No. 2, supra, ¶¶ 66–67 ("The Tribunal considers that the nationality of a ship is a question of fact to be determined, like other facts in dispute before it, on the basis of evidence adduced by the parties"); The *Grand Prince* case (Belize v. France), Prompt Release, ITLOS Case No. 8, Judgment of Apr. 20, 2001, ¶ 66, 125 Int'l L. Rep. 251. In an application for prompt release, the applicant has the burden of establishing the vessel's nationality.

75. See 46 U.S.C. § 12134. No similar evidentiary effect is given to a vessel issued a certificate of numbers under 46 U.S.C. ch. 123, even though such "numbered vessels" are a "vessel of the United States." See 46 U.S.C. § 116. By contrast, in some applications foreign registry documents may be given conclusive effect. See, e.g., 18 U.S.C. § 2285(e)(2) (effect of nationality documents for submersible and semisubmersible vessels).

76. Historically, the ship's flag has been deemed prima facie evidence of its nationality. Colombos, supra, at 291–93.

77. See 18 U.S.C. § 2285(d); 46 U.S.C. § 70502(e).

78. Oppenheim's International Law, vol. 1, § 261 (Hersch Lauterpacht ed., 8th ed. 1958).

79. 1958 Convention on the High Seas, supra, art. 6.

vessels that have been assimilated to a vessel without a nationality.[80] These "stateless" vessels are a matter of serious global concern because they are commonly engaged with illegal trafficking operations and illegal, unregulated, and unreported (IUU) fishing.[81] When a vessel is without nationality, either in fact or by assimilation, it has neither direct nor derivative rights to navigate. In fact, courts have labeled such vessels "international pariahs."[82] As such, they lose what would otherwise be the protection of exclusive flag state jurisdiction while on the high seas. If a vessel is genuinely stateless, there is in fact no flag state to exercise effective jurisdiction and control over the vessel or to grant consent to another state to take enforcement action. By contrast, a vessel assimilated to statelessness by virtue of having made false or inconsistent nationality claims, or refusing to make any nationality claim at all, might in fact be entitled to fly the flag of a state and would still be subject to that state's jurisdiction and control. Moreover, that state could consent to a boarding or other law enforcement action. However, the conduct of the vessel may justify another state in deeming it a stateless vessel for enforcement purposes.

1. Statelessness

A vessel "has the nationality" of the state whose flag it is entitled to fly.[83] Ships are required by the LOS Convention to "sail under the flag of one State only."[84] The vessel's flag state is required to issue the vessel documents that attest to its right to fly that state's flag.[85] Accordingly, a vessel is without a nationality (stateless) if it is not entitled to fly any state's flag.[86] A vessel may be entitled to fly the state's flag either as a result of registration or on some other basis, such as meeting the "numbering" or state registration requirement in the United States.[87] Reasonable suspicion that a vessel is stateless may justify a right of visit under Article 110.

Under the U.S. Maritime Drug Law Enforcement Act, the issue of whether a vessel was, at the time of the enforcement action, without a nationality goes to the preliminary question of jurisdiction, and is therefore decided by the court, not the jury.[88] It must be proven by a preponderance of the evidence.[89] Several ITLOS cases brought to obtain the prompt release of seized

80. Restatement FRLUS § 522 n.7; 70 Am. Jur.2d, Shipping § 12 (vessels without nationality); Commander's Handbook, supra, ¶¶ 3.11.2.3, 3.11.2.4, & 4.4.4.1.5.

81. Ted L. McDorman, Stateless Fishing Vessels, International Law and the U.N. High Seas Fisheries Conference, 25 J. Mar. L. & Com. 531 (1994).

82. See, e.g., U.S. v. Caicedo, 47 F.3d 370, 371 (9th Cir. 1995); U.S. v. Marino-Garcia, 679 F.2d 1373 (11th Cir. 1982).

83. LOSC art. 91(1); U.S. v. Arra, 630 F.2d 836 (1st Cir. 1980).

84. LOSC art. 92(1). Article 92 of the 1982 LOS Convention is virtually identical with Article 6 of the 1958 Convention on the High Seas.

85. LOSC art. 91(2); Restatement FRLUS § 501 n.3.

86. See LOSC art. 92(2); Andrew Anderson, Jurisdiction over Stateless Vessels on the High Seas: An Appraisal under Domestic and International Law, 13 J. Mar. L. & Com. 323 (1982); Whiteman, 9 Digest of International Law, supra, at 6, 7, 21, 25, 26, 34–35; What Constitutes "Vessel without Nationality," So As to Be Subject to Jurisdiction of United States under Maritime Drug Law Enforcement Act, 46 U.S.C.A. § 70502(d)(1), and Predecessor Statutes, 63 A.L.R. Fed. 2d 411.

87. 46 U.S.C. § 116 defines a "vessel of the United States" as a vessel documented under 46 U.S.C. chapter 121, numbered under 46 U.S.C. chapter 123, or titled under the laws of a state. Any such "vessel of the United States" would be entitled to fly the U.S. flag.

88. See Coast Guard Authorization Act of 1996, Pub. L. No. 104-324, § 1138, 110 Stat. 3901, 3988–89, codified at 46 U.S.C. § 70504(a) (jurisdiction over a vessel under the MDLEA is not an element of the offense but rather a matter to be determined solely by the court). Before 1996, the courts held that whether a vessel was stateless was to be determined by the jury. See U.S. v. Rosero, 42 F.3d 166 (3d Cir. 1994) (citing cases from the First, Fifth, and Eleventh Circuits). See also U.S. Department of Justice, U.S. Attorneys' Manual, Title 9, Criminal Resource Manual, ¶ 666, "Proof of Territorial Jurisdiction" (citing the trend to treat certain "jurisdictional facts" that do not bear on guilt as nonelements of the offense, and therefore as issues for the court rather than the jury, and to require proof by only a preponderance).

89. U.S. v. Matos-Luchi, 627 F.3d 1, 5 (1st Cir. 2010). The dissenting judge in the case argued that the beyond a reasonable doubt standard should be applied. Id. at 13–15 (Lipez, J. dissenting).

vessels have involved enforcement actions by one state against a foreign vessel with apparent registration irregularities. Those cases required the tribunal to determine as a preliminary matter whether the vessel had the nationality of the state bringing the action on its behalf. In doing so, ITLOS has generally given a wide measure of deference to flag state assertions that a given vessel did meet the state's registration requirements.

2. Assimilation to Statelessness

The LOS Convention stipulates that a ship that sails under the flags of two or more states, using them according to convenience, may not claim any of the nationalities in question with respect to any other state, and may be assimilated to a ship without a nationality.[90] Two important issues are left unclear by that provision. First, it does not specify the immediate and longer-term effect of a decision to "assimilate" a vessel to statelessness. Is a vessel assimilated to statelessness thereafter treated in all respects the same as a vessel that is truly stateless? On this question, it should be noted that Article 92(2) textually limits its application to "any *other* state," thus apparently ruling out any effect on the states whose flags were in fact flown or claimed. The second question left unanswered by the article is what acts constitute "sailing under the flags of two or more states"? The answer to those questions requires resort to treaty interpretation principles.

Treaty interpretation begins with a search for the plain meaning of an otherwise undefined term, in light of its context. The LOS Convention uses the verb "assimilate" in two articles: Article 92 on statelessness and Article 102 on pirate ships. In neither case is the meaning clear. The common nonlegal meaning of the term is "to incorporate, absorb, or transform." Under that meaning, a vessel assimilated to statelessness would be incorporated or absorbed into the class of stateless vessels. However, for the reasons discussed below, that is probably not the intended meaning of Article 92. Rather, the intent appears to be that a vessel assimilated to statelessness may be treated by states other than the flag state "as if" it is stateless, even if it actually is properly registered in and entitled to fly the flag of another state. International cases applying the term support that interpretation. In the *S.S.* Lotus case, the PCIJ reasoned that a vessel can be "assimilated" to the territory of its flag state.[91] The court did not appear to be suggesting that the vessel was part of the flag state's territory as a matter of law. Rather, by operation of a useful legal fiction, the court was explaining that a vessel may be treated "as if" it is the territory of the flag state. Resort to the larger LOS Convention context lends additional support to that interpretation. For example, if the assimilation language is contrasted with the more consequential language of Article 99, which provides that "any slave taking refuge on board any ship, whatever its flag, shall *ipso facto* be free,"[92] it seems clear that a vessel or person "assimilated" into a class is something less than one that is ipso facto a member of the class.

The plain language of Article 91(1) must also be considered. It provides that "ships *shall have the nationality* of the State whose flag they are entitled to fly."[93] That same article and the associated cases decided by international tribunals confer on the flag state the sole competency to fix the conditions "for the right to fly its flag." The assignment of sole competency to the flag

---

90. LOSC art. 92(2). See also Restatement FRLUS § 501 cmt. c; Tullio Treves, Flags of Convenience before the Law of the Sea Tribunal, 6 San Diego Int'l L.J. 179 (2004).
91. The S.S. *Lotus*, supra, ¶ 65 ("A corollary of the principle of the freedom of the seas is that a ship on the high seas is assimilated to the territory of the State the flag of which it flies, for, just as in its own territory, that State exercises its authority upon it and no other State may do so").
92. This anachronistic provision, which assumes that international law (which deems the ban on slavery a peremptory norm) would countenance that a person might not otherwise be "free," dates back to the 1890 General Act of Brussels, July 2, 1890.
93. Article 91(1) does not add limiting language, such as "unless those on board the vessel have committed acts justifying a state in assimilating the vessel to one without a nationality."

state casts serious doubt on arguments that a third state may, by the discretionary act of assimilation, negate a vessel's nationality and bind another state to its action. Finally, Article 92(2) limits application of the assimilation rule to "any *other* State," thereby excluding the claimed flag states. Thus, a vessel assimilated to statelessness is not ipso facto stateless,[94] because as between the flag state and the vessel and its owner, the flag state may continue to treat the vessel as possessing flag state nationality. The other state may, however, deem it stateless for law enforcement purposes (just as a vessel "constructively present" in a zone may be subject to enforcement action *as if* it actually were in that zone) and treat it no more favorably than vessels that are in fact stateless.[95]

One judge characterized the assimilation provision as a sanction, "effectively penalizing vessels that attempt to evade law enforcement authority on the high seas."[96] Logically, that means that the ship that commits the predicate acts in Article 92(2) (discussed in the following section) can be boarded under the right of visit in Article 110 because there is suspicion that it is stateless. Case law in the U.S. courts has borne this out.

In describing the actions that justify assimilation, the 1982 LOS Convention essentially carries forward Article 6 of the 1958 Convention on the High Seas. Neither convention supplies a complete statement of the law. Resort must therefore be made to state practice as evidence of customary international law.

The U.S. Maritime Drug Law Enforcement Act (MDLEA), reflecting the practice of a state that is "specially affected" by drug trafficking, incorporates Article 6 of the 1958 Convention on the High Seas as a source of law on assimilation.[97] The MDLEA lists three scenarios that render a vessel stateless;[98] however, the effect of the act does not stop there. Drawing on the MDLEA's legislative history, courts have held that the examples of statelessness in section 70502(d) do not exhaust the possible grounds that may warrant a finding that the vessel is legally stateless.[99] In *United States v. Victoria*, then Circuit Judge (now U.S. Supreme Court Justice) Stephen Breyer held that a vessel sailing without a flag flying and that failed to respond to multilingual inquiries about its nationality was a "vessel without nationality," and thus subject to U.S. counterdrug laws, even though it was near the coast of Colombia at the time of the interdiction.[100] While still on the Third Circuit, Judge (now Supreme Court Justice) Samuel Alito similarly took a broad view of the test for statelessness under the MDLEA. In his opinion for the circuit court in *U.S. v. Rosero*, Judge Alito held that the statutory definition in section 70502(d) was not exhaustive, and that vessels that would be stateless as a matter of customary international law are stateless for purposes of the MDLEA, even on grounds not expressly included in the statute.[101]

State practice regarding acts justifying assimilation can be distilled down to a three-pronged test. A vessel commits an act justifying another state in assimilating the vessel to statelessness if it:

---

94. See Meyers, Nationality of Ships, supra, at 322.
95. See Matos-Luchi, 627 F.3d at 16–17 (Lipez, J. dissenting). See also id. at 17–20 (examining the distinction between "genuine statelessness" and "deemed statelessness").
96. Id.
97. See also 16 U.S.C. §§ 1802(44) & 2432(11) (stateless fishing vessels); 33 C.F.R. § 107.200 (defining stateless vessels for purposes of prohibition on unauthorized entry into Cuban territorial waters); George H. W. Bush, Exec. Order 12,807, May 24, 1992 (interdiction of illegal aliens). Paragraph 2(b)(2) of the order extends the maritime alien migrant interdiction order to "vessels without nationality or vessels assimilated to vessels without nationality in accordance with paragraph (2) of Article 6 of the Convention on the High Seas of 1958 (U.S. T.I.A.S. 5200; 13 U.S.T. 2312)." By contrast, the U.S. statute implementing the Convention for the Suppression of Unlawful Acts against the Safety of Maritime Navigation (SUA convention) does not extend jurisdiction to stateless vessels. See 18 U.S.C. § 2280(b).
98. See 46 U.S.C. § 70502(d).
99. Matos-Luchi, 627 F.3d at 4 (citing S. Rep. No. 99-530 at 15–16 and H.R. Rep. No. 96-323 at 23–24).
100. U.S. v. Victoria, 876 F.2d 1009 (1st Cir. 1989).
101. See U.S. v. Rosero, 42 F.3d 166 (3d Cir. 1994).

1. Makes a nationality claim that is denied by the claimed state.[102] A vessel gets one opportunity to properly and truthfully claim a flag. If the claimed state of registry denies that the vessel is entitled to fly its flag, the master or person in charge does not get a second chance to get it right.

2. Fails to make any nationality claim. Article 92(1) imposes an affirmative requirement on vessels to sail under the flag of one (and only one) state.[103] Customary law holds that "it is not enough that a vessel have a nationality; she must claim it and be in a position to provide evidence of it."[104]

3. Claims more than one nationality (inconsistent or contradictory claims). Under U.S. law, a claim of nationality or registry is made only by possession on board the vessel and production of documents evidencing the vessel's nationality in accordance with Article 5 of the 1958 Convention on the High Seas; flying its flag state's ensign or flag; or a verbal claim of nationality or registry by the master or person in charge of the vessel.[105]

Other indicia that have been cited as acts that may justify assimilation include the absence of anyone admitting to be the master; invalidly changing flags during the voyage; using removable signboards showing different vessel names, home ports, or both; and displaying no name, flag, or other identifying characteristics. The cases do not distinguish a deliberate attempt to deceive law enforcement from the inadvertent or negligent failure of an ill-informed or confused master to make a correct claim of nationality. However, something more than mere inadvertence is suggested by the qualifying phrase "using them according to *convenience*" in Article 92(2) of the LOS Convention.

It is also important to distinguish acts that do not justify assimilation. Violating the flag state's conditions on registration by, for example, failing to timely perfect or renew a vessel's registration, seizure by a third state, or placing the vessel under the command of a noncitizen[106] are not included in the U.S. provisions regarding invalidation of a vessel's registration. In fact, U.S. law expressly provides for the continued application of certain U.S. laws in cases of invalidated documentation, making it clear that loss of documentation does not render the vessel beyond the reach of U.S. law.[107] The ITLOS cases involving prompt release actions have been similarly liberal with respect to documentation irregularities, again highlighting the distinct questions of the current validity of the vessel's registration and its entitlement to fly a state's flag.

3. Consequences of Stateless Status

As a matter of international law, vessels that are genuinely stateless are denied the navigation rights and the benefits of exclusive flag state jurisdiction extended to properly flagged vessels. In

---

102. Under the MDLEA, a claim of registry may be verified or denied by radio, telephone, or similar oral or electronic means. The denial of such claim of registry by the claimed flag state is conclusively proved by certification of the U.S. secretary of state or the secretary's designee. 46 U.S.C. § 70502(d)(2).

103. Matos-Luchi, 627 F.3d at 5 ("under international law, every vessel must sail under the flag of one and only one state; those that sail under no flag or more than one flag enjoy no legal protection" [citing Oppenheim's International Law, vol. 1, § 261, at 595–96]).

104. Matos-Luchi, 627 F.3d at 6 (quoting Anderson, Stateless Vessels, supra, at 336–37). The court held that "the controlling question is whether at the point at which the authorities confront the vessel, it bears the insignia or papers of a national vessel or its master is prepared to make an affirmative and sustainable claim of nationality." Id.

105. 46 U.S.C. § 70502(e). See also 18 U.S.C. § 2285(d) (rule on submersible and semisubmersible vessels).

106. 46 U.S.C. § 12135.

107. 46 U.S.C. § 12136.

holding that a stateless vessel has no rights under the law of the sea, the court of appeals in *United States v. Cortes* explained that "the freedom of navigation on the open sea is freedom for such vessels only as sail under the flag of a State. . . . To secure the protection afforded merchant vessels on the high seas, a vessel must accept the duties imposed by registration. This the [defendant's vessel] failed to do; her crew cannot complain of the results."[108] Suspicion that a vessel is without nationality may justify a right of visit by a warship or other law enforcement vessel (see chapters 8 and 11). A right-of-visit boarding under Article 110 of the LOS Convention is an act of "interference" with the vessel's navigation, not an assertion of jurisdiction. If it turns out the vessel is in fact stateless or the enforcing state properly assimilates it to statelessness, however, the dominant view, supported by substantial state practice without apparent objection and by suggestive treaty provisions,[109] is that the state may then, as a matter of international law, exercise jurisdiction over the vessel.[110] With regard to such vessels, "no question of comity nor of any breach of international law can arise, if there is no State under whose flag the vessel sails."[111]

When a vessel is not in fact stateless, but was assimilated to that status by the acts of those on board, what are the flag state's continuing rights and interests in the vessel? Returning to the earlier-mentioned pirate ship example, Article 104 suggests that, at least for piracy, any question regarding the vessel's retention or loss of nationality is determined by the flag state. Thus, piratical acts by those on board a vessel do not necessarily strip the flag state of its relationship to the vessel. Similarly, false or deceptive nationality claims by operators on board a vessel that justify an assimilation by a second state should not strip the vessel's flag state of its rights and obligations under international or domestic law.

The distinction between a vessel that is in fact stateless and one that was assimilated to statelessness will perhaps prove consequential in a future case in which the flag state of a vessel that is in fact properly registered and entitled to fly a state's flag, but has been assimilated to statelessness by another state, brings an action for prompt release of the vessel or otherwise asserts claims on the vessel's behalf. The tribunal would then have to determine whether the case is admissible.[112] A 2007 ITLOS decision involving the fishing vessel *Tomimaru* suggests reluctance on the part of the tribunal to strip a vessel of its nationality. In that case, ITLOS held that judicial "confiscation" (i.e., a punitive seizure) of a vessel for violation of the coastal state's fisheries law renders the application for prompt release "without object," because it transfers title to the confiscating

---

108. U.S. v. Cortes, 588 F.2d 106, 110 (5th Cir. 1979) (citing Oppenheim's International Law, vol. 1, at 546). See also U.S. v. Rosero, 42 F.3d 166, 171 (3d Cir. 1994); U.S. v. Acosta Valdez, 84 F. Supp.2d, 237, 239 (D.P.R. 1999).

109. Maritime conventions that suggest jurisdiction over stateless vessels on the high seas include the 1988 UN Convention against Illicit Traffic in Narcotic Drugs and Psychotropic Substances (art. 17(2)), the UN Convention against Transnational Organized Crime (TOC convention) Protocol against the Smuggling of Migrants (art. 8(1)), and the Straddling Fish Stocks Agreement (art. 21(17). Admittedly, all three provisions are vague on the issue.

110. Restatement FRLUS § 522 n.7. The alternate view is that a stateless vessel is not, by virtue of its stateless condition alone, subject to the jurisdiction of every state. See, e.g., Churchill & Lowe, supra, at 214. The authors argue for an examination of the recognized bases for jurisdiction under international law, including the territoriality, nationality, protective, and passive personality principles. Jurisdiction may also be founded on treaty sources, including Articles 99 and 108 of the LOS Convention and other conventions calling for suppression of certain activities at sea, such as the 1988 UN Convention against Illicit Traffic in Narcotic Drugs and Psychotropic Substances.

111. Molvan v. Attorney General for Palestine, 1948, A.C. 351, 369 (Privy Council).

112. The case for preserving the option of a flag state to assert diplomatic protection on behalf of one of its vessels that has been assimilated to statelessness by another state is more compelling in situations in which the master, crew, or vessel owner are denied the opportunity to raise international law defenses in criminal actions against them (or forfeiture actions against the vessel) in the assimilating state's domestic courts, as is the case under the MDLEA.

state; however, the seizure does not in itself result in a change in the vessel's nationality.[113] If a judicial order of confiscation does not by itself affect a vessel's nationality, it seems unlikely that an enforcing state's decision to assimilate it to statelessness would have a greater effect.[114]

Under Article 92(2), the decision whether to assimilate a vessel to a vessel without nationality is discretionary (i.e., it "may be" assimilated).[115] Moreover, the fact that international law permits a state to exercise jurisdiction over a stateless vessel does not by itself mean that enforcement vessels of a given state may do so. The enforcing vessel's flag state must have exercised its prescriptive jurisdiction to reach such vessels. Thus, for example, international law would not preclude an enforcement action against a stateless vessel engaged in drug trafficking on the high seas, but absent a U.S. statute like the MDLEA that criminalizes conduct by traffickers on stateless vessels the Coast Guard would have no law to enforce against the vessel.

4. U.S. Law Regarding Stateless Vessels

High-seas drift net fishers and illegal narcotics and migrant smugglers commonly use vessels that are in fact stateless or attempt to deceive law enforcement of their true registry to preempt boardings with the flag state's consent. The practice has generated a substantial body of U.S. case law on stateless vessels. The MDLEA provides an elaborate definition of a "vessel without nationality"[116] and makes such vessels subject to the jurisdiction of the United States for purposes of the prohibitions it lists.[117] The MDLEA definition of vessels subject to the jurisdiction of the United States also applies to fisheries violations under the Magnuson-Stevens Act.[118] Federal courts in the previously cited *Victoria* and *Rosero* cases held that the three circumstances set out in the MDLEA that will render a vessel "without nationality" (i.e., stateless) do not exhaust the possibilities, and that a vessel that is stateless as a matter of international law is also stateless under the MDLEA. The MDLEA further lists the means by which a vessel makes a claim of nationality or registry,[119] an important consideration in assimilating a vessel to statelessness for making inconsistent claims of nationality or failing to make a claim of nationality.

To avoid detection by maritime law enforcement vessels and aircraft, some of the newer smuggling techniques for high-value cargoes such as cocaine employ fully submersible vessels and self-propelled semisubmersible vessels. Congress addressed that threat vector in the Drug Trafficking Vessel Interdiction Act of 2008 (DTVIA),[120] one section of which provides that

---

113. ITLOS' reluctance to render a vessel's connection to its flag state legally inadequate is evident in The *Tomimaru* (Japan v. Russia) ITLOS Case No. 15 (Aug. 6, 2007), ¶¶ 70–76; noted in Bernard H. Oxman, Case Report, 102 Am. J. Int'l L. 316 (2008). Contra The *Grand Prince* (Belize v. France) ITLOS Case No. 8, (Apr. 20, 2001), ¶¶ 61, 77, 93 (application for prompt release dismissed on the ground that applicant failed to establish that it was the flag state at the time of the application). The vessel's provisional registration had expired. Additionally, Belize, the putative flag state, had subsequently deregistered the vessel.

114. As the ITLOS judgment in the *M/V Saiga* case demonstrates, the actual conduct of the putative flag state toward the vessel is an important consideration in determining the vessel's nationality. The M/V *Saiga* No. 2, supra, ¶ 68.

115. The permissive approach in Article 92(2) differs from the "assimilation" mechanism in Article 102, which addresses the status of warships engaged in piracy. Under Article 102, the assimilation is automatic ("are assimilated"). Article 102 of the 1982 LOS Convention is virtually identical with Article 16 of the 1958 Convention on the High Seas.

116. 46 U.S.C. § 70502(d).

117. 46 U.S.C. § 70502(c)(1)(A) (vessel without nationality); 46 U.S.C. § 70502(c)(1)(B) (vessel assimilated to a vessel without nationality).

118. 16 U.S.C. §§ 1801(44) & 2432(11).

119. 46 U.S.C. § 70502(e).

120. Pub. L. No. 110-407 (2008). The DTVIA was codified in 46 U.S.C. §§ 70501, 70502, & 70508, and 18 U.S.C. § 2285.

"whoever knowingly operates, or attempts or conspires to operate, by any means, or embarks in any submersible vessel or semi-submersible vessel that is without nationality and that is navigating or has navigated into, through, or from waters beyond the outer limit of the territorial sea of a single country or a lateral limit of that country's territorial sea with an adjacent country, with the intent to evade detection, shall be fined under this title, imprisoned not more than 15 years, or both."[121] In targeting stateless submersibles, the act reverses the normal burden of proof in criminal trials by treating the vessel's nationality as an affirmative defense and requiring the defendant to prove, by a preponderance of the evidence, that the submersible or semisubmersible vessel was lawfully registered and therefore not subject to the act.[122]

Although Congress has taken the position that stateless vessels engaged in drug trafficking or the use of high-seas drift nets are subject to U.S. jurisdiction,[123] some U.S. circuit courts of appeal have held that extraterritorial application of a criminal statute to those on board a foreign vessel violates the due process clause of the U.S. Constitution if the offense charged lacks an adequate nexus to the United States.[124] The restriction has not been applied to U.S. nationals (citizens or resident aliens) on board a stateless vessel.[125] The relationship between the nexus requirement and international law limits on state jurisdiction was examined by a federal circuit court of appeals in 1995. The court explained that "principles of international law are useful as a rough guide in determining whether application of the [MDLEA] would violate due process," and that a nexus requirement, imposed as a matter of due process, makes sense when the "rough guide" of international law also requires a nexus.[126] The court then distinguished stateless vessels, explaining that "international law restrictions on the right to assert jurisdiction over foreign vessels on the high seas and the concomitant exceptions have no applicability in connection with stateless vessels [because such] vessels are 'international pariahs.' By attempting to shrug the yoke of any nation's authority, they subject themselves to the jurisdiction of all nations solely as a consequence of the vessel's status as stateless."[127] In rejecting the defendant's due process objection to prosecution by the United States, the court explained:

> A defendant [on a properly flagged vessel] would have a legitimate expectation that because he has subjected himself to the laws of one nation, other nations will not be entitled to exercise jurisdiction without some nexus. . . . As a matter of comity and fairness, such an intrusion should not be undertaken absent proof that there is a connection between the criminal conduct and the United States

---

121. 18 U.S.C. § 2285(a). See also U.S. v. Ibarguen-Mosquera, 634 F.2d 1370 (11th Cir. 2011) (upholding conviction of stateless semisubmersible crew under the DTVIA over a due process clause objection).

122. 18 U.S.C. § 2285(e).

123. 46 U.S.C. §§ 70501–70507; 16 U.S.C. § 1802(44); Restatement FRLUS § 522 n.7.

124. See U.S. v. Klimavicius-Viloria, 144 F.3d 1249, 1257 (9th Cir. 1998) (explaining that the nexus requirement for application of criminal statutes serves the same function as the minimum contacts requirement for personal jurisdiction in civil suits). See also A. Mark Weisburd, Due Process Limits on Federal Extraterritorial Legislation?, 35 Colum. J. Transnat'l L. 379 (1997). One commentator points out the irony of invoking extraterritorial application of the Constitution to defeat extraterritorial application of a criminal statute. Curtis A. Bradley, Universal Jurisdiction and U.S. Law, 2001 Univ. Chi. Legal Forum 323, 338.

125. U.S. v. Caicedo, 47 F.3d 370 (9th Cir. 1995); U.S. v. Alvarez-Mena, 765 F.2d 1259 (5th Cir. 1985). In addition, some courts have held that the nexus requirement is unnecessary when the flag state consented to an assertion of U.S. jurisdiction. U.S. v. Cardales, 168 F.3d 548 (1st Cir. 1999); U.S. v. Martinez-Hidalgo, 993 F.2d 1052, 1056 (3d Cir. 1993). The Ninth Circuit disagrees, and requires a nexus even under those circumstances. Klimavicius-Viloria, 144 F.3d at 1257.

126. U.S. v. Caicedo, 47 F.3d at 371–72; U.S. v. Cardales, 168 F.3d at 553; U.S. v. Ibarguen-Mosquera, 634 F.3d 1370, 1378 (11th Cir. 2011).

127. U.S. v. Caicedo, 47 F.3d at 371 (citations and internal quotations omitted).

sufficient to justify the United States' pursuit of its interests. But where a defendant attempts to avoid the law of all nations by travelling on a stateless vessel, he has forfeited these protections of international law and can be charged with the knowledge that he has done so.[128]

Whether that rationale adequately explains why a constitutionally required nexus (in contrast to one that might be required by international law) is not required with respect to foreign nationals on a stateless vessel might reasonably be questioned. Perhaps anticipating that question, the court also pointed out that the defendants could not identify a single state where their drug trafficking would be lawful. Accordingly, any argument that they were not given constitutionally adequate notice that they could be haled into a court and prosecuted for their activity was unpersuasive.

F. UNMANNED MARINE VEHICLES

Although they have so far attracted less attention than their aerial counterparts, unmanned marine vehicles (UMVs) are increasingly being designed for and constructed and employed in a wide variety of commercial, scientific, and military applications. UMV capability and activity is not limited to the United States, and demand for UMVs is rapidly growing. Mindful that the expected rapid evolution in UMV design and applications argues against a detailed analysis of the treatment of UMVs under international law at this time, this section is limited to a brief discussion of the issues raised by their use in the maritime domain.

The LOS Convention's failure to define "vessels" has led some to question how the convention will be applied to UMVs.[129] Their growing use and the variety of their designs, capabilities, and applications highlight the importance of the inquiry. Much of the attention so far has centered on whether UMVs have the same navigation rights as more traditional vessels and whether naval or other government-owned and government-operated UMVs enjoy the same sovereign immunity protections as warships and other public vessels. For their part, the maritime law enforcement community sees UMVs (and their aerial counterparts) as both an asset that can be harnessed to enhance their mission performance and a threat that is increasingly being exploited by criminal organizations to avoid detection. Thus, a naval commander might be wondering whether a particular military UMV can navigate an international strait in transit passage, and if so what its obligations are under the applicable collision avoidance regulations. By contrast, a coast guard patrol boat commander might be asking whether a UMV suspected of smuggling contraband is a "vessel," and if so whether it can be boarded on the high seas only if a right of visit is legally justified or the UMV's flag state consents.

It bears repeating that a given craft's classification engenders both primary-order and second-order consequences. The second-order consequences on jurisdiction over the craft are mentioned above. With respect to primary-order consequences, a vessel is not an ordinary chattel, like a buoy, crab pot, or oceanographic research device. A vessel has a nationality and must carry appropriate documents to that effect. Most are entered in a registry. A vessel answers to its flag state, which has a positive obligation to exercise jurisdiction and control over it. Presumably, a vessel has a master and crew (who are on board). The master must ensure that the vessel adheres to the rules on collision avoidance and has a duty to come to the aid of other mariners in distress. Under the Uniform Code of Military Justice, a service member may be prosecuted for

---

128. Id. at 372–73 (citations omitted).
129. See Dalton, Future Navies, supra, 59 Nav. War Coll. Rev. at 22–25; Andrew H. Henderson, Murky Waters: The Legal Status of Unmanned Undersea Vehicles, 53 Nav. L. Rev. 55 (2006).

improperly hazarding any "vessel" of the armed forces.[130] In many nations, maritime liens can attach to a vessel, rendering the vessel liable in rem for certain torts and contracts, and it can be arrested and sold to satisfy a judgment. States may not discriminate in form or fact against the "ships" of any state.[131] Finally, a craft denominated a "vessel" may be subject to applicable safety and pollution prevention regulations.

The classification of UMVs entails a two-step inquiry. In the first step, the inquiry focuses on the claim made by the state of "nationality," to the extent such craft can be said to possess nationality. That is, does the state of nationality treat the craft as a vessel? The second step focuses on the extent to which the state's claim is consistent with international law, or has been accepted by other states as a matter of international law,[132] and is therefore opposable to other states.

1. The 2007 U.S. Assertion on UMVs

The current edition of the *Commander's Handbook on the Law of Naval Operations*, jointly issued by the U.S. Navy, Coast Guard, and Marine Corps in 2007, divides UMVs into two classes. The first class consists of unmanned surface vehicles (USVs), which are defined as watercraft that are either autonomous or remotely navigated and may be launched from surface, subsurface, or aviation platforms.[133] The second class includes unmanned underwater vehicles (UUVs), which are defined as underwater craft that are either autonomous or remotely navigated and may be launched from surface, subsurface, or aviation platforms.[134] The UUV definition excludes towed systems, hard-tethered devices, systems not capable of fully submerging, semisubmersible vehicles, and bottom crawlers. Despite the fact the *Commander's Handbook* denominates USVs and UUVs "vehicles" rather than vessels, the three services asserted in 2007 that USVs and UUVs engaged exclusively in government, noncommercial service are sovereign immune craft,[135] and that they enjoy the same navigation rights as vessels.[136]

Research in open sources in 2012 failed to uncover any objections to the U.S. assertion that UMVs enjoy the navigation rights and immunities of manned vessels during the five years following publication of the 2007 *Commander's Handbook*. It is also noteworthy that three of the twenty-two states that participated in the biennial Rim of the Pacific exercises in 2012 announced they would be deploying UMVs during the exercises,[137] without any apparent objection or comment by any other state. Several explanations for the absence of objections to UMV operations suggest themselves. One obvious explanation is that other states have already accepted that the meaning of "vessel" in the 1982 LOS Convention is broad enough to include UMVs. A second possibility is that, just as flag states have been given broad discretion to determine the requirements for registration and the right to fly the national flag, they have similar discretion to determine whether UMVs should be classified as vessels and regulated under the regime for those craft. Thus, a craft will be deemed a vessel if it meets the flag state's criteria for vessel status. Finally, a new customary norm might have already emerged, largely shaped by the rapidly developing state practice with respect to UAVs and their treatment as aircraft.

---

130. Uniform Code of Military Justice, art. 110, 10 U.S.C. § 910.

131. See, e.g., LOSC arts. 24(1)(b) & 42(2).

132. A state that persistently objects to a developing rule of customary law is not bound by the new rule; however, such objections must be made while the rule is developing.

133. Commander's Handbook, supra, ¶ 2.3.4.

134. Id. ¶ 2.3.5.

135. Id. ¶ 2.3.6. USV/UUV status does not depend on the status of the launch platform.

136. Id. ¶ 2.5.2.5. The *Handbook* does not specify whether the conclusion is based on customary or conventional law.

137. Australia, New Zealand, and the United States listed UMVs in their inventory. The Australian and New Zealand entries were listed as autonomous unmanned vehicles.

2. Analysis

Much of the analysis on the characterization of UMVs so far has fallen prey to the initial assumption that the terms "vessel" and "ship" have a single meaning and that the question whether UMVs are "vessels" is subject to a single binary answer: all UMVs are either vessels for all purposes or they are not vessels for any purpose. In fact, the prudent answer is that whether a given UMV is a "vessel" depends on two broad inquiries. The first concerns the context and application at issue. It focuses on the purpose of the classification and the consequences of including or excluding some or all UMVs from the class.[138] The second inquiry calls for application of the purpose-based definition to the design and operating characteristics of the particular UMV under examination. Given the diversity in UMV designs and operating modes, a single characterization that would apply to the entire class of unmanned surface and undersea vehicles, both existing and those yet to be developed, is at best premature and probably unwise.[139]

A recurring threshold inquiry in approaching UMV issues will be whether the question of classification is governed by customary or conventional law. If the latter, the relevant convention or treaty articles must be examined to determine if they include a treaty-specific definition (as does the 1972 International Regulations for Preventing Collisions at Sea convention (COLREGS) and whether the term "vessel" or "ship" is being used in an unrestricted or restricted sense. Given that the LOS Convention uses the terms "ship" and "vessel" in both the unrestricted and restricted senses, the broader meaning should be applied anywhere the convention uses one of the terms without a qualifying restriction.[140]

A logical starting point for the unrestricted definition is the irreducible core of each of the specialized, restricted definitions. In the United States, that core definition, reflected in 1 U.S.C. § 3, is "every description of water-craft or other artificial contrivance used or capable of being used as a means of transportation on the water." Turning to the meaning of the term under international law, some might question whether the unrestricted definition should be limited to vehicles with a transportation function, given that the broad freedom-of-navigation articles are not limited to vessels engaged in "transportation." Even in the United States, a recently enacted statute on stolen vessels defines a vessel as "any watercraft or other contrivance used or designed for transportation or navigation on, under, or immediately above, water." By adding "navigation" to the "transportation" function of the watercraft the new definition would seem to eliminate any doubt as to whether UMVs are included.[141] Similarly, a study by the American Branch of the International Law Association concluded that the transportation function requirement should

---

138. On the domestic level, this factor distinguishes the *Dutra* and *Lozman* cases examined in section A above. *Stewart v. Dutra Construction Co.* involved a personal injury claim by an engineer who was seeking specialized compensation as a maritime worker on the theory that the dredge on which he was employed at the time of his injury was a vessel. By contrast, *Lozman v. City of Riviera Beach* concerned enforcement of a maritime lien against a floating home.

139. For example, the *SeaFox* UUV designed to locate and destroy mines (self-destructing in the process) functions much like a smart torpedo.

140. This is consistent with the Navy judge advocate general's approach to the question of unmanned aerial overflight rights. See Department of the Navy, Office of the Judge Advocate General (Code 10), Memorandum for the Naval Warfare Development Command on the Use of Unmanned Aerial Vehicles (UAVs) while Transiting the Strait of Hormuz, Ser. 103/337 (Apr. 20, 2005) (unclassified). The memo first observes that "international law provisions on the right of transit passage are silent on whether unmanned vehicles are contemplated in the definition of 'aircraft.'" Next it notes that international law instruments go to great lengths to define specialized terms such as "military aircraft," "civil aircraft," and "auxiliary aircraft." It then makes the logic argument that anywhere the convention refers to "aircraft" without qualification "one must reasonably conclude that the term 'aircraft' includes all vehicles capable of flight, both manned and unmanned."

141. 18 U.S.C. § 2311.

be eliminated. Thus, the ILA's suggested definition for "vessel" is any "human-made device, including submersible vessels, capable of traversing the sea."[142] That definition may be too open-ended, however. For example, a torpedo is a "human-made device" that is "capable of traversing the sea," but few would argue that such weapons meet the definition of a vessel.

The sounder approach to an unrestricted vessel definition would be to require that the watercraft be capable of transportation or navigation. If, however, the transportation function is included in the definition, the follow-on question is "transportation of what?" Must the craft transport people or cargo, or would a craft that carries only sensors or communications equipment meet the definition? Warships are ships even though they do not transport passengers or cargo. They do, however, transport the equipment and weapons essential to their security function, as well as the crew to operate them. If it is assumed that the transportation requirement refers to the carriage of something that has a functional value other than the craft itself, that functional definition would include craft that carry (i.e., transport) sensors and other equipment that enhance or extend the user's capabilities and for which navigation rights are essential to its function.

a. Treaty Construction and Application

For states that are party to the LOS Convention, analysis begins with the text of the convention and the accepted canons of treaty interpretation. Article 31 of the Vienna Convention on the Law of Treaties instructs that a treaty is to be interpreted in good faith in accordance with the ordinary meaning to be given to the terms of the treaty in their context and in the light of its object and purpose.[143] Account shall also be taken of any subsequent practice in the application of the treaty that establishes the agreement of the parties regarding its interpretation.[144] Recourse may be had to supplementary means of interpretation, including the preparatory work of the treaty and the circumstances of its conclusion, in order to confirm the meaning resulting from the application of Article 31, or to determine the meaning when the interpretation according to Article 31 leaves the meaning ambiguous or obscure or leads to a result that is manifestly absurd or unreasonable.[145] When a treaty has been authenticated in two or more languages, as the LOS Convention was, the text is equally authoritative in each language, and the terms of the treaty are presumed to have the same meaning in each authentic text.[146]

Because the LOS Convention incorporates by reference the IMO conventions that constitute "generally accepted international" regulations, rules, and standards,[147] various of its articles arguably incorporate relevant definitions of "ships" or "vessels" from the SOLAS, MARPOL, and COLREGS conventions. Each defines the term "ship" or "vessel" somewhat differently, to best serve the convention's object and purpose. The purpose and object of a convention setting out rules on collision avoidance is best served by a broad construction of the class of vessels to which it applies, while the purpose and object of a convention on ship registration or maritime liens and mortgages might call for a narrower construction that focuses on commercial shipping and the needs of creditors. The default, unrestricted use of the terms "vessel" and "ship" in the LOS Convention must be broad enough to include both applications.

---

142. See Walker, Definitions for the Law of the Sea, supra, at 55–61, 300–301.
143. Vienna Convention on Treaties, supra, art. 31.
144. Id. art. 31(b)(3)(b).
145. Id. art. 32.
146. Id. art. 33; LOSC art. 320.
147. See, e.g., LOSC arts. 94(4)(c), 94(5), 210(6), & 211(2).

Most of the LOS Convention articles on navigation use the terms "ship" and "vessel" in the unrestricted sense. The high-seas freedom to "navigate" (Article 87) and "sail" (Article 90); the right of innocent passage (Article 17), which is within the "rules applicable to all ships"; and the right of transit passage for "all ships and aircraft" all incorporate the unrestricted definition. Article 20 limits the manner of innocent passage for "submarines and other underwater vehicles," a subset of the larger class of "vessels." Neither term is defined. It is significant, however, that both submarines and "other underwater vehicles" are addressed in the subsection on "rules applicable to all ships," and both classes are required to travel on the surface and "show their flag," indicating that however underwater vehicles are distinguished from submarines, they too must sail under a state's flag. The issue whether a UMV is entitled to exercise freedom of navigation on the high seas under Article 90 would be analyzed by applying the unrestricted term "ship" to the UMV.[148] By contrast, whether that UMV has sovereign immunity under either Article 95 or 96 would be analyzed by applying the restricted definitions found in Articles 29, 32, and 96.

b. Customary International Law Analysis

For states that are not party to the 1982 LOS Convention, questions concerning UMVs will be governed by a mix of customary law and conventions other than the LOS Convention (e.g., COLREGS), depending on the nature of the inquiry. A customary law analysis would also be necessary to determine if a new norm applicable to UMVs has emerged outside the LOS Convention framework. The three U.S. maritime services declared the U.S. position on selected aspects of the UMV question in the 2007 *Commander's Handbook* and have acted consistently with that position, without apparent protest by other states, for more than five years.

Congress' position with respect to submersible and semisubmersible vessels in the MDLEA will be relevant to any inquiry regarding state practice. Congress defined those vessels in a way that includes both manned and unmanned watercraft.[149] It then criminalized the operation of such craft if "stateless," an implied declaration of Congress' intent that unmanned submersible and semisubmersible watercraft be treated as vessels that must comply with the law of the sea requirements for establishing nationality.

The majority position (as reflected in the 2000 ILA report on customary law) is that to establish a new rule of customary law extending navigation rights to UMVs (if not already covered by LOS Convention or existing customary law), the rule proponent would need to demonstrate widespread and public state practice. Acts do not count as state practice if they are not public,[150] and the practices of one or two states with UMVs will not necessarily support a claim of navigation rights under customary law. At the time of this writing, no such systematic study has been done.

From the U.S. point of view, the general definition provided in 1 U.S.C. § 3 ("every description of water-craft or other artificial contrivance used or capable of being used as a means of transportation on the water") is likely to be given substantial weight. The U.S. Supreme Court has held that this is the default definition in U.S. law.[151] To be sure, there are other, purpose-

---

148. An additional consideration is whether, in construing the terms, states and international tribunals must or should defer to the flag state's decision if it chooses to register the UMV as a vessel.
149. 46 U.S.C. § 70502(f).
150. ILA, Committee on Formation of Customary (General) International Law: Final Report of the Committee 15 (2000).
151. Stewart v. Dutra Const. Co., 543 U.S. 481, 490 (2005) (1 U.S.C. § 3 supplies the default definition of "vessel" throughout the U.S. Code, unless the context indicates otherwise).

specific definitions in the U.S. Code, just as there are in international vessel registration, safety, pollution prevention, arrest, and limitation-of-liability conventions.

G. STATUS OF AIRCRAFT

Aircraft, both manned and unmanned, are now commonly launched from military and commercial vessels. Applications include logistics support; crew and passenger transport; intelligence, surveillance, and reconnaissance (ISR); search and rescue; law enforcement; force protection; and other national defense missions. The vessel-aircraft partnership requires that the seagoing officer be familiar with the status of those aircraft and any restrictions on their operations at sea.

Chapter 5 addresses the overflight rights of aircraft, including the distinction between national airspace (the airspace over a state's internal waters, territorial sea, and archipelagic waters) and international airspace (all airspace seaward of any state's territorial sea). The right of overflight above the high seas is expressly recognized in Article 87 of the LOS Convention and is extended into the airspace over the EEZ by Article 58(1) (air defense identification zones and flight information regions extending into international airspace are examined in chapter 6). In addition, civil and military aircraft enjoy a right of transit passage and archipelagic sea-lanes passage in their normal mode of operation over international straits and archipelagic sea-lanes. Aircraft do not have a right of innocent passage, however, and save in cases of force majeure or distress, have no right to enter a nation's airspace absent the state's consent (subject to the transit and archipelagic sea-lanes rights described above).

International law broadly distinguishes between civil and state aircraft. Article 17 of the Chicago Convention on Civil Aviation provides that "aircraft have the nationality of the State in which they are registered."[152] The convention applies only to civil aircraft; state aircraft are not included. The Chicago Convention does not define state aircraft, but it does stipulate that aircraft used in military, customs, and police services shall be deemed to be state aircraft.[153] While the Chicago Convention is comparatively generous in granting to civil aircraft the right to overfly national airspace, no such rights are accorded to state aircraft or to pilotless aircraft.[154]

The rights and responsibilities of aircraft are only briefly addressed in the LOS Convention. Generally, the LOS Convention's navigation articles do not distinguish between civil and military aircraft or manned and unmanned aircraft.[155] Some law enforcement actions (e.g., hot pursuit, right-of-visit boardings, and pirate ship seizures) can be carried out only by military or other specially authorized and marked aircraft.[156] The LOS Convention does not define the term "military aircraft"; nor does it directly address the sovereign immunity of military or other state aircraft.[157] The *San Remo Manual* defines "military aircraft" for purposes of the law of naval

---

152. Chicago Convention on Civil Aviation, supra, art. 17. International Civil Aviation Organization Doc. 7300/9. See also Restatement FRLUS § 501 n.10.

153. Chicago Convention on Civil Aviation, supra, art. 3(b).

154. Id. art. 8. At this writing, the U.S. Federal Aviation Administration is reportedly relaxing restrictions on unmanned aerial vehicle flights in U.S. national airspace. Currently, civil or military UAV operation in U.S. national airspace requires a certificate of authorization (COA) from the FAA.

155. One exception is found in Article 39 of the LOS Convention, which requires civil aircraft in transit passage to "observe the Rules of the Air established by the International Civil Aviation Organization as they apply to civil aircraft"; however, with respect to state aircraft, it provides that they "will normally comply with such safety measures and will at all times operate with due regard for the safety of navigation." Article 39 applies mutatis mutandis to aircraft in archipelagic sea-lanes passage. See LOSC art. 54.

156. See, e.g., LOSC arts. 107, 110(4)–(5), & 111(5).

157. One exception is Article 236 of the LOS Convention, which exempts from the requirements of Part XII on protection of the marine environment "aircraft owned or operated by a State and used, for the time being, only on government non-commercial service."

warfare as "aircraft operated by commissioned units of the armed forces of a State having the military marks of that State, commanded by a member of the armed forces and manned by a crew subject to regular armed forces discipline."[158] The *Commander's Handbook* adopts the same definition.[159] The *Handbook* also includes unmanned aerial vehicles in that definition.[160] Finally, the *Handbook* provides a brief overview of the navigational rules for aircraft.[161] Additional guidance is available in chapter 4 of *Air Force Operations and the Law*.

Owing to the strict regulations governing military flights in foreign airspace, Navy and Coast Guard vessel and aircraft commanders must be familiar with applicable regulations for obtaining clearance for aircraft to fly over or land in foreign territory and to fly over foreign territorial seas.[162] Aircraft-equipped vessels intending to visit a foreign port must specifically request clearance to fly aircraft in the host nation's airspace. Aircraft commanders are generally required to confirm that such clearance has been received, even when another unit or entity is responsible for obtaining clearances. If clearance is not received, the aircraft may not fly, except to the extent a right of transit or archipelagic sea-lanes passage exists.

The status and immunities of military and auxiliary aircraft[163] are not addressed in the LOS Convention with the same detail as the status and immunities of warships.[164] Articles 42 and 236 do recognize the sovereign status of state aircraft.[165] As sovereign instrumentalities,[166] military and auxiliary aircraft are entitled to the privileges and immunities customarily accorded warships and naval auxiliaries under international law.[167] Absent agreement to the contrary, those

---

158. San Remo Manual, supra, ¶ 13(j). The Manual also provides a definition of "auxiliary aircraft," "civil aircraft," and "civil airliners." See also Commander's Handbook, supra, ¶ 2.4.1.

159. Commander's Handbook, supra, ¶ 2.4.1.

160. Id. ¶ 2.4.4. See also Department of Defense, DoD Directive 4540.1. Unmanned aerial vehicles (UAVs) are defined as pilotless aircraft that are either autonomous or remotely piloted and may be launched from surface or aviation platforms or land bases. Commander's Handbook, supra, ¶ 2.4.4. UAVs may also be launched from submarines or UUVs. The Air and Missile Warfare Manual categorizes military UAVs as "military aircraft." See Harvard University Program on Humanitarian Policy and Conflict Research, Manual on International Law Applicable to Air and Missile Warfare, May 15, 2009, available at http://www.ihlresearch.org/amw/manual/ (accessed Feb. 1, 2013). Reportedly, there were no objections among the drafting parties to that characterization.

161. Commander's Handbook, supra, ¶ 2.9.3.

162. See DoD, Foreign Clearance Guide, DoD Directive 4500.54E (Dec. 28, 2009). U.S. Coast Guard aircraft follow DoD foreign clearance procedures. U.S. Coast Guard, Air Operations Manual, ¶ 3.A.9, COMDTINST M3710.1G (Feb. 2013).

163. Auxiliary aircraft are state aircraft, other than military aircraft, that are owned or under the exclusive control of the armed forces. Such aircraft are also exempt from foreign search and inspection. See Commander's Handbook, supra, ¶ 2.4.3.

164. Like the 1982 LOS Convention, the draft UN Convention on Jurisdictional Immunities of States and Their Property (2004) expressly addresses the immunity of state-owned and state-operated vessels (Article 16), but it provides no similar express recognition for state-owned or state-operated aircraft. It does, however, exempt "property of a military character or used or intended for use in the performance of military functions" (Article 21(b)).

165. It is sometimes asked why the *transit* passage regime (and, by incorporation under Article 54, the archipelagic sea-lanes passage regime) recognizes the immunity of state aircraft but no similar recognition is included in the *innocent* passage articles (which give extensive treatment to the immunity of warships and other government vessels). The answer, of course, is that aircraft do not enjoy a right of innocent passage (and therefore would not be addressed in the innocent passage articles); however, they do have rights under the other two passage regimes. That may also explain why the sovereign immunity of military aircraft is not as well developed in the LOS Convention as the immunities of warships.

166. Commander's Handbook, supra, ¶ 2.4.2. The 1919 Paris Convention was the only air law instrument to expressly codify the rule that military aircraft are entitled to "the privileges which are customarily accorded to foreign ships of war." Convention relating to the Regulation of Aerial Navigation, art. 32, Oct. 13, 1919, 297 L.N.T.S. 173 (1922).

167. U.S. Air Force, Air Force Operations and the Law: A Guide for Air, Space and Cyber Forces 71 (2009), available at http://www.afjag.af.mil/library/ (accessed Feb. 1, 2013). See also Thomas A. Geraci, Overflight, Landing Rights, Customs, and Clearances, 7 Air Force L. Rev. 155 (1994).

privileges and immunities include exemption from duties and taxation;[168] immunity from search, seizure, and inspections; and any other exercise of jurisdiction by the host nation over the aircraft, personnel, equipment, or cargo on board. Foreign officials may not board military or other state aircraft without the consent of the aircraft commander.[169] U.S. military aircraft commanders are generally instructed not to authorize boarding, search, seizure, inspection, or similar exercises of jurisdiction by foreign authorities except by direction of the appropriate service headquarters or the U.S. embassy in the country concerned. However, *U.S. Navy Regulations* requires aircraft commanders to comply with applicable U.S. or foreign quarantine laws and to afford every assistance to U.S. or foreign health officials, insofar as permitted by the requirements of military necessity and security.[170] Should an aircraft commander decline to certify the aircraft's compliance with the foreign state's customs, immigration, or quarantine requirements, the foreign state authorities may direct the aircraft to depart. Sunken military aircraft retain their sovereign immunity unless the flag state relinquishes or abandons title to the aircraft. Indeed, the same is true for all sovereign property, including unmanned vehicles, test missiles, and practice torpedoes.[171] As a consequence, military aircraft cannot be salvaged without the consent of the flag state.

---

168. The U.S. government policy on the exemption from duties and taxation is set out in the DoD Foreign Clearance Guide, supra, ¶ C2.1.7.
169. U.S. Navy Regulations, supra, art. 0860.
170. Id. art. 0859; see also Commander's Handbook, supra, ¶ 3.2.3.
171. Commander's Handbook, supra, ¶ 3.9.

Marine Stewardship and International Law

The prevailing twenty-first-century marine stewardship ethic calls for a balanced and sustainable use of the oceans and their resources while at the same time preserving the marine environment and protecting it against threats from pollution, climate change, ocean acidification, harmful algal blooms, hypoxia, habitat destruction, marine debris, and the spread of marine pathogens and invasive species. Elements of the marine stewardship ethic can be found in the 1972 Stockholm Declaration,[1] the 1987 Brundtland Report,[2] the Rio Declaration of Principles agreed to at the 1992 UN Conference on Environment and Development,[3] and the 2010 U.S. National Ocean Policy.[4] To some degree, those elements have already been incorporated into the law of the sea, both through the 1982 LOS Convention and in the various treaties, codes, and resolutions developed under the auspices of the International Maritime Organization (IMO),[5] the UN Environment Program (UNEP), and the FAO Committee on Fisheries. The stewardship ethic also informs the ecosystem-based management approach.[6] Effective maritime safety and security regimes further stewardship goals by preventing incidents, whether accidental or intentional, that might result in harm to the marine environment.

Comprehensive coverage of the growing field of international environmental law would require a volume in itself. No such coverage is attempted here.[7] Rather, this chapter focuses on those aspects of international law that relate directly to the oceans and are likely to be of particular relevance to the seagoing officer. Section A examines the international law addressing marine pollution, and section B addresses the sustainable use of marine living resources.[8] The materials in both sections are supplemented by the chapters that describe the particular legal regime applicable in each of the ocean zones.

---

1. Declaration of the United Nations Conference on the Human Environment, U.N. Doc. A/Conf.48/14/Rev. 1 (1973); 11 I.L.M. 1416 (1972). See The Stockholm Declaration and Law of the Marine Environment (Myron H. Nordquist et al. eds., 2003). The 1972 conference led the United Nations to establish the UN Environment Program in Nairobi, Kenya.
2. Our Common Future: Report of the World Commission on Environment and Development (1987), U.N. Doc. A/42/427, Annex (1987) (commonly referred to as the Brundtland Report, in honor of the commission's chair).
3. Rio Declaration on Environment and Development, 31 I.L.M. 874 (1992).
4. Exec. Order 13,547, Stewardship of the Ocean, Our Coasts, and the Great Lakes, July 19, 2010, 75 Fed. Reg. 43023 (July 22, 2010).
5. Convention on the Inter-governmental Maritime Consultative Organization, Mar. 6, 1948, 9 U.S.T. 621, 289 U.N.T.S. 48.
6. See generally Lawrence Juda, International Law and Ocean Use Management: The Evolution of Ocean Governance (1996). But see Bernard Oxman, The Territorial Temptation, 110 Am. J. Int'l L. 830, 848 (2006) (highlighting the "territorializing" effect of spatial planning).
7. See generally Shipping, Law and the Marine Environment in the 21st Century (Richard Caddell & Rhidian Thomas eds., 2013).
8. The inherent tension in the concept of sustainable development was examined by the ICJ in 1997. See The Gabčíkovo-Nagymaros Project, 1997 I.C.J. 41, 78 (Sept. 25).

A. POLLUTION OF THE MARINE ENVIRONMENT

Earth's marine ecosystems are in trouble, particularly those near densely populated coasts. The threat vectors are familiar to most mariners. In their 2001 *A Sea of Troubles* report, the Group of Experts on Scientific Aspects of Marine Environmental Protection (GESAMP) catalogued a growing list of "pressures and effects" that threaten the environmental integrity of the oceans.[9] Similarly, the U.S. Commission on Oceans Policy found that "coastal waters are one of the nation's greatest assets, yet they are being bombarded with pollution from all directions."[10] The 2011 release of more than 10,000 tons of contaminated cooling water from Japan's crippled Fukushima nuclear plant reactors, which contained levels of iodine-131 at least one hundred times greater than the legal limit allowed for sea discharge, and the island-size debris field that started coming ashore on U.S. beaches in 2012 are prime examples.

Progress in the legal regimes for protection of the marine environment and responsible conservation and management of marine resources is too often made only in response to front-page disasters or exposés. Spills from the tankers *Torrey Canyon* (1967), *Argo Merchant* (1976), *Amoco Cadiz* (1978), and *Exxon Valdez* (1989) focused attention on the risks posed by oil transport by sea.[11] Offshore oil exploration and production activities came under close scrutiny following the 1969 spill from an oil production platform off the Santa Barbara coast, the much larger 1979–80 spill from the Ixtoc oil well in Mexico's Bay of Campeche, and more recently the 2010 *Deepwater Horizon* oil spill in the Gulf of Mexico. The collapse of key fisheries off the Grand Banks and Georges Banks and precipitous declines in global marine mammal populations and tuna stocks may be a signal that some species have already passed the point of no return.

It is customary to trace the developing law of marine pollution to the ICJ judgment in the *Corfu Channel* case or even to the earlier *Trail Smelter* international arbitration decision.[12] Together, the cases established the *sic utere tuo ut alienum non laedas* principle, which declares that a state may not knowingly allow its territory to be used in a manner that causes harm to another state.[13] Importantly, the *Trail Smelter* case concerned only transboundary air emissions emanating from a smelter in Canada that flowed across the border and caused environmental harm in the United States.[14] At the time, international law had little to say about intrastate pollution, leaving that subject to the domestic law of the affected states.

One of the first treaties on marine oil pollution was agreed to four years before the 1958 Geneva conventions on the law of the sea were completed.[15] The 1954 "OILPOL" Convention, which narrowly dealt with vessel-source oil pollution, was superseded by the more comprehensive MARPOL Convention in 1978.[16] In 1972 a second marine environmental

---

9. Group of Experts on Scientific Aspects of Marine Environmental Protection, A Sea of Troubles, GESAMP Reports and Studies No. 70 (2001).

10. U.S. Commission on Ocean Policy, An Ocean Blueprint for the 21st Century 2004 (July 22, 2004).

11. See R. Michael M'Gonigle & Mark W. Zacher, Pollution, Politics and International Law (1979).

12. Corfu Channel case (U.K. v. Albania) 1949 I.C.J. 4 (Apr. 9) (holding that every state has an "obligation not to allow knowingly its territory to be used for acts contrary to the rights of other States"). Trail Smelter case (U.S. v. Canada), ¶ 157, 3 Rep. Int'l Arb. Awards 1905 (1941). See generally Restatement FRLUS § 601 n.1.

13. See Restatement FRLUS § 601, Introductory Note (sources of environmental law). See also Advisory Opinion on the Legality of the Threat or Use of Nuclear Weapons, ¶ 29, 1996 I.C.J. 226 (July 8).

14. See Convention on Long-Range Transboundary Air Pollution, Nov. 13, 1979, 34 U.S.T. 3043, 1302 U.N.T.S. 217.

15. International Convention on the Prevention of Pollution of the Sea by Oil [hereinafter "OILPOL"], May 12, 1954, 12 U.S.T. 2989, 327 U.N.T.S. 3.

16. International Convention for the Prevention of Pollution of the Sea by Vessels [hereinafter "MARPOL Convention"], Nov. 2, 1973, T.I.A.S. No. 10561, 1340 U.N.T.S. 184, as amended by 1978 Tanker Safety and Pollution Prevention Protocol, June 1, 1978, 1340 U.N.T.S. 61. See generally Alan Tan, Vessel-Source Marine Pollution: The Law and Politics of International Regulation (2006).

protection treaty, the London Dumping Convention, was adopted to address the deliberate at-sea disposal of wastes and other matter, other than ship-generated wastes (which are regulated under MARPOL).[17]

The four 1958 Geneva conventions only briefly addressed protection of the marine environment. The Convention on the High Seas included just two articles on pollution. One required states to promulgate regulations to prevent oil discharges from ships and pipelines and to control pollution from seabed activities.[18] The other addressed the dumping of radioactive wastes and pollution from activities involving radioactive materials or other harmful agents.[19] The Convention on the Territorial Seas and the Contiguous Zone recognized the right of a coastal state to exercise the control necessary to prevent or punish infringements of its "sanitary" regulations within its territorial sea.[20] The Convention on the Continental Shelf obligated states to undertake in safety zones (if they chose to establish them) "all appropriate measures for the protection of the living resources of the sea from harmful agents."[21]

Reflecting growing concern over the deteriorating condition of the marine environment and emergence of the developing marine stewardship ethic, Part XII of the 1982 LOS Convention devotes some forty-five articles to preservation and protection of the marine environment. The convention has been described as the strongest comprehensive environmental treaty now in existence or likely to emerge for quite some time.[22] Part XII begins by solemnly declaring that all states have an obligation to protect and preserve the marine environment.[23] Consistent with the stewardship ethic, the convention sets a broad marine pollution prevention charter. Article 1 defines "pollution of the marine environment" as the introduction by man, directly or indirectly, of substances or energy into the marine environment, including estuaries, which results or is likely to result in deleterious effects, including harm to living resources and marine life, hazards to human health, hindrance of marine activities, impairment of water quality, or reduction of amenities.

Close inspection of Part XII and the complementary marine environmental protection treaties reveals a strong preference for pollution prevention and reduction over after-the-fact response and mitigation. Moreover, the scope of pollution "response" is increasingly being viewed as extending beyond mere removal of pollutants to include full restoration of the affected marine environment to the maximum extent possible. The "polluter pays" principle serves that remedial goal by requiring the polluter to fully internalize the costs of the polluting incident. For the most part, the LOS Convention's approach to marine pollution is based on the zones defined

---

17. Convention on the Prevention of Marine Pollution by Dumping of Wastes and Other Matter [hereinafter "London Dumping Convention"], Dec. 29, 1973, 26 U.S.T. 2403, T.I.A.S. No. 8165.

18. 1958 Convention on the High Seas, supra, art. 24.

19. Id. art. 25.

20. The debate over the extent to which marine pollution measures fall within the class of "sanitary" regulations contemplated by the contiguous zone regime was to some extent mooted by the creation of the EEZ regime, where the coastal state has jurisdiction with regard to protection and preservation of the marine environment.

21. 1958 Convention on the Continental Shelf, supra, art. 5.

22. Bernard H. Oxman, The Future of the United Nations Convention on the Law of the Sea, 88 Am. J. Int'l L. 488, 496 (1994).

23. LOSC art. 192. See also Restatement FRLUS §§ 601 & 603. The LOS Convention does not define "marine environment," despite its importance in the application of Part XII and to the availability of provisional measures under Article 290(1). The International Seabed Authority gave the term "marine environment" an expansive interpretation. See ISA, Regulations on Prospecting and Exploration for Polymetallic Nodules in the Area, Reg. 2(2), ISBA/6/A/18 (2000).

according to their distance from the baseline, without regard to the boundaries of relevant eco-systems, rather than the now widely embraced ecosystem-based management approach.[24]

The 1982 LOS Convention was never intended to serve as the sole or complete legal regime for protection of the marine environment. Rather, it was drafted to serve as a flexible international framework within which existing or subsequently enacted treaties governing particular activities may be implemented globally.[25] Additionally, to the extent relevant authorities may also be found in customary international law, the LOS Convention's Preamble saves such customary law as well.[26] In nearly all cases, the LOS Convention and the related treaties operate in harmony with each other. When potential or actual conflicts develop, however, the LOS Convention's "supremacy clauses" subordinate those other international agreements to the LOS Convention.[27] The one exception is the UN Charter, which by its terms supersedes any other conflicting treaty,[28] including the LOS Convention.

1. State Obligations to Protect the Marine Environment

The core organizing principle of Part XII of the LOS Convention is that all states have an obligation to protect and preserve the marine environment.[29] At the same time, states have the sovereign right to exploit their natural resources,[30] and to engage in any number of legally protected activities in the oceans. Those activities are, however, subject to the convention articles on protection of the marine environment and the general duty of states to exercise due regard for the interests of other states and carry out their activities in a manner that does not constitute an abuse of rights.[31] To promote and facilitate compliance, executive department agencies in the United States, including the Navy and Coast Guard, have promulgated environmental protection and compliance policies for their personnel.[32]

Part XII of the LOS Convention is organized into eleven sections (the complete text is reproduced in appendix C). Sections 1–4 address general obligations of states. Section 5 is broken down into the six main sources of ocean pollution: land-based activities, continental shelf exploration and exploitation, seabed mining, ocean dumping, vessel-source pollution, and marine pollution from or through the atmosphere. Section 6 addresses marine environmental protection enforcement measures. Section 7 prescribes safeguards applicable to those enforcement measures. Section 8, consisting of a single article, addresses enhanced protections for ice-covered

---

24. See Lawrence Juda & Timothy Hennessey, Governance Profiles and the Management of the Uses of Large Marine Ecosystems, 32 Ocean Dev. & Int'l L. 41–67 (2001).

25. UN Division for Ocean Affairs and the Law of the Sea, The Law of the Sea: Protection and Preservation of the Marine Environment, U.N. Sales No. E.90.V.3 (1990).

26. LOSC, Preamble, ¶ 8 ("affirming that matters not regulated by this Convention continue to be governed by the rules and principles of general international law") & art. 293. The continuing relevance of customary law was recognized by ITLOS in the *M/V Saiga* case, in which it cited Article 293 before turning to customary law to address the use of force by the Ghanaian enforcement vessel.

27. See LOSC arts. 293 & 311. LOSC Article 237 stipulates that the provisions of Part XII are without prejudice to other special conventions and agreements that relate to the protection and preservation of the marine environment. Accordingly, "special conventions" that relate to the protection and preservation of the marine environment come within the scope of Article 237, not Article 311. See United Nations Convention on the Law of the Sea 1982: A Commentary, vol. V, at 243 (Myron H. Nordquist et al. eds., 1989). Additionally, Article 51(1) of the LOS Convention assigns priority to certain preexisting agreements regarding archipelagic waters.

28. UN Charter, supra, art. 103.

29. LOSC art. 192.

30. Id. art. 193.

31. Id. art. 300.

32. See, e.g., U.S. Navy, Environmental Readiness Program Manual OPNAVINST 5090.1 (series); U.S. Coast Guard, Commanding Officer's Environmental Guide, COMDTPUB P5090.1 (series).

areas in the EEZ. Section 9 briefly deals with responsibility and liability (largely relegating the subjects to other sources of international law). Section 10 saves the application of sovereign immunity principles. Section 11 sets out the method for resolving potential conflicts between the Part XII articles and any other applicable treaties or agreements.

a. General Obligations of States

The 1982 LOS Convention expressly requires *action*: all states must take the necessary measures to prevent, reduce, and control pollution of the marine environment from any source, using the best practicable means at their disposal and in accordance with their capabilities (a principle referred to as "common but differentiated responsibility").[33] Those measures must include necessary steps to control pollution from the use of technologies under the state's jurisdiction and to control and prevent the introduction of alien species to an area of the marine environment where they may cause significant harm.[34] In taking pollution control measures, a state may not shift or transfer damage from one area of the marine environment to another or attempt to transform one type of pollution into another.[35]

The convention repeatedly calls for *cooperation*: all states must cooperate on a regional and global basis, directly or through competent international organizations such as the IMO, to formulate international rules and standards to prevent, reduce, and control pollution.[36] In the *Straits of Johor* case, ITLOS reiterated that the "duty to cooperate is a fundamental principle in the prevention of pollution of the marine environment under Part XII of the Convention and general international law."[37] A commonly used framework for regional cooperation is a "regional seas" agreement formed under the auspices of the UN Environment Program[38] and encouraged by Agenda 21.[39] In addition, a number of states have entered into regional port state control (PSC) agreements to promote vessel safety and control vessel-source pollution. The PSC framework is introduced in chapter 4 and is more fully developed below.

The Convention calls for *foresight*: it requires states to observe, measure, evaluate, and analyze, using scientific methods, the risks or effects of pollution of the marine environment.[40] In particular, states must keep under surveillance the effects of any activities they permit, or in which they engage, in order to determine whether those activities are likely to pollute the marine environment.[41] In addition, if a state believes that a planned activity under its jurisdiction or control may cause substantial pollution of or significant and harmful changes to the marine environment, it is required to assess the potential effects of the activity on the marine environment

---

33. LOSC art. 194(1).

34. Id. art. 196.

35. Id. art. 195. This prohibition may be implicated when in situ burning is used to remove oil from the oceans, potentially resulting in significant air pollution.

36. See, e.g., id. arts. 197 (general duty to cooperate), 208(5) (duty to cooperate in establishing rules and standards governing pollution from seabed activities subject to national jurisdiction), & 211(1) (duty to cooperate in establishing rules and standards governing pollution by ocean dumping).

37. Land Reclamation by Singapore in and around the Straits of Johor (Malaysia v. Singapore), Provisional Measures, ITLOS Case No. 12, Order of Oct. 8, 2003, ¶ 92, 126 Int'l L. Rep. 487. The Joint Declaration in the case by ad hoc Judges Oxman and Hossain provides a well-crafted framework for meaningful and effective cooperation.

38. See UN Environment Program, Regional Seas Program, available at http://www.unep.org/regionalseas/ (accessed Feb. 1, 2013).

39. Chapter 17 of Agenda 21 applies to enclosed and semi-enclosed seas. See Agenda 21, June 16, 1992, 31 I.L.M. 874 (1992). Article 17.119 of Agenda 21 urges states to strengthen and extend relevant UNEP Regional Seas programs.

40. LOSC art. 204.

41. Id. art. 204(2).

and communicate reports of the results of such assessments to the cognizant international organi-zation.[42] Finally, recognizing that even the best prevention programs may fail, states are required to develop contingency plans for responding to pollution incidents.[43]

The convention requires due *consideration* for other states: states are charged with an obliga-tion to take all necessary measures to ensure that activities under their jurisdiction or control are conducted in a manner that guards against pollution damage to other states, and that pollution arising from incidents or activities under their jurisdiction or control does not spread beyond the areas where they exercise sovereign rights.[44] If a state becomes aware that the marine environ-ment is in imminent danger of being damaged or has been damaged by pollution, it is required to immediately notify other states likely to be affected by such damage, as well as the relevant competent international organizations.[45] The LOS Convention encourages states to promote scientific and technical assistance, giving priority to developing states.[46]

The convention requires a *comprehensive* approach: the state's antipollution measures must address all sources of pollution of the marine environment,[47] including the release of pollutants from land-based sources, from or through the atmosphere and by dumping, pollution from ves-sels, pollution from installations used in exploration or exploitation of the natural resources of the seabed, and pollution from other installations operating in the marine environment.[48]

Finally, the convention requires a *rigorous* approach: marine pollution regulations must be grounded in scientific criteria,[49] and in most cases the state's pollution prevention, reduction, and control measures must be no less effective in addressing those sources than generally accepted international standards.[50] This requirement seeks to discourage the "race to the bottom," which might otherwise tempt states to reduce their level of environmental protection in order to pro-mote economic goals.

b. Potential for Misuse of Marine Environmental Protection Jurisdiction

The environmental protection obligations of states extend throughout the marine environment; however, the LOS Convention adopts a zonal approach in allocating the obligations and juris-diction of states with respect to such protection. Not surprisingly, the convention's approach to marine environmental protection across the zones seeks to strike an appropriate balance between the interests of coastal states and flag states. As chapter 6 on the EEZ regime highlights, however, some coastal states may be tempted to use their jurisdiction with regard to protection and preser-vation of the marine environment to limit or even deny navigation and other freedoms preserved in the EEZ regime, in the same way that some states exploit the concept of conditions on port

---

42. Id. arts. 205 & 206. See also Pulp Mills on the River Uruguay (Argentina v. Uruguay), 2010 I.C.J. 14, 49 I.L.M. 1123 (2010).

43. LOSC art. 199. Interstate cooperation in pollution contingency planning and response is facilitated by the Inter-national Convention on Oil Pollution Preparedness, Response and Co-operation [hereinafter "OPRC"], Nov. 30, 1990, S. Treaty Doc. No. 102-11, 1891 U.N.T.S. 51 (1991). The OPRC Convention addresses international cooperation and mutual assistance, pollution reporting, oil pollution emergency plans, research and development, and oil spill preparedness and response. It is supplemented by a 2000 protocol for incidents involving hazardous and noxious substances.

44. LOSC art. 194(2).

45. Id. art. 198.

46. Id. arts. 202 & 203.

47. Id. art. 194(3).

48. Id. art. 194(3).

49. Id. art. 201.

50. See Bernard H. Oxman, The Duty to Respect Generally Accepted International Standards, 24 N.Y. J. Int'l L. & Politics 109 (1991).

entry. When coupled with the potential for ITLOS to order provisional measures to "prevent serious harm to the marine environment" and arguments for an increasingly rigorous "precautionary principle," this expansive view of the coastal state's marine environmental protection jurisdiction has raised concerns on the part of some flag states over the potential for Part XII of the LOS Convention to be used to limit or exclude foreign vessel navigation or other legitimate activities in the EEZ.[51]

c. State Obligations to Control Pollution from Vessels

A 2001 GESAMP report demonstrates that, contrary to popular belief, vessels are now a comparatively small source of oil pollution in the marine environment, responsible for between 10 and 15 percent of marine pollution.[52] Nevertheless, as the 1989 *Exxon Valdez* and 2010 *Deepwater Horizon* incidents demonstrate, vessel-source and vessel-caused pollution incidents are among the most visible and closely scrutinized events, and have been the subject of numerous pollution prevention, response, liability, and compensation laws.[53]

Ship wastes of concern to ocean stewards include fuel and cargo oil; toxic or harmful liquid and bulk cargoes; radioactive substances; black water (sewage); gray water (nonsewage waste water); ballast water that may contain oil residues, pathogens, or nonnative species; air pollution from propulsion and auxiliary machinery; ozone-depleting substances (ODSs); volatile organic compounds (VOCs); greenhouse gases (GHGs); toxic antifouling paints; and solid wastes (i.e., garbage), including persistent plastics. Emerging concerns over vessel-generated noise that may be harmful to marine fauna, especially marine mammals, and even ships themselves when disposed of, are receiving increasing international attention.

The flag state's obligations and the concept of port state control over foreign vessels are discussed in chapters 9 and 4 respectively. This section focuses on regulatory measures to prevent and control marine pollution. The LOS Convention sets out an elaborate scheme for vessel-source marine pollution prevention and discharge prohibitions that allocates prescriptive and enforcement jurisdiction among flag states, coastal states, and port states. The convention's "framework" character, however, means that many of the details will be prescribed by other complementary agreements developed under the auspices of competent international organizations or in diplomatic conferences. The keystone treaty for controlling vessel-source pollution is MARPOL 73/78, as amended. MARPOL addresses vessel-source waste streams in six annexes:[54]

- Annex I: Prevention of Pollution by Oil
- Annex II: Control of Pollution by Noxious Liquid Substances in Bulk
- Annex III: Pollution by Harmful Substances Carried by Sea in Packaged Form
- Annex IV: Prevention of Pollution by Sewage from Ships

---

51. See George V. Galdorisi & Kevin R. Vienna, Beyond the Law of the Sea 154–56 (1997).
52. See GESAMP, A Sea of Troubles, GESAMP Reports and Studies No. 70 (2001); Estimates of Oil Entering the Marine Environment from Sea-Based Activities, GESAMP Reports and Studies No. 74, (2007). In evaluating the relative contributions reported in the latter report, note that Report 74 is limited to sea-based activities and therefore excludes the contributions of land-based and atmospheric sources and ocean dumping.
53. The LOS Convention also assigns responsibilities to the "flag states" of aircraft. See, e.g., LOSC art. 212. Those responsibilities are beyond the scope of this book.
54. The MARPOL Convention is implemented in the United States by the Act to Prevent Pollution by Ships (APPS), 33 U.S.C. §§ 1901–1914. The act expressly requires that it be carried out in accordance with international law. See 33 U.S.C. § 1912.

- Annex V: Prevention of Pollution by Garbage from Ships[55]
- Annex VI: Prevention of Air Pollution from Ships

Amendments to Annex V that went into effect in 2013 imposed tighter restrictions on vessel garbage discharges. Annex VI presently addresses sulfur- and nitrogen-oxide emissions and VOC and ODS emissions. Additional measures to address GHG emissions are under development. Antifouling paints and other coatings are the subject of the 2001 International Convention on the Control of Harmful Anti-fouling Systems on Ships. Ballast water is to be addressed by the 2004 International Convention for the Control and Management of Ships' Ballast Water and Sediments, if and when it enters into force. Similarly, recycling retired vessels will be addressed by the 2009 Hong Kong International Convention for the Safe and Environmentally Sound Recycling of Ships, if it attracts sufficient ratifications to enter into force.

i. Prescriptive Jurisdiction over Vessel-Source Pollution

Part XII of the LOS Convention is organized with the distinction between the state's jurisdiction to prescribe laws and its jurisdiction to enforce those laws in mind (see chapter 1). Section 5 of Part XII addresses the prescriptive jurisdiction of flag, coastal, and port states; and Section 6 defines the respective states' enforcement jurisdiction. In approaching these materials it will be helpful to distinguish prevention measures from discharge prohibitions.[56] Vessel construction, design, equipment, manning, training, and operating regulations all seek to prevent incidents that might result in pollution. By contrast, discharge prohibitions seek to deter discharges by prescribing sanctions for those responsible for discharges that occur despite prevention measures. As a general rule, flag states have broad responsibility for both categories. The competency of coastal states lies mainly, but not exclusively, in discharge prohibitions. Port states increasingly play a role in both categories of antipollution measures under both the LOS Convention and MARPOL.

The LOS Convention reaffirms the long-established principle that primary responsibility for regulating vessel safety lies with flag states.[57] Along with the right to grant national registry to ships comes the attendant international duty to take adequate measures to ensure that those vessels meet standards that are at least as strict as the generally accepted international standards designed to promote marine safety and pollution prevention goals.[58] The LOS Convention does not define the "generally accepted international standards" (GAIS), but with respect to vessel pollution measures, the phrase is understood to refer to the family of widely ratified treaties developed under the auspices of the competent international organizations, including most prominently the IMO.[59] The GAIS of concern in this chapter are of two kinds: safety measures, such as SOLAS, STCW, and COLREGS; and pollution prevention and discharge prohibition measures, most prominently in MARPOL and its six annexes. MARPOL limits a vessel's dis-

---

55. MARPOL Convention Annex V was amended in 2012 to limit all discharges other than food waste. Annex V discharges must be recorded in the Garbage Record Book.
56. The distinction is also important in maritime preemption analysis in the United States. Compare Askew v. American Waterways Operators Inc., 411 U.S. 325 (1973) (challenging a Florida pollution liability measure) with Ray v. Atlantic Richfield Corp., 435 U.S. 151 (1978) (challenging Washington's tanker pollution prevention measures).
57. Restatement FRLUS § 603 cmt. b.
58. See John Mansell, Flag State Responsibility: Historical Development and Contemporary Issues (2009).
59. See Restatement FRLUS § 601 cmt. b. The GAIS include, at a minimum, the MARPOL, SOLAS, STCW, COLREGS, and Load Lines Conventions and the International Convention concerning Minimum Standards in Merchant Ships (ILO No. 147), all of which have been ratified by more than 90 percent of the flag states.

charge of oil, sewage, solid waste, and air pollutants and imposes record-keeping requirements to facilitate enforcement.[60] The GAIS also include international rules relating to prompt notification to coastal states whose coastline or related interests may be affected by incidents, including maritime casualties, that involve discharges or the likelihood of a discharge. Although a flag state is free to establish national standards that exceed the GAIS, few states do so.[61]

The coastal state's prescriptive jurisdiction over pollution prevention and control in its adjacent waters varies by zone. In the state's territorial sea, the coastal state is limited to the GAIS with respect to vessels in *transit* passage.[62] With respect to vessels in *innocent* passage, the coastal state is limited to the GAIS that relate to the construction, design, equipment, and manning of foreign vessels, subject always to the obligation not to hinder innocent passage.[63] Within its EEZ, a coastal state has jurisdiction to prescribe measures to protect and preserve the marine environment.[64] However, it is limited to the GAIS for pollution prevention with respect to foreign vessels within its EEZ,[65] except in those areas where it can be demonstrated to the IMO that the GAIS would not provide an adequate level of protection (see section A.2 below). Coastal states may prescribe "conditions on entry" applicable to foreign vessels bound for their ports (see chapter 4), and those conditions sometimes exceed the GAIS.

The coastal state may also employ certain operational control measures to prevent pollution by vessels. For example, the LOS Convention authorizes states, acting through the IMO, to establish, where appropriate, vessel-routing systems to minimize the threat of accidents that might cause pollution.[66] The coastal state's jurisdiction is broader in its territorial sea, extending even to vessels in innocent or transit passage.[67] Because states enjoy full sovereignty within their internal waters and ports, the LOS Convention does not in itself limit the port state's prescriptive jurisdiction over vessels other than public vessels. Nevertheless, treaties constituting the GAIS, such as the SOLAS and MARPOL Conventions, may limit states that are party to those treaties to the standards set by the treaty, precluding the state from prescribing more stringent measures for foreign vessels flying the flag of another state party.

ii. Enforcement Jurisdiction over Vessel-Source Pollution

Prescriptive jurisdiction is a necessary but not a sufficient precondition for the exercise of enforcement jurisdiction (see chapter 1). As a matter of international law, a state cannot enforce a law enacted in excess of the state's prescriptive jurisdiction.[68] However, even a law enacted in strict compliance with such limits might not be enforceable at a given time or in a particular location. Thus, a flag state cannot take enforcement action against one of its vessels or nationals

---

60. Falsification of MARPOL-required Oil Record Books and Garbage Record Books is a common basis for enforcement actions by port states.

61. In response to President Clinton's Regulatory Reinvention Initiative, the U.S. Coast Guard embarked on a program in 1995 to modify its regulations on navigational safety and marine engineering in order to harmonize them with international standards such as SOLAS, and to allow fuller use of new technologies. See Coast Guard, Presidential Regulation Review, 60 Fed. Reg. 28,376 (1995); Coast Guard, Harmonization with International Safety Standards, 61 Fed. Reg. 58,804 (1996).

62. LOSC art. 42(1)(b).

63. Id. arts. 21(1)(f), 21(2), & 211(4).

64. Id. arts. 56(1)(b)(iii) & 211(4)–(5).

65. Id. art. 211(5).

66. Id. art. 211(1).

67. See, e.g., id. arts. 21(1)(f), 22, 23, 41, & 42(1)(a)–(b).

68. This limitation is not true as a matter of domestic law in the United States. A constitutional law is enforceable as a matter of U.S. law even if it exceeds the international law limits on prescriptive jurisdiction. If, however, the statute is ambiguous, the courts will endeavor to construe it in a manner that does not conflict with international law.

while in a foreign port in the absence of the port state's consent,[69] and a coastal state might have to delay enforcement action against a foreign vessel suspected of violating its pollution laws while in the EEZ until the vessel enters one of its ports. At the same time, under circumstances in which a coastal or port state might not otherwise have enforcement jurisdiction, the flag state may consent to such an exercise. Finally, it should be noted that enforcement action against foreign vessels may be exercised only by warships, military aircraft, or other ships or aircraft clearly marked and identifiable as being on government service and authorized to that effect.[70]

a) Enforcement by Flag States

As with prescriptive jurisdiction, the 1982 LOS Convention allocates enforcement jurisdiction among flag, coastal, and port states. The principal responsibility for enforcing vessel-source pollution regulations lies with the flag state, regardless of where the violation occurred;[71] however, the flag state may not carry out enforcement actions in another state's territory without that state's consent.

The LOS Convention requires flag states to verify the vessel's compliance with the applicable GAIS for the prevention, reduction, and control of pollution of the marine environment both before granting the vessel its registration and periodically thereafter.[72] Verification must be performed through inspections by qualified surveyors.[73] Certificates attesting to compliance must be issued to the vessel and carried on board.[74] Those certificates must be accepted by other states as evidence of the condition of the vessel unless there are clear grounds for believing that the vessel's condition does not substantially correspond with the particulars of the certificates.[75] Flag states are further required to adopt laws and regulations and take other measures necessary for their implementation and to provide for the effective enforcement of the applicable GAIS, irrespective of where a violation occurs.[76] When one of its vessels is alleged to have committed a violation of the GAIS, the flag state is required to conduct an immediate investigation and, where appropriate, institute penalty proceedings.[77] In conducting its investigation, the flag state may request the assistance of any other state whose cooperation could be useful in clarifying the circumstances of the case.[78] Flag states are required to ensure that any penalties they impose are adequate in severity to discourage violations.[79] When the investigation and any further penalty proceedings are complete, the flag state is required to notify the competent international organization (the IMO) of the outcome.[80]

---

69. The use of extradition procedures to obtain the presence of persons for prosecution who are located in another state is briefly discussed in chapter 11.
70. LOSC art. 224.
71. Id. art. 217(4).
72. Id. art. 217(1). See also LOSC art. 94(4)(a). The flag state must prohibit a vessel from sailing until it complies with the GAIS on design, construction, equipment, and manning. LOSC art. 217(2).
73. Surveys are normally conducted by inspectors of the flag state authority (such as the U.S. Coast Guard) or a classification society acting as a recognized organization. See, e.g., 46 U.S.C. § 3316 (authority of U.S. Coast Guard to delegate certain inspection duties to classification societies).
74. LOSC art. 217(3). These include, for example, the International Load Line Certificates, SOLAS Cargo and Passenger Vessel Safety Construction and Safety Equipment Certificates, and the MARPOL International Oil Pollution Prevention Certificate (IOPCC). See, e.g., 33 U.S.C. § 1904 (MARPOL certificates).
75. LOSC art. 217(3). The United States generally recognizes those certificates on the basis of reciprocity. See 46 U.S.C. § 3303. But see 46 U.S.C. § 3711 (requiring additional certificates of compliance for foreign tankers).
76. LOSC art. 217(1).
77. Id. art. 217(4) & (6).
78. Id. art. 217(5).
79. Id. art. 217(8).
80. Id. art. 217(7). That information must be made available to all states.

b) Enforcement by Coastal States

The coastal state's enforcement with respect to foreign vessels varies by zone, the nature and magnitude of the incident, and the level of certainty that a violation has occurred.[81] Coastal states are empowered to enforce antipollution rules within their internal waters and their territorial sea, subject to the rules on innocent and transit passage described in chapter 5. Within its EEZ, the coastal state is generally limited to enforcing laws consistent with the GAIS.[82]

Article 220 of the LOS Convention sets out a complex pollution enforcement scheme that was likely easier to draft than it will be to construe and apply.[83] The scheme establishes limits on the timing and location of enforcement activities involving foreign vessels. Enforcement actions range from less intrusive "inquiries" directed at the ship to determine its identity, port of registry, last and next port of call, and information related to the possible violation to more intrusive boardings, inspections, and even detentions.[84] Failure to provide the requested information may justify additional enforcement measures. The greatest latitude is given to enforcing states when the foreign vessel is voluntarily in one of its ports.[85] Article 220 is more restrictive when the foreign vessel is navigating at the time of the contemplated investigation and enforcement actions. Table 2 summarizes the coastal state's jurisdiction to conduct pollution investigations involving foreign vessels while they are navigating in the state's territorial sea or EEZ (for further details, consult the text of Article 220 in appendix C).

Few categories of violations justify at-sea enforcement by the coastal state under Article 220. Some must await the vessel's arrival in port. In fact, the convention requires states to develop procedures that will help avoid unnecessary physical inspections of vessels at sea.[86] Coastal states' enforcement actions are also subject to the "safeguards" described below. Those safeguards include a remedy for illegal enforcement actions that delay the vessel. Accordingly, where the

TABLE 2. **Coastal State Jurisdiction to Conduct Pollution Investigations**

Violation Location	Magnitude of Spill	Level of Certainty	Actions Authorized	LOS Convention Article
Territorial Sea	Any	Clear grounds for believing	Physical inspection	220(2)
EEZ	Any	Clear grounds for believing	Require information	220(3)
EEZ	Substantial discharge that causes or threatens significant pollution	Clear grounds for believing	Physical inspection	220(5)
EEZ	Major damage	Clear objective evidence	Institute "proceedings," including detention	220(6)

81. Id. art. 220. See Restatement FRLUS § 604(3) cmt. d; International Law Association, Committee on Coastal State Jurisdiction relating to Marine Pollution, Final Report (E. Franckx & E. J. Molenaar, rapporteurs), in International Law Association, Report of the 69th Conference (2000).

82. LOSC art. 220(3).

83. See UN Division for Ocean Affairs and the Law of the Sea, The Law of the Sea: Enforcement by Coastal States: Legislative History of Article 220 of the United Nations Convention on the Law of the Sea, U.N. Sales No. 05.V.14 (2005).

84. LOSC art. 220.

85. Id. art. 220(1).

convention requires "clear grounds for believing" or "clear objective evidence," or evidence that the discharge was "substantial" or caused or had the potential to cause "major" damage, the prudent enforcement official will memorialize the basis for concluding that the necessary predicate exists, just as a police officer must do to obtain a search warrant.

c) Enforcement by Port States

Because they intrude less on the vessel's navigation, investigation and enforcement actions are less restricted when a foreign vessel voluntarily enters one of the enforcing state's ports or moors at one of its offshore terminals. When a foreign vessel is voluntarily within a port of a state, that state may exercise the investigatory and enforcement powers of the coastal state with respect to any violation by the vessel while in the state's own waters.[87] In addition, the port state may undertake investigations and, where the evidence so warrants, institute proceedings in respect of any discharge by the foreign vessel in violation of GAIS while on the high seas.[88] Under some circumstances, the port state may also investigate violations in the waters of a third state.[89] Investigatory responsibilities are further defined by the MARPOL Convention. If requested, the records of the port state's investigation must be forwarded to the flag state or to the coastal state in whose waters the violation occurred.[90]

The LOS Convention also grants states authority to inspect foreign vessels voluntarily in their ports to determine if they are in compliance with applicable international rules and standards relating to seaworthiness of vessels.[91] If a vessel is not in compliance and its unseaworthiness threatens damage to the marine environment, the coastal state has a duty to detain the vessel until the condition is corrected. This authority, together with the broader port state control regime, is examined in chapter 4.

iii. Measures to Avoid Pollution Arising from Maritime Casualties

The law of the sea exhibits a strong preference for prevention over response. The duty of a port state to intervene in cases involving unseaworthy foreign vessels has already been mentioned. The LOS Convention also reaffirms the authority of coastal states under customary and conventional international law[92] to intervene in marine casualties occurring in waters beyond their territorial sea when necessary to abate actual or threatened pollution damage to their coastline

---

86. Id. art. 228(2).

87. Id. art. 220(1).

88. Id. art. 218(1). See also UN Division for Ocean Affairs and the Law of the Sea, The Law of the Sea: Enforcement by Port States: Legislative History of Article 218 of the United Nations Convention on the Law of the Sea, U.N. Sales No. 02.V.11 (2002).

89. LOSC art. 218(2) & (3) (no proceedings in respect of a discharge violation in the waters of another state may be instituted unless requested by that state, the flag state, or a state damaged or threatened by the discharge violation, or unless the violation has caused or is likely to cause pollution in the internal waters, territorial sea, or EEZ of the state instituting the proceedings).

90. LOSC art. 218(4).

91. Id. art. 219. The port state may require the vessel to proceed to the nearest appropriate repair yard. The vessel must be permitted to resume its voyage once the condition is corrected.

92. See LOSC art. 221(1). The right of a coastal state to intervene in the adjacent waters dates back to the 1969 International Convention relating to Intervention on the High Seas in Cases of Oil Pollution Casualties [hereinafter "1969 Intervention Convention"], Nov. 29, 1969, 26 U.S.T. 765, T.I.A.S. No. 8068, 970 U.N.T.S. 211, as supplemented by the 1973 Protocol relating to Intervention on the High Seas in Cases of Marine Pollution by Substances Other than Oil. See also 33 U.S.C. §1471 (U.S. implementing act). The 1969 Intervention Convention was a response to the 1967 T/V *Torrey Canyon* grounding off the coast of Cornwall and the subsequent British Royal Air Force actions to destroy the vessel in an attempt to mitigate the effects of the 120,000 tons of crude oil the vessel spilled.

or related resources[93] from pollution or threat of pollution following upon a maritime casualty[94] or acts relating to such a casualty, which may reasonably be expected to result in major harmful consequences.[95]

iv. Safeguards in Vessel Enforcement Measures

The LOS Convention strikes a balance between the port and coastal state's interest in protecting their waters and the flag state's interest in facilitating the safe and efficient operation of its vessels. Accordingly, the port and coastal states' Part XII enforcement powers are subject to important safeguards. These safeguards are supplemented by provisions for securing the prompt release of vessels and their crews under Part XV of the convention. This section summarizes the safeguards prescribed by the LOS Convention. Additional safeguards may be found in many of the IMO conventions, including MARPOL and SOLAS. LOS Convention safeguards include the following:

- A prohibition on discrimination against vessels by flag[96]
- A duty to notify the vessel's flag state and consular officials[97]
- A duty to guard against actions that might endanger navigation safety[98]
- A duty to avoid unduly delaying the vessel[99]
- Procedural safeguards applicable to the investigation[100]
- A duty to release the vessel upon the posting of security[101] except where the vessel's release might unreasonably endanger the marine environment[102]
- Procedural safeguards applicable to actions to impose penalties[103]
- Flag state primacy in cases of violations beyond the territorial sea[104]
- A duty to compensate for unlawful or excessive enforcement actions[105]

The LOS Convention limits the kind of penalties a state may impose on foreign vessels and their crews. If the violation occurred beyond the coastal state's territorial sea, sanctions are

---

93. "Related interests" are defined in Article I(4) of the 1969 International Convention.
94. "Maritime casualty" is defined in Article I(1) of the 1969 Intervention Convention to include vessel collisions, stranding or other incident of navigation, or other occurrences on board a vessel or external to it resulting in material damage or imminent threat of material damage to a vessel or its cargo.
95. LOSC art. 221.
96. Id. art. 227.
97. Id. art. 231.
98. Id. art. 225 (states shall not endanger the safety of navigation or otherwise create any hazard to a vessel, or bring it to an unsafe port or anchorage, or expose the marine environment to an unreasonable risk).
99. Id. art. 226(1)(a). Any physical inspection of a foreign vessel is limited to an examination of such certificates, records, or other documents as the vessel is required to carry by the GAIS or of any similar documents which it is carrying; further physical inspection of the vessel may be undertaken only after such an examination and only when: (1) there are clear grounds for believing that the condition of the vessel or its equipment does not correspond substantially with the particulars of those documents, (2) the contents of such documents are not sufficient to confirm or verify a suspected violation, or (3) the vessel is not carrying valid certificates and records.
100. Id. art. 223. The LOS Convention also prescribes a three-year statute of limitations. Id. art. 228(2).
101. Id. art. 226(1)(b). See also id. art. 292 (judicial authority to order prompt release).
102. Id. art. 226(1)(c).
103. Id. art. 230(3). See also id. art. 223.
104. Id. art. 228(1).
105. Id. art. 232. See, e.g., 33 U.S.C. § 1904(h) (compensation for loss or damage when vessel is unreasonably detained or delayed for MARPOL investigation).

limited to monetary penalties (thus excluding a sentence of imprisonment).[106] If the pollution violation occurred in the coastal state's territorial sea, the state is similarly limited to monetary penalties, unless the act was willful and serious.[107] In either zone, the U.S. Act to Prevent Pollution from Ships (APPS), which implements the MARPOL Convention, authorizes the court to award up to one-half of any fine assessed against a violator to the person who provided the information that led to the conviction.[108] Violations of laws other than discharge prohibitions, such as the prohibition on making false statements to investigators, witness tampering, or spoliation of evidence, may trigger more severe penalties, including a sentence of imprisonment.[109] The U.S. Senate has proposed two understandings respecting the convention's limits on penalties for pollution violations that clarify the U.S. position on permissible penalties. Among other things, the Senate understanding lists some of the factors that may be used to determine whether a pollution violation was "willful," "serious," or both, as well as the categories of violations that are not subject to the LOS Convention's limits on punishments, such as obstruction of justice and false statement.[110]

d. State Obligations to Control Pollution from Source Other than Vessels

In contrast to the elaborate regime for vessel-source pollution, the LOS Convention provides only a rough framework for addressing pollution by dumping, atmospheric pollution, land-based pollution, and pollution from activities on the continental shelf or deep seabed. In general, the coastal states must adopt rules and standards respecting pollution by dumping and from seabed activities within national jurisdiction that are no less effective than international standards.[111]

i. Pollution by Dumping

For many years, a belief in the ocean's unlimited capacity to assimilate wastes led to widespread dumping of sewage sludge, solid waste, and even radioactive wastes and discarded chemical weapons. The 1958 Convention on the High Seas and the 1972 London Dumping Convention signaled a slow retreat from that mentality. That retreat was hastened by the 1996 Protocol to the London Convention discussed below.

Article 1 of the LOS Convention defines "dumping" as "any deliberate disposal of wastes or other matter from vessels, aircraft, platforms or other man-made structures at sea" and "any deliberate disposal of vessels, aircraft, platforms or other man-made structures at sea."[112] That

---

106. LOSC art. 230(1). One court held that the United States is bound by this limitation even as a nonparty to the LOS Convention. See U.S. v. Royal Caribbean Cruises Ltd., 1998 A.M.C. 1841 (D. P.R. 1997). Although the court's reasoning is flawed, the same result might follow from 33 U.S.C. § 1912 (requiring that APPS be applied consistently with international law).

107. LOSC art. 230(2).

108. 33 U.S.C. § 1908(a).

109. See, e.g., U.S. v. Royal Caribbean Cruise Lines, 11 F. Supp. 2d 1358 (S.D. Fl. 1998) (upholding criminal penalties for false statements in Oil Record Book relating to foreign vessel's discharge outside the U.S. territorial sea); U.S. v. Jho, 534 F.3d 398, 406 (5th Cir. 2008) (upholding conviction of foreign vessel crewmember for knowingly failing to maintain Oil Record Book).

110. See S. Exec. Rpt. No. 110-09, understandings 11 & 12 (reprinted in appendix D).

111. See LOSC arts. 208(3), 210(6). By contrast, the 1958 Convention on the High Seas required only that states take into account any existing treaty provisions or international standards and regulations in drawing up regulations applicable to their vessels on the high seas. 1958 Convention on the High Seas, supra, art. 24.

112. LOSC art. 1. This restriction was raised in response to plans to dispose of unwanted drill or production rigs by toppling them in place (e.g., the 1995 *Brent Spar* controversy). The question is now addressed in Article 1 of the 1996 Protocol to the London Convention, which adds to the definition of "dumping" "any abandonment or toppling at site of platforms or other man-made structures at sea, for the sole purpose of deliberate disposal."

definition expressly excludes the disposal of wastes or other matter incidental to or derived from the normal operations of vessels, aircraft, platforms, or other man-made structures at sea. It also excludes the placement of matter for a purpose other than the mere disposal thereof, provided that such placement is not contrary to the aims of the convention. Vessel-source waste disposal and discharges from ocean outfalls are not included in the definition of "dumping."

The LOS Convention requires states to adopt laws to prevent, reduce, and control pollution of the marine environment by dumping.[113] Those laws must be no less effective than the global rules and standards.[114] The London Convention is widely recognized to be the principal source of those global rules and standards.[115] Dumping within the territorial sea and the EEZ or onto the continental shelf may not be carried out without the express consent of the coastal state.[116] Enforcement jurisdiction over ocean dumping may be exercised by the flag state, the coastal state (with regard to dumping within its territorial sea or its EEZ or onto its continental shelf), or by any state with regard to acts of loading of wastes within its territory.[117] A state is not required to institute enforcement proceedings if another state has already done so.

The once common practice of dumping land-generated wastes into the sea is largely being phased out by those states that have ratified the 1996 Protocol to the London Convention.[118] At the same time, several dumping issues have yet to be fully resolved. For example, some people have advocated iron fertilization in carefully selected ocean waters as a means to mitigate climate impacts and, to a lesser extent, ocean acidification caused by increasing levels of atmospheric carbon dioxide, positing that doing so would stimulate the production of phytoplankton and lead to an increased uptake of atmospheric carbon dioxide in the course of photosynthesis. Opponents of this untested measure have cast serious doubt on both its probable efficacy and its legality. Another atmospheric carbon reduction concept involves sequestration of carbon dioxide generated by terrestrial energy facilities and industrial operations in deep ocean waters or the seabed. Both proposals raise "dumping" issues, and both remain controversial.[119] The IMO, which serves as the secretariat for the London Convention and its 1996 protocol, continues to monitor both proposals.[120] Another issue of recent debate is the placement of functional military or industrial facilities on the high seas and whether such placements might fall within the ocean dumping regime. Close reading of the carefully worded LOS Convention's definition of dumping makes it clear, however, that placement of any matter for a purpose other than mere disposal does not constitute ocean dumping, as long as it is not contrary to the aims of the LOS Convention or the London Convention.[121] Accordingly, placement of a military or industrial facility or device designed to serve an ongoing function would no more constitute dumping than would the instal-

---

113. LOSC art. 210(1). See generally UN Division for Ocean Affairs and the Law of the Sea, The Law of the Sea: Pollution by Dumping, U.N. Sales No. E.85.V.12 (1985).

114. LOSC art. 210(6).

115. The London Dumping Convention is implemented in the United States by the Ocean Dumping Act, Titles I & II of the Marine Protection, Research and Sanctuaries Act, 33 U.S.C. §§ 1401–1421.

116. LOSC art. 210(5).

117. Id. art. 216.

118. 1996 Protocol to the Convention on the Prevention of Marine Pollution by Dumping of Wastes and Other Matter, Nov. 7, 1996. S. Treaty Doc. No. 110-5, S. Exec. Rpt. 110-21. The protocol was signed by the United States on March 31, 1998, and entered into force on March 24, 2006; however, as of February 2013 the United States is not a party.

119. A 2006 amendment to annex I of the 1996 Protocol to the London Convention addresses carbon sequestration.

120. See, e.g., Assessment Framework for Scientific Research Involving Ocean Fertilization, IMO Res. LC-LP.2 (2010), Oct. 15, 2010.

121. LOSC art. 1(5)(b)(ii); 1996 Protocol to the London Convention, supra, art. 1.2.2.

lation of a submarine cable.[122] At the same time, however, establishment of an installation, device, or artificial island in the EEZ would fall within the coastal state's jurisdiction.

ii. Pollution from Land-Based Sources

Land-based sources are responsible for more than 40 percent of the pollution of the oceans.[123] Of particular concern is the waterborne discharge of agricultural pesticides and nutrients (nitrogen and phosphorus), both of which have been implicated as a leading cause of coastal "dead zones."[124] Despite the magnitude of the problem, the international law on prevention and control of land-based pollutants is at best primitive.[125] The LOS Convention only briefly addresses the problem, and the complementary frameworks lack substantive standards.

The LOS Convention's rather timid approach to global land-based pollution consists of three prescriptions. First, it establishes a duty to undertake cooperative action to "endeavor to establish" global and regional rules, standards, and practices to control land-based pollution.[126] Second, it imposes a general duty to adopt laws to prevent and control pollution from such land-based sources, including rivers, estuaries, pipelines, and outfall structures.[127] When feasible, states are encouraged to harmonize their policies at the appropriate regional level.[128] A number of states have, in fact, entered into regional treaties addressing land-based pollution. Finally, the convention requires states to enforce their own laws and regulations and to take measures necessary to implement any applicable international rules and standards.[129]

iii. Pollution from Seabed Activities Subject to National Jurisdiction

Chapter 7 describes the legal regime applicable to the coastal state's continental shelf, where the coastal state has the sovereign right to explore and exploit the shelf's natural resources. In carrying out those activities, coastal states are required to adopt and enforce laws and regulations to prevent, reduce, and control pollution of the marine environment arising from or in connection with seabed activities subject to their jurisdiction and from artificial islands, installations, and structures under their jurisdiction.[130] Those regulations must be no less effective than the applicable GAIS.[131]

---

122. Any "disposal" of such installations or devices when deactivated would, however, fall within the definition of "dumping."

123. See Group of Experts on Scientific Aspects of Marine Environmental Protection, Reports and Studies No. 71: Protecting the Oceans from Land-Based Activities (2001).

124. In 2011, the Gulf of Mexico hypoxic "dead" zone off the mouth of the Mississippi River measured 6,765 square miles. It reached its largest extent in 2002, when it measured more than 8,400 square miles.

125. See, e.g., Convention for the Prevention of Marine Pollution from Land-Based Sources, June 4, 1974, 1546 U.N.T.S. 119 (1974). See also Montreal Declaration on the Protection of the Marine Environment from Land-Based Activities, Nov. 30, 2001, 48 Law of the Sea Bull. 55 (2002).

126. LOSC art. 207(4). No binding global regime for preventing or controlling land-based pollution has yet been adopted, relegating the problem to regional or national approaches.

127. LOSC art. 207(1) & (2). States are required to adopt laws and regulations to prevent, reduce, and control pollution of the marine environment from land-based sources, including rivers, estuaries, pipelines, and outfall structures, taking into account internationally agreed rules, standards, and recommended practices and procedures.

128. Id. art. 207(3).

129. Id. art. 213.

130. Id. art. 208. See also International Maritime Organization, IMO Res. A.672(16), Oct. 19, 1989 (Guidelines and Standards for the Removal of Offshore Installations and Structures on the Continental Shelf and Exclusive Economic Zone).

131. LOSC art. 208(3). The noise generated by continental shelf activities and its effect on marine mammals is a growing concern that has not yet been addressed by the GAIS.

iv. Pollution from Seabed Mining Activities in the Area

The legal regime applicable to mining activities on the deep seabed beyond national jurisdiction ("the Area") is briefly addressed in chapter 7. Article 145 of the LOS Convention expressly addresses requirements to protect the marine environment from harm by activities in the Area. It requires the International Seabed Authority to adopt appropriate rules, regulations, and procedures to prevent, reduce, and control pollution and other hazards to the marine environment,[132] and to protect and conserve natural resources of the Area and prevent damage to the flora and fauna of the marine environment. The ISA, through its council, is given broad discretionary powers to assess the potential environmental impact of a given deep seabed mining operation, recommend changes, formulate rules and regulations, establish a monitoring program, and to issue emergency orders to prevent serious environmental damage.

Any "plan of work" submitted to the ISA by a seabed miner must be accompanied by an assessment of the potential environmental impacts of the proposed activities and a description of a program for oceanographic and baseline environmental studies.[133] The ISA has authority to disapprove areas for exploitation when substantial evidence indicates a risk of serious harm to the marine environment, and to issue emergency orders, which may include orders for the suspension or adjustment of operations, to prevent serious harm to the marine environment arising out of activities in the Area.[134]

States are liable for any damage caused by their own seabed mining enterprise or by contractors under their jurisdiction.[135] In 2011 the Seabed Disputes Chamber of ITLOS, at the request of the ISA, issued a far-reaching advisory opinion on state responsibility for activities in the Area.[136] The opinion addressed issues of state responsibility and liability and examined the precautionary approach and the duty to conduct prior environmental impact assessments.[137]

v. Pollution from or through the Atmosphere

Atmospheric sources contribute more than 30 percent of the total volume of marine pollution. The LOS Convention requires states to adopt and enforce laws and take other measures to prevent, reduce, and control pollution of the marine environment from or through the atmosphere. Those laws must extend to the state's sovereign airspace and to its vessels and aircraft and take into account internationally agreed-on rules and standards.[138] States are also required to adopt laws and regulations and take other measures necessary to implement applicable international rules and standards established through competent international organizations or diplomatic conferences to prevent, reduce, and control pollution of the marine environment from or through the atmosphere.[139] Notwithstanding the reference to international rules and standards,

---

132. The convention requires "particular attention" to the need for protection from the harmful effects of activities in the Area such as drilling, dredging, excavation, disposal of waste, construction, and operation or maintenance of installations, pipelines, and other devices related to activities. LOSC art. 145(a).

133. Part XI Implementation Agreement, supra, § 1, art. 7.

134. LOSC art. 162(2)(w) & (x).

135. Id. art. 139.

136. Responsibilities and Obligations of States Sponsoring Persons and Entities with Respect to Activities in the Area, Request for Advisory Opinion Submitted to the ITLOS Seabed Disputes Chamber, ITLOS Case No. 17, Advisory Opinion of Feb. 1, 2011, 50 I.L.M. 458 (2011).

137. See id. ¶¶ 107–20 (state responsibility), ¶¶ 125–35 (the precautionary approach), and ¶¶ 141–50 (environmental impact assessments).

138. LOSC arts. 212 (prescription) & 222 (enforcement). See, e.g., Convention on Long-Range Transboundary Air Pollution, supra.

139. LOSC art. 222.

no binding global regime for preventing or controlling pollution of the marine environment from or through the atmosphere (other than vessel-source air pollution) has yet been adopted, relegating the problem to regional or national approaches.

2. Enhanced Environmental Protection for Vulnerable Ecosystems

The LOS, SOLAS, and MARPOL Conventions, alone or in combination with the family of regional seas agreements, provide a framework for enhanced protection of uniquely vulnerable or sensitive marine ecosystems. When used in combination, enhanced vessel safety and pollution prevention measures and discharge limitations or prohibitions can, together with measures to limit the harvest of living marine resources, provide an effective regime for protecting or restoring marine ecosystems. Increasingly, the approach adopts an area-based management framework.[140]

The LOS Convention includes a positive requirement for states to take measures necessary to protect and preserve rare or fragile ecosystems as well as the habitat of depleted, threatened, or endangered species and other forms of marine life.[141] Article 211(6) of the convention permits the coastal state, working through the IMO, to prescribe heightened standards for particularly sensitive sea areas (PSSAs) in their EEZ. A PSSA is a particular, clearly defined area within the EEZ where oceanographic and ecological conditions require the adoption of special mandatory measures for the prevention of pollution from vessels.[142] Vessel restrictions pursuant to the PSSA regime may complement or be included within a broader marine protected area designation, which contemplates all relevant resource activities and pollution sources.

MARPOL establishes a process for designating certain defined waters as "special areas" or "emission control areas," where discharges or vessel air emissions that would otherwise be permitted under the global standards set by the MARPOL Convention and its annexes are restricted or even prohibited. Enclosed or semi-enclosed seas are sometimes designated no-discharge special areas under one or more of the MARPOL annexes and may be designated a PSSA.[143]

Chapter V of the SOLAS Convention complements the LOS Convention framework by providing authority and a process for promulgating ships' reporting and routing systems and other safety-of-navigation rules to promote safety of life at sea, efficient navigation, and protection of the marine environment.[144] Such measures have been employed off the U.S. Atlantic Coast to protect endangered whale species. Under its SOLAS authority, the IMO is the approval authority for areas to be avoided, precautionary areas, recommended routes, two-way routes, and deepwater routes, as well as vessel reporting schemes.[145] Any given routing or reporting measure may be recommended or mandatory, and may be applied selectively to certain categories of ships or to ships carrying certain cargoes. Coastal states or regions may petition the IMO for these enhanced standards for PSSAs and apply them in their coastal waters.

3. Environmental Protection for Polar Regions

The Antarctic region is a continent surrounded by oceans, while the Arctic is an ocean surrounded by continents. The signal characteristics of each "cryosphere" region are their remoteness,

---

140. Some international organizations and NGOs have recommended that up to 20 percent of the oceans be set aside in a system of marine protected areas.
141. LOSC art. 194(5); Restatement FRLUS § 603 cmt. d & n.6.
142. LOSC art. 211(6). The coastal state must first consult with the IMO and any other concerned states. Id.
143. See LOSC, arts. 194(5), 211(6); IMO, IMO Res. A.982(24), Dec. 11, 2005 (Revised Guidelines for the Identification and Designation of Particularly Sensitive Sea Areas).
144. See generally IMO, Ships' Routeing, IMO Pub. 927 (10th ed. 2010).
145. IMO, IMO Res. A.572(14), General Provisions on Ships' Routeing, Nov. 20, 1985.

extreme weather, persistent ice, vulnerable ecosystems, and paucity of infrastructure. To varying degrees, both regions are undergoing dramatic physical change due to climate change and ocean acidification. International law approaches to the two regions differ significantly.[146]

a. The Arctic

The Arctic Ocean is the smallest and shallowest of the world's five major oceans. It is surrounded by the European, Asian, and North American continents and two strategically important islands, Greenland and Iceland. Its shrinking ice pack, increasing acidity, and a seasonally significant hole in the Arctic ozone layer—and the effect of all three changes on Arctic ecosystems—are matters of serious global concern.

In evaluating navigation rights and coastal state regulatory jurisdiction in Arctic waters, the first step is to correctly determine the classification of the particular waters under consideration. Any of the classifications described in the previous chapters could potentially be applicable. A given water area might constitute ordinary internal waters not subject to passage rights (LOS Convention Articles 2 and 8(1)); internal waters enclosed by a lawful straight baseline and subject to innocent passage rights (Articles 2 and 8(2)); territorial seas subject to a suspendable right of innocent passage (Articles 2, 3, 17, and 211(4)); a strait used for international navigation and subject to transit passage rights (Articles 34–44 and 233) or nonsuspendable innocent passage rights (Article 45); a contiguous zone (Article 33); an EEZ, which might qualify for heightened protection under Articles 211(6) or 234; a semi-enclosed sea, where cooperation of the bordering states is encouraged (Articles 122 and 123); or the high seas. Those regimes are subject to the sovereign immunity restrictions in Articles 29–32, 95, 96, and 236. Other than Article 234, on "ice-covered areas," each of those articles is examined in earlier chapters or sections of this chapter. Accordingly, this section focuses on Article 234. At the outset, it must be emphasized that Article 234 does not apply to all ice-covered areas; it is limited by its terms to areas within a state's EEZ. Additionally, the Article 220 limitations on the coastal state's enforcement jurisdiction and the exemption for sovereign immune vessels under Article 236 apply equally to coastal state regulations based on Article 234.[147]

Article 211 sets out the coastal state's prescriptive jurisdiction over vessels in its EEZ. In most cases, the coastal state is limited to generally accepted international rules and standards established through the competent international organization or general diplomatic conference.[148] The LOS Convention provisions for heightened measures for PSSAs are described above. Article 234 prescribes a distinct protective regime for ice-covered areas. It permits coastal states to adopt and enforce nondiscriminatory laws and regulations for the prevention, reduction, and control of marine pollution from vessels in ice-covered areas within the limits of the EEZ, where particularly severe climatic conditions and the presence of ice covering such areas for most of the year create obstructions or exceptional hazards to navigation, and pollution of the marine environment could cause major harm to or irreversible disturbance of the ecological balance.[149] In prescribing and enforcing such laws and regulations the coastal state must base its decisions

---

146. See generally Donald R. Rothwell, The Polar Regions and the Development of International Law (1996).
147. Notwithstanding Article 236, Canada's Northern Canada Vessel Traffic Services Zone Regulations (NORDREGS), as issued in 2010, do not include an exemption for foreign sovereign immune vessels. In a letter to the Canadian Department of Transport dated March 29, 2010, the United States protested the regulations on that ground, among others.
148. LOSC art. 211(5).
149. Id. art. 234.

on the best available scientific evidence and exercise due regard for navigation and the protection and preservation of the marine environment.

Neither "ice-covered areas" nor "severe climatic conditions" is defined in the convention.[150] In construing those terms, while also giving full effect to the requirement for the coastal state to exercise due regard for navigation, it is noteworthy that, in contrast to Article 211(6) for PSSAs, nothing in Article 234 requires coastal states to consult with the IMO and other concerned states in developing measures for ice-covered areas in their EEZ.[151] The omission of any requirement to consult with the IMO prior to imposing measures that exceed or are inconsistent with generally accepted international rules and standards suggests a construction of Article 234 that limits its application to those areas and time periods that meet all of the criteria set out in Article 234. That is, the area must be experiencing "severe climatic conditions" and be "covered" by ice "most of the year." Thus, in areas where sea ice is retreating and is no longer present for most of the year, the area falling within Article 234 would also be shrinking. In addition, ice must create either an "obstruction" or an "exceptional" hazard to navigation. Coastal states seeking to protect Arctic waters within their EEZ that do not meet all of those criteria, but where pollution "could cause major harm to or irreversible disturbance of the ecological balance" (the fifth criteria), should refer to the criteria and the procedures prescribed by Article 211(6), including its requirement for prior consultation with the IMO, before prescribing protection measures that exceed the generally accepted international standards. At the same time, concerned states may seek to progressively develop the generally accepted international rules and standards for vessels operating in polar waters. Those rules and standards would then be applicable to vessels operating in covered waters under Article 211(5), thus obviating or at least lessening the need to rely on Article 211(6) or 234. A comprehensive code applicable in all polar waters would also avoid a patchwork approach treating ice-covered waters differently from noncovered waters.

In 1991 eight Arctic states (Canada, Denmark, Finland, Iceland, Norway, Russia, Sweden, and the United States) and six Arctic indigenous communities formed the Arctic Council, partly to address the prospect of increased shipping and oil and gas activities in the Arctic and the risks they pose to the fragile Arctic environment.[152] In 2011 the Arctic Council member states concluded an agreement addressing SAR operations in the region—the council's first legally binding agreement.[153] That same year, the Arctic Council ministers established a task force to develop an international instrument on Arctic marine oil pollution preparedness and response. The council adopted the agreement prepared by the task force at the council's May 2013 meeting.[154] The member states have also been active within the IMO in promoting development of a Mandatory Polar Code for shipping that would apply to Arctic and Antarctic waters. The proposed code will amend existing international conventions such as SOLAS, MARPOL, and STCW in order to address the unique threats and challenges posed by polar navigation.[155] Presumably, some or

150. See United Nations Convention on the Law of the Sea 1982: A Commentary, vol. IV, at 392–98 (Myron H. Nordquist et al. eds., 1991). Article 234 was negotiated directly by the USA, USSR, and Canada. Id.
151. In fact, Canada did not consult with the IMO before promulgating its NORDREGS in 2010.
152. See Arctic Council, Arctic Marine Shipping Assessment Report (2009); E. J. Molenaar, Arctic Marine Shipping: Overview of the International Legal Framework, Gaps and Options, 8 J. Transnat'l L. & Pol'y 289 (2009) (Symposium: Arctic Law in an Era of Climate Change).
153. Arctic Council, Agreement on Cooperation in Aeronautical and Maritime Search and Rescue in the Arctic, May 12, 2011, 50 I.L.M. 1119 (2011).
154. Arctic Council, Agreement on Cooperation on Marine Oil Pollution Preparedness and Response in the Arctic, May 15, 2013, available at http://www.state.gov/r/pa/prs/ps/2013/05/209406.htm (accessed May 17, 2013).
155. See IMO MEPC/MSC, Guidelines for Ships Operating in Arctic Ice-Covered Waters (2002) (under review, with a view to adopting a mandatory Polar Code); IMO, Guidelines for Voyage Planning for Passenger Ships Operating in Remote Waters, IMO Res. A.999(25) (2007).

all of the code will codify or ripen into generally accepted international rules and standards for
polar waters.

b. Antarctica

Antarctica is the fifth-largest continent. Some 98 percent of the continent is covered by ice. Antarctica is surrounded by the Southern Ocean (the ocean area south of 60 degrees south latitude).
A number of contiguous and distant nations (not including the United States) have asserted
territorial claims to portions of Antarctica;[156] however, since 1959 all such claims have been suspended under the terms of the Antarctic Treaty.[157] The United States is a party to the 1959 Convention and does not recognize the validity of claims to the Antarctic continent or to the adjacent
territorial seas or airspace.

The 1959 treaty provides that Antarctica "shall be used for peaceful purposes only"; and that
"any measures of a military nature, such as the establishment of military bases and fortifications,
the carrying out of military maneuvers, as well as the testing of any type of weapons" are prohibited.[158] Jurisdiction over activities in the treaty area is based on nationality, not territoriality.[159] All
stations and installations, and all ships and aircraft at points of discharging or embarking cargo or
personnel in Antarctica, are subject to inspection by designated foreign observers.[160] The United
States does not conduct classified activities in Antarctica, and all classified material is removed
from U.S. ships and aircraft prior to visits to the continent (and before the arrival of any foreign
observers). The treaty does not, however, affect in any way the high-seas freedoms of navigation
and overflight in the Antarctic region.

Article 234 of the LOS Convention on ice-covered areas does not apply to Antarctica, which
is governed instead by its own system of treaties (and where EEZ claims are not generally recognized). Fishing in the treaty area is governed by the Convention on the Conservation of Antarctic Marine Living Resources.[161] Commercial whaling activity is prohibited within the Southern
Ocean Whale Sanctuary established by the International Whaling Commission in 1994.[162]

Since 1998 the "Madrid" Protocol on Environmental Protection to the Antarctic Treaty,[163]
to which the United States is a party, provides an important legal framework. The protocol and
its six annexes designate Antarctica as a natural reserve devoted to peace and science, and set
forth basic principles and detailed mandatory rules applicable to human activities in Antarctica,
including an obligation to conduct prior environmental assessments and to accord priority to
scientific research.[164] The protocol also established a fifty-year moratorium on activities related

---

156. Such claims are typically justified on the basis of discovery, contiguity, or the "sector" theory.

157. The Antarctic Treaty System (ATS) consists of a family of treaties that began with the 1959 treaty. See Antarctic
    Treaty, art. I, Dec. 1, 1959, 12 U.S.T. 794, 402 U.N.T.S. 71. See also Restatement FRLUS § 601 n.5; Christopher
    C. Joyner, The Antarctic Treaty System and the Law of the Sea—Competing Regimes in the Southern Ocean? 10
    Int'l J. Marine & Coastal L. 301 (1995).

158. Commander's Handbook, supra, ¶¶ 2.6.5.2 & 10.2.2.3.

159. Antarctic Treaty, supra, art. VIII.

160. Id. art. VII.

161. See also Convention on the Conservation of Antarctic Marine Living Resources, May 21, 1980, 33 U.S.T. 3476,
    1329 U.N.T.S. 47.

162. See International Convention for the Regulation of Whaling, art. V(1)(c), Dec. 2, 1946, 62 Stat. 1716, 161
    U.N.T.S. 74. In 1986 the International Whaling Commission imposed a global moratorium on commercial
    whaling, subject to an exception for the taking of whales for "scientific" purposes.

163. Protocol on Environmental Protection to the Antarctic Treaty [hereinafter "Madrid Protocol"], Oct. 4, 1991, S.
    Treaty Doc. 102-22, 30 I.L.M. 1455 (1991). The protocol entered into force in 1998.

164. A sixth annex will address liability arising from environmental emergencies. See 2005 Annex VI to Protocol to the
    Protocol on Environmental Protection to the Antarctic Treaty; Liability Arising from Environmental Emergen-
    cies, 45 I.L.M. 5 (2006).

to mineral resources other than scientific research.[165] Violations of the 1988 Protocol on Environmental Protection are enforceable under the U.S. Act to Prevent Pollution from Ships.[166]

4. Public Vessel Responsibility for Marine Pollution and Sovereign Immunity

Chapter 9 addresses the status of vessels and the rule of sovereign immunity of public vessels. In addition, the complementary marine pollution conventions typically exempt public vessels. The marine environmental protection articles in Part XII of the LOS Convention do not apply to warships, naval auxiliaries, other vessels, or aircraft owned or operated by a state and used, for the time being, only on government noncommercial service.[167] However, the flag state for such vessels or aircraft must ensure that their public vessels and state aircraft act in a manner consistent, so far as is reasonable and practicable, with the convention.[168] It should also be noted that the sovereign immunity of public vessels and state aircraft from enforcement actions by other states does not insulate the vessel's flag state from international responsibility for harms caused by its public vessels.[169] Chapter 14 provides a general overview of the international law of state responsibility. The next section provides a brief summary of the more specific rules on state responsibility and liability for marine pollution.

5. Responsibility and Liability for Marine Pollution

Responsibility and financial liability for marine pollution raise two distinct questions: the responsibility and liability of private parties, such as shipowners, and the responsibility of states, either as flag states or as port and coastal states. State responsibility and liability may in turn be further divided into the state's direct liability when a state actor, public vessel, or state aircraft was responsible for the pollution incident; and indirect liability, in which it is alleged that a state failed to take legally required measures to prevent a pollution incident by a nonstate actor.[170] The distinct question of state liability for wrongful enforcement measures is discussed above.

This chapter has outlined the many obligations of states to protect and preserve the marine environment. States are responsible for any failure to fulfill their international obligations[171] and may be required to make reparation for any failure to do so.[172] To that end, they are required to ensure that recourse is available within their legal systems for prompt and adequate compensation or other relief in respect of damage caused by pollution of the marine environment by natural or juridical persons under their jurisdiction.[173]

Close reading of the LOS Convention reveals that, consistent with the convention's "framework" approach, the drafters made no attempt to comprehensively address pollution-related liabilities. Nothing in the LOS Convention limits the institution of civil proceedings for claims

---

165. Madrid Protocol, supra, arts. 7 & 25.
166. 33 U.S.C. §§ 1901, 1903, 1907, & 1908.
167. LOSC art. 236.
168. Id. See, e.g., 33 U.S.C. § 1902(e) (compliance with MARPOL by exempted ships).
169. LOSC art. 31. Following the January 17, 2013, grounding of the USS *Guardian* (MCM-5) on Tubbataha Reef (a UNESCO World Heritage site home to about 500 species of fish and 350 species of coral as well as whales, dolphins, sharks, turtles, and breeding seabirds), the Philippine government assessed a $1.5 million "fine" against the United States for damage to the reef.
170. See Restatement FRLUS § 601 cmt. d. In its 2011 advisory opinion, the ITLOS Seabed Disputes Chamber was careful to distinguish the question of responsibility from liability.
171. LOSC art. 235(1).
172. Id. art. 232. Restatement FRLUS § 604.
173. LOSC art. 235(2).

for loss or damage resulting from pollution of the marine environment.[174] Moreover, the LOS Convention provisions regarding responsibility and liability for damage do not preclude application of existing rules and the development of further rules regarding responsibility and liability under international law.[175]

With the objective of ensuring prompt and adequate compensation for damage caused by pollution of the marine environment, states are required to cooperate in developing and implementing international law relating to responsibility and liability for the assessment of and compensation for damage, together with procedures for payment of adequate compensation, such as compulsory insurance or compensation funds.[176] International regimes for vessel-source pollution liability include the 2001 International Convention on Civil Liability for Bunker Oil Pollution Damage[177] and two conventions covering liability for oil cargo discharges: the 1969 International Convention on Civil Liability for Oil Pollution Damage (CLC)[178] and the 1992 Protocol to the International Convention on the Establishment of an International Fund for Compensation for Oil Pollution Damage.[179] The 1996 International Convention on Liability and Compensation for Damage in Connection with the Carriage of Hazardous and Noxious Substances (HNS) and its 2010 protocol address nonoil cargoes. For the most part, the United States has rejected international pollution liability regimes in favor of domestic regimes, such as the Oil Pollution Act of 1990 and the 1980 Comprehensive Response, Compensation and Liability Act (CERCLA) for releases of hazardous substances.

6. Environmental Protection and the Law of Armed Conflict

The law of armed conflict (LOAC) is examined in chapter 13. One LOAC treaty component is relevant in this chapter on protection of the marine environment.[180] The 1977 Convention on the Prohibition of Military or Any Other Hostile Use of Environmental Modification Techniques (ENMOD) prohibits military or any other hostile use of environmental modification techniques having widespread, long-lasting, or severe effects as the means of destruction, damage, or injury to any other state party.[181] The intentional destruction of offshore oil structures by Iraq in the 1991 Gulf War resulting in catastrophic oil spills in the northern Arabian Gulf provoked widespread international condemnation. Such intentional acts might also constitute a war crime in those states that are party to the Rome Statute of the International Criminal Court.[182]

---

174. Id. art. 229.

175. Id. art. 304.

176. Id. art. 235(2) & (3).

177. International Convention on Civil Liability for Bunker Oil Pollution Damage [hereinafter "Bunker Convention"], Mar. 23, 2001, 40 I.L.M. 1493 (2001). The United States is not a party.

178. International Convention on Civil Liability for Oil Pollution Damage [hereinafter "CLC"], Nov. 29, 1969, 973 U.N.T.S. 3, 9 I.L.M. 45 (1970), as amended. The United States is not a party.

179. Convention on the Establishment of an International Fund for Compensation for Oil Pollution Damage [hereinafter "Fund Convention"], Dec. 18, 1971, 1110 U.N.T.S. 57, 11 I.L.M. 284 (1972), as amended. The United States is not a party.

180. See generally U.S. Naval War College, International Law Department, Protection of the Marine Environment during Armed Conflict, 69 Nav. War Coll. Int'l L. Studies (1996).

181. Convention on the Prohibition of Military or Any Other Hostile Use of Environmental Modification Techniques [hereinafter "ENMOD"], art. 1, May 18, 1977, 31 U.S.T. 333, 1108 U.N.T.S. 151. See also Restatement FRLUS § 601 n.7.

182. Rome Statute of the International Criminal Court, art. 8(2)(b)(iv), July 17, 1998, 2187 U.N.T.S. 90, 37 I.L.M. 1002 (1998). The United States is not a party.

B. CONSERVATION AND MANAGEMENT OF LIVING MARINE RESOURCES

Earlier chapters on the territorial sea, EEZ, continental shelf, and high seas describe the legal regimes for living marine resource exploitation in those zones. This section surveys some of the stewardship issues applicable to all of those zones.[183] Those issues arise as a result of exploitation practices that are proving to be unsustainable.[184] They include overfishing;[185] excessive bycatch of nontarget species (including seabirds, marine mammals, and other endangered marine species); and fishing gear or techniques that destroy habitat, such as bottom trawling and the use of poisons and explosives to harvest coral reef species. This section will also expand on the developing regime for sustainable fisheries on the high seas. The international organization responsible for these issues is the FAO and its Committee on Fisheries. On occasion, the UN General Assembly has also stepped in, as it did in 1991 when it called for a global moratorium on fishing with large-scale drift nets on the high seas, which are notorious for their excessive bycatch of seabirds and marine mammals.[186]

The LOS Convention imposes no conservation and management obligations on states with respect to living marine resources in their territorial sea or on their continental shelf. Such obligations are, however, imposed on coastal states with respect to the resources in their EEZ and on all states with respect to the resources of the high seas. Many believed that the widespread application of the EEZ regime under the 1982 LOS Convention would avert the "tragedy of the commons" in those waters.[187] Unfortunately, whether due to lack of information or insufficient will, the advent of EEZs has so far failed to halt the decline of fish stocks. The LOS Convention was a progressive step toward achieving the goal of sustainable fisheries, but much remained to be done. The 1992 UN Conference on Environment and Development (UNCED), convened in Rio de Janeiro a decade after the LOS Convention was completed, served as the critical next step. The 1992 "Earth Summit" produced two important treaties and two "soft law" instruments that advanced the sustainable use agenda. The UN Framework Convention on Climate Change[188] and the Convention on Biological Diversity[189] are both vital treaty components in the international environmental law regime and have enduring relevance in the oceans. The two soft law instruments, the Rio Declaration of Principles and Environment and Development, and Agenda 21: the Program of Action for Sustainable Development (chapter 17 of which is devoted to the oceans and seas),[190] are both important in themselves and for the other legal instruments and

---

183. For a detailed examination, see William T. Burke, The New International Law of Fisheries: UNCLOS 1982 and Beyond (1994); Stuart M. Kaye, International Fisheries Management (2001); Jose A. de Yturriaga, The International Regime of Fisheries: From UNCLOS 1982 to the Presential Sea (1997).

184. The stakes are high and the temptation to fish unsustainably is great. In 2013 a single bluefin tuna reportedly sold at a Tokyo fish auction for $1.76 million.

185. The FAO reports that nearly 70 percent of the 600 fish stocks it monitors are either fully exploited or overexploited. Another 8 percent are depleted or recovering from depletion. Declining fish stocks, together with excess fishing capacity—often exacerbated by government subsidies—results in more and more efficient vessels chasing fewer and smaller fish. Data on fisheries is reported by the FAO Committee on Fisheries annually. See FAO, The State of the World Fisheries and Aquaculture (produced annually), available at www.fao.org (accessed Feb. 1, 2013).

186. G.A. Res. 46/215, U.N. Doc. A/RES/46/215 (Dec. 20, 1991) (Large-Scale Pelagic Driftnet Fishing and Its Impact on the Living Marine Resources of the World's Oceans and Seas). The assembly's resolution is not legally binding.

187. Garrett Hardin, The Tragedy of the Commons, 162 Science 1243–48 (Dec. 13, 1968).

188. United Nations Framework Convention on Climate Change [hereinafter "UNFCCC"], May 9, 1992, S. Treaty Doc No. 102-38, 1771 U.N.T.S. 107, 165, 31 I.L.M. 849 (1992). The United States is a party.

189. Convention on Biological Diversity, June 5, 1992, S. Treaty Doc. 103-20. 1760 U.N.T.S. 79, 31I.L.M. 818 (1992). The United States is not a party.

190. UN Conference on Environment and Development, Agenda 21: The United Nations Program of Action, June 16, 1992, 31 I.L.M. 874 (1992).

actions they led to. One of those instruments, the Straddling Fish Stocks and Highly Migratory Fish Stocks Agreement, is examined in chapter 6. The FAO High Seas Fishing Compliance Agreement is introduced in chapter 8. The latter agreement is implemented in the United States by the High Seas Fishing Compliance Act.[191] A third instrument, the FAO Code of Conduct for Responsible Fisheries,[192] finds application in all fisheries, including those in the sovereign waters of the states.

The FAO Code of Conduct consists of twelve articles. Article 6 sets out the code's principles, many of which closely parallel the UNCED Declaration of Principles. They include an affirmation that the right to fish carries with it the obligation to do so in a responsible manner so as to ensure effective conservation and management of the living aquatic resources. Additionally, conservation and management decisions for fisheries should be based on the best scientific evidence available, while also taking into account traditional knowledge of the resources and their habitat, as well as relevant environmental, economic, and social factors. It calls on fisheries management organizations to apply a precautionary approach widely and to promote the use of selective and environmentally safe fishing gear and practices. It also calls on states to protect and rehabilitate critical fisheries habitats in marine and freshwater ecosystems. Although the FAO Code of Conduct remains a soft law instrument, and therefore is not legally enforceable, it serves as an important benchmark to guide states and international organizations in drafting legal regimes for sustainable fisheries.

The LOS Convention largely sidesteps the controversy surrounding whaling, including subsistence harvests by indigenous peoples and "scientific" whaling. Article 120 addressing marine mammals on the high seas incorporates by reference Article 65 on the same subject in the EEZ. In turn, Article 65 stipulates: "Nothing in this Part restricts the right of a coastal State or the competence of an international organization, as appropriate, to prohibit, limit or regulate the exploitation of marine mammals more strictly than provided for in this Part. States shall co-operate with a view to the conservation of marine mammals and in the case of cetaceans shall in particular work through the appropriate international organizations for their conservation, management and study." Consistent with its domestic Marine Mammal Protection Act, the United States has taken a strong preservationist position on whaling. The draft Senate understanding states that "the United States understands that article 65 of the Convention lent direct support to the establishment of the moratorium on commercial whaling, supports the creation of sanctuaries and other conservation measures, and requires States to cooperate not only with respect to large whales, but with respect to all cetaceans."[193]

---

191. Pub. L. No. 112-90, codified at 16 U.S.C. §§ 5501–5509.

192. FAO Code of Conduct for Responsible Fisheries, Oct. 31, 1995, FAO Doc. 95/20/REV/1; U.N. Sales No. E98.V.11 (Oct. 31, 1995).

193. See S. Exec. Rpt. No. 110-09, understanding 18 (reprinted in appendix D).

Maritime Law Enforcement

Most seagoing officers are acutely aware that the maritime domain suffers from a chronic security, safety, and stewardship deficit. That deficit prompted the U.S. Coast Guard to launch its three-part commitment to protect those on the sea, to protect against threats from the sea, and to protect the sea itself.[1] All three mission areas require a wide-ranging at-sea law enforcement presence.

This book has repeatedly emphasized the importance of regime effectiveness in achieving public order on the oceans. To achieve its purposes a legal regime must be both adequate in its prescriptions and effectively enforced. Unfortunately, we continue to suffer from a number of regime pathologies. A few regimes (e.g., nonproliferation) suffer from prescriptive inadequacies, but a far more common and persistent problem is inadequate enforcement. Regime architecture has so far failed to provide a credible deterrent to conduct that undermines the public order of the oceans. Some lay the blame on the rule of exclusive flag jurisdiction and the prevalence of flag-of-convenience registries, some of which effectively operate as "flags of immunity" for unscrupulous operators. Others simply point to the practical difficulties of policing the vast ocean expanse.

Maritime law enforcement (MLE) "constabulary" operations,[2] together with maritime security operations (MSO) by warships, seek to provide the needed deterrent and close the security, safety, and stewardship deficit. The MLE operations examined in this chapter overlap with several MSO missions examined in chapter 12; however, MLE focuses more specifically on threats posed by private actors rather than states, transnational terrorist organizations, and weapons proliferators. MLE operations are also directed toward a very specific end game: arrest and prosecution of those who violate the laws. This chapter surveys three categories of crimes that command the time and attention of twenty-first-century MLE forces: maritime counterdrug operations, irregular migration by sea, and marine environmental and natural resource crimes. Maritime counterproliferation, counterterrorism, counterpiracy, and UN Security Council resolution enforcement operations are examined in chapter 12. What follows builds on the framework laid in earlier chapters. In particular, it distinguishes between prescriptive and enforcement jurisdiction, and distinguishes both forms of jurisdiction from the authority of agencies and their officers to exercise the nation's law enforcement powers. The final sections of the chapter examine the problems increasingly posed by noncompliant vessels and the human rights dimensions of maritime law enforcement. Both subjects overlap with the materials on the use of force necessary to compel compliance or in self-defense in chapter 13.

---

1. U.S. Coast Guard, Coast Guard Pub. 3-0, Operations, at 3 (Feb. 2012). See also U.S. Coast Guard Strategy for Maritime Safety, Security and Stewardship (Jan. 19, 2007).
2. Maritime law enforcement refers to armed intervention by uniformed boarding officers to deter, detect, and suppress violations of applicable laws.

A. THE DUTY TO COOPERATE IN SUPPRESSING CRIMINAL ACTIVITIES

Maritime safety, security, and protection of the marine environment are shared responsibilities that require international cooperation. The law of the sea calls on all states, including flag states, to cooperate in suppressing a variety of activities deemed inimical to the public order. Since the nineteenth century all states have had an obligation to cooperate in the suppression of piracy.[3] In the twentieth century, a requirement for all states to cooperate in suppressing illicit traffic in narcotic drugs and psychotropic substances was added.[4] Similarly, states now have a duty to suppress unauthorized broadcasting from the high seas.[5] Finally, the LOS Convention requires states to cooperate to conserve and manage living marine resources on the high seas[6] and to protect and preserve the marine environment.[7] Flag states also have an individual responsibility to prevent and punish the transport of slaves in ships authorized to fly their flag; however, the LOS Convention does not impose a more general duty to cooperate in the suppression of slavery or slave trade or transport.[8] More specific cooperation duties have been imposed on states by other treaties, particularly the family of multilateral terrorism conventions and those developed under the auspices of the International Maritime Organization, Food and Agriculture Organization, UN Environment Program, and UN Office of Drugs and Crime.

Transnational organized crime has emerged as another grave concern. The UN General Assembly called attention to the magnitude of the threat in a recent resolution on the law of the sea. In that resolution the assembly:[9]

> *Notes* that transnational organized criminal activities are diverse and may be interrelated in some cases and that criminal organizations are adaptive and take advantage of the vulnerabilities of States, in particular coastal and small island developing States in transit areas, and calls upon States and relevant intergovernmental organizations to increase cooperation and coordination at all levels to detect and suppress the smuggling of migrants and trafficking in persons, in accordance with international law; [and]
>
> *Recognizes* the importance of enhancing international cooperation at all levels to fight transnational organized criminal activities, including illicit traffic in narcotic drugs and psychotropic substances, within the scope of the United Nations instruments against illicit drug trafficking, as well as the smuggling of migrants and trafficking in persons and criminal activities at sea falling within the scope of the United Nations Convention against Transnational Organized Crime.

The UN Convention against Transnational Organized Crime and its three protocols is one of several conventions that prescribe means and methods for interstate cooperation in suppressing crimes of transnational concern.[10] One such means, bilateral or multilateral boarding or

---

3. See LOSC art. 100.
4. See, e.g., id. art. 108.
5. Id. art. 109. See also 47 U.S.C. § 301. Unauthorized broadcasting refers to the transmission of radio or television signals from a ship or offshore facility and intended for receipt by the general public, contrary to international regulations.
6. LOSC arts. 117–119.
7. Id. art. 197.
8. Id. art. 99.
9. G.A. Res 66/72, at 20, ¶¶ 104–05, U.N. Doc. A/66/L.21 (Nov. 28, 2011).
10. For the U.S. approach, see The White House, Strategy to Combat Transnational Organized Crime, July 25, 2011, available at http://www.whitehouse.gov/sites/default/files/microsites/2011-strategy-combat-transnational -organized-crime.pdf (accessed Feb. 1, 2013).

ship-rider agreements, is examined below. A second option to enhance international cooperation in criminal matters is provided by the web of mutual legal assistance treaties (MLATs). The United States has entered into more than fifty such agreements.[11] MLATs received formal recognition in Article 7 of the 1988 UN Convention against Illicit Traffic in Narcotic Drugs and Psychotropic Substances.[12] MLAT terms differ from state to state, but most typically provide for the taking of evidence or statements from persons in another state party, transferring custody of suspects, executing searches or seizures, and providing information and evidentiary items.

Increasingly, treaties on crimes of international concern include "extradite or prosecute" (*aut dedere aut judicare*) clauses that obligate states parties to prosecute persons found within their jurisdiction who are suspected of committing one of the crimes specified in the treaty or to deliver them to another state for prosecution. In the United States most extraditions are carried out pursuant to a bilateral treaty and generally involve the U.S. Department of State and the federal courts.[13] Less formal methods of delivery include deportation of aliens to the requesting state and informal rendition (delivering an individual without the judicial formalities of an extradition).[14]

B. LAW ENFORCEMENT AUTHORITY

While *jurisdiction* is governed by both international and domestic law, *authority* to enforce those laws is largely a matter of domestic law. Jurisdiction refers to a government's right to exercise legal authority over persons, vessels, and territory. States and their subsidiary governments are said to have jurisdiction. That jurisdiction is exercised by agencies, public vessels, and officials to whom the state has granted authority. In some cases, the LOS Convention places limits on how the state may allocate authority. For example, the convention restricts some enforcement actions to warships or other authorized and marked government vessels.

Congress and the president have designated the U.S. Coast Guard as the nation's lead federal agency for maritime law enforcement. In carrying out its MLE operations, the Coast Guard often works with components of the Department of Defense (DoD). The involvement of DoD components raises issues under the U.S. *posse comitatus* laws and regulations; however, the *posse comitatus* rule is one of domestic law only. Indeed, most nations rely heavily, even exclusively, on their navies for maritime law enforcement. Finally, applicable service directives, operations, and tasking orders and rules of engagement may restrict authority or make its exercise in some circumstances subject to prior approval, a statement of no objection (SNO), or interagency coordination procedures.

1. U.S. Coast Guard Law Enforcement Authority

Alexander Hamilton, considered by many to be the father of the modern U.S. Coast Guard, wrote in Federalist Paper No. 12 that "a few armed vessels, judiciously stationed at the entrances

---

11. See U.S. Department of State, Bureau of International Narcotics and Law Enforcement Affairs, 2012 International Narcotics Control Strategy Report, Mar. 7, 2012 (listing fifty-six MLAT states), available at http://www .state.gov/j/inl/rls/nrcrpt/2012/vol2/184110.htm (accessed Feb. 1, 2013).
12. UN Convention against Illicit Traffic in Narcotic Drugs and Psychotropic Substances [hereinafter "1988 UN Convention on Drugs"], art. 7, Dec. 20, 1988, S. Treaty Doc. No. 101-4, 1582 U.N.T.S. 165, 28 I.L.M. 493 (1989). MLAT agreements concluded under Article 7 of the 1988 UN Drugs Convention should not be confused with bilateral boarding agreements, discussed later in this chapter.
13. See 18 U.S.C. §§ 3181–3196; Restatement FRLUS §§ 475–478.
14. Within the United States, an irregular rendition or abduction is not necessarily a bar to prosecution. See Collins v. Frisbie, 342 U.S. 519 (1952); Ker v. Illinois, 119 U.S. 436 (1886); U.S. v. Alvarez-Machain, 504 U.S. 655 (1992).

of our ports, might at a small expense be made useful sentinels of the law." Later, as the nation's first secretary of the treasury, Hamilton presided over the launch of the U.S. Revenue Cutter Service, the forebear of today's multimission Coast Guard. MLE operations play a role in at least six of the eleven missions assigned to the Coast Guard.[15] The Coast Guard carries out its MLE missions in cooperation with an array of federal, state, and local agencies, using a variety of vessels, aircraft, and other assets.

In assessing its operational readiness, the Coast Guard carefully considers its authorities, capabilities, competencies, capacities, and partnerships. The Coast Guard's organizational law enforcement authority is set out in 14 U.S.C. § 2, which provides in relevant part that:

> the Coast Guard shall enforce or assist in the enforcement of all applicable Federal laws on, under, and over the high seas and waters subject to the jurisdiction of the United States; shall engage in maritime air surveillance or interdiction to enforce or assist in the enforcement of the laws of the United States; shall administer laws and promulgate and enforce regulations for the promotion of safety of life and property on and under the high seas and waters subject to the jurisdiction of the United States covering all matters not specifically delegated by law to some other executive department.

The service's law enforcement authority is further defined and then assigned to certain qualifying "boarding officers" by 14 U.S.C. § 89(a), which provides that:

> the Coast Guard may make inquiries, examinations, inspections, searches, seizures, and arrests upon the high seas and waters over which the United States has jurisdiction, for the prevention, detection, and suppression of violations of laws of the United States.
>
> For such purposes, commissioned, warrant, and petty officers may at any time go on board of any vessel subject to the jurisdiction, or to the operation of any law, of the United States, address inquiries to those on board, examine the ship's documents and papers, and examine, inspect, and search the vessel and use all necessary force to compel compliance.
>
> When from such inquiries, examination, inspection, or search it appears that a breach of the laws of the United States rendering a person liable to arrest is being, or has been committed, by any person, such person shall be arrested or, if escaping to shore, shall be immediately pursued and arrested on shore, or other lawful and appropriate action shall be taken. . . .
>
> [I]f it shall appear that a breach of the laws of the United States has been committed so as to render such vessel, or the merchandise, or any part thereof, on board of, or brought into the United States by, such vessel, liable to forfeiture, or so as to render such vessel liable to a fine or penalty and if necessary to secure such fine or penalty, such vessel or such merchandise, or both, shall be seized.

---

15. 6 U.S.C. § 468 lists eleven U.S. Coast Guard missions, divided into two categories: (1) "non–homeland security missions," which include marine safety, search and rescue, aids to navigation, living marine resources (fisheries law enforcement), marine environmental protection, and ice operations; and (2) "homeland security missions," which include ports, waterways, and coastal security; drug interdiction; migrant interdiction; defense readiness; and other law enforcement.

Law enforcement operations by the U.S. maritime forces are conducted in accordance with applicable service directives and doctrine, which may include the U.S. Coast Guard's *Maritime Law Enforcement Manual*; the U.S. Coast Guard/U.S. Navy *Maritime Counter-drug and Alien Migrant Interdiction Operations Manual*;[16] and, in some cases, the U.S. Navy/U.S. Coast Guard *Maritime Interception Operations* tactics, techniques, and procedures publication.[17] Access to all three is restricted to official uses, and discussion of their content in this book is limited to the releasable portions.[18]

Congress or the president may choose to limit an agency's law enforcement authority. For example, the 1976 Mansfield Amendment to the 1961 Foreign Assistance Act prohibits U.S. federal law enforcement officers from participating in certain direct counternarcotics enforcement actions in foreign territory.[19] However, that restriction does not apply to maritime law enforcement operations conducted in the territorial sea or archipelagic waters of another state with that state's consent.[20] Congress has been more explicit in addressing the role of DoD service branches in MLE.

2. Posse Comitatus Act

In contrast to Congress' broad delegation of law enforcement authority to the Coast Guard, the 1878 Posse Comitatus Act (PCA) and the associated *posse comitatus* regulations restrict the use of DoD military elements.[21] The present codification of the act provides that "whoever, except in cases and under circumstances expressly authorized by the Constitution or Act of Congress, willfully uses any part of the Army or the Air Force as a posse comitatus or otherwise to execute the laws shall be fined under this title or imprisoned not more than two years, or both."[22] The statutory prohibition on Army and Air Force participation has been extended to the Navy and Marine Corps.[23] Importantly, however, it does not apply to the U.S. Coast Guard or to National Guard units operating under state control.

The PCA was designed to limit the use of federal military personnel to enforce civil and criminal laws, largely in reaction to well-documented abuses during the post–Civil War Reconstruction period. The U.S. Department of Justice has adopted a comprehensive three-part test

---

16. U.S. Coast Guard/U.S. Navy, Maritime Counter-drug and Alien Migrant Interdiction Operations Manual COMDTINST M16247.4A (series)/NWP 3–07.4M (unclassified, but for official use only). In case of conflict between the Coast Guard/Navy Maritime Counter-drug and Alien Migrant Interdiction Operations Manual and the MLE Manual, the MLE Manual takes precedence. Of course, both must conform to controlling constitutional or statutory laws.

17. U.S. Navy/Coast Guard Maritime Interception Operations, NTTP 3–0711M/COMDTINST M3330.1M (Apr. 2008) (unclassified, but for official use only).

18. A useful resource on MLE issues is U.S. Coast Guard, Model Maritime Operations Guide (Apr. 21, 2003), available at http://www.uscg.mil/international/affairs/MMOG/English/ (accessed Feb. 1, 2013). Chapter 2 of the Model Guide includes materials on law enforcement, international law, fisheries law enforcement, marine protected species, drug interdiction, and migrant interdiction.

19. See 22 U.S.C. § 2291(c)(1) ("No officer or employee of the United States may directly effect an arrest in any foreign country as part of any foreign police action with respect to narcotics control efforts, notwithstanding any other provision of law").

20. See 22 U.S.C. § 2291(c)(4). The "exception for maritime law enforcement" provides that, with the agreement of a foreign country, the prohibition does not apply with respect to maritime law enforcement operations in the territorial sea or archipelagic waters of that country. See also Coast Guard MLE Manual, supra, ¶ 5.B.3.

21. Commander's Handbook, supra, ¶ 3.11.3.

22. 18 U.S.C. § 1835. The original act of June 18, 1878, is available at 20 Stat. 152.

23. See 10 U.S.C. § 375; Department of Defense, DoD Cooperation with Civilian Law Enforcement Officials, DoD Directive 5525.5 (Jan. 15, 1986), ¶ 2.1 (defining the "military services").

to determine whether an act or activity violates the PCA:[24] (1) the PCA is violated when civilian law enforcement authorities make "direct active use" of military personnel to execute the laws; (2) the PCA may be violated when the use of military personnel pervades the activities of civilian law enforcement;[25] and (3) the PCA is violated if military authorities subject civilians to military regulations, proscriptions, or compulsions.

Although the DoD military services are not permitted to take a "direct" role in law enforcement activities in the United States, it is DoD policy to cooperate with civilian law enforcement officials (including the Coast Guard) to the extent practical. That policy is implemented "consistent with the needs of national security and military preparedness, the historic tradition of limiting direct military involvement in civilian law enforcement activities, and the requirements of applicable law."[26] The somewhat complex domestic law questions posed by the PCA and DoD policy are beyond the scope of this book on international law;[27] however, it can be said that the PCA and implementing DoD directives generally leave a wide scope for DoD assistance in maritime interdiction activities outside the territorial boundaries of the United States.[28] Naval officers are no doubt aware, for example, of the DoD's close cooperation in gathering and disseminating maritime intelligence and the long-standing program of joint U.S. Navy warship/U.S. Coast Guard law enforcement detachment (LEDET) operations.[29] The proactive partnership extends beyond the Navy and Coast Guard, and now includes all of the DoD services and other executive branch agencies.

One of the signal success chapters in U.S. counterdrug operations has been the Joint Interagency Task Forces (JIATF). JIATF South, located in Key West, Florida, detects, sorts, and monitors targets of counterdrug interest and then turns them over to enforcement vessels under the designated operational commander. Over its more than twenty years of operations it has developed into an effective mechanism for dealing with a well-defined threat. JIATF West, located in Hawaii, performs a similar function for the western Pacific. Intelligence elements of the naval services have also come together to form the National Maritime Intelligence-Integration Office (formerly the National Maritime Intelligence Center) in Suitland, Maryland. The NMIO neither collects nor produces intelligence. Rather, its mission is to overcome the historical barriers to information sharing.

C. JURISDICTION TO PRESCRIBE

The state's jurisdiction to prescribe laws (legislative jurisdiction) is distinct from its jurisdiction to enforce those laws and the jurisdiction of the state's courts to adjudicate civil and criminal

24. See U.S. Department of Justice, Office of Legal Counsel, Effect of Posse Comitatus Act on Proposed Detail of Civilian Employee to the National Infrastructure Protection Center, May 26, 1998, available at http://www.justice.gov/olc/pca1fnl.htm (accessed Feb. 1, 2013).
25. DoD Directive 5525.2, ¶ 3.1.1, includes the Coast Guard in the definition of "civilian agency."
26. Id. ¶ 4; 10 U.S.C. § 379.
27. Christopher A. Abel, Not Fit for Sea Duty: The Posse Comitatus Act, the United States Navy, and Federal Law Enforcement at Sea, 1 Wm. & Mary L. Rev. 445 (1990). For possible PCA waivers, see U.S. Attorneys' Manual, Criminal Resource Manual §§ 1613–14.
28. See DoD Directive 5525.2, supra, ¶ 8.1 and enclosure E4 (distinguishing between direct assistance within the United States and outside it); U.S. Department of Justice, Office of Legal Counsel, Memorandum to National Security Council on Extraterritorial Effect of the Posse Comitatus Act, Nov. 3, 1989, 13 Op. Off. Legal Counsel 321 (1996); Commander's Handbook, supra, ¶¶ 3.11.3–3.11.4; CJCS Instruction 2430.01A, Support of High Seas Driftnet Fisheries Enforcement (June 6, 2002).
29. See, e.g., 10 U.S.C. § 124 (designating DoD as the lead federal agency for the detection and monitoring of aerial and maritime transit of illegal drugs into the United States).

cases.[30] Jurisdiction to prescribe is a necessary precondition to the exercise of enforcement jurisdiction, but it is not always sufficient.[31] Enforcement might have to await the violator's return to the prescribing state's territory or necessitate the defendant's extradition from the foreign state.[32] Jurisdiction may be exclusive or concurrent (or, as some prefer, "parallel"). Mention has also been made of treaty-based jurisdiction. A treaty may confer on the states parties jurisdiction to prescribe and enforce laws consistent with the terms of the treaty. Examples may be found in the family of treaties on terrorism (including the SUA Convention, discussed in chapter 12), which impose an obligation to prescribe laws implementing the treaties' prohibitions and to prosecute individuals who violate those laws or to extradite them to another state for prosecution.

Customary international law recognizes six bases, or "principles," of prescriptive jurisdiction.[33] The first and most widely accepted basis is the territoriality principle, which recognizes that a state is competent under international law to apply its domestic law to persons, property, and acts within its territory. The second principle, a variant of territorial jurisdiction, extends jurisdiction to extraterritorial acts that have an effect within the state's territory (alternately referred to as effects-based jurisdiction or objective territoriality). Under the third principle, nationality, a state may prescribe laws applicable to its nationals even when they are located outside the state. The fourth basis of jurisdiction, the passive personality principle, provides that a state has jurisdiction to prescribe laws applicable to extraterritorial conduct injuring one of its nationals.[34] The United States has relied on that basis to criminalize assaults on U.S. passengers on foreign-flag cruise ships.[35] The fifth basis of jurisdiction, the protective principle, recognizes that a state may extend its laws extraterritorially to protect vital state interests, such as the state's national security or core governmental functions or interests. U.S. courts have relied on the protective principle in upholding prohibitions on passport fraud and counterfeiting.[36]

The last recognized basis for extraterritorial jurisdiction is the universality principle (introduced in chapter 1). The universality principle is a unique basis for a state to exercise jurisdiction in that it permits a state to prescribe penal laws respecting conduct even if that conduct has no nexus with the enforcing state.[37] For example, the fact that a pirate

---

30. Restatement FRLUS §§ 401 & 522.
31. Id. § 431(1).
32. R.M.S. *Titanic* Inc. v. Haver, 171 F.3d 943 (4th Cir. 1999) (explaining that "the *jus gentium*, the law of all maritime nations, is easy to define and declare. But its enforcement must depend on persons or property involved in such a declaration coming into the zone of power of participating nations").
33. The jurisdictional bases are described in the Draft Convention on Research in International Law of the Harvard Law School, Jurisdiction with respect to Crime, 29 Am. J. Int'l L. 435, 467 (Supp. 1935). See also Restatement FRLUS § 402. Some writers combine subjective territorial and objective territorial jurisdiction into a single category, and therefore refer to the "five bases" of jurisdiction. Objective territorial jurisdiction, better known as "effects" jurisdiction, is now so commonly cited and discussed, however, that it deserves to be listed as a sixth category.
34. Some courts question application of the passive personality basis of jurisdiction in cases in which the victim was not targeted because of nationality. See, e.g., U.S. v. Vasquez-Velasco, 15 F.3d 833, 841 (9th Cir. 1994).
35. 18 U.S.C. § 7(8); 18 U.S.C. § 2241(a); U.S. v. Neil, 312 F.3d 419 (9th Cir. 2002) (upholding the conviction of a non-U.S. national who, while serving as a crewmember on a Panamanian-flag cruise ship located in the Mexican territorial sea, molested an American passenger). See also Florida v. Stepansky, 761 So.2d 1027, 2000 A.M.C. 1893 (Florida Supreme Ct.) (upholding conviction of a U.S. citizen who, while serving in the crew of a Liberian cruise ship, committed burglary and attempted sexual assault on a U.S. national), cert. denied, 531 U.S. 959 (2000).
36. U.S. v. Birch, 470 F.2d 808 (4th Cir. 1972); U.S. v. Pizzarusso, 388 F.2d 8, 10 (2d Cir. 1968) (upholding conviction of non-U.S. national for knowingly making a false statement to a U.S. consular officer in Canada in conjunction with a visa application). But see U.S. v. Robinson, 843 F.2d 1, 3 (1st Cir. 1988) (questioning the "overly broad" reading of protective jurisdiction).
37. See Restatement FRLUS §§ 404 & 403; Curtis A. Bradley, Universal Jurisdiction and U.S. Law, 2001 Univ. Chi. Legal Forum 323. It is noteworthy that section 403 of the Restatement, which enumerates the "reasonableness" limits on a state's exercise of the other five bases of jurisdiction, does not apply to crimes of universal jurisdiction.

ship flies a foreign flag, sails with a foreign crew, and harms no nationals of the enforcing state is no bar to that state prescribing and enforcing laws against such conduct even when the prohibited activities take place outside the enforcing state's waters.[38] The commonly cited rationale for this expansive jurisdictional reach is that the conduct involved renders the violator *hostis humani generis*—the enemy of all humankind. Universal jurisdiction is said (with obvious circularity) to extend to "offenses recognized by the community of nations as of universal concern."[39] As the discussion below explains, the principal point of disagreement is not so much whether there is a class of crimes for which jurisdiction is "universal," but rather which crimes are included in that class.[40] The president of the ICJ concluded in a 2002 ruling that customary international law knows of only one true case of universal jurisdiction: piracy.[41] China apparently agrees, while noting that its domestic law makes it difficult to exercise universal jurisdiction even over piracy.[42] Other authorities suggest that war crimes and genocide are also crimes of universal jurisdiction.[43] As the recent history of piracy prosecution has demonstrated, universal jurisdiction presents additional interpretive problems when extended beyond the principals who actually committed the piratical acts to accessories and to those who, while not accessories, provide material support to those who commit crimes of universal jurisdiction and to conspiracies and attempts to commit those crimes.

Any application of universal jurisdiction principles must acknowledge that people (and in rare cases juridical entities such as corporations), not vessels, commit crimes. While it is true that a vessel may be used to commit or facilitate a crime, and may therefore be subject to arrest, seizure, and even forfeiture, the criminal statute is enforced against the individuals who engaged in the conduct. A cruise ship might be carrying a passenger known to be a notorious pirate, whose conduct might subject him to universal jurisdiction, but a state other than the cruise ship's flag state could not invoke universal jurisdiction to board the vessel on the high seas to arrest him without the flag state's consent.[44] It should also be noted that the competence to prescribe laws prohibiting conduct can be "universal," but the competence to enforce that law will still be territorially limited. For example, a vessel engaged in piracy under international law could not be boarded and seized by a warship while the vessel was in the territorial sea of another state, absent the coastal state's consent or when authorized by the UN Security Council.[45]

38. In an 1818 decision the U.S. Supreme Court rejected an interpretation of the U.S. piracy statute that would have extended its application to an incident that occurred on a foreign ship while on the high seas and having no other connection to the United States. U.S. v. Palmer, 16 U.S. (3 Wheat.) 610, 630 (1818). At the time, territoriality and nationality were viewed as the only legitimate bases of jurisdiction. See The *Apollon*, 22 U.S. (9 Wheat.) 362, 371 (1824) (holding that no nation's law can justly extend beyond its own territories, except insofar as regards its own citizens).
39. Restatement FRLUS § 404.
40. Bradley, Universal Jurisdiction, supra, at 324 & 329. See also Matter of Demjanjuk, 776 F.2d 571 (6th Cir. 1975) (extradition of alleged Nazi war criminal to stand trial in Israel).
41. Arrest Warrant case (Dem. Rep. Congo v Belgium), 2002 I.C.J. Rep. 3, 38 (Apr. 11) (opinion of ICJ president Guillaume). In the United States, however, the statutes criminalizing torture and genocide (as amended in 2007) also reflect universal jurisdiction. See 18 U.S.C. §§ 1091(d)(5) & 2340A.
42. Chi Manjiao, A Note on China's Legal and Operational Responses to International Piracy, 44 Ocean Dev. & Int'l L. 113, 117, & n.51 (2013).
43. Restatement FRLUS § 404.
44. In 2004, to effect the arrest of organized crime boss Jose Miguel Battle Jr., a U.S. Coast Guard boarding team operating from the USS *Thomas S. Gates* (CG-51) boarded the Bahamian-flag cruise ship *Celebrity Summit* on the high seas. The operation was conducted with the consent of the flag state and the cooperation of the vessel's owner. See Larry Lebowitz, Accused Godfather of Cuban Gambling Organization Arrested on Cruise Ship, MiamiHerald.com, Mar. 19, 2004.
45. Security Council resolutions authorizing such actions in Somali waters are discussed in the piracy materials in chapter 12.

Some offenses may be universally condemned and even made the subject of a widely held prosecute-or-extradite obligation, yet still not be a crime of universal jurisdiction. Crimes prohibiting "terrorist" acts have been cited by the courts as examples. Similarly, the 1988 UN Convention against Illicit Traffic in Narcotic Drugs and Psychotropic Substances—ratified by more than 180 states—requires states parties to criminalize certain drug-related activities, provide for severe penalties, and cooperate with other states in enforcement and extradition. Article 108 of the LOS Convention—ratified by more than 160 states—requires all states parties to cooperate in the suppression of illicit drug trafficking. It further provides that any state that has reasonable grounds for believing that a ship flying its flag is engaged in such trafficking may request the cooperation of other states to suppress it. However, neither the 1988 UN Drug Convention nor the 1982 LOS Convention declared that maritime drug trafficking is a crime of universal jurisdiction (or a basis in itself for exercising a right of visit).

Despite the potentially global reach of a flag state's prescriptive jurisdiction as a matter of international law, national courts do not always favor extraterritorial application of domestic laws.[46] In the United States, Congress has the power to define and punish piracy and felonies committed on the high seas, as well as crimes "against the law of nations."[47] In addition, Congress has the authority to regulate interstate and foreign commerce,[48] and to implement the admiralty and maritime jurisdiction.[49] Finally, Congress has the power to enact legislation necessary and proper to implement a treaty to which the United States is a party.[50] Notwithstanding that broad grant of legislative power, U.S. courts have adopted a presumption that Congress does not intend that U.S. statutes will apply extraterritorially.[51] Importantly, the presumption does not apply to criminal statutes, which are, as a class, not logically dependent on their locality for the government's jurisdiction,[52] such as those involving U.S.-flag vessels. Criminal laws that apply in the "special maritime and territorial jurisdiction of the United States" plainly fall in that category. Similarly, Congress made clear its intent that the Maritime Drug Law Enforcement Act applies extraterritorially, even in cases involving foreign vessels and nonnationals.[53] In the absence of explicit provision in a statute for extraterritorial application, the courts will apply canons of construction to determine the statute's reach. The courts will begin with a presumption that an act of Congress is constitutional[54] and that Congress did not intend to violate principles of

---

46. For example, two nineteenth-century Supreme Court decisions held that federal criminal jurisdiction does not attach to offenses committed by and against foreigners on foreign vessels. See U.S. v. Holmes, 18 U.S. (5 Wheat.) 412 (1890); U.S. v. Palmer, 16 U.S. (3 Wheat.) 281, 288 (1818).

47. U.S. Const. art. I, § 8, cl. 10. The U.S. Supreme Court has interpreted that clause to contain three distinct grants of power: (1) the power to define and punish piracies, (2) the power to define and punish felonies committed on the high seas, and (3) the power to define and punish offenses against the law of nations. U.S. v. Bellaizac-Hurtado, 700 F.3d 1245, 1248 (11th Cir. 2012). But see U.S. v. Flores, 289 U.S. 137 (1933) (the power to define and punish piracy does not preclude additional jurisdiction over admiralty and maritime matters). See also Eugene Kontorovich, The "Define and Punish" Clause and the Limits of Universal Jurisdiction, 103 Nw. U. L. Rev. 149 (2009).

48. U.S. Const. art. I, § 8, cl. 3.

49. U.S. Const. art. III, § 2; Romero v. Int'l Terminal Operating Co., 358 U.S. 354, 360–61 (1959) (construing the Article III admiralty and maritime jurisdiction clause to confer three separate powers, including the power for Congress "to revise and supplement the law within the limits of the Constitution").

50. Missouri v. Holland, 252 U.S. 416 (1920).

51. Kiobel v. Royal Dutch Petroleum Co., 133 S. Ct. 1659 (2013); U.S. v. Mitchell, 553 F.2d 996 (5th Cir. 1977) (holding that the Marine Mammal Protection Act prohibition on taking marine mammals did not apply to a U.S. citizen while in Bahamian waters).

52. See U.S. v. Bowman, 260 U.S. 94 (1922). But see Morrison v. Nat'l Australia Bank, 130 S. Ct. 2869, 2881 (2010) (applying the presumption against extraterritoriality in *all* cases).

53. 46 U.S.C. §§ 70502 & 70503(b).

54. See Immigration and Naturalization Service v. Chadha, 462 U.S. 919, 944 (1982). See also Ashwander v. Tennessee Valley Auth., 297 U.S. 288, 341 (1935) (Brandeis, J., concurring).

international law.[55] More specifically, the *Charming Betsy* canon of construction instructs that in applying the terms of an ambiguous statute the court will not construe it "to violate the law of nations if any other possible construction remains."[56] To effectuate the canon, courts may refer to the above-listed customary and conventional international law bases for a state to extend application of its laws beyond its territory. When, however, Congress makes plain its intent that a statute is to apply extraterritorially, courts must enforce the statute as written, even if the statute exceeds the nation's jurisdiction under international law,[57] unless the statute violates the Constitution.[58]

D. MARITIME CRIMES

Maritime criminal law, both international and domestic, has evolved significantly over the centuries. The field includes many of the same categories of violent and property crimes encountered ashore, as well as such uniquely maritime crimes as piracy,[59] barratry,[60] scuttling,[61] mutiny,[62] and the failure to heave to.[63] This chapter focuses on three maritime crime "clusters" that form the core missions of many of the world's maritime constabulary services: the slavery/human trafficking/migrant smuggling crime cluster, drug trafficking, and the environmental/natural resource crime cluster. Counterpiracy, counterterrorism, and counterproliferation, which have emerged as significant components of the naval forces' maritime security operations mission, are examined in chapter 12.

The 1982 LOS Convention is the centerpiece of the law of the sea but not its sole source; other treaties and customary international law supplement it. The family of treaties prohibiting trafficking in narcotic and psychotropic drugs is a familiar supplementary regime. Another supplementary regime recognizes that maritime crimes are increasingly transnational in their planning, financing, coordination, execution, and effects. Because transnational organized crime presents unique challenges to states, the UN Convention on Transnational Organized Crime (TOC Convention) and its three protocols were developed under the auspices of the UN Office on Drugs and Crime.[64] The TOC Convention is introduced below, followed by an examination of the protocols on migrant smuggling and human trafficking. A third supplementary treaty regime examined in this chapter addresses marine environmental and living resource crimes, including illegal, unregulated, and unreported (IUU) fishing and the use of large-scale drift nets

---

55. McCulloch v. Sociedad Nacional de Marineros de Honduras, 372 U.S. 10, 21–22, (1963); Restatement FRLUS § 114.

56. Murray v. The Schooner *Charming Betsy*, 6 U.S. (2 Cranch) 64, 118 (1804). The purpose of the *Charming Betsy* canon is to avoid the negative "foreign policy implications" of violating the law of nations. Weinberger v. Rossi, 456 U.S. 25, 32 (1982). The canon comes into play only when Congress' intent is ambiguous. U.S. v. Yousef, 327 F.3d 56, 92 (2d Cir. 2003). See also Curtis A. Bradley, The *Charming Betsy* Canon and Separation of Powers: Rethinking the Interpretive Role of International Law, 86 Geo. L. J. 479 (1997).

57. See Cabrera-Alvarez v. Gonzales, 423 F.3d 1006, 1009 (9th Cir. 2005) (holding that "Congress has the power to legislate beyond the limits posed by international law"); U.S. v. Aguilar, 883 F.2d 662, 679 (9th Cir. 1989).

58. See, e.g., U.S. v. Bellaizac-Hurtado, 700 F.3d 1245, 1258 (11th Cir. 2012) (holding that Congress exceeded its constitutional power under the "define and punish" clause when it extended the MDLEA to violations in a foreign state's territorial waters).

59. 18 U.S.C. § 1651.

60. 18 U.S.C. § 1656.

61. 18 U.S.C. § 2275.

62. 18 U.S.C. § 2193.

63. 18 U.S.C. § 2237.

64. See David McLean, Transnational Organized Crime: A Commentary on the UN Convention and Its Protocols (2007). The U.S. Senate gave its advice and consent to the TOC Convention in 2005, while also attaching understandings and declarations limiting its application to states within the United States. See S. Treaty Doc. No. 108-16.

on the high seas. The 1988 Convention for the Suppression of Unlawful Acts against the Safety of Maritime Navigation (SUA Convention) and its 2005 protocol are examined in chapter 12 in conjunction with the materials on counterterrorism and counterproliferation. Although each of these treaty regimes defines the elements of a variety of maritime crimes, as a matter of international law, none of these "international" crimes comes within the jurisdiction of the ICC, whose jurisdiction is presently limited to war crimes, genocide, and crimes against humanity.[65] As a result, these maritime crimes (as well as the crime of piracy) are prosecuted in national courts.

1. Illicit Traffic in Narcotic Drugs or Psychotropic Substances

The UN Office on Drugs and Crime (UNODC) characterizes drug trafficking as a global illicit trade involving the cultivation, manufacture, distribution, and sale of substances that are subject to drug prohibition laws. UNODC compiles data on the production, use, and interdiction of six categories of drugs: cannabis (both herbal and resin), opiates, opioids, cocaine, amphetamine-type substances, and Ecstasy. Worldwide annual cocaine consumption is estimated at 470 metric tons, with the United States accounting for about 165 tons of that. Although Colombia has long been the principal source of cocaine trafficked to North America, Colombian production declined more than 60 percent from 2001 to 2010,[66] while production in Bolivia and Peru saw significant increases. Cocaine produced in South America is transported to the United States by air, sea, and land border routes. A single shipment might involve all three transportation modes. Maritime smuggling modes include everything from container, bulk cargo, and cruise ships to fishing and recreational vessels (often fitted with hidden compartments) and even submersible craft. Cocaine bound for the United States is typically transported from a South American source country (Colombia or Peru) to Mexico or Central America by sea, and then goes by land to the U.S. border. Air drops to waiting "go fast" boats are common in some theaters, particularly between the Bahamas and Florida.

Because the threat posed by drug trafficking and related crimes is transnational, well-organized, and well-financed, an effective response must likewise be multinational. Serious efforts to stem trafficking in narcotic drugs and psychotropic substances by sea began in the 1960s. Since then, the nature of the smuggled drugs and the criminal enterprises engaged in their production and transport, as well as the methods used by smugglers and interdiction forces, have undergone significant changes.[67] Ruthless and well-armed drug-trafficking organizations pose a risk different in both degree and kind from other more common and uncoordinated maritime crimes. To meet the enforcement challenge, joint and interagency counterdrug operations are now common.[68]

a. UNODC Treaties on Narcotic Drugs and Psychotropic Substances

Multilateral efforts to suppress drug trafficking can be traced back to the Single Convention on Narcotic Drugs of 1961.[69] The framework was expanded and refined by general suppression

---

65. Rome Statute of the International Criminal Court, art. 5, July 7, 1998, 2187 U.N.T.S. 3.
66. The U.S. Office of National Drug Control Policy (ONDCP) reports that Colombian cocaine production declined from 700 metric tons in 2001 to 270 metric tons in 2010, a 61 percent decline. See The White House, National Drug Control Strategy 31 (2012), available at http://www.whitehouse.gov/sites/default/files/ondcp/2012_ndcs.pdf (accessed Feb. 1, 2013).
67. Charles M. Fuss Jr., Sea of Grass: The Maritime Drug War 1970–1990 (1996).
68. See, e.g., Chairman, Joint Chiefs of Staff, Joint Pub. 3-07.4, Joint Counterdrug Operations (2007); Commander's Handbook, supra, ¶ 3.11.4.
69. Single Convention on Narcotic Drugs, Mar. 30, 1961, 18 U.S.T. 1407, 520 U.N.T.S. 204, as amended by the

conventions in 1971[70] and 1988,[71] along with the 1982 LOS Convention.[72] The UNODC describes the 1961, 1971, and 1988 narcotic drug conventions as mutually supportive and complementary. By 2012, more than 180 states, including the United States, had ratified the 1988 UN Convention against Illicit Traffic in Narcotic Drugs and Psychotropic Substances. The 1961, 1971, and 1988 treaties were an important first gesture toward a multilateral response. The real test of a treaty regime, however, is the effectiveness of its implementation by the states parties. Reversing the global drug abuse epidemic requires the concerted efforts of source states, consumption states, flag states, and the states in whose financial system the money proceeds are laundered.

The 1988 UN Convention on Drugs has particular relevance to the MLE community. It extends the drug control regime to precursor ingredients while also establishing measures to combat illicit drug trafficking and related money laundering. The convention strengthened the framework of international cooperation in criminal matters with its provisions on extradition and mutual legal assistance. Article 17 of the 1988 convention addresses illicit maritime drug trafficking.

ARTICLE 17. Illicit Traffic by Sea

1. The Parties shall co-operate to the fullest extent possible to suppress illicit traffic by sea, in conformity with the international law of the sea.
2. A Party which has reasonable grounds to suspect that a vessel flying its flag or not displaying a flag or marks of registry is engaged in illicit traffic may request the assistance of other Parties in suppressing its use for that purpose. The Parties so requested shall render such assistance within the means available to them.
3. A Party which has reasonable grounds to suspect that a vessel exercising freedom of navigation in accordance with international law, and flying the flag or displaying marks of registry of another Party is engaged in illicit traffic may so notify the flag State, request confirmation of registry and, if confirmed, request authorization from the flag State to take appropriate measures in regard to that vessel.
4. In accordance with paragraph 3 or in accordance with treaties in force between them or in accordance with any agreement or arrangement otherwise reached between those Parties, the flag State may authorize the requesting State to, inter alia:
   a. Board the vessel;
   b. Search the vessel;
   c. If evidence of involvement in illicit traffic is found, take appropriate action with respect to the vessel, persons and cargo on board.
5. Where action is taken pursuant to this article, the Parties concerned shall take due account of the need not to endanger the safety of life at sea, the security of the vessel and the cargo or to prejudice the commercial and legal interests of the flag State or any other interested State.

1972 Protocol Amending the Single Convention on Narcotic Drugs, 1961. The 1961 Single Convention lists "narcotic drugs" in Schedules I and II.
70. Convention on Psychotropic Substances, Feb. 21, 1971, 32 U.S.T. 543, 1019 U.N.T.S. 175.
71. The 1988 UN Convention on Drugs extends the prohibitions to the drug precursors listed in tables I and II of the convention.
72. The IMO has also contributed useful guidance on suppressing maritime trafficking in drugs, psychotropic substances, and precursor chemicals. See IMO, Guidelines for the Prevention and Suppression of Drugs, Psychotropic Substances and Precursor Chemicals on Ships Engaged in International Maritime Traffic, IMO Res. A.872(20) (1997), revised by IMO Res. A.985(24)/Rev.1 (2006).

6. The flag State may, consistent with its obligations in paragraph 1 of this article, subject its authorization to conditions to be mutually agreed between it and the requesting Party, including conditions relating to responsibility.

7. For the purposes of paragraphs 3 and 4 of this article, a Party shall respond expeditiously to a request from another Party to determine whether a vessel that is flying its flag is entitled to do so, and to requests for authorization made pursuant to paragraph 3. At the time of becoming a Party to this Convention, each Party shall designate an authority or, when necessary, authorities to receive and respond to such requests. Such designation shall be notified through the Secretary-General to all other Parties within one month of the designation.

8. A Party which has taken any action in accordance with this article shall promptly inform the flag State concerned of the results of that action.

9. The Parties shall consider entering into bilateral or regional agreements or arrangements to carry out, or to enhance the effectiveness of, the provisions of this article.

10. Action pursuant to paragraph 4 of this article shall be carried out only by warships or military aircraft, or other ships or aircraft clearly marked and identifiable as being on government service and authorized to that effect.

11. Any action taken in accordance with this article shall take due account of the need not to interfere with or affect the rights and obligations and the exercise of jurisdiction of coastal States in accordance with the international law of the sea. United Nations Convention against Illicit Traffic in Narcotic Drugs and Psychotropic Substances, art. 17, Dec. 20, 1988, 1582 U.N.T.S. 95, 28 I. L.M. 497 (1989).

The Article 17 provision for multilateral and bilateral boarding agreements has been a clear game-changer in international efforts to stem maritime drug trafficking. The boarding agreements the United States has entered into with other regional states are discussed in the section on enforcement jurisdiction below.

b. 1982 LOS Convention Articles on Drug Trafficking

The 1982 LOS Convention addresses drug trafficking in Articles 27 and 108. In addition, as a "customs" issue, the import, export, or transshipment of drugs is relevant to the foreign vessel's right of innocent passage under Article 19(2)(g), the scope of the coastal state's regulatory authority over vessels in passage under Article 21(1)(h) and Article 42(1)(d), the contiguous zone regime in Article 33, and jurisdiction with respect to artificial islands and structures in the EEZ or on the continental shelf.[73] Beyond the contiguous zone, vessels are subject to the exclusive jurisdiction of their flag state on drug-trafficking matters, absent consent.

A foreign vessel found loading or unloading any commodity in the territorial sea in violation of the coastal state's customs laws is not entitled to innocent passage status (see chapter 5).[74] The coastal state is entitled to prevent any passage that is not innocent.[75] Additionally, the coastal state's regulatory authority over vessels in innocent or transit passage extends to measures to prevent infringement of the customs law,[76] and the Article 27 precatory limits on the coastal state's

---

73. LOSC arts. 60(2) & 80.
74. Id. art. 19(2)(g).
75. Id. art. 25(1).
76. Id. arts. 21(1)(h) & 42(1)(d).

exercise of criminal jurisdiction over vessels in passage do not apply when enforcement is necessary for the suppression of illicit traffic in narcotic drugs or psychotropic substances.[77] Finally, it should be noted that the LOS Convention's provisions for "prompt release" of seized vessels and their crews do not apply to drug-trafficking offenses.[78]

The impediments to an effective maritime drug-trafficking regime lie not in restrictions on prescriptive jurisdiction but rather in limits on enforcement jurisdiction. Courts have upheld extraterritorial prescriptive jurisdiction over maritime drug trafficking under both the effects and protective principles. Drug trafficking is not a crime of universal enforcement jurisdiction, however, and there is no right of visit with respect to foreign vessels suspected of engaging in it. Although the right of hot pursuit from the territorial sea or contiguous zone under Article 111 and the associated doctrine of constructive presence have been applied in cases involving drug trafficking by foreign-flag vessels, the rule of exclusive flag state jurisdiction over vessels on the high seas continues to shield some drug traffickers from enforcement actions.

Under Article 108 of the LOS Convention all states have a duty to cooperate in the suppression of illicit traffic in narcotic drugs and psychotropic substances engaged in by ships on the high seas contrary to international conventions.[79] Article 108 thus informs the flag state's obligation to exercise effective jurisdiction and control over its vessels under Article 94. The flag state's obligations extend to the vessel itself, its master and crew, and any cargo or passengers it carries. When the flag state is unable to immediately exercise jurisdiction and control, Article 108 provides that if it has reasonable grounds for believing that a ship flying its flag is engaged in illicit traffic in narcotic drugs or psychotropic substances, the flag state may request the cooperation of other states to suppress such traffic, a provision also included in Article 17(2) of the 1988 UN Convention on Drugs. The LOS Convention does not address the reverse situation, in which a state having grounds for believing that a foreign-flag vessel is engaged in drug trafficking could request the cooperation of the flag state in suppressing the illicit traffic; however, Article 17(3) of the UN Convention on Drugs provides the missing mechanism.

c. U.S. Maritime Drug Law Enforcement Act

President Richard Nixon launched the nation's "war on drugs" in 1971. Within the United States, the Office of National Drug Control Policy, established in 1988, coordinates the nation's drug abuse prevention and control program, with overall direction provided by the National Drug Control Strategy. The national strategy documents the success of the joint maritime interdiction and law enforcement efforts and sets an ambitious goal of reducing cocaine transport through the U.S.-bound transit zone by 40 percent between 2012 and 2015. The strategy explains:

> For over two decades, the U.S. interagency law enforcement, intelligence, and military team, coordinated through JIATF South, has worked together with partner nations to stem the flow of illicit drugs through the Western Hemisphere. The Panama Express Program (PANEX), a multi-agency task force dedicated to disrupting and dismantling major maritime drug transport organi-

---

77. Id. art. 27(1)(d).
78. Because Article 292 prompt release actions are limited to circumstances in which the LOS Convention requires the coastal state to release a seized vessel on payment of reasonable security, and those requirements are found only in Part V (Article 73) and Part XII (Article 226), some states have sought to obtain a vessel's release for violations not covered by those articles by invoking the court's power to order "provisional measures" under Article 290. See, e.g., The ARA *Libertad* Case (Argentina v. Ghana), Provisional Measures, ITLOS Case No. 20, Order of Nov. 20, 2012.
79. LOSC art. 108; Restatement FRLUS § 522 cmt. d & n.4.

zations based in South and Central America, has contributed to the interdiction of over 850 tons of cocaine in international waters destined for the United States or its Southern neighbors. PANEX has resulted in over 2,100 individuals being brought to the United States for prosecution—with a 97 percent conviction rate. The Administration has maintained a national goal to remove 40 percent of documented cocaine movement through the transit zone by the year 2015.[80]

Within the United States, the principal legal regime addressing drug trafficking by sea is set out in the Maritime Drug Law Enforcement Act.[81] The MDLEA opens with Congress' findings that (1) trafficking in controlled substances on board vessels is a serious international problem, is universally condemned, and presents a specific threat to the security and societal well-being of the United States; and (2) operating or embarking in a submersible vessel or semisubmersible vessel without nationality and on an international voyage is a serious international problem; facilitates transnational crime, including drug trafficking and terrorism; and presents a specific threat to the safety of maritime navigation and the security of the United States.[82]

The MDLEA prohibits the intentional manufacture or distribution, or possession with intent to manufacture or distribute, of a controlled substance on board a "vessel of the United States," a "vessel subject to the jurisdiction of the United States," or any other vessel with respect to an individual who is a citizen of the United States or a resident alien of the United States.[83] The criminal prohibitions on maritime drug trafficking were extended to self-propelled semisubmersible (SPSS) and fully submersible vessels (FSV) in the Drug Trafficking Vessel Interdiction Act of 2008.[84] The MDLEA provides a list of "practices commonly recognized as smuggling tactics," which may provide "prima facie evidence of intent" to use a vessel in a manner to make it subject to forfeiture under the act.[85] It also permits seizure and forfeiture of vessels designed for smuggling even if no contraband was found on the vessel at the time of boarding.[86] Criminal penalties for MDLEA violations range from five years to life imprisonment.[87] Sentences may be enhanced if the defendant used or possessed a firearm or failed to comply with an order to heave to. Congress limited the MDLEA defendant's standing to raise international law defenses, thus relegating allegations that the enforcement action violated international law to the involved nation-states.[88]

2. Slave Transport, Human Trafficking, Migrant Smuggling, Refugees, and Asylum

The second maritime crime cluster includes three crimes involving the transport or movement of people by sea, together with the closely associated rights of refugees and the law of asylum. Although all three of the crimes—slave transport, human trafficking, and migrant smuggling—

80. National Drug Control Strategy, supra, at 36.
81. Maritime Drug Law Enforcement Act, 46 U.S.C. §§ 70501–70508. The current act has its roots in Pub. L. No. 96-350, § 2, Sept. 15, 1980, which largely obviated prosecution under 21 U.S.C. § 955a.
82. 46 U.S.C. § 70501.
83. 46 U.S.C. § 70503. See also Commander's Handbook, supra, ¶ 3.11.4.
84. Pub. L. No. 110-407 (2008). The DTVIA was codified in 46 U.S.C. §§ 70501, 70502, 70508; and 18 U.S.C. § 2285. See also Coast Guard MLE Manual, supra, ¶ 5.C.2 & 5.E.1; Brian Wilson, Submersibles and Transnational Criminal Organizations, 17 Ocean & Coastal L. J. 35 (2011). The 2012 edition of the U.S. Coast Guard/U.S. Navy, Maritime Counter-drug and Alien Migrant Interdiction Operations Manual contains updated guidance and procedures for SPSS and FSV interdictions.
85. 46 U.S.C. § 70507(b).
86. Id. See also Coast Guard MLE Manual, supra, ¶ 5.C.1; 19 U.S.C. § 1703.
87. 46 U.S.C. § 70506, incorporating the penalties in 21 U.S.C. § 960(b).
88. 46 U.S.C. § 70505.

are universally condemned and prohibited by widely ratified treaties, none of the three is subject to universal jurisdiction. Only one of the three (the slave trade) gives rise to a right of visit under Article 110 of the LOS Convention.

a. Border Control Issues Raised by Visitors and Migrants

Persons who are not citizens or nationals come to a state as visitors or as migrants. Lawful visitors arrive at airports, seaports, or other authorized ports of entry and present their passport and, unless waived, a nonimmigrant entry visa. Presumably, visitors will depart the state when the reason for their visit has concluded or will apply for a change in status. By contrast, migrants seek not merely to visit but to relocate to the destination state. They do so for a variety of reasons. Many simply seek a better quality of life or to unite with other family members. Some migrate to escape armed violence, natural disasters, famine, or even genocide. Others—potential refugees— seek to escape persecution in their state of origin. A few arrive as victims of human trafficking or slavery, and some come to the state to commit crimes or acts of terrorism or espionage.

Migrants entering in accordance with "regular" immigration procedures generally arrive at a designated port of entry with the appropriate identity and entry documents. In the United States such immigrants may later qualify for lawful permanent resident (LPR) status or citizenship by naturalization. "Irregular" immigration refers to entry or attempted entry without complying with the formalities of regular migration. A small number of irregular migrants enter the country as stowaways on unsuspecting vessels or aircraft.[89] Irregular migrants who can afford it might arrange for surreptitious passage with individuals or organized criminal groups who engage in migrant smuggling for profit. Of particular concern to the seagoing officer are migrants who openly attempt the voyage by vessel, often in large numbers. Those migrants are sometimes intercepted at sea by patrol craft. Some are immediately repatriated by the intercepting state. Others are first prescreened for possible asylum claims or given a hearing to determine if they are removable. A few may be paroled and permitted to remain.[90]

This second cluster of MLE mission areas poses a variety of challenges to maritime law enforcement and maritime interception operations forces. A vessel engaged in slave transport, human trafficking, or migrant smuggling might initially present itself as a distress case, humanitarian relief event, law enforcement incident, noncompliant vessel boarding, or some combination of the four. The intercepting vessel might be called on to execute its rescue and assistance bill or to mobilize a "takedown" team (to overcome boarding resistance) and boarding party and even a large-scale emergency medical care detail. Accordingly, the commander must be mindful of his or her duty of rescue (recalling the USS *Dubuque* incident and the commanding officer's court-martial cited in chapter 8), law enforcement jurisdiction, rules of engagement or on the use of force, obligations with respect to recovered persons and asylum seekers, and, of course, any requirements for interagency coordination and communication with operational or tactical commanders.

b. Slavery, Slave Trading, and Human Trafficking

Although slavery has long been outlawed, pockets of the practice persist. Slavery-like human trafficking practices, including debt bondage and forced labor and prostitution, remain a serious and more common problem, one that is not always easy to distinguish from true slavery.

---

89. Stowing away is a felony in the United States. See 18 U.S.C. § 2199. See also 8 U.S.C. §§ 1281–1287. The owner of a vessel or aircraft bringing an alien to the United States must pay the costs of detaining and maintaining the alien pending his or her removal. 8 U.S.C. § 1231(c)(3).

90. On the discretionary power of the secretary of homeland security to parole migrants, see 8 U.S.C. § 1182(d)(5)(A) & 8 C.F.R. § 212.5.

Efforts to eradicate slavery began in the early nineteenth century.[91] Great Britain outlawed the slave trade in 1807, and the United States followed the next year.[92] Courts in both countries issued important decisions on the nature and limits of jurisdiction over slave ships.[93] Treaty-based prohibitions on slavery and the slave trade began with the 1815 Treaty of Paris.[94] It was followed in 1926 by the Convention to Suppress the Slave Trade and Slavery,[95] and the 1956 UN Supplementary Convention on the Abolition of Slavery, the Slave Trade, and Institutions and Practices Similar to Slavery.[96] Legal "ownership" of the victim distinguishes slavery under international law from other forms of "enslavement" such as debt bondage and forced prostitution, a distinction discussed further in the section below on human trafficking. The Slavery Convention of 1926 defined slavery as "the status or condition of a person over whom any or all of the powers attaching to the right of *ownership* are exercised."[97] The "slave trade" is defined in Article 7 of the 1956 Supplementary Convention to include, among other acts, "every act of trade or transport in slaves, by whatever means of conveyance." The United States has enacted criminal statutes prohibiting participation in the slave trade.[98]

The widely ratified 1966 International Covenant on Civil and Political Rights confirmed the abolition of slavery and the slave trade.[99] The prohibitions on slavery and the slave trade are widely considered to be peremptory (*jus cogens*) norms, from which no derogation is permitted.[100] Both the 1958 Convention on the High Seas and the 1982 LOS Convention require states to take effective measures to prevent and punish the transport of slaves in ships authorized to fly their flag and to prevent the unlawful use of their flag for that purpose.[101] The *Restatement (Third) of Foreign Relations Law of the United States* refers to slavery as a crime of universal jurisdiction.[102] It is important to note, however, that that oft-cited and frequently misunderstood section of the

---

91. For a detailed history of the efforts to eradicate the slave trade, see Louis B. Sohn, Peacetime Use of Force on the High Seas, 64 U.S. Nav. War Coll. Int'l L. Studies 38, 39–59 (1991). See also John Bassett Moore, A Digest of International Law, vol. II, § 310 (1906).

92. Act Prohibiting Importation of Slaves, March 2, 1807, 2 Stat. 426. See also Slave Trade Act, ch. 51, 2 Stat. 70 (1800) (prohibiting U.S. vessels to engage in slave trade between other nations); Slave Trade Act, ch. 91, 3 Stat. 450 (1818).

93. In *Le Louis*, 2 Dods. 210 (British High Court of Admiralty, 1817); The *Antelope*, 23 U.S. (10 Wheat.) 66 (1825). The brig *Le Louis* was a French-flag slaver that was seized by the British warship *Queen Charlotte*. In the course of the boarding, the crew of *Le Louis* killed twelve members of the *Queen Charlotte* boarding party. The admiralty court concluded that there was no lawful basis for the boarding; therefore, the crew's action in violently resisting the boarding was not unlawful.

94. Definitive Treaty between Great Britain, Austria, Prussia and Russia, and France, Nov. 15, 1815, reprinted in British & Foreign State Papers, vol. 3 (1838). The "additional article" to the treaty pledged that to achieve their commitment to "complete and universal abolition of the Slave Trade," the contracting parties should "without loss of time, . . . [find] the most effectual measures for the entire and definitive abolition of a Commerce so odious, and so strongly condemned by the laws of religion and of nature."

95. Convention on Suppression of Slave Trade and Slavery, Sept. 25, 1926, 46 Stat. 2183, T.S. No. 778, 60 L.N.T.S. 253, as amended by the protocol of Dec. 7, 1953, 7 U.S.T. 479, T.I.A.S. 3532.

96. Supplementary Convention on the Abolition of Slavery, the Slave Trade, and Institutions and Practices Similar to Slavery, Sept. 7, 1956, 18 U.S.T. 3201, 266 U.N.T.S. 40.

97. 1926 Convention on Suppression of Slave Trade and Slavery, supra, art. 1(1) (emphasis added).

98. U.S. criminal statutes on slavery and the slave trade are now codified in 18 U.S.C. §§ 1581–1588. For examples of early enforcement action by the U.S. Revenue Cutter Service, see The *Merino*, 22 U.S. (9 Wheat.) 391 (1824); and The *Slavers*, 69 U.S. (2 Wall.) 350 (1864).

99. International Covenant on Civil and Political Rights [hereinafter "ICCPR"], art. 8(1), Dec. 16, 1966, S. Treaty Doc. No. 95-20, 999 U.N.T.S. 171.

100. Restatement FRLUS § 102 n.6.

101. 1958 Convention on the High Seas, supra, art. 13; LOSC art. 99; United Nations Convention on the Law of the Sea 1982: A Commentary, vol. III, at 72–86 (Myron H. Nordquist et al. eds., 1995).

102. Restatement FRLUS § 404.

Restatement addresses only *prescriptive* jurisdiction.[103] A later section of the *Restatement* makes it clear that *enforcement* jurisdiction over slavers is not universal.[104] While suspicion that a foreign vessel on the high seas is engaged in the slave trade may provide grounds for exercising a right-of-visit boarding under Article 110 of the LOS Convention,[105] the convention does not permit seizure of the foreign vessel if the suspicions are confirmed,[106] as it does with respect to piracy. Thus, the recourse for a boarding team exercising a right of visit on discovering that a properly registered foreign vessel is indeed engaged in the slave trade is to notify the vessel's flag state and perhaps to request its consent to take appropriate action against the vessel.

"Human trafficking" refers to the illegal trade in human beings. The TOC Convention's 2000 Protocol to Prevent, Suppress and Punish Trafficking in Persons, especially Women and Children, provides the international legal framework for suppressing human trafficking.[107] It defines human trafficking as

> the recruitment, transportation, transfer, harboring or receipt of persons, by means of the threat or use of force or other forms of coercion, of abduction, of fraud, of deception, of the abuse of power or of a position of vulnerability or of the giving or receiving of payments or benefits to achieve the consent of a person having control over another person, for the purpose of exploitation. Exploitation shall include, at a minimum, the exploitation of the prostitution of others or other forms of sexual exploitation, forced labor or services, slavery or practices similar to slavery, servitude or the removal of organs.[108]

The protocol goes on to explain that consent of a victim to the intended exploitation is irrelevant to the existence of a trafficking offense when the trafficker used a threat or use of force or other forms of coercion, abduction, fraud, deception, the abuse of power, or a position of vulnerability. The protocol applies only to transnational trafficking that involves an organized criminal group.[109] It requires parties to the protocol to criminalize human trafficking and extend protection to victims of such trafficking.[110] It also encourages parties to consider adopting legislative or other measures that will permit victims of trafficking to remain in the party's territory, temporarily or permanently.[111]

Although "slavery" is one of the forms of "exploitation" listed in the protocol's definition of human trafficking, the definition also includes forced labor or services and practices similar to

---

103. The section refers to the state's jurisdiction to "define and prescribe punishment" for the listed offenses of "universal jurisdiction." See 18 U.S.C. §§ 1585–1587.

104. Restatement FRLUS § 522 cmt. d & n.3.

105. Except when supported by prior intelligence, it is difficult to imagine vessel approach scenarios that would provide the approaching enforcement vessel a reasonable ground to believe that the vessel being approached is engaged in the slave trade, thus justifying a right-of-visit boarding.

106. Compare LOSC art. 105 ("every State" may enforce piracy prohibition) with LOSC art. 99 (no similar provision for vessels engaged in the slave trade).

107. Protocol to Prevent, Suppress and Punish Trafficking in Persons, Especially Women and Children, Supplementing the UN Convention against Transnational Organized Crime [hereinafter "Human Trafficking Protocol"], adopted by the UN Nov. 15, 2000, 2237 U.N.T.S. 319 (No. 39574), 40 I.L.M. 335, 377–85 (2001). See also Anne T. Gallagher, The International Law of Human Trafficking (2010).

108. Human Trafficking Protocol, supra, art. 3.

109. Id. art. 4.

110. Id. art. 5. The relevant U.S. criminal statute on human trafficking is codified in 18 U.S.C. § 1590. Sex trafficking is prohibited by 18 U.S.C. § 1591.

111. Human Trafficking Protocol, supra, art. 7. In 2000 Congress enacted the Victims of Trafficking and Violence Protection Act, 22 U.S.C. § 7101 Note, which established the "T" nonimmigrant status for victims of certain severe forms of trafficking.

slavery and servitude.[112] Thus, slavery and the slave trade might constitute human trafficking, but not all forms of human trafficking constitute slavery or the slave trade. The distinction is important in construing and applying Article 110 on the right of visit—which does not extend to human-trafficking cases. There are also important distinctions between human trafficking and migrant smuggling. Relatively few victims of human trafficking are transported by migrant smugglers. It is reportedly far more common for them to travel singly or in small numbers via common carriers (using legitimate or forged travel documents), which are generally unaware the passenger is a victim of trafficking.[113] Similarly, migrant smugglers are not necessarily also human traffickers; in the typical case the "client's" obligation to the migrant smuggler generally does not extend beyond a payment for transportation services.

c. Irregular Immigration and Migrant Smuggling

The International Covenant on Civil and Political Rights affirms that all persons have "the right to leave any country, including [their] own."[114] While that suggests a right to emigrate from one's state of origin or residence, it does not create a corresponding right to enter another state as an immigrant. It is, in fact, incontestable that border control is an incident of the state's sovereignty.[115] With a few exceptions for individuals who may qualify as refugees, immigration is governed by the laws and policies of the destination state.

Irregular immigration entries and attempted entries have created acute concern in many regions. Italy and Spain have both experienced serious irregular maritime migration influxes by people in search of a pathway to EU states. In the Southern Hemisphere, Australia has long been a favored regional destination for irregular migrants, as is the United States in the Americas. Dennis Noble has written a comprehensive history of the U.S. Coast Guard's maritime migrant interdiction experience from 1959 to the present.[116] His book recounts, for example, the mass migration episode triggered by Fidel Castro's 1980 decree that anyone who wanted to leave Cuba was to be given free access to depart from the seaport of Mariel. In what became known as the "Mariel Boatlift," some 124,000 Cuban migrants entered the United States in a flotilla of vessels, quickly overwhelming the resources of southern Florida. Similar mass migrations to the United States occurred in 1993 (prompting Operation Able Manner, involving the interdiction of 25,000 Haitian migrants) and 1994 (prompting Operation Able Vigil, involving the interdiction of 31,000 Cuban migrants).

Maritime migrant interdiction and enforcement is carried out under direction provided by the U.S. Coast Guard *Maritime Law Enforcement Manual* and the Coast Guard/U.S. Navy *Maritime Counter-drug and Alien Migrant Interdiction Operations Manual.* Drawing on lessons learned from the earlier mass migrations from Cuba and Haiti, the U.S. Department of Homeland Security prepared the Vigilant Sentry operation plan in preparation for possible similar incidents in the Caribbean region.

---

112. Human Trafficking Protocol, supra, art. 3(a).
113. Article 11 of the Human Trafficking Protocol requires parties to take measures to address the role of common carriers in preventing human trafficking.
114. ICCPR, supra, art. 12(2).
115. Patricia Mallia, Migrant Smuggling by Sea 24 (2010) ("Maritime interception is based on the classical understanding that a State has complete sovereign authority over a defined territory and, thus, the plenary power to determine who crosses its borders").
116. Dennis L. Noble, The U.S. Coast Guard's War on Human Smuggling (2011).

d. Immigration and the 1982 LOS Convention

The LOS Convention addresses immigration in five articles. Article 19(2)(g) excludes from innocent passage any vessel that loads or unloads any person contrary to the immigration laws and
regulations of the coastal state while in the territorial sea. The coastal state may take the necessary measures to prevent such noninnocent passage. Articles 21(1)(h) and 42(1)(d) extend the
coastal state's regulatory authority over vessels in passage in the territorial sea to laws to prevent
infringement of the coastal state's immigration laws. Article 33 provides that in its contiguous
zone the coastal state may exercise the control necessary to prevent or punish infringement of
its immigration laws in its territory or the territorial sea. Finally, the coastal state has exclusive
jurisdiction over immigration matters with respect to artificial islands and structures in the EEZ
or on the continental shelf.[117] Beyond the contiguous zone, vessels are subject to the exclusive
jurisdiction of their flag state on immigration-related matters, absent consent. Neither illegal
migration nor migrant smuggling is a crime of universal jurisdiction, and there is no right of
visit regarding vessels suspected of engaging in either offense. However, the right of hot pursuit
from the territorial sea or contiguous zone under Article 111 and the associated doctrine of constructive presence may be applied in cases involving migrant smuggling or illegal migration by
foreign-flag vessels.

e. The TOC Convention Protocol on Migrant Smuggling

The TOC Convention's Protocol on Alien Smuggling defines "alien smuggling" as "the pro-
curement, in order to obtain, directly or indirectly, a financial or other material benefit, of the
illegal entry of a person into a State Party of which the person is not a national or a permanent
resident."[118] "Illegal entry" is further defined as a border crossing without complying with the
necessary requirements for legal entry into the receiving state.[119] The protocol requires parties to criminalize migrant smuggling; however, its application is limited to offenses that are
transnational in nature and involve an organized criminal group.[120] Under the protocol, criminal
penalties are imposed only on the smuggler, not the migrant,[121] and only when the smuggling is
intentional and carried out to obtain, directly or indirectly, a financial or other material benefit.[122]
Thus, "rescuers" who recover migrants at sea and transport them to another state do not fall
within the protocol's prohibition (though domestic laws may impose restriction on their entry).
Parties to the protocol are required to preserve the rights of the persons being smuggled and to
protect them against violence by the smuggler.[123] The UNODC prepared a model law to assist
parties in implementing the protocol.[124]

The Migrant Smuggling Protocol requires parties to cooperate to the fullest extent possible
to prevent and suppress the smuggling of migrants by sea, in accordance with the international

117. LOSC arts. 60(2) & 80.
118. Protocol against the Smuggling of Migrants by Land, Sea and Air, supplementing the UN Convention against
    Transnational Organized Crime [hereinafter "Migrant Smuggling Protocol"], art. 3, adopted by UN Nov. 15,
    2000, 2241 U.N.T.S. (No. 39574), 40 I.L.M. 335, 385–94 (2001).
119. Id. art. 3.
120. Id. art. 4.
121. Id. art. 5.
122. Id. art. 6.
123. Id. art. 16.
124. UN Office on Drugs and Crime, Model Law against the Smuggling of Migrants, available at http://www.unodc
    .org/documents/human-trafficking/Model_Law_Smuggling_of_Migrants_10–52715_Ebook.pdf (accessed July 1,
    2012).

law of the sea.[125] It also calls on the parties, including migrant source states, to strengthen their border controls to prevent and detect migrant smuggling.[126] Like the 1988 UN Drug Convention, the Migrant Smuggling Protocol requires states to cooperate in enforcement. Cooperation may include requesting and granting consent to enforcement actions by, for example, entering into bilateral boarding agreements.[127] When the grounds for enforcement measures prove to be unfounded, the vessel must be compensated for any loss or damage sustained, provided that the vessel has not committed any act justifying the measures.[128]

f. U.S. Law and Policy on Maritime Interdiction of Irregular Migrants and Migrant Smugglers

The U.S. maritime migrant interdiction program includes both a preventive border control and security component and an at-sea maritime law enforcement component. Particular encounters with vessels transporting migrants might also involve a distress and rescue component. In the United States, the Coast Guard is the lead agency for all three components, working closely with the Department of Homeland Security's border and transportation security directorate and the U.S. Customs and Border Protection (CBP), Immigration and Customs Enforcement (ICE), and U.S. Citizenship and Immigration Services (USCIS). The president has also directed the DoD to provide assistance.[129] DoD assistance is coordinated through the cognizant combatant commander.

The U.S. Supreme Court has long recognized that it is "an accepted maxim of international law that every sovereign nation has the power, as inherent in sovereignty and essential to self-preservation, to forbid the entrance of foreigners within its dominions, or to admit them only in such cases and upon such conditions as it may see fit to prescribe."[130] The broad and "undoubted" powers of the federal government over immigration matters, resting in part on its "inherent power as sovereign to control and conduct relations with foreign nations," was reaffirmed as recently as 2012.[131] Congress has exercised that authority in a series of immigration and nationality acts, while also delegating broad implementation powers to the president and agencies within the executive branch. As a matter of domestic law, when the president exercises that authority by official acts, such as an executive order, "customary international law is inapplicable."[132]

The Immigration and Nationality Act (INA) provides the primary U.S. statutory regime for immigration matters.[133] The act makes it a crime to enter or attempt to enter the United States without complying with the applicable immigration rules.[134] Notwithstanding the prohibition,

---

125. Migrant Smuggling Protocol, supra, art. 7.

126. Id. art. 11(1).

127. Id. arts. 8, 9, & 17.

128. Id. art. 9(2).

129. George W. Bush, Delegation of Responsibilities concerning Undocumented Aliens Interdicted or Intercepted in the Caribbean Region, Exec. Order 13,276, ¶ 1(c)(ii), Nov. 15, 2002, 67 Fed. Reg. 69,985 (2002) (DoD assistance in cases of "mass migration"); William Clinton, Alien Smuggling, Presidential Decision Directive 9 (June 18, 1993) (now declassified).

130. Fong Yue Ting v. U.S., 149 U.S. 698, 705 (1893). See also Chae Chan Ping v. U.S. (The Chinese Exclusion Case), 130 U.S. 581, 606–07 (1889); Knauff v. Shaughnessy, 338 U.S. 537, 542–43 (1950).

131. Arizona v. U.S., 132 S. Ct. 2492, 2499 (2012).

132. See Galo-Garcia v. INS, 86 F.3d 916, 918 (9th Cir. 1996); Gisbert v. U.S. Attorney General, 988 F.2d 1437, 1448 (5th Cir. 1993).

133. Immigration and Nationality Act of 1952, June 27, 1952, Pub. L. No. 82-414, 66 Stat. 163, codified as amended at 8 U.S.C. §§ 1101–1537.

134. See 8 U.S.C. §§ 1185(a)(1) & 1325. Smuggled aliens (other than Cubans or those who enter as stowaways) who enter illegally are subject to expedited removal procedures. See Illegal Immigration Reform and Responsibility Act of 1996; 8 U.S.C. § 1225.

prosecution is generally reserved for repeat offenders, those who attempt to enter after having been previously removed,[135] and those who present false documents.[136]

The INA delegates considerable powers to the president, including the power to suspend entry of aliens.[137] In 1981, partly in response to the 1980 Mariel Boatlift experience, President Reagan issued Presidential Proclamation 4865,[138] which suspended the entry of undocumented migrants to the United States from the high seas. The 1981 Reagan proclamation was followed by President George H. W. Bush's Executive Order 12,807 in 1992, which directed the Coast Guard to enforce the suspension of maritime entry by interdicting U.S.-bound migrants at sea and returning them to their state of origin or departure.[139] With some modifications, the "interdict and repatriate" policy remains in effect today. The policy has been closely scrutinized by the U.S. Department of Justice[140] and was upheld by the U.S. Supreme Court in 1993.[141] That same year President Clinton issued Presidential Decision Directive 9, which directs:

> The U.S. government will take the necessary measures to preempt, interdict and deter alien smuggling into the U.S. Our efforts will focus on disrupting and dismantling the criminal networks which traffic in illegal aliens. We will deal with the problem at its source, in transit, at our borders and within the U.S. We will attempt to interdict and hold smuggled aliens as far as possible from the U.S. border and to repatriate them when appropriate. We will seek tougher criminal penalties both at home and abroad for alien smugglers. We will seek to process smuggled aliens as quickly as possible.[142]

Consistent with the TOC Convention Protocol on Migrant Smuggling, migrant smuggling is a crime in the United States.[143] Violations are potentially punishable by substantial criminal penalties and may subject violators who are not U.S. citizens to removal (formerly called deportation).[144] However, difficulties in proving a violation (particularly in obtaining witnesses) and the comparatively light sentences that are typically imposed on those convicted have so far failed to provide an adequate deterrent for those looking to engage in a crime with a 70 percent success rate that can earn them up to $10,000 per "passenger" for a single night's run from Cuba to the Florida coast. Congress has so far failed to enact legislation that would provide the needed

---

135. See 8 U.S.C. § 1326(a) (reentry after deportation).

136. See, e.g., 18 U.S.C. § 1546 (fraud involving immigration documents).

137. See, e.g., 8 U.S.C. § 1182(e).

138. Ronald Reagan, High Seas Interdiction of Illegal Aliens, Proclamation 4865, 46 Fed. Reg. 48107, 3 C.F.R. 50–51 (1981–83 Comp.). The proclamation was accompanied by Exec. Order 12,323, which was superseded by Exec. Order 12,807, discussed below.

139. George H. W. Bush, Interdiction of Illegal Aliens, Exec. Order 12,807, 57 Fed. Reg. 23,133 (1992).

140. See U.S. Department of Justice, Office of Legal Counsel, Memorandum for the Attorney General, Immigration Consequences of Undocumented Aliens' Arrival in United States Territorial Waters, Oct. 13, 1993, 17 Op. Off. Legal Counsel 77; U.S. Department of Justice Office of Legal Counsel, Memorandum for David A. Martin, General Counsel, Immigration and Naturalization Service, Rights of Aliens Found in U.S. Internal Waters, Nov. 21, 1996, 20 Op. Off. Legal Counsel 381 (1996). OLC opinions are binding on agencies of the federal government.

141. Sale v. Haitian Centers Council, 509 U.S. 155 (1993). See also Gary W. Palmer, Guarding the Coast: Alien Migrant Interdiction Operations at Sea, 29 Conn. L. Rev. 1565 (1997).

142. Presidential Decision Directive 9, supra, at 1.

143. 8 U.S.C. § 1324(a)(2) (alien smuggling for commercial gain); U.S. v. Kendrick, 682 F.3d 974 (11th Cir. 2012). See also Coast Guard MLE Manual, supra, ¶ 6.C.2. Any failure to heave to on being ordered to do so is a separate offense under 18 U.S.C. § 2237, with significant sentence enhancements applicable to migrant smugglers.

144. See 8 C.F.R. pt. 1240.

deterrent.[145] In what might be characterized as a gap-filling attempt to prevent U.S. smugglers from traveling from the United States to Cuba in order to smuggle Cuban migrants to the United States, the Coast Guard promulgated 33 C.F.R. part 108, prohibiting "unauthorized entry into Cuban waters." Operators of vessels subject to U.S. jurisdiction who knowingly violate the regulation are subject to civil penalties and criminal penalties of up to ten years.[146]

g. Refugees, Asylum Seekers, and the Non-Refoulement Rule

Under U.S. immigration law, irregular migrants who "arrive" in U.S. territory are, consistent with due process guarantees, subject to formal or expedited removal proceedings before they can be returned to their state of nationality or departure. However, irregular migrants have no right to a removal hearing unless and until they actually land in the United States.[147] That rule helps explain what is commonly referred to as the "feet-wet/feet-dry" policy. To obtain the procedural rights of an "arrived" migrant it is not enough to be brought on board a U.S.-flag vessel or to enter the U.S. territorial sea or internal waters; the migrant must actually land (i.e., qualify for feet-dry status) in U.S. territory. As a result, undocumented migrants intercepted before they land in U.S. territory may be repatriated directly, without a removal hearing, assuming their state of nationality, origin, or some third state will accept them.

The feet-wet/feet-dry policy applies to all undocumented migrants, but it works to the particular advantage of Cuban migrants who meet the feet-dry test. The 1994 U.S.-Cuba Migrant Accords agreement,[148] as amended in 1995, provides that "Cuban migrants *intercepted at sea* by the United States and attempting to enter the United States will be taken to Cuba." The accords make no provision for repatriating those who make it to U.S. territory. Because they cannot be repatriated to Cuba under the accords (and because the state of origin must consent to any repatriation), migrants who satisfy the feet-dry test are generally paroled into the United States and may then legally remain. Under the 1966 Cuban Adjustment Act,[149] the U.S. attorney general has the discretion to grant lawful permanent resident status to any Cuban migrant who remains physically present in the United States for at least one year, even if the individual entered illegally.[150]

Although perhaps "irregular" in their attempt to gain entry into the destination state, some migrants encountered at sea might be entitled to request and receive asylum by the intercepting state or a third state. The Universal Declaration of Human Rights declares that every person has the right to seek and enjoy asylum from persecution.[151] Article 1 of the 1951 Convention on Refugees (as amended) defines a refugee as a "person who owing to a well-founded fear of being

---

145. The U.S. Coast Guard and Department of Justice drafted a comprehensive proposal for a "maritime alien smuggling law enforcement and sentence enhancement act" that would have prescribed a minimum three-year sentence and a fine of up to $100,000. A decline in the use of this mode of migrant smuggling by 2013 rendered the legislation temporarily moot.

146. Coast Guard MLE Manual, supra, ¶ 6.C.4.

147. See, e.g., Xin-Chang Zhan v. Slattery, 55 F.3d 732 (2d Cir. 1995).

148. See Cuba–United States: Joint Statement on Normalization of Migration, Building on the Agreement of September 9, 1994, 35 I.L.M. 327, 329 (stating that "migrants rescued at sea attempting to enter the United States will not be permitted to enter the United States, but instead will be taken to safe haven facilities outside the United States"); U.S. Department of State, Cumulative Digest of United States Practice in International Law 1991–1999 at 59. See Coast Guard MLE Manual, supra, figure 6-1 (Operational Procedures re Cuban Repatriation).

149. 8 U.S.C. § 1255.

150. See Memorandum from Doris Meissner, Commissioner, Immigration and Naturalization Service, Eligibility for Permanent Residence under the Cuban Adjustment Act Despite Having Arrived at a Place Other than a Designated Port-of-Entry (Apr. 19, 1999), U.S. Citizenship & Immigration Services, Field Adjudicator's Manual, app. 23-4.

151. UN Universal Declaration of Human Rights, art. 14(1), Dec. 10, 1948, G.A. Res. 217 (III), U.N. Doc. A/777.

persecuted for reasons of race, religion, nationality, membership of a particular social group or political opinion, is outside the country of his nationality and is unable or, owing to such fear, is unwilling to avail himself of the protection of that country; or who, not having a nationality and being outside the country of his former habitual residence as a result of such events, is unable or, owing to such fear, is unwilling to return to it."[152]

A refugee is entitled to seek asylum and should not be returned to his or her country "where his life or freedom would be threatened" (*non-refouler*).[153] Independently, Article 3 of the Convention against Torture provides that no state party to that convention will "expel, return ('refouler') or extradite a person to another State where there are substantial grounds for believing that he would be in danger of being subjected to torture."[154] The U.S. understanding of Article 3 is that "substantial grounds" exist "if it is more likely than not that he would be tortured."[155] The U.S. Navy and Coast Guard have each issued detailed directives to the fleet regarding the relevant laws and service policies and procedures for handling requests for asylum.[156] Service judge advocates and Department of Homeland Security legal advisers and asylum specialists stand ready to assist the fleet in applying those laws and policies.

The United States has determined that the asylum protections do not apply to migrants intercepted outside territories under the exclusive jurisdiction of the United States.[157] That interpretation is not universally accepted.[158] Although under its interpretation of the convention the United States is not legally required to provide asylum to migrants intercepted at sea, its policy and practice is to guard against returning migrants to countries where they will be subject to persecution. Accordingly, Presidential Directive 9 directs that migrants intercepted at sea will be "fairly assessed and/or screened by appropriate authorities to ensure protection of bona fide refugees."[159] In practice, most migrants are prescreened at sea to determine whether the individual

---

152. Convention relating to the Status of Refugees, art. 1, Jul. 28, 1951, 19 U.S.T. 6259, 189 U.N.T.S. 137, as amended by the Protocol relating to the Status of Refugees, Jan. 31, 1967, 606 U.N.T.S. 267.

153. Article 33(1) of the Convention on Refugees provides that "no Contracting State shall expel or return ('refouler') a refugee in any manner whatsoever to the frontiers of territories where his life or freedom would be threatened on account of his race, religion, nationality, membership of a particular social group or political opinion." See also Refugee Act of 1980, Pub. L. No. 96-212, 94 Stat. 102 (amending the INA).

154. Convention against Torture and Other Cruel, Inhuman or Degrading Treatment or Punishment, Dec. 10, 1984, 1465 U.N.T.S. 85, 23 I.L.M. 1027 (1984), as modified, 24 I.L.M. 535 (1985). In the United States, "torture" is defined in 18 U.S.C. § 2340 & 8 C.F.R. § 208.18(a). The convention's *non-refouler* rule (implemented in part by 8 C.F.R. § 208.16(c)) applies only to torture, not to cruel, inhuman, or degrading treatment or punishment. But see Detainee Treatment Act § 1003, Pub. L. No., Title X; 119 Stat. 2739 (prohibiting cruel, inhuman, or degrading treatment or punishment of any person "under the physical control of the United States Government, regardless of nationality or physical location").

155. See S. Treaty Doc. No. 100-20 (Senate consent given Oct. 27, 1990). See also U.S. reservations, declarations, and understandings, Convention against Torture and Other Cruel, Inhuman or Degrading Treatment or Punishment, Cong. Rec. S17486-01 (daily ed., Oct. 27, 1990).

156. U.S. Navy Regulations, supra, art. 0914; Commander's Handbook, supra, ¶ 3.3 (asylum and temporary refuge) (highlighting critical difference between Department of Navy policy and U.S. Coast Guard policy); U.S. Navy/Coast Guard, Maritime Interception Operations, appendix H, ¶¶ H.13 & 1.5.12 (Pre-planned Response for Asylum Request); Coast Guard MLE Manual, supra, ¶¶ 6.B.1.a, 6.B.2.c, 6D.4 & appendix L.

157. Exec. Order 12,807, Preamble, ¶ 2 (Article 33 of the Refugee Convention does not extend to "persons located outside the territory of the United States"); Sale v. Haitian Centers Council, 509 U.S. 155, 178–83 (1992); Commander's Handbook, supra, ¶ 3.3.1.3.

158. See, e.g., Hirsi Jamaa et al. v. Italy, 51 I.L.M. 423 (Eur. Ct. Human Rights 2012) (holding that Italy breached the prohibition on *non-refoulement* by repatriating migrants interdicted at sea to Libya). The ECHR ruling and its "control" test for applying *non-refoulement* outside the state's territory would arguably extend to the flag state of a vessel that discovered a stowaway. Because the vessel is subject to the flag state's jurisdiction and control, the *non-refoulement* obligation arguably attaches for those states party to the European convention.

159. Presidential Decision Directive 9, supra, at 1–2.

has a credible fear of persecution or torture only if they make a verbal or physical claim of fear of persecution if they are returned to their state of origin or departure.[160] In those circumstances, the migrant will be given a preliminary screening by a U.S. Citizenship and Immigration Services asylum prescreening officer.[161]

3. Resource and Environmental Crimes, High-Seas Drift Nets, and IUU Fishing

At more than seven billion, Earth's population is already putting a severe strain on ocean resources and the marine environment. In some regions competition for marine resources has already taken a violent and sometimes fatal turn. Confrontations between fishermen and marine patrol vessels, between warships and other patrol vessels of states contesting each other's maritime claims (or fishing vessels acting as belligerent proxies for their state), and even between environmental direct action groups and fishing vessels or oil and gas exploration and development activities are far too common. Canada's 1995 seizure of the Spanish F/V *Estai* while on the high seas, without Spain's consent,[162] and which involved the use of force by one NATO member against the fishing vessel of another NATO member,[163] demonstrates the lengths to which some states will go in order to protect fish stocks important to the nation. Similarly, the decision by EU states to accelerate the ban on single-hull oil tankers from their EEZs following the T/V *Erika* (1999) and *Prestige* (2002) oil spills, and the EU's threat to forcibly remove vessels that fail to comply, even though doing so would violate the limits on the coastal state's jurisdiction under the LOS Convention and tarnish the EU's reputation as a strict adherent to the rule of law,[164] demonstrate the highly charged domestic politics of environmental protection. There is every reason to believe that the conflict over access to marine resources and protection of the marine environment will present an escalating global security challenge for maritime patrol forces.

Living marine resources (LMR) conservation and management, and in some cases preservation of marine protected species such as whales, is a highly specialized and regionally specific area of study. Because most fish are harvested in waters subject to the sovereignty, sovereign rights, or jurisdiction of a coastal state, most of the LMR regime lies in domestic law, enacted in accordance with the rules and standards discussed in the materials on the EEZ regime. As the domestic fleets of coastal states increasingly expanded their harvesting capacity relative to the allowable catch, foreign fishing vessels were excluded from most nearshore fisheries and sought out new opportunities on the high seas, where a vessel might never see an enforcement officer from its flag state. Unsustainable fishing practices, often taking the form of illegal, unregulated, or unreported fishing, put severe pressure on target species and those associated with or dependent on the target species.

Several international frameworks seek to promote responsible and sustainable fishing on the high seas and on transboundary stocks that could be harvested in waters of one or more

---

160. Exceptions apply to migrants from certain states identified in paragraph 6.D.3 of the MLE Manual. "Credible fear" is defined in 8 U.S.C. § 1225(b)(1)(B)(v).

161. Coast Guard MLE Manual, supra, ¶ 6.D.3.

162. Rebecca Bratspies, Finessing King Neptune: Fisheries Management and the Limits of International Law, 25 Harv. Envt'l L. Rev. 213 (2001).

163. Spain attempted to challenge Canada's use of force against the F/V *Estai* in the ICJ, but the court dismissed the application for lack of jurisdiction after Canada made a last-minute change to its declaration on ICJ jurisdiction. Fisheries Jurisdiction case (Spain v. Canada), 1998 I.C.J. 432 (Dec. 4).

164. Article 211(5) of the LOS Convention requires the coastal state to conform its pollution prevention laws to generally accepted international rules and standards. The generally accepted international rules and standards in the MARPOL Convention still permitted single-hull tanker vessels. Thus, the EU banned some tankers that met the generally accepted international standards. See Alan Boyle, EU Unilateralism and the Law of the Sea, 21 Int'l J. Marine & Coastal L. 15 (2006).

coastal states or on the high seas. One of the early multilateral conservation agreements that occupies much of the time of patrol forces in the Southern Ocean is the 1980 Convention on the Conservation of Antarctic Marine Living Resources.[165] In 1991 the UN General Assembly passed a broadly supported but nonbinding resolution calling for a moratorium on the use of large-scale high-seas drift nets.[166] More than two decades later, however, maritime patrol forces in the North Pacific still encounter vessels engaged in that highly indiscriminate and destructive fishing practice. Prompted by the 1992 UN Conference on Environment and Development, the UN General Assembly convened a diplomatic conference in 1993 to draft the Straddling Fish Stocks Agreement. That same year the FAO brokered the High Seas Fishing Compliance Agreement.[167] Those global agreements are complemented by a family of regional agreements on the conservation and management of tuna and other migratory species and anadromous species. The members of the International Convention for the Regulation of Whaling,[168] for example, agreed to a moratorium on whale harvests in 1982. Japan, however, has relied on an exception for "scientific" whaling to continue harvests.

The marine environmental regimes of greatest maritime law enforcement interest include the MARPOL Annex I (oil) and Annex V (garbage) discharge prohibitions and recording-keeping requirements and the London Dumping Convention.[169] Transportation by sea of hazardous waste without the necessary permits might also implicate the Basel Convention.[170] Enforcement of each of those environmental protection regimes is generally carried out under domestic laws implementing the conventions. The U.S. Act to Prevent Pollution by Ships (APPS) implements MARPOL in the United States.[171] The high number of APPS prosecutions for MARPOL violations in the United States is surprising, particularly considering the severity of the penalties that are typically imposed. The U.S. Ocean Dumping Act implements the nation's obligations under the London Dumping Convention.[172] Transportation of hazardous waste in the United States is governed by the Resource Conservation and Recovery Act, which does not yet fully implement U.S. obligations under the Basel Convention.[173]

E. JURISDICTION TO ENFORCE

Maritime law enforcement operations are by their nature multifaceted. On any given day MLE patrol forces might find themselves "interfering" with a vessel's navigation, taking "necessary

---

165. Convention on the Conservation of Antarctic Marine Living Resources [hereinafter "CCAMLR"], May 21, 1980, 33 U.S.T. 3476, 1329 U.N.T.S. 47.

166. G.A. Res. 46/215, U.N. Doc. A/RES/46/215 (1991). U.S. implementing statutes can be found at 16 U.S.C. §§ 1826, 1826a–1826g. U.S. Department of State, Cumulative Digest of United States Practice in International Law 1991–1999, at 1725.

167. The FAO High Seas Fishing Compliance Agreement was implemented in the United States by 16 U.S.C. §§ 5501–5509. See also Cumulative Digest of United States Practice in International Law 1991–1999, supra, at 1739.

168. International Convention for the Regulation of Whaling, Dec. 2, 1946, 62 Stat. 1716, T.I.A.S. No. 1849, 161 U.N.T.S. 162.

169. The 1972 London Dumping Convention has been amended several times and renamed the "London Convention." The London Convention and its 1996 protocol are examined in chapter 10.

170. Basel Convention on the Control of Transboundary Movements of Hazardous Wastes and Their Disposal, Mar. 22, 1989, U.N. Doc. UNEP/WG.190/4, 28 I.L.M. 649, 657 (1989).

171. 33 U.S.C. §§ 1901–1915. The United States may also cooperate with the vessel's flag state or with another state in whose water a discharge occurred, as provided for in MARPOL and the LOS Convention.

172. 33 U.S.C. §§ 1401–1421. The ODA was enacted as Titles I & II of the 1972 Marine Protection, Research and Sanctuaries Act.

173. See Mark Bradford, The United States, China and the Basel Convention on the Transboundary Movements of Hazardous Wastes and Their Disposal, 8 Fordham Envt'l L. Rev. 305 (2011).

steps" to prevent a breach of conditions of port entry, exercising the "control" necessary to prevent or punish customs and immigration laws in the contiguous zone, exercising "enforcement jurisdiction," rendering law enforcement "assistance" to a flag state or coastal state with jurisdiction, or carrying out similar activities pursuant to consent by the vessel's master. Any exercise of MLE authority will almost certainly involve an armed boarding team who will conduct an initial safety inspection of the vessel. Enforcement activities might necessitate the use of reasonable force to compel compliance when the act of control or interference is authorized by the LOS Convention or the flag state, or in defense of enforcement vessels, boats, aircraft, and personnel. On occasion, vessels involved in maritime crimes or transporting migrants are so unseaworthy and present such a hazard to navigation that they are destroyed in the interests of safety.[174]

Three overarching principles govern the exercise of maritime enforcement jurisdiction. The first is the well-established principle that a vessel's flag state has jurisdiction over its vessels wherever those vessels are located. Flag state jurisdiction over nonsovereign immune vessels is concurrent when the vessel is located in another state's ports or coastal waters; however, the flag state cannot exercise its jurisdiction in the territory of another state without that state's consent. The second principle is that warships, naval auxiliaries, and other vessels and aircraft owned or operated by a state and used only on noncommercial activities enjoy sovereign immunity. The final principle is that in times of peace a vessel on the high seas is subject to the exclusive jurisdiction of the flag state, subject to such exceptions expressly provided for in the LOS Convention or other international treaties.[175]

Enforcement jurisdiction decisions call for the examination and analysis of factual, legal, and operational issues.[176] Factual issues include the flag of the vessel, visible indicia of that nationality (or another nationality), the act or activity in which the vessel is engaged, the vessel's location at the time of the act or activity, and the nationality of the individuals on board and their role as master, person in charge, or crewmember. Relevant legal issues include, at a minimum, jurisdiction, authority, and any applicable basis for consent and the scope of that consent. Operational issues are confronted in all phases of the interception, beginning with the approach and initial observation phase and continuing through the inquiry, boarding, search, and release or seizure phases. Operational decisions are guided by applicable techniques, tactics and procedures publications, rules of engagement, orders from the operational or tactical commander, and requirements for prior interagency coordination or a statement of no objection. Even when there is clear jurisdiction and authority for an at-sea boarding, in some cases the better course of action might be to defer the boarding and inspection until the vessel arrives in a port. Indications that the vessel might not comply with boarding orders or that those on board might actively oppose the boarding, perhaps requiring the enforcement vessel to use force to compel compliance or in self-defense, must be considered in the go/no-go decision to board.

---

174. The Coast Guard has statutory authority to "destroy or tow into port sunken or floating dangers to navigation." 14 U.S.C. § 88(a)(4); U.S. Coast Guard Regulations, supra, art. 4-2-21. The destruction of vessels used in criminal activities can raise evidentiary issues or give rise to property loss claims by the owner. See, e.g., U.S. v. Revolorio-Ramo, 468 F.3d 771 (11th Cir. 2006) (rejecting due process violation claim by defendant after the USS *Boone* (FFG-28) destroyed defendant's seized fishing vessel when the Coast Guard LEDET determined it posed a hazard to navigation); Montego Bay Imports Ltd. v. U.S., 10 Cl. Ct. 806 (Claims Court, 1986).

175. LOSC art. 92(1).

176. See generally U.S. Department of Justice, U.S. Attorneys' Manual, Title 9, Criminal Resources Manual, section 670 ("maritime jurisdiction"). Within the MLE context, jurisdiction turns on three factors: the substantive law, the status and flag of the vessel, and the vessel's location.

1. Flag State Jurisdiction

The flag state has a positive obligation to exercise effective jurisdiction and control over its vessels (see chapters 8 and 9) regardless of those vessels' location.[177] When such vessels enter the internal waters, archipelagic waters, territorial sea, contiguous zone, or EEZ of another state, however, they are subject to the coastal state's sovereignty, sovereign rights, or jurisdiction, depending on the vessel's location and status. Prescriptive jurisdiction in such cases may be shared concurrently between the coastal state and the flag state. By contrast, enforcement jurisdiction is usually vested in one state on an exclusive or primary basis.

Properly registered vessels sailing on the high seas are subject to the exclusive enforcement jurisdiction of their flag state. As the PCIJ explained in the *S.S.* Lotus dispute between France and Turkey, it is "certainly true that—apart from certain special cases which are defined by international law—vessels on the high seas are subject to no authority except that of the State whose flag they fly."[178] One prominent commentator has taken the view that in any case in which an exception to the general rule is asserted, the burden of proof falls on the party relying on the exception.[179] The customary law principle relied on in the *S.S.* Lotus case was later codified in the 1958 Convention on the High Seas[180] and the 1982 LOS Convention, although the articles in those conventions speak in terms of "jurisdiction" rather than "authority."[181] Article 92(1) of the LOS Convention now provides that "ships shall sail under the flag of one State and, save only in exceptional cases expressly provided for in international treaties or in this Convention, shall be subject to its exclusive jurisdiction on the high seas. A ship may not change its flag during a voyage or while in a port of call, save in the case of a real transfer of ownership or change in registry."[182]

Some flag states fail to fulfill their obligation to exercise effective jurisdiction and control for reasons of inability or unwillingness. In assessing the magnitude of any breach of the flag state's obligation, the distinction between the unable and the unwilling is critical. A flag state may be unable to fully discharge its obligations because it lacks the resources or the vessel is in a remote location. Under such circumstances, the flag state can meet its obligation to exercise effective jurisdiction and control and to suppress illicit activities by requesting assistance through the capacity-building programs of organizations such as the IMO or cooperation and assistance from an "able" state with an asset in the area. That cooperation and assistance may take the form of a boarding, inspection, and search followed by detention, arrest, and seizure if requested or authorized by the flag state. The "unwilling" state presents a thornier question of state responsibility and may invite intervention, countermeasures, or legal challenges by other states.

The exercise of U.S. enforcement powers against foreign-flag vessels can create contentious foreign relations issues for the state, particularly if force is used to overcome the vessel's

---

177. Restatement FRLUS § 502 cmts. a & d. See also U.S. v. Rodgers, 150 U.S. 249, 266 (1893); U.S. v. Flores, 289 U.S. 137, 153 (1933).
178. The S.S. *Lotus* case (France v. Turkey), 1927 P.C.I.J. (ser. A) No. 9 (Sept. 7), at 25.
179. Colombos, supra, at 311; Henry W. Halleck, International Law 239 (S. Baker ed., 3d ed. 1967). See also Churchill & Lowe, supra, at 12 (treating the principle of exclusive flag-state jurisdiction as a "residual presumption for the resolution of doubtful claims." They explain that "here any doubt over the existence of the non–flag state's rights is settled in favor of exclusiveness of the flag state's jurisdiction, by reference to the general principle"; id.).
180. 1958 Convention on the High Seas, supra, art. 6.
181. LOSC art. 91.
182. Id. art. 92; Restatement FRLUS § 522. The predecessor article in the 1958 Convention on the High Seas was held not to be self-executing. Accordingly, an individual could not assert a violation of the article as a defense to prosecution. See U.S. v. Postal, 589 F.2d 862, 873 (5th Cir. 1979).

resistance.[183]Accordingly, since Presidential Directive 27 was issued in 1978,[184] the concerned U.S. federal agencies are required to consult and coordinate on certain nonmilitary actions with the potential to affect the nation's foreign affairs. In 2006, PD-27 was supplanted by the Maritime Operational Threat Response (MOTR) Plan for threats in the maritime domain.[185] Additionally, within the Coast Guard certain enumerated enforcement actions (including boarding, seizure, and the use of force involving foreign vessels) may require the on-scene forces to obtain a "statement of no objection" (SNO) from the Coast Guard commandant or another flag officer. Those internal requirements and procedures can be found in service directives and manuals.[186]

2. Exceptions to Exclusive Flag State Jurisdiction

For centuries, some states have dispatched their vessels to patrol distant waters. Such patrols were indispensable in regions where piracy and slave trading flourished. The need for patrol vessels is no less urgent today. Jurisdiction to enforce laws in the maritime domain is governed by both international law and by the enforcing state's constitution and statutes. This section examines the conventional and customary international laws applicable to maritime law enforcement operations. Two distinct issues affect enforcement operations involving foreign vessels. The first concerns acts of "interference" with the foreign flag vessel's navigation.[187] The principal LOS Convention rule relevant to such interferences is Article 110, which prohibits "acts of interference" with foreign-flag vessels on the high seas except where the act of interference derives from powers conferred by a treaty or is "justified" by one of the five grounds listed in Article 110. The second issue involves the exercise of jurisdiction over the vessel. The relevant LOS Convention rule is Article 92(1), which provides that a vessel on the high seas is subject to the "exclusive" jurisdiction of its flag state save in exceptional cases expressly provided for in the LOS Convention or another treaty.

Close inspection of the LOS Convention demonstrates that even in the case of lawfully registered vessels, the flag state's jurisdiction or authority over its vessels while on the high seas during peacetime is not always "exclusive."[188] While preserving the primacy of flag state jurisdiction, the LOS Convention permits non–flag states to "interfere" with vessels on the high seas under limited circumstances.[189] The chapeau to Article 110 begins with a general prohibition on

---

183. For the most part, international law is directly implicated only in incidents involving conduct directed against the nationals, vessels, or aircraft of another state. See Postal, 589 F.2d at 870 ("the boarding of a vessel on the high seas by its flag state is not an international event. The consequences are solely a domestic matter. The boarding of a foreign vessel is, of course, a matter of international concern that might call for more restraint on the part of the boarding state"). See also Skiriotes v. Florida, 313 U.S. 69, 73 (1941) (holding that the United States "is not debarred by any rule of international law from governing the conduct of its own citizens upon the high seas or even in foreign countries when the rights of other nations or their nationals are not infringed").

184. See Presidential Directive 27, Procedures for Dealing with Non-military Incidents (Jan. 19, 1978). The need for closer interagency consultation and coordination was made manifest in the 1970 asylum request incident involving the Lithuanian seaman Simas Kudirka. See Algis Ruksenas, Day of Shame (1973).

185. MOTR is a network of integrated national-level maritime command centers, including the U.S. Coast Guard Command Center, designed to achieve coordinated, unified, and timely and effective planning and maritime command and control. See DoD Inst. 3020.48 (Mar. 6, 2009); Coast Guard MLE Manual, supra, appendix D.

186. Coast Guard MLE Manual, supra, appendix D.

187. Robert C. F. Reuland, Interference with Non-national Ships on the High Seas: Peacetime Exceptions to the Exclusivity of Flag-State Jurisdiction, 22 Vand. J. Transnat'l L. 1161 (1989).

188. For excerpts of the Department of State memorandum on maritime interdiction and law enforcement, including the exceptions to exclusive flag state jurisdiction on the high seas, see U.S. Department of State, Digest of United States Practice in International Law 1989–1990, at 448–52.

189. Few would argue that "interference" with a merchant vessel on the high seas is tantamount to a use of armed force against the territorial integrity or political independence of a state, in violation of Article 2(4) of the UN

states other than the flag state from interfering with a vessel's navigation. It then recognizes that such acts may, however, be authorized by the LOS Convention itself or by the "power conferred by treaty." Although some sources opine that the term "treaty" should be limited to written agreements between states,[190] nothing in the text of the article supports such a limitation. In fact, there is no textual or contextual reason to conclude that Article 110 was meant to exclude oral agreements between states.[191] Oral international agreements, while not common, can constitute valid and binding "treaties."[192] The United States has long recognized the validity of ad hoc oral ship-boarding agreements with flag states.[193] Moreover, the state's oral or written consent will estop it from later asserting that the boarding encroached on the right waived.[194]

A flag state might choose to go beyond authorizing another state to merely interfere with one of its vessels; it might take the further step of waiving its primary jurisdiction or even affirmatively ceding or transferring its jurisdiction to a second state.[195] In language that roughly parallels the "interference" regime in Article 110, the Article 92 "jurisdiction" rule acknowledges that exceptions to flag state exclusivity may arise within the convention itself or some other international agreement. While not constituting an exception to the rule of flag state exclusivity in themselves, other conventions such as the UN Convention on Narcotic Drugs, the Straddling Fish Stocks Agreement, and the Human Trafficking and Illegal Migrant Smuggling Protocols invite their states parties to enter into boarding agreements. Similarly, UN Security Council resolutions imposing economic embargoes may override the flag state's exclusive jurisdiction, though that power has rarely been exercised.[196]

The six recognized exceptions to the rule of exclusive flag state jurisdiction are examined in chapter 8. MLE operations commonly rely on four of them: (1) enforcement actions against stateless vessels or vessels that may be assimilated to statelessness, (2) actions taken with the consent of the flag state, (3) actions taken with the consent of the master, and (4) consent by a third state in whose waters the foreign flag vessel is located. The other two exceptions, universal jurisdiction over piracy and pirate vessels and actions taken under authority of a UN Security Council resolution, are examined in chapter 12.[197] Because the right of visit is, strictly speaking, not an "exception" to the rule that a vessel on the high seas is subject to the exclusive jurisdiction

---

Charter. Indeed, the civil remedies provisions for unjustified boardings or detentions incorporated into the LOS Convention evince intent to bring such actions within the umbrella of state responsibility for acts in violation of international law.

190. Vienna Convention on Treaties, supra, art. 2(1)(a).

191. See Marjorie M. Whiteman, 14 Digest of International Law 5 (1968) (no rule requires treaties to be in writing). See also U.S. Department of Justice, Office of Legal Counsel, Seizure of Foreign Ships on the High Seas Pursuant to Special Arrangements, 4B Op. Off. Legal Counsel 406 (1980).

192. Restatement FRLUS § 301 cmt. b.

193. See Whiteman, 9 Digest of International Law, supra, 65–66; 46 U.S.C. § 70502(c)(2)(A).

194. Under the ILC Draft Articles on State Responsibility, valid consent by a state to a given act by another state precludes the wrongfulness of the act in relation to the consent-granting state, to the extent that the act remains within the limits of consent. See Draft Articles on Responsibility of States for Internationally Wrongful Acts [hereinafter "ILC Draft Articles on State Responsibility"], art. 20, adopted by the ILC at its Fifty-third Session (2001), U.N. GAOR, 53d Sess., Supp. No. 10, U.N. Doc. A/56/10 (2001), reprinted in 2000 Y.B. Int'l L. Comm'n, vol. II, pt. 2, at 65–71, U.N. Doc. A/CN.4/SER.A/2000/Add.1 (pt. 2).

195. U.S. v. Robinson, 843 F.2d 1, 3 & 4 (1st Cir. 1988) (holding that the flag state's consent to an enforcement action precluded any defense that the United States lacked jurisdiction under international law); see also Restatement FRLUS § 522 cmt. e (under the U.S. view, "interference with a ship that would otherwise be unlawful under international law is permissible if the flag state has consented").

196. The validity of interdictions under authority of the Security Council resolutions turns mainly on the text of the resolution.

197. In the United States, enforcement actions relying on universal jurisdiction may require interagency coordination and an SNO from higher authority.

of its flag state, but rather the basis for a limited right to interfere with the vessel, it is examined separately in section F below.

a. Stateless Vessels

In the United States the decision whether to treat a vessel as stateless (see chapters 8 and 9) may be subject to interagency coordination and statement of no objection requirements. Of particular importance in the MLE context is the rule that a vessel's status as a stateless vessel or one assimilated to statelessness is also an element in several U.S. maritime crime regimes, including the MDLEA,[198] the Magnuson-Stevens Fishery Conservation Management Act,[199] the Alien Migrant Interdiction executive order,[200] and the regulation banning entry of U.S. vessels into Cuban waters.[201] Statelessness is also an element of the crime in cases involving submersible or semisubmersible vessels engaged in narcotics trafficking.[202]

b. Flag State Consent: Bilateral and Multilateral Boarding Agreements

Written bilateral and multilateral treaties authorizing foreign vessel boardings in waters beyond national jurisdiction have become increasingly common.[203] The United States has concluded dozens of MLE agreements with flag states under the frameworks provided by the 1988 UN Drug Convention,[204] the Protocol against the Smuggling of Migrants,[205] and the Proliferation Security Initiative. Enforcement cooperation agreements may also be concluded under the framework established by the 1995 Straddling Fish Stocks Agreement[206] and the 2005 protocol to the SUA Convention.[207] Such agreements may be in written form or entered into orally on a case-by-case basis.[208] The Coast Guard now serves as the executive agent for more than fifty standing bilateral agreements on maritime law enforcement.[209]

198. 46 U.S.C. § 70502(c).

199. 16 U.S.C. §§ 1802(44) & 2342(11).

200. Exec. Order 12,807, supra, section 2, ¶ (b)(2).

201. 33 C.F.R. § 107.200 (defining stateless vessels for purposes of the prohibition of unauthorized entry into Cuban waters).

202. 46 U.S.C. § 2285(a).

203. See generally Coast Guard MLE Manual, supra, ¶ 2.C.2; U.S. Department of State, Cumulative Digest of U.S. Practice in International Law 1981–1988, supra, vol. II, at 1386–99.

204. 1988 UN Convention on Narcotic Drugs, supra, art. 17. As of 2012, the United States had entered into counterdrug agreements with twenty-five states. For public access to the agreements in force, see U.S. Department of State, List of Maritime Counter Narcotics Law Enforcement Agreements Signed by the United States as of August 2005, available at http://www.state.gov/s/l/2005/87199.htm (accessed Feb. 1, 2013). See also Roach & Smith, Excessive Maritime Claims, supra, at appendix 16.

205. Migrant Smuggling Protocol Article 17 ("agreements and arrangements") provides that "States Parties shall consider the conclusion of bilateral or regional agreements or operational arrangements or understandings aimed at: Establishing the most appropriate and effective measures to prevent and combat the conduct set forth in article 6 of this Protocol; or Enhancing the provisions of this Protocol among themselves." Executive Order 12,807 requires the Coast Guard to obtain flag state consent to interdict foreign vessels on the high seas believed to be smuggling aliens. 3 C.F.R. pt. 303 (1992). For an example of such an agreement, see Agreement between the Government of the United States of America and the Government of the Dominican Republic concerning Maritime Migration Law Enforcement, May 20, 2003, 2003 UST Lexis 32.

206. Straddling Fish Stocks Agreement, supra, arts. 20, 21, & 60. In presenting the agreement to the Senate, Secretary of State Warren Christopher emphasized that the agreement "remains faithful to the general principle of international law that States other than the flag State may only take fisheries enforcement action against a vessel on the high seas with the consent of the flag State." President's Message to the Senate Transmitting Agreement for Implementation of the Law of the Sea Convention, XII, S. Treaty Doc. No. 104-24 (1996), at xii.

207. 2005 SUA Protocol, supra, art. 8 (adding Article 8bis to the SUA Convention).

208. Digest of U.S. Practice in International Law 1989–1990, supra, at 450. Depending on the form of the agreement (oral or written), interagency coordination or an SNO might be required before boarding.

209. Coast Guard MLE Manual, supra, ¶ 3.D. The majority of the agreements are for counterdrug operations; however, three (Bahamas, Dominican Republic, and Haiti) extend to irregular migration.

Under 22 U.S.C. § 2291(a) the president is authorized to conclude agreements with other countries to control illegal drug trafficking. Those agreements take a variety of forms. A few are multilateral,[210] but most are bilateral. They include: (1) ship-rider agreements, in which one state agrees to place an enforcement officer on board the patrol vessel of the other to take necessary enforcement action against vessels flying the flag of or located in the waters of the ship-rider's state; (2) ship-boarding agreements, in which the flag state gives its prior consent to boardings under circumstances falling within the terms and geographic boundaries set out in the agreement; and (3) "presumed consent" agreements, in which the parties agree that the intercepting state will first contact the flag state and request its consent to board, and that consent may be presumed if the flag state does not object in the time set out in the agreement.[211] Flag state consent may extend to boardings on the high seas or to vessels flying the consenting state's flag while in innocent passage through a coastal state's territorial sea (essentially waiving the innocent passage protection).

Recent bilateral boarding agreements entered into under the Proliferation Security Initiative (discussed in chapter 12) reveal a developing distinction in the nature and scope of the flag state's consent. For example, Article 5 of the agreements between the United States and two major flag states, Liberia and the Marshall Islands, characterizes the flag state as having the "*primary* right to exercise jurisdiction" over its vessels on the high seas, while recognizing that the flag state's right can be "waived." In addition to waiving its right to exercise enforcement jurisdiction, the flag state may "authorize" the other state to either assist the flag state in enforcing its laws against the vessel or to enforce the boarding state's own laws against the vessel.[212] Some commentators refer to the last-mentioned authorization as an act that "cedes" or "transfers" enforcement jurisdiction from the flag state, whose jurisdiction is primary, to a boarding state with concurrent jurisdiction, much as states confer prescriptive, investigative, or enforcement powers on an international organization.

As a matter of U.S. law, a flag state's consent may, depending on the particular statute, render the vessel "subject to the jurisdiction of the United States" and its crew subject to prosecution in U.S. courts. For example, Congress defined the phrase "vessel subject to the jurisdiction of the United States" in the MDLEA to include "a vessel registered in a foreign nation where the flag nation has consented or waived objection to the enforcement of United States law by the United

---

210. See, e.g., Agreement concerning Co-operation in Suppressing Illicit Maritime and Air Trafficking in Narcotic Drugs and Psychotropic Substances in the Caribbean Area, Apr. 10, 2003, available at http://www.state.gov/s/l/2005/87198.htm (accessed Feb. 1, 2013); Council of Europe Agreement on Illicit Traffic by Sea, Implementing Article 17 of the UN Convention against Illicit Traffic in Narcotic Drugs and Psychotropic Substances, Jan. 31, 1995, 29 L. Sea Bull. 62 (not yet in force).

211. See Cumulative Digest of United States Practice in International Law 1991–1999, supra, at 1604–05; Coast Guard MLE Manual, supra, ¶ 3.D; Joseph E. Kramek, Bilateral Maritime Counter-drug and Immigration Interdiction Agreements: Is This the World of the Future?, 31 U. Miami Inter-Am. L. Rev. 121, 133–34 (2000); Ben Bowling, Policing the Caribbean: Transnational Security Cooperation in Practice (2010).

212. Agreement between the Government of the United States and the Government of the Republic of the Marshall Islands concerning Cooperation to Suppress the Proliferation of Weapons of Mass Destruction, Their Delivery Systems, and Related Materials by Sea, art. 5, August 13, 2004:

Jurisdiction of the Parties. In all cases covered by Article 4 concerning the vessels of a Party located seaward of any State's territorial sea, that Party shall have the primary right to exercise jurisdiction over a detained vessel, cargo or other items and persons on board (including seizure, forfeiture, arrest, and prosecution), provided, however, that the Party with the right to exercise primary jurisdiction may, subject to its Constitution and laws, *waive* its primary right to exercise jurisdiction and *authorize* the enforcement of the other Party's law against the vessel, cargo or other items and persons on board.

Emphasis added. Available at http://www.state.gov/t/isn/trty/35237.htm (accessed Feb. 1, 2013).

States."[213] The MDLEA recognizes the validity of both flag state consent and waiver.[214] The act provides that flag state consent may be obtained by radio, telephone, or similar or electronic means.[215] U.S. courts have upheld enforcement actions against foreign vessels and crews based on boardings conducted with the consent of the flag state.[216] They have also held that the Coast Guard may legally detain a vessel while awaiting consent of the flag state to exercise jurisdiction over the vessel.[217]

c. Consent by Vessel Master

Although the term "consensual boarding" is commonly used to refer to a boarding based on consent by the vessel's flag state, the coastal state in whose waters the vessel is located, or the master or person in charge, in some usages the term refers only to the master's consent. Consent by a vessel's master, a private individual, must be distinguished from boarding authorization from a state having jurisdiction over the vessel. Consent by the master justifies the boarding state in taking actions, including boarding the vessel, which would, in the absence of the master's consent, constitute an "interference" with the vessel's navigation. The master's consent does not bind the flag state or affect the flag state's jurisdiction over the vessel.[218] It should also be noted that some states, such as the United Kingdom, object to boardings of their vessels on the high seas based only on consent of the master. The rationale typically offered for that position—a position at odds with considerable state practice—is that the right of noninterference with navigation attaches to the flag state, not the vessel owner or master, and that only the flag state may legally consent to boardings. The sounder view is that any boarding carried out with the master's consent does not constitute interference with the vessel's navigation or fishing rights and, because it does not constitute an exercise of jurisdiction by the boarding state, does not encroach on the flag state's jurisdiction over its vessels.[219] In practice, even the United Kingdom appears to tacitly accept this interpretation in its maritime security operations, as demonstrated by the common practice of its warships in boarding foreign vessels based on an "invitation" from the master or person in charge.[220]

As with all consensual boardings or searches, those conducted on the basis of the master's consent are limited in their reach to the scope of the consent. In most cases, if the master withdraws consent, the boarding must be terminated. If, however, during a consensual boarding the

---

213. 46 U.S.C. § 70502(c)(1)(C). The same definition is applied to fishing violations. See 16 U.S.C. §§ 1802(44) & 2342(11).

214. See, e.g., 46 U.S.C. § 70502(c)(1)(A), defining "vessel subject to the jurisdiction of the United States" to include vessels registered in a foreign nation when the flag nation has consented or waived objection to U.S. enforcement actions. The agreement may be formal or informal. U.S. v. Robinson, 843 F.2d 1, 10–11 (1st Cir. 1988) (Breyer, J.).

215. 46 U.S.C. § 70502(c)(2)(A).

216. U.S. v. Suerte, 291 F.3d 366 (5th Cir. 2002); U.S. v. Bustos-Useche, 273 F.3d 622 (5th Cir. 2001); U.S. v. Romero-Galue, 757 F.2d 1147 (11th Cir. 1985) ("nothing in international law prohibits two nations from entering into a treaty, which may be amended by other arrangement, to extend the customs waters and the reach of domestic law of one of the nations into the high seas"). See also Restatement FRLUS § 522 cmt. e.

217. U.S. v. Kahn, 35 F.3d, 426, 430 (9th Cir. 1994).

218. Digest of U.S. Practice in International Law 1989–1990, supra, at 449 (concluding that no enforcement jurisdiction, such as arrest or seizure, may be exercised during a consensual boarding of a foreign-flag vessel without the permission of the flag state [whether or not the master consents], even if evidence of illegal activities is discovered).

219. In other maritime contexts, such as salvage and general average, the consent of the master of the vessel, as an agent of necessity, binds the cargo interests as well. See, e.g., 1989 SALCON, supra, art. 6(2).

220. First-person accounts indicate that the "invitation" is commonly rewarded with some form of aid or supplies, such as bottled water.

boarding team develops an independent basis for exercising jurisdiction and control, law enforcement actions may continue even if consent is withdrawn or is otherwise terminated. Although MLE boardings are as rule preceded by an initial safety inspection of the vessel to identify any threats to the boarding party, in a consensual boarding such inspections require the master's consent. Finally, it should again be emphasized that consent by the vessel's master does not in itself confer jurisdiction over the vessel as a matter of international or U.S. law.[221]

d. Coastal State Consent

It is well established that no state—including the flag state—may, in the absence of consent, carry out law enforcement activities in the territory of another state, including the state's territorial sea.[222] Enforcement actions in the territorial sea of another state based on consent by a coastal state are less common than those based on flag state consent. Nevertheless, such agreements already serve an important function in contemporary efforts to combat illegal smuggling. For example, some of the bilateral agreements referred to above include "pursuit and entry" provisions that allow an enforcing state to enter the territorial waters of the coastal state in pursuit of a vessel. The statutory definition of a "vessel subject to the jurisdiction of the United States" includes vessels in the territorial waters of a foreign nation if the nation consents to the enforcement of U.S. law by the United States.[223] U.S. Courts have, until quite recently, upheld U.S. enforcement actions in a foreign state's territorial sea based on coastal state consent.[224]

In evaluating the role and effect of coastal state consent to a boarding by the flag state or a third state, be mindful of the principle that, as a matter of international law, the boarding state has no greater rights or jurisdiction than the coastal state would have under the circumstances (unless the boarding state is also the flag state or it has the joint consent of the flag state). The derivative nature of its authority means that the enforcing state's vessel is limited in its jurisdiction over the pursued vessel not only by the scope of the coastal state's consent but also by any applicable innocent and transit passage doctrines that might limit the coastal state's jurisdiction over foreign vessels.

F. RIGHT-OF-VISIT BOARDINGS

In the first half of the twentieth century the United States found itself virtually alone in the world in prohibiting the import or sale of alcoholic beverages. During the maritime "Rum War" that took place during the 1919–33 Prohibition era,[225] U.S. enforcement vessels frequently encountered ships of foreign registry engaged in alcohol smuggling. Hovering vessel rules (a rough precursor to the contiguous zone), the constructive presence doctrine, and right of hot pursuit and

---

221. Cf. 46 U.S.C. § 70502(c); 18 U.S.C. § 7 (defining the special maritime and territorial jurisdiction of the United States).
222. Restatement FRLUS § 432(2) (a state's law enforcement officers may exercise their functions in the territory of another state only with the consent of that state, given by duly authorized officials of that state).
223. 46 U.S.C. § 70502(c)(1)(E).
224. See U.S. v. Conroy, 589 F.2d 1258 (5th Cir. 1979) (Coast Guard enforcement actions against a U.S.-flag vessel in Haitian territorial sea). But see U.S. v. Bellaizac-Hurtado, 700 F.3d 1245, 1258 (11th Cir. 2012) (holding that Congress exceeded its constitutional power under the "define and punish" clause when it extended the MDLEA to violations in a foreign state's territorial waters).
225. The Volstead National Prohibition Act of 1919, enacted to implement the 18th Amendment, prohibited, inter alia, the importation of "intoxicating liquors." As later amended, it was extended to waters up to twelve nautical miles offshore. It was repealed in 1933. The leading test case was Maul v. U.S., 274 U.S. 501 (1927) (upholding seizure of a rum-running vessel thirty-four nautical miles off the U.S. coast for a "customs" violation).

boarding agreements with selected flag states were a partial response to the foreign vessel threat. The dominant view as late as 1950, however, was that while states had long accepted a right of approach to a foreign vessel, there was no follow-on international law right of visit during peacetime (other than for foreign vessels suspected of damaging submarine cables).[226] Such a right was one of the progressive developments of the 1958 Convention on the High Seas.

In the second half of the twentieth century, as traffickers turned from alcohol to narcotic and psychotropic drugs, the right of approach was again pressed into service—along with the new right of visit—in response to traffickers' attempts to avoid interdiction by concealing or misrepresenting their vessel's nationality or even leaving the vessel unregistered.[227] The resurgence of piracy beginning in the late 1970s gave new relevance to the right of visit, while the short-term nuisance posed by unauthorized broadcasting and the need for the corresponding visit right had largely faded before the 1982 LOS Convention was opened for signature. As maritime trafficking in weapons and human migrants becomes more common, and maritime terrorism persists as a growing global concern, some advocate an expanded right of approach. The reformists' suggestions generally take one of two approaches. The first recognizes the limited nature of the existing right and advocates amendments to the rule or new supplementary regimes to address the rule's perceived shortfalls. The second approach eschews the amendment path and argues instead for an expansive interpretation of the existing rules on visit rights respecting piracy or slave transport to meet new threats posed by maritime terrorism and human trafficking.

1. Current Understanding of the Right of Visit

Article 110 recognizes a right of visit in five situations:[228] reasonable ground for suspecting that (1) the ship is engaged in piracy; (2) the ship is engaged in the slave trade; (3) the ship is engaged in unauthorized broadcasting and the flag state of the warship has jurisdiction under article 109; (4) the ship is without nationality;[229] and (5) though flying a foreign flag or refusing to show its flag, the ship is of the same nationality as the warship.[230] Two of those grounds, unauthorized broadcasting and statelessness, were not included in the 1958 Convention on the High Seas. The right of visit in cases of suspicion of unauthorized broadcasting is not universal; only states that would potentially have jurisdiction over an unauthorized broadcasting offense under Article 109 may exercise the related right of visit.[231] The right of visit includes the right to use necessary force to compel compliance or in self-defense. Self-defense measures extend to those necessary to ensure the boarding team's safety during the visit, such as an initial safety inspection.

---

226. Article X of the 1884 Convention for the Protection of Submarine Cables conferred on warships a limited right to board vessels suspected of damaging or interfering with submarine cables on the high seas, in order to inspect their documentation.
227. See Gerhard O. W. Mueller & Freda Adler, Outlaws of the Ocean, chs. 3–8 (1985); Andrew W. Anderson, In the Wake of the *Dauntless:* The Background and Development of Maritime Interdiction Operations, in The Law of the Sea: What Lies Ahead?, at 21 (Thomas A. Clingan ed., 1988).
228. Resort to the Article 110 right of visit is unnecessary in the enforcing state's territorial sea, contiguous zone, or EEZ if the vessel is otherwise subject to the state's jurisdiction in those zones.
229. A right-of-visit boarding is warranted when there are no indicators of nationality or when there is clear, articulable evidence indicating that the indicators or claims of nationality are false or conflicting.
230. In U.S. v. Ricardo the court held that the Coast Guard could reasonably believe that a vessel that failed to fly a flag or otherwise exhibit its nationality, had English speakers on board, and was in proximity to the United States and bearing toward it was a U.S. vessel and was justified in exercising a right of visit. U.S. v. Ricardo, 619 F.2d 1124, 1130 n.4 (5th Cir. 1980).
231. LOSC art. 110(1)(c).

It bears repeating that for each of the five listed grounds, any exercise of the right must be based on "reasonable ground for suspecting" that the vessel falls into the named category. The right of visit is, like consent by the master, an exception to the noninterference rule in Article 110, not a basis for jurisdiction. Once the boarding team has addressed the initial safety issues, the boarding begins with verification of the ship's "right to fly its flag." If "suspicion remains after the documents have been checked," the boarding team "may proceed to a further examination on board the ship, which must be carried out with all possible consideration." When the basis for boarding is suspicion that the vessel is stateless or of the same nationality as the enforcement vessel, that further examination may include inspection of the vessel's "main beam" or other location where the ship's official number should be stamped. The onboard examination typically continues until either there are no longer any reasonable grounds for suspecting the vessel's claim of nationality or the examination is completed, either confirming or dispelling the original suspicion.

If the suspicions are confirmed, all but one of the grounds for the right of visit (suspicion the vessel is engaged in the slave trade) may lead to an assertion of jurisdiction by the visiting ship. If evidence supports a finding that the vessel is indeed stateless or of the same flag as the enforcing state, jurisdiction may be asserted on that basis. By contrast, if the ship's nationality is confirmed, consent to further enforcement action must be sought from the flag state (unless previously granted through a bilateral agreement with the flag state). If the "suspicions prove to be unfounded, and provided that the ship boarded has not committed any act justifying them," the boarding state must compensate the boarded vessel for any loss or damage from the right-of-visit boarding. The fact that suspicions turned out to be wrong, however, does not mean that they were "unfounded." To demonstrate that the visit was well founded, the prudent commanding officer of the warship will memorialize the basis for the original suspicions and any acts committed by the ship boarded that may have created or failed to allay those suspicions before sending over the boarding team.

2. Arguments for an Expanded Right of Visit

Like Article 22 of the 1958 convention, in listing the bases for right-of-visit boardings Article 110 of the LOS Convention lacks the critical "inter alia" found in the chapeaux of other articles of the convention.[232] The omitted "inter alia" strongly suggests that the Article 110 list is exhaustive and that any new bases for interference will have to be grounded on new international agreements or an amendment to the article.[233] The limited Article 110 visit regime has left some commentators unsatisfied. A few have argued for a more liberal interpretation of the elements of piracy to loosen the "private ends" and two-ship requirements in Article 101 of the LOS Convention. Others have argued that the right of visit in cases of suspected slave transport should similarly be given a more expansive interpretation, to permit its extension to maritime human trafficking of victims of debt bondage or forced prostitution.[234] Others espouse a broader vision

---

232. In enumerating the freedoms of the high seas, the chapeau to Article 87 includes an "inter alia" modifier, indicating that the list is not exhaustive. In describing the duties of the flag states, Article 94(3) follows the same approach. Thus, by omitting that qualifier from Article 110 (and Article 19(2)), the drafters signaled that the list is exhaustive.

233. The opening clause of Article 110 ("except where acts of interference derive from power conferred by *treaty*") forecloses additional exceptions based on customary law. The treaty exceptions would, of course, bind only parties.

234. Samuel Pyeatt Menefee, The Smuggling of Refugees by Sea: A Modern Day Maritime Slave Trade, 2 Regents J. Int'l L. 1 (2003–04).

of non–flag state enforcement to meet the growing challenge of IUU fishing on the high seas.[235] Another suggestion calls for a new right of visit to enforce UN Security Council resolutions, even when the council did not expressly provide such a right in the resolution.[236]

Neither an amendment to Article 110 to add new grounds for a visit boarding nor general acceptance by states of the previously mentioned arguments for liberal interpretation of the existing rule seems likely in light of the respective state interests. As one treatise astutely observed, "*many* states have flagged merchant vessels; *few* have the resources to conduct at-sea interdictions."[237] That asymmetry, and perceptions regarding the identities of the states that do "have the resources to conduct at-sea interdictions," best explains why the majority of flag states are unlikely to loosen their grip on exclusive jurisdiction over vessels on the high seas, through either an expanded right of visit or new crimes of universal jurisdiction. Moreover, exclusive flag state jurisdiction over vessels on the high seas is considered to be one of the general principles of international law, and any doubtful case involving a possible conflict between exclusive flag state jurisdiction and a lesser principle is likely to be resolved in favor of flag state jurisdiction.[238] Consistent with that general principle, recent international agreements and state practice rely instead on individualized flag state consent, either through carefully drafted standing agreements or on an ad hoc basis. Perhaps in the future a Security Council resolution will authorize a right of visit to facilitate the universal goal of halting the proliferation of WMD. It seems unlikely, however, that the right of visit will be extended to human- and drug-trafficking cases. Accordingly, efforts to promote more effective compliance and enforcement might more profitably focus on other options, including some combination of multilateral and bilateral enforcement agreements and lawful countermeasures directed at states that fail to meet their obligations with respect to their vessels.

G. RIGHT OF HOT PURSUIT AND THE DOCTRINE OF CONSTRUCTIVE PRESENCE

The right of hot pursuit and the associated constructive presence doctrine may extend the coastal state's jurisdiction under some circumstances.[239] Both practices developed under the customary law and found frequent (and contentious) application during the tumultuous U.S. Prohibition era. The right of hot pursuit was later codified in Article 23 of the Convention on the High Seas and then Article 111 of the 1982 LOS Convention.[240] The constructive presence doctrine is not expressly set out in the 1982 LOS Convention; however, its validity is established in part by the incorporation of its essential elements in Article 111(4) on hot pursuit. The right of hot pursuit still serves an important role in facilitating effective enforcement, particularly against fishing vessels that commit violations in the outer waters of the state's EEZ. Constructive presence has been rendered less important by the seaward expansion of coastal state jurisdictional zones under the 1982 LOS Convention.

---

235. Rosemary G. Rayfuse, Non–Flag State Enforcement in High Seas Fisheries (2004).
236. The Restatement takes the position that "it may be suggested that the right to inspect and seize foreign ships be extended to ships carrying stolen nuclear materials or escaping terrorists, but the present international law on the subject is unclear." Restatement FRLUS § 522 n.6.
237. Douglas Guilfoyle, Shipping Interdiction and the Law of the Sea 25 (2009) (emphasis added).
238. Churchill & Lowe, supra, at 12.
239. On hot pursuit, see LOSC art. 111. See also United Nations Convention on the Law of the Sea 1982: A Commentary, vol. III, at 247–60 (Myron H. Nordquist et al. eds., 1995); on "constructive presence," see The Grace and Ruby, 283 F. 475 (D. Mass. 1922); Churchill & Lowe, supra, at 215; William C. Gilmore, Hot Pursuit and Constructive Presence in Canadian Law Enforcement, 12 Marine Pol'y 105 (1988).
240. See Robert C. Reuland, The Customary Right of Hot Pursuit onto the High Seas: Annotations to Article 111 of the Law of the Sea Convention, 33 Va. J. Int'l L. 557 (1993).

1. The Law of Maritime Hot Pursuit

The right of hot pursuit is one of two "jurisdiction extenders" available to the coastal state (the other being constructive presence). Briefly summarized, Article 111 stipulates that the hot pursuit of a foreign ship may be undertaken when the coastal state has "good reason to believe" that the ship has violated the laws and regulations of that state while physically (or constructively) present in waters over which the coastal state has jurisdiction.[241] Historically, the right of hot pursuit has also been invoked in cases in which the enforcing vessel's jurisdiction is conferred by a treaty or other special arrangement, which by its terms imposed geographic limits on its exercise.[242] The right may be exercised only by warships (including submarines)[243] or military aircraft, or other ships or aircraft clearly marked and identifiable as being on government service and authorized to that effect.[244]

Resort to hot pursuit is unnecessary if the vessel is of the same flag as the enforcing vessel, is stateless, or the flag state has consented to a boarding. Vessels and aircraft enjoying sovereign immunity are, of course, not subject to hot pursuit.[245] The patrol craft's operational tasking orders or rules of engagement may limit the exercise of hot pursuit or require prior approval by higher authority before it is commenced or the enforcement boarding is conducted. Finally, in many states, a vessel's failure to heave to when signaled by the patrol vessel may constitute an additional offense under that state's domestic law. Such offenses are discussed in the noncompliant vessel section below.

Article 111 prescribes detailed prerequisites for a lawful hot pursuit. ITLOS has ruled that all of the conditions listed in Article 111 must be met for a hot pursuit to be lawful.[246] Hot pursuit must be commenced when the foreign ship or one of its boats is within the internal waters, archipelagic waters, territorial sea, contiguous zone, or EEZ of the pursuing state, and may be continued outside those waters only if the pursuit is "continuous" (i.e., not interrupted).[247] The coastal state's enforcement vessel or aircraft must first "satisfy itself" that the pursued ship (or one of its boats or other craft working as a team and using the pursued ship as a mother ship) is within the limits of the relevant jurisdictional zone (e.g., territorial sea, contiguous zone, or EEZ).[248]

---

241. LOSC art. 111. See generally Whiteman, 4 Digest of International Law, supra, 67. For an early case on point, see The King v. The Ship *North*, 37 S.C.R. 385 (Canadian Supreme Ct., 1905–06).

242. See, e.g., The *Newton Bay*, 30 F.2d 444 (E.D.N.Y. 1928); The *Vinces*, 20 F.2d 164 (E.D.S.C. 1927). Both actions involved vessels subject to the U.S./U.K. liquor prohibition enforcement agreement. Convention for the Prevention of Smuggling of Intoxicating Liquors, Jan. 23, 1924, 43 Stat. 1761, T.S. No. 685.

243. See LOSC art. 29 (defining "warship"). See also Nicholas Poulantzas, The Right of Hot Pursuit in International Law 196 (2d ed. 2002) (the author takes the position that the submarine must surface).

244. When hot pursuit is effected by an aircraft, the aircraft giving the order to stop must itself actively pursue the ship until a ship or another aircraft of the coastal state arrives to take over the pursuit, unless the aircraft is itself able to arrest the ship.

245. The issue would arise when a government-owned vessel claims to be engaged in noncommercial "marine scientific research" when by all outward appearances it is engaged in fishing or whaling.

246. M/V *Saiga* (St. Vincent & the Grenadines v. Guinea), ITLOS Case No. 2, Judgment of July 1, 1999, ¶ 146, 38 I.L.M. 1323 (1999).

247. If the foreign ship is within a contiguous zone, the pursuit may be undertaken only if there has been a violation of the rights for the protection of which the zone was established. The right also applies to violation of law and regulations in the EEZ or on the continental shelf, including safety zones around continental shelf installations, but only to the extent that such laws and regulations are consistent with the LOS Convention.

248. LOSC art. 111(4). The pursuing vessel might "satisfy itself" of the vessel's position by relying on position information provided by another reliable source. Moreover, given the widespread use of ECDIS systems that record vessel positions, courses, and speeds, an electronic confirmation will often be available once the vessel is boarded. Note that the coastal state may take enforcement action against foreign vessels for violations of the coastal state's customs, fiscal, sanitation, and immigration laws in the state's territorial sea even after the vessel "flees" to the contiguous zone, without relying on the right of hot pursuit. See LOSC art. 33.

Before the pursuit is begun, the pursued vessel must be given a "visual or auditory signal" to stop at a distance that enables it to be seen or heard by the foreign ship.[249] State practice and associated cases recognize that the pursuing vessel may use reasonable and necessary force to compel compliance.[250] If the pursued ship is stopped or arrested under circumstances that did not justify hot pursuit, the vessel must be compensated for any loss or damage sustained.[251]

The contemporary exercise of a right of hot pursuit raises four issues. The first concerns the requirement to signal the vessel by "visual or auditory" means before beginning the pursuit. This requirement has been rendered anachronistic in the era of reliable radio communications.[252] Some commentators have therefore concluded that the signaling requirement can be met by radiotelephone signals, even if given before the enforcing vessel comes within sight.[253] The second issue relates to the requirement that the pursuit be "continuous." Before radar and similar electronic tracking methods (and recoverable vessel electronic position, course, and speed data) became widely available, continuous contact meant continuous visual contact. In periods of darkness or low visibility such continuous visual contact might be impossible. The question therefore arises whether continuous contact by electronic means, such as radar, satisfies the requirements of the rule.[254] The U.S. view has long been that visual or radar contact satisfies the rule. Moreover, short gaps in observations due to horizon distance, weather, darkness, or other intervening causes (including stopping to retrieve contraband jettisoned by the fleeing vessel)[255] do not constitute an interruption of hot pursuit, as long as the pursuing vessel can reliably identify the fleeing vessel.[256] The third issue concerns the possible role of unmanned aerial and marine vehicles and systems in a hot pursuit.

A fourth and less common issue concerns what might be called a "tag team" approach to hot pursuit—passing off the pursuit to another vessel or aircraft. Two Australian-led long-distance hot pursuit cases illustrate the importance of the issue. Each highlights the operational challenges posed by hot pursuit in EEZ fisheries enforcement situations, particularly when the speed differential between the pursuing and pursued vessels is small. In late March 2001, enforcement vessels pursued the Togo-flag fishing vessel *South Tomi* for fourteen days, covering a distance of more than three thousand nautical miles. In the second case, in August 2003, several enforcement vessels pursued the Uruguay-flag fishing vessel *Viarsa 1* for three weeks and over a distance of nearly four thousand nautical miles. The two cases raised several legal issues, including the legality of passing the pursuit to enforcement vessels of a third state in order to maintain continuous pursuit ("multilateral hot pursuit"). It is clear from the text of Article 111 that hot pursuit can be transferred between warships and other qualifying enforcement vessels and aircraft of the state that originally initiated the pursuit. The LOS Convention is silent, however, on whether pursuit

249. LOSC art. 111(4).
250. The use of force in hot pursuit cases is examined in chapter 13.
251. LOSC art. 111(8). A finding that hot pursuit was not justified as a matter of international law will not necessarily bar a subsequent prosecution of the offenders in U.S. courts. See 46 U.S.C. § 70505 (precluding international law defenses in MDLEA prosecutions).
252. One rationale offered for limiting the signal to visual or auditory means is the need to guard against an exercise of pursuit by enforcement vessels that are not visible to the pursued vessel. If, however, the pursued vessel was signaled to stop when pursuit began, it is not clear how it would thereafter be prejudiced by the fact that it cannot continuously see the pursuing vessel or aircraft.
253. See e.g., McDougal & Burke, supra, at 897.
254. Id. at 323–24.
255. The King v. The Ship *North*, supra, 11 Ex. C.R. 143–44 (1905), aff'd, 37 S.C.R. 385 (1905–06).
256. The *Newton Bay*, 36 F.2d 729, 731 (2d Cir. 1929) (upholding hot pursuit even though the pursuing vessel was "unable always to see or apprehend [the pursued vessel] while she was dodging in the darkness").

can be passed to qualified vessels or aircraft of a third state when it can be demonstrated that those technologies or techniques provide the same level of protection against misidentification as the means presently incorporated into the law.[257] Another constraint imposed by the LOS Convention that might prove decisive in such long-distance pursuits is that the right of hot pursuit ceases as soon as the pursued ship enters the territorial sea of its own state or of a third state,[258] unless the coastal state authorizes entry into its waters. Entry into the EEZ or contiguous zone of the flag state does not require termination of hot pursuit; however, the potential for conflict with the coastal state or the vessel's flag state remains a possibility.[259]

2. Constructive Presence

The doctrine of constructive presence is a legal construct that permits a coastal state to assert jurisdiction over a vessel that remains just outside its territorial reach and relies on contact boats to transport contraband or migrants ashore.[260] By working with contact boats to violate the coastal state's laws while remaining outside the coastal state's waters, the mother ship is not *actually* present but is deemed *constructively* present. Just as the law treats a vessel assimilated to statelessness "as if" it is stateless, a vessel constructively present in the coastal state's waters is treated "as if" it were actually present. This hovering vessel tactic was widely used during the Prohibition era, when foreign mother ships carrying liquor hove to just beyond U.S. customs waters and one or more small craft came out to meet the mother ship, offload the contraband, and speed it ashore. Drug traffickers and migrant smugglers use the same technique.

Commentators have identified two approaches to interpreting the constructive presence doctrine.[261] The distinction between the two approaches turns on whether the mother ship uses its own boats to transport its contraband or relies instead on other boats, typically based ashore, to come out to meet the mother ship and transport the contraband. The narrower "simple" approach holds that a vessel is constructively present in the coastal state's waters only when it uses its own boats. The broader "extensive" approach holds that the mother ship is constructively present whether it relies on its own boats or on shore-based boats or aircraft to transport the contraband. The United States has adopted the extensive approach.[262] Article 111(4) supports that broader view. In limiting the right of hot pursuit, it requires the pursuing ship to satisfy itself that the ship pursued "or one of its boats *or other craft working as a team and using the ship pursued as a mother ship*" is within the relevant jurisdictional zone.[263] The italicized portion describes the applicable constructive presence doctrine and does not limit its application to situations involving the mother ship's own boats.

---

257. See Erik Jaap Molenaar, Multilateral Hot Pursuit and Illegal Fishing in the Southern Ocean: The Pursuits of the *Viarsa 1* and the *South Tomi*, 19 Int'l J. Marine & Coastal L. 19, 32 (2004) (arguing in favor of permitting pursuit to be transferred between vessels of different states).

258. LOSC art. 111(3).

259. See Eugene R. Fidell, Enforcement of the Fisheries Conservation and Management Act of 1976: The Policeman's Lot, 52 Wash. L. Rev. 513, 572 (1977).

260. McDougal & Burke, supra, at 909–14; Colombos, supra, at 173–75; Churchill & Lowe, supra, at 133–34, 215–16. In the United States, enforcement actions relying on constructive presence may require interagency coordination and an SNO from higher authority.

261. Churchill & Lowe, supra, at 133.

262. Practical difficulties with the narrow view are apparent given the wide geographic expanse of the coastal state zones and limited patrol resources available to most states. One obvious issue concerns the difficulties a lone enforcing vessel or aircraft would encounter in having to prove that the contact boat was indeed one of the mother ship's own boats before it could commence hot pursuit.

263. LOSC art. 111(4) (emphasis added).

In some regions, the "mother aircraft" has replaced the mother ship in drug transport. Aircraft transport baled shipments of drugs that are dropped to high-speed contact boats in prearranged locations beyond the target state's territorial sea. The contact boats then speed the contraband to the target state. While extension of the constructive presence doctrine has not been formally extended to reach the transporting aircraft in such cases, and a host of operational difficulties and legal restrictions on the use of weapons against civil aircraft in flight would make enforcement on a constructive presence or hot pursuit theory difficult,[264] the use of the phrase "boats or other craft working as a team" in Article 111 lends some support to suggestions that constructive presence might extend beyond vessel-to-vessel operations.[265]

Extension of the coastal state's territorial sea to twelve nautical miles and its contiguous zone up to twenty-four nautical miles under the 1982 LOS Convention has largely obviated the need to rely on constructive presence to assert jurisdiction over so-called mother ships. At the same time, the greater distances make the use of contact boats more problematic (and dangerous for migrant smuggling) and present new challenges for law enforcement units to prove the connection between the mother ship and the putative contact boats.

H. NONCOMPLIANT VESSEL BOARDINGS

The term "noncompliant vessel" (NCV) refers to a vessel subject to examination that refuses to heave to after being lawfully ordered to do so. The frequency and severity of passive and active resistance to maritime law enforcement activities, particularly in the western Pacific, have become matters of grave concern. Several incidents involving violent resistance by Chinese fishermen have resulted in deaths of fishermen and enforcement officers alike. Under some circumstances, maritime patrol vessels have been required to defend their vessels and boarding teams against violent NCV tactics. Elsewhere, NCVs present vexing use-of-force issues because maritime patrol forces are (if their rules of engagement permit) increasingly using a variety of means and methods to stop or disable NCVs to permit boarding. New challenges will likely be presented in the coming years by noncompliant submersible and semisubmersible vessels.

1. Tactical Responses to the NCV Threat

The violence that occurred with NCVs during the maritime Rum War has been well documented (see chapter 13 for cases that involved the use of force by or against rum-runners). More recently, maritime patrol forces have met with a variety of NCV tactics in their counterdrug and alien migrant interdiction operations. Applicable service doctrine and rules of engagement or on the use of force increasingly draw a three-category distinction between compliant and noncompliant vessels and opposed boardings. Boardings involving NCVs or actual opposition to the boarding team present greater challenges and risks to the boarding team. Accordingly, enforcement actions against NCVs or vessels likely to oppose the boarding are, if carried out at all (after a thorough risk-gains assessment), generally conducted by specially trained and equipped "takedown" teams that will likely be subject to carefully tailored rules of engagement or use-of-force rules.

The U.S. Coast Guard launched Operation New Frontier (ONF) in 1999 in partial response to the NCV challenge posed by drug-trafficking vessels. ONF tactics by specially equipped and embarked helicopters employing airborne use of force and the cutter's over-the-horizon

---

264. The Chicago Convention on Civil Aircraft's prohibition on the use of weapons against civil aircraft in flight is discussed in chapter 13.
265. See LOSC art. 111(4).

small boats span a continuum that runs from verbal commands and warning shots to nonlethal use-of-force weapons and techniques to disable the vessel.[266] Use-of-force issues are examined in chapter 13.

2. Additional Penalties for Noncompliant Vessel Operators

Congress has responded to the NCV threat with new legislation. In 2006 Congress enacted the prohibition now codified in 18 U.S.C. § 2237(a)(1),[267] which makes it a felony for the master, operator, or person in charge of a vessel of the United States or subject to the jurisdiction of the United States to knowingly fail to obey an order by an authorized federal law enforcement officer to heave to.[268] Failure to heave to is also one of the factors considered in vessel seizure and forfeiture actions, even if no contraband is found during the boarding.[269] The 2006 statute defines "heave to" as "to cause a vessel to slow, come to a stop, or adjust its course or speed to account for the weather conditions and sea state to facilitate a law enforcement boarding." The statute further prohibits acts that forcibly resist, oppose, prevent, impede, intimidate, or interfere with a boarding or other law enforcement action authorized by federal law.[270] Depending on their conduct, other crewmembers might be chargeable as aiders and abettors.[271] Violations of the heave-to law are punishable by fines and up to five years' imprisonment. Certain aggravated violations can carry a life sentence. Whether punishment for a failure to heave to is subject to the LOS Convention's prohibition against sentences of imprisonment for "violations of fisheries laws and regulations" in the EEZ has not been authoritatively determined; however, the U.S. Senate's proposed understanding on marine pollution penalties suggests that the convention does not preclude harsher penalties.[272]

I. HUMAN RIGHTS CONSTRAINTS AND CONSIDERATIONS

International human rights law plays an increasingly important role in maritime affairs, particularly in maritime law enforcement. Human rights are protected both by safeguards incorporated into the 1982 LOS Convention and by other multilateral and bilateral maritime agreements, as well as a large body of international human rights law. In the United States, three issues are commonly raised with human rights law. The first concerns whether a given treaty or article within the treaty to which the United States is a party is self-executing under U.S. law and creates a private right of action. The second concerns the question whether any protections provided by human rights treaties exceed those already available under U.S. domestic law. For example, in ratifying some treaties, the United States has attached an "understanding" that the standards of protection set out in the treaty are equivalent to those already set out in the U.S. Constitu-

---

266. Disabling fire is defined as the firing of ordnance at a vessel with the intent to disable it with minimum injury to personnel or damage to the vessel. Properly used, disabling fire does not constitute deadly force.

267. Reducing Crime and Terrorism in America's Seaports Act, Pub. L. 109-177, Title III, § 303(a), Mar. 9, 2006, 120 Stat. 233, codified as amended at 18 U.S.C. § 2237. The violation is limited to cases in which the vessel is "subject to the *jurisdiction* of the United States" and might technically not apply to a right-of-visit boarding.

268. U.S. v. Santana-Perez, 619 F.3d 117, 121 (1st Cir. 2010) (holding that conviction requires proof that defendant was aware of and understood the Coast Guard's order to heave to).

269. 46 U.S.C. § 70507(b) (listing practices commonly recognized as smuggling tactics).

270. Assaulting a federal official is also punishable under 18 U.S.C. § 111.

271. U.S. v. Santana-Perez, 619 F.3d at 122.

272. See LOSC arts. 73(3) & 230(1). The Senate's draft proposed understanding strictly construes this limitation. See Senate Committee on Foreign Relations, Report on the United Nations Convention on the Law of the Sea, S. Exec. Rpt. No. 110-9, understanding 12 (reprinted in appendix D).

tion. Finally, Congress has on occasion statutorily precluded defenses based on international law. For example, the MDLEA expressly provides that a failure to comply with international law in MDLEA enforcement actions is not a defense to prosecution.[273]

The peacetime law of the sea—both conventional and customary—incorporates several established limits on states taking enforcement actions against vessels and their crews.[274] The domestic laws of enforcing states commonly impose even greater restrictions. The LOS Convention provides some general safeguards, including, for example, a general prohibition on discriminatory treatment. Under what some loosely refer to as a "rule of reasonableness" implied in Article 300 of the LOS Convention,[275] enforcing states are held to be limited in their enforcement actions to measures that are reasonably necessary.[276] The reasonableness limit is nowhere more evident or more important than in the rules regarding the use of force. The LOS Convention also requires that the enforcing state notify the flag state when one of its vessels has been arrested or detained.[277] The notification requirements are even more specific in cases in which the coastal state is contemplating the exercise of criminal jurisdiction over a person on board a vessel in innocent passage.[278] The convention requires that if the enforcing state detains a foreign vessel for a possible violation of the enforcing state's laws, it shall promptly release the vessel and its crew upon the posting of reasonable security for any penalty that may be imposed for the violation.[279] To the extent feasible, innocent cargo should be released for transshipment to its consignee or owner. Enforcement actions taken under the authority of a bilateral ship-boarding treaty, the TOC Convention's Protocol on Migrant Smuggling, and the SUA Protocol may be subject to additional safeguards set out in those agreements.[280]

Other international law instruments detail additional rights. The rights of refugees and asylum seekers are examined above in section D.2.g on maritime migration. The larger international human rights regime begins with the 1948 UN Universal Declaration of Human Rights (UDHR). Although the UDHR is not legally binding, many of its elements were later incorporated into binding treaties. The International Covenant on Civil and Political Rights (ICCPR)[281]

---

273. 46 U.S.C. § 70505.
274. Bernard H. Oxman, Human Rights and the United Nations Convention on the Law of the Sea, 36 Colum. J. Transnat'l L. 399 (1997).
275. Article 300 provides that "States Parties shall . . . exercise the rights, jurisdiction and freedoms recognized in this Convention in a manner which would not constitute an abuse of right." See also Barcelona Traction, Light & Power Co. Ltd. (Belgium v. Spain), ¶ 93, 1970 I.C.J. 3 (Feb. 5) (in all fields of international law, "it is necessary that the law be applied reasonably").
276. Chief Justice John Marshall explained the rationale for a rule of reasonableness more than two centuries ago. See Church v. Hubbard, 6 U.S. (2 Cranch) 187, 235 (1804) (reasoning that other states will oppose measures that are unreasonable, but if a state's enforcement measures are "reasonable and necessary to secure their laws from violation, they will be submitted to").
277. See, e.g., LOSC arts. 73(4) & 231. Similar requirements to notify the vessel's flag state are included in some of the IMO-sponsored conventions.
278. LOSC art. 27(3). If the master of the vessel so requests, the coastal state is required to notify a diplomatic agent or consular officer of the flag state before taking action. Concurrent notification is acceptable in cases of emergency.
279. LOSC arts. 73, 220, & 292.
280. See, e.g., 2005 SUA Protocol, supra, art. 8bis, ¶ 8; Bilateral WMD Shipboarding Agreement, U.S.-Liberia, arts. 4, 8, 9, & 12–14, available at http://www.state.gov/t/isn/c27733.htm (accessed Feb. 1, 2013).
281. ICCPR, supra, arts. 9, 10, 14, & 15. The United States ratified the ICCPR in 1992 subject to a number of reservations, understandings, and declarations. See S. Rep. 102-123 (1992); 138 Cong. Rec. 8070 (1992). It was ratified "on the express understanding that it was not self-executing and so did not itself create obligations enforceable in the federal courts." Sosa v. Alvarez-Machain, 542 U.S. 692, 735 (2004). See also Serra v. Lapin, 600 F.3d 1191 (9th Cir. 2010) (holding that the ICCPR is not self-executing, and even if it were, it does not purport to serve as a source of private rights); U.S. v. Duarte-Acero, 296 F.3d 1277 (11th Cir. 2002) (holding that the ICCPR applies to the United States only when the affected person is both within U.S. territory *and* subject to U.S. jurisdiction).

and the Vienna Convention on Consular Relations[282] may be relevant if crewmembers or others on board the vessel are detained or prosecuted.[283] Importantly, the human rights and consular notification obligations under those conventions have the potential to involve states other than the flag state of the vessel.[284] Finally, in any case in which one or more individuals are suspected of having committed an offense that is subject to an obligation to prosecute or extradite the individual, still another class of states may become involved in the follow-on enforcement measures through requests for extradition.

---

282. Vienna Convention on Consular Relations, art. 36, Apr. 24, 1963, 21 U.S.T. 77, 596 U.N.T.S. 261.
283. The solicitude shown by ITLOS for the human rights of vessel crewmembers has been remarkable. See Bernard H. Oxman, The International Tribunal for the Law of the Sea, in Bringing New Law to Ocean Waters 285, 291–92 (David D. Caron & Harry N. Scheiber eds., 2004).
284. Article 292 of the LOS Convention limits standing for actions seeking prompt release of a vessel or its "crew" to the flag state or a party acting on behalf of the flag state.

12

Military Activities in the Maritime Domain

The oceans are reserved for peaceful purposes.[1] That does not mean, however, that the oceans have been demilitarized.[2] In fact, peace on the oceans has long depended on military activities at sea. Witness, for example, the multinational counterpiracy fleet of warships and military aircraft presently operating off the coast of Somalia. The final report by the UN secretary-general's High-Level Panel on Threats, Challenges and Change lists six interconnected threats to international peace and security: interstate armed conflict, internal armed conflicts, weapons of mass destruction, terrorism, transnational organized crime, and economic and social threats.[3] Those threats to international peace and security flow all too easily across three operating domains: areas under the target nation's own control, areas under another nation's control, and areas beyond any nation's control. All three domains have a maritime component.

The state's first obligation is to protect its citizens. Defense of the homeland is the prime directive for the nation's armed forces. At the same time, however, the security interests of the modern state now extend beyond defense of its maritime and land borders against armed attack. All states share an interest in a level of public order in the oceans sufficient to provide the safety and security on which their territorial integrity, freedom of navigation, economic prosperity, and the health and viability of their marine ecosystems depend. In pursing those interests, states must aim for an optimal balance between unilateral and multilateral action, between force and diplomacy,[4] between sovereignty and legitimacy, and between certainty and mere possibility of the threat.

The contemporary maritime security climate has entered the "counter-x" era, in which the naval and maritime constabulary fleets, aircraft, and the associated forces of the world—increasingly cooperating through combined, joint, and interagency task forces—are engaged in counterpiracy, counterproliferation, counterterrorism, and counternarcotics operations in the maritime domain. At the same time, the security situation is increasingly characterized by gaps, seams, and ambiguities, which are sometimes expressed as dichotomous choices between what might roughly be called the law enforcement approach to maritime security examined in chapter 11 and the military approach to maritime security discussed in this chapter. In fact, it is no choice at all. As the more recently developed "hybrid model" demonstrates, we must embrace both options

---

1. LOSC art. 301.
2. Despite its broad "peaceful uses" caption, Article 301 of the LOS Convention does little more than restate Article 2(4) of the UN Charter.
3. See UN, A More Secure World, Report of the Secretary-General's High-Level Panel on Threats, Challenges and Change (2004), available at http://www.un.org/secureworld/ (accessed Feb. 1, 2013).
4. See Ken Booth, Law, Force and Diplomacy at Sea (1985).

if we are to achieve global maritime security. The operational concepts set out in naval doctrine and the implementing naval tactics, techniques, and procedures provide the necessary guidance.[5]

This chapter continues the binary peace-war approach to international law first adopted by Hugo Grotius in *De Jure Belli ac Pacis* (*The Laws of War and Peace*) and later adopted by the U.S. Navy, Marine Corps, and Coast Guard in the *Commander's Handbook on the Law of Naval Operations*. Part I of the *Commander's Handbook* (chapters 1–4) covers the law of peacetime naval operations; part II examines the law of naval warfare. Peacetime naval operations, particularly peacetime maritime security operations, implicate some of the same issues examined in chapter 11 on maritime law enforcement. In fact, the *Commander's Handbook* explains that part I is complemented by the more definitive guidance on maritime law enforcement promulgated by the U.S. Coast Guard.

A. "MILITARY ACTIVITIES" DEFINED

It is clear from the numerous references to warships and the exemption from compulsory dispute settlement procedures for "military activities" that the 1982 LOS Convention's drafters understood that states have conducted, and will continue to conduct, military activities in the maritime domain.[6] By implication, there must therefore be a set of military activities that do not violate the convention's peaceful uses restrictions. The corollary, and one embraced in the title to part I of the *Commander's Handbook*, is that some military activities—indeed, most contemporary military activities—are governed by the peacetime law of the sea. At the same time, however, the convention saves the application of "other rules of international law,"[7] including the law of naval warfare and other rules on the use of force examined in chapter 13. The *Commander's Handbook* makes clear that the materials in part II of the *Handbook*, on the law of naval warfare, apply whenever naval forces are employed in armed conflict, and it affirms the long-established U.S. policy to apply the law of armed conflict to all circumstances in which the armed forces of the United States are engaged in combat operations, regardless of whether such hostilities are declared or otherwise designated "war."[8]

The LOS Convention refers to "military activities" but does not define them. No international tribunal has yet construed the term, and the United States has eschewed any attempt at a fixed definition. The ordinary meaning of "military activities" necessarily includes activities by warships or military aircraft on, under, and over the water in support of national security objectives. At the same time, Article 298 suggests that an even broader meaning might be intended by the convention. It permits a state to exempt from the convention's compulsory dispute

---

5. "Naval" doctrine, which is applicable to all three of the U.S. naval services, is the foundation on which naval tactics, techniques, and procedures are built. Doctrine articulates the operational context that governs the employment of naval forces. Doctrine is subject to policy, treaties, and legal constraints. See Naval Doctrine Pub. 1: Naval Warfare, Foreword and iii (Mar. 2010) (promulgated jointly by the Chief of Naval Operations, Commandant of the Marine Corps, and Commandant of the Coast Guard).

6. See UN Disarmament Study Series—The Naval Arms Race, Report of the Secretary-General, ¶ 188, U.N. GAOR, 40th Sess., Annexes, Agenda Item 68(b), U.N. Doc. No. A/40/535 (1985) (concluding that nothing in the LOS Convention prohibits military activities that are consistent with the principles of international law embodied in the UN Charter, in particular with Articles 2(4) and 51). The report goes on to conclude that "in the exercise of the right of collective self-defense it is clear that parties to [collective] security arrangements may use force upon the high seas, within the limits prescribed by international law, to protect their armed forces, public vessels or aircraft." Id. ¶ 178.

7. See, e.g., LOSC arts. 87(1) & 58(3).

8. Commander's Handbook, supra, Preface, at 19.

settlement procedures (discussed in chapter 15) "disputes concerning military activities, *including military activities by government vessels and aircraft engaged in non-commercial service.*"[9]

Inspection of joint and naval doctrine provides a sense of the breadth of possible U.S. military activities. Joint Publication 3-0 ("Operations") divides military operations into three categories: (1) military engagement, security cooperation, and deterrence;[10] (2) crisis response and limited contingency operations; and (3) major combat operations and campaigns.[11] Those three broad categories subsume a range of missions, including homeland defense; combating weapons of mass destruction; chemical, biological, radiological, and nuclear consequence management; combating terrorism; counterinsurgency; foreign internal defense; noncombatant evacuation; personnel recovery;[12] peace operations; stability operations; counterdrug operations; civil support; and foreign humanitarian assistance.[13] A recent U.S. Navy description listed security force assistance operations, in which forward-deployed Navy ships—often deployed in carrier strike groups (CSGs) or amphibious ready groups (ARGs)—exercise and work with foreign navies, coast guards, and maritime constabulary forces to improve their ability to conduct maritime security operations and engage in civic assistance and disaster relief operations. As "military activities," those operations may be exempted from the LOS Convention's compulsory dispute settlement provisions under Article 298.[14] In addition, maritime interception operations in support of UN Security Council resolutions fall within both the optional exemption for military activities and a second optional exemption for disputes involving matters over which the council is exercising its functions under the UN Charter.[15]

Several of the missions listed in Joint Publication 3-0 overlap with the maritime law enforcement activities covered in chapter 11, presenting a challenge to those seeking to distinguish maritime law enforcement operations from military activities. The fact that some states employ their navies in maritime law enforcement operations further complicates the challenge in distinguishing the two activities. In fact, no bright line separates the two. Warships are authorized by the LOS Convention to execute selected law enforcement actions at sea. The U.S. Coast Guard, one of the five branches of the U.S. armed forces,[16] is the lead federal agency for maritime law enforcement, yet it is transferred to the Department of the Navy when the nation goes to war.[17] At the same time, notwithstanding the Posse Comitatus Act's ban on taking a direct role in law

---

9. LOSC art. 298(2)(b) (emphasis added).
10. Deterrence is furthered by such naval activities as forward presence and a show of force.
11. Chairman, Joint Chiefs of Staff, Joint Pub. 3-0, Joint Operations, at V-2 (2011). The Senate's proposed understanding on the LOS Convention focuses on common maritime "military activities, such as anchoring, launching and landing of aircraft and other military devices, launching and recovering water-borne craft, operating military devices, intelligence collection, surveillance and reconnaissance activities, exercises, operations, and conducting military surveys."
12. Ronzitti Natalino, Rescuing Nationals Abroad through Military Coercion and Intervention on Grounds of Humanity (1985); Lillich on the Forcible Protection of Nationals Abroad, 77 U.S. Nav. War Coll. Int'l L. Studies (2002). Rescue of nationals may be characterized as an exercise of self-help countermeasures rendered necessary by the fact that the intervened-in state is unable or unwilling to protect the intervening state's nationals, or as an exercise of the inherent right of self-defense.
13. Many of these operations are governed by more specific joint publications. See, e.g., Chairman, Joint Chiefs of Staff: Joint Pub. 3-03, Joint Interdiction (2011); Joint Pub. 3-07.4, Joint Counterdrug Operations (2007); Joint Pub. 3-26, Counterterrorism (2009); Joint Pub. 3-07.2, Antiterrorism (2010); Joint Pub. 3-40, Combating Weapons of Mass Destruction (2009).
14. At this writing, twenty-three of the fifty-four states that have made compulsory dispute declarations have invoked Article 298 to exclude military activities. The exempting states include four of the P-5 (China, France, Russia, and the United Kingdom), as well as U.S. neighbors Canada, Mexico, and Cuba.
15. LOSC art. 298(1)(c).
16. 10 U.S.C. § 101(a)(4); 14 U.S.C. § 1 (the Coast Guard "is at all times an Armed Force of the United States").
17. 14 U.S.C. § 3. See also U.S. Coast Guard, Coast Guard Pub. 3-0, Operations (2012).

enforcement operations, Navy warships can be seen temporarily flying the U.S. Coast Guard ensign when operating with a Coast Guard law enforcement detachment in support of counterdrug operations. These seams and overlaps may explain why the LOS Convention's optional exclusion from compulsory dispute settlement procedures for "disputes concerning military activities" goes on to include "disputes concerning law enforcement activities" in regard to the exercise of certain sovereign rights.[18]

The broad array of operations and activities that might be carried out by members of the U.S. armed forces, including the Coast Guard, poses a serious challenge to those who might be called on to determine which of those operations and activities constitute "military activity" under the LOS Convention and which do not. Perhaps for that reason the U.S. Senate Committee on Foreign Relations' draft resolution of advice and consent on the LOS Convention recommended that the United States exercise the option under Article 298(1)(b) to exempt military activities (and certain law enforcement activities) from the convention's compulsory dispute settlement procedures, while at the same time declaring that "each State Party has the exclusive right to determine whether its activities are or were 'military activities' and that such determinations are not subject to review."[19]

Three interrelated military activities—intelligence activities, special operations, and the use of maritime zones—are carried out in both peacetime and during armed conflicts. These are examined below before the chapter turns to peacetime and naval warfare activities. The visit, board, search, and seizure (VBSS)[20] framework is also employed in both peacetime maritime security operations and to enforce the law of neutrality and blockade during armed conflicts; however, the two applications differ in important ways and are therefore examined separately.[21]

B. INTELLIGENCE ACTIVITIES IN THE MARITIME DOMAIN

"Intelligence" refers to the product resulting from the collection, exploitation, processing, integration, analysis, evaluation, and interpretation of available information. Seagoing officers are insatiable information consumers.[22] Since the first vessel went to sea, seagoing officers have sought out information on a range of matters that affected their safety. Their very lives depended on it. Early mariners were necessarily part geographer, part navigator, part oceanographer, and part meteorologist. The information they obtained on their vessel's position, the weather, navigation features and hazards, and port conditions and customs was indispensable to the success of their voyage. The kind and quality of information sought by mariners may have changed over the millennia, but the seagoing officer's thirst for information about the maritime environment has not abated. That information is acquired, analyzed, and applied to questions involving voyage planning and navigation, vessel safety and security, and force protection, and in the planning and execution of maritime law enforcement and maritime security missions and naval warfare.

---

18. LOSC art. 298(1)(b).
19. Senate Committee on Foreign Relations, Report on the United Nations Convention on the Law of the Sea, S. Exec. Rpt. No. 110-09, declaration 2 (reprinted in appendix D).
20. VBSS is defined as the "procedures by which U.S. forces conduct maritime interception operations in order to determine the true character of vessels, cargo, and passengers." See Department of the Navy, Office of the Chief of Naval Operations, Navy Supplement to the DoD Dictionary of Military and Associated Terms (2010). The naval dictionary's definition does not distinguish between peacetime VBSS and belligerent VBSS.
21. Peacetime VBSS operations are governed by U.S. Navy/Coast Guard, Maritime Interception Operations, NTTP 3-07.11M/COMDTINST M3330.1 (Apr. 2008) and, to the extent they include maritime law enforcement by the Coast Guard, the U.S. Coast Guard Maritime Law Enforcement Manual, COMDTINST M16247.1. VBSS operations during armed conflicts are governed by the law of naval warfare.
22. R. Taylor, The Haven-Finding Art: A History of Navigation from Odysseus to Captain Cook (1971).

Reduced to its simplest terms, intelligence is knowledge and foreknowledge of the world; the prelude to decision and action by U.S. policymakers and other intelligence consumers. No one would deny that timely and reliable intelligence is indispensable to national security. Such classic military texts as Sun Tzu's *Art of War* and Clausewitz's *On War* recognize the indispensability of intelligence to the state's security and defense.[23] Intelligence is equally important in contemporary maritime security and law enforcement operations for both mission accomplishment and force protection. For that reason, intelligence activities are carried out in times of peace and war. Intelligence is now highly specialized and increasingly dependent on new technologies. It is acquired through a variety of means and methods operating across all five operating domains: land, water (surface, subsurface, and seabed), air, space, and cyberspace.[24]

1. The U.S. Intelligence Community

The U.S. Intelligence Community (IC) consists of sixteen members and is led by the director of national intelligence.[25] The Central Intelligence Agency, perhaps the best-known member of the IC, is an independent agency of the U.S. government. The other fifteen elements are offices or bureaus within federal executive departments. DoD members include the Defense Intelligence Agency, National Geospatial-Intelligence Agency, National Reconnaissance Office, National Security Agency, and the four service intelligence commands. Intelligence functions are also carried out at the combatant commander and numbered fleet levels, other commands, and in various fusion centers. Navy and Coast Guard intelligence components staff the National Maritime Intelligence Integration Office in Suitland, Maryland, to more effectively integrate maritime intelligence.

2. Intelligence Collection in the Maritime Domain

In the post–September 11, 2001, security environment, characterized by the pervasive and widely dispersed threat of asymmetric attacks on military and civilian targets, the United States promulgated a family of maritime security plans under the overall framework of the National Strategy for Maritime Security.[26] The National Plan for Maritime Domain Awareness is of particular relevance.[27] It defines the maritime domain as "all areas and things of, on, under, relating to, adjacent to, or bordering on a sea, ocean, or other navigable waterway, including all maritime-related activities, infrastructure, people, cargo, and vessels and other conveyances." Acquiring the necessary awareness of such a broad domain requires a significant at-sea information and intelligence collection effort.

---

23. Sun Tzu, The Art of War (ca. 476–221 BCE); Carl von Clausewitz, On War (1836) (Michael Howard & Peter Paret transl. & eds., 1976).
24. See generally Chairman, Joint Chiefs of Staff, Joint Pub. 2-0, Joint Intelligence (2007); U.S. Navy, Naval Doctrine Pub. 2, Naval Intelligence (1994); U.S. Coast Guard, Coast Guard Pub. 2-0, Intelligence (2010).
25. 50 U.S.C. § 401a(4). See generally Office of the General Counsel, Office of the Director of National Intelligence, Intelligence Community Legal Reference Book (2012).
26. The White House, The National Strategy for Maritime Security (2007), available at http://www.nmic.gov/docs/HSPD13_MaritimeSecurityStrategy.pdf (accessed Feb. 1, 2013). See also Presidential Policy Directive 18 (PDD-18), Maritime Security, Aug. 14, 2012 (reaffirming the National Strategy for Maritime Security).
27. National Maritime Domain Awareness Plan for the National Strategy for Maritime Security, Dec. 2013, available at http://www.whitehouse.gov/sites/default/files/docs/national_maritime_domain_awareness_plan.pdf (accessed Jan.18, 2014).

In contrast to domestic law,[28] international law neither prohibits the collection of intelligence nor expressly confers a right to engage in such activities.[29] Intelligence-gathering activities in another state's territory or national airspace are likely to draw a swift response, perhaps including prosecution under the state's domestic espionage laws.[30] The LOS Convention briefly addresses intelligence activities in the articles on innocent passage. Article 19 stipulates that "any act aimed at collecting information to the prejudice of the defense or security of the coastal State" (i.e., intelligence collection) renders a foreign vessel's passage noninnocent.

Outside of the express provision on intelligence activities in Article 19, the convention does not limit intelligence activities. Intelligence activities are not among the enumerated high-seas freedoms listed in Article 87, but that list of freedoms was not meant to be exhaustive. So long as intelligence activities are carried out with due regard for the interests of other states in their exercise of the freedom of the high seas and other rights under the convention, and do not violate the peaceful use rule, nothing in the LOS Convention prohibits them. The rule on high-seas freedoms was sorely tested in 1968 when naval vessels of the Democratic People's Republic of Korea (DPRK; i.e., North Korea) fired on and then seized the USS *Pueblo* (AGER-2)—an intelligence collection vessel—and its crew. The United States asserted that at the time of the encounter the *Pueblo* was on the high seas, more than twelve nautical miles from the Korean baseline. North Korea, which claims a fifty-nautical-mile security zone, disputed that.[31]

Assuming that intelligence activities are a nonenumerated yet preserved high-seas freedom under Article 87 and customary international law, that right is applicable in the EEZ of a foreign state under Article 58(1) of the convention. Nevertheless, some states dispute the right of foreign vessels to collect intelligence in the EEZ, with China being among the most outspoken and provocative.[32] Objections are generally based on one of three grounds. First, some states insist that it is a military activity,[33] but then incorrectly assert that a coastal state may restrict all military activities in the EEZ. Second, others invoke the coastal state's jurisdiction over marine scientific research in the EEZ and assert that intelligence activities fall within the MSR regime, requiring the coastal state's consent. A third objection (invoked by China in the 2001 EP-3 aircraft force majeure incident) argues that surveillance activities violate the requirement to give due regard to the coastal state's economic interests in the EEZ.[34] The United States has consistently rejected all three arguments.

---

28. See, e.g., U.S. National Security Act, 50 U.S.C. § 403-4a (authorizing intelligence activities by the Central Intelligence Agency); 18 U.S.C. §§ 793 & 794 (criminalizing crime of espionage).

29. On the issue of spying during times of armed conflict, see Commander's Handbook, supra, ¶¶ 12.8 & 12.9.

30. In 1960 the Soviet Union shot down a U-2 spy plane flying over Soviet airspace piloted by Francis Gary Powers, a former U.S. Air Force captain. The U-2 was flying 65,000 feet above the Sverdlovsk nuclear facility, 1,300 miles inside Soviet airspace. Powers bailed out and was captured by the Soviets. He was convicted by the Soviets of espionage and sentenced to ten years' imprisonment.

31. See Oliver J. Lissitzyn, Electronic Reconnaissance from the High Seas and International Law, 61 U.S. Nav. War Coll. Int'l L. Studies 563–71 (1980). The USS *Pueblo*'s officers and crew were held captive in a North Korean POW camp for eleven months. The ship itself is still held by North Korea.

32. China's apparently intentional interference with the flight of a U.S. Navy EP-3E and the operations of the USNS *Bowditch* (T-AGS 62) in 2001 and the USNS *Impeccable* (T-AGOS 23) in 2009 are perhaps the best known. See Jonathan G. Odom, The True "Lies" of the *Impeccable* Incident, 18 Mich. State J. Int'l Law 1–42 (2010).

33. Federal law broadly distinguishes between defense operations (Title 10 of the U.S. Code) and intelligence activities (Title 50 of the U.S. Code). The distinction has important congressional oversight implications, as the former activities are generally within the purview of the House and Senate committees on the armed forces, while the latter fall under the select committees on intelligence. Both, however, are "military activities" under international law.

34. See U.S. Department of State, Digest of United States Practice in International Law 2001, at 703–11.

Neither the LOS Convention nor the analogous rules of customary law confers on the coastal state authority to prohibit intelligence activities as a "military activity": In response to the first claimed rationale, The United States has consistently declared its understanding that within the EEZ "all States enjoy high seas freedoms of navigation and overflight and all other internationally lawful uses of the sea related to these freedoms, including, *inter alia*, military activities, such as anchoring, launching and landing of aircraft and other military devices, launching and recovering water-borne craft, operating military devices, intelligence collection, surveillance and reconnaissance activities, exercises, operations, and conducting military surveys."[35] That position was clear throughout the UNCLOS III negotiations on the convention's EEZ articles and has been a consistent element of U.S. freedom-of-navigation challenges to excessive maritime claims.

Intelligence activities do not fall within the category of marine scientific research, over which the coastal state has jurisdiction: In response to the second rationale, the United States has declared its understanding that marine scientific research does not include military activities, including military surveys or hydrographic surveys.[36] Although the 1982 LOS Convention does not define "marine scientific research," the convention offers substantial textual and structural support for the distinction between marine scientific research, which falls within the coastal state's jurisdiction when carried out in its EEZ, and military and hydrographic surveys, which do not.

Intelligence activities do not categorically violate the duty of states to conduct activities in a foreign state's EEZ with due regard for the interests of the coastal state: In response to the "due regard" complaint, the United States has asserted that surveys do not interfere with any of the coastal state's protected sovereign rights or jurisdiction in the EEZ.[37] Categorical statements regarding the consistency or inconsistency of an activity with the "due regard" duty demonstrate a misunderstanding of the duty. Properly conducted, a due regard analysis begins with a recognition that states other than the coastal state have a number of reserved rights in the EEZ, including those set out in Article 58 or otherwise reserved under customary international law. The analysis then applies the "due regard" standard to the actual conduct of those reserved activities on a case-by-case basis.

C. SPECIAL OPERATIONS IN THE MARITIME DOMAIN

"Special operations" can be defined as operations conducted in hostile, denied, or politically sensitive environments to achieve military, diplomatic, informational, and/or economic objectives by employing military capabilities for which there is no broad conventional force requirement.[38] In addition to combat engagements, special operations forces (SOF) are selectively employed in peacetime missions such as counterproliferation and counterpiracy (mostly in hostage rescue operations).[39] Opposed boardings typically employ SOF or Marine Corps special operations

---

35. S. Exec. Rpt. No. 110-09, understanding 4 (reprinted in appendix D).

36. Id. understanding 5.

37. One commentator interprets the phrase "due regard" as having two components: an awareness and consideration of other states' interests component, and a balancing component. More specifically, the requirement of due regard in Article 58(3) means, according to the author, "that other states, in exercising their rights and performing their duties, must *inter alia* be aware of and consider the rights and duties of the coastal State in its EEZ. [Those] other States must balance their rights and duties against the rights and duties of the coastal State in its EEZ." See Walker, Definitions for the Law of the Sea, supra, at 180. Arguably, the proposed definition's requirement to conduct a "balancing" of interests is closer to the former "reasonable regard" standard than the current "due regard" requirement.

38. See generally Chairman, Joint Chiefs of Staff, Joint Pub. 3-05, Special Operations, (2011).

39. Employment of SOF in activities that could eventually lead to an arrest and criminal prosecution potentially raises issues concerning *posse comitatus* restrictions on DoD forces, constitutional criminal procedure, evidence gathering

capable (SOC) teams. The teams may also be used in noncompliant boardings. SOF typically operate in small elements (relative to conventional forces) to conduct missions independently. The operations can be designed to handle specific contingencies, such as seizing weapons of mass destruction in failed-state scenarios, combat search and rescue, or the training and coordination of foreign military personnel. Recent SOF operations that attracted global attention include the 2009 rescue of the *Maersk Alabama* master held by Somali pirates and the 2011 Osama bin Laden capture-or-kill mission. An even more complex 2012 SEAL team operation to rescue two U.S. aid workers held hostage by Somali pirates received less attention.[40]

Activities by military SOF (under Title 10 of the U.S. Code), which may include direct action, unconventional warfare, foreign internal defense, psychological operations, and counterterrorism,[41] are distinguished from "covert activities" by intelligence agencies under the National Security Act (Title 50 of the U.S. Code). A "covert activity" is defined as "an activity or activities of the United States Government to influence political, economic, or military conditions abroad, where it is intended that the role of the United States Government will not be apparent or acknowledged publicly."[42] The term does not include "traditional" military or law enforcement activities or routine support of such activities.[43] Historically, most U.S. covert activities have been conducted by the CIA. The National Security Act assigns to the CIA four intelligence collection, analysis, and coordination duties, and a fifth mission to "perform such other functions and duties related to intelligence affecting the national security as the President or the National Security Council may direct."[44] Executive Order 12,333 implements the statutory provision, authorizing the CIA to "conduct special activities approved by the President."[45] It further provides that "no agency except the CIA (or the Armed Forces of the United States in time of war declared by Congress or during any period covered by a report from the President to the Congress under the War Powers Resolution (87 Stat. 855) may conduct any special activity unless the President determines that another agency is more likely to achieve a particular objective."[46] Although such activities are less likely to take place in the maritime domain,[47] the distinction between intelligence and military activities is an important one for the seagoing officer to understand, particularly as the United States increasingly takes a joint/interagency "whole of government" approach to the nation's challenges, threats, and opportunities.

D. UNMANNED MILITARY VEHICLES

New technologies and their applications have long been an important factor in the evolution of the international law of the sea. Unmanned aerial and marine vehicle systems are rapidly transforming the naval and law enforcement operating environment.[48] There are more than 5,000 unmanned aircraft systems in the U.S. inventory, and more than 12,000 unmanned ground systems were deployed to Iraq and Afghanistan. While the inventory of sea-based unmanned and

---

    and chain of custody, and the availability of SOF personnel to testify at trial that are beyond the scope of this book.

40. Jeffrey Gettleman, U.S. Swoops In to Free 2 from Pirates in Somali Raid, NY Times, Jan. 25, 2012.
41. See 10 U.S.C. § 167(j), which defines the authority of U.S. Special Operations Command.
42. 50 U.S.C. § 413b(e).
43. Id.
44. 50 U.S.C. § 403-3(d).
45. Exec. Order 12,333 (July 2008), 3 C.F.R. 200 (1981), reprinted in 50 U.S.C. § 401(3.4)(h).
46. Exec. Order 12,333, supra, ¶ 1.7(a)(4). See Andru E. Wall, Demystifying the Title 10–Title 50 Debate: Distinguishing Military Operations, Intelligence Activities and Covert Operations, 3 Harv. Nat'l Security J. 85 (2011).
47. See John Piña Craven, The Silent War: The Cold War and the Battle beneath the Sea (2001).
48. See DoD, Unmanned Systems Integrated Roadmap FY 2013-2038 (2013).

robotic systems is substantially smaller, due in part to the more demanding marine environment, the prospects for future growth are favorable. A 2009 report by the Chief of Naval Operations Strategic Studies Group (*The Unmanned Imperative*)[49] concluded that unmanned vehicle technologies and automated networks will be an important basis of the future Navy.[50] The littoral combat ship was, in fact, designed to carry and work with a variety of unmanned systems. Seagoing officers are therefore increasingly likely to operate with unmanned aerial and marine systems and must be alert to the potential legal issues posed by their use (see chapter 9 on unmanned marine systems and their navigation rights).

Unmanned aerial, land, and marine systems are already in wide use in intelligence, surveillance, and reconnaissance (ISR) roles. Accordingly, the above discussion of intelligence activities in the marine environment is equally relevant to unmanned systems. Unmanned systems are also playing an important role in maritime counterdrug operations. Missile-equipped Predator and Reaper drones became the weapon of choice during the Obama administration's war on al Qaeda and the Taliban. Generally operated remotely by combat systems officer "pilots" under the direction and control of the CIA, the drones typically launch from airfields in Djibouti and Afghanistan to carry out their "targeted killing" missions in Afghanistan, Pakistan, Yemen, and Somalia. Sources estimate that the drone program has targeted up to three thousand individuals, the vast majority during the Obama administration's first term. Issues regarding the use of force from unmanned systems, including the Obama administration's legal justifications for their use, are examined in chapter 13.

E. MARITIME OPERATIONAL ZONES

Maritime operational zones are designated ocean areas and superjacent airspace in which a nation purports to restrict the freedom of navigation and/or overflight of other users or otherwise affect the exercise of those freedoms.[51] A variety of labels have been attached to such area-based approaches to safety and security.[52] Some of the zones apply in peacetime, some in crisis situations, and some only during an armed conflict. Most zones are fixed and of limited duration; however, some may be permanent, and moving zones have been used to provide a protective area around vessels in transit.[53]

An invaluable reference for understanding and applying maritime zones is the U.S. Naval War College's *Maritime Operational Zones Manual*,[54] an unofficial publication prepared by the college's international law department that is widely recognized for its thorough treatment of the subject. The *MOZ Manual*'s organization provides an excellent overview of area-based "zonal" approaches to regulating maritime activities. It begins with an overview of the coastal state's

---

49. U.S. Department of the Navy, Chief of Naval Operations Strategic Studies Group XXVIII Report: The Unmanned Imperative, Dec. 2009 (unclassified but for official use only).

50. U.S. Department of the Navy, Chief of Naval Operations Strategic Studies Group XXVIII Report: The Unmanned Imperative, Dec. 2009 (unclassified but for official use only). See also Robert Morris & Capt. Paul S. Fischbeck, Disruptive Technologies: The Navy's Way Forward, 138 U.S. Nav. Inst. Proc. 68–72 (Nov. 2012).

51. Commander's Handbook, supra, ¶¶ 4.5, 7.8, & 7.9.

52. Other possible area-based "zones" include no-fly zones (imposed in Libya in 2011 by Security Council Resolution 1973) and nuclear-free zones (see paragraph 2.6.6 of the Commander's Handbook). The United States has also promulgated naval defensive sea areas, some of which remain in effect. See 32 C.F.R. § 761.3.

53. The dilemma presented in using such moving zones is that other vessels are not able to avoid the zone unless the protected vessel's position and intended course and speed are disclosed, and such disclosures make a determined assailant's task easier.

54. U.S. Naval War College, Int'l L. Dep't, Maritime Operational Zones Manual (Feb. 1, 2006), available at http://www.usnwc.edu/getattachment/b7c60abb-a03d-4236-9cf5-01e98951333e/Maritime-Operational-Zones-Manual (accessed Feb. 1, 2013).

authority in peacetime to temporarily suspend innocent passage and to promulgate MOZs and other control mechanisms in its waters or national airspace, including safety zones, security zones, regulated navigation areas, naval vessel protection zones, restricted waterfront areas, danger zones, air defense identification zones, and naval defensive sea areas. It then examines warning areas for military exercises and weapons testing during peacetime. Next, the manual describes two zones used to control the sea and airspace activities in crisis or "brink of war" conditions, including the cordon sanitaire and quarantine.[55] Three categories of area-based controls under the law of naval warfare are then covered, including blockades, control over the immediate area of operations, and wartime exclusion zones. The final category includes zones that may be used pursuant to UN Security Council resolutions, such as maritime interception zones.

Maritime operational zones are subject to several general restrictions. For example, MOZs that purport to regulate warships or military aircraft are not permitted under the LOS Convention or customary law. Although a nation may temporarily suspend innocent passage in its territorial sea for security reasons, in peacetime it may not establish a permanent security zone beyond the territorial sea that limits freedom of navigation and overflight of foreign ships and aircraft.[56] Nevertheless, some nations have established security zones beyond the territorial sea that purport to regulate activities of warships and military aircraft.[57] The parameters vary, but provisions may require prior permission or notification, may limit the number of vessels or aircraft or their operational activities, and may even exclude foreign warships and military aircraft entirely.

Maritime *warning* zones are, as the name suggests, zones of warning, not zones of exclusion. In contrast to purported coastal state security zones beyond the territorial sea, maritime warning zones are ocean areas that are temporarily declared to be dangerous to ships, aircraft, or both, typically because of military exercises or weapons testing. Although warning zones do not assert sovereignty over the affected area, and foreign ships and aircraft are not required to remain outside the zone, they do warn of danger and thereby discourage use of that area for navigation or overflight during the specified period. Such temporary warning zones must be announced in advance, typically through a notice to mariners (NOTMAR), notice to airmen (NOTAM), Hydro-Atlantic (HYDROLANT) or Hydro-Pacific (HYDROPAC) message, and the Global Maritime Distress and Safety System. The United States has relied on maritime warning zones to support naval operations in areas of ongoing tensions or hostilities, effectively creating "bubbles" of air and sea space within which the United States requested approaching ships and aircraft to identify themselves and maintain communications. Ships and aircraft entering the defined area without communicating were warned that they "may be held at risk by US defensive measures." The United States has not used fixed distances recently, but it continues to issue warnings.[58]

As force protection measures, maritime warning zones are not necessarily governed by the imminent threat standard applicable to the exercise of self-defense.[59] However, such measures must be evaluated and applied in conjunction with the applicable rules of engagement.[60] Indeed,

---

55. Commander's Handbook, supra, ¶ 4.4.8.

56. Id. ¶ 1.6.4.

57. See Annotated Supplement to the Commander's Handbook, supra, table A1–11 (listing nineteen such states).

58. Commander's Handbook, supra, ¶¶ 2.4.3.1 & 4.4.7. For examples of zone notices issued by the United States in 2003 and 2004, see appendix A (HYDROLANT 597/03), appendix B (Maritime Liaison Office Bahrain Advisory Bulletin 06-03), and appendix C (HYDROPAC 795/2004) of the Commander's Handbook.

59. See U.S. Navy, Antiterrorism/Force Protection, NTTP 3-07.2.1, rev. A (2004) (unclassified but for official use only); Commander's Handbook, supra, ¶ 2.6.3.

60. The 1904 Dogger Bank incident, in which Russian warships mistakenly fired on unarmed British fishing vessels, highlights the risks of linking rules of engagement solely to the proximity of contacts that have not been positively

rules of engagement for maritime forces may adopt a zone-based approach to the use of force,[61] and a vessel's refusal to comply with zone-based force protection measures will be relevant in determining whether the vessel is engaging in a hostile act or demonstrating hostile intent.

Zone-based force protection measures can be controversial. For example, on July 16, 2012, an embarked security team on the USNS *Rappahannock* (T-AO 204) fired on a 50-foot vessel powered by 3 outboard engines after it disregarded warnings and rapidly closed on the oiler near Jebel Ali, United Arab Emirates. When the vessel approached to within 1,200 yards of *Rappahannock* the vessel's security team executed a series of nonlethal, preplanned responses, in accordance with Navy force protection procedures.[62] The *Rappahannock*'s crew repeatedly attempted to warn the vessel's operators to turn away by signals and a warning shot. When those efforts failed to deter the approaching vessel and it closed to within 90 yards, the *Rappahannock* apparently concluded that the approaching vessel demonstrated hostile intent, and its security team fired rounds from a .50-caliber machine gun in an attempt to disable the vessel, inadvertently killing one of its crewmembers and injuring three others.

Maritime *exclusion* zones, which are employed during hostilities, do more than warn of the risk of unintended targeting. They threaten the use of force against any ship or aircraft entering the zone. Critics of such zones are apt to call them "kill zones" or "free fire zones" because belligerents are supposedly freed of the constraints of distinction and proportionality. By contrast, advocates argue that they are designed and used to protect neutrals and noncombatants by encouraging them to remain outside an area of combat operations.

During an armed conflict, international law permits belligerents to apply special restrictions on the activities of neutral ships and aircraft to ensure that they are not aiding the enemy.[63] The complete exclusion of neutral ships and aircraft from declared areas is not clearly supported by international law, however, particularly if the zone is not limited to a relatively small area so as not to interfere unreasonably with the neutrals' rights under international law.[64] The Royal Navy's total exclusion zone (TEZ) employed during the Falklands War is an example of an exclusion zone most would consider illegal under international law.[65]

Should a belligerent establish an exclusion zone, the same body of law applies both inside and outside the zone.[66] For example, lawful targets of the enemy located outside neutral territory can be engaged without respect to the geographic limits of the exclusion zone.[67] However, a belligerent cannot be absolved of its duties under the law of armed conflict by establishing

identified. The Russian fleet admiral had reportedly instructed his ships that "no vessel of any sort whatsoever must be allowed to get in amongst the fleet." See Richard Ned Lebow, Accidents and Crises: The Dogger Bank Affair, 31 Nav. War Coll. Rev. 66 (1978).

61. See, e.g., Int'l Inst. of Humanitarian Law, Sanremo Handbook on Rules of Engagement [hereinafter "Sanremo ROE Handbook"] (Nov. 2009), at 45, available through the U.S. Naval War College's Stockton Portal (Operational Resources), http://usnwc.libguides.com/LOAC-IHL (accessed Jan. 1, 2013).

62. See U.S. Navy, Antiterrorism/Force Protection, NTTP 3-07.2.1, supra.

63. Commander's Handbook, supra, ¶¶ 7.8 & 7.9.

64. As a legal matter, when zones are defined to exclude the ships and aircraft of all nations, and not just those of an opposing belligerent, they encroach on the navigation and overflight rights of ships and aircraft from countries not involved in the conflict.

65. Both Argentina and the United Kingdom promulgated exclusion zones during the war. Initially, the United Kingdom claimed a 200-nautical-mile maritime exclusion zone that applied only to Argentine warships and naval auxiliaries, then replaced it with a 200-nautical-mile total exclusion zone that applied to naval and merchant vessels of other states as well as Argentine vessels. When hostilities ceased, the TEZ was replaced with a 150-nautical-mile Falkland Islands Protective Zone. See generally William J. Fenrick, The Exclusion Zone Device in the Law of Naval Warfare, 24 Canadian Y.B. Int'l L. 91 (1986).

66. San Remo Manual, supra, ¶ 105.

67. A U.K. submarine engaged the ARA *General Belgrano* even though the Argentine warship was well outside the two-hundred-nautical-mile U.K. exclusion zone at the time.

zones that might adversely affect the legitimate uses of defined areas of the sea.[68] Moreover, the extent, location, and duration of the zone and the measures imposed must not exceed what is strictly required by military necessity and the principles of proportionality.[69] The belligerent is also required to give due regard to the rights of neutral states to exercise legitimate uses of the seas and must provide safe passage through the zone for neutral vessels and aircraft where the geographical extent of the zone significantly impedes free and safe access to the ports and coasts of a neutral state and in other cases where normal navigation routes are affected, except where military requirements do not permit such accommodations.

F. LAW OF PEACETIME NAVAL OPERATIONS

The LOS Convention provides the framework for the peacetime use of the oceans.[70] That framework requires that all states must, in exercising their rights and performing their obligations under the convention, refrain from any threat or use of force against the territorial integrity or political independence of any state, or in any manner inconsistent with the principles of international law embodied in the UN Charter.[71] Although some would interpret the "peaceful purposes" articles expansively, to banish all military activities from the oceans, that interpretation is not supported by the text of the LOS Convention and its negotiating history. Indeed, it is difficult to imagine how the core purpose of the UN Charter to "maintain international peace and security" could be achieved without military activities at sea. When the U.S. Senate Committee on Foreign Relations reported out the LOS Convention for advice and consent, it included its understanding that nothing in the convention, including provisions referring to "peaceful uses," impairs a state's inherent right of individual or collective self-defense or rights during armed conflict.[72] More generally, nothing in the LOS Convention drafting history suggests that the "peaceful uses or purposes" articles were intended to nullify the existing law of naval operations (any more than the UN Charter abolished the law of armed conflict) or force navies to stay at home when compelling security concerns require a forward deployed presence. Nor will the peaceful use articles force navies to expose their vessels, aircraft, and crews to unnecessary risks by forgoing the intelligence-gathering and force protection measures essential to the deployed units' safety and security.[73]

1. Maritime Security Operations and the Law

Maritime security operations are one of the six core competencies of the naval forces.[74] In the broadest sense, particularly among the partner nations who answered the call in the early years of the twenty-first century following a series of terrorist and pirate attacks and the partial

---

68. San Remo Manual, supra, ¶ 106.

69. Id.

70. See, e.g., LOSC arts. 301 & 88; see also Restatement FRLUS § 521 cmt. b.

71. LOSC art. 301. See Bernard H. Oxman, The Regime of Warships under the United Nations Convention on the Law of the Sea, 24 Va. J. Int'l L. 809 (1984); Boleslaw A. Boczek, Peaceful Purposes Provisions of the United Nations Convention on the Law of the Sea, 20 Ocean Dev. & Int'l L. 359 (1989).

72. S. Exec. Rpt. No. 110-09, understanding 1 (reprinted in appendix D).

73. China, North Korea, Iran, Pakistan, Brazil, India, Malaysia, and others have challenged U.S. military operations in their EEZ as being inconsistent with the LOS Convention and customary law. Statement of Rear Adm. William L. Schachte, USN (Ret.), Senate Committee on Foreign Relations Hearings on the United Nations Convention on the Law of the Sea, Oct. 14, 2003, S. Exec. Rpt. 108-10, at 64 (Mar. 11, 2004).

74. NDP-1, Naval Warfare, supra, at 25. The other five are forward presence, deterrence, sea control, power projection, and humanitarian assistance/disaster response (HA/DR).

breakdown of the nonproliferation regime, maritime security operations seek to preserve, restore, or enhance security in the maritime environment and to promote stability and global prosperity.[75] They have been carried out through a combination of national, bilateral, and multilateral forces. Maritime security operations embrace missions designed to counter maritime-related terrorism, weapons proliferation, transnational crime, piracy, environmental destruction, and illegal seaborne immigration. As such, they complement the counterterrorism and security efforts of regional states and seek to impede the use of the maritime environment as a venue or medium for attack or to transport personnel, weapons, or other material. MSO activities overlap with and draw on theater security cooperation, maritime interception, expanded maritime interception, and law enforcement operations.[76]

The National Strategy for Maritime Security, jointly developed by the DoD and the Department of Homeland Security and promulgated by the president in 2005, sought to address the troublesome seam between peacetime law enforcement operations and the deployment of armed force against large-scale threats in or from the maritime domain.[77] The traditional binary approach, based on the belief that the two paradigms for peace and war are mutually exclusive, has proven wholly unsatisfactory. The peace side of the security operations spectrum (displayed in figure 8) seeks to maintain order through law enforcement activities carried out with due respect for human and civil rights. Law enforcement is reactive, and privacy interests limit the scope and use of intelligence. Military involvement in law enforcement operations raises *posse comitatus* issues (discussed in chapter 11). By contrast, the war side of the spectrum is governed by the law of armed conflict and relies heavily on intelligence. Both ends depend on credible deterrence for their success. It is important to note that the most legitimate end-game for maritime security missions in the eyes of many is an arrest and prosecu-

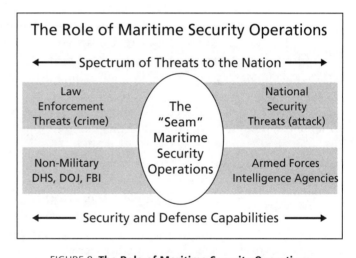

FIGURE 8. **The Role of Maritime Security Operations**

tion, which requires law enforcement authority. The choice of platform and the uniforms worn by boarding teams can have a significant impact on perceived legitimacy.

---

75. Chapters 3 and 4 of the Commander's Handbook provide an overview of the law of peacetime naval operations. The working definition of "maritime security operations" is set out in the Naval Operations Concept as "those tasks and operations conducted to protect sovereignty and maritime resources, support free and open seaborne commerce, and to counter maritime related terrorism, weapons proliferation, transnational crime, piracy, environmental destruction, and illegal seaborne migration." Naval Operations Concept 2010, (2010), at 35. The execution of MSOs must be carried out by personnel with law enforcement authority and jurisdiction, which is one of the U.S. Coast Guard's contributions to the National Fleet Policy agreement.
76. See generally Douglas Guilfoyle, Shipping Interdiction and the Law of the Sea (2009).
77. The U.S. Coast Guard is the lead federal agency for maritime homeland security. U.S. Northern Command has responsibility for homeland defense of the continental USA, Alaska, and the surrounding waters out to five hundred nautical miles. See Commander's Handbook, supra, ¶ 3.12.

2. Peacetime Visit, Board, Search, and Seizure

Vessel interceptions and boardings by naval vessels are generally carried out by visit, board, search, and seizure (VBSS) teams drawn from components of the U.S. naval forces.[78] Boarding teams from U.S. Navy platforms may include Navy, Marine Corps, and Coast Guard personnel. Coast Guard interception and boarding teams may also operate from Coast Guard boats or cutters or from allied naval vessels. In most cases, Coast Guard law enforcement detachments (LEDETs) on naval vessels serve under the operational or tactical control of the cognizant Coast Guard command authority when conducting boardings.[79] In cases not calling for law enforcement measures, however, the LEDET may operate under DoD control, drawing on the Coast Guard's statutory authority to provide assistance to other agencies.[80] Boarding team composition and operations must be adapted to the mission and the perceived threat level, including the extent to which the suspect vessel and its crew are cooperative.

Boardings generally fall into one of three categories: compliant vessel boardings, noncompliant vessel boardings, and opposed boardings. A compliant vessel boarding is one in which the suspect vessel complies with the directions of the on-scene commander, there is no apparent passive or active resistance measures, and there is no intelligence to indicate a threat.[81] By contrast, a noncompliant vessel (NCV) boarding is one in which there is no intelligence data to indicate a threat, but the vessel employs active or passive measures to prevent or impede the boarding phase of the operation, and any or all of the following conditions are met: the vessel fails to comply with warship's directions, and passive measures in place are intended to delay, impede, complicate, or deter the access to spaces required for control of the vessel, but measures can be overcome by mechanical means. Opposed boardings are those in which any or all of the following conditions are present: active or passive resistance measures are in place and are clearly intended to inflict serious bodily harm or death to the boarding team; the suspect vessel has demonstrated an intent to actively oppose the boarding by inflicting serious bodily harm or using deadly force against the boarding team; intelligence indicates a possible threat to inflict serious bodily harm or death to the boarding team; or any demonstration of hostile action, including the threatening display of weapons.

The Navy/Coast Guard NTTP publication *Maritime Interception Operations* draws on the above distinction between compliant boardings, noncompliant boardings, and opposed boardings. The publication further breaks down noncompliant vessel boardings into two levels based on the anticipated threat level. SOF or other specially trained and designated assault and boarding teams will normally conduct opposed boardings and may conduct NCV vessel boardings.

3. Maritime Interception Operations

The *Maritime Interception Operations* publication, which applies only in peacetime, outlines the naval tactics, techniques, and procedures (NTTP) used to conduct unilateral or joint maritime interception operations and VBSS operations and serves as the doctrinal basis for U.S. multinational operations.[82] The NTTP it describes do not apply to naval blockade or neutrality enforcement boardings during armed conflicts. Although the publication was jointly promulgated by the

---

78. As used here, the term "U.S. naval forces" includes the Navy, Marine Corps, and Coast Guard. See NDP-1, Naval Warfare, supra, at iii.
79. See 10 U.S.C. § 379.
80. 14 U.S.C. § 141.
81. Maritime Interception Operations, NTTP 3-07.11M, supra, at 1–2.
82. Id.

Navy and Coast Guard, Coast Guard boarding teams conduct their MLE boardings in accordance with the Coast Guard *Maritime Law Enforcement Manual*.

Maritime interception operations (MIO)[83] by U.S. naval forces are conducted to deny suspect vessels access to specific ports for import or export of prohibited goods to or from a specific nation or nations or non-state-sponsored organizations, for purposes of peacekeeping or to enforce sanctions.[84] In contrast to law enforcement operations,[85] MIO are considered military missions. Peacetime MIO activities are conducted in accordance with international law, including the rules on enforcement jurisdiction. The *Commander's Handbook* lists nine legal bases for conducting MIO, all but two of which (belligerent right of visit and inherent right of self-defense) apply in peacetime MIO.[86]

The authority to conduct MIO is normally found in resolutions, lawful orders, or other directives of the UN Security Council or some other competent national or regional authority. Expanded MIO (EMIO) are maritime interception operations to intercept targeted personnel or material that pose an imminent threat to the United States or coalition members. Maritime counterproliferation interdiction (MCPI) is the use of naval forces to combat the proliferation of weapons of mass destruction, including nuclear, biological, and chemical weapons; their delivery systems; and related material. VBSS operations are the procedures by which forces conduct MIO, EMIO, and MCPI boardings and searches in order to determine the true character and nature of vessels, cargo, and passengers.

The UN Charter assigns the fifteen-member Security Council primary responsibility for the maintenance of international peace and security.[87] The council generally acts under the authority conferred by Chapter VI (pacific settlement of disputes) or Chapter VII (actions in response to threats to the peace, breaches of the peace, and acts of aggression).[88] If it finds, pursuant to Article 39, that a situation threatens international peace or constitutes a breach of the peace or an act of aggression, the council has the authority to, inter alia, impose an economic embargo (and interrupt rail, sea, and air communications) under its Article 41 authority.[89] If, on the other hand, it finds that Article 41 measures will be or have been inadequate, the council may impose more severe measures under Article 42, including blockade or the use of armed force. Alternatively, it may simply authorize the use of "all necessary means" to restore international peace and security. Because the UN does not have its own armed force (or law enforcement

---

83. The MIO acronym has been used to refer alternatively to maritime interdiction operations and maritime *interception* operations. The term "interdiction" has a negative connotation for some states.

84. Chairman, Joint Chiefs of Staff, DoD Dictionary of Military and Associated Terms, Joint Pub. 1-02 defines maritime interception operations as the "efforts to monitor, query, and board merchant vessels in international waters to enforce sanctions against other nations such as those in support of United Nations Security Council Resolutions and/or prevent the transport of restricted goods."

85. Law enforcement operations (LEO) are a specialized form of interception operations. The Coast Guard is the lead agency for maritime LEO. DoD personnel are generally precluded by the Posse Comitatus Act from direct involvement in LEO.

86. Commander's Handbook, supra, ¶ 4.4.4.1. The other seven bases for conducting MIO include operations pursuant to Security Council resolutions, flag state consent, master's consent, right of visit, stateless vessels, conditions on port entry, and bilateral/multilateral agreements.

87. UN Charter, supra, art. 24(1).

88. The General Assembly is delegated limited dispute settlement (peacekeeping) authority under Chapter VI. See UN Charter, supra, arts. 34 & 35; see also id. arts. 11, 12, & 14.

89. Most commentators reject the notion that the laws of neutrality are relevant in the context of an embargo or blockade imposed by the Security Council under Chapter VII. In 1945 the French government was the first to take the position that no nation could be neutral with respect to actions by a state in violation of the UN Charter. See Documents of the United Nations Conference on International Organizations, vol. 6, at 312, 400–401 (1945); Commander's Handbook, supra, ¶ 4.4.4.1.1.

agency),[90] enforcement measures are ordinarily carried out by member states.[91] The Security Council determines whether the enforcement of its decision will be undertaken by all member states or only by those it designates.[92] The applicable Security Council resolution will generally define the means that the participating states may employ to carry out the enforcement measures imposed by the resolution.[93]

The history of UN Security Council resolutions imposing selective or full embargoes against states embroiled in armed conflict or other grave security circumstances now spans more than four decades.[94] The resolutions have taken a number of forms. A 1966 resolution imposed a maritime blockade and authorized the use of force to enforce it.[95] Another authorized seizure and forfeiture of vessels and cargoes found to be in violation of the resolution.[96] Recent Chapter VII measures, including those imposed in response to conflicts in the former Yugoslavia[97] and in Iraq,[98] required prolonged maritime enforcement measures. Very few Chapter VII resolutions have authorized participating states to take extraterritorial enforcement measures against nonnationals (i.e., high-seas boardings) or to conduct enforcement operations in the territorial sea of a state without the coastal state's consent.[99] Whether express authorization is required for third-party enforcement of a mandatory Chapter VII measure, without flag state consent, remains a subject of dispute.[100] One view holds that a warship would not be acting unlawfully if it boarded

---

90. The charter envisioned that member states would enter into agreements with the UN to make armed forces, assistance, and facilities available to the Security Council, under plans to be developed with the assistance of a Military Assistance Committee. See UN Charter, supra, arts. 43 & 45. In the nearly seventy-year history of the UN, however, no such agreements have been concluded.

91. All members of the UN are required to accept and carry out the decisions of the Security Council. UN Charter, supra, arts. 25 & 49.

92. Id. art. 48.

93. See generally U.S. Department of Justice, Office of Legal Counsel, Memorandum for Alan J. Kreczko, Special Assistant to the President and Legal Adviser to the National Security Council, Placing of United States Armed Forces under United Nations Operational or Tactical Control, May 8, 1996, 20 Op. Off. Legal Counsel 182 (1996).

94. See Alfred H. A. Soons, Enforcing the Economic Embargo at Sea, in United Nations Sanctions and International Law 307–08 (W. Gowlland-Debbas ed., 2001) (identifying fourteen such resolutions, six of which entailed maritime enforcement measures); Robin R. Churchill, Conflicts between United Nations Security Council Resolution and the 1982 United Nations Convention on the Law of the Sea, and Their Possible Resolution, 84 U.S. Nav. War Coll. Int'l L. Studies 143 (2008); Richard Zeigler, Ubi Sumus? Quo Vadimus? Charting the Course of Maritime Interception Operations, 43 Nav. L. Rev. 1 (1996).

95. S.C. Res. 221, U.N. Doc. S/RES/221 (Apr. 9, 1966) (concerning the situation in southern Rhodesia). The resolution authorized the use of force to enforce the blockade on the port of Beira.

96. See, e.g., S.C. Res. 820, ¶ 25, U.N. Doc. S/RES/820 (Apr. 17, 1993) (in response to the Bosnian crisis, directing that vessels in violation "shall be impounded and, where appropriate, they and their cargoes may be forfeited to the detaining state"). Such authority is rare. More commonly, vessels in violation of the embargo are diverted or otherwise prevented from delivering cargo to the target state.

97. See, e.g., S.C. Res. 1160, U.N. Doc. S/RES/1160 (Mar. 31, 1998) (¶ 8 imposed an embargo on arms and related materiel of all types, but it did not authorize boardings by states other than the flag state). A 1999 announcement by NATO states of plans to interdict oil shipments into Yugoslavia through the Strait of Otranto proved controversial.

98. See, e.g., S.C. Res. 665, U.N. Doc. S/RES/665 (Aug. 25, 1990) (calling upon member states that have deployed maritime forces to the Iraq-Kuwait theater to use such measures as are necessary to halt all inward and outward maritime shipping, in order to inspect and verify their cargoes and destinations, to ensure compliance with the embargo imposed by Resolution 661).

99. There are reports that vessels assigned to the Multinational Interception Forces, possibly from Australia, may have pursued ships suspected of violating the UN embargo on Iraq into the territorial sea of neighboring Iran. See Lois E. Fielding, Maritime Interception Centerpiece of Economic Sanctions in the New World Order, 53 La. L. Rev. 1191, 1223–24 & n.182 (1993).

100. See Soons, supra, at 316–17 (identifying two views on the question). See also Commander's Handbook, supra, ¶ 4.1.1.

and diverted a foreign ship to enforce a Security Council resolution, even if the resolution did not expressly provide for third-party enforcement.[101] The United States rejected that view in a 2009 incident involving the North Korean cargo ship *Kang Nam I*, which was suspected of transporting materials in violation of Security Council Resolution 1874.

Three sets of Chapter VII resolutions issued by the Security Council since 1991 impose both individual state obligations and duties to cooperate in suppressing global terrorism and WMD proliferation.[102] Each resolution triggers the UN Charter's Article 1 obligation for all states to take effective collective measures to prevent and remove threats to the peace and the Article 2 obligation to refrain from giving assistance to any state and, by necessary implication, any nonstate entity against which the UN is taking preventive or enforcement action.[103] Resolution 1373 calls upon states to cooperate "particularly through bilateral and multilateral arrangements and agreements, to prevent and suppress terrorist attacks and take actions against perpetrators of such acts."[104] Resolution 1526, which directly responded to the September 11, 2001, attacks on the United States, among other things calls on flag states to prevent the direct or indirect supply or transfer of arms or related materials and the use of their vessels or aircraft in the transport of arms and related materials to the individuals or organizations on a "consolidated list" that includes the Taliban; al Qaeda; and other individuals, groups, undertakings, and entities associated with them.[105] The obligation of flag states to prevent the use of their vessels or aircraft to transport arms and related material to those on the consolidated list is clearly mandatory under Resolution 1617.[106] Moreover, individuals or entities that supply, sell, or transfer arms and related material to those on the consolidated list will be deemed to be "associated with" al Qaeda or the Taliban.[107] Resolution 1540, discussed below, calls upon all states to "take cooperative action to prevent illicit trafficking in nuclear, chemical or biological weapons, their means of delivery, and related materials."[108] The Security Council has also passed a family of resolutions seeking to halt and reverse nuclear weapons programs in North Korea and Iran.

Not every activity that threatens international peace and security is a violation of domestic law. Put another way, not every successful MIO boarding will lead to a law enforcement action, as the December 2002 interception of the *M/V So San* by Spanish and U.S. naval patrol forces in the western Indian Ocean demonstrated. Exercising a right of visit under Article 110, VBSS teams discovered fifteen Scud ballistic missiles, missile components, and propellant being shipped from North Korea to the Mideast.[109] Because the vessel was not in violation of any applicable Spanish or U.S. domestic law, however, it was released to deliver its cargo to Yemen.

---

101. See Soons, supra, at 317. Professor Soons relies on the duty of all states to comply with resolutions of the Security Council and concludes that if the flag state fails to comply, third-party action may be justified as a lawful countermeasure or, alternatively, under the principle of necessity.

102. The principal resolutions of interest include 687 (Iraq), 1172 (affirming that the proliferation of WMD constitutes a threat to international peace and security), 1373, 1540, and 1617. See also Jochen Frowein & Nico Kirsch, introduction to Chapter VII, in The Charter of the United Nations: A Comment 701–16 (Bruno Simma et al. eds., 2d ed. 2002).

103. UN Charter, supra, arts. 1(1) & 2(5).

104. S.C. Res. 1373, ¶ 3(c) U.N. Doc. S/RES/1373 (Sept. 28, 2001). The "calls upon" language indicates that the action called for is not mandatory.

105. S.C. Res. 1526, ¶ 1(c), U.N. Doc. No. S/RES/1526 (Jan. 30, 2004).

106. S.C. Res. 1617, ¶ 1(c), U.N. Doc. No. S/RES/1617 (July 29, 2005).

107. Id. ¶ 2.

108. S.C. Res. 1540, ¶ 8, U.N. Doc. No. S/RES/1540 (Apr. 28, 2004).

109. The facts are taken primarily from U.S. Department of State, Digest of United States Practice in International Law 2002, at 1052–57.

4. Combating Piracy

The recorded history of piracy stretches back more than two millennia. Pirates raided the fleets of the Assyrian kings and Alexander the Great. The Roman emperor Julius Caesar was reportedly taken hostage by pirates. Cicero famously condemned pirates as *hostis humani generis*—the enemies of all humankind.[110] In his *Mare Liberum*, published in 1609, Hugo Grotius recognized that the unique criminal jurisdiction over pirates dated back to Roman times.[111] By the time Daniel Defoe wrote his *General History of the Robberies and Murders of the Most Notorious Pyrates* in 1724, the "Golden Age" of piracy had terrorized the coasts of the New World for nearly three decades, and the law's treatment of the pirate had grown increasingly harsh. London's Newgate Prison, a swift and summary trial, and a gallows on the bank of the Thames awaited any pirate captured and returned to England.

By 1925, however, the incidence of piracy was so insignificant that a writer for the *Harvard Law Review* questioned the continued need for a law of piracy.[112] The answer to that question came in the late 1970s, when piracy incidents began to surge, particularly in the Straits of Singapore and Malacca. By 1983 the International Maritime Organization felt compelled to urge all states to give the "highest priority" to measures to prevent and suppress acts of piracy and armed robbery against ships, and in 1992 the International Maritime Bureau (IMB) established the Piracy Reporting Center in Kuala Lumpur, Malaysia. Today, annual statistics collected by the IMB demonstrate that the rumors of piracy's death were greatly exaggerated.[113] In 2012 the IMB Piracy Reporting Center received 297 reports of pirate attacks throughout the world (down from 439 attacks in 2011 and 445 in 2010), of which 28 resulted in the ship being hijacked. As this chapter was being written, pirates in Somalia were holding 8 vessels and 127 crewmember hostages for ransom.[114] Resurgent ransom piracy—often leading to torture and/or death of the hostages—has turned some areas of the world into virtual war zones. The pirates' tactics, the accompanying violence, and the geographic range of their operations sorely test the limits of the traditional law enforcement approach.

In most regions, pirates focus on robbing the vessel and its crew. The more ambitious ones might hijack the ship and later sell its cargo or even the ship itself. Early piracy off the Somali coast typically followed that pattern, in some cases preying on cargo ships carrying World Food Program relief supplies to Somalia. Taking advantage of the "safe havens" available in the many lawless regions of Somalia,[115] the pirates soon shifted to ransom piracy. Pirates now forcibly board merchant or fishing vessels at sea, take the crew hostage, and force them to sail the ship into Somali waters, where the ship and crew remain, sometimes within sight of multinational patrol vessels offshore, until the vessel's owner ransoms the vessel and crew.[116] When an owner

---

110. See Marcus Tullius Cicero, *De Republica* bk. III (ca. 54–51 BCE; Clinton Walker Keyes trans., 1928).
111. Hugo Grotius, *Mare Liberum* (The Freedom of the Seas: or the Right Which Belongs to the Dutch to Take Part in the East Indian Trade), at 35 (1608; Ralph Van Deman Magoffin trans., James Brown Scott ed., 1916).
112. Edwin D. Dickinson, Is the Crime of Piracy Obsolete?, 38 Harv. L. Rev. 334 (1925).
113. Periodic reports are compiled by the International Maritime Bureau, Piracy Reporting Center, available at http://www.icc-ccs.org/ (accessed Feb. 1, 2013).
114. International Chamber of Commerce, Piracy Reporting Center, Piracy and Armed Robbery News and Figures, available at http://www.icc-ccs.org/piracy-reporting-centre/piracynewsafigures (accessed Feb. 1, 2013).
115. From 1992 to 2000 Somalia had no functioning government. In 2000 the Transitional Federal Government (TFG) gained general recognition among other states; however, many areas of the country are not under TFG control.
116. In contrast to the stated policy of most states never to negotiate with terrorists or give in to their demands, payment of multimillion-dollar ransoms to Somali pirates was common. Intelligence suggests that some of the

refuses or delays more than the pirates think reasonable, the hostages may be tortured or killed. Pirates have tortured or killed hostages in publicized reprisals to deter rescue attempts.

Early pirate attacks occurred in waters immediately off the coast of Somalia. When the ships' track lines were moved further offshore to avoid the pirates, the pirates adjusted, moving increasingly east and south and ranging two hundred nautical miles or more seaward. Their methods also grew increasingly bold and violent. In 2005 a boatload of pirates attacked the cruise ship *Seabourn Spirit* with machine guns and rocket-propelled grenades one hundred nautical miles off the coast of Somalia. In 2011 four Americans who were cruising the Indian Ocean on their sailboat *The Quest* were shot dead by pirates in full view of U.S. Navy ships coming to rescue them. The month before, in a particularly bloody rescue of the cargo ship *Samho Jewelry* in the Arabian Sea by South Korean commandos, eight pirates armed with assault rifles and antitank missiles were killed by the rescue team—but not before one of the pirates shot the ship's master in the abdomen in an apparent demonstration meant to deter future rescue attempts.

In the early phases of counterpiracy operations off the Horn of Africa, distinguishing opportunistic pirates from subsistence fishermen in a region where even legitimate fishermen carry weapons for self-defense was a daunting challenge. As pirate bands moved further offshore and staged their operations from mother ships, that presented less of a challenge.

U.S. Maritime Administration (MARAD) piracy advisories for the waters immediately off the coast of Somalia have now been extended well eastward into the Arabian Sea and Indian Ocean. The MARAD advisories designate certain "high-risk waters" and call on transiting vessels to employ best management practices to protect against pirate attacks off the coast of Somalia.[117] In 2009 the Contact Group on Piracy off the Coast of Somalia (CGPCS) was established, pursuant to UN Security Council Resolution 1851. The CGPCS coordinates actions among states and organizations to suppress piracy off the coast of Somalia. The forum brings together more than sixty states and international organizations working toward the prevention of piracy off the Somali coast.

The piracy epidemic off the Somali coast also prompted a broad multinational military response.[118] The multinational Combined Maritime Forces (CMF) was established in 2002 to promote security, stability, and prosperity across approximately 2.5 million square miles of international waters including the Gulf of Aden, the Southern Red Sea, and the Indian Ocean. CMF oversees three combined task forces whose missions are to defeat terrorism, prevent piracy, and encourage regional cooperation to promote a safe maritime environment. In January 2009 CMF stood up Combined Task Force 151 to conduct counterpiracy operations in the greater Gulf of Aden, a patrol area estimated to extend over 1.1 million square miles. Drawing on the vessels and maritime patrol aircraft and intelligence apparatus provided by volunteer states,[119] the task force's stated mission is to actively deter, disrupt, and suppress piracy in order to protect global maritime security and secure freedom of navigation for the benefit of all nations. Command of CTF 151 has rotated among the Danish, South Korean, Pakistani, Thai, Turkish, and U.S.

---

ransom payments found their way to Somali warlords or terrorist organizations. Richard Lough, Piracy Ransom Cash Ends Up with Somali Militants, Reuters, Jul. 6, 2011 (quoting a UN official report that "links between armed pirate gangs and Somalia's al Qaeda–affiliated rebels were gradually firming").

117. See, e.g., U.S. Maritime Administration, Best Management Practices for Protection against Somalia Based Piracy, version 4 (2011), available at http://www.marad.dot.gov/documents/Piracy_Best_Management_Practices.pdf (accessed Feb. 1, 2013).

118. See Tullio Treves, Piracy, Law of the Sea, and Use of Force: Developments off the Coast of Somalia, 20 Eur. J. Int'l L. 399 (2009).

119. Some states operate outside the CMF framework to protect ships flying their flag, leaving general maritime security enforcement to the more community-minded states. See Martin N. Murphy, International Cooperation against Piracy: China's Role, Problems and Prospects, 11 World Mar. Univ. J. Mar. Aff. 71 (2012); Chi Manjiao, A Note on China's Legal and Operational Responses to International Piracy, 44 Ocean Dev. & Int'l L. 113 (2013).

navies, among others. CTF 151's efforts are supplemented by units assigned to NATO's Operation Ocean Shield and the EU's Naval Force Somalia and its Operation Atalanta. The naval presence, together with the increasing use of armed private security service forces on board transiting vessels, has significantly reduced the incidence of attacks, but it is too soon to tell whether those gains will prove to be lasting if the deployed naval forces are scaled down or the armed security guards are removed from the transiting ships. So long as the lawless regions of Somalia provide pirates with a safe haven and shipowners and their insurers pay multimillion-dollar ransoms to obtain release of their ships and crews, geopolitical realities in the area favor the pirates.[120] Although a few pirates have been captured, prosecuted, and sentenced to long periods of confinement, many have been the happy beneficiaries of a "catch and release" policy adopted by some patrolling states to free them from the unpleasant, politically charged, and legally risky business of detainee operations.[121]

a. Historical Development of the Law of Piracy

International lawyers are prone to wince at the all-too-common solecisms involving the use of the term "piracy." "Piracy" has become the epithet of choice for virtually any maritime crime about which the speaker feels strongly. Thus, environmental groups condemn "pirate fishing vessels" and "pirate whaling ships." European states referred to high-seas radio broadcasters as "pirate radio." The United States condemned the Cambodian Navy's 1975 seizure of the U.S. merchant vessel *Mayaguez* as an act of piracy. The 1985 hijacking of the cruise ship *Achille Lauro* by Palestinian terrorists and the murder of a disabled American passenger was similarly labeled piracy.[122] In fact, none of those incidents constitutes an act of piracy under international law. For international lawyers, the solecisms are more than a mere pedantic quarrel with an imprecise use of terminology. True piracy under international law (piracy *jure gentium*),[123] in contrast to other maritime violence, is a crime of universal jurisdiction. It is, in fact, the oldest and most widely accepted crime to qualify as one over which all states have jurisdiction, without regard to the flag of the involved vessels or the nationality of the pirates or their victims.

The laws of piracy date back more than two millennia.[124] Efforts to codify the law formally began in 1932 when the Group on Research in International Law of Harvard Law School published a Draft Convention and Comment on Piracy.[125] The draft convention consisted of nineteen articles and an extensive commentary derived principally from the group's review of various scholarly writings on the subject of piracy. In 1949, some seventeen years after the publication of

120. Martin N. Murphy, Small Boats, Weak States, Dirty Money: Piracy and Maritime Terrorism in the Modern World (2009).
121. Some patrolling states are limited to "disrupt and deter" measures. Under that approach, captured pirates are generally transported ashore by the patrol ship's small boat and then released. The pirate vessel is typically destroyed. See generally Commander's Handbook, supra, ¶ 4.6. See also Douglas Guilfoyle, Counter-piracy Law Enforcement and Human Rights, 59 Int'l Comp. L. Q. 141–69 (2010). Warships of EU member states must, of course, be mindful of the ruling of the European Court of Human Rights in the Hirsi Jamaa et al. v. Italy, 51 I.L.M. 423 (Eur. Ct. Human Rights 2012) case discussed in chapter 11 and its liberal test for "effective control" in *non-refoulement* matters.
122. See Malvina Halberstam, Terrorism on the High Seas: The *Achille Lauro*, Piracy and the IMO Convention on Maritime Safety, 82 Am. J. Int'l L. 269–310 (1988).
123. "Piracy" under international law must be distinguished from the broader definition used by the IMB and in the statutes of many coastal states, which may include piracy-like offenses in the territorial sea or other armed violence not amounting to piracy under Article 101 of the LOSC.
124. Restatement FRLUS § 522 cmt. c & n.2.
125. Harvard Research in International Law, Draft Convention on Piracy, reprinted in 26 Am. J. Int'l L. 739 (Supp. 1932); Dickinson, Is the Crime of Piracy Obsolete?, supra (discussing doctrinal confusion about piracy as an international or municipal crime).

the Harvard Group's Draft Convention, the International Law Commission appointed a working group to draft a convention for the high seas that would include articles on piracy. The ILC report contained just six articles on piracy, all of which closely followed those developed by the Harvard Group.[126] After extensive debate and further deliberations, the full ILC drew up a final report containing eight articles on piracy and issued it to the UN General Assembly. Subject to a few nonsubstantive changes, the ILC's draft piracy provisions were codified by the UNCLOS I conferees in the 1958 Convention on the High Seas.

b. Piracy under the 1982 LOS Convention

The modern provisions on the international law of piracy are set out in Articles 100–107 of the 1982 LOS Convention.[127] Article 100 charges all states with a duty to cooperate in the repression of piracy on the high seas or in areas outside the territorial jurisdiction of any state.[128] The LOS Convention defines piracy in Article 101 as any illegal acts of violence, *or* any illegal acts of detention, *or* any act of "depredation," a term that covers plundering and pillaging.[129] Article 101 then limits the crime of piracy to acts committed for private ends. This requirement continues to be a source of contention, as courts and scholars examine application of the piracy definition to public or political acts, on the one hand, and private acts, on the other, particularly with respect to terrorist acts and, more recently, violent environmental protest activities.[130] Article 101 also perpetuates the requirement that two vessels be involved in order for an act to qualify as piracy. For example, acts committed on a ship on the high seas by its own crew or passengers and directed only against the ship itself, like the 1985 *Achille Lauro* hijacking, are not acts of piracy, even when the purpose of the perpetrators was to seize the ship.

Article 101 contains an important geographical limitation. To fall within its purview, the act must take place on the high seas or "in a place outside the jurisdiction of any State."[131] Thus, Article 101 excludes what might otherwise be piratical acts from its definition when they take place in the territorial sea of a state.[132] Of course, the coastal state could choose to enforce purely domestic "piracy" laws within its territorial sea; however, such offenses would not be subject to universal jurisdiction. Whether similar acts committed in the EEZ constitute piracy requires an examination of Article 58(2) of the convention. It incorporates Articles 88–115 into the EEZ

---

126. Jean Pierre Adrien François (special rapporteur), Regime of the High Seas (1954), U.N. Document A/CN.4/79, 1954 Y.B. Int'l L. Comm'n, vol. II, at 7 (original in French).

127. See also Commander's Handbook, supra, ¶ 3.5; Guilfoyle, Shipping Interdiction and the Law of the Sea, supra, ch. 4.

128. LOSC art. 100.

129. Id. art. 101. See also Marjorie M. Whiteman, 6 Digest of International Law § 5 (1968).

130. In 1961 Portuguese rebels captured the Portuguese cruise ship *Santa Maria* while off the coast of Venezuela to protest the rule of Antonio Salazar, raising questions whether their acts were committed for private or political ends. For an early U.S. case examining insurgents under the law of piracy, see The *Ambrose Light*, 25 F. 408 (S.D.N.Y. 1885). In early 2013 a U.S. court of appeals held that violent acts by Sea Shepherd Conservation Society vessels directed against Japanese whaling vessels in the Southern Ocean constituted piracy under Article 101 of the LOS Convention. See Institute of Cetacean Research v. Sea Shepherd Conserv. Soc'y, 708 F.3d 1099 (9th Cir. 2013). Similarly, in 1986 the Belgian Court of Cassation held that a Greenpeace vessel had committed piracy against a Dutch vessel believed to be guilty of pollution when Greenpeace attacked it, because the act of violence was "in support of a personal point of view" and not political. Castle John v. NV *Mabeco*, (Belg. Ct. Cassation, Dec. 19, 1986), 77 Int'l L. Rep. 537, 540 (1986).

131. This refers chiefly to "acts committed by a ship or aircraft on an island constituting *terra nullius* or on the shore of an unoccupied territory."

132. A U.S. federal court applied the twelve-nautical-mile limit on the territorial sea even when the coastal state purported to claim a wider sea. See U.S. v. Ahmed Muse Salad, Order of Nov. 29, 2012, 2012 WL 6097444 (E.D. Va. 2012).

regime, insofar as they are not incompatible with the other EEZ articles. Accordingly, the major-ity view is that the high-seas piracy articles (100–107) are applicable in the EEZ.[133]

Article 103 defines a "pirate ship" as one that is intended by those in dominant control to be used for the purposes of committing one of the piratical acts described in Article 101, even if it has not yet done so. Similarly, a ship remains a pirate ship after commission of a piratical act as long as it remains under the control of the persons who committed the act, without regard to their present intention.

c. Piracy as a Universal Crime

As defined in Article 101 of the LOS Convention, the crime of piracy is subject to universal prescriptive, enforcement, and adjudicative jurisdiction.[134] Article 105 of the LOS Convention provides an exception to the general rule that a ship is subject to the exclusive enforcement juris-diction of its flag state on the high seas by permitting every state to seize pirate ships or ships taken by piracy, and to arrest and seize the persons and property on board. That jurisdiction may be exercised on the high seas, in the EEZ, or in any place beyond the jurisdiction of any state. Seizures of pirate ships may be carried out only by warships or military aircraft, or other ships or aircraft clearly marked and identifiable as being on government service and authorized to that effect.[135] Where the seizure has been effected without adequate grounds, the state making the seizure is liable to the flag state of the ship or aircraft for any loss or damage caused by the seizure.[136]

When disposing of the seized property and punishing the pirates, Article 105 implies that the courts of the state that carried out the seizure will apply national law. Thus, the piracy regime under the LOS Convention, while defining piracy as an "international" crime, suggests that domestic law is to be applied with respect to determining punishments and property disposition. Some states engaged in counterpiracy patrols welcomed the Security Council's recognition of the need to address the destruction of pirate vessels and equipment in order to better suppress the ongoing crimes.

d. Piracy as a Threat to International Peace and Security

Piracy in the Straits of Malacca and Singapore, the Gulf of Aden, and the Gulf of Guinea has attracted increasing attention by the regional states, the UN and IMO, and the cognizant com-batant commanders. Sixteen Asian states established the Regional Co-operation Agreement on Combating Piracy and Armed Robbery against Ships in Asia (ReCAAP) in 2004 to promote interstate cooperation and capacity building.[137] ReCAAP operates an information-sharing center in Singapore. Other concerned states instituted the Code of Conduct concerning the Repression

---

133. United Nations Convention on the Law of the Sea: A Commentary, vol. III, at 196–223 (Myron Nordquist ed., 1995).

134. As early as 1927, Judge John Bassett Moore explained that with respect to piracy under the law of nations, "there has been conceded a universal jurisdiction, under which the person charged with the offence may be tried and punished by any nation into whose jurisdiction he may come." The S.S. *Lotus* case (France v. Turkey), 1927 P.C.I.J. (ser. A) No. 9 (Sept. 7), ¶¶ 248–50 (Moore, J. dissenting). The courts of Kenya and the Seychelles have adjudicated a number of piracy cases involving foreign nationals interdicted and arrested by the maritime patrol forces of CTF 151 and the European Union. In October 2012 the Kenyan Court of Appeal ruled that the state's courts have jurisdiction to try foreign pirates caught in international waters.

135. LOSC art. 107.

136. Id. art. 106.

137. Regional Co-operation Agreement on Combating Piracy and Armed Robbery against Ships in Asia, 2398 U.N.T.S. 199, 44 I.L.M. 829 (2005).

of Piracy and Armed Robbery against Ships in the Western Indian Ocean and the Gulf of Aden (the Djibouti Code) in 2009.[138] The code addresses capacity building, training, information sharing, apprehension and prosecution of pirates, and protection of victims. The code also calls for establishment of three regional information-sharing centers. In early 2013, in response to the growing number of piracy and armed robbery incidents in the Gulf of Guinea,[139] which some predict will soon overtake the Horn of Africa as the leading piracy hotspot, seven regional states,[140] in cooperation with the EU, launched the Critical Maritime Routes in the Gulf of Guinea Program. The program seeks to improve the safety and security of the main regional shipping routes by providing training and other capacity-building measures and by establishing a regional information-sharing network.

In late 2007 the IMO Assembly passed a resolution calling on the Somali TFG to advise the UN Security Council that the TFG would consent to foreign warships entering Somalia's territorial sea to suppress the pirate attacks.[141] The TFG consented on February 27, 2008, and on June 2, 2008, the UN Security Council issued Resolution 1816 finding that incidents of piracy and armed robbery against vessels in the territorial waters of Somalia and the high seas off the coast of Somalia constitute a threat to international peace and security in the region (focusing mainly on the threat to peace in Somalia). Exercising its powers under Chapter VII of the UN Charter, the council authorized "all necessary means" to suppress acts of piracy and armed robbery at sea.[142] It also affirmed that international law, as reflected in the 1982 LOS Convention, sets out the legal framework applicable to combating piracy and armed robbery. At the same time, however, the council took note of the TFG's urgent request for assistance in securing the territorial and international waters off the coast of Somalia for the safe conduct of shipping and navigation. In response to that request, the council authorized, for an initial period of six months, foreign vessels "co-operating with the TFG in the fight against piracy and armed robbery at sea" to enter the territorial waters of Somalia for the purpose of repressing acts of piracy and armed robbery.[143] The initial six-month authorization has been extended several times. Resolution 1851 went a step further, authorizing operations "in Somalia" (not just in Somalia's territorial sea), with the TFG's consent, but added a somewhat puzzling requirement that any actions taken under the resolution must be consistent with international humanitarian law.[144] In response to a growing piracy problem off the opposite coast of Africa, the Security Council adopted resolutions in 2011 and 2012 to address piracy in the Gulf of Guinea, but neither resolution grants new enforcement authority.[145]

---

138. IMO, Resolution C102/14 (April 3, 2009), annex.

139. In early 2013, Worldwide Threat to Shipping Reports compiled by the U.S. Navy's Office of Naval Intelligence (http://www.oni.navy.mil/Intelligence_Community/piracy.htm) reported that piracy and armed robbery incidents off Africa's west coast now outnumber those on the east coast. Many of the west coast incidents occurred in the ports or nearshore territorial waters of Nigeria and would therefore not constitute piracy under the LOS Convention.

140. The seven states are Benin, Cameroon, Equatorial Guinea, Gabon, Nigeria, São Tomé and Principe, and Togo.

141. IMO, IMO Doc. A 25/Res.1002 (Dec. 6, 2007).

142. S.C. Res. 1816, U.N. Doc. S/RES/1816 (June 2, 2008).

143. The Security Council authorization addresses the concern that Somalia lacks an effective government to grant consent to counterpiracy actions in the state's territorial sea. The temporary authority provided by S.C. Res. 1816 has been extended several times. See, e.g., S.C. Res. 1846, U.N. Doc. S/RES/1846 (Dec. 2, 2008).

144. S.C. Res. 1851, U.N. Doc. S/RES/1851 (Dec. 16, 2008). The reference to international humanitarian law (also known as the law of armed conflict) is puzzling because the counterpiracy operations do not constitute an armed conflict. One possible explanation is that the council was preserving the application of LOAC to the ongoing noninternational armed conflict in Somalia.

145. See, e.g., S.C. Res. 2018, U.N. Doc. S/RES/2018 (Oct. 31, 2011); S.C. Res. 2039, U.N. Doc. S/RES/2036 (Feb. 29, 2012).

e. Piracy under U.S. Law

Piracy is the only crime expressly named in the U.S. Constitution's "define and punish" article.[146] The United States has enacted two statutory responses to piracy. One concerns the use of the armed forces to protect U.S. shipping from pirate attacks; the other criminalizes the act of piracy, providing a basis for arrest and prosecution. The statute criminalizing piracy was among the first passed by the U.S. Congress. It provides that "whoever, on the high seas, commits the crime of piracy as defined by the law of nations, and is afterwards brought into or found in the United States, shall be imprisoned for life."[147] Notwithstanding its general reluctance to confer law enforcement powers on the armed forces, Congress also authorized the president to employ "public armed vessels" to protect merchant vessels of the United States and their crews from pirate attacks—one of the earliest statutes authorizing the employment of the armed forces against nonstate actors.[148] The antipiracy statutes go to on authorize the president to instruct those armed public vessels to seize pirate ships and to "retake any vessel of the United States or its citizens, which may have been unlawfully captured on the high seas."[149] A recently enacted federal "self-help" statute authorizing U.S. vessels to "oppose and defend" themselves against pirate attacks is examined in chapter 13.

5. Combating International Terrorism

The maritime domain has not been spared by transnational terrorist groups. The 2000 attack on the USS *Cole* (DDG-67) while it was taking on fuel in the port of Aden, Yemen, took the lives of seventeen crewmembers and injured thirty-eight more.[150] In 2002 terrorists belonging to the al Qaeda affiliate Aden-Abeyan Islamic Army used a small boat loaded with explosives to attack the French tanker *Limburg* as it transited past the Yemeni coast. One crewman was killed and more than 200,000 gallons of crude oil were released into the sea. On February 27, 2004, members of Abu Sayyaf planted a bomb on the Philippine-flag *Superferry 14*, killing more than one hundred of its passengers. Two months later, when an unidentified dhow approached Iraq's Khawr Al Amaya Oil Terminal, the USS *Thunderbolt* (PC-10), which was assigned to protect the offshore platform, dispatched a seven-member U.S. Navy and Coast Guard boarding team to intercept the dhow. As the boarding team approached the dhow in the *Thunderbolt*'s rigid hull inflatable boat, the dhow's crew detonated the onboard explosives meant for the platform, killing three members of the boarding team and wounding four others. Al Qaeda in Iraq claimed responsibility for the attack. In 2010 the terrorist group Abdullah Azzam Brigades attacked the T/V *M Star*, driving a small boat loaded with explosives into the laden supertanker as it navigated the Strait of Hormuz.

---

146. U.S. Const. art. I, § 8, cl. 10 ("Congress shall have the power to define and punish Piracies and Felonies committed on the High Seas, and Offenses against the Law of Nations").

147. 18 U.S.C. § 1651. This statute has recently been subject to intensive judicial scrutiny in federal prosecutions of pirates captured off the Horn of Africa. One recent case held that because the statute defines piracy by reference to the law of nations, its meaning evolves as the law of nations evolves. See U.S. v. Dire, 680 F.3d 446 (4th Cir. 2012) (holding that Congress intended to define piracy as a universal jurisdiction crime and incorporate a definition of piracy that changes with advancements in the law of nations). See also U.S. Department of State, Digest of United States Practice in International Law 2010, at 103.

148. 33 U.S.C. § 381. Counterpiracy operations by U.S. naval forces may require interagency coordination under the Maritime Operational Threat Response (MOTR) Plan. See Coast Guard MLE Manual, supra, appendix D.

149. 33 U.S.C. § 382. See also 33 U.S.C. §§ 384 &385 (seizure and condemnation of pirate ships).

150. Al Qaeda members Abd al-Rahim al-Nashiri and Abu Ali al-Harithi were later identified as key planners in the attack. Al-Nashiri was captured in late 2002 and faces criminal prosecution in the United States. Al-Harithi was reportedly killed in a Predator strike.

UN member states and the Security Council responded to these and other terrorist attacks with a variety of treaties and resolution-based measures. The family of UN conventions to combat terrorism follows a common pattern, requiring their states parties to criminalize the covered conduct and prosecute any person within their territory suspected of committing such an offense or extraditing them to another state for prosecution.[151] In addition, terrorism has been addressed by the UN Security Council in a number of resolutions that target terrorists' ability to travel and access to funds. The U.S. strategy for combating terrorism takes a defeat, deny, diminish, and defend approach.[152] It seeks to reduce both the scope and the capability of transnational terrorist organizations by attacking their sanctuaries, leadership, command, control, and communications; denying them sponsorship, support, and sanctuary; and diminishing the underlying conditions that terrorist organizations seek to exploit.

Transnational terrorism has been identified as a threat to international peace and security. A terrorist attack may also give rise to a right of individual and collective self-defense, subject to the necessity and proportionality constraints imposed under the *jus ad bellum*.[153] The LOS Convention does not directly address the threats posed by international terrorism. The gap in international law became apparent after the 1985 hijacking of the Italian cruise ship *Achille Lauro* by Palestinian terrorists. To close that gap, at least in part, a diplomatic conference convened under the auspices of the IMO drafted the 1988 Convention for the Suppression of Unlawful Acts against the Safety of Maritime Navigation (SUA Convention).[154] The SUA Convention entered into force in 1991 and by 2012 had some 160 parties. It is important to keep in mind, however, that while much of the LOS Convention reflects customary international law, the same cannot be said of the SUA Convention. The SUA Convention is binding only on states that are party to it. Although it is widely ratified, to this author's knowledge, no one has suggested that the SUA Convention has passed into customary law, such that it would be binding even on nonparties.

Covered offenses under the 1988 SUA Convention include any of the following when the act is done unlawfully and intentionally and is likely to endanger the safety of navigation: seizing a ship by force or intimidation; acts of violence against persons on board a ship; destroying or causing damage to a ship or its cargo; placing a device on board a ship that is likely to destroy or damage it; destroying, seriously damaging, or interfering with navigational facilities; communicating false information that endangers the safety of navigation; and injuring or killing a person in connection with any of the listed acts.[155] All states that are party to the SUA Convention are required to make the listed offenses punishable by appropriate penalties under their domestic law. The SUA Convention also allocates jurisdiction over the listed offenses. Generally, the flag

---

151. Tokyo Convention on Offences Committed On Board Aircraft (1963); Hague Convention for the Suppression of Unlawful Seizure of Aircraft (1970); Montreal Convention for the Suppression of Unlawful Acts against Civil Aviation (1971); New York Convention on Crimes against Internationally Protected Persons (1973); International Convention against the Taking of Hostages (1979); Convention on the Physical Protection of Nuclear Material (1980); Convention for the Suppression of Unlawful Acts against Safety of Civil Aviation (1988); Rome Convention for Suppression of Unlawful Acts against Safety of Maritime Navigation (1988); Protocol for Suppression of Unlawful Acts against Safety of Fixed Platforms Located on the Continental Shelf (1988); Convention on the Marking of Plastic Explosives (1991); Convention for the Suppression of Terrorist Bombing (1997); Convention for the Suppression of the Financing of Terrorism (1999); Convention for the Suppression of Acts of Nuclear Terrorism (2005).

152. The White House, The National Strategy for Combating Terrorism (2006), available at http://www.hsdl.org/ ?view&did=466588 (accessed Feb. 1, 2013).

153. Specially trained and equipped Marine Corps Fleet Antiterrorism Security Teams (FAST) are deployable on short notice for rapid response to terrorist threats or attacks.

154. See Commander's Handbook, supra, ¶ 3.14.

155. 1988 SUA Convention, supra, art. 3.

state has jurisdiction over offenses committed on vessels flying its flag, and the coastal state has jurisdiction over offenses in its territorial sea.[156] A state whose nationals were seized, threatened, injured, or killed may also assert jurisdiction. The SUA Convention includes the familiar "punish or extradite" requirement when an offender is found in the territory of a state party.[157] It is implemented in the United States by the International Maritime and Port Security Act.[158]

UN Security Council Resolution 731, issued in 1992 shortly after bombs planted by Libyan operatives destroyed Pan American Airlines flight 103 over Lockerbie, Scotland, and UTA flight 722 over the Sahara Desert, recognized the "right of all states to protect their nationals from acts of international terrorism that constitute threats to international peace and security." UN Security Council Resolution 1368, issued in response to the September 11, 2001, attacks, begins by announcing the council's determination to "combat by all means threats to international peace and security," and then recognizes the inherent right of individual or collective self-defense and stresses that those responsible for aiding, supporting, or harboring the perpetrators, organizers, and sponsors of these acts will be held accountable.[159] A few weeks later the council unequivocally condemned the terrorist attacks of September 11 and reaffirmed that acts of international terrorism constitute a threat to international peace and security.[160]

6. Combating Proliferation of WMD and Delivery Systems

Proliferation of nuclear, biological, and chemical weapons and their component parts and missile-delivery systems is a matter of grave concern. The 1982 LOS Convention does not address the illicit transport of weapons of mass destruction (WMD). Accordingly, the substantive bases for suppressing WMD proliferation must be found outside the law of the sea.[161] Those bases include national laws, multilateral export control regimes, UN Security Council resolutions, and a 2005 protocol to the SUA Convention.[162]

The U.S. National Strategy to Combat Weapons of Mass Destruction is built on three pillars: counterproliferation to combat WMD use, strengthened nonproliferation to combat WMD proliferation, and consequence management to respond to WMD use.[163] The strategy acknowledges that effective interdiction operations, enabled and enhanced through strengthened international cooperation, are essential to the success of the counterproliferation pillar. Strengthening international cooperation is the goal behind the Proliferation Security Initiative, through which participating states pool their authorities, capabilities, and competencies to combat the proliferation of WMD and their delivery systems. The initiative seeks to address the threats posed by both states and nonstate actors of proliferation concern.

---

156. Id. art. 6.
157. Id. arts. 6(4) & 10(1).
158. International Maritime and Port Security Act, Pub. L. No. 99-399, 100 Stat. 889 (1986); Violent Crime Control and Law Enforcement Act of 1994, Pub. L. No. 103-322, Title VI, § 60019(a), 108 Stat. 1975-1977 (1994) (codified in part at 18 U.S.C. §§ 2280–2281).
159. S.C. Res. 1368, U.N. Doc. S/RES/1368 (Sept. 12, 2001).
160. S.C. Res. 1373, U.N. Doc. S/RES/1373 (Sept. 28, 2001).
161. See generally Guilfoyle, Shipping Interdiction and the Law of the Sea, supra, ch. 9; Craig H. Allen, Maritime Counterproliferation Operations and the Rule of Law (2007).
162. The regime might one day be supplemented by the Draft Arms Trade Treaty, adopted by a UN-sponsored conference on March 27, 2013. See U.N. Doc. A/CONF.217/2013/L.3, Annex. If the treaty enters into force, it will restrict trade in "conventional arms," to include everything from warships and combat aircraft to missiles and missile launchers, as well as their component parts and munitions.
163. The White House, The National Strategy to Combat Weapons of Mass Destruction (2002), available at http://www.hsdl.org/?view&did=860 (accessed Feb. 1, 2013).

a. WMD Proliferation as a Threat to International Peace and Security

The UN Security Council has assumed a growing role in countering the proliferation of weapons of mass destruction and their delivery systems. Partly in response to the discovery that the Abdul Qadeer Kahn network, which operated out of Pakistan between the 1980s and 2004, was selling nuclear weapons technology and equipment to North Korea, Libya, and Iran[164] using components obtained or assembled in Europe, Dubai, and Malaysia,[165] the Security Council unanimously adopted Resolution 1540 in 2004. Exercising its Chapter VII authority, the council affirmed that the proliferation of nuclear, chemical, and biological weapons and their means of delivery pose a threat to international peace and security.[166] Recognizing that nuclear terrorism potentially poses one of the gravest threats to international security, Resolution 1540 obliges states to refrain from supporting, by any means, nonstate actors from developing, acquiring, manufacturing, possessing, transporting, transferring, or using WMD and their delivery systems. The resolution also established a committee within the UN to monitor implementation of the resolution. The 1540 committee's charge has been extended by several subsequent resolutions.[167]

The Security Council also found that nuclear and missile-delivery programs by North Korea and Iran pose a similar threat to international peace and security and imposed significant restrictions on their imports and exports. Enforcing the Security Council's import and export restrictions, as well as the complementary restrictions imposed at the national level, requires a substantial maritime component.

North Korea ratified the 1968 Treaty on the Non-proliferation of Nuclear Weapons (NPT) in 1985,[168] but then withdrew in 2003 and expelled the International Atomic Energy Agency's (IAEA) compliance inspectors. It subsequently developed and tested missiles on July 4, 2006, and its first nuclear device on October 9, 2006. In response, the Security Council unanimously passed Resolution 1695, condemning the tests and imposing sanctions on North Korea.[169] Shortly thereafter, the council established the Resolution 1718 Sanctions Committee to monitor compliance with those sanctions.[170] Three years later the Security Council adopted Resolution 1874, imposing significant new sanctions on North Korea, in response to its second nuclear device test in 2009.[171] In 2013, in response to North Korea's December 12, 2012, rocket launch, the council unanimously voted to tighten existing sanctions and add new ones.[172] Undeterred, North Korea conducted a third nuclear device test on February 12, 2013,[173] prompting still another resolution by the council.[174]

---

164. Paul Reynolds, Pakistan Leaks Prompt Western Resolve, BBC News.com, Feb. 5, 2004.
165. William J. Broad & David E. Sanger, The Bomb Merchant: Chasing Dr. Kahn's Network, NY Times, Dec. 26, 2004, at A1.
166. The legislative nature of the resolution has been questioned. See, e.g., Stefan Talmon, The Security Council as World Legislature, 99 Am. J. Int'l L. 175 (2005); Daniel H. Joyner, Non-proliferation Law and the United Nations System: Resolution 1540 and the Limits of the Power of the Security Council, 20 Leiden J. Int'l L. 489 (2007).
167. See, e.g., S.C. Res. 1673 (2006); S.C. Res. 1810 (2008); S.C. Res. 1977 (2011); S.C. Res. 2055 (2012).
168. Treaty on the Non-proliferation of Nuclear Weapons [hereinafter "NPT"], July 1, 1968, 21 U.S.T. 483, T.I.A.S. No. 6839, 729 U.N.T.S. 161.
169. S.C. Res. 1695, U.N. Doc. S/RES/1695 (July 15, 2006).
170. S.C. Res. 1718, U.N. Doc. S/RES/1718 (Oct. 14, 2006).
171. S.C. Res. 1874, U.N. Doc. S/RES/1874 (June 12, 2009). See also Exec. Order 13,570, Prohibiting Certain Transactions with respect to North Korea (Apr. 18, 2011).
172. S.C. Res. 2087, U.N. Doc. S/RES/2087 (Jan. 22, 2013).
173. The United States condemned the test as a violation of Resolutions 1718, 1874, and 2087.
174. S.C. Res. 2094, U.N. Doc. S/RES/2094 (Mar. 7, 2013).

Iran ratified the NPT in 1970 and remains a party to it. In response to allegations that Iran was engaged in undeclared nuclear activities in violation of the NPT, the IAEA launched an investigation that concluded in 2003 that Iran had systematically failed to meet its obligations under its NPT.[175] In 2006 the IAEA reported Iran's failure to comply with the NPT safeguards to the UN Security Council, which then imposed sanctions.[176] Resolution 1929, passed by the council in 2010, reaffirmed the threats posed by Iran's nuclear enrichment program and increased the sanctions imposed by the council's earlier resolutions.[177] The sanctions imposed on Iran by the Security Council joined a growing body of U.S. statutes, regulations, and presidential executive orders imposing sanctions on Iran that date back to the American embassy hostages crisis of 1979.[178] In addition, the United States and member states of the EU, among others, have imposed an interlocking matrix of sanctions relating to Iran's nuclear, missile, energy, shipping, transportation, and financial sectors.

Compliance with Security Council resolutions applicable to Iran is monitored by the Council's Resolution 1737 Sanctions Committee. Suspected violations of the resolutions are referred to the committee for investigation. For example, after the Yemeni Coast Guard intercepted an inbound vessel transporting a large shipment of explosives, mortars, rocket-propelled grenades, IED precursors, and man-portable antiaircraft missiles from Iran to Yemeni insurgents on January 23, 2013, Sana'a reported the incident to the Security Council committee as a probable violation of resolutions prohibiting arms exports from Iran.[179]

Despite the seriousness of the threat posed to international peace and security, none of the Security Council resolutions on the proliferation of WMD and their delivery systems have so far authorized enforcing states to board foreign flag vessels on the high seas to verify their compliance with trading restrictions imposed by the resolution. Nor does the Article 110 right of visit apply to such boardings (unless the vessel's nationality is questionable). When the acknowledged threat posed by WMD proliferation (or maritime terrorism) is compared with offenses like unauthorized broadcasting, it might seem odd to not include at least a right of visit in cases involving Security Council resolution enforcement addressed to those threats. While the logic is compelling for many, the short answer is that it has not yet proved to be compelling for the members of the Security Council. In the absence of such authority in the applicable resolutions, concerned states have turned to cooperative frameworks that encourage and facilitate information sharing, resource pooling, and, if appropriate, consensual boardings.

b. The Proliferation Security Initiative

The Proliferation Security Initiative (PSI) marked its tenth anniversary in May 2013. The one hundred plus participating states have all committed to undertake measures to interdict illicit transfers of weapons of mass destruction and missile-related items, exchange relevant

175. See IAEA, Implementation of the NPT Safeguards Agreement in the Islamic Republic of Iran, Nov. 10, 2003, IAEA Doc. GOV/2003/75. See also IAEA Docs. GOV/2003/63 (Aug. 26, 2003) and GOV/2003/40 (June 6, 2003).
176. See, e.g., S.C. Res. 1696 (2006); S.C. Res. 1737 (2006); S.C. Res. 1747 (2007); S.C. Res. 1803 (2008) and 1835 (2008).
177. S.C. Res. 1929, U.N. Doc. S/RES/1929 (June 9, 2010).
178. The Department of State's Office of Economic Sanctions Policy and Implementation and the Department of Treasury's Office of Foreign Assets Control (OFAC) are jointly responsible for implementing U.S. sanctions programs. U.S. sanctions on Iran impose broad restrictions on imports from Iran and on the export, sale, or supply of goods, technology, or services to Iran or to the government of Iran (including a multitude of entities listed in 31 C.F.R. § 560.304), unless licensed by OFAC. See, e.g., Iranian Transactions Regulations, 31 C.F.R. pt. 560.
179. See S.C. Res. 1747, ¶ 5. Similar issues concern Iranian arms shipments to Syria and to Hezbollah and Hamas.

information, and strengthen legal authorities to conduct interdictions. In 2011 the PSI-endorsing states launched a new initiative, led by the PSI Operational Experts Group, designed to build critical capabilities and practices for interdicting WMD. Endorsing states also conduct exercises, workshops, and other activities to improve their capacities to fulfill their PSI commitments. The PSI states carry out a variety of intelligence and enforcement actions in furtherance of initiative goals. All PSI interdictions are carried out in accordance with the Statement of Interdiction Principles.[180] The principles affirm a commitment to "establish a more coordinated and effective basis through which to impede and stop shipments of WMD, delivery systems, and related materials flowing to and from states and non-state actors of proliferation concern,"[181] while adhering to "national legal authorities and relevant international law and frameworks, including the UN Security Council." The PSI does not provide the participating states with any new legal authority or jurisdiction to conduct counterproliferation operations. Rather it relies on existing authorities while pledging to work to further develop those authorities.[182] The UN secretary-general has praised the PSI,[183] and the UN High-Level Panel on Threats, Challenges and Change report encouraged all states to join the PSI.[184] The PSI is not without its critics, but no one has yet identified any operation conducted under the PSI framework that violated the LOS Convention or other applicable international law.

The PSI encourages states to cooperate in their counterproliferation efforts. That cooperation takes the form of training, exercises, and an exchange of views. In addition, flag states are encouraged to authorize other states that are willing and able to carry out PSI investigation and enforcement activities to enter into agreements to that effect. The United States has concluded treaties with eleven flag states that grant qualified rights to board vessels to implement the PSI.[185] The agreements are modeled after existing agreements used for counternarcotics boardings (discussed in chapter 11). Expedited flag state approval provisions are a key element in the agreements. Interestingly, the PSI agreements are couched in terms of the flag state having the "primary right to exercise jurisdiction," but that right can be waived.[186]

Coastal state cooperation and consent could prove to be just as important to the success of PSI operations as the flag state agreements. For example, a vessel suspected of transporting WMD or delivery systems to state or nonstate actors of proliferation concern that was originally intercepted on the high seas might attempt to flee into the territorial sea of a third state to escape pursuit. Under existing law, the pursuing vessel could not continue its pursuit in the territorial sea of the coastal state in the absence of consent by that state. To facilitate cooperation and

---

180. Interdiction Principles for the Proliferation Security Initiative, Sept. 4, 2003, available at http://www.state.gov/t/isn/c27726.htm (accessed Feb. 1, 2013). See also Commander's Handbook, supra, ¶ 4.4.5; Chairman, Joint Chiefs of State, Instruction 3520.02A, Proliferation Security Initiative (PSI) Activity Program (2007).

181. The PSI participating states have not designated which states are "of proliferation concern." Resolution 1540 makes it clear that any proliferation involving nonstate actors is a matter of proliferation concern. Security Council resolutions regarding the nuclear weapons, delivery systems, and fissile material development programs by Iran and North Korea render both states of proliferation concern. Whether other states pose "proliferation concerns" might be determined by reviewing the operations of the A. Q. Khan network and examining reports presented to the Security Council's Resolution 1540 Committee.

182. Among those legal authorities is the state's inherent right to take necessary and proportionate steps in individual and collective self-defense in response to an armed attack or the imminent threat of an armed attack.

183. See Kofi Annan, March 10, 2006, speech in Madrid to the International Summit on Democracy, Terrorism and Security ("I applaud the efforts of the Proliferation Security Initiative to fill a gap in our defenses").

184. High-Level Panel on Threats, Challenges and Change, Final Report, supra, at 45.

185. The eleven states are Antigua and Barbuda, Bahamas, Belize, Croatia, Cyprus, Liberia, Malta, Marshall Islands, Mongolia, Panama, and Saint Vincent and the Grenadines. See U.S. Department of State, Proliferation Security Initiative, Ship Boarding Agreements, available at http://www.state.gov/t/isn/c27733.htm (accessed Feb. 1, 2013).

186. See, e.g., Bilateral WMD Ship Boarding Agreement, U.S.-Liberia, art. 5, available at http://www.state.gov/t/isn/c27733.htm (accessed Feb. 1, 2013).

consent, states participating in PSI operations "pool" their respective authorities and capabilities by drawing on the jurisdiction and enforcement resources of flag, coastal, and port states. Although information relevant to enforcement is often shared, the reluctance to disclose intelligence that will reveal a state's sources and methods, or that comes from another state that has not consented to disclosure, may frustrate the consent process if the flag state insists on full disclosure of the basis for the requesting state's suspicion that a vessel is engaged in illicit activity.

c. The 2005 Protocol to the SUA Convention

The IMO launched a major counterproliferation measure in 2001, when it put the 1988 SUA Convention under review.[187] The review efforts came to fruition in 2005, when a diplomatic conference approved the text of a new protocol to the SUA Convention.[188] The 2005 protocol entered into force for the United States and other states parties in 2010. By the end of 2012, 22 of the 160 states parties to the 1988 SUA Convention had ratified the protocol.

When more widely and effectively implemented, the 2005 protocol will criminalize the transport of WMD, their delivery systems, and related materials on vessels at sea.[189] The protocol calls attention to the "international will" to combat terrorism in all its forms and manifestations, as expressed in UN Security Council Resolutions 1368 and 1373. It also cites Resolution 1540 as evidence of the urgent need for all states to take additional effective measures to prevent the proliferation of WMD and their means of delivery. The protocol significantly expands the authority of states other than the vessel's flag state to conduct boardings, creating an expanded "right of visit," but only among parties to the protocol.[190] It also addresses the use of force in such visits. A state party in which a person suspected of committing an offense under the SUA Convention is found will have a duty to prosecute the individual or extradite that person to another state with jurisdiction to do so.[191] The protocol further instructs that none of the offenses should be considered a "political offense" for the purposes of extradition.[192] The protocol will also require states parties to afford one another assistance in connection with criminal proceedings brought in respect of offenses under the amended SUA Convention.[193]

G. LAW OF NAVAL WARFARE

U.S. naval forces operate throughout the range of military operations, but their raison d'être, according to Naval Doctrine Publication 1 on Naval Warfare, is "to defend the Nation and project combat power in war."[194] This book, however, focuses on the peacetime law of the sea.[195]

---

187. See IMO, Review of Measures and Procedures to Prevent Acts of Terrorism Which Threaten the Security of Passengers and Crews and the Safety of Ships, Res. A.924(22) (Nov. 20, 2001).
188. 2005 SUA Protocol, supra. The U.S. attached one reservation, five understandings, and a declaration that, with one exception, the protocol is self-executing. See S. Treaty Doc. No. 110-08, S. Ex. Rept. 110-25. See also Digest of U.S. Practice in International Law 2002, supra, at 104–10.
189. See 2005 SUA Protocol, supra, art. 4(5)–(7) (adding new offenses in Articles 3*bis*, 3*ter*, and 3*quater* to the SUA Convention). See also 18 U.S.C. §§ 2283 & 2284 (criminalizing the knowing transport of a terrorist or WMD on any U.S.-flag vessel or foreign vessel subject to U.S. jurisdiction or on the high seas).
190. 2005 SUA Protocol, supra, art. 8(2) (adding Article 8*bis* to the SUA Convention); Natalie Klein, The Right of Visit and the 2005 Protocol on the Suppression of Unlawful Acts against the Safety of Maritime Navigation, 35 Denver J. Int'l L. & Policy 287 (2007).
191. 2005 SUA Protocol, supra, art. 6, ¶ 3 (providing a substitute Article 6, ¶ 4 to the SUA Convention).
192. Id. art. 10 (adding Article 11*bis* to the SUA Convention). Offenses under the protocol are also deemed to be included as extraditable offenses in any extradition treaty existing between the states parties.
193. Id. art. 11 (providing a substitute Article 12, ¶ 1 to the SUA Convention).
194. NDP 1, Naval Warfare, supra, at iv.
195. The law of naval warfare is covered in chapters 5–12 of the Commander's Handbook. Many of the relevant source materials are accessible through the U.S. Naval War College's "Stockton e-Portal." http://usnwc.libguides.com/LOAC-IHL (accessed Feb. 1, 2013).

Readers seeking coverage of the means and methods of naval warfare, targeting, and the use of deception are encouraged to refer to the more specialized sources.[196] What follows is an examination of several crossover effects of armed conflicts on peacetime maritime operations. While international armed conflicts obviously pit the belligerents against each other, they also impose obligations and potentially onerous burdens on neutral states. The preamble to the 1909 Declaration concerning the Laws of Naval War (the London Declaration) called attention to the deleterious effect on "peaceful commerce" that ensues "in the unfortunate event of a naval war."[197]

The following sections examine several naval warfare practices that affect third states, including blockades, the law of neutrality, and the associated concepts of contraband and the right of visit, board, search, and capture. Chapter 13 examines issues involving the use of force at sea. It should be noted here that the law of naval warfare was developed in the context of *international* armed conflicts. Application of the law of neutrality and blockade in noninternational armed conflicts has not been authoritatively determined.

Seams and overlaps between peacetime naval operations and the various doctrines of naval warfare are a source of persistent confusion. In approaching these materials it is important to avoid confusing the peacetime right of visit under the 1982 LOS Convention discussed in chapter 11 and section F.2 of this chapter with the belligerents' right of visit and search to ensure compliance with the law of neutrality under the law of naval warfare or to enforce a blockade against the enemy. At the same time, when law enforcement activities by warships and constabulary forces confront organized criminal organizations and armed groups, the risks posed by the confrontation might bear many of the hallmarks of a classic naval confrontation. Indeed, America's first naval expeditionary "war" was against the pirates of the Barbary Coast.[198]

1. Derogation of LOS Convention during Armed Conflicts

Treaty drafters have largely avoided directly addressing the relationship between the centuries-old law of naval warfare and the more recently codified peacetime law of the sea.[199] For example, in contrast to the Chicago Convention on Civil Aviation,[200] the LOS Convention has no general derogation clause to address questions regarding possible suspension of treaty obligations during war or a declared national emergency. As a result, the question whether some or all of the LOS Convention can be suspended in time of armed conflict cannot be authoritatively

---

196. Parts of the materials in the following sections were adapted from authoritative statements in the Commander's Handbook on the Law of Naval Operations and the black letter rules in the San Remo Manual on International Law Applicable to Armed Conflicts at Sea. See also Jane Gilliland Dalton, A Comparison between the San Remo Manual and the U.S. Navy's Commander's Handbook, 36 Israeli Y.B. Human Rights 71 (2006); The Law of Naval Warfare (Natalino Ronzitti ed., 1988).

197. Declaration concerning the Laws of Naval War [hereinafter "London Declaration"], 208 Consol. T.S. 338 (1909). Presumably, "war" referred to an international armed conflict, not noninternational armed conflicts.

198. See Joseph Wheelan, Jefferson's War: America's First War on Terror, 1801–1805 (2003); Ivan W. Toll: The Epic History of the Founding of the U.S. Navy ch. 2 (2006).

199. See International Law Commission, Draft Articles on the Effects of Armed Conflicts on Treaties, adopted by the ILC at its sixty-third session, in 2011. Article 7 and the accompanying annex of the draft suggest the categories of treaties that should continue in force during an armed conflict. For U.S. comments on the draft articles, see Digest of United States Practice in International Law 2010, supra, at 155.

200. Chicago Convention on Civil Aviation, supra, art. 89 (war and emergency conditions) provides that "in case of war, the provisions of this Convention shall not affect the freedom of action of any of the contracting States affected, whether as belligerents or as neutrals. The same principle shall apply in the case of any contracting State which declares a state of national emergency and notifies the fact to the Council." See also 1923 Statute on the International Regime of Maritime Ports, supra, art. 16 (derogation of port access provisions with respect to belligerents and neutrals during wartime).

answered by resort to the LOS Convention.[201] A textual and structural analysis of the LOS Convention reveals that it does contain at least four provisions that address derogation. Article 25 permits a coastal state to temporarily suspend the right of innocent passage in some circumstances during peacetime. By contrast, Articles 44, 45, and 54 (incorporating Article 44) prohibit the coastal state from suspending transit or archipelagic sea-lanes passage. Logically, one could invoke the *expressio unius est exclusio alterius* canon of construction and argue that the convention drafters knew how to incorporate a derogation contingency when they felt it was warranted, and that by including one for suspension of innocent passage while prohibiting suspension in three other situations they knowingly rejected other possible derogations. Others call such arguments simplistic and note that the convention drafters were simply distinguishing between suspendable transit rights and nonsuspendable transit rights, without attempting to comprehensively address the question of derogation in times of armed conflict. Although the issue has not been addressed by the courts, at least two conclusions have wide support. First, the baseline and jurisdictional zones set out in the LOS Convention and state claims consistent with the convention fully apply during armed conflict. As a consequence, "neutral waters" under the law of naval warfare now extend to the twelve-nautical-mile territorial sea and to archipelagic waters claimed under the convention. A second conclusion, adopted in the *San Remo Manual*, is that the passage rights set out in the convention are, with minor exceptions, equally available to belligerents during armed conflicts.[202] Although belligerents enjoy a right of innocent, transit, and archipelagic sea-lanes passage,[203] the general prohibition on belligerents engaging in "hostile" activities or seeking "sanctuary" in neutral waters now extends up to twelve nautical miles seaward of all neutral states and in neutral archipelagic waters.[204] Those limitations do not apply, however, in the EEZ of a neutral state.[205]

Some issues remain contested. Those who take a strict stand against any derogation argue that an international or noninternational armed conflict does not affect the states' rights and obligations under the LOS Convention, most particularly with respect to neutrals.[206] That would mean, for example, that flag states, if neutral, would continue to have exclusive jurisdiction over their vessels and that belligerents could not lawfully board them to enforce the various specialized laws associated with naval warfare, including blockade, neutrality, contraband, or to enforce maritime operational zones. The issue was discussed but not resolved during the 1980–88 Iran-Iraq War.

Commentators are divided on the issue. One expert commentator examining the relationship between the LOS Convention and laws of naval warfare observed that "international law is in disarray as to whether war terminates or suspends treaties; most sources, considering the

---

201. The Vienna Convention on the Law of the Treaties addresses suspension and termination of treaty obligations. Recognized grounds include a fundamental change of circumstances; however, the Vienna Convention does not directly address situations involving armed conflicts. See Vienna Convention on Treaties, supra, art. 73 (sidestepping the issue). Much of the current research on derogation focuses on international human rights law during armed conflict.

202. San Remo Manual, supra, ¶¶ 29 & 33. See also id. ¶ 19.

203. Id. ¶ 15; Commander's Handbook, supra, ¶ 7.3.

204. San Remo Manual, supra, ¶ 14, 15. Prohibited "hostile" actions are enumerated in ¶ 16.

205. Commander's Handbook, supra, ¶ 7.3.8.

206. See, e.g., Mark W. Janis, Neutrality, 64 U.S. Nav. War Coll. Int'l L. Studies 148 (1991). See also A. V. Lowe, The Commander's Handbook on the Law of Naval Operations and the Contemporary Law of the Sea, 64 U.S. Nav. War Coll. Int'l L. Studies 109, 130–31 (1991) (concluding that "it is by no means clear that the traditional Laws of War retain their validity today").

pacta sunt servanda principle, emphasize suspension."[207] He concluded, however, that Articles 293 and 311 of the LOS Convention preserve application of "other" rules of international law not incompatible with the LOS Convention, save application of the law of armed conflict, including the law of naval warfare and the law of maritime neutrality."[208] By contrast, another respected commentator, writing in 1991, concluded that the UN Charter "terminated" the customary law of neutrality.[209] So long as the United States remains a nonparty to the 1982 LOS Convention while declaring that most of the convention reflects customary international law, the question is not strictly whether an outbreak of hostilities permits the suspension or termination of rights and obligations under the LOS Convention, but rather the relationship between the customary international law of the sea and the conventional and customary law of naval warfare.

2. Blockade

Blockades, the maritime equivalent of a terrestrial siege, have been employed by maritime powers against their enemies for centuries.[210] Like the neutrality enforcement measures discussed below, blockades can have a dramatic effect on neutral states and their vessels.[211] Historically, blockades have been considered an act of war.[212] Blockades are also among the "enforcement" measures the UN Security Council may impose when acting under its Chapter VII authority, as necessary to maintain or restore international peace and security.[213] Some observers thus view blockades by belligerent nations as relics of a Napoleonic Wars mindset that have no place in the UN Charter era unless authorized by the UN Security Council. The charter, however, recognizes the inherent right of self-defense, and states have continued the practice in the decades following the charter's entry into force. In the Korean conflict, naval forces supporting South Korea successfully used a relatively close-in blockade of both coasts of North Korea. During the last two weeks of the Indo-Pakistani war in 1971, the Indian navy maintained a blockade of more than 180 nautical miles of East Pakistan's coastline. In the 1982 Falkland Islands armed conflict between the United Kingdom and Argentina, the British declared a blockade of Argentina's 1,500-mile coastline and announced that any Argentine warship or plane found more than 12 nautical miles from its coast would be regarded as hostile and subject to attack. In 2012

---

207. George K. Walker, Professionals' Definitions and States' Interpretive Declarations (Understandings, Statements, or Declarations) for the 1982 Law of the Sea Convention, 21 Emory Int'l L. Rev. 461, 495, n.182 (2007).

208. Id. at 492, quoting the International Law Association (American Branch) Law of the Sea Committee's interpretation.

209. Janis, Neutrality, supra, at 148. State practice in the ensuring decades and the Palmer Commission report (discussed below) all cast doubt on Professor Janis' 1991 conclusion.

210. See Colombos, supra, §§ 814–17 (sixteenth- and seventeenth-century origins). See also Wolff Heintschel von Heinegg, Naval Blockade and International Law, in Naval Blockades and Seapower Strategies and Counter-Strategies, 1805–2005, at 10–22 (Bruce A. Elleman & S. C. M. Paine eds., 2006); John Bassett Moore, A Digest of International Law, vol. VII, ch. XVII (1906); U.S. Nav. War Coll., Maritime Operational Zones, supra, at 4-20– 4-30.

211. Professor O'Connell devotes a chapter to "economic warfare at sea," which includes the law of neutrality and blockade. O'Connell, supra, vol. II, ch. 30. There is an important distinction between the two bodies of law, however, and one that is overlooked even by the Commander's Handbook (which includes blockade in the chapter on neutrality). The purpose of law of neutrality is to protect neutral states, vessels, and their crews. By contrast, the law of blockade is a tool employed by belligerents to wage war against an enemy.

212. President Kennedy reportedly sought to avoid the legal consequences of declaring a blockade by using the term "quarantine" during the Cuban Missile Crisis with the Soviet Union and Cuba. According to Ted Sorenson, Kennedy's close friend and speech writer, the principals chose to call it a quarantine (because it was limited and selective), the lawyers called it a blockade, and Khrushchev called it high-seas piracy. See Commander's Handbook, supra, ¶ 4.4.8 (distinguishing quarantines and blockades).

213. UN Charter, supra, art. 42.

Argentina turned around and threatened a blockade of the Falkland Islands to pressure the United Kingdom to abandon its sovereignty over the islands. In the 2006 conflict between Israel and Hezbollah fighters in Lebanon, Israel, imposed a blockade on Lebanon.[214]

Blockades are imposed during war (what today is termed "international armed conflict") by a cordon of ships stationed off the entrance to an enemy port or coast for the purpose of preventing vessels from entering or leaving.[215] The ability of the Royal Navy to blockade Britain's enemies during the Napoleonic War is widely regarded as decisive in Britain's eventual victory. Although the purpose of a blockade remains the same today, advances in weapons, vessels, aircraft, and even spacecraft have led to a change in methods.

The 1909 London Declaration acknowledged the legality of blockades in time of "war."[216] The twenty-two articles in Chapter I of that declaration set out the legal requirements for a blockade, most of which remain valid today. Any blockade must be applied impartially to the vessels of all states. The blockade must be declared, and notice must be given to all belligerents and neutral states.[217] The cessation, temporary lifting, reestablishment, extension, or other alteration of a blockade must be likewise declared and notified. The declaration must specify the commencement, duration, location, and extent of the blockade and the period within which vessels of neutral states may leave the blockaded coastline. A blockade must not bar access to the ports and coasts of neutral states. A blockade is illegal if its sole purpose is to starve the civilian population or deny it other objects essential for its survival.[218] Similarly, a blockade would be deemed disproportionate if damage to the civilian population is, or may be expected to be, excessive in relation to the concrete and direct military advantage anticipated from the blockade.[219]

To be legal, any blockade must be effective.[220] Nominal or notional blockades are illegal. An effective blockade is one that ensures that a ship attempting to breach it will probably be captured. A blockade may be enforced and maintained by a combination of means and methods. Merchant vessels reasonably believed to be breaching a blockade are subject to capture by the blockading state's warships or military aircraft.[221] A merchant vessel that, after prior warning, resists capture may be attacked. A vessel that breached or attempted to breach a blockade is subject to condemnation by a prize court. If, however, the prize court determines that the vessel was not subject to capture, established principles of state responsibility require the seizing state to make reparation, just as it would for an unjustified exercise of the peacetime right of visit or hot pursuit.[222]

Israel's interdiction of the so-called Gaza Flotilla in 2010 is among the most closely scrutinized recent blockade enforcement actions. In response to repeated Palestinian rocket attacks on Israeli cities and civilian targets after Hamas came to power in 2007, Israel imposed a blockade on the Hamas-controlled Gaza Strip.[223] On May 31, 2010, maritime interdiction forces of the

214. See HYDROLANT message No. 1308/2006(56) (notifying all shipping that within the area specified in the HYDROLANT "Israeli naval Ships will not allow entrance or exit of any ship to or from this closure area").
215. Commander's Handbook, supra, ¶ 7.7. For an examination of the law of blockade and cyber warfare, see the Tallinn Manual on the International Law Applicable to Cyber Warfare 200 (Michael N. Schmitt et al. eds., 2013).
216. London Declaration, supra, Pt. I.
217. San Remo Manual, supra, ¶¶ 93–101.
218. If the civilian population of the blockaded territory is inadequately provided with food and other objects essential for its survival, the blockading party must allow free passage of foodstuffs and other essential supplies. San Remo Manual, supra, ¶ 103.
219. Id. ¶ 102.
220. This requirement dates back to the 1856 Declaration of Paris.
221. Commander's Handbook, supra, ¶ 7.10.
222. See, e.g., LOSC arts. 110 & 111.
223. After Israel pulled out of Gaza, ending its occupation, it classified the continuing cross-border conflict with Hamas-controlled Gaza an international armed conflict.

Israeli Defense Forces (IDF) intercepted six foreign vessels on the high seas roughly fifty nautical miles off the coast of Gaza to enforce that blockade. The six vessels were carrying nearly seven hundred crewmembers, pro-Palestinian activists, and journalists, along with supplies destined for Hamas-controlled Gaza. The Israelis' boarding of the MV *Mavi Marmara* was violently opposed by those on board. On their first attempt to board by small boat, the Israeli officers were beaten back with cold weapons. Boarding team members vertically inserted by helicopter were similarly met by violent opposition. By the time the vessel was brought under control, nine Turkish nationals on the *Mavi Marmara* were dead and a number of Israeli boarding team members and *Mavi Marmara* crewmembers were injured.

Reactions to the Israeli interdiction were immediate and reflexively negative, particularly within the human rights components of the United Nations. Criticisms of Israel generally took two forms: the first condemned the high-seas interdiction itself as a violation of international law not justified by the law of blockade; the second criticized Israel's use of force to carry out that interdiction. Little was said about the responsibility of the flotilla organizers or the *Mavi Marmara*'s crew, who violently opposed the boarding.[224] Nor was Turkey's responsibility as the vessel's flag state scrutinized.[225] Investigations by three different bodies came to conflicting conclusions regarding the lawfulness of the conduct.[226] The Turkel and Palmer inquiries concluded that the blockade was lawful under international law, but only the Turkel inquiry concluded that Israel's use of force was consistent with international law standards. The third inquiry, conducted by the UN Human Rights Council, condemned all aspects of Israel's enforcement action, as one would have predicted given its historical stance on Israel and the less-than-neutral title of its inquiry.[227]

3. Neutrality

Neutrality is the condition of a state or government that has elected to refrain from taking any part in an armed conflict between other states.[228] It is also a condition of immunity from invasion by the belligerents or their use of its territory. Switzerland and the Vatican City are permanently

---

224. The report of the UN secretary-general's Palmer Commission did question the motivations of the flotilla organizers, stating that "there exist serious questions about the conduct, true nature and objectives of the flotilla organizers, particularly IHH." The commission recognized that the IDF were met with "organized and violent resistance from a group of passengers" on boarding the vessel and that force was necessary for purposes of self-defense, but concluded that "the loss of life and injuries resulting from the use of force by Israeli forces during the take-over of the *Mavi Marmara* was unacceptable." See Report of the Secretary-General's Panel of Inquiry on the 31 May 2010 Flotilla Incident, September 2011, available at http://www.un.org/News/dh/infocus/middle_east/Gaza_Flotilla_Panel_Report.pdf (accessed Feb. 1, 2013).

225. The responsibility of flag states to exercise effective jurisdiction and control over their vessels is discussed in chapter 9. The obligations of neutral states with respect to their nationals were confirmed in the CSS *Alabama* claims arbitration decision discussed below.

226. The four-member Turkel Committee (named after its chair, a retired justice of the Israeli Supreme Court) appointed by the government of Israel found that the actions of the IDF in the raid and Israel's naval blockade of Gaza were legal as a matter of international law and accused the group of "IHH activists" of having armed themselves and conducting hostilities "in an organized manner." The Palmer Commission, appointed by the UN secretary-general, determined that Israel's blockade of the Gaza Strip was legal, but that the "decision to board the vessels with such substantial force at a great distance from the blockade zone and with no final warning immediately prior to the boarding was excessive and unreasonable."

227. UN Human Rights Council, Report of the International Fact-Finding Mission to Investigate Violations of International Law, Including International Humanitarian and Human Rights Law, Resulting from the Israeli Attacks on the Flotilla of Ships Carrying Humanitarian Assistance, U.N. Doc. A/HRC/15/21 (Sept. 27, 2010).

228. Commander's Handbook, supra, chapter 7; John Bassett Moore, A Digest of International Law vol. VII, ch. XVIII (1906).

neutral,[229] as is the Panama Canal.[230] Other states adopt a neutral posture with respect to a particular belligerency.[231] When a state adopts the policy of neutrality, it assumes certain obligations toward the belligerents.[232] As long as it fulfills those obligations impartially, it has certain rights that must be respected by the belligerents.[233]

Many of the rights and duties of neutrals and belligerents are concerned with measures directed against commerce. Commerce restrictions on neutrals were a contentious issue in the early years of the American Republic. Despite President George Washington's 1793 declaration of neutrality in the war between Great Britain and France, U.S. merchants and vessels continued to trade with the belligerents. Countermeasures by France and Great Britain against U.S. vessels were among the causes of the Quasi War with France (1798–1800) and the War of 1812 with Great Britain (1812–15).[234] Similarly, German attacks on neutral American merchant and passenger vessel shipping in the early years of World War I and World War II—often by submarine and without prior warning—were among the factors that drew the United States into those wars.

Under the law of naval warfare, a belligerent warship may ensure the neutral character of merchant ships outside neutral territory. That is, it may ensure that the merchant vessel is not carrying contraband in support of the enemy. In 2002, for example, Israeli commandos intercepted the M/V *Karine A*, a cargo ship flying the Tonga flag that was found to be carrying 50 tons of rockets, missiles, mortars, and mines from Iran to Gaza.[235] In late 2009 Israel intercepted the M/V *Francorp*, a German-owned vessel flying the Antigua-Barbuda flag that was carrying some 320 tons of weapons to Hezbollah fighters in Lebanon,[236] in violation of UN Security Council Resolution 1701.[237]

The law of maritime neutrality was largely codified in the 1907 Hague Convention XIII.[238] Briefly summarized, neutral merchant vessels are subject to capture outside neutral waters if they are engaged in any of the activities that are impermissible for neutrals,[239] or if it is determined as a result of visit and search or by other means that they: (1) are carrying contraband; (2) are

---

229. A permanently neutralized state must be distinguished from a state that has declared its neutrality with respect to a particular conflict. Switzerland was neutralized by the Congress of Vienna in 1815 and has maintained its neutrality ever since. Austria unilaterally declared its neutralized status by a constitutional statute in 1955.

230. See Treaty concerning Permanent Neutrality and Operation of the Panama Canal, arts. I & II, Sept. 7, 1977, 33 U.S.T. 1, T.I.A.S. No. 2966, 232 U.N.T.S. 289.

231. This is a contentious issue best left to books devoted to the law of naval warfare.

232. A claim by the United States that Great Britain violated its duties as a neutral by failing to exercise due diligence to prevent a British shipbuilder from supplying a warship (the *Alabama*) to the Confederacy during the Civil War was settled by international arbitration, resulting in an award of $15.5 million in damages to the United States.

233. San Remo Manual, supra, ¶ 7 (neutral states may lend assistance to a state that has been the victim of an act of aggression or a breach of the peace).

234. Alexander Hamilton warned in Federalist No. 11 that "a nation, despicable in its weakness, forfeits even the privilege of being neutral." In an attempt to avoid confrontations with Britain and France, the United States passed nonintercourse and neutrality acts prohibiting U.S. nationals and vessels from violating neutrality laws.

235. See James Bennet, Seized Arms Would Have Vastly Extended Arafat Arsenal, NY Times (Jan. 12, 2002).

236. See Richard Boudreaux, Israel Seizes Ship with Alleged Hezbollah-Bound Arms, LA Times (Nov. 4, 2009).

237. S.C. Res. 1701, ¶ 15, U.N. Doc. No. S/RES/1701 (Aug. 11, 2006).

238. Hague Convention (XIII) concerning the Rights and Duties of Neutral Powers in Naval War, Oct. 18, 1907, 36 Stat. 2415, reprinted in Documents on the Law of War 127 (Adam Roberts & Richard Guelff eds., 3d ed. 2002).

239. Merchant vessels flying the flag of neutral states may not be attacked unless they: (1) are believed on reasonable grounds to be carrying contraband or breaching a blockade, and after prior warning they intentionally and clearly refuse to stop, or intentionally and clearly resist visit, search, or capture; (2) engage in belligerent acts on behalf of the enemy; (3) act as auxiliaries to the enemy s armed forces; (4) are incorporated into or assist the enemy's intelligence system; (5) sail under convoy of enemy warships or military aircraft; or (6) otherwise make an effective contribution to the enemy's military action, e.g., by carrying military materials, and it is not feasible for the attacking forces to first place passengers and crew in a place of safety. Unless circumstances do not permit, they are to be given a warning so that they can reroute, offload, or take other precautions. San Remo Manual, supra, ¶ 67.

on a voyage especially undertaken with a view to the transport of individual passengers who are embodied in the armed forces of the enemy; (3) are operating directly under enemy control, orders, charter, employment, or direction; (4) present irregular or fraudulent documents, lack necessary documents, or destroy, deface, or conceal documents; (5) are violating regulations established by a belligerent within the immediate area of naval operations; or (6) are breaching or attempting to breach a blockade. In a decision later overturned by the U.S. Supreme Court on other grounds, the U.S. Court of Appeals for the Second Circuit held that Argentina violated the law of neutrality by attacking a neutral merchant vessel in international waters during the Falkland Islands conflict.[240]

The U.S. Constitution authorized Congress to grant letters of marque and reprisal that authorized their holders—privateers—to capture enemy prizes.[241] Some observers have inaccurately characterized privateering as government-sanctioned piracy by private vessels and their operators for profit,[242] but it was extensively relied on to disrupt enemy shipping in the early days of the American Republic when the nation's fleet of warships was quite small.[243] Privateering was abolished in the Paris Declaration of 1856.[244]

4. Contraband

The law of neutrality permits a belligerent warship to intercept contraband goods destined for the enemy.[245] Contraband is defined as goods that are ultimately destined for territory under the control of the enemy and may be susceptible for use in armed conflict.[246] Contraband goods are divided into two categories: absolute and conditional. Absolute contraband consists of goods that are used primarily for war or goods whose very character makes them destined to be used in war. Conditional contraband consists of goods that are equally susceptible of use either for peaceful or for warlike purposes (sometimes called "dual use" goods). Absolute contraband may be seized by a belligerent warship or aircraft if it is destined to territory under control of the enemy. Conditional contraband is subject to seizure if it is destined for the use of an enemy government or enemy armed forces. In order to exercise the right of capture the belligerent must have published a contraband list.[247] The precise nature of a belligerent's contraband list may vary according to the particular circumstances of the armed conflict. Contraband lists must be reasonably specific.

---

240. Cases concerning the boarding of neutral vessels during armed conflicts were examined by the court of appeals in Amerada Hess Shipping Corp. v. Argentine Republic, 830 F.2d 421 (2d Cir. 1987) (examining cases back to Talbot v. Janson, 3 U.S. (3 Dall.) 133, 161 (1795) and The *Lusitania*, 251 F. 715, 732–36 (S.D.N.Y. 1918)).

241. U.S. Const. art. I, § 8, cl. 11.

242. Several crucial factors distinguished privateers and pirates. A privateering vessel was at all times subject to the jurisdiction and control of its flag state and had an obligation to comply with applicable flag state law. Only enemy ships or neutral ships that violated a blockade or the law of neutrality were subject to capture. Privateers were subject to punishment for illegal or excessive use of force and had to bring any captured vessel before a prize court to obtain a legal award. See David J. Bederman, The Feigned Demise of Prize, 9 Emory Int'l L. Rev. 31 (1995); Donald A. Petrie, The Prize Game (1999).

243. C. Kevin Marshall, Putting Privateers in Their Place: The Applicability of the Marque and Reprisal Clause to Undeclared Wars, 64 U. Chi. L. Rev. 953 (1997). During the Revolutionary War, the Continental Congress and the states issued some two thousand privateering commissions.

244. Paris Declaration respecting Maritime Law, Apr. 16, 1856, reprinted in Documents on the Law of War 47, 49 (Adam Roberts & Richard Guelff eds., 3d ed. 2002) ("privateering is, and remains, abolished"). Although the United States was not a party to the Paris Declaration, President William McKinley later declared that the nation would adhere to its rules as a matter of policy. Proclamation No. 8, 30 Stat. 1770, 1771 (1898).

245. See Restatement FRLUS § 521 n.1; Commander's Handbook, supra, ¶ 7.4.

246. San Remo Manual, supra, ¶ 148.

247. Id. ¶ 149.

Goods not on the belligerent's contraband list are "free goods," and therefore not subject to capture.[248]

5. The Belligerents' Right of Visit, Board, Search, and Seizure

Article 110 of the LOS Convention confers on a state's warships and other duly authorized public vessels the "right" to approach and visit vessels on the high seas under certain circumstances, even though the state might not have jurisdiction to prescribe and enforce laws against the vessel visited. Similarly, the law of naval warfare provides that belligerent warships[249] and military aircraft have a right to visit and search merchant vessels[250] outside neutral waters when there are reasonable grounds for suspecting that they are subject to capture.[251] Such operations are employed to identify and capture enemy vessels, enforce a blockade against the enemy, or intercept contraband goods destined for the enemy.[252] The two "visit" rights share common terminology but differ in important respects. First, the predicate for each differs. Article 110 of the LOS Convention enumerates the sole grounds for exercising a peacetime right of visit, while the right under the law of naval warfare is largely based on customary law. A second distinction concerns the vessels authorized to exercise the right. The peacetime right of visit under Article 110 can be conducted by warships or other specially authorized and marked government vessels of any state, while the belligerent right of visit and search is limited to warships (or military aircraft) of a belligerent. Third, if a visit and search at sea is deemed hazardous or impracticable, the belligerent warship can divert the intercepted vessel to a location where the boarding can be safely conducted.[253] No similar right to compel the visited vessel to divert has been recognized under the peacetime right of visit. Fourth, the consequences differ. A peacetime right of visit might lead to an assertion of jurisdiction and perhaps seizure of the vessel, arrest of the crew, and adjudication; the belligerent right of visit leads to "capture" and a proceeding in prize or to release of the vessel. Even though a common VBSS bill is used for both peacetime and belligerent operations,[254] the applicable techniques, tactics and procedures, and rules of engagement used in a belligerent VBSS operation will almost certainly differ in important respects from the peacetime VBSS. *Maritime Interception Operations* (NTTP 3-07.11M), discussed above in section

---

248. "Free goods" include religious objects; articles intended exclusively for the treatment of the wounded and sick and for the prevention of disease; clothing, bedding, essential foodstuffs, and means of shelter for the civilian population in general; items destined for prisoners of war; goods otherwise specifically exempted from capture; and other goods not susceptible for use in armed conflict.

249. Under the law of naval warfare, a "warship" is defined as "a ship belonging to the armed forces of a State bearing the external marks distinguishing the character and nationality of such a ship, under the command of an officer duly commissioned by the government of that State and whose name appears in the appropriate service list or its equivalent, and manned by a crew which is under regular armed forces discipline." San Remo Manual, supra, ¶ 13(g).

250. A "merchant vessel" is "a vessel, other than a warship, an auxiliary vessel, or a State vessel such as a customs or police vessel, that is engaged in commercial or private service." San Remo Manual, supra, ¶ 13(i).

251. Commander's Handbook, supra, ¶ 7.6.

252. San Remo Manual, supra, ¶¶ 118–19. See also Wolff Heintschel von Heinegg, Visit, Search, Diversion, and Capture in Naval Warfare: Part I, The Traditional Law, 29 Canadian Y.B. Int'l L. 283 (1991); Wolff Heintschel von Heinegg, Visit, Search, Diversion, and Capture in Naval Warfare: Part II, Developments since 1945, 30 Canadian Y.B. Int'l L. 89 (1992); Joseph Lohengrin Frascona, Visit, Search, and Seizure on the High Seas (1938); James Whitman, An Inquiry into the Right of Visit or Approach by Ships of War (1858).

253. Commander's Handbook, supra, ¶ 7.6.1(5); San Remo Manual, supra, ¶ 119.

254. See U.S. Navy, Standard Organization and Regulations Manual (SORM), OPNAVINST 3120.32D (July 16, 2012), ¶ 6.3.21 (Visit and Search, Boarding and Salvage, and Prize Crew Bill).

F.3, does not apply to VBSS operations conducted under the law of naval warfare.[255] Nevertheless, the thorough coverage of VBSS procedures in the NTTP publication will no doubt prove useful in planning and executing belligerent VBSS operations.

A neutral merchant vessel is exempt from the exercise of the right of visit and search if (1) it is bound for a neutral port; (2) it is under the convoy of an accompanying neutral warship of the same nationality or a neutral warship of a state with which the flag state of the merchant vessel has concluded an agreement providing for such convoy; (3) the flag state of the neutral warship warrants that the neutral merchant vessel is not carrying contraband or otherwise engaged in activities inconsistent with its neutral status; and (4) the commander of the neutral warship provides, if requested by the commander of an intercepting belligerent warship or military aircraft, all information as to the character of the merchant vessel and its cargo as could otherwise be obtained by visit and search.[256]

A belligerent exercising the right of visit signals the merchantman to stop,[257] and a visit, board, search, and seizure team under the command of one of the warship's officers is sent over from the warship. The VBSS team boards the vessel and examines its documents to determine its registry, ports of departure, and destination and the nature of its cargo and mission. If the documentary examination satisfies the VBSS team that the vessel and its cargo are not subject to capture, they make an appropriate entry of the visit in the vessel's log and depart. If, on the other hand, the ship's documents arouse suspicion as to their authenticity or suggest that its cargo, destination, or mission would subject the vessel to capture, a search may be made. If visit and search at sea is impracticable or unsafe, the vessel may be directed to an appropriate area or port in order to exercise the right of visit and search.[258] If the ship's papers or the search reveals that the vessel is liable to capture, it is taken to port for adjudication by a prize court.[259]

---

255. Given the belligerents' primary focus on warfighting and the infrequency of belligerent VBSS operations, it is not surprising that the peacetime VBSS tactics, techniques, and procedures are better developed than their law of naval warfare counterpart.

256. San Remo Manual, supra, ¶ 120.

257. If a merchantman resists, the warship may act forcibly and may, if absolutely necessary, sink it. An *enemy* merchantman's right to resist visit is recognized by international law, and the consequences of such an act are the risks of damage and loss that the captain chooses to take. A neutral does not have this right. Forcible resistance or flight by a neutral merchant ship may be treated by a belligerent warship as a suspicious circumstance justifying its capture.

258. San Remo Manual, supra, ¶ 121.

259. The federal district courts have jurisdiction over prize cases. See 28 U.S.C. § 1333(2). The act of capturing a vessel does not in itself vest title in the capturing nation. The title remains in trust with the captor until there has been adjudication by a prize court. Destruction of a neutral prize is therefore lawful only under the most unusual circumstances.

13

Use of Force in the Maritime Domain

Perhaps no decision made by naval and coast guard officers is more consequential than the decision to use force. History has repeatedly demonstrated that the use of force or the threat to use force against another state or one of its vessels or aircraft can trigger reprisals and even precipitate armed conflict. The use of force without legal justification or in a manner that is illegal may also lead to state responsibility under international law, liability under the state's domestic laws, and disciplinary action against those responsible.

An examination of the use of force at sea can be divided into three distinct inquiries. The first concerns the use of armed force in combat operations, which is the focus of the law of naval warfare and section A of this chapter. The second inquiry focuses on the use of force by warships, military aircraft, and other public vessels and military and other state aircraft in "constabulary" law enforcement operations against nonstate actors. Such "police" force actions are addressed in section B. Police force is distinguished from "countermeasures" taken by one state against another state that has breached an international law obligation (discussed in chapter 14). By contrast, the use of force in law enforcement operations is generally directed against nonstate actors. The third inquiry, addressed in section C, concerns the use of force in self-defense by nonstate actors and would include, for example, the use of force by crewmembers or onboard private maritime security service providers to repel an attempt by pirates or other armed attackers to board or take control of a vessel or offshore platform.[1]

A. ARMED FORCE AT SEA

Theorists commonly posit four possible approaches to preserving global order: hegemony, balance of power, collective security, and world government.[2] The UN Charter adopted the collective security approach, by which any breach of or threat to international peace or security is to be met with swift and effective collective suppression measures.[3] Although the logic of collective security is brilliant, its implementation has fallen short of the mark. Even when the Security Council has acted, the response has typically been neither swift nor effective, thus undermining

---

1. In 1873 the U.S. Supreme Court ruled that a citizen of the United States enjoys a constitutionally protected privilege to "demand the care and protection of the Federal government over his life, liberty, and property when on the high seas." The Slaughterhouse Cases, 83 U.S. (16 Wall.) 36, 79 (1873).
2. See generally Robert J. Art & Kenneth Neal Waltz, The Use of Force: Military Power and International Politics (7th ed. 2009); Colin S. Gray, War, Peace and International Relations (2007); Paul D. Miller, Five Pillars of American Grand Strategy, 54 Survival: Global Politics and Strategy 7–44 (Oct. 2012).
3. The UN Charter's collective security scheme rests on three pillars: prohibition on the use of force (Article 2(4)); the duty of the Security Council to deal with acts of aggression, breaches of the peace, and threats to the peace (Articles 39–42); and express reservation of the right of individual and collective self-defense until the Security Council can take effective action to suppress and remove the threat (Article 51).

the approach's deterrent value. As a result, for the first five decades under the UN Charter, states were legally committed to collective security while "peace" was maintained through a mostly bipolar balance of power and a web of collective self-defense agreements. Although theorists still struggle to characterize the post–Cold War environment, most agree that the risks posed to global order, including the growing threat posed by nonstate actors, are no less pervasive and no less likely to place heavy demands on global maritime security forces.[4]

The legal regime governing the use of armed force has historically been divided into the *jus ad bellum* (legal restrictions on the resort to armed force)[5] and the *jus in bello*, or law of armed conflict (legal restrictions on the means and methods of warfare and treatment on combatants and civilians). Any examination of the use of force must include the rules of engagement (ROE), which combine the law of armed conflict with policy and operational goals to provide direction on the employment of force by the nation's combat forces. Relevant guidance for U.S. warships and naval aircraft in the use of armed force at sea can be found in the *Commander's Handbook on the Law of Naval Operations* and the unofficial but highly respected *San Remo Manual on International Law Applicable to Armed Conflicts at Sea*.[6]

1. Jus ad Bellum

Legal restrictions on the use of armed force, or the *jus ad bellum*, consist of conventional and customary international law sources and, in some cases, resolutions of the UN Security Council. Since 1945, any examination of the international law limitations on the use of armed force begins with the UN Charter and its nonaggression norm. Additional nonbinding guidance may be found in resolutions of the UN General Assembly and interpretive decisions by international tribunals. Military measures that might otherwise violate the nonaggression norm may be authorized by the UN Security Council acting under its Chapter VII power to take or authorize states to take action necessary to maintain or restore international peace and security.

a. The Nonaggression Norm

Article 2(4) of the UN Charter prohibits the use of armed force or the threat to use armed force against the territorial integrity or political independence of any state, or in any other manner inconsistent with the purposes of the UN.[7] This nonaggression norm has its roots in the Covenant of the League of Nations,[8] the Kellogg-Briand Pact,[9] and elements of the just war theory.[10]

---

4. See, e.g., Quadrennial Defense Review (2010); National Security Strategy (2010); and the 2012 Defense Strategic Guidance ("Sustaining U.S. Global Leadership: Priorities for 21st Century Defense").
5. *Jus ad bellum* (or *jus contra bellum*) was historically distinguished from the *jus duellum*, which concerned the use of force by nonstate actors. Once the legal monopoly on the use of armed force is wrested from the state's control, existing distinctions between war and crime break down. See Martin van Creveld, The Rise and Decline of the State 399–408 (1999).
6. San Remo Manual, supra. The 1994 manual was later supplemented with a second publication addressing noninternational armed conflicts; however, it does not address law of naval warfare issues. See International Institute of Humanitarian Law, The Manual on the Law of Non-international Armed Conflict with Commentary (2006).
7. UN Charter, supra, art. 2(4). See also Yoram Dinstein, War, Aggression and Self-Defence (5th ed. 2011).
8. Covenant of the League of Nations, art. 12, June 28, 1919, 225 Consol. Treaty Series 188.
9. General Treaty for the Renunciation of War as an Instrument of National Policy [hereinafter the "Kellogg-Briand Pact"], Aug. 27, 1928, 46 Stat. 2343, T.S. No. 795, 94 L.N.T.S. 57. The United States did not ratify the Covenant of the League of Nations; however, it did ratify the Kellogg-Briand Pact.
10. The "just war" theory or doctrine, now largely rejected by legal academics, is rooted in theological writings, including those of Saint Thomas Aquinas. See Michael Walzer, Just and Unjust Wars: A Moral Argument with Historical Illustrations (2006). See also Gareth Evans, When Is It Right to Fight? 46 Survival: Global Politics and Strategy 59 (2004).

Those authorities condemn wars of "aggression" but are less clear in distinguishing acts of aggression from legitimate uses of armed force.

In 1974 the UN General Assembly attempted to define "aggression" by resolution.[11] The assembly's nonbinding resolution largely repeats Article 2(4) of the UN Charter, stating that aggression is the use of armed force by a state against the sovereignty, territorial integrity, or political independence of another state, or in any other manner inconsistent with the Charter of the United Nations, as defined by the resolution. The resolution then goes on to examine particular applications of that nonaggression norm.[12] For example, under the General Assembly's definition, an "attack by the armed forces of a State on the land, sea or air forces, or marine or air fleets of another State" constitutes aggression.[13] In 2010 parties to the Rome Statute of the International Criminal Court met in Kampala, Uganda, to draft a definition of "aggression" for purposes of criminal prosecutions under the Rome Statute.[14] The ICJ has also addressed the nonaggression norm on several occasions, two of which involved cases brought against the United States.[15]

b. The Inherent Right of Self-Defense

The inherent right of all states to use armed force in self-defense is recognized in Article 51 of the UN Charter:

> Nothing in the present Charter shall impair the inherent right of individual or collective self-defense if an armed attack occurs against a Member of the United Nations, until the Security Council has taken measures necessary to maintain international peace and security. Measures taken by Members in the exercise of this right of self-defense shall be immediately reported to the Security Council and shall not in any way affect the authority and responsibility of the Security Council under the present Charter to take at any time such action as it deems necessary in order to maintain or restore international peace and security.[16]

Article 51 does not *grant* a right of individual and collective self-defense. Rather, it recognizes an inherent right that predates the UN Charter. More than two centuries ago, the U.S. Supreme Court recognized the right of a state to "secure itself from injury" through actions on the high

---

11. UN General Assembly, Definition of Aggression, G.A. Res. 3314 (XXIX), U.N. Doc. A/RES/3314 (Dec. 14, 1974). The closely related nonintervention norm introduced in chapter 1 and reflected in Article 2(7) of the UN Charter is broader than the nonaggression norm.

12. Questions regarding the applicability of Articles 2(4) and 51 to "cyber attacks" are addressed in the Tallinn Manual on the International Law Applicable to Cyber Warfare (Michael N. Schmitt et al. eds., 2013).

13. G.A. Res. 3314 (XXIX), supra, ¶ 3(d).

14. The tentative definition of "aggression" developed at the 2010 Kampala review conference draws on General Assembly Resolution 3314. The Kampala definition will be revisited in 2017. See generally Michael P. Scharf, Universal Jurisdiction and the Crime of Aggression, 53 Harv. Int'l L. J. 358 (2012).

15. Armed Activities on the Territory of the Congo (Dem. Rep. Congo v. Uganda), 2005 I.C.J. 116 (Dec. 19); Military and Paramilitary Activities in and against Nicaragua (Nicaragua v. U.S.), 1986 I.C.J. 14 (June 27); Oil Platforms case (Iran v. U.S.), 2003 I.C.J. 161 (Nov. 6). The majority's reasoning and conclusions in the Oil Platforms case have been called into question. See William H. Taft IV, Self-Defense and the Oil Platforms Decision, 29 Yale J. Int'l L. 295 (2004) (criticizing the court for its excursion into obiter dictum and its treatment of the armed attack and self-defense issues).

16. UN Charter, supra, art. 51. See also Encyclopedia of Public International Law, vol. 4, at 361 (Rudolph Bernhardt ed., 2000) ("Self-Defence").

seas beyond the state's own waters.[17] A leading American nineteenth-century international law scholar described the state's right of self-preservation as an absolute right lying at the foundation of all of the state's other rights.[18] The ICJ confirmed the inherent nature of the right of self-defense in its 1986 judgment in the *Nicaragua Military and Paramilitary Activities* case, in which it held that the UN Charter confirms the established customary law rule on self-defense without purporting to supervene the existing rule.[19]

The use of force in self-defense is subject to the customary law limits of necessity, proportionality, and immediacy.[20] Particular applications may also be limited by treaty. For example, following the 1983 Korean Airlines flight 007 incident, in which the Soviet Union shot down a civil airliner carrying 269 passengers and crew that had strayed into Soviet airspace, the states parties to the Chicago Convention on Civil Aviation adopted a protocol to that convention that generally prohibits the use of weapons against civil aircraft in flight.[21] The use of hijacked civilian airliners in the September 11, 2001, attacks on the World Trade Center and the Pentagon prompted a reexamination of the 1984 protocol.[22] Commentators pointed out that the protocol's ban on the use of weapons against civil aircraft is qualified by a provision stipulating that it must not be "interpreted as modifying in any way the rights and obligations of States set forth in the Charter of the United Nations,"[23] thus preserving the inherent right of self-defense under Article 51 of the charter.[24]

The balance struck by the prohibition in Article 2(4) and the self-defense right in Article 51 has been debated almost from the UN Charter's inception. The charter was founded on a belief in the promise of the previously mentioned "collective security" measures, to be administered primarily by the Security Council and carried out by member states or forces made available to the council by member states under Article 43 agreements. For a variety of reasons—most commonly, decisions by one or more of the ideologically divided permanent Security Council members to veto enforcement measures—the promise was never fulfilled.[25] The failure of the collective security approach forced states to continue to rely on individual and collective self-defense, or to turn to the General Assembly when the Security Council failed to take the needed action.[26] Judge Philip Jessup was one of the first to acknowledge the conditional relationship

---

17. See Church v. Hubbard, 6 U.S. (2 Cranch) 187, 234–35 (1804) (Marshall, C.J.) (upholding legality of Portugal's seizure of a U.S. vessel off the coast of Brazil).

18. Henry Wheaton, Elements of International Law with a Sketch of the History of the Science 81 (1st ed. 1836).

19. See Military and Paramilitary Activities, supra, at 94 (it cannot "be held that article 51 is a provision which 'subsumes and supervenes' customary international law").

20. Advisory Opinion on Legality of the Threat or Use of Nuclear Weapons, 1996 I.C.J. 226 (July 8). The court explained that those limits apply under customary law and Article 51. Id. at ¶ 41.

21. Chicago Convention on Civil Aviation, supra, art. 3*bis* ("every State must refrain from resorting to the use of weapons against civil aircraft in flight"); Commander's Handbook, supra, ¶ 4.4.2. See also Gerald F. FitzGerald, The Use of Force against Civil Aircraft: The Aftermath of the KAL Flight 007 Incident, 22 Can. Y.B. Int'l L. 291 (1984); John T. Phelps II, Aerial Intrusions by Civil and Military Aircraft in Time of Peace, 107 Mil. L. Rev. 255 (1985).

22. Andrew S. Williams, The Interception of Civil Aircraft over the High Seas in the Global War on Terror, 59 Air Force L. Rev. 73 (2007).

23. Chicago Convention on Civil Aviation, supra, art. 3*bis*.

24. Use of force in self-defense by U.S. forces would be subject to the standing rules of engagement (SROE) and its definitions of "hostile act" and demonstrated "hostile intent."

25. Two commentators observed that "we are operating under a set of rules governing the use of force that were framed for a very different world. . . . These rules can continue to serve us well only if they are revised and updated to meet a new set of threats." Lee Feinstein & Anne-Marie Slaughter, A Duty to Prevent, 83 Foreign Aff. 136, 150 (2004).

26. Collective self-defense of a state following an armed attack by another state (e.g., Kuwait following Iraq's invasion in 1990) must be distinguished from providing military assistance to the de facto state government engaged in an internal armed conflict.

between the "surrender" of some elements of the customary right of self-help and the promise that collective security would step in to fill the void.[27] Thus, to the extent that the Security Council and its military staff committee were unable to timely respond to a threat to a state,[28] forcible self-help might still be necessary and lawful.[29] Later writers openly condemned the failure of the UN Charter–based collective security regime to effectively remove threats to international peace and security and called for a reexamination of the limits on the noncollective use of force by member states.[30] State practice appears to be headed in that direction. In the words of one commentator, Article 2(4) is shrinking while Article 51 is expanding.[31]

Customary law recognizes the state's right of anticipatory self-defense.[32] However, the status of the customary right of anticipatory self-defense vis-à-vis Articles 2(4) and 51 and the contours of such a right in situations short of an armed attack are a matter of dispute.[33] For most states, being forced to absorb a first blow before responding is unacceptable, particularly if the blow might be delivered by a nuclear weapon or an untreatable strain of deadly virus. On the other hand, some feel that a strict test is essential to guard not only against the aggressive use of force, in violation of the UN Charter, but also an anticipatory use of force that turns out to have been unnecessary.

Historically, claims to a right of anticipatory self-defense have been tested by the standards articulated by Secretary of State Daniel Webster in the *Caroline* incident. The incident concerned the 1837 entry into the United States by British forces, who destroyed the *Caroline* after concluding that it was being used to assist Canadians in their rebellion against the British. The United States and Great Britain were not at war at the time. In an exchange of notes on the question of Britain's responsibility for the vessel's destruction, Secretary Webster articulated the U.S. standard for anticipatory self-defense: the use of armed force before, but in anticipation of, an armed attack is legally justified only if "the necessity of that self-defense is instant, overwhelming, and leaving no choice of means, and no moment for deliberation."[34] The *Caroline* standard thus looks at both the imminence of the attack and the necessity of the use of force to preempt that attack.[35]

---

27. Philip C. Jessup, A Modern Law of Nations 162 (1952).
28. The General Assembly famously recognized the Security Council's failure to discharge its primary responsibility for international peace and security on behalf of the member states in the 1950 "Uniting for Peace" resolution. See UN, General Assembly, Uniting for Peace, G.A. Res. 337V (Nov. 3, 1950).
29. Richard B. Lillich, Forcible Self-Help under International Law, 62 U.S. Nav. War Coll. Int'l L. Studies 129, 135 (1980).
30. Robert F. Turner, Operation Iraqi Freedom: Legal and Policy Considerations, 27 Harv. J. L. & Public Pol'y 765, 767 (2004) (concluding that "unenforced international law will not maintain the peace"). For an examination of the problems with a "mechanical" interpretation of Article 2(4), see W. Michael Reisman, Criteria for the Lawful Use of Force in International Law, 10 Yale J. Int'l L. 279 (1985).
31. Philip Bobbitt, The Shield of Achilles: War, Peace, and the Course of History 474 (2002).
32. The legality of anticipatory self-defense measures was accepted by the UN High Level Panel on Threats, Challenges and Change. See A More Secure World: Our Shared Responsibility, U.N. Doc. A/59/565 (2004), ¶ 188 (recognizing that under "long established international law" a state may take military action in response to an "imminent" threat of attack, subject to the related rules of necessity and proportionality).
33. Michael J. Glennon, Why the Security Council Failed, 82 Foreign Aff. 16 (2003); Jack M. Beard, America's New War on Terror: The Case for Self-Defense under International Law, 25 Harv. J. L. & Pub. Pol'y 559 (2002). See also The Chatham House Principles of International Law on the Use of Force in Self-Defence, 55 Int'l & Comp. L. Q. 963 (2006).
34. Letter from Daniel Webster to Lord Ashburton (Aug. 6, 1842), quoted in John Bassett Moore, A Digest of International Law, vol. 2, at 412 (1906) [hereinafter "The Caroline"].
35. Under SROE, U.S. forces may respond with armed force to hostile acts or demonstrated hostile intent. Some states have adopted narrower rules that permit the use of force in self-defense only in response to a hostile act.

The chief deficiency in the *Caroline* standard, and one easily explained by the circumstances of the incident itself, is that it focuses almost entirely on the imminence of the blow, without factoring in the magnitude of the harm likely to flow from it.[36] The threat to Great Britain posed by a small inland steamboat used to transport men and munitions across the Niagara River was not great. The potential magnitude of the harm is, of course, the distinguishing characteristic of weapons of mass destruction, particularly nuclear weapons or the most threatening biological agents. Modern risk analysis approaches consider the probability of an event and its magnitude, as well as the time required to employ protective countermeasures.[37] Those considerations informed the controversial 2002 National Security Strategy of the United States, which was written shortly after the September 11, 2001, attacks and concluded that "the greater the threat, the greater is the risk of inaction—and the more compelling the case for taking anticipatory action to defend ourselves, even if uncertainty remains as to the time and place of the enemy's attack."[38]

Like other forms of self-help countermeasures, self-defense has mostly been confined to acts by and against states, and not individuals, terrorist organizations, or organized criminal syndicates; however, the threat posed by twenty-first-century international terrorism has challenged the orthodox view. Attacks by nonstate actors on the Marine barracks in Lebanon (1983), the Khobar Towers U.S. Air Force dormitory in Saudi Arabia (1996), the USS *Cole* in Yemen (2000), the Pentagon (2001), and al Qaeda's unsuccessful 2005 rocket attack on U.S. Navy warships in Aqaba[39] demonstrate terrorists' willingness to attack even military targets.[40] Armed confrontations between Israel and Hezbollah and Hamas groups and the attack from sea on civilian targets in Mumbai, India, by Pakistani militants provide additional examples of the threat level posed by nonstate actors. It is important to note that nothing in Article 51 suggests that only armed attacks by nation-states (as opposed to armed groups) trigger the inherent right of self-defense. Indeed, the leading case on the law of anticipatory self-defense, which arose out of the destruction of the vessel *Caroline*, involved a British military expedition against nonstate actors in the United States.[41] More important, following the September 11, 2001, attacks by al Qaeda, nearly all of the relevant international and national authorities agreed that the right of individual and collective self-defense applied.[42] Armed groups and their leaders have been the subject of Chapter VII measures

---

36. See Commander's Handbook, supra, ¶ 4.4.3.1.

37. See Myres S. McDougal, The Soviet-Cuban Quarantine and Self-Defense, 57 Am. J. Int'l L. 588, 597–98 (1963) (arguing that the justification for self-defense measures turns on both the imminence of the threat and its "degree," particularly when the degree of the attack may preclude effective resort to nonviolent measures).

38. White House, National Security Strategy of the United States of America, Sept. 17, 2002. Although the 2002 National Security Strategy (NSS) did not specify the form of action the United States would take (e.g., law enforcement, diplomatic, intelligence, economic, or military), most critics assumed it referred only to the use of armed force. The need to take action even in cases involving "uncertainty" as to the time and place of attack (what critics characterized as an illegal "preventative" use of force before any attack was "imminent") would later characterize one line of criticism by the 9/11 Commission of government inaction and its collective "failure of imagination." See National Commission on Terrorist Attacks on the United States, The 9/11 Commission Report (2004), ch. 8: "The System Was Blinking Red." In subsequent revisions to the NSS, the criticized language was largely removed.

39. Al Qaeda Claim for Red Sea Attacks, CNN News.com, Aug. 19, 2005. The warships, the amphibious assault ships USS *Ashland* (LSD-48) and USS *Kearsarge* (LHD-3), were in port with members of the 26th Marine Expeditionary Unit to conduct joint training with Lebanon when they were attacked with Katyusha rockets.

40. Id. See also Michael N. Schmitt, Responding to Transnational Terrorism under the *Jus ad Bellum:* A Normative Framework, 56 Nav. L. Rev. 1 (2008).

41. The Caroline, supra, at 409.

42. See, e.g., UN Security Council Resolutions 1368 & 1373. Member states of the North Atlantic Treaty Organization (NATO) and Organization of American States (OAS) alliances also invoked the relevant articles in those collective self-defense treaties. See also Commander's Handbook, supra, ¶ 5.1.2.3; U.S. Department of Justice, Office of Legal Counsel, The President's Constitutional Authority to Conduct Military Operations against

imposed by the Security Council on several occasions. Resolution 1267, adopted in 1999, identifies by name Osama bin Laden as a threat to international peace and security. Similarly, Resolutions 1373 and 1540 address threats to international peace and security by nonstate actors.
Surprisingly, however, a majority of the judges on the ICJ suggested that the right of self-defense
does not apply to attacks by armed groups.[43] The court offered no reasoning for its puzzling
conclusion and did not attempt to reconcile its conclusion with the text of Article 51, historical
cases such as the *Caroline*, or resolutions issued by the UN Security Council in the wake of the
September 11, 2001, attacks.

The United States has consistently taken the position that a terrorist attack may give rise
to the right of individual and collective self-defense, subject to the necessity and proportionality
constraints imposed under the *jus ad bellum*, and to the applicable law of armed conflict. In a key
2010 policy announcement, Harold Koh, legal adviser to the U.S. Department of State, clarified
the U.S. position on the use of force, particularly with regard to the use of armed unmanned
aerial vehicles (UAVs) in foreign territories. He announced that any future decision by the United
States to use force will be based on three factors: (1) the immediacy of the threat to the United
States, (2) the sovereign interests of the target or host state that are at stake, and (3) whether that
target/host state is able and willing to effectively suppress the threat against the United States.[44]
The policy was affirmed by the U.S. attorney general, Eric Holder, in a speech on March 5, 2012,
in which he emphasized that the United States is

> at war with a stateless enemy, [and] because the United States is in an armed
> conflict, we are authorized to take action against enemy belligerents under
> international law. The Constitution empowers the President to protect the
> nation from any imminent threat of violent attack. And international law rec-
> ognizes the inherent right of national self-defense. None of this is changed
> by the fact that we are not in a conventional war. Our legal authority is not
> limited to the battlefields in Afghanistan . . . the use of force in foreign territory
> would be consistent with these international legal principles if conducted, for
> example, with the consent of the nation involved—or after a determination that
> the nation is unable or unwilling to deal effectively with a threat to the United
> States.[45]

c. UN Security Council Authorization

Article 39 of the UN Charter provides that the Security Council "shall determine the existence
of any threat to the peace, breach of the peace, or act of aggression and shall make recommendations, or decide what measures shall be taken in accordance with Articles 41 and 42, to maintain

---

Terrorists and Nations Supporting Them, Sept. 25, 2001; Sir Daniel Bethlehem, Self-Defense against an Imminent or Actual Armed Attack by Nonstate Actors, 106 Am. J. Int'l L. 770 (2012).

43. See Advisory Opinion on the Legal Consequences of the Construction of a Wall in the Occupied Palestinian Territory, International Court of Justice, ¶ 139, 2004 I.C.J. 136 (Jul. 9) (concluding that the UN Charter provisions
on self-defense had "no relevance" to Israel's construction of a security barrier because Israel did "not claim that
the attacks against it are imputable to a foreign State").

44. Harold Hongju Koh, Legal Adviser, U.S. Department of State, Address at the Annual Meeting of the American
Society of International Law, Washington, D.C., Mar. 25, 2010, available at http://www.state.gov/s/l/releases/
remarks/139119.htm (accessed Feb. 1, 2013).

45. See Attorney General Eric Holder Speaks at Northwestern University School of Law, March 5, 2012, available at
http://www.justice.gov/iso/opa/ag/speeches/2012/ag-speech-1203051.html (accessed Feb. 1, 2013).

or restore international peace and security." Article 41 governs measures not involving the use of armed force. Those measures may include "complete or partial interruption of economic relations and of rail, sea, air, postal, telegraphic, radio, and other means of communication, and the severance of diplomatic relations." Should the Security Council determine that the Article 41 measures would be inadequate or they have proved to be inadequate, the council may invoke Article 42 and order "such action by air, sea, or land forces as may be necessary to maintain or restore international peace and security [including] demonstrations, blockade and other operations by air, sea or land forces of the member states." All UN member states agree to accept and carry out decisions of the Security Council.[46] On at least one occasion the council has authorized the use of force to enforce the blockade it imposed.[47] In addition to its enforcement powers under Articles 41 and 42, the Security Council also has the power under Article 40 to impose provisional measures to prevent escalation of the situation. Actions taken by states in accordance with the Security Council's Chapter VII measures, including actions involving the use of armed force when authorized by the council under Article 42, do not violate Article 2(4).

d. An Exception for Humanitarian Intervention?

Advocates of a "responsibility to protect" (R2P) norm have argued in favor of an exception to the nonaggression and nonintervention norms when necessary, as a last resort, to stop what will otherwise be massive human rights violations.[48] As commonly described, the R2P rests on three pillars. The first is that states have the primary responsibility to protect their populations from mass atrocities. Second, the international community has a responsibility to assist the state in fulfilling its primary responsibility. Finally, if a particular state fails to protect its population from mass atrocities and peaceful measures have failed, the international community has a responsibility to intervene, including through coercive measures such as economic sanctions.[49] Military intervention is considered the last resort. If military intervention is authorized by the UN Security Council exercising its Chapter VII powers and the intervention is confined to the scope of that authorization, no Article 2(4) issue is presented. In contrast, interventions in the absence of such an authorization (or measures that exceed the scope of the authorization) and not justified under the law of self-defense can pose a potential Hobson's choice between the moral course of action and the legal course of action.

Rather than claim a right under international law to engage in humanitarian intervention without Security Council authorization,[50] some states might prefer the "immaculate violation" alternative. When humanitarian considerations impel a state to act in violation of international

---

46. UN Charter, supra, art. 25. One U.S. court has held that a Security Council resolution is not self-executing in the United States. Diggs v. Richardson, 555 F.2d 848 (D.C. Cir. 1976).

47. S.C. Res. 221, Apr. 9, 1966 (question concerning the situation in southern Rhodesia). The resolution authorized the use of force to enforce the blockade on the port of Beira.

48. The ICJ has rejected the argument that human rights violations justify use of force. Military and Paramilitary Activities, supra, at 271. In its earlier decision in the Corfu Channel case, the court stated that it "can only regard the alleged right of intervention as the manifestation of a policy of force, such as has, in the past, given rise to most serious abuses and such as cannot, whatever the present defects in international organization, find a place in international law." The Corfu Channel case (U.K. v. Albania) 1949 I.C.J. 1, 35 (Apr. 9).

49. See generally Jared Genser et al., The Responsibility to Protect (2011); United Nations, 2005 World Summit Outcome, U.N. Doc. A/60/L.1 (2005), ¶¶ 138–39, available at http://daccess-ods.un.org/TMP/6748730 .54027557.html (accessed Feb. 1, 2013).

50. "Humanitarian intervention" may be defined as the threat or use of force across state borders by a state (or a group of states) aimed at preventing or ending widespread and grave violations of the human rights of individuals other than the intervening state's own citizens, without the permission of the state within whose territory force is applied.

law, the state could attempt to justify or rationalize its actions under existing international law, or it could take the path followed by some NATO states when they deployed armed force against Serbian forces to halt the atrocities in Kosovo.[51] The approach is called the "immaculate violation" because the act's illegality is admitted but the intervention is defended as legitimate.[52] At the same time, confessing that the act violated international law—essentially, pleading guilty, subject to extenuating circumstances—avoids the risk that an intervention defended on dubious legal grounds might cast doubt on or even supplant the existing rules on nonaggression and nonintervention.[53]

2. *Jus in Bello*

Characterizing an action involving the use of force as an application of armed force (in contrast to police or constabulary force) carries with it several important legal consequences. If the situation is one of armed conflict, the use of force is governed by the law of armed conflict. The law of armed conflict (LOAC), variously called the *jus in bello*, law of war,[54] and international humanitarian law, refers to the body of law that regulates the actual conduct of armed conflict. The LOAC is principally set out in the Hague Rules,[55] the four Geneva conventions of 1949,[56] and a body of customary international law.[57] The LOAC distinguishes between combatants and civilians

---

51. See Albert Legault, NATO Intervention in Kosovo: The Legal Context, Canadian Armed Forces J. (spring 2003), at 63–66. See also The Clinton Administration, in Shaping Foreign Policy in Times of Crisis 124–25 (Michael P. Scharf & Paul R. Williams eds., 2010); Michael J. Glennon, Limits of Law, Prerogatives of Power: Interventionism after Kosovo 13–35 (2001) (concluding that NATO's Kosovo campaign violated the UN Charter).

52. Public statements by Tony Blinken, President Barack Obama's deputy national security adviser, in September 2013 regarding the possible justification for an armed reprisal against Syria for the alleged use of chemical weapons against insurgents took the position that the use of force in the absence of a Security Council resolution would be illegal under international law but legitimate.

53. Discrepant practice with respect to a treaty can be interpreted in several different ways: (1) a violation of the treaty, leaving its existing meaning intact and rendering the offending state responsible for any harm caused by the breach; (2) some evidence of practice establishing the agreement of the parties regarding the treaty's interpretation under Article 31(b)(3) of the Vienna Convention on Treaties; or (3) a modification of the treaty as between the particular states (see, e.g., Article 311 of the LOSC). See Military and Paramilitary Activities in and against Nicaragua (Nicaragua v. U.S.), 1986 I.C.J. 14, 98 (June 27) (state conduct inconsistent with a rule will not constitute practice supporting a new rule or exception when it has generally been treated as a breach of the existing rule). See also William H. Taft IV, International Law and the Use of Force, 36 Geo. J. Int'l L. 659, 662 (2004).

54. The U.S. Department of Defense defines the "law of war" as "that part of international law that regulates the conduct of armed hostilities. It is often called the 'law of armed conflict.' The law of war encompasses all international law for the conduct of hostilities binding on the United States or its individual citizens, including treaties and international agreements to which the United States is a party, and applicable customary international law." DoD, The Law of War Program, DoD Directive 2311.01E, May 9, 2006. See generally Gary D. Solis, The Law of Armed Conflict: International Humanitarian Law in War (2010); Yoram Dinstein, The Conduct of Hostilities under the Law of International Armed Conflict (2d ed. 2010).

55. "Hague Rules" refers to the conventions and regulations respecting the laws and customs of war adopted at peace conferences held at The Hague in 1899 and 1907. They are collected in Documents on the Laws of War (Adam Roberts & Richard Guelff eds., 3d ed. 2000).

56. Geneva Convention for the Amelioration of the Condition of the Wounded and Sick in Armed Forces in the Field [Geneva Convention I], Aug. 12, 1949, 6 U.S.T. 3114, 75 U.N.T.S. 31; Geneva Convention for the Amelioration of the Condition of the Wounded, Sick and Shipwrecked Members of Armed Forces at Sea [Geneva Convention II], Aug. 12, 1949, 6 U.S.T. 3217, T.I.A.S. 3363, 75 U.N.T.S. 85; Geneva Convention Relative to the Treatment of Prisoners of War [Geneva Convention III], Aug. 12, 1949, 6 U.S.T. 3316, 75 U.N.T.S. 135; Geneva Convention Relative to the Protection of Civilian Persons in Time of War [Geneva Convention IV], Aug. 12, 1949, 6 U.S.T. 3516, 75 U.N.T.S. 287.

57. Application of customary law in LOAC is saved by use of Martens' clauses in the various treaties. See, e.g., Laws and Customs of War on Land (Hague IV), Oct. 18, 1907, Preamble, ¶ 8. A list of the "sources" of the LOAC is included in the Commander's Handbook (¶ 5.5), which also discusses the limited application of international human rights law in armed conflicts (¶ 5.6).

and includes provisions for detention of captured enemy combatants and even civilians in some circumstances. In a rare grant of authority to a nongovernmental organization, the International Committee for the Red Cross is charged with responsibility for promoting and ensuring respect for the 1949 Geneva conventions.[58]

It is a fundamental principle of the LOAC that those rules apply regardless of whether the conflict itself is "legal" under the *jus ad bellum*. DoD policy unequivocally requires compliance with the LOAC during all armed conflicts, however such conflicts are characterized, and in all other military operations.[59] Under the LOAC, any use of armed force is constrained by the principles of military necessity, distinction, proportionality, and humanity.[60] Roots of the modern LOAC can be found in the advice Talleyrand reportedly offered to Napoleon in 1806 that "nations ought to do to one another in peace, the most good, and in war, the least evil possible."[61] Consistent with that advice, it is well established that whenever armed force is used, the choice of means and methods is not unlimited.[62] That rule is reflected in LOAC instruments.[63] Grave violations of the LOAC may be prosecuted as war crimes and may fall within the jurisdiction of the ICC.[64] Less serious violations might be punishable under the various articles of the Uniform Code of Military Justice (UCMJ).

3. Rules of Engagement

Rules of engagement are "directives that a government may establish to delineate the circumstances and limitations under which its own naval, ground, and air forces will initiate and/or continue *combat* engagement with enemy forces."[65] Adequate ROE appropriate to the situation are vital to mission success and protection of U.S. and allied assets. An unexcused failure to obey controlling ROE is punishable as an orders violation under the UCMJ.[66] Additionally, a service member who violates the applicable ROE may lose affirmative defenses to assault or homicide charges under the UCMJ.[67] At the same time, however, the fact that official conduct may have violated applicable ROE or an internal agency directive does not mean the conduct violated international law.[68]

In the United States, a distinction is drawn between ROE for combat operations and the rules and policies on the use of force in noncombat engagements. The latter category includes

58. See Commander's Handbook, supra, ¶ 6.2.2. The International Committee for the Red Cross was founded by Henry Dunant in 1863 and is headquartered in Geneva.
59. Commander's Handbook, supra, ¶ 5.3 (citing DoD Directive 2311.01).
60. Advisory Opinion, Legality of the Threat or Use of Nuclear Weapons, 1996 I.C.J. 226, 245 (July 8). See also Commander's Handbook, supra, ¶ 5.3; Restatement FRLUS § 905.
61. Charles Maurice de Talleyrand was a French diplomat. His advice to Napoleon originated in the writings of Montesquieu.
62. See, e.g., Protocol for the Prohibition of the Use in War of Asphyxiating, Poisonous or Other Gases, and of Bacteriological Methods of Warfare, June 17, 1925, 26 U.S.T. 571, 94 L.N.T.S. 65.
63. See, e.g., Hague Convention IV Regulations Annex, art. 22, Oct. 18, 1907.
64. See 18 U.S.C. § 2441.
65. See DoD Dictionary, Joint Pub. 1-02, supra (emphasis added). See also Sanremo ROE Handbook, supra, at 1.
66. UCMJ, art. 92, 10 U.S.C. § 892.
67. Self-defense is an affirmative defense under the Uniform Code of Justice. Rule for Courts-Martial (R.C.M.) 916(e), Manual for Courts Martial (2002). A similar rule applies in cases brought before the International Criminal Court. To prevail on a defense of self-defense before the ICC, the conduct must have been a "reasonable" response to an imminent and unlawful use of force. Rome Statute of the ICC, supra, art. 31(1)(c). The Rome Statute also limits the defense of obedience to orders. Responsibility for crimes falling within the Rome Statute is excluded only if (a) the person acting under a legal obligation to obey orders did not know the order was unlawful, and (b) the order was not manifestly unlawful. Rome Statute of the ICC, supra, art. 33.
68. See U.S. v. Hensel, 699 F.2d 18, 28, 29 (1st Cir. 1983).

the U.S. Coast Guard Use of Force Policy (CGUFP) applicable to law enforcement activities and the rules on the use of force (RUF) for DoD elements engaged in civil support and homeland security missions that do not call for the traditional use of armed force.[69] All three rule sets address the active use of force to accomplish the respective missions. Each also addresses the use of force in self-defense. Self-defense is further broken down into national, unit, and individual self-defense.

Although much of ROE doctrine and guidance is classified, a few general comments can be made. ROE are commonly characterized as a command and control tool. The ROE applicable to a given situation are typically promulgated by national and subordinate command authorities and may include rules promulgated by joint or combined command authorities. They can include permissive articles (e.g., "the use of X is authorized") or restrictive articles ("you may not use X"). ROE include both self-defense and mission accomplishment rules, and any supplemental rules of engagement for specific operations, missions, or projects. Self-defense is distinguished from many force protection (FP) measures by the fact that some FP measures are precautionary and are not tested by the "imminence" standard and the presence of a hostile act or demonstrated hostile intent.[70]

The three commonly cited bases relied on in drafting ROE are national policy objectives, operational requirements, and applicable laws. ROE must always conform to the relevant international and national law, including the law of armed conflict. For strategic, operational, and policy reasons, however, the commander may elect to promulgate ROE that are more restrictive than international or national law.[71] Accordingly, compliance with the ROE should constitute compliance with the applicable law.

The U.S. SROE were approved by the president and the secretary of defense and promulgated by the chairman of the Joint Chiefs of Staff. Combatant commanders may augment the SROE as necessary to reflect changing political and military policies, threats, and missions specific to their area of responsibility. Such augmentations to the standing rules are approved by the president, the secretary of defense, or both and are promulgated by the Joint Staff, as annexes to the SROE.[72]

Unless otherwise directed by the secretary of defense, the SROE apply to all military operations and contingencies and routine military department functions, as well as air and maritime homeland defense missions conducted within U.S. territory and territorial seas.[73] Although the U.S. Coast Guard is one of the five armed forces,[74] it falls under the Department of Homeland Security, not the DoD. Nevertheless, under some circumstances the DoD's SROE are also applicable to U.S. Coast Guard units and personnel. Those circumstances are listed in the U.S. Coast Guard *Maritime Law Enforcement Manual*.[75]

The SROE do not limit a commander's inherent obligation and authority to take appropriate action, using all necessary means available, in self-defense of the commander's unit and

---

69. See Chairman, Joint Chiefs of Staff, Standing Rules of Engagement for U.S. Forces, CJCS Inst. 3121.01B (June 13, 2005), ¶ 3.b. Sections of the instruction are classified; however, Enclosure A, which sets out the standing rules of engagement for self-defense, is unclassified, as are the enclosures setting out the rules on the use of force.

70. See U.S. Navy, Antiterrorism/Force Protection, NTTP 3-07.2.1, rev. A (2004) (unclassified but for official use only).

71. For example, applicable ROE might limit engagement of targets beyond visual range or impose stricter limits on collateral casualties or damage.

72. Commander's Handbook, supra, at 19 & ¶ 4.4.3.2.

73. See CJCS Inst. 3121.01B, supra, Encl. A, ¶ 1(a). An exception is included for U.S. forces under the operational control of a multinational force. Id. ¶ 1(f).

74. 14 U.S.C. § 1.

75. Coast Guard MLE Manual, supra, ch. 4, ¶ B.1 (note).

other U.S. forces in the vicinity.[76] The U.S. Navy has long emphasized that the commanding officer has both the right and the obligation to defend his or her unit.[77] The duty to defend the unit was implicated in the prosecution of three officers of the USS *Stark* (FFG-31) following a 1987 missile attack on the frigate by an Iraqi fighter. Other cases that raised the issue include the 1988 Iranian airliner incident involving the USS *Vincennes* (CG-49) and the 2000 attack on the USS *Cole* (DDG-67) during a refueling stop in Yemen. The findings of a Navy court of inquiry convened by CINCPAFLT to investigate the conduct of the USS *Pueblo* (AGER-2) following the warship's forcible seizure by North Korea in 1968 are instructive. In recommending that the commanding officer be court-martialed, the court members concluded that he "decided to surrender his ship when it was completely operational without offering any resistance. He just didn't try—this was his greatest fault. . . . He failed in every way to take any immediate and aggressive protective measures and to counter-attack in accordance with his instructions when attacked by the North Koreans. . . . He made no apparent effort to resist seizure of his ship. . . . He permitted his ship to be boarded and searched while he still had the power to resist."[78]

The right of self-defense is subject to the twin constraints of necessity and proportionality.[79] "Necessity" for the use of force in self-defense exists when a hostile act occurs or when the target exhibits hostile intent. "Proportionality" in the self-defense context refers to measures that are reasonable in intensity, duration, and magnitude in relation to the perceived or demonstrated threat, based on all the facts known to the commander at the time. The SROE emphasize that "all necessary means available and all appropriate actions" may be used in self-defense.[80] Although the meaning of that phrase under the SROE is classified, it can be said that when the hostile force no longer represents an imminent threat, the right to self-defense ends.

B. USE OF FORCE IN MARITIME LAW ENFORCEMENT

The introduction to this chapter highlights the distinction between the two common usages of the term "force." When the UN Charter speaks of "force" in Article 2(4), it is referring to armed military force (aggressive and defensive) by one state against another state or, in some cases, an armed group. "Force" is also used to refer to the means used by authorized warships and other government vessels and military and other state aircraft and their authorized personnel to compel individuals to comply with law enforcement measures.[81] Such "police force" is not directed

---

76. CJCS Inst. 3121.01B, supra, Encl. A, ¶ 3.a.

77. See, e.g., Article 0914 of the U.S. Navy Regulations ("On occasions when injury to the United States or to citizens thereof is committed or threatened in violation of the principles of international law or in violation of rights existing under a treaty or other international agreement, the senior officer present . . . shall take such action as is demanded by the gravity of the situation. In time of peace, action involving the use of force shall be taken only in consonance with the provisions of [Article 0915]"). Article 0915 limits the use of force against another state to cases of self-defense against hostile acts or hostile intent directed against the unit and, when appropriate, in defense of U.S. citizens, their property, and U.S. commercial assets in the vicinity. See also Joseph H. Elred, The Use of Force in Hostage Rescue Missions, 56 Nav. L. Rev. 251 (2008).

78. U.S. Navy, Findings of Fact, Opinions and Recommendations of a Court of Inquiry [USS *Pueblo* incident], available at http://www.usspueblo.org/Court_of_Inquiry/Court%20&%20SECNAV%20findings.pdf (accessed Feb. 1, 2013). See also Code of Conduct for Members of the U.S. Armed Forces, art. II ("I will never surrender of my own free will. If in command, I will never surrender the members of my command while they still have the means to resist").

79. Id. ¶ 4; Sanremo ROE Handbook, supra, at 3–6 & appendix 5.

80. CJCS Inst. 3121.01B, supra, ¶ 4(a).

81. See Louis Sohn, Peacetime Use of Force on the High Seas, 64 U.S. Naval War Coll. Int'l L. Studies 38 (1991).

against a state and does not constitute "armed force,"[82] nor does it violate the LOS Convention provisions reserving the seas for "peaceful purposes"[83] and requiring states to refrain from the use of force in any manner inconsistent with the UN Charter.[84] Nonetheless, it is possible that some acts conducted in the course of a law enforcement operation against a vessel might be construed as an act of aggression.[85]

The use of force in maritime law enforcement operations arises in at least five distinct applications: (1) force used against a noncompliant vessel, to slow or stop the vessel in order to facilitate boarding; (2) force used against individuals on board the vessel who are opposing the boarding team's embarkation; (3) force used in unit self-defense by the enforcement vessel against the suspect vessel; (4) force used in unit self-defense by the enforcement vessel against a third vessel that is attempting to thwart the enforcement action; and (5) force used in individual self-defense by the boarding team against individuals on the boarded vessel after the team boards. Force in the first two categories "to compel compliance" roughly corresponds to mission accomplishment ROE; the latter three correspond to the SROE on self-defense.

As the number of violent law enforcement encounters rises and vessel crews grow bolder or more desperate, the need to resort to force to board noncompliant vessels or in self-defense by the enforcement vessel or its boarding team is likely to grow as well.[86] The 2010 Israeli interdiction of the MV *Mavi Marmara* when it attempted to breach the Gaza blockade and the numerous violent encounters between Japanese and Korean patrol vessels and Chinese fishing vessels in the Yellow Sea and East China Sea demonstrate that an "opposed" boarding may require a combination of both force necessary to compel compliance and force in self-defense.

1. International Law Sources

The exercise of law enforcement authority outside the territorial limits of the state is limited under international law.[87] The use of force in actions not constituting an armed conflict may be authorized or limited by treaty,[88] such as a multilateral or bilateral boarding agreement,[89] or by customary international law.[90] For the most part, international law is directly implicated only

---

82. Myres S. McDougal, Authority to Use Force on the High Seas, 61 U.S. Nav. War Coll. Int'l L. Studies 551, 557–58 (1979) (concluding that the use of force in law enforcement activities does not constitute forcible countermeasures); Ivan A. Shearer, Problems of Jurisdiction and Law Enforcement against Delinquent Vessels, 35 Int'l & Comp. L. Q. 320 (1986).

83. LOSC art. 88.

84. Id. art. 301.

85. In its dispute with Canada over Canada's seizure of the Spanish F/V *Estai* on the high seas in 1995, Spain argued that Canada's use of warning shots to stop the vessel constituted a use of force in violation of Article 2(4) of the UN Charter. Fisheries Jurisdiction case (Spain v. Canada), ¶ 78, 1998 I.C.J. 432 (Dec. 4) (declining jurisdiction). However, nothing in the decision by the ICJ in that case or by ITLOS in the *M/V Saiga No. 2* case, discussed below, suggests that either tribunal considered the use of force in stopping and boarding a nonpublic vessel to be an "armed attack" or a violation of Article 2(4) of the UN Charter or Article 301 of the LOS Convention.

86. Not all "force" involves the use of weapons. For example, when the Italian warship *Sibilla* encountered the Albanian migrant-smuggling vessel *Kater I Rades* in the Adriatic Sea thirty-five nautical miles off the coast of Italy and attempted to turn the smuggler back with close-aboard maneuvers, the vessels collided, killing fifty-eight persons on the *Rades*. See Xhavara and Others v. Italy and Albania, European Ct. Human Rights (Jan. 11, 2001). Such vessel-to-vessel shouldering and ramming cases appear to be on the rise in disputed Asian waters.

87. See, e.g., LOSC art. 73 (limiting enforcement measures available to coastal state in the EEZ).

88. See Straddling Fish Stocks Implementation Agreement, supra, art. 22 (limiting the use of force in fisheries enforcement actions).

89. The European Council's legislation authorizing the Operation Atalanta counterpiracy operations off the coast of Somalia expressly authorized the use of force. See European Council, Council Joint Action 2008/851/CFSP of 10 November 2008 (Article 2(d) addresses the use of force).

90. See generally Guilfoyle, Shipping Interdiction and the Law of the Sea, supra, at 271–93.

in incidents involving conduct by one state directed against the nationals, vessels, or aircraft of another state.[91] However, international human rights law, including the International Covenant on Civil and Political Rights (ICCPR), might apply to a state's conduct when directed at one of its own nationals.[92]

When an interception and boarding is carried out under authority of a multilateral or bilateral agreement, the agreement itself may authorize or limit the use of force. Such is the case with several boarding agreements entered into by the United States and authorizing counterdrug or counterproliferation boardings.[93] Any use of force other than in self-defense is therefore restricted to measures authorized by the treaty, as modified by any later case-specific verbal agreements. The interplay of conventional and customary law on the use of force in maritime law enforcement operations is demonstrated by three leading cases.[94] The first case, concerning the vessel *I'm Alone*, arose under a bilateral boarding treaty but also briefly examines the use of force under customary law.

a. The *I'm Alone* (1929)

The starting point for examining the international law limits on the use of force against a foreign vessel by maritime law enforcement authorities is the arbitration commission decision in the dispute that arose out of the sinking of the auxiliary-powered schooner *I'm Alone* on March 22, 1929.[95] The U.S. Coast Guard cutter *Wolcott* intercepted the British-flag (Canadian-registered) vessel *I'm Alone* on March 20, 1929, when it was anchored between eight and fifteen nautical miles off the coast of Louisiana (the distance offshore was disputed by the parties). A 1924 treaty between the United States and Great Britain authorized the United States to board British-flag vessels suspected of liquor smuggling while in close proximity to the U.S. coast.[96] Both governments agreed that the *I'm Alone* was "unquestionably" a notorious smuggling vessel that transported liquor from Belize and the Bahamas for delivery to contact boats off the U.S. coast while staying just outside the U.S. territorial sea.[97] The contact boats then ran the liquor ashore, in violation of the National Prohibition Act. When the cutter *Wolcott* approached, the master of the *I'm Alone* protested that the U.S. Coast Guard had no jurisdiction over his vessel, weighed anchor, and began to flee southwest toward Mexico. The *Wolcott* fired across the vessel's bow and into the rigging, but the *I'm Alone* continued to flee. Over the next two days, the *Wolcott* followed the vessel in hot pursuit, eventually enlisting the assistance of two other Coast Guard

---

91. See U.S. v. Postal, 589 F.2d 862, 870 (5th Cir. 1979) (holding that "the boarding of a vessel on the high seas by its flag state is not an international event. The consequences are solely a domestic matter. The boarding of a foreign vessel is, of course, a matter of international concern that might call for more restraint on the part of the boarding state").

92. See ICCPR, supra, art. 2(1) (requiring states parties to protect the defined rights of all individuals "within its territory and subject to its jurisdiction"). See also Restatement FRLUS § 701. Application might turn on reservations and exception entered and the extent to which the convention is deemed to be self-executing.

93. See, e.g., U.S.-Liberia Bilateral WMD Boarding Agreement (Article 9 addresses the use of force), available at http://www.state.gov/t/isn/trty/32403.htm (accessed Feb. 1, 2013).

94. A fourth case, involving Israel's interdiction of the so-called Gaza flotilla in 2010 was, as a blockade enforcement action, governed by the law of armed conflict. The incident is examined in chapter 12.

95. The diplomatic correspondence, claims, and briefs exchanged between the two governments are reprinted in U.S. Department of State, Arbitration Series No. 2 (vols. 1–7), *I'm Alone* case (1931–35).

96. Convention for the Prevention of Smuggling of Intoxicating Liquors (U.S.–Great Britain), Jan. 23, 1924, 43 Stat. 1761, 27 L.N.T.S. 181, reprinted in the *I'm Alone* case, supra, vol. 1, annex B. Article II of the convention provided the United States jurisdiction to board British vessels beyond U.S. waters when within a distance from the coast the target vessel could traverse in one hour.

97. Under customary international law, by acting as a "mother ship" supplying contraband to contact boats in violation of U.S. laws, the *I'm Alone* was arguably "constructively present" in U.S. waters.

cutters, the *Dexter* and the *Hamilton*. On March 22, 1929, after the chase had taken the vessels more than two hundred miles from the U.S. coast, the cutter *Dexter* closed in on the *I'm Alone* and once again ordered the vessel to heave to for boarding. After the master refused, the *Dexter* fired across the vessel's bow and then into the sails and rigging. The *Dexter* then ceased fire and once again ordered the vessel to stop, warning that it would be sunk if it did not. According to the Coast Guard account, the master of the *I'm Alone* brandished a pistol and told the *Dexter* that he would forcibly resist any attempt to board his vessel. The *Dexter* then resumed fire, this time into the hull of the *I'm Alone*, which sank about thirty minutes later. The master and crew of the *I'm Alone* jumped into the water as the vessel sank. The Coast Guard recovered all but one of the crew. One crewman, a French national, drowned before he could be recovered.

The arbitration panel appointed by the United States and Canada concluded that, assuming the United States had jurisdiction over the *I'm Alone* under the 1924 treaty, the Coast Guard was justified in using "necessary and reasonable force for the purpose of effecting the objects of boarding, searching, seizing and bringing into port the suspected vessel; and if sinking should occur incidentally, as a result of the exercise of necessary and reasonable force for such purpose, the pursuing vessel might be entirely blameless."[98] The commissioners went on to conclude, however, that the cutter's act of intentionally sinking the *I'm Alone* was not justified under either the 1924 treaty or any other principle of international law.[99]

Three observations are in order. First, the commission resolved the case under what its members understood to be the prevailing international law standard. Second, the "reasonable and necessary force" standard articulated by the commissioners applied to all phases of the interception, from boarding through seizure.[100] Finally, the commission did not attempt to flesh out its "reasonable and necessary" standard, other than to draw a distinction between a sinking that was incidental and one that was intentional; nor did it explain whether the nature of the suspected offense (liquor smuggling) was a factor to be considered in weighing the necessity or proportionality of the force used. It was sufficient for the commissioners to determine that the Coast Guard's decision to intentionally sink the *I'm Alone* under the circumstances exceeded that standard.

b. The *Red Crusader* (1961)

A second frequently cited law enforcement use of force case arose out of a 1961 enforcement action against the British fishing vessel *Red Crusader* by the Danish frigate *Niels Ebbesen*.[101] On May 21, 1961, the trawler *Red Crusader* and several other fishing vessels were sighted near the Danish Faeroe Islands. The parties disputed the *Red Crusader*'s exact position and whether it was

---

98. Joint Interim Report of the Commissioners, The *I'm Alone* case (1933), supra, vol. 6, at 5.

99. Id. Ultimately, compensation was denied to the owners on the ground that they were U.S. nationals, but the arbitrators ordered the United States to apologize and pay $25,000 in compensation to the United Kingdom for its insult to the U.K. flag. Joint Final Report of the Commissioners, The *I'm Alone* case (1935), supra, vol. 7, at 3–4.

100. Part V of the LOS Convention, which governs enforcement of marine resource laws in the EEZ, similarly limits "enforcement measures" available to the coastal state to those "necessary"; however, it appears to take a broad view of necessity. Article 73 provides that the coastal state is authorized to "take such measures, including boarding, inspection and judicial proceedings, *as may be necessary to ensure compliance* with the laws and regulations adopted in conformity with this Convention." LOSC art. 73 (emphasis added). This is functionally equivalent to the standard in 14 U.S.C. § 89 (authorizing "all necessary force to compel compliance"). Spain took a narrower view of Article 73 in its dispute with Canada over the 1995 seizure of the F/V *Estai*. Spain's counsel suggested in oral argument that because Article 73 does not expressly authorize the use of force, any use of force would violate international law. Fisheries Jurisdiction case (Spain v. Canada) (Oral argument for Spain by Counsel Sanchez on June 9, 1998), at http://www.icj-cij.org/icjwww/idocket/iec/iecframe.htm (accessed Feb. 1, 2013).

101. The *Red Crusader* case (U.K. v. Denmark), Commission of Enquiry, Mar. 23, 1962, 35 Int'l L. Rep. 485 (1962). The two governments agreed to establish a commission of inquiry to determine the vessel's location at the time of interception.

engaged in fishing. On sighting the *Red Crusader*, the *Niels Ebbesen* signaled it to stop by signal searchlight and siren. When those signals went unheeded, the Danes fired a blank 40-mm warning shot across the *Red Crusader*'s bow. The *Red Crusader* stopped, and the *Niels Ebbesen* sent over a boarding party. The master of the *Red Crusader* was notified that his vessel was under arrest and was told to follow the *Niels Ebbesen* into port. A two-man custody crew was placed on board the *Red Crusader*. After initially complying with the Danish frigate's instructions, the master of the *Red Crusader* changed his mind, locked up the custody crew, and attempted to flee with the embarrassed hostages.

When the *Red Crusader*'s attempted flight became apparent to the commanding officer of the *Niels Ebbesen*, the frigate fired two 127-mm warning shots (one astern and one to starboard), accompanied almost immediately by a sound signal (Morse code "K") to stop. Two minutes later, it fired warning shots ahead of and to port of the *Red Crusader*, again closely followed by a whistle signal to stop. Fifteen minutes later, as the *Red Crusader* continued to flee, the *Niels Ebbesen* fired solid (nonexplosive) shots at the vessel's scanner, mast, masthead light, hull, and stem while interspersing further warnings by loudhailer to stop. The vessel was damaged but not sunk, and no one was injured. Britain protested the Danes' action.

The commission of inquiry later appointed by the two governments to investigate the matter determined:

> (1) In opening fire at 03.22 hours up to 03.53 hours, the Commanding Officer of the *Niels Ebbesen* exceeded legitimate use of armed force on two counts: (a) firing without warning of solid gun-shot; (b) creating danger to human life on board the *Red Crusader* without proved necessity, by the effective firing at the *Red Crusader* after 03.40; (2) The escape of the *Red Crusader* in flagrant violation of the order received and obeyed, the seclusion on board the trawler of an officer and rating of *Niels Ebbesen*, and Skipper Wood's refusal to stop may explain some resentment on the part of Captain Sølling. Those circumstances, however, cannot justify such violent action; and (3) The Commission is of the opinion that other means should have been attempted, which, if duly persisted in, might have finally persuaded Skipper Wood to stop and revert to the normal procedure which he himself had previously followed.[102]

The commission did not specify what other, nondeadly means would have been appropriate in this fisheries enforcement action. Nor did it categorically rule out a use of force that might create a danger to human life, at least in cases of "proved necessity."[103]

The commission was also asked to examine the propriety of the conduct of the British naval vessel HMS *Troubridge*, which intervened in the confrontation. The Danish government initially protested that the *Troubridge* had interfered with legitimate law enforcement measures by Denmark by interposing itself between the other two vessels. Although Denmark withdrew parts of the question from the commission, the commission nevertheless offered its opinion that *Troubridge* "made every effort to avoid any recourse to violence between *Niels Ebbesen* and *Red Crusader*."[104] The commission went on to opine that "such an attitude and conduct were

---

102. Id. at 499.
103. The use of the phrase "proved necessity" suggests that the burden of proof was on Denmark.
104. This conclusion may mean nothing more than that if the fleeing vessel's flag state intervenes and persuades the vessel to stop, the use of force is no longer necessary. Had the British intervention permitted the *Red Crusader* to escape, it is unlikely that it would have been excused.

impeccable."[105] The two governments later agreed to mutually waive all claims and charges arising out of the incident.[106]

c. The M/V *Saiga* (1997)

A more recent decision examining the international law limits on the use of force in a maritime law enforcement boarding was issued in 1999 by the International Tribunal for the Law of the Sea.[107] The case was initiated by the flag state, Saint Vincent and the Grenadines, against the Republic of Guinea, in its capacity as a coastal state. It arose out of the forcible arrest by Guinea of the Saint Vincent–flag vessel M/V *Saiga*, a coastal tanker that refueled fishing vessels at sea. On the day before the incident, the *Saiga* had delivered fuel to three fishing vessels in waters twenty-two nautical miles offshore from Guinea. The *Saiga* then moved to a position just outside the Guinean EEZ to await the arrival of several more vessels in need of fuel. At about 0800 on October 28, 1997, the *Saiga* was, in the words of the tribunal, "attacked" by Guinean patrol boat *P35* for an alleged violation of customs laws. Armed officers from the *P35* boarded the *Saiga*, seized the vessel, and arrested the master and crew, firing their weapons at various times in the process. The *Saiga* was taken to Conakry, where the master was detained and the crewmembers' travel documents were confiscated. Two crewmen who were injured by gunfire during the boarding were later allowed to travel to Dakar for medical treatment.

The tribunal's first ruling in the matter concerned Saint Vincent's application for prompt release of the *Saiga* and its crew on the posting of reasonable security.[108] The second decision concerned the merits and addressed a number of issues, including the use of force by the Guinean enforcement vessel. Saint Vincent argued that Guinea's use of force in stopping and boarding the vessel was excessive and unreasonable, pointing out that the *Saiga* was an unarmed tanker that was almost fully laden with gas oil.[109] The vessel was riding low in the water (and therefore easily boarded) and was capable of a speed of no more than ten knots. The crew offered no resistance. Saint Vincent also called the tribunal's attention to the fact that the *P35* fired live ammunition, using solid shot from large-caliber automatic weapons. In response, Guinea asserted that the *P35* crew's actions were neither unreasonable nor unnecessary because the *Saiga* refused all visual, auditory, and radio signals to stop. In its ruling, the tribunal explained that "although the Convention does not contain express provisions on the use of force in the arrest of ships, international law, which is applicable by virtue of article 293 of the Convention, requires that the use of force must be avoided as far as possible and, where force is unavoidable, it must not go beyond what is reasonable and necessary in the circumstances. Considerations of humanity must apply in the law of the sea, just as they do in other areas of international law."[110]

The tribunal concluded that the Guinean patrol vessel fired live ammunition at the *Saiga* without first issuing any of the signals and warnings required by international law and practice. Once on board the *Saiga*, Guinean enforcement personnel fired their weapons indiscriminately, despite the fact that the crew of the *Saiga* offered no resistance and did not threaten the boarding

---

105. The *Red Crusader*, supra, 35 Int'l L. Rep. at 500.
106. Id.
107. M/V *Saiga* (St. Vincent & the Grenadines v. Guinea), ITLOS Case No. 2, Judgment of July 1, 1999, 38 I.L.M. 1323 (1999).
108. See M/V *Saiga* (St. Vincent & the Grenadines v. Guinea), ITLOS Case No. 1, Prompt Release of Dec. 4, 1997, 37 I.L.M. 360 (1998). After the tribunal ruled on Saint Vincent's prompt release request, the parties entered into a special agreement to have the tribunal hear the merits. Accordingly, there was no examination of whether Guinea's enforcement actions potentially fell within an exception to compulsory dispute settlement.
109. The M/V *Saiga* No. 2, supra, ¶ 153.
110. Id. ¶ 155.

team. In the process, two of the *Saiga* crewmembers were seriously injured and vital equipment in the vessel's radio room and engine room was damaged. The tribunal ordered the government of Guinea to make reparation to the vessel's flag state. It relied in part on the I'm Alone and Red Crusader cases as the basis for its ruling and held that Guinea's use of force before and after the boarding was excessive and endangered human life.[111]

The tribunal identified at least two steps an enforcing vessel must take before using force against a noncompliant vessel.[112] First, the noncompliant vessel must be given an auditory or visual signal to stop using internationally recognized signals. If the signals are not heeded, the enforcing vessel is justified in firing one or more warning shots across the bow of the vessel in a manner likely to attract attention. If the warning shots also go unheeded, the enforcing vessel is justified, as a last resort and after further warning the noncompliant vessel, in using disabling fire.[113]

In ruling against Guinea, the tribunal referred to the enforcement provisions in the 1995 Straddling Fish Stocks Agreement,[114] which was not in effect at the time of the decision, and in any event would not have been controlling in the *Saiga* dispute, which did not involve fisheries. Article 21 of the Straddling Fish Stocks Agreement provides a mechanism for states other than the flag state to exercise fisheries enforcement authority over foreign vessels on the high seas. Article 22 calls on parties conducting enforcement measures to ensure that their duly authorized fisheries inspectors "avoid the use of force except when and to the degree necessary to ensure the safety of the inspectors and where the inspectors are obstructed in the execution of their duties."[115] The tribunal concluded that Article 22 reaffirmed the "basic principle concerning the use of force in the arrest of a ship at sea."[116] Had the tribunal looked to other possible rules or standards to guide its decision, it might have also examined Article 225 of the LOS Convention. Although that article appears in Part XII on protection of the marine environment, the actual text suggests that it has a wider application. It provides that "in the exercise under this Convention of their powers of enforcement against foreign vessels, States shall not endanger the safety of navigation or otherwise create any hazard to a vessel, or bring it to an unsafe port or anchorage, or expose the marine environment to an unreasonable risk."

Assuming the Article 225 standard is relevant, whatever the prohibition on "hazarding" the suspect vessel or "endangering" the safety of navigation might mean, the tribunal's judgment in the *M/V* Saiga case does not suggest that the LOS Convention prohibits all use of force to stop a noncompliant vessel. At the same time, a tribunal examining the question today might also look to the use-of-force provisions of the 2005 Protocol to the Convention for the Suppression of Unlawful Acts against the Safety of Maritime Navigation. The protocol limits the use of force by enforcement units and personnel to "the minimum degree of force which is necessary and reasonable in the circumstances."[117]

---

111. Id. ¶ 153.

112. Id. ¶ 156. How these safeguards will be applied to submersible and semisubmersible drug-trafficking vessels, where visual warnings and warning shots may not be practical, has yet to be determined.

113. The tribunal ultimately concluded, on conflicting assertions, that Guinea had failed to warn the *Saiga* before opening fire. Id. ¶ 157. If warnings were given, the *P35* did not document the warnings by audiotape or videotape.

114. Straddling Fish Stocks Agreement, supra, art. 22.

115. Id. art. 22(1)(f). Before extending the Article 22 limits outside the fisheries enforcement context it might be useful to consider that some fisheries enforcement regimes do not even permit boarding officers to be armed while conducting boardings. Unarmed boardings would be unrealistic for vessels that might be engaged in trafficking in narcotics, weapons, or humans, and any use of force policy must recognize the differing risk levels presented in the various contexts.

116. The *M/V Saiga* No. 2, supra, ¶ 156.

117. 2005 SUA Protocol, supra, art. 8*bis* (9).

d. UN Guidance Documents

The increasing use of deadly force in maritime interdiction and enforcement actions highlights the need for further development and clarification on the international limits on such actions.[118] It is clear that customary law prohibits firing into a vessel without warning. Additionally, using gunfire to intentionally sink a fleeing vessel suspected of smuggling illegal liquor, at least without first attempting to disable it, violates the established rule that force must be necessary and reasonable. Such gunfire would almost certainly pose a threat to the lives of those on board.[119] But the precise contours of the legal limits on the use of police force at sea remain unclear.[120] In contrast to U.S. law, international law has so far failed to recognize explicitly that the level of force that is reasonable and appropriate under the circumstances will vary according to the nature of the violation and the impact alternative enforcement approaches will have on the legal regime's effectiveness.[121] Force levels appropriate in interdicting a vessel engaged in narcotics trafficking might well be inappropriate to one suspected of violating fisheries or customs laws. Similarly, the shared interest in interdicting a WMD shipment under circumstances that threaten international peace and security could justify force levels that would be deemed excessive in response to a less threatening vessel. To be accurate, any contemporary statement of customary law must also account for a significant amount of recent state practice—particularly in the counterpiracy operations and fisheries enforcement encounters in East Asian waters—that is not easily reconciled with the broad statements made by ITLOS in the *M/V* Saiga case.

Prominent commentators have adopted the position that international law, as articulated by the arbitral tribunal in the I'm Alone case and the 2005 SUA Protocol, permits states to use only the "minimum force" necessary to compel compliance.[122] That "minimum" force standard (as contrasted with "reasonable" force) is generally consistent with UN doctrine. The *Basic Principles on the Use of Force and Firearms by Law Enforcement Officials* was adopted by the United Nations for enforcement operations ashore.[123] Drawing on Article 3 of the UN Code of Conduct for Law Enforcement Officials,[124] the *Basic Principles* states that "law enforcement officials may use force only when strictly necessary and to the extent required for the performance of their duty."[125] It generally argues against the use of firearms and asserts:

> Governments and law enforcement agencies should develop a range of means
> as broad as possible and equip law enforcement officials with various types of

---

118. See Tim Zimmermann, If World War III Comes, Blame Fish, U.S. News & World Rep. (Oct. 21, 1996), at 59–60. The United Kingdom dispatched naval frigates to protect British fishing boats during the several "cod wars" with Iceland from 1958 to 1976. See also D. P. O'Connell, The International Law of the Sea, vol. II, at 1071–72 n.67 (Ivan A. Shearer ed., 1984) (collecting cases and protests involving the use of force against U.S. vessels and those of other states).

119. The use of force to intentionally sink a vessel with persons on board would constitute "deadly force" (force that is likely to cause death or serious physical injury). The standards for the use of deadly force are much more stringent than those applicable to the use of disabling fire to stop a noncompliant vessel.

120. Recent decisions by the ICJ highlight the importance of clarifying the burden and quantum of proof in such cases. See Oil Platforms, supra (Separate Opinion of Judge Higgins, ¶¶ 30–39).

121. The LOS Convention prescribes an effectiveness standard for enforcement. See, e.g., LOSC art. 94(1) (establishing flag state's duty to "effectively" exercise its jurisdiction and control).

122. Churchill & Lowe, supra, at 461; see also O'Connell, supra, at 1071–74 (also relying on the I'm Alone case).

123. Basic Principles on the Use of Force and Firearms by Law Enforcement Officials [hereinafter "Basic Principles"], U.N. Doc. E/CN.15/1996/16/Add.2 (1990).

124. UN Code of Conduct for Law Enforcement Officials [hereinafter "Code of Conduct"], adopted by the UN General Assembly, G.A. Res. 34/169, Dec. 17, 1979, U.N. Doc. A/RES/34/169 (1979).

125. That standard is generally consistent with Article 2(2) of the European Human Rights Convention, which provides a narrow exception to the protection-of-life guarantee for the use of "force which is no more than absolutely necessary" under one of three listed circumstances, including self-defense and defense of others.

weapons and ammunition that would allow for a differentiated use of force and firearms. These would include the development of non-lethal incapacitating weapons for use in appropriate situations, with a view to increasingly restraining the application of means capable of causing death or injury to persons. For the same purpose, it should also be possible for law enforcement officials to be equipped with self-defensive equipment such as shields, helmets, bullet-proof vests and bullet-proof means of transportation, in order to decrease the need to use weapons of any kind.[126]

The commentary accompanying the *Code of Conduct* emphasizes that the use of force by law enforcement officials should be exceptional. Although the *Basic Principles* is not in itself binding, an argument can be made that when the UN Security Council authorizes enforcement measures under Article 41, with the proviso that such measures shall be carried out "in conformity with international standards," the applicable standards might be construed to include the *Basic Principles* and *Code of Conduct* documents if the measures taken are in the nature of law enforcement actions.

It should be noted that the *I'm Alone* minimum force rule was adopted in the context of force used to "compel compliance" with law enforcement measures, not force used in self-defense. Thus, measures to board a noncompliant vessel or to overcome resistance in an opposed boarding would be governed by that standard. By contrast, the weight of authority rejects the "minimum force" standard in self-defense situations in favor of a "reasonable force" standard. Both applications now commonly employ a variety of nonlethal weapons and tactics.[127]

2. U.S. Coast Guard Use-of-Force Authorities

Although the focus of this book is international law, a brief examination of relevant U.S. law and policy on the use of force in at-sea law enforcement actions will provide context. Throughout the approach and boarding phases of a maritime law-enforcement encounter, U.S. law and policy distinguish the use of force to carry out the boarding, search, and seizure (i.e., force to compel compliance) from the use of force in self-defense. A host of statutes and service directives and doctrines control the use of force in such circumstances. Prominent service directives providing doctrine and tactics, techniques, and procedures (TTP) include the U.S. Coast Guard *Maritime Law Enforcement Manual*, the U.S. Navy/Coast Guard *Maritime Interception Operations* TTP manual, and the rules of engagement.

a. Use of Force to Compel Compliance: Noncompliant Vessels

14 U.S.C § 89 establishes the general law enforcement authority of U.S. Coast Guard boarding officers and authorizes such officers to "use all necessary force to compel compliance." In exercising the authority conferred by that statute, Coast Guard personnel and, in some situations,

---

126. Basic Principles, supra, ¶ 2. The European Court of Human Rights held that the government of Turkey bore responsibility for failing to equip its security forces with non-lethal force equipment when they responded to a large internal civil disturbance, leaving the forces no alternative to the use of deadly force. Güleç v. Turkey, [1998] Eur. Ct. H.R. 21593/93, at ¶¶ 71, 73 & 83.

127. Nonlethal weapons include propeller-fouling devices, water cannons, long-range acoustic devices, laser dazzlers, rubber bullets, beanbag rounds, stun guns, and chemical irritants. A relatively new entry is the LA51 signal and warning device, which is fired from a 12-gauge military shotgun. Even nonlethal means might kill. On Oct. 16, 2012, in the Yellow Sea, a Chinese fisherman died while resisting arrest after being struck by a rubber bullet fired by a South Korean coast guard officer. The use of nonlethal weapons in armed conflicts is examined in the Commander's Handbook (¶ 9.1).

supporting DoD platforms and personnel, must comply with the Coast Guard's Use of Force Policy (see section A.3 above). The CGUFP is set out in the agency's *Maritime Law Enforcement Manual*. Although public access to the CGUFP provisions of the *Coast Guard MLE Manual* is restricted, the guidance on the use of force provided in Coast Guard's Port Security Advisory 03-09, discussed in section C below, is indicative of the service's views on the relevant law and policy on self-defense.[128]

Noncompliant vessels (NCVs) may require law enforcement vessels and aircraft to use force to compel compliance with directions to facilitate boarding. Although the definition of "noncompliant vessel" varies, the term generally refers to a vessel that fails to comply with the boarding directions given by the patrol craft and uses active or passive measures, such as refusing to heave to, to prevent or impede the boarding phase of the operation.[129] Some NCVs present the additional challenge of an "opposed boarding," a term that refers to situations in which active or passive measures are in place and intended to inflict serious bodily harm or death on the boarding team or to otherwise demonstrate a hostile intent toward the boarding team.[130]

Not all NCVs require the use of force to facilitate the boarding. For example, a low-freeboard vessel traveling at a relatively slow speed might be safely boarded even without the cooperation of the master or crew. With other NCVs, a boarding team might be vertically inserted by helicopter, obviating the use of force to stop or slow the vessel. If such nonforcible measures are unavailable or ineffective, a patrol vessel might use a combination of warning shots and disabling fire to induce or compel a determined NCV to take the necessary steps to facilitate boarding. Warning shots are a signal and do not constitute the use of force. If resort to disabling fire is required, it is important that any force be directed against the suspect vessel, not those on board. Properly conducted, disabling fire is employed in a manner that will disable a NCV without creating a risk of death or serious bodily injury to anyone on board; while it is a use of force, it does not constitute the use of deadly force.

As amended in 2004, 14 U.S.C. § 637, as amended in 2004, addresses the use of force to stop a vessel "liable to seizure or examination" by the Coast Guard.[131] It authorizes disabling fire under limited circumstances and provides for indemnity of commanding officers called on to use disabling fire.[132] Disabling fire may be used against vessels subject to "examination" or "seizure." Until recently, the federal statute governing the Coast Guard's use of force against NCVs expressly required that warning shots be fired before employing disabling fire. Any failure to first fire warning shots might have stripped the commanding officer of the indemnity provided by the statute. A 2004 amendment to 14 U.S.C. § 637 introduced an exception to the requirement. The amended statute no longer requires that warning shots be given before disabling fire if the person in command of the enforcing vessel determines that the firing of a warning signal would unreasonably endanger persons or property in the vicinity of the vessel to be stopped.[133] It is important not to read too much into the 2004 amendment. To meet the standards set by international law

---

128. U.S. Coast Guard, Port Security Advisory—Piracy (03-09), Guidance on Self-Defense or Defense of Others by U.S. Flagged Commercial Vessels Operating in High Risk Waters.

129. Maritime Interception Operations, NTTP 3-07.11M, supra, ¶ 1.2.5.

130. Id. ¶ 1.2.6. Opposed boardings are generally conducted by special operations forces, special operations capable forces, or other specially trained and designated forces.

131. 18 U.S.C. § 2237(a)(1) makes it a felony offense for the master, operator, or person in charge of a vessel of the United States, or a vessel subject to the jurisdiction of the United States, to knowingly fail to obey an order by an authorized federal law enforcement officer to heave to.

132. The indemnity also extends to those acting under that commanding officer's direction for any penalties or actions for damages arising out of the action. 14 U.S.C. § 637(b).

133. 14 U.S.C. § 637(a)(2).

for the use of force in maritime enforcement actions, the use of disabling fire without prior warning shots would still have to be preceded by an effective means of warning the fleeing vessel that force will be used if it fails to comply with the enforcing vessel's orders.[134]

U.S. Navy and other non–Coast Guard units operating under Coast Guard tactical control conducting law enforcement support operations follow the CGUFP for employing warning shots and disabling fire. Under those circumstances, the provisions and immunities of 14 U.S.C. § 637 extend to the naval unit.[135] Although their "for official use only" designation precludes disclosure of the CGUFP provisions applicable to the use of force against NCVs, it can be said that they address both the conditions for, and modalities of, using force to stop a vessel in a law enforcement situation. Use of force against NCVs generally follows the familiar multistep approach that progresses from low-level measures such as verbal commands and warnings up to disabling fire. In applying the CGUFP it is important to recognize that U.S. practice differs in some respects from the practices of other nations. Some states categorically reject the use of force to stop NCVs for minor offenses or for offenses not involving public safety. Other states merely apply the twin principles of necessity and proportionality in determining whether the use of force is appropriate to overcome a vessel's noncompliance. A final consideration in the United States is that any use of force other than in self-defense may require case-specific approval by the operational or tactical commander, who might decline to approve the use of force even in situations in which it would be permitted under the CGUFP.

One of the more successful NCV countermeasure programs began when the U.S. Coast Guard launched its Operation New Frontier (ONF) program in 1999. ONF forces employ specially equipped helicopters deployed from the Coast Guard's Helicopter Interdiction Squadron (HITRON) to patrol cutters on station in selected drug-trafficking routes. HITRON helicopters carried a Barrett M107 .50-caliber sniper rifle that can be used to disable the engines of fleeing vessels, permitting boarding by the cutter's crew.[136] Similar disabling tactics are employed by the Coast Guard's cutter-launched over-the-horizon (OTH) pursuit boats.[137] While successful against the commonly encountered "go fast" boats equipped with multiple outboard engines, such tactics are of limited utility with heavily built craft, such as commercial fishing or merchant vessels, and submerged vessels.

b. Use of Force in Self-Defense

The CGUFP also includes provisions for the use of force in self-defense. Like the SROE, it recognizes the commanding officer's inherent right and obligation to exercise self-defense in response to active aggression or immediate danger. Force used in unit self-defense must adhere

---

134. In Lewin v. U.S., the court of appeals rejected the defendant's claim that because the Coast Guard had failed to fire warning shots before firing into his vessel, unintentionally killing another crewman, the defendant was justified in resisting the boarding with "force." Although the court concluded that the former statutory requirement to fire warning shots should be "rigidly administered" "for the good of the service," it also concluded that it was "perfectly clear that the defendant knew his boat was being chased." Lewin v. U.S., 62 F.2d 619, 620 (1st Cir. 1933).

135. 14 U.S.C. § 637(c). By the terms of the statute, it applies to naval surface vessels (or aircraft) on which one or more members of the Coast Guard are assigned pursuant to 10 U.S.C. § 379. See also Commander's Handbook, supra, ¶ 3.11.5.2.

136. Coast Guard MLE Manual, supra, appendix S. One recorded fatality involving the airborne use of force occurred in January 2010 when a helicopter deployed from a Coast Guard cutter patrolling in the eastern Pacific off the coast of Guatemala used disabling fire to stop a *panga* boat smuggling cocaine and a ricochet killed the boat's operator.

137. Coast Guard MLE Manual, supra, appendix S. OTH crew training is administered by the Joint Maritime Training Center at Marine Corps Base Camp Lejeune, N.C.

to the CGUFP; however, the NCV use-of-force limitations referred to above do not apply to vessel-on-vessel use of force in self-defense. Such vessel-on-vessel defense issues apply to both the parent warship or cutter and its small boat used to transport the boarding party. The vulnerability of small craft used for boardings was demonstrated by the fatal 2012 attack on a Coast Guard cutter's small boat by the operators of a *panga*-type vessel of interest, killing a chief petty officer on the Coast Guard small boat.[138]

Unless otherwise directed by the commanding officer, Coast Guard unit personnel may exercise individual self-defense, including defense of others. They are generally authorized to use the force reasonably necessary under the circumstances to defend themselves or others from physical harm. The provisions applicable to the use of force against individuals adopt the use-of-force continuum approach that distinguishes between nondeadly force and deadly force. Only that force reasonably necessary under the circumstances may be used. Force must not be used when the assigned duties can be discharged without the use of force. However, there is no duty to retreat to avoid law enforcement situations justifying the use of force, including deadly force. There is no requirement that the force used in individual self-defense be of equal or lesser force than the force used by an aggressor. Nor it is limited to the "minimum force necessary." However, any force used in self-defense must be both necessary and reasonable.

C. USE OF FORCE IN SELF-DEFENSE BY NONSTATE ACTORS

A third maritime use-of-force inquiry concerns self-defense by nonstate actors. One application that is attracting growing attention is the use of force by vessel crews or vessels' onboard privately contracted armed security personnel to repel an attempt by pirates to board or take control of the vessel.[139] This third use-of-force issue is principally governed by the domestic laws of the involved state or states, not by international law. Congressional authorization for U.S. merchant vessels to use force to repel such attacks dates back to 1819.[140] A 2009 U.S. Coast Guard Port Security Advisory succinctly summarizes the law on self-defense and defense of others for mariners facing piracy and other armed attacks at sea in certain "high-risk waters."[141] In that advisory, the Coast Guard made it clear that its intent was to "restate existing law" on the subject. Other Coast Guard port security advisories have provided guidance on related subjects, such as the carriage of weapons[142] and the minimum guidelines for contracted security services for U.S.-flag vessels operating in certain designated high-risk waters.[143]

---

138. The incident involving the U.S. Coast Guard Cutter *Halibut*'s rigid hull inflatable boat occurred on December 2, 2012, off the California coast. The *panga* operators, both Mexican nationals, were later apprehended and charged with various crimes, including murder of an officer of the United States while that officer was engaged in his official duties and assaulting a federal officer with a deadly and dangerous weapon. See also MLE Manual, supra, ¶ 4.B.3.b.5 & appendix J.
139. See Brian Wilson, The Somali Piracy Challenge: Operational Partnering, the Rule of Law, and Capacity Building, 9 Loy. U. Chi. Int'l L. Rev. 45, 60–62 (2011). The IMO issued its Guidelines for Private Maritime Security Companies (PMSCs) Providing Privately Contracted Armed Security Personnel on Board Ships. See ISO/PAS 28007:2012. The guidelines, issued under the auspices of the International Organization for Standardization, address professional certification, PMSC company requirements, PMSC company management, and deployment considerations.
140. The Protection against Piracy Act (Act of March 3, 1819, 3 Stat. 510) authorized merchant vessels to oppose and defend against aggression by a private armed vessel.
141. U.S. Coast Guard, Port Security Advisory—Piracy (03-09), Guidance on Self-Defense or Defense of Others by U.S. Flagged Commercial Vessels Operating in High Risk Waters.
142. U.S. Coast Guard, Port Security Advisory—Piracy (04-09, revision 4), International Traffic in Arms Regulations.
143. U.S. Coast Guard, Port Security Advisory—Piracy (05-09, revision 1), Minimum Guidelines for Contracted Security Services for Vessels Operating in High Risk Waters.

Questions regarding the use of force in self-defense by nonstate actors at sea are primarily governed by domestic law. Under U.S. law, a provision inserted by Congress in the 2010 Coast Guard Authorization now authorizes the victim vessel to use force in such cases. It provides that

> the commander and crew of any merchant vessel of the United States, owned wholly, or in part, by a citizen thereof, may oppose and defend against any aggression, search, restraint, depredation, or seizure, which shall be attempted upon such vessel, or upon any other vessel so owned, by the commander or crew of any armed vessel whatsoever, not being a public armed vessel of some nation in amity with the United States, and may subdue and capture the same; and may also retake any vessel so owned which may have been captured by the commander or crew of any such armed vessel, and send the same into any port of the United States.[144]

The statute only provides authority as a matter of U.S. law, and will not necessarily preclude civil or criminal actions in another nation.[145] A dispute between India and Italy following an at-sea shooting incident that took the lives of two Indian fishermen on February 15, 2012, demonstrates the potential for conflicting claims of jurisdiction and applicable law in such incidents. The Italian marines, who were providing security for the Italian tanker *Enrica Lexie*, believed the Indians were pirates preparing to attack the vessel and fatally shot them. The incident took place off the coast of the southern Indian state of Kerala. Italy protested India's exercise of jurisdiction over the incident, claiming the shooting occurred in international waters thirty-three nautical miles off the Indian coast. At this writing in late 2013, the two Italian marines are sequestered in the Italian embassy in New Delhi awaiting trial by India.

Concerns over actual or perceived abuses by private military contractors, particularly in combat theaters, led to the adoption of the Code of Conduct for Private Security Providers in 2010. Fifty-eight providers signed on to the newly completed code, including some who provide maritime security services.[146] By subscribing to the code, a company agrees to "adopt Rules for the Use of Force consistent with applicable law and the minimum requirements contained in the section on Use of Force in this Code." The referenced code section on the use of force provides that:

> 30. Signatory Companies will require their Personnel to take all reasonable steps to avoid the use of force. If force is used, it shall be in a manner consistent with applicable law. In no case shall the use of force exceed what is strictly necessary, and should be proportionate to the threat and appropriate to the situation.
>
> 31. Signatory Companies will require that their Personnel not use firearms against persons except in self-defense or defence of others against the imminent threat

---

144. Pub. L. No. 111-281, Oct. 15, 2010, § 912, 124 Stat. 2905. The 2012 Coast Guard and Marine Transportation Act requires government agencies to provide armed security personnel to U.S. vessels carrying certain government-impelled cargoes while in transit through high-risk waters or to reimburse vessel owners or operators for the cost of providing such security. See 46 U.S.C. § 55305.
145. 33 U.S.C. § 383. See also 76 Fed. Reg. 39,411 (July 6, 2011) (Coast Guard discussion on implementation of self-defense measures).
146. See International Code of Conduct for Private Security Service Providers, Nov. 10, 2010, available at http://www.news.admin.ch/NSBSubscriber/message/attachments/21143.pdf (accessed Feb. 1, 2013).

of death or serious injury, or to prevent the perpetration of a particularly serious crime involving grave threat to life.

32. To the extent that Personnel are formally authorized to assist in the exercise of a state's law enforcement authority, Signatory Companies will require that their use of force or weapons will comply with all national and international obligations applicable to regular law enforcement officials of that state and, as a minimum, with the standards expressed in the *United Nations Basic Principles on the Use of Force and Firearms by Law Enforcement Officials* (1990).

Although the code is not legally binding, by adopting the "strictly necessary" standard rather than the "reasonably necessary" standard, together with a pledge to "take all reasonable steps" to avoid the use of force altogether, the code may be viewed as evidence of the industry standard in negligence claims against security service providers for the use of force.

State Responsibility, Remedies, and Countermeasures

This chapter examines the circumstances under which one state may enforce its rights when the state or one of its nationals is harmed by another state's violation of international law. The inquiry implicates questions of state responsibility and liability, together with the law of sovereign immunity. In this context, "responsibility" refers to the state's primary obligations to adhere to international law, and "liability" refers to the state's secondary obligations, namely, the consequences of a breach of the primary obligation.[1] Article 235 of the 1982 LOS Convention briefly addresses "responsibility and liability." In examining those terms, the ITLOS Seabed Disputes Chamber concluded that, as used in the 1982 LOS Convention, the term "responsibility" has the same meaning as in the ILC Articles on State Responsibility.[2]

Mindful of the distinction between responsibility and liability,[3] this chapter briefly surveys international and U.S. laws applicable to claims for damage allegedly caused by a state before turning to the law of state responsibility. In addition to the above-cited Draft Articles on State Responsibility, prepared and adopted by the ILC in 2001,[4] a second important, but presently nonbinding, reference that guides any examination of state responsibility, liability, and immunities is the 2004 UN Convention on Jurisdictional Immunities of States and Their Properties.[5]

A. PRIVATE CLAIMS FOR DAMAGES

Seagoing officers on both sides of the maritime security and law enforcement transaction (i.e., enforcement vessel officers and those on the vessels subject to enforcement action) must be

---

1. See Responsibilities and Obligations of States Sponsoring Persons and Entities with Respect to Activities in the Area, Request for Advisory Opinion Submitted to the ITLOS Seabed Disputes Chamber, ITLOS Case No. 17, Advisory Opinion of Feb. 1, 2011, ¶ 66, 50 I.L.M. 458 (2011).
2. Id., ¶ 67.
3. State liability may attach for violations of international law or for acts or omissions in which a state's domestic law imposes a duty to compensate one harmed by the state's act or omission. The fact that sovereign immunity exempts the state from another state's enforcement measures or judicial jurisdiction does not negate the state's responsibility for violating an applicable international or domestic law. It simply requires resort to alternative means for adjustment.
4. Draft Articles on Responsibility of States for Internationally Wrongful Acts [hereinafter "ILC Draft Articles on State Responsibility"], adopted by the ILC at its Fifty-third Session (2001), U.N. GAOR, 53d Sess., Supp. No. 10, U.N. Doc. A/56/10 (2001), reprinted in 2000 Y.B. Int'l L. Comm'n, vol. II, pt. 2, at 65–71, U.N. Doc. A/CN.4/SER.A/2000/Add.1 (Part 2). The Draft Articles are analyzed in Symposium: The ILC's State Responsibility Articles, 96 Am. J. Int'l L. 773–890 (2002).
5. See UN Convention on Jurisdictional Immunities of States, 44 I.L.M. 803 (2005) (not yet in force). The Immunities Convention was drafted by the ILC and a working group chartered by the UN General Assembly. The United States participated actively in the treaty negotiations but has neither signed nor ratified it.

mindful of the potential magnitude of the commercial losses that can result from maritime security and law enforcement scenarios. For example, the direct and indirect costs of a one-week
delay of a container ship loaded with cargo destined for consignees who rely on just-in-time
deliveries from their supply chains could carry a staggering price tag. The friction costs to the
global trade and transportation system if such occurrences were anything more than isolated and
exceptional would be far more damaging.

Claims by private parties for damages caused by an act or omission attributable to a state
might be filed in the defendant state's own courts, the courts of the injured party, or those of a
third state. Private suits against states for damages need not necessarily be based on a violation of
international law. On the contrary, such suits nearly always rely on domestic law rules.[6] Claimants suing governments in U.S. courts may face a number of potential defenses not available to
nongovernment defendants, including sovereign immunity and the closely related act-of-state
doctrine.[7]

Despite ongoing attempts to establish uniform international standards for state sovereign
immunity and its exceptions,[8] the standards continue to vary from state to state, giving claimants
an incentive to litigate their claims in the most favorable forum (forum shop). The UN Convention on Jurisdictional Immunities of States and Their Properties, which will apply when a claim
against a state is brought in the domestic courts of another state, would establish a presumption
in favor of immunity in such cases. Article 5 of the Immunities Convention provides that "a
state enjoys immunity, in respect of itself and its property, from the jurisdiction of the courts
of another State subject to the provisions of the present Convention."[9] It then goes on to list a
number of exceptions to the general rule,[10] including one addressed specifically to ships owned
or operated by the state and engaged in noncommercial activities.[11] The position taken by the
Immunities Convention reflects the "restrictive view" of sovereign immunity,[12] which subjects
the commercial transactions of states and their instrumentalities to the same rules that govern
transactions by nonstate entities.[13] Claims arising out of the activities of warships and other government-operated vessels not engaged in commercial activities are *not* included in the exception
to the general rule on immunity.[14] Accordingly, the Immunities Convention would bar private

---

6. Potential "tort" theories include acts by government officers without, or in excess of, legal authority. See, e.g., LOSC art. 232.
7. With some exceptions, the judicially created act-of-state doctrine bars a court from reviewing the legality of the governmental acts of a foreign state taken within that state's territory. See Banco Nacional de Cuba v. Sabbatino, 376 U.S. 398 (1964); W. S. Kirkpatrick & Co. v. Envt'l Tectonics Corp. 493 U.S. 682 (1990). The doctrine is characterized as a rule of decision for the courts that is not required by international law or the principle of sover-eign immunity.
8. Sovereign immunity limits the jurisdiction of domestic courts over claims against a foreign state and precludes most enforcement measures by another state. See Jurisdiction Immunities of the State (Germany v. Italy), 2012 I.C.J. (Feb. 3) (holding that a state cannot be sued in the courts of another state, even for alleged serious human rights violations). The ICJ also held that the fact that the acts alleged may have violated a *jus cogens* norm does not override the rule on sovereign immunity. Id. ¶ 97.
9. See UN Convention on Jurisdictional Immunities of States, supra, art. 5.
10. Id. arts. 7–9 & pt. III.
11. Id. art. 16.
12. The U.S. Department of State adopted the restrictive theory in 1952. See Letter from Jack B. Tate, Acting Legal Adviser, U.S. Dep't of State, to Philip B. Perlman, Acting U.S. Att'y (May 29, 1952), reprinted in 26 Dep't St. Bull. 984 (1952).
13. David P. Stewart, The UN Convention on Jurisdictional Immunities of States and Their Property, 99 Am. J. Int'l L. 194 (2005).
14. UN Convention on Jurisdictional Immunities of States, supra, art. 16. Article 16 preserves the immunity of war-ships, naval auxiliaries, and other state-owned or state-operated vessels used only in government noncommercial service.

parties from asserting claims for damages arising out of a maritime security or law enforcement operations by a warship or other government vessel.

Depending on the location of a maritime security or law enforcement boarding and its outcome, the U.S. sovereign immunity waiver statutes might be less restrictive than the Immunities Convention. The statutory scheme for claims against nation-states in the United States distinguishes between claims against the U.S. federal government and those against the government of a foreign state.[15] Suits in U.S. courts against foreign governments must generally fall within one of the immunity exceptions set out in the Foreign Sovereign Immunities Act.[16] When the harm was caused by a vessel or an agent of the U.S. federal government, relevant sovereign immunity waivers may be found in the Federal Tort Claims Act,[17] Suits in Admiralty Act,[18] Public Vessels Act (PVA),[19] or Foreign Claims Act.[20] Additionally, the Tucker Act may provide a cause of action in cases in which the federal government takes private property (such as a vessel or its cargo) without paying just compensation.[21] Although federal officers and employees are generally immune from a personal suit for common law torts committed in the scope of their office or employment,[22] the U.S. Supreme Court has created a private right of action for persons injured by the "constitutional torts" of federal officers.[23]

B. INTERNATIONAL LAW OF STATE RESPONSIBILITY

State responsibility and liability are established by both conventional and customary international law sources. Those international sources have developed against several background principles, including the widely followed, but imperfectly defined, doctrine of sovereign immunity adverted to above. A state responsibility claim arises when an act or omission attributable to a state violates a duty owed under international law to another state and causes injury to the claimant state or one of its nationals.[24] The doctrine of state responsibility has no application in a claim between a state and its own nationals or vessels. On the state-to-state level, reparations for acts or omissions in violation of international law can be sought through a variety of processes ranging from diplomatic negotiations to formal adjudications before international tribunals. Those are discussed in chapter 15. Alternatively, as the previous section described, an injured shipowner or

---

15. Suits against individual states within the United States and the related Eleventh Amendment issues are beyond the scope of this examination.

16. 28 U.S.C. § 1605. See also Restatement FRLUS ch. 5. The FSIA provides the sole basis for obtaining jurisdiction over foreign sovereigns; such claims may not be brought under the Alien Tort Statute. Argentine Republic v. Amerada Hess Shipping Corp., 488 U.S. 428 (1989).

17. See generally Lester S. Jayson, Handling Federal Tort Claims: Administrative and Judicial Remedies (2012).

18. 46 U.S.C. §§ 30901–30918.

19. 46 U.S.C. §§ 31101–31113. See also Koohi v. U.S., 976 F.2d 1328 (9th Cir. 1992) (dismissing PVA claims arising out of incident in which the USS *Vincennes* mistakenly shot down an Iranian airliner after the court concluded that the FTCA's exception, in 28 U.S.C. § 2680(j), for "any claim arising out of combatant activities of the military or naval forces, or the Coast Guard, during time of war" also applies to PVA claims).

20. 10 U.S.C. § 2734. A claim may be allowed only if it did not arise from action by an enemy or result directly or indirectly from an act of the armed forces of the United States in combat. See 10 U.S.C. § 2724(b)(3).

21. 28 U.S.C. § 1491. The Tucker Act's waiver of sovereign immunity does not extend to claims based on violations of customary international law. Al-Qaisi v. U.S., 103 Fed. Cl. 439, 444 & n.6 (Fed. Cl. 2012). Moreover, a foreign citizen with no connection to the United States has no right to compensation under the Fifth Amendment for a taking that occurs in a foreign country. Atamirzayeva v. U.S., 524 F.3d 1320 (Fed. Cir. 2008).

22. See, e.g., 28 U.S.C. § 2679(b); 46 U.S.C. § 30904.

23. Bivens v. Six Unknown Named Agents of the Federal Bureau of Narcotics, 403 U.S. 388 (1971). See also Harlow v. Fitzgerald, 457 U.S. 800, 809 (1982) (recognizing qualified immunity of federal officers from claims under the *Bivens* doctrine).

24. See Marjorie M. Whiteman, 8 Digest of International Law ch. 24 (1965).

cargo shipper might seek compensation for harm caused by the state through national courts. In fact, the requirement for exhaustion of local remedies (examined in chapter 15) requires that the injured shipowner first seek relief in the responsible state.

1. Customary International Law of State Responsibility

The law of state responsibility is still largely defined by customary law. The ICJ articulated the principle of state responsibility in the 1928 *Chorzów Factory* case, in which the court explained that "it is a principle of international law, and even a general conception of law, than any breach of an engagement involves an obligation to make reparations," even if the underlying treaty does not expressly mention such a duty.[25] The responsible state is under an obligation to make full reparation for the injury caused by the internationally wrongful act.[26] The court recently reaffirmed that rule in *Armed Activities on the Territory of the Congo* when it declared that it is "well established in general international law that a state which bears responsibility for an internationally wrongful act is under an obligation to make full reparation for the injury caused by that act."[27]

2. The ILC Draft Articles on State Responsibility

For roughly five decades, the ILC developed and then debated what has come to be called the Draft Articles on State Responsibility. The current version of the Draft Articles, which represent both a codification of existing customary law (distilled from judicial decisions such as the 1928 *Chorzów Factory* case) and progressive development of the law, is founded on the principle that every internationally wrongful act of a state entails the international responsibility of that state.[28] An internationally wrongful act consists of an act or omission attributable to the state under international law that constitutes a breach of an international obligation of the state.[29] Eight of the ILC Draft Articles are devoted to attribution principles.[30] The obligations on which a state responsibility claim may be predicated may be owed to another state, a group of states, an international organization, or "to the international community as a whole" (i.e., an *erga omnes* obligation).[31]

Whether an act or omission is internationally wrongful is governed solely by international law.[32] Internationally wrongful acts can consist of a violation of customary international law, a treaty, the UN Charter, or a mandatory resolution of the UN Security Council. An internationally wrongful act can also consist of a failure to act when international law requires it. For example, the arbitration tribunal's decision in the *CSS Alabama* case recognized the duty of a state (in this case a neutral state) to exercise due diligence to prevent harm to another state by its

---

25. Factory at Chorzów (Germany v. Poland), 1928 P.C.I.J. (ser. A) No. 17, at 29 (Sept. 13). The court held that "reparation must, as far as possible, wipe out all the consequences of the illegal act and reestablish the situation which would, in all probability, have existed if that act had not been committed." Id. at 47.

26. ILC Draft Articles on State Responsibility, supra, art. 31. See also The *Virginius* case (1873), reported in John Bassett Moore, A Digest of International Law, vol. 2, at 895 (1906) (claim concerning Spanish warship's interdiction of a U.S.-flag vessel being used to transport arms to Spanish-held Cuba and the execution of fifty-three of its crewmembers).

27. Armed Activities on the Territory of the Congo (Dem. Rep. Congo v. Uganda), Judgment, ¶ 259, 2005 I.C.J. 116 (Dec. 19).

28. ILC Draft Articles on State Responsibility, supra, art. 1.

29. Id. art. 2.

30. Id. arts. 4–11.

31. Id. arts. 33, 42(b), & 48.

32. Id. art. 3. See also id. art. 32.

nationals.[33] A state's act or omission does not constitute a breach of an international obligation unless the state is bound by the obligation at the time the act or omission occurs.[34] The temporal element in that standard will be relevant when one of the states is no longer bound by a treaty due, for example, to a material breach by the other party, impossibility of performance, or under the *rebus sic stantibus* rule.[35]

3. Defenses to Responsibility

A state's conduct will not give rise to responsibility when it was justified by consent, self-defense, force majeure, distress, or necessity. In addition, countermeasures taken by a state in conformity with customary international law are not wrongful (in the ILC's language, these are "circumstances precluding wrongfulness").[36] Countermeasures as a self-help remedy are discussed in section D below. The defense of consent is self-explanatory.[37] Of course, the act complained of must fall within the scope of the consent. The defense of self-defense is limited by the ILC Draft Articles to lawful measures taken in conformity with the UN Charter.[38] Under the ILC's formulation, force majeure is the occurrence of an irresistible force or of an unforeseen event, beyond the control of the state, making it materially impossible in the circumstances to perform the obligation.[39] The ILC Draft Articles limit the defense of "distress" to situations in which human life is in danger.[40] Historically, distress under maritime law is broader than the ILC's version, and the so-called Good Samaritan doctrine is more forgiving than the relevant ILC Draft Article.[41] Although the defense of necessity is recognized in the ILC Draft Articles,[42] the relevant article reflects a very narrow construction of the defense by the ICJ.[43]

---

33. John Bassett Moore, History and Digest of the International Arbitrations to which the United States has been a Party, vol. I, at 653, 656–57 (1898); Thomas Willing Balch, The *Alabama* Arbitration (1900).

34. ILC Draft Articles on State Responsibility, supra, art. 13. In the Gabčíkovo-Nagymaros Project (Hungary/Slovakia), the ICJ highlighted the need to distinguish those issues controlled by the law of treaties (e.g., a treaty's validity and the grounds for suspension or termination) from those issues governed by the law of state responsibility (e.g., whether breach of a treaty may be "excused" on grounds of necessity). Id. at ¶ 47, 1997 I.C.J. 3 (Sept. 27).

35. See Vienna Convention on Treaties, supra, arts. 60–62. The *rebus sic stantibus* doctrine refers to circumstances in which one party seeks to avoid a treaty obligation by arguing there has been a fundamental change of circumstances not foreseen by the parties when they entered into the treaty. Id. art. 62.

36. ILC Draft Articles on State Responsibility, supra, art. 22 ("The wrongfulness of an act of a State not in conformity with an international obligation towards another State is precluded if and to the extent that the act constitutes a countermeasure taken against the latter State in accordance with" Articles 49–54 of the Draft Articles).

37. Id. art. 20 ("Valid consent by a State to the commission of a given act by another State precludes the wrongfulness of that act in relation to the former State to the extent that the act remains within the limits of that consent").

38. Id. art. 21. ("The wrongfulness of an act of a State is precluded if the act constitutes a lawful measure of self-defence taken in conformity with the Charter of the United Nations").

39. Id. art. 23 ("The wrongfulness of an act of a State not in conformity with an international obligation of that State is precluded if the act is due to *force majeure*, that is the occurrence of an irresistible force or of an unforeseen event, beyond the control of the State, making it materially impossible in the circumstances to perform the obligation"). The force majeure article does not apply if the situation is due to the conduct of the state invoking it or the state assumed the risk of that situation occurring.

40. Id. art. 24 ("The wrongfulness of an act of a State not in conformity with an international obligation of that State is precluded if the author of the act in question has no other reasonable way, in a situation of distress, of saving the author's life or the lives of other persons entrusted to the author's care"). This distress article does not apply if the situation of distress is due to the conduct of the state invoking it or the act in question is likely to create a comparable or greater peril.

41. See LOSC art. 98. See also 46 U.S.C. § 2302(c) (conferring "Good Samaritan" immunity on rescuers in maritime assistance cases).

42. ILC Draft Articles on State Responsibility, supra, art. 25; Robert D. Sloane, On the Use and Abuse of Necessity in the Law of State Responsibility, 106 Am. J. Int'l L. 447 (2012).

43. Gabčíkovo-Nagymaros Project (Hungary v. Slovakia), 1997 I.C.J. 7 (Sept. 25). The case is examined in section D below, in conjunction with The *M/V Saiga* case decided by ITLOS.

C. REMEDIES IN STATE RESPONSIBILITY CASES

When one state has committed an international wrongful act that harmed another state (or its national), the law of state responsibility generally calls for reparation.[44] Reparation may be voluntarily made, either formally or by way of ex gratia compensation without admitting fault.[45] When a state is unable to timely obtain reparation from the state in breach, it might resort to self-help measures. In evaluating the options available for obtaining redress it should be noted that a state's responsibility and liability and the process for obtaining remedies might be limited by international agreement, such as an applicable status of forces agreement.[46]

It is well established that every internationally wrongful act of a state entails the international responsibility of that state.[47] The responsible state is under an obligation to make full reparation for the injury caused by the internationally wrongful act.[48] Reparation may include restitution, compensation, or satisfaction.[49] The goal of reparation is to restore the injured party to the status quo ante as much as possible.[50] The Draft Articles take the position that in cases in which compensation is the appropriate form of reparation, it should cover any financially assessable damage, including lost profits and interest.[51] The Draft Articles also adopt a form of comparative fault, providing that the amount of compensation will take into account the extent to which a negligent act or omission by the injured state, or a person or entity for whom reparation is sought, contributed to the injury.[52] Importantly, the Draft Articles do not apply where and to the extent that responsibility is governed by special rules of international law (*lex specialis*).[53] The 1982 LOS Convention includes such provisions. They are examined in section E below.

D. SELF-HELP REMEDIES: COUNTERMEASURES

An important second category of "remedies" to be considered is variously referred to as "self-help" or "countermeasures." One treatise writer observes that self-help measures in response to a violation of the state's rights under international law are not the exception to the rule, but rather the predominant choice of injured states.[54] Countermeasures overlap somewhat with the "necessity" exemption from state responsibility.[55] For example, Great Britain's decision to destroy the

---

44. If the internationally wrongful conduct is continuing, the offending state has a duty to cease the conduct. ILC Draft Articles on State Responsibility, supra, art. 30.

45. See Restatement FRLUS § 902 cmt. h. Examples include U.S. ex gratia payments following the accidental bombing of the Chinese embassy in 1999 during the Kosovo interdiction and the USS *Vincennes*' mistaken attack on a commercial Iranian airliner in 1988. Aerial Incident of 3 July 1988 (USA v. Iran), 1996 I.C.J. 9 (Feb. 22) (order removing case from ICJ docket after parties notified court they had settled the dispute).

46. See, e.g., NATO Status of Forces Agreement, art. VIII, June 19, 1951, 4 U.S.T. 1972, T.I.A.S. 2846 (as amended).

47. ILC Draft Articles on State Responsibility, supra, art. 1.

48. Id. art. 31. The Draft Article includes a controversial provision calling for compensation for damage "whether material or *moral*." Id. art. 31(b) (emphasis added).

49. Id. art. 34.

50. The requirement to provide satisfaction might call for extraordinary measures in some cases. For example, following the 2001 collision between the USS *Greeneville* (SSN-772) and the Japanese fishing training vessel *Ehime Maru* nine miles off Hawaii, the United States raised the sunken fishing vessel to permit Japan to remove the remains of the nine deceased crewmembers and their effects.

51. ILC Draft Articles on State Responsibility, supra, arts. 36 & 38. Compare this standard with the more restrictive "pecuniary" loss compensation standard in Article 12 of the UN Convention on Jurisdictional Immunities of States.

52. ILC Draft Articles on State Responsibility, supra, art. 39.

53. Id. art. 55.

54. Peter Malanczuk, Akehurst's Modern Introduction to International Law 3–4 (7th rev. ed. 1999).

55. See ILC Draft Articles on State Responsibility, supra, art. 25.

T/V *Torrey Canyon* to mitigate pollution damage to its coast (a self-help measure) was justified at the time on the grounds of necessity.[56]

The customary law of countermeasures applies only to breaches of international law by states, not legal violations by nonstate actors;[57] however, this limitation may change as nonstate actors increasingly become subjects of international law. Indeed, if, as the Security Council determined following the September 11, 2001, attacks, states may use force in self-defense against nonstate actors, a fortiori they should be able to employ nonforcible countermeasures against them.

International law has long recognized that a state injured by the breach of an international law obligation owed to it by another state has the option of responding with self-help or by seeking redress through a recognized dispute settlement procedure.[58] Many believe that self-help countermeasures are necessitated by the absence of a global executive or court with compulsory jurisdiction.[59] Extrajudicial self-help measures have a long pedigree in the domestic law of many states, including such well-recognized common law self-help remedies as ejection of trespassers and recovery of chattels, which may be invoked against private actors. In a 1997 decision, the ICJ confirmed the state's right to employ nonforcible countermeasures while noting that countermeasures must meet several conditions to be justifiable.[60] Like provisional measures (discussed in chapter 15), countermeasures can be employed in combination with more formal dispute settlement measures to preserve the status quo or prevent irreversible harm.[61]

The customary right to invoke unilateral or self-help remedies (what one commentator refers to as the "muscular version of what is practically required to enforce international norms")[62] includes the forcible countermeasures[63] of rescue, reprisal, intervention, and self-defense, as well as nonforcible measures of rebuke, retorsion, and nonforcible reprisals.[64] "Rescue" is distinguished from "intervention" in that the former is directed at the protection of the

---

56. Self-defense was also cited, perhaps because military aircraft were employed to destroy the vessel, which some might interpret as the use of armed force under Article 2(4) of the UN Charter.

57. Actions by nonstate actors may, however, be attributed to a state or may have been made possible by a state's breach of its duty to exercise effective control over the entity, and might therefore give rise to a right of self-help against that state. See ILC Draft Articles on State Responsibility, supra, arts. 4–11.

58. See generally Marjorie M. Whiteman, 12 Digest of International Law ch. 36 (1971). Countermeasures have been applied in response to three categories of international law violations: (1) violations that harmed the state employing the countermeasures or one of its nationals; (2) violations of an *erga omnes* obligation owed to the community nations as a whole; and (3) violations, usually of international human rights law, that harmed the target state's own citizens.

59. See Myres S. McDougal, Authority to Use Force on the High Seas, 61 U.S. Nav. War Coll. Int'l L. Studies 551, 555 (1979) ("International law has depended largely upon the unorganized, unilateral making and enforcement of law by nation-states"); Report of the International Law Commission to the General Assembly, 2000 Y.B. Int'l L. Comm'n, vol. II, pt. 2, at 53, ¶ 308.

60. The Gabčíkovo-Nagymaros Project, 1997 I.C.J. 41, 56–57 (Sept. 25). The court explained that countermeasures may be taken only in response to an internationally wrongful act by another state. Such measures must be taken against the offending state, the target state must be given notice, and an opportunity to cure and any countermeasures must be proportionate. Id. ¶¶ 83–85. Additionally, any countermeasures must be applied consistently with Articles 2 and 33 of the UN Charter.

61. See ILC Draft Articles on State Responsibility, supra, art. 52(2) (the injured state may take such urgent countermeasures as may be necessary to preserve its rights). But see United States Diplomatic and Consular Staff in Tehran case (USA v. Iran), 1980 I.C.J. 3, 43 (May 24), in which the ICJ criticized the United States for resorting to self-help measures to free the hostages while the case was before the court. See also ILC Draft Articles on State Responsibility, supra, art. 52 (taking the same position).

62. David J. Bederman, Counterintuiting Countermeasures, 96 Am. J. Int'l L. 817, 818 (2002).

63. See Restatement FRLUS § 905.

64. Malcolm N. Shaw, International Law 1023 (6th ed. 2008) (concluding that nonforcible reprisals "may still be undertaken legitimately").

rescuing state's own nationals while the latter is generally directed at the safety of the nationals of other states, most often the nationals of the intervened-in state.[65] The *Restatement* cites the Israel Defense Force's 1976 hostage rescue operation at the Entebbe airport in Uganda as an example of a lawful, forcible self-help measure.[66] Other examples include the rescue of the U.S. crewmen of the M/V *Mayaguez* and the unsuccessful attempt to rescue the U.S. diplomatic staff held hostage for more than one year by Iran.[67]

A "retorsion" is the adoption by one state of an unfriendly and harmful act that is nevertheless lawful as a method of retaliation against the injurious legal activities of another state.[68] Familiar examples include suspension of trade or port access privileges, loss of foreign aid, and severance of diplomatic relations. Reprisals, in contrast, are illegal acts that have been adopted by one state in retaliation for the commission of an earlier illegal act by another state.[69] For example, when the U.S. diplomatic and consular staffs were seized and held hostage in Iran in 1979, President Carter exercised his authority under the U.S. International Emergency Economic Powers Act to seize Iran's assets on deposit in the United States.[70] The preconditions for exercising the peacetime right of reprisal were set out in the *Naulilaa Incident* arbitration.[71] They include the existence of a prior act contrary to international law by the target state, a requirement for a prior unsatisfied demand by the acting state, and proportionality between the reprisal and the offense.[72] Such countermeasures may not violate peremptory norms or nonderogable human rights.

Although the use of forcible countermeasures is now constrained by the UN Charter,[73] which requires all states to settle their disputes by peaceful means[74] and prohibits the threat or use of force against the territorial integrity or political independence of a state,[75] the right to engage in countermeasures, not including the use of armed force, has not been extinguished.[76] Any countermeasures chosen must, however, be necessary to terminate or remedy the violation or to prevent a further violation, and they must be proportionate to the violation and the injury suffered.[77]

65. Historically, interventions have also been undertaken for the intervening state's benefit. See The Corfu Channel case (U.K. v. Albania) 1949 I.C.J. 1, 4, 35 (Apr. 9) (considering, but ultimately rejecting, Britain's argument that it had a right to intervene and clear mines in the Albanian territorial sea to facilitate the safe passage of U.K. warships during peacetime).
66. See Restatement FRLUS § 905 cmt. g.
67. See generally Commander's Handbook, supra, ¶ 3.10.1.1. See also 22 U.S.C. § 1732; Thomas E. Behuniak, The Seizure and Recovery of S.S. *Mayaguez:* A Legal Analysis of United States Claims, 82 Mil. L. Rev. 41 (1978).
68. See Restatement FRLUS § 905 cmt. f.
69. Shaw, supra, at 1023. In its coverage of countermeasures, the ILC does not include those retorsions that do not constitute a violation of international law.
70. International Emergency Economic Powers Act (IEEPA), Oct. 28, 1977, Title II of Pub. L. No. 95-223, 91 Stat. 1626 (codified at 50 U.S.C. §§ 1701–1707).
71. Concerning the Responsibility of Germany for Damage Caused in the Portuguese Colonies of South Africa (Portugal v. Germany), Arbitral Decision of July 31, 1938, 2 Rep. Int'l Arb. Awards 1011 (1949). The distinct law and policy governing belligerent reprisals during armed conflicts is examined in the Commander's Handbook (¶ 6.2.4). See also Advisory Opinion on the Legality of the Threat or Use of Nuclear Weapons 1996 I.C.J. 226, 246 (July 8) (concluding that armed reprisals in time of peace are unlawful).
72. Air Services Agreement of 27 March 1946 (USA v. France), 54 Int'l. L. Rep. 304 (1978) (holding that countermeasures must be proportionate to the prior illegal act, in terms of both the damages the illegal act caused and the importance of the principle at stake).
73. See Restatement FRLUS § 904(2); ILC Draft Articles on State Responsibility, supra, art. 50(1)(a).
74. UN Charter, supra, arts. 2(3) & 33; LOSC arts. 280 & 281.
75. UN Charter, supra, art. 2(4); LOSC art. 301.
76. See Gabčíkovo-Nagymaros Project (Hungary v. Slovakia), Judgment, ¶ 83, 1997 I.C.J. 7, 55 (Sept. 25); Oil Platforms (Iran v. USA) 2003 I.C.J. 161, 332 (separate opinion of Judge Simma) (Nov. 6) (citing the ICJ's decision in the *Nicaragua* case for the proposition that proportionate countermeasures short of a use of "armed force" may be used in response to the use of force by another state not rising to the level of an armed attack).
77. See Restatement FRLUS § 905; ILC Draft Articles on State Responsibility, supra, art. 51.

Countermeasures may be taken in response to a state's actions in violation of international law or its failure to act when required by international law. For example, states have the primary obligation to protect foreign nationals, vessels, and aircraft in their territory, including their territorial sea.[78] When the state is unable or unwilling to discharge its responsibility, the flag state may be justified in employing proportionate countermeasures, such as rescue or noncombatant evacuation operations,[79] to protect its nationals, without awaiting the state's consent.[80] Because such operations by U.S. armed forces raise a variety of critical legal, political, and diplomatic considerations, they are closely scrutinized and planned at the highest level.

The *Restatement* largely reflects the above-described customary law of self-help countermeasures. It provides that a state victim of a violation of an international obligation by another state may resort to countermeasures that might otherwise be unlawful, if such measures are necessary to terminate the violation or prevent further violation or to remedy the violation. Such countermeasures must not be out of proportion to the violation and the injury suffered.[81] The ILC Draft Articles on countermeasures (which have proven controversial)[82] are more narrowly circumscribed than the *Restatement* formulation.[83] In its comments on the ILC Draft Articles, the U.S. government singled out the articles on countermeasures as among its "most serious concerns" and went on to explain that the draft countermeasures articles impose restrictions not supported by customary international law.[84] More specifically, it stated that "the United States continues to believe that the restrictions in Articles 50 to 55 that have been placed on the use of countermeasures do not reflect customary international law or state practice, and could undermine efforts by states to peacefully settle disputes. We therefore strongly believe these articles should be deleted."[85]

In distinguishing between forcible and nonforcible countermeasures, it must be emphasized that the term "forcible countermeasures" does not include those in which "police force" is used against a private entity or vessel to carry out law enforcement measures. The international law scholar Myres McDougal, for example, carefully distinguishes the use of force in law enforcement measures taken against private actors from forcible self-help and self-defense measures taken against states for violations of international law.[86]

---

78. In waters seaward of any state's territorial sea, the flag state or other state of nationality has the primary duty to defend its vessels, aircraft, and nationals; however, other states may assist as an exercise of the inherent right of collective defense.

79. The safe and efficient evacuation of U.S. government officials, their families, and U.S. citizens from a foreign nation when their lives are endangered by war, civil unrest, or human-made or natural disasters. Commander's Handbook, supra, ¶ 3.10.3.

80. Id. ¶ 3.10.1.1. On occasion, foreign warships have been forced to rely on self-help measures when the port state was unable or unwilling to provide needed security with respect to environmental protestors.

81. Restatement FRLUS § 905. See also Shaw, supra, at 708.

82. See Bederman, supra; Philip Allott, State Responsibility and the Unmaking of International Law, 29 Harv. J. Int'l L. J. 1 (1988).

83. Although the ILC Draft Articles on State Responsibility acknowledge that some countermeasures are lawful, in the opinion of the U.S. Department of State, the drafters take a narrow view of the range of permissible countermeasures. See U.S. Department of State, Digest of United States Practice in International Law 2002, at 364–71. The countermeasures articles have been characterized as "lightning rods of criticism and controversy" and are likely as much a product of progressive development as a codification effort. See Bederman, supra, at 827–28.

84. U.S. Department of State, Draft Articles on State Responsibility, Comments of the Government of the United States of America, Mar. 21, 2001, available at http://www.state.gov/documents/organization/28993.pdf (accessed Feb. 1, 2013).

85. Id. at 2.

86. See McDougal, Authority to Use Force, supra, at 557–58. See also Alfred H. A. Soons, Enforcing the Economic Embargo at Sea, in United Nations Sanctions and International Law 307, 311–12, & 321, n.45 (W. Gowlland-Debbas ed., 2001) (distinguishing the use of "police force" in maritime interception operations from the use of

E. STATE RESPONSIBILITY UNDER THE LAW OF THE SEA CONVENTION

The 1982 LOS Convention, which qualifies as *lex specialis* (specialized law) under the ILC Draft Articles framework,[87] sets out a number of specific rules that impose responsibility on states.[88] For example, the convention expressly addresses state responsibility and liability for enforcement actions that are unlawful or exceed those reasonably required in the light of available information.[89] At the same time, the convention "saves" customary law rules regarding responsibility and liability for damage.[90] Accordingly, the bases for establishing state responsibility set out in the ILC Draft Articles may be relevant in cases arising under the LOS Convention, at least to the extent that the Draft Articles accurately reflect customary law. Additionally, bilateral boarding agreements entered into by the United States with certain flag states often include provisions establishing safeguards and limiting the use of force, and procedures for presenting claims and for resolving disputes between the parties.[91]

1. Admissible Claims under the LOS Convention

The LOS Convention expressly recognizes a state's responsibility for damage caused by its warships and other government-operated vessels.[92] The flag state is generally not responsible, however, for damage caused by nongovernment recreational or commercial vessels flying its flag, because those acts are ordinarily not attributable to the state. The LOS Convention also imposes responsibility for a state's failure to fulfill its obligations concerning protection of the marine environment and for the state's conduct of marine scientific research activities.[93] Finally, the LOS Convention includes a number of responsibility articles that address a state's unjustified interference with foreign vessels. The LOS Convention articles are supplemented by safeguards incorporated into several maritime conventions, including SOLAS and MARPOL, which require states to provide compensation for excessive delay or unwarranted enforcement actions.[94]

The basis for responsibility under the LOS Convention for interference with foreign vessels varies from article to article; however, the common theme that any interference must be founded on a sufficient level of suspicion of wrongful activity runs throughout. The fact that no evidence or insufficient evidence of an actual violation of applicable law by the vessel, master, owner, or crew is discovered does not necessarily mean the boarding state's actions violated international law, giving rise to state responsibility. It is important in each case to examine the basis for the boarding. For example, if the vessel was boarded out of suspicion that it was engaged in piracy, Article 106 of the LOS Convention provides that the boarding state must compensate the

---

"armed force" and concluding that potential measures taken under Article 41 of the UN Charter can include police force). Some states would consider the use of armed force against any vessel flying their flag an attack on the state, justifying the exercise in self-defense. However, the use of "police force" in the course of a legitimate law enforcement action involving a foreign vessel is generally not included.

87. ILC Draft Articles on State Responsibility, supra, art. 55.
88. Other treaties, including, for example, those in the IMO and World Trade Organization–GATT families, as well as bilateral friendship, commerce, and navigation treaties and bilateral investment treaties, may impose international obligations the breach of which could implicate state responsibility.
89. See, e.g., LOSC art. 106, 110(3), 111(8), & 232.
90. Id. art. 304; see also *M/V Saiga* (St. Vincent & the Grenadines v. Guinea), ITLOS Case No. 2, Judgment of July 1, 1999, ¶¶ 169–73, 38 I.L.M. 1323 (1999) (applying the above-cited *Chorzów Factory* standard under Article 304 of the LOS Convention).
91. See, e.g., U.S.-Liberia WMD Shipboarding Agreement, arts. 8, 9 13, & 14, available at http://www.state.gov/t/isn/c27733.htm (accessed Feb. 1, 2013).
92. LOSC art. 31.
93. Id. arts. 235 & 263.
94. See SOLAS Convention, supra, art. 19(f); MARPOL Convention, supra, art. 7.

vessel for any loss or damage caused by the seizure if the seizure was "effected without adequate ground."[95] By contrast, liability for the exercise of a right of visit attaches only if the "suspicions prove to be unfounded, and provided that the ship boarded has not committed any act justifying them."[96] When a ship has been stopped or arrested "in circumstances which do not justify the exercise of hot pursuit, it shall be compensated for any loss of damage that may have been thereby sustained."[97] Finally, when enforcement measures undertaken under Part XII of the LOS Convention to protect the marine environment are "unlawful or exceed those reasonably required in light of available information," the enforcing state is liable for any loss or damage attributable to the enforcement action."[98]

2. State Responsibility for Failure to Act

States bear responsibility for their warships and other government vessels, but generally not for nongovernment vessels flying their flag. However, customary law recognizes that a breach of international law may also consist of the failure to act when international law imposes a duty to do so.[99] With regard to omissions by flag states, the *Restatement* has adopted the somewhat controversial position that "any state that has, or whose nationals have, suffered a loss as a result of the failure of a flag state to exercise proper jurisdiction and control may present an international claim for damages against the flag state."[100] Under the *Restatement* view, a state that fails to carry out its obligations under Article 94 of the LOS Convention would thus bear international responsibility for any harm suffered by the breach. However, efforts to obtain reparations for injuries caused by a flag state's failure to exercise due diligence in controlling its vessels might be frustrated by the LOS Convention, which provides a relatively weak and potentially time-consuming mechanism for other states to respond to the failure of a flag state to effectively carry out its obligation to exercise control and jurisdiction over vessels flying its flag.[101] It is not clear whether the very limited recourse provided in the LOS Convention would preclude an injured state from taking proportionate countermeasures, such as restricting port access or imposing additional conditions on port entry, if the flag state fails to take the remedial action called for in Article 94 of the LOS Convention.

An advisory opinion issued by the ITLOS Seabed Disputes Chamber in 2011 examines the state's responsibility and liability for failing to carry out its obligations.[102] The chamber's discussion of the sponsoring state's obligation to exercise due diligence and the distinction between a state's responsibility and its liability may well find application beyond questions involving activities in the seabed. Similar arguments for state responsibility based on a failure to act might be made in cases involving the breach of a universal obligation imposed by a UN Security Council resolution that causes harm to another state.

---

95. LOSC art. 106.
96. Id. art. 110(3).
97. Id. art. 111(8).
98. Id. art. 232 ("States shall be liable for damage or loss attributable to them arising from measures taken [under Part XII] when such measures are unlawful or exceed those reasonably required in light of available information. State shall provide for recourse in their courts for actions in respect of such damage or loss").
99. ILC Draft Articles on State Responsibility, supra, art. 2.
100. See Restatement FRLUS § 502 cmt. f (citing Article 235 of the LOS Convention).
101. LOSC art. 94(6) provides that "a State which has clear grounds to believe that proper jurisdiction and control with respect to a ship have not been exercised may report the facts to the flag state. Upon receiving such a report, the flag State shall investigate the matter and, if appropriate, take action necessary to remedy the situation."
102. Responsibilities and Obligations of States Sponsoring Persons and Entities with Respect to Activities in the Area, Request for Advisory Opinion Submitted to the ITLOS Seabed Disputes Chamber, ITLOS Case No. 17, Advisory Opinion of Feb. 1, 2011, Part III, ¶¶ 175–77, 50 I.L.M. 458 (2011).

3. Defenses to State Responsibility under the LOS Convention

A number of defenses might be raised in response to an admissible claim under the LOS Convention. Presumably, all of the defenses recognized in the Draft Articles on State Responsibility, including consent, self-defense, force majeure, distress, and necessity, are available under the LOS Convention, which saves the application of consistent customary international law. In addition, the LOS Convention recognizes situation-specific rights to employ self-help countermeasures (discussed in section F.4 below). In considering those self-help countermeasures under the LOS Convention, bear in mind that ITLOS examined and ultimately rejected a "necessity" defense in the *M/V* Saiga case. The tribunal cited the ICJ's decision in the *Gabčíkovo-Nagymaros Project*[103] before "endorsing" the conditions for invoking the necessity defense in the ILC Draft Articles on State Responsibility.[104] It is too soon to tell whether that decision portends that the tribunal will largely follow the narrower and somewhat controversial ILC Draft Articles on countermeasures.

4. Remedies under the LOS Convention

The LOS Convention provides a number of primary rules of conduct that may serve as the grounds for state responsibility,[105] several secondary rules on liability,[106] and prescribes a duty to provide compensation;[107] however, it only briefly addresses the measure of reparation.[108] In the *M/V* Saiga case, ITLOS implicitly adopted the ILC's Draft Articles on State Responsibility on reparations.[109] The Draft Articles recognize a duty to cease conduct that violates international law[110] and to make reparations for any injury caused by an internationally wrongful act by the state. The preferred remedy for a breach is restitution—reestablishing the conditions that existed before the wrongful act was committed (i.e., a return to the status quo ante).[111] To the extent that restitution is excused or does not make good the damages sustained, the responsible state is required to provide compensation.[112] In the ITLOS decision in the *M/V* Saiga case it is noteworthy that the tribunal, applying the Draft Articles, held that the right to reparation extended to the damage suffered directly by the flag state as well as damage or other loss suffered by the vessel and all persons involved or interested in its operations, and that the measure of damages included loss of profits and other economic losses.[113] It should also be noted that the provisions of the LOS Convention requiring prompt release of seized vessels and crews and compensation for delay are more specific than the ILC Draft Articles and therefore constitute *lex specialis* under

---

103. The M/V *Saiga* No. 2, supra, ¶¶ 132–36 (citing the ICJ's decision in the *Gabčíkovo-Nagymaros Project* case).

104. Id. ¶ 134. The tribunal noted that the ICJ had earlier concluded that Article 33 of the ILC Draft Articles on State Responsibility reflects customary law. Id. The tribunal's opinion suggests that the burden of proof is on the state asserting the justification. The ICJ took a similar position in the U.S. assertion of a self-defense justification in the Oil Platforms case (Iran v. U.S.) 2003 I.C.J. 161 (Nov. 6).

105. See, e.g., LOSC art. 31.

106. Id. arts. 106 & 232. See also id. art. 235.

107. Id. arts. 110(3) & 111(8).

108. See, e.g., LOSC arts. 110(3), 111(8), & 232 (compensation for unjustified enforcement measures).

109. The M/V *Saiga* No. 2, supra, ¶ 171.

110. ILC Draft Articles on State Responsibility, supra, art. 30; Restatement FRLUS § 901 cmt. c & n.2.

111. ILC Draft Articles on State Responsibility, supra, art. 35. Restitution is not required when it is not materially possible or it involves a burden out of all proportion to its benefits.

112. Id. art. 36.

113. The M/V *Saiga* No. 2, supra, ¶ 172. Compensation was awarded for injury to persons, unlawful arrest, detention, or other forms of ill treatment, and damage to or seizure of property. Id.

Article 55 of the ILC Draft Articles.[114] Additionally, the LOS Convention provides a procedure for obtaining provisional relief when, for example, the state committing the wrongful conduct has failed to cease that conduct.[115]

The 1982 LOS Convention recognizes some self-help measures. For example, Article 25 provides that a coastal state may take the "necessary steps" within its territorial sea to "prevent" passage that is not innocent. Such steps may include the use of force when necessary.[116] Although warships enjoy sovereign immunity, Article 30 recognizes that a coastal state may "require" a warship to leave the coastal state's territorial sea if the warship fails to comply with regulations applicable in those waters, and it may use any force necessary to compel the warship to do so.[117] Additionally, Article 221 recognizes the existing right of a coastal state to "take and enforce" measures beyond their territorial sea to protect their coastline or related interests" from pollution or the threat of pollution.[118] Such measures must be proportionate to the actual or threatened damage posed. By their terms, all three articles contemplate the possibility that the coastal state may resort to extrajudicial countermeasures against foreign vessels without incurring state responsibility.[119]

---

114. See, e.g., LOSC arts. 73, 106, 110(3), 111(8), 232, & 304. The LOS Convention's *lex specialis* rules override the more general rules set out in the Draft Articles.
115. Id. art. 279. See, e.g., Southern Bluefin Tuna Cases (New Zealand v. Japan; Australia v. Japan), Provisional Measures, ITLOS Cases Nos. 3 & 4, Order of Aug. 27, 1999, 38 I.L.M. 1624 (1999); The MOX Plant Case (Ireland v. United Kingdom), Provisional Measures, ITLOS Case No. 10, Order of Dec. 2, 2001, 41 I.L.M. 405 (2002).
116. See generally Churchill & Lowe, supra, at 99. Article 25 is in subsection A of section 3, and therefore applies to all ships, including warships. Accordingly, the "necessary steps" could be taken against a state's warship, making it a true self-help measure.
117. Churchill & Lowe, supra, at 99 (concluding that the coastal state may use force to expel a warship for violations of "customs, navigation and pollution" laws); Commander's Handbook, supra, ¶ 2.5.2.1.
118. An often-cited example of such a countermeasure is the destruction of the stranded oil tanker *Torrey Canyon* by British Royal Air Force warplanes to abate the pollution threat posed by the tanker.
119. It is noteworthy that Article 219 of the LOS Convention, which provides authority for measures relating to seaworthiness of vessels, limits measures by states other than the flag state to "administrative measures."

15

Dispute Resolution Forums and Procedures

The previous chapters have identified countless bases for potential conflicts over access to and use of the oceans. Territorial claims involving baselines and boundaries and claims to historic bays and islands have frequently been the source of protracted and sometimes bitter disputes, even in the post–UN Charter era. "Bumping" incidents between vessels or aircraft and the use of force by or against fishing vessels, tankers, or offshore oil platforms have on occasion been cited as a *casus belli* leading to, or nearly leading to, armed conflict. Despite a clear mandate in the UN Charter for states to settle their disputes by peaceful means, in such a manner that international peace and security is not endangered,[1] the record since 1945 is far from perfect. Explanations vary, but two challenges stand out: how to persuade all states to accept peaceful dispute settlement procedures that will be effective,[2] and how to ensure effective compliance with the resulting judgment. The 1982 LOS Convention seeks to address those issues through its requirement that most, but not all, disputes arising under the convention be subject to the compulsory dispute settlement authority of an international court or to binding international arbitration.

A comprehensive examination of international dispute settlement is beyond the scope of this book for the seagoing officer; however, a general background in the resolution of interstate disputes will prove useful before the text turns to specific procedures set out in the 1982 LOS Convention. States have developed a wide variety of methods to resolve disputes ranging from informal negotiation at one end to formal arbitration or adjudication at the other. The latter forms are often referred to as "third-party" dispute settlement procedures because they directly involve outsiders in the process.

This chapter focuses on the settlement of "public" international disputes between states, to the exclusion of "private" (mostly commercial) international disputes, although the distinction between the two is not always clear. For example, nonstate actors have standing, under some circumstances, to appear before a tribunal with competency over disputes involving the deep seabed. Similarly, a nonstate actor may appear before a tribunal "on behalf of" a flag state in an action seeking prompt release of a privately owned vessel or its crew (discussed below). Moreover, many of the disputes arising under the LOS Convention will involve allegations by or against private entities, such as shipowners, whose claims might be pursued in national forums or espoused by the state of nationality. For example, state X might board, search, and seize a merchant vessel registered in state Y while that vessel was in transit passage through state X's waters. If it turns out that the actions of state X violated the LOS Convention, the owner of the seized vessel might have a claim for damages against state X. Additionally, state Y might have

---

1. UN Charter, supra, art. 2(3). See also LOSC art. 279.
2. Advisory Opinion on the Status of the Eastern Carelia, 1923 P.C.I.J. (ser. B) No. 5, at 27 ("It is well established in international law that no State can, without its consent, be compelled to submit its disputes with other States either to a mediation or arbitration, or to any other kind of pacific settlement").

claims against state X, both for its own damages as the flag state and on behalf of the injured vessel owner. Section A of this chapter addresses the first class of claims; section B examines the second.

A. PRIVATE CLAIMS AND THE EXHAUSTION-OF-LOCAL-REMEDIES REQUIREMENT

When a state's violation of international law injures a private party, such as a vessel owner or crewmember, the injured party will ordinarily have a claim for damages against the responsible state. Such claims might be brought in the national courts of the responsible state or in those of another state. Injured private parties face several possible hurdles in pursuing claims on their own. In contrast to states, private parties generally do not have standing to bring their own claims in an international court. They must instead rely on their state to espouse the claim. The injured party might also find that any claim in the national courts must surmount applicable laws governing the sovereign immunity of states.[3] Through several statutory schemes described in chapter 14, the U.S. government has waived its sovereign immunity in selected circumstances.[4] U.S. federal courts also provide a forum for some private claims against foreign governments[5] and individuals who commit a tort in violation of international law.[6] Nevertheless, private litigation against sovereign states is fraught with problems arising from the sovereign immunity doctrine.

Notwithstanding the doctrine of sovereign immunity, international law generally, and the LOS Convention in particular, requires a party to exhaust local remedies before recourse against the responsible state in an international forum.[7] Generally, the exhaustion requirement applies only in cases in which the state is espousing a claim on behalf of one of its nationals (commonly referred to as an exercise of "diplomatic protection"). In such circumstances the injured national generally must first exhaust available administrative and judicial remedies as available in the state responsible for the injury before the injured individual's state may espouse a claim on the national's behalf. Exhaustion is not always required. For example, ITLOS has held that exhaustion is not required as a precondition to bring an action for prompt release of a vessel or crew under Article 292 of the LOS Convention.[8] Additionally, the ICJ has ruled that exhaustion is not required in cases in which the applicant state is asserting a violation of its own internationally protected rights while also espousing a claim on behalf of one of its nationals.[9]

---

3. In the United States, the political question doctrine might also be invoked to dismiss the claim. See, e.g., Aktepe v. U.S., 105 F.3d 1400 (11th Cir. 1997) (dismissing, as a nonjusticiable political question, a claim against the United States brought after the USS *Saratoga* (CV-3) mistakenly fired two Sea Sparrow missiles at the Turkish destroyer TCG *Muavenet* during a NATO exercise, resulting in several injuries and deaths).

4. See, e.g., Federal Tort Claims Act, Public Vessels Act, Suits in Admiralty Act and Foreign Claims Act (discussed in chapter 14).

5. See Foreign Sovereign Immunities Act, 28 U.S.C. §§ 1330, 1441(d), 1602–1611. Limitations on such suits are discussed in chapter 14.

6. Alien Tort Statute, 28 U.S.C. § 1350. In Kiobel v. Royal Dutch Pet. Co., 133 S. Ct. 1659 (2013) the Court limited the Alien Tort Statute's application in cases involving conduct outside the United States.

7. LOSC art. 295. The ICJ has held that the burden of proof is on the resisting state to prove that the injured individual failed to exhaust local remedies. See Elettronica Sicula S.p.A. (U.S. v. Italy), 1989 I.C.J. 15 (July 20).

8. The *Camouco* case (Panama v. France), Prompt Release, ITLOS Case No. 5, Judgment of Feb. 7, 2000, 39 I.L.M. 666 (2000) (reasoning that Article 292 provides for an independent remedy and is not an appeal against a decision by a national court).

9. Avena and Other Mexican Nationals (Mexico v. U.S.), Merits, ¶ 40, 2004 I.C.J. 12, 27–28 (Mar. 31).

B. METHODS FOR RESOLVING DISPUTES BETWEEN STATES

International law favors dispute avoidance over dispute resolution.[10] For example, the LOS Convention includes a number of provisions calling on states to cooperate, consult, or notify other states—particularly with regard to issues concerning the conservation and management of living marine resources and the protection of the marine environment. It also requires all states to exercise good faith in carrying out their obligations under the convention and to exercise the rights, jurisdiction, and freedoms recognized in the convention in a manner that would not constitute an abuse of rights.[11] ITLOS has emphasized the importance of cooperation and has shown a readiness to order parties to enter into consultations, exchange information concerning the risks and effects of the proposed activities, and devise ways to deal with them.[12]

Despite all required consultations, notifications, and coordination, a disagreement may ripen into an "international dispute" that must be adjusted.[13] Chapter VI of the UN Charter requires all such disputes to be settled by peaceful means, which may include negotiation, inquiry, mediation, conciliation, arbitration, judicial settlement, resort to regional agencies, or arrangements or other peaceful means of the parties' choosing.[14] Negotiation is the favored method of adjusting disputes. Negotiation may be carried out by formal diplomatic channels, through "competent authorities" other than the diplomatic corps, through lower-level contacts (including military to military), or by "back channel" means. The ICJ has suggested that the states' obligations may entail a duty to conduct themselves in such a manner that the negotiations are "meaningful."[15]

Negotiations may be supplemented by access to the "good offices" of a third party who facilitates further negotiations without necessarily taking a formal role in resolving the conflict. Should the good offices be provided by a respected head of state or the UN secretary-general, the pressure on the parties to reach agreement is increased. A third party might also agree to act as a mediator. Mediation takes a variety of forms, but they have in common that the mediator's role is to assist the parties in reaching an agreed resolution. The mediator might propose the terms of such an agreement; however, the parties remain free to reject any such proposal.[16]

Third parties may also be called up to serve an inquiry or conciliation role. An inquiry commission may, for example, be tasked with finding facts that the parties to the conflict can use in reaching a resolution. Following an attack by the Russian navy on unarmed British fishing vessels, a respected inquiry commission served such a fact-finding role, and was credited with

---

10. A useful starting point for dispute avoidance and resolution is the UN General Assembly's 1970 Declaration of Principles of International Law concerning Friendly Relations and Co-operation among States in Accordance with the Charter of the United Nations. G.A. Res. 2625 (XXV), U.N. GAOR 25th Sess., Supp. No. 18, Annex (Oct. 24, 1970), U.N. Doc. A/8028 (1971).

11. LOSC art. 300.

12. Land Reclamation by Singapore in and around the Straits of Johor (Malaysia v. Singapore), Provisional Measures, ITLOS Case No. 12, Order of Oct. 8, 2003, ¶ 92, 126 Int'l L. Rep. 487.

13. "International dispute" is a term of art under the UN Charter. While not defined in the charter, it is generally understood to refer to an authentic disagreement between states that is appropriately concrete, specific, and contested, and has risen to the level that requires peaceful adjustment. For its part, ITLOS has defined a dispute as simply a "disagreement on a point of law or fact, a conflict of legal views or of interests." Southern Bluefin Tuna Cases (New Zealand v. Japan; Australia v. Japan), Provisional Measures, ITLOS Cases Nos. 3 & 4, Order of Aug. 27, 1999, ¶ 44, 38 I.L.M. 1624 (1999). See also Restatement FRLUS § 902 n.7; Mavrommatis Palestine Concessions (Greece v. Great Britain), 1924 P.C.I.J. (Ser. A) No. 2 (Aug. 30), at 11.

14. UN Charter, supra, art. 33(1). See also J. G. Merrills, International Dispute Settlement (4th ed. 2005).

15. North Sea Continental Shelf cases (Fed. Rep. Germany v. Denmark/Fed. Rep. Germany v. Netherlands), 1969 I.C.J. 3, 47 (Feb. 20).

16. See, e.g., UN Secretary-General: Ruling Pertaining to Differences between France and New Zealand Arising from the *Rainbow Warrior* Affair, 26 I.L.M. 1346 (1987). France later breached the mediated agreement and New Zealand sought arbitration. *Rainbow Warrior* Arbitration (New Zealand v. France) 82 Int'l L. Rep. 499 (1990).

helping the parties avoid escalation of the conflict.[17] Conciliation bodies (which grew out of the commissions of inquiry provided for by the Hague Conventions of 1899 and 1907 and the Bryan Treaties of 1913–14)[18] generally go beyond mere fact-finding and provide a nonbinding proposed resolution of the conflict.

International courts and arbitral tribunals offer another option for dispute resolution. The so-called horizontal international legal system is often criticized, however, for lacking a court or tribunal with compulsory jurisdiction over disputes between and among states. Thus, the disputing states must generally agree to submit their dispute to the court or tribunal. As is more fully discussed below, the LOS Convention seeks to reduce the categories of disputes for which no compulsory settlement procedures are prescribed. The convention's articles and annexes build upon centuries of experience with international arbitration and adjudication.

1. Arbitration of Disputes between States

International arbitration differs from the previously described methods of dispute settlement in that it is generally more formal and results in a resolution that is binding on the parties. Arbitral panels, commonly composed of three or five arbitrators, draw their terms of reference from a *compromis*, the agreement to submit a claim to arbitration or adjudication prepared by the parties. Accordingly, the parties largely control the level of formality.

Arbitration has unique strengths and drawbacks in comparison with adjudication by a standing international court. Generally, the parties are given more flexibility in defining the composition and procedures of the tribunal, the location of the proceedings, and the questions presented. Flexibility has a price: the cost of arbitration for the parties can be quite high because the parties must pay their own costs as well as the expenses of arbitration and compensation for the arbitrators. The parties may also choose to keep the arbitration proceedings and their outcome confidential, a feature that has drawn criticism from advocates of transparency. Although some argue that arbitration generally proceeds with greater dispatch than adjudications in courts, the recent record does not necessarily support that assertion.

Public international arbitration has a long history. Several questions left undecided by the so-called Jay Treaty between the United States and Great Britain following the Revolutionary War were referred to arbitration.[19] Similarly, the 1814 Treaty of Ghent following the War of 1812 called for arbitration of certain disputes left unresolved. The arbitration between the United States and Great Britain for the latter's responsibility, as a neutral state, regarding the Confederate ship *Alabama* remains an important case in the law of state responsibility.[20] Arbitration has been employed successfully to resolve a number of maritime disputes, including those

17. The Dogger Bank Incident (Great Britain v. Russia), Hague Ct. Rep. (Scott) 403 (Comm'n Inquiry 1905). See also *Red Crusader* Incident (U.K. v. Denmark) Hague Ct. Rep. (Scott) (Comm'n Inquiry 1962).
18. See the (first) Hague Convention for the Pacific Settlement of Disputes, July 29, 1899, 187 Consol. Treaty Series 410; and (second) Hague Convention for the Pacific Settlement of Disputes, Oct. 18, 1907, 205 Consol. Treaty Series 233. Soon after taking office as secretary of state under President Woodrow Wilson, William Jennings Bryan negotiated a series of twenty-eight treaties calling for arbitration of disputes among states.
19. The Jay Treaty arbitration agreements produced 536 arbitral awards between 1799 and 1804 dealing with such issues as territorial delimitations and claims for seizure of ships at sea. See Treaty of Amity, Commerce and Navigation, (U.S.–Great Britain), Nov. 19, 1794, 8 Stat. 116. See also Treaty of Paris (U.S.–Great Britain), Sept. 3, 1783, 48 Consol. Treaty Series 487.
20. See Treaty of Washington (U.S.–Great Britain), May 8, 1871, 17 Stat. 863; *Alabama* Claims case (1871/2), in John Bassett Moore, History and Digest of the International Arbitrations to which the United States has been a Party, vol. I, at 653 (1898); Tom Bingham, *Alabama* Claims Arbitration, 54 Int'l & Comp. L.Q. 1 (2005). The arbitrators ultimately ordered Great Britain to pay the United States $15.5 million in reparations.

over access to the Newfoundland lobster fishery (United Kingdom/France 1891) and over fur seals in the Bering Sea (United States/United Kingdom 1892). More recently, the arbitral tribunal constituted under the terms of the Algiers Accords to adjust claims between Iran and the United States is generally held up as an example of relatively successful large-scale arbitration. Since 1981, the Iran Claims Tribunal has reportedly received more than five thousand claims and has made awards totaling more than $2 billion.

Recognizing the value of third-party dispute resolution bodies, states have established several international courts and arbitral tribunals. The Permanent Court of Arbitration, which was established in 1899 by the Hague Convention for the Pacific Settlement of International Disputes and sits at the Peace Palace in The Hague, is not really a court, but rather an organization with a panel of arbitrators nominated to hear disputes among states. Each party to the Permanent Court of Arbitration may nominate up to four arbitrators to serve on the panel. As cases arise, arbitrators are then selected from the master list. One drawback to this and any other ad hoc arbitration approach is that arbitration panels selected on an ad hoc basis are less likely to develop a common body of law or jurisprudence than is a standing court.

2. Adjudication of Disputes between States

Adjudication—dispute settlement by courts—is distinguished from arbitration by the fact that the decision is rendered by the judges or justices of a standing court. Disputes between states may come before an international court such as the ICJ or ITLOS, or before a regional court. The commonly used, though technically incorrect term "World Court" refers collectively to the Permanent Court of International Justice and its successor, the International Court of Justice. The PCIJ, which sat in The Hague, began to function in 1932 as the judicial organ of the League of Nations. Like the ICJ, the PCIJ was created by and operated under a "Statute" of the court that set out the court's jurisdiction and procedures. The PCIJ's decisions, including the seminal *S.S. Lotus* case, are frequently cited to this day.

The ICJ, one of the six principal organs of the United Nations,[21] sits at the Peace Palace in The Hague and comprises fifteen judges who serve nine-year terms. The court sits without a jury. If the facts of the case are disputed, the judges determine the relevant facts, though some tribunals make use of scientific or other experts and masters. The Statute of the ICJ is annexed to the UN Charter. Only states have standing to bring contentious cases before the ICJ. In 1978 the court's rules were amended to permit decisions by special "chambers" composed of three or more judges (typically five).[22] The avowed purpose of the amendment was to "attract more business" to the court. Decisions by special chambers are treated as decisions by the full court.[23]

Article 36 of the Statute of the ICJ sets out the court's jurisdiction. Jurisdiction is always based on the consent of states.[24] Absent consent, a state may not be compelled to adjudicate a case before the court. A state may consent to ICJ jurisdiction through three principal means: by special agreement (usually by filing a *compromis*), by becoming party to a treaty that includes a provision (called a "compromissory clause") conferring jurisdiction over disputes arising under the treaty on the ICJ, or by making a declaration under the so-called optional clause in Article 36(2) of the ICJ Statute. Jurisdiction under the optional clause extends to all legal disputes

---

21. UN Charter, supra, art. 93.
22. See ICJ Statute, supra, art. 26 (providing for special chambers composed of judges whose number is determined by the court with the approval of the parties).
23. Id. art. 27.
24. See generally Marjorie M. Whiteman, 12 Digest of International Law 1252–1351 (1971).

concerning the interpretation of a treaty; any question of international law; the existence of any fact that would, if established, constitute a breach of an international obligation; and the nature or extent of the reparation to be made for the breach of an international obligation.

The ICJ's "optional" compulsory jurisdiction is limited to states that have consented in advance by filing a declaration in accordance with Article 36(2) of the ICJ Statute.[25] Demonstrating the reluctance of states to accept the jurisdiction of international courts, only about one-third of the UN member states (and only one of the permanent members of the Security Council) have done so,[26] and several of those states have made their consent subject to limiting exceptions.[27]

Under Article 94(1) of the UN Charter, all members have an obligation to abide by an ICJ decision binding on them. If a state fails to do so, an aggrieved party may apply to the UN Security Council for enforcement. Any of the council's permanent members can effectively veto an enforcement measure, which might explain in part why the Security Council has never exercised its power to enforce ICJ judgments.[28]

The United States originally agreed to the ICJ's optional clause jurisdiction under Article 36(2), subject to two reservations, including the Connally Amendment, by which the United States declined ICJ compulsory jurisdiction over "disputes with regard to matters which are essentially within the domestic jurisdiction of the U.S., as determined by the U.S.A."[29] In 1985 the United States revoked its Article 36(2) declaration and withdrew from the ICJ's compulsory jurisdiction.[30] It is, however, still subject to the ICJ's jurisdiction under Article 36(1) for treaties in force with compromissory clauses that call for ICJ jurisdiction over disputes arising under the treaties.[31] In addition, the United States may submit a dispute to the ICJ by special agreement. This option was exercised in 1981 when the United States and Canada referred their maritime boundary dispute involving the Gulf of Maine to a special chamber of the ICJ.[32]

The ICJ is empowered to adjudicate "contentious" cases and, in limited circumstances, to provide advisory opinions. When the UN Charter was drafted, consideration was given to conferring a power of "judicial review" on the ICJ that would empower the court to serve as the "ultimate authority to interpret the Charter"; however, that proposal was rejected.[33] With rare exceptions, only a state that was injured directly or indirectly by another state's violation of an international legal obligation has standing before the ICJ.[34] Under Article 96 of the UN Charter, the other principal organs of the UN (e.g., the General Assembly and Security Council) and

---

25. Although Article 36 refers to jurisdiction under the optional clause as "compulsory," it is in fact grounded on the prior consent of the states involved.

26. As of 2013, only sixty-nine states had accepted the ICJ's compulsory jurisdiction. See ICJ, Declarations Recognizing the Jurisdiction of the Court as Compulsory, available at http://www.icj-cij.org/jurisdiction/index .php?p1=5&p2=1&p3=3 (accessed Mar. 1, 2013).

27. Restatement FRLUS § 903 n.2.

28. See, e.g., United States Diplomatic and Consular Staff in Tehran (U.S. v. Iran), 1980 I.C.J. 3 (May 24).

29. The second reservation (drafted by Senator Arthur Vandenberg) concerned disputes arising under multilateral treaties. Restatement FRLUS § 903 n.3.

30. U.S. Department of State Letter and Statement concerning Termination of Acceptance of Compulsory I.C.J. Jurisdiction, Oct. 7, 1985, 24 I.L.M. 1742 (1985); Restatement FRLUS § 903 n.3. The decision came less than one year after the ICJ ruled that it had jurisdiction over the United States in a complaint brought by Nicaragua. Military and Paramilitary Activities (Nicaragua v. U.S.), Jurisdiction, 1984 I.C.J. 14 (Nov. 26).

31. After the United States withdrew its Article 36 declaration accepting the ICJ's compulsory jurisdiction, several cases were brought against the United States under compromissory clauses in the Vienna Convention on Consular Relations and in a treaty of friendship, commerce, and navigation.

32. Delimitation of Maritime Boundary in the Gulf of Maine Area (U.S./Canada), 1984 I.C.J. 246 (Oct. 12).

33. Certain Expenses of the United Nations, Advisory Opinion of 20 July 1962, 1962 I.C.J. 151, 168 (July 20).

34. A narrow exception exists for violations of legal duties owed to the community of nations as a whole (*erga omnes* obligations). Restatement FRLUS § 903 cmt. a.

certain of its specialized agencies may request advisory opinions from the court.[35] The court's advisory opinion role has been used to clarify important "constitutional" questions regarding the charter.[36] Recently, however, the court has come under criticism for also using its power to issue advisory opinions in a way that appears to be designed to circumvent a state's refusal to consent to the court's jurisdiction for contentious cases.[37]

The role of regional courts in international disputes is growing, particularly among the member states of the EU. In addition, several ad hoc tribunals (the Nuremberg and Tokyo war crimes tribunals and the International Criminal Tribunal for the former Yugoslavia) and standing courts (most recently, the International Criminal Court) have been created to exercise jurisdiction over individuals charged with committing crimes under international law.[38] Nevertheless, the vast majority of judicial decisions involving questions or application of international law are heard in the courts of the nation-states. The role of national courts is often supplemented by decisions of administrative agencies or commissions.

C. DISPUTE SETTLEMENT PROVISIONS IN THE 1958 GENEVA CONVENTIONS

Some observers viewed the failure of the four 1958 Geneva conventions on the law of the sea to include provisions for compulsory, binding dispute settlement procedures as a significant flaw. A dispute settlement provision in Article 9 of the Convention on Fishing and Conservation of the Living Resources of the High Seas that required certain disputes to be referred to an ad hoc commission was of limited use because few states were parties to that convention.[39] The Optional Protocol of Signature concerning the Compulsory Settlement of Disputes applicable to the other three conventions was ratified by only thirty-seven states, and the United States was not among them.[40] No cases were ever referred to the ICJ under the 1958 conventions' Optional Protocol. Despite the general absence of compulsory dispute settlement procedures in the 1958 Geneva conventions, however, a number of significant decisions involving disputes under the law of the sea found their way to the ICJ during the 1958 Geneva conventions era.

D. DISPUTE SETTLEMENT PROVISIONS IN THE 1982 LOS CONVENTION

Provisions for the settlement of disputes arising out of an international treaty are on occasion contained in a separate optional protocol—as they were for the principal 1958 Geneva conventions. Parties to the treaty may therefore choose to be bound by those provisions or not, by accepting or rejecting the protocol. The 1982 LOS Convention is organized differently, with the mechanisms for the settlement of disputes incorporated into the treaty itself, from which no "reservations" are permitted. The convention does, however, include a number of automatic and optional exclusions from its compulsory dispute settlement procedures.

---

35. Restatement FRLUS § 903 cmt. h.
36. See, e.g., Advisory Opinion on Reparations for Injuries Suffered in the Service of the United Nations, 1949 I.C.J. 174 (Apr. 11); Advisory Opinion on Certain Expenses of the United Nations, 1962 I.C.J. 151 (July 20).
37. Compare Advisory Opinion on the Status of the Eastern Carelia, 1923 P.C.I.J. (ser. B) No. 5 (July 23) (refusing to issue an advisory opinion in a matter concerning the Soviet Union, which had not accepted the court's jurisdiction) with Advisory Opinion on Legal Consequences of Construction of a Wall in the Occupied Palestinian Territory, 2004 I.C.J. 136 (July 9) (no similar reluctance to intervene when the nonconsenting state is Israel).
38. Under its founding statute, the ICC has jurisdiction over the international crimes of genocide, crimes against humanity, war crimes, and (once defined) aggression. See Rome Statute of the International Criminal Court, supra, art. 5.
39. Convention on Fishing and Conservation of the Living Resources of the High Seas, art. 9, Apr. 29, 1958, 17 U.S.T. 138, 559 U.N.T.S. 285.
40. U.N. Doc. No. A/CONF.13/L.57 (1958), UNCLOS I, II Off. Rec. 145; 450 U.N.T.S. 169.

During the drafting of the 1982 LOS Convention, a significant number of states initially opposed binding decisions by third-party judges or arbitrators, insisting, as many of them did in the 1958 UNCLOS I negotiations, that disputes could best be resolved by direct negotiation between the states. Others, pointing to a history of failed negotiations and long-standing disputes sometimes leading to use of force, argued that the best chances for peaceful settlement lay in the willingness of states to bind themselves in advance to accept the decisions of judicial or arbitral bodies, at least with respect to certain categories of disputes.

The UNCLOS III negotiations produced a combination of the two approaches that many commentators regard as remarkably creative. For those disputes in which direct negotiations between the parties, together with the convention's "general procedures" for dispute resolution, fail to produce a resolution, the convention provides the disputing states with a choice of four forums: (1) submission of the dispute to ITLOS (a court created by the LOS Convention), (2) adjudication by the ICJ, (3) submission to binding "general" international arbitration, or (4) submission to a "special" arbitration tribunal with expertise in specific types of disputes.[41] All four forums involve a binding third-party settlement, in which an agent other than the parties directly involved in the dispute issues a decision, which the parties are committed in advance to respect. The four forums share in the application of a number of important structural and procedural provisions; however, each is also governed by provisions uniquely applicable to that particular forum.

1. Structure of Part XV of the LOS Convention

The dispute settlement procedures for the 1982 LOS Convention are set out in Part XV, Annexes V–VIII, and several articles scattered throughout the remainder of the convention.[42] Part XV is divided into three sections: Section 1 provides the general rules for settling disputes arising under the convention; Section 2 lays out the procedures for obtaining a binding decision from a court or tribunal; and Section 3 enumerates the categories of disputes that are not subject to the procedures in Section 2 but are nonetheless still subject to the procedures in Section 1. As is discussed more fully below, some categories are automatically excluded from the Section 2 procedures. Others are excluded from Section 2 only if the state involved has, by "declaration" (not reservation), exercised its option to exclude them.

2. Section 1 General Provisions Applicable to All Disputes

The provisions in Section 1 of Part XV are binding only on states parties to the convention, which are required by the LOS Convention (and the UN Charter) to settle any dispute between them concerning the interpretation or application of the convention by peaceful means.[43] Although with most issues the dispute settlement provisions are compulsory among parties to the

---

41. See generally Natalie Klein, Dispute Settlement in the UN Convention on the Law of the Sea (2005). Thirty-three of the 165 states that are party to the LOS Convention declared that ITLOS is their first choice of forum (none of the 5 permanent members of the Security Council has done so); 20 declared the ICJ as their first choice; and 10 declared special or general arbitration. By failing to make a declaration, the other 102 states parties implicitly defaulted to general arbitration. See LOSC art. 287(3). See UN Division of Ocean Affairs and Law of the Sea, Settlement of Disputes Mechanism Choice of Procedure (Recapitulative Table updated Feb. 15, 2013), available at http://www.un.org/Depts/los/settlement_of_disputes/choice_procedure.htm#Choice%20of%20procedure (accessed May 1, 2013).

42. See, e.g., LOSC Part XI, arts. 186–91. See also UN Division of Ocean Affairs and Law of the Sea, Digest of International Cases on the Law of the Sea, U.N. Sales No. E.07.V.5 (2007).

43. LOSC art. 279.

convention, the convention has preserved considerable flexibility. States remain free to agree at any time to settle a dispute between them by any peaceful means of their choosing.[44] If the states have agreed to seek settlement of the dispute by a peaceful means of their own choice, the Section 1 procedures apply only when no settlement has been reached.[45] Parties to a dispute arising under the LOS Convention are required to expeditiously exchange views regarding its settlement by negotiation or other peaceful means.[46] ITLOS has held, however, that a state party is not obliged to pursue these Section 1 procedures if it has concluded that the possibility of settlement has been exhausted.[47]

3. Section 2 Compulsory Procedures for Binding Decisions by Courts or Tribunals

In cases in which no settlement has been reached through the procedures in Section 1, the dispute may be submitted at the request of either party to the court, tribunal, or arbitral panel having jurisdiction under Section 2,[48] subject to the exemption provisions of Section 3 (discussed below). When signing, ratifying, or acceding to the convention, or at any time thereafter, a state is free to choose, by means of a written declaration (referred to as "the election"), among four forums for the settlement of disputes concerning the interpretation or application of the convention.[49] A party to a dispute not covered by a declaration in force will be deemed to have accepted general arbitration under Annex VII. If the parties to a dispute have accepted the same procedure for the settlement of the dispute, it may be submitted only to that procedure, unless the parties later reach a different agreement for that particular dispute. If they have not accepted the same procedure, it will be submitted to Annex VII general arbitration.

A court or tribunal selected under Article 287 is given jurisdiction over any dispute concerning the interpretation or application of the LOS Convention that is submitted to it.[50] It also has jurisdiction over any dispute concerning the interpretation or application of an international agreement related to the purposes of the convention that is submitted to it in accordance with the agreement. Only a state with standing may assert a claim for diplomatic protection.[51] In most cases, a state has standing to assert such a claim only on behalf of one of its nationals (individuals and juridical entities such as corporations) and vessels and aircraft flying its flag. It is now accepted that a vessel's flag state may assert claims not only on behalf of the vessel but also on behalf of the vessel's crew and passengers, even if those individuals are not nationals of the flag state.[52]

---

44. Id. art. 280.
45. Id. art. 281. See Bernard H. Oxman, Complementary Agreements and Compulsory Jurisdiction, 95 Am. J. Int'l L. 277 (2001).
46. LOSC art. 283.
47. The MOX Plant case (Ireland v. U.K.), Provisional Measures, ITLOS Case No. 10, Order of Dec. 2, 2001, ¶ 60, 41 I.L.M. 405 (2002).
48. LOSC art. 286.
49. Id. art. 287.
50. Id. art. 288.
51. See Draft Articles on State Responsibility, supra, art. 42. See also Barcelona Traction, Light & Power Co. Ltd. (Belgium v. Spain), 1970 I.C.J. 3 (Feb. 5). A relevant exception is the provision in Article 292 of the LOS Convention permitting actions for the prompt release of detained vessels and their crews to be brought "by or on behalf of the flag State."
52. The M/V Saiga case (St. Vincent and the Grenadines v. Guinea), Merits, ITLOS Case No. 2, Judgment of July 1, 1999, ¶ 106, 38 I.L.M. 1323 (1999). See also Restatement FRLUS § 502 cmt. h & § 902(2).

4. Section 3 Limitations and Exceptions to Rules on Binding Decisions

Section 3 of Part XV enumerates the categories of disputes that are not subject to the otherwise compulsory procedures in Section 2, but which are nonetheless still subject to the procedures in Section 1. The exceptions from the compulsory dispute settlement provisions of the convention were of considerable importance to some states (including the United States) during the UNCLOS III negotiations that would likely not have agreed to compulsory dispute settlement without those exemptions. The exceptions are generally set out in Articles 297 ("imitations on applicability of section 2") and 298 ("optional exceptions to applicability of section 2"). They are admittedly complex. Some categories of disputes are automatically excluded by Article 297 from the Section 2 procedures. Others are excluded only if the state involved has exercised its option under Article 298 to exclude them. It is not entirely clear what role the Article 297 and 298 exceptions play in the prima facie jurisdiction determination necessary for a court or tribunal to order provisional measures for the prompt release of a vessel.[53]

Article 297 automatically *excludes* from the convention's compulsory dispute settlement procedures all but three categories of disputes concerning the interpretation or application of the convention with regard to the exercise by a coastal state of its sovereign rights or jurisdiction. Under the first "exception" to the Article 297 exclusion, the compulsory procedures will apply when it is alleged that a coastal state acted in contravention of the convention's provisions in regard to the freedoms and rights of navigation, overflight, or the laying of submarine cables and pipelines, or in regard to other internationally lawful uses of the sea specified in Article 58. Second, the compulsory procedures will apply when it is alleged that a state has, in exercising the aforementioned freedoms, rights, or uses, acted in contravention of the convention or of laws or regulations adopted by the coastal state in conformity with the convention and other rules of international law. The final exception provides that the compulsory dispute settlement procedures will apply in cases alleging that a coastal state has acted in contravention of international rules for the protection of the marine environment. All other categories of disputes concerning the interpretation or application of the convention with regard to the exercise by a coastal state of its sovereign rights or jurisdiction are excluded. It must be emphasized that the third "exception" above is a narrow one and does not render all marine environmental protection disputes involving a coastal state subject to the compulsory procedures. The third exception applies only when it is alleged that the coastal state acted in contravention of "specified international rules and standards for the protection and preservation of the marine environment which are applicable to the coastal state and which have been established by [the LOS] Convention or through a competent international organization or diplomatic conference in accordance with [the LOS] Convention."[54]

Article 297 goes on to provide that, as a general rule, disputes concerning the interpretation or application of the provisions of the convention with regard to marine scientific research are subject to the Section 2 procedures for binding decisions. However, the coastal state is not obliged to accept Section 2 procedures for the settlement of disputes arising out of a decision to deny consent for MSR in accordance with Article 246 or a decision to order suspension or cessation of an MSR project under Article 253.

Disputes concerning the interpretation or application of the convention with regard to fisheries must generally be settled in accordance with Section 2, except that the coastal state need not accept the submission of disputes relating to its sovereign rights over the living resources in

53. See Klein, Dispute Settlement in the UN Convention on the Law of the Sea, supra, at 67–69.
54. LOSC art. 297(c).

the EEZ or their exercise, including its discretionary powers for determining the allowable catch, its harvesting capacity, the allocation of surpluses to other states, and the terms and conditions established in its conservation and management laws and regulations.[55] Those exemptions must, however, be read in conjunction with the dispute settlement provisions of the Straddling Fish Stocks Agreement for states that are party to that agreement.[56]

In addition to the limitations described above, Article 298 provides states parties with the option of excluding certain other disputes from the binding dispute settlement procedures. It provides that a state may declare that it does not accept the Section 2 procedures with respect to one or more of the following categories of disputes:

- disputes (with some exceptions) concerning the interpretation or application of Articles 15, 74, and 83 relating to sea boundary delimitations, or those involving historic bays or titles;

- disputes concerning military activities, including military activities by government vessels and aircraft engaged in noncommercial service;[57]

- disputes concerning law enforcement activities relating to the exercise of sovereign rights or jurisdiction excluded from the jurisdiction of a court or tribunal under Article 297, paragraph 2 (marine scientific research) or 3 (fisheries); and

- disputes in respect of which the UN Security Council is exercising the functions assigned to it by the UN Charter.

In submitting the LOS Convention to the Senate for its advice and consent on the question of accession to the treaty in 1994, President Clinton indicated that he intended to exercise the options concerning dispute settlement recommended by Secretary of State Warren Christopher.[58] Secretary Christopher had recommended that the United States elect to have all three categories of disputes listed in Article 298 exempted from the convention's binding dispute settlement procedures.[59] The Senate Committee on Foreign Relations adopted the president's proposal.[60] The draft resolution explains: "The United States further declares that its consent to accession to the Convention is conditioned upon the understanding that, under article 298(1)(b),

---

55. The U.S. Senate understanding declares: "The United States understands that, with respect to articles 61 and 62, a coastal State has the exclusive right to determine the allowable catch of the living resources in its exclusive economic zone, whether it has the capacity to harvest the entire allowable catch, and to establish the terms and conditions under which access may be granted. The United States further understands that such determinations are, by virtue of article 297(a)(3), not subject to binding dispute resolution under the Convention." Senate Committee on Foreign Relations, Report on the United Nations Convention on the Law of the Sea, S. Exec. Rpt. No. 110-09, understanding 17 (reprinted in appendix D).

56. See Agreement for the Implementation of the Provisions of the United Nations Convention on the Law of the Sea of 10 December 1982 relating to the Conservation and Management of Straddling Fish Stocks and Highly Migratory Fish Stocks, Aug. 4, 1995, 2167 U.N.T.S. 88, 34 I.L.M. 1542 (1995).

57. In its review of the LOS Convention the Senate Committee on Foreign Relations reported its conclusion that intelligence activities were included within the class of "military activities" that may be excluded from the convention's compulsory dispute settlement provisions. S. Exec. Rpt. No. 110-09, supra, declaration 2 and understanding 4(A) (reprinted in appendix D).

58. ITLOS emphasized the restricted scope of this exemption in *Arctic Sunrise* (The Netherlands v. Russia), ITLOS Case No. 22, Provisional Measures, Order of Nov. 22, 2013. The tribunal also signaled its readiness to apply international human rights law in maritime law enforcement cases.

59. See Warren Christopher, Letter of Submittal of Sept. 23, 1994, S. Treaty Doc. No. 103-39, at ix–x.

60. See S. Exec. Rpt. No. 110-09, understanding 2 (reprinted in appendix D).

each State Party has the exclusive right to determine whether its activities are or were 'military activities' and that such determinations are not subject to review."[61]

All four of the other permanent members of the UN Security Council have similarly elected to exercise their prerogative reserved by Article 298 to exempt military and law enforcement activities from the compulsory dispute settlement procedures in Section 2 of Part XV.[62]

Questions concerning the application of Article 297 and Article 298 are sure to arise in cases in which the parties dispute the nature of the action, with one party to the dispute characterizing the claim in a way that falls within an exemption while the other characterizes it in a way that falls outside the exemption. The approach of the ICJ in the *Fisheries Jurisdiction* case (Spain v. Canada) suggests how a court or tribunal might approach such jurisdictional disputes.[63] The case arose out of Canada's interdiction of the Spanish trawler *Estai* on the high seas. In filing its application, Spain asserted the ICJ had jurisdiction by virtue of Canada's "optional clause" declaration conferring jurisdiction on the ICJ under Article 36(2) of the ICJ Statute.[64] Canada contested jurisdiction on the ground that a recent substitute Article 36(2) declaration included a reservation against certain fishery disputes.[65] The ICJ began by noting that the two states characterized the dispute differently.[66] Spain argued that the dispute concerned Canada's impermissible exercise of jurisdiction over a Spanish vessel on the high seas, and Canada characterized the dispute as one involving fishery conservation and management issues. After examining the application and the written and oral pleadings (which must specify the "subject of the dispute"), the ICJ found that "the essence of the dispute" was whether the acts of Canada on the high seas violated Spain's rights under international law. It then examined Canada's recently filed reservation to its Article 36(2) declaration, interpreting the words "in a natural and reasonable way," and concluded that the dispute was one "arising out of" and "concerning" conservation and management measures.[67] The ICJ then ruled that the dispute did fall within Canada's reservation and that the court therefore lacked jurisdiction.

Two features of the ICJ's *Fisheries Jurisdiction* decision are noteworthy. First, the ICJ did not employ a presumption for or against jurisdiction in the case. Indeed, the court observed that "the establishment or otherwise of jurisdiction is not a matter for the parties but for the Court

---

61. For an explanation of the administration's position, see Letter of William H. Taft IV, Legal Adviser of the Department of State, to Foreign Relations Committee Chairman Richard G. Lugar dated Mar. 1, 2004, reprinted in U.S. Department of State, Digest of United States Practice in International Law 2004, at 676–77. The ICJ examined the effect of a self-judging jurisdiction clause in Certain Norwegian Loans (France v. Norway), 1957 I.C.J. 34 (July 6) & 48 (Lauterpacht, J. concurring opinion). See also Merills, International Dispute Settlement, supra, at 190 (concluding that whether a state can rely on an Article 297 or 298 exemption in a particular case "is not a matter to be decided by the state unilaterally").

62. On August 25, 2006, China filed an Article 298 notice with the UN secretary-general that effectively excludes military and law enforcement activities from the compulsory dispute resolution articles. China stated: "Declaration under article 298: The Government of the People's Republic of China does not accept any of the procedures provided for in Section 2 of Part XV of the Convention with respect to all the categories of disputes referred to in paragraph 1 (a) (b) and (c) of Article 298 of the Convention." See http://www.un.org/Depts/los/convention_agreements/convention_declarations.htm (accessed Feb. 1, 2013). Canada and Mexico have similarly exercised their Article 298 options. Argentina invoked Article 298 to exempt military activities from the CDS procedure when it ratified the convention in 1995, but in 2012, shortly before filing an application against Ghana for its judicial seizure of the tall ship ARA *Libertad*, Argentina withdrew its Article 298 election "with immediate effect."

63. 1998 I.C.J. 432 (Dec. 4).

64. Id. at 435.

65. Id. at 438–39. The court quoted paragraph 2(d) of the substitute declaration.

66. Id. at 446.

67. Id. at 454.

itself."[68] Second, in construing Canada's reservation it adopted a liberal interpretation, largely owing to the reservation's use of the phrase "disputes arising out of or concerning" the specified fishery conservation and management measures. The court noted that the "words of the reservation exclude not only disputes whose immediate 'subject matter' is the measures in question and their enforcement, but also those '*concerning*' such measures."[69] The jurisdiction limitations and exceptions in Articles 297 and 298 similarly employ the "concerning" qualifier.

5. Preliminary Proceedings

Article 294 of the LOS Convention provides a court or tribunal with the power to terminate a case at an early stage if it finds that the asserted claim constitutes an abuse of legal process or is prima facie unfounded. Such determinations may be made at the request of a party or on the tribunal's own initiative (*proprio motu*). The negotiating history of Article 294 documents that some states, particularly coastal states, believed that without this means of protecting against "harassment through frivolous complaints," they would be forced to defend against too many cases before international courts and tribunals, "stretching thin their financial resources and skilled manpower."[70] The time it can take an international tribunal to reach a decision on jurisdictional challenges under ordinary circumstances demonstrates the need for an early, expedited disposition rule in the LOS Convention. In the *Fisheries Jurisdiction* case between Spain and Canada, for example, it took the ICJ more than three and one-half years to dismiss the case, even though Canada objected that the court "manifestly lacks jurisdiction" less than one month after Spain filed the application.[71]

6. Provisional Measures

Contentious cases between states may include distinct phases calling for (1) decisions by the court on an application for provisional measures or prompt release of a vessel and crew, (2) a determination on whether the tribunal has jurisdiction over the underlying claims, and (3) a judgment on the merits. Provisional measures pending a final decision are limited to two situations: such measures are necessary to preserve the rights of the parties to the dispute or to prevent serious harm to the marine environment.[72] Article 290 of the LOS Convention sets out the procedures for obtaining provisional measures. They may be prescribed, modified, or revoked only at the request of a party to the dispute and after both parties have been given an opportunity to be heard. They may be modified or revoked as soon as the circumstances justifying them have

---

68. Id. at 450. The court added: "That being so, there is no burden of proof to be discharged in the matter of jurisdiction." Id.

69. Id. at 458 (emphasis in original).

70. United Nations Convention on the Law of the Sea 1982: A Commentary, vol. V, at 76 (Myron H. Nordquist et al. eds., 1989).

71. 1998 I.C.J. at 435. In a more recent dispute involving a preliminary objection under Article 79 of the ICJ's rules, two and one-half years elapsed between the filing of the application and the order of dismissal. Application of the International Convention on the Elimination of All Forms of Racial Discrimination (Georgia v. Russia), 2011 I.C.J. (Apr. 1).

72. The M/V *Saiga* case (St. Vincent and the Grenadines v. Guinea), Provisional Measures, ITLOS Case No. 2, Order of Mar. 11, 1998; Land Reclamation by Singapore in and around the Straits of Johor (Malaysia v. Singapore), Provisional Measures, ITLOS Case No. 12, Order of Oct. 8, 2003, 126 Int'l L. Rep. 487; The M/V *Louisa* Case (St. Vincent and the Grenadines v. Spain), Provisional Measures, ITLOS Case No. 18, Order of Dec. 23, 2010 (denying provisional measures after finding that Spain's safeguards respecting the seized Vincentian vessel adequately protected the marine environment).

changed or ceased to exist. The parties to the dispute are required to comply promptly with any provisional measures prescribed.[73]

Pending constitution of an arbitral tribunal to which a dispute is being submitted, any court or tribunal agreed on by the parties or, failing such agreement, ITLOS, may prescribe, modify, or revoke provisional measures, but only if the "urgency of the situation so requires."[74] Once constituted, the tribunal to which the dispute has been submitted may modify, revoke, or affirm those provisional measures. ITLOS's power to prescribe provisional measures has been invoked on several occasions. In one of its early cases, Australia and New Zealand sought provisional measures against Japanese boats fishing for southern bluefin tuna pending arbitration of the merits by another tribunal.[75] Similarly, Ireland sought provisional measures from ITLOS against the pending construction of a metal oxide (MOX) plant by the United Kingdom.[76] In a 2003 case, Malaysia applied to ITLOS for provisional measures against a reclamation project by Singapore.[77] In 2012 Argentina successfully petitioned ITLOS to invoke its power to impose provisional measures to secure the release of the Argentine sail training ship ARA *Libertad*, which had been effectively seized by Ghana to enforce a foreign civil judgment.[78]

7. Prompt Release Actions

Articles 73 and 226 of the LOS Convention expressly require that foreign vessels (but not aircraft) and their crews be promptly released on the posting of reasonable security.[79] Article 292 provides a judicial enforcement mechanism in cases in which the enforcing state fails to comply. More specifically, it prescribes the procedures for enforcing the convention's provisions calling for the prompt release of vessels and crews.[80] "Prompt release cases"—most brought on behalf of owners of vessels allegedly engaged in illegal fishing—constitute roughly half of the ITLOS docket. The application for release may be made only by or on behalf of the flag state of the vessel. The expanded rule on standing in prompt release actions has been called into question because attorneys for private litigants have increasingly started to appear before the tribunal only nominally "on behalf of" the flag state.

In considering what constitutes "reasonable" security, ITLOS has held that it will examine the gravity of the offense, the penalties imposed or which may be imposed under the laws of the detaining state, the value of the detained vessel and the seized cargo, the amount of the bond imposed by the detaining state, and the form of the bond. The tribunal has emphasized that the

---

73. Article 41 of the ICJ Statute empowers that court to enter provisional measures as well; however, in contrast to Article 290 of the LOSC, Article 41 of the ICJ Statute does not expressly indicate that the measures are binding on the parties. The ICJ has stated, however, that its orders on provisional measures have binding effect. See LaGrand case (Germany v. U.S.), Judgment, ¶ 109, 2001 I.C.J. 466, 506 (June 27).

74. LOSC art. 290(5).

75. Southern Bluefin Tuna Cases (New Zealand v. Japan; Australia v. Japan), Provisional Measures, ITLOS Cases Nos. 3 & 4, Order of Aug. 27, 1999, 38 I.L.M. 1624 (1999).

76. The MOX Plant case (Ireland v. U.K.), Provisional Measures, ITLOS Case No. 10, Order of Dec. 2, 2001, 41 I.L.M. 405 (2002).

77. Land Reclamation by Singapore in and around the Straits of Johor (Malaysia v. Singapore), Provisional Measures, ITLOS Case No. 12, Order of Oct. 8, 2003, 126 Int'l L. Rep. 487.

78. The ARA *Libertad* case (Argentina v. Ghana), ITLOS Case No. 20, Provisional Measures, Order of 15 December 2012.

79. Consular relations treaties may also require that the flag state of the vessel, the state of nationality of the crew, or both be notified.

80. See, e.g., LOSC arts. 73 & 226.

value of the vessel is not, by itself, controlling.[81] The tribunal has also ruled that additional non-financial measures, such as a requirement to participate in a vessel-monitoring system (VMS) or to conform to an international fishery conservation regime, could not be considered as components of the bond or other financial security for the purposes of Article 292 of the convention.[82]

8. Applicable Law and Proceedings

A court or tribunal having jurisdiction[83] over an LOS Convention dispute will apply the convention and other rules of international law not incompatible with the convention.[84] If all relevant parties so agree (at best a remote possibility), however, the court or tribunal may decide a case *ex aequo et bono* (by what is fair and good). "Other rules of international law" include both treaties and customary international law.[85] In construing and applying the LOS Convention or any other treaty, the tribunal or court will be guided by the Vienna Convention on the Law of Treaties, which requires that treaties be interpreted in good faith, in accordance with the ordinary meaning given to its terms and context in light of the treaty's object and purpose.[86] If the meaning remains unclear, resort may be had to the treaty's negotiating history (*travaux préparatoires*).[87]

E. COURTS AND ARBITRAL TRIBUNALS UNDER THE 1982 LOS CONVENTION

Article 287 of the LOS Convention permits states parties to elect among forums for resolving disputes arising under the convention. The ICJ, described in section B of this chapter, continues to play an important role in resolving law of the sea disputes, particularly with respect to maritime boundary delimitations. ITLOS and the special and general arbitration forum options are discussed below. Regardless of the forum chosen, any decision rendered by a court or tribunal having jurisdiction under Part XV is final and must be complied with by all the parties to the dispute.[88]

1. Arbitration under the LOS Convention

Article 287 of the LOS Convention outlines two distinct approaches to arbitration. The procedures for general arbitration are set out in Annex VII. Special arbitration is described in Annex

---

81. See, e.g., The *Camouco* case (Panama v. France), Prompt Release, ITLOS Case No. 5, Judgment of Feb. 7, 2000, ¶¶ 67–69, 39 I.L.M. 666 (2000); The *Monte Confurco* case (Seychelles v. France), Prompt Release, ITLOS Case No. 6, Judgment of Dec. 18, 2000, ¶¶ 71–76, 125 Int'l L. Rep. 203. See generally Erik Franckx, "Reasonable Bond" in the Practice of the International Tribunal for the Law of the Sea, 32 Cal. W. Int'l L. J. 303 (2002).

82. The *Volga* case (Russia v. Australia), Prompt Release, ITLOS Case No. 11, Judgment of Dec. 23, 2002, 42 I.L.M. 159 (2003).

83. Although states parties have the burden of proving any facts necessary to establish the court's jurisdiction, the court, not the parties, bears the ultimate burden of proof on its jurisdiction. See Fisheries Jurisdiction (Spain v. Canada), 1998 I.C.J. 432, 450 (Dec. 4).

84. LOSC art. 293. The phrase "other rules of international law" is examined in Walker, Definitions for the Law of the Sea, supra, at 267–72. The "applicable law" applied by the court should not be confused with the bases for the tribunal's jurisdiction. The tribunal's jurisdiction must be based on "the interpretation or application" of the 1982 LOS Convention or another international agreement related to the purposes of the LOS Convention and which is submitted in accordance with that other agreement. See LOSC art. 288. Thus, although the tribunal might apply customary international law as a rule of decision in a case, it would not have jurisdiction over a claim arising solely under customary law.

85. The *M/V Saiga* No. 2, supra, ¶ 155.

86. Vienna Convention on Treaties, supra, art. 31.

87. Id. art. 32.

88. LOSC art. 296.

VIII. Special arbitration is limited to disputes involving fisheries, protection and preservation of the marine environment, marine scientific research, and navigation, including pollution by vessels and dumping. In both general and special arbitration, the arbitral panel is composed of five arbitrators, preferably drawn from lists maintained by either the UN secretary-general (Annex VII arbitrators) or a specialized agency (Annex VIII arbitrators).[89] Decisions are decided by a majority vote of the five members and are final and binding on the parties.[90] Unless the arbitral tribunal decides otherwise, the parties pay the expenses of the tribunal, including the arbitrators' compensation.

In submitting the LOS Convention to the U.S. Senate for its advice and consent on the question of accession to the treaty in 1994, President Clinton indicated that he intended to exercise the options concerning dispute settlement recommended by Secretary of State Warren Christopher, who had recommended that the United States elect to have all disputes falling within the subject matters qualifying for special arbitration under Annex VIII resolved using that method and all other disputes resolved by general arbitration under Annex VII, thereby rejecting either of the international courts.[91] In the forwarding recommendation by the Senate Committee on Foreign Relations, the committee adopted the Clinton proposal.[92]

2. International Tribunal for the Law of the Sea

ITLOS is the specialized international forum established by the LOS Convention for the peaceful settlement of disputes.[93] The tribunal is headquartered on the banks of the Elbe River in Hamburg, Germany, but it may sit and exercise its functions elsewhere whenever it considers such a move desirable. The tribunal's composition, jurisdiction, and procedures are set out in Part XV, the Statute of the Tribunal in Annex VI, and the tribunal's rules.[94] ITLOS is composed of twenty-one judges (compared with fifteen on the ICJ) elected by states parties to the LOS Convention from among persons with competence in the law of the sea and who collectively represent the principal legal systems of the world.[95] The first election was held in August 1996. All hearings before the tribunal are open to the public unless the tribunal decides otherwise or the parties demand that the public not be admitted.

In hearing a dispute, all available members of the tribunal may sit, although a quorum of only eleven members is required to constitute the tribunal. Disputes and applications submitted are heard by a quorum of the full tribunal, by the Seabed Disputes Chamber (as its name suggests, a specialized forum for dispute involving the Area), or, when the parties request, by a special chamber of the tribunal. Like the ICJ, ITLOS sits without a jury, with the judges determining both

---

89. LOSC Annex VII, art. 2; Annex VIII, art. 2. In Annex VII arbitrations each party appoints one arbitrator and the other three are appointed by agreement of the parties or, failing agreement, by the president of ITLOS. Annex VII, art. 3. In Annex VIII arbitrations each party appoints two arbitrators. The fifth, who serves as president, is appointed by agreement or, failing agreement, by the UN secretary-general.

90. LOSC Annex VII, art. 8; Annex VIII, art. 4. An important difference between the two arbitral options is that decisions in specialized Annex VIII arbitration are rendered by experts in such subjects as navigation and fisheries.

91. Clinton, Letter of Transmittal of Oct. 7, 1994, S. Treaty Doc. No. 103-39, supra, at iii–iv; Christopher, Letter of Submittal of Sept. 23, 1994, S. Treaty Doc. No. 103-39, supra, at ix–x.

92. See S. Exec. Rpt. No. 110-09, understanding 1 (reprinted in appendix D).

93. The ITLOS yearbooks are a valuable resource in determining the tribunal's organization, competence, and procedures. The yearbooks also provide a compilation of the Article 287 forum elections by the states parties. The tribunal's decisions are available online through the tribunal's web site: http://www.itlos.org/.

94. The relevant documents, including the Rules of the Tribunal, are available on the ITLOS web site: http://www.itlos.org/ (accessed Feb. 1, 2013).

95. LOSC Annex VI, arts. 2 & 3.

the facts and the law and issuing judgment. In accordance with Article 293, the tribunal will apply the provisions of the LOS Convention and other rules of international law not incompatible with the convention in deciding disputes submitted to it.[96] Decisions of the tribunal are final; however, they are binding only between the parties in respect of the particular dispute.[97] Each party normally bears its own litigation costs (as in the U.S. system) unless the tribunal decides otherwise.[98] In contrast to arbitration, however, the parties do not have to bear the tribunal's costs.

The tribunal will form special chambers for dealing with particular disputes if the parties so request. The composition of such chambers is determined by the tribunal with the approval of the parties. Additionally, the tribunal may form such other chambers, composed of three or more of its members, as it considers necessary for dealing with particular categories of disputes. Examples include the seven-judge chambers for disputes involving the marine environment and fisheries disputes. Special chambers drawn from ITLOS judges potentially provide several advantages over arbitration. The parties have considerable control over the composition of the ad hoc chamber and the questions to be decided, and at the same time have the benefit of having their dispute decided by experienced jurists and the advantage of practicing under the tribunal's carefully drafted rules. Finally, states parties do not have to bear the costs of proceedings before the tribunal or one of its chambers.

The tribunal has jurisdiction over all disputes and all applications submitted to it in accordance with the LOS Convention and all matters specifically provided for in any other agreement that confers jurisdiction on the tribunal.[99] Such "other agreements" include, for example, disputes arising under the 1995 Implementation Agreement on Straddling Fish Stocks, the 1996 Protocol to the London (Dumping) Convention, the 2000 Convention on the Conservation and Management of Highly Migratory Fish Stocks in the Western and Central Pacific Ocean, and the 2001 Convention on Underwater Cultural Heritage.

Given the breadth of the convention's subject matter, the tribunal's jurisdiction over maritime issues is broad, although not unlimited. Nevertheless, some of the tribunal's decisions to date and public statements by judges have raised concerns that the court is taking an expansive view of its jurisdiction. One of the ITLOS judges, for example, publicly argued that the tribunal has the power to exercise what some might call ancillary or pendent jurisdiction over nonmaritime claims. In a 2002 address at the United Nations, Judge Eiriksson asserted that "questions of marine delimitation would often relate to disputes over sovereignty over land territory and the tribunal would be required to pronounce on such questions in reaching a decision."[100]

ITLOS has the power to prescribe provisional measures (discussed above). The tribunal also has special jurisdiction over prompt release cases. Although neither the LOS Convention nor the ITLOS annex confers a general authority on the tribunal to issue advisory opinions, Article 191 of the convention authorizes the ITLOS Seabed Disputes Chamber to give advisory opinions at the request of the International Seabed Authority Assembly or Council. The ITLOS Seabed Disputes Chamber recently exercised its power to issue an advisory opinion in a case concerning state responsibility for activities in the Area (discussed below).[101] Additionally, Article 138 of the

---

96. Id. Annex VI, art. 23.

97. Id. Annex VI, art. 33.

98. Id. Annex VI, art. 34.

99. Id. Annex VI, art. 21.

100. Gudmundur Eiriksson, DOALOS/UNITAR Briefing on Developments in Ocean Affairs and the Law of the Sea: Settlement of Disputes II, International Tribunal for the Law of the Sea, Sept. 25–26, 2002, at 3.

101. Responsibilities and Obligations of States Sponsoring Persons and Entities with Respect to Activities in the Area, Request for Advisory Opinion submitted to the ITLOS Seabed Disputes Chamber, ITLOS Case No. 17, Advisory Opinion of Feb. 1, 2011, 50 I.L.M. 458 (2011).

ITLOS Rules provides that "the Tribunal may give an advisory opinion on a legal question if an international agreement related to the purposes of the Convention specifically provides for the submission to the tribunal of a request for such an opinion."[102]

Whether the LOS Convention will be successful in promoting efficient and principled resolution of disputes is uncertain. The adaptability of the available forums is promising. Arbitration and adjudication are drawing closer together as courts proceed in special chambers of judges largely selected by the parties to the dispute and as the procedures adopted by arbitration panels look more and more like the rules adhered to in courts. Some members of the international tribunals worry, however, that the proliferation of international courts and arbitral tribunals is undermining the goal of uniform interpretation and application of international law, particularly the law of the sea.[103] The current framework does in fact raise the risk of conflicting decisions, even in the same case, as when, for example, ITLOS is called on to adjudicate a request for prompt release or provisional measures and an arbitral tribunal later hears the merits and comes to a decision that conflicts with the one issued by ITLOS.[104] Although uniformity in interpreting and applying the LOS Convention is certainly desirable, concerns over uniformity and consistency must be evaluated in light of the equally forceful argument that global order is enhanced by a system that provides for a wide array of methods to peacefully settle disputes among states.

F. DISPUTE SETTLEMENT PROVISIONS IN RELATED TREATIES

A number of other treaties that address law of the sea issues include provisions for settling disputes by adjudication or arbitration. They include, for example, the 1969 High Seas Pollution Intervention Convention, 1996 Protocol to the London Dumping Convention, SUA Convention, Straddling Fish Stocks Agreement, and MARPOL Convention. Disputes arising under Article V of the GATT, which provides certain access rights for foreign vessels, and parallel provisions in treaties of friendship, commerce, and navigation would likely fall under that treaty's compromissory clause.

As the *Southern Bluefin Tuna* dispute between New Zealand, Australia, and Japan demonstrated, the interplay between two treaty dispute resolution regimes can introduce complications. Article 311(2) of the LOS Convention contains what some have characterized as a "supremacy clause," which suggests that in cases in which the states' obligations under the LOS Convention conflict with obligations arising under another applicable agreement, the LOS Convention controls, except on matters falling within the purview of Part XII of the convention concerning protection of the marine environment.[105] On occasion this interpretation might be in tension

---

102. ITLOS, Rules of the Tribunal (ITLOS/8), as amended, art. 138, available at http://www.itlos.org/start2_en.html (accessed Feb. 1, 2013).

103. See, e.g., Tullio Treves, Judicial Lawmaking in an Era of "Proliferation" of International Courts and Tribunals: Development or Fragmentation of International Law? in Developments of International Law in Treaty Making, 587 (Rüdiger Wolfrum & Volker Roben eds., 2005). See also Rosalyn Higgins, A Babel of Judicial Voices? Ruminations from the Bench, 55 Int'l & Comp. L. Q. 791 (2006); Bruno Simma, Fragmentation in a Positive Light, 25 Mich. J. Int'l L. 845 (2004).

104. The *Southern Bluefin Tuna* case is sometimes cited as an example. In that case, ITLOS found prima facie jurisdiction and imposed provisional measures, which were later vacated by the arbitration panel. See Arbitral Tribunal Constituted under Annex VII of the UN Convention on the Law of the Sea (Award on Jurisdiction and Admissibility, 2000), 39 I.L.M. 1358 (2000). In fact, however, the two tribunals applied differing jurisdictional tests. ITLOS needs only to find prima facie jurisdiction to impose provisional measures, while the court or arbitral tribunal deciding the merits must make a finding of unreserved jurisdiction. See Klein, Dispute Settlement in the UN Convention on the Law of the Sea, supra, at 61–69.

105. The relevant rule for conflicts involving Part XII of the LOSC is in Article 237.

with the *lex specialis* canon, which provides that in cases of conflict the special rule controls over the general rule.[106] The *lex posteriori derogat priori* canon introduced in chapter 1, under which the rule made later in time prevails, might also come into play.[107] Finally, disputes raising interstate boundary questions might call for application of the *uti possidetis* principle.[108] It must be emphasized, however, that so long as the terms of the other agreement are "compatible" with those of the LOS Convention, effect will be given to both.[109]

---

106. The canon does not suggest that "general" law is automatically displaced whenever a "special" rule is found to apply. See, e.g., Southern Bluefin Tuna case (Australia & New Zealand v. Japan), Arbitral Tribunal Award of Aug. 4, 2000, ¶ 52, 39 I.LM. 1359 (2000).

107. United Nations Convention on the Law of the Sea 1982: A Commentary, vol. V, at 243 (Myron H. Nordquist et al. eds., 2002).

108. The *uti possidetis* (as you possess) principle stands for the proposition that a state's borders are to be respected, even with respect to newly independent states. See, e.g., The Frontier Dispute (Burkina Faso v. Mali), 1986 I.C.J. 554 (Dec. 22); Land and Maritime Boundary (Cameroon v. Nigeria), 2002 I.C.J. 303 (Oct. 10).

109. The other agreement might also address conflicts. See, e.g., Implementation Agreement on Straddling Fish Stocks, supra, Annex 2, ¶ 7 (providing that the LOS Convention prevails in cases of conflict); Part XI Implementation Agreement, supra, art. 2 (in case of conflict, the Part XI Implementation Agreement controls).

Conclusion

International law is no less salient for today's seagoing officers than it was for John Paul Jones and his contemporaries. Indeed, despite the greater ease of access to expert legal advice, even while at sea, today's seagoing officers are likely to find themselves frequently referring to and interpreting a growing body of international law on subjects ranging from navigation rights to collision avoidance rules, piracy, maritime safety and security, asylum, pollution prevention, and naval warfare. Naval service regulations require officers to comply with those laws.

The body of international law for the maritime domain comprises a web of treaties and customary law rules governing navigation, maritime safety, protection of the marine environment and the conservation and management of its resources, marine scientific research, and the maritime law enforcement and security and defense measures essential to preserving order on the oceans. That web of international law is anchored in the 1982 Convention on the Law of the Sea, the fundamental text for ocean space for its 166 states parties. The legion of experts attending the UNCLOS III sessions between 1973 and 1982 accomplished a feat not likely to be repeated: they produced a robust and widely accepted "constitution" for the oceans. The international organizations established by the 1982 LOS Convention, including the International Tribunal for the Law of the Sea, the International Seabed Authority, and the Commission on the Limits of the Continental Shelf, join the United Nations and several maritime international organizations such as the International Maritime Organization to more effectively implement the global maritime legal regime.

The global maritime legal regime will be called on to address a number of persistently recurring and newly emerging issues. Many have been identified in the preceding chapters, including maritime criminal activity; maritime security threats posed by state and nonstate actors; illegal, unregulated, and unreported fishing; and adaptation of the existing regime to such subjects as Arctic navigation and resource extraction activities, the rapid emergence of LNG-fueled vessels and unmanned marine vehicles, cyber warfare at sea, ocean acidification, climate change, and rising sea levels. Perhaps no challenge will prove more consequential for public order of the oceans than that of realizing the full potential of the LOS Convention's scheme for peacefully settling disputes arising under the Convention.

In the United States—a dualist nation that views international and domestic laws as distinct bodies—interpretation and application of international law presents unique challenges. Grappling with questions regarding which treaty provisions are self-executing and the relationship between customary international law and treaties (self-executing and non-self-executing), federal statutes and regulations, executive and military orders by the president, and judicial decisions has become a recurring feature of U.S. maritime relations and operations that challenges even the most experienced judge advocates.

Because the United States is one of the few states that have yet to ratify or accede to the 1982 Law of the Sea Convention, and does not appear likely to do so in the near future, lawyers advising U.S. clients must become adept at identifying and explaining the relationship between the conventional law rules set out in the 1982 LOS Convention and customary international law, as well as the legal effect of those customary law rules codified in that convention in the U.S. domestic law system. Given the U.S. Supreme Court's subordination of customary international law to treaties and domestic law in the 1900 *Paquete* Habana case, the fact that the far-reaching and consequential "law of the sea" remains largely a body of customary law for the United States undermines its effectiveness as a rule of decision within the U.S. legal system.

On the international plane, although abiding by the 1982 LOS Convention's articles entails few legal and diplomatic risks for the United States, claiming the rights and privileges of the convention will, at the very least, raise questions regarding the nation's good faith and, more problematically, is likely to necessitate continued diplomatic and operational assertions to preserve those rights. Those assertions must at present be based not on claims to rights guaranteed to all parties by the convention, but rather on a weaker claim that the United States enjoys those same rights as a matter of customary law. Moreover, while navigation-minded states that are party to the convention defend its carefully drafted articles against persistent threats posed by the claims of other states to various forms of creeping jurisdiction or treaty nullification, the United States will continue to find its credibility as a co-defender of the law of the sea's rights and freedoms compromised by its nonparty status.

Supreme Court Justice Oliver Wendell Holmes Jr. observed that the life of the law is driven not by logic but rather by experience. With all due respect for the great common-law jurist and thrice-wounded Civil War veteran, the life of international law is driven by logic *and* experience. The most able international lawyers must therefore combine both qualities. Fortunately, the United States boasts a large, professional, and dedicated team of international and operational law experts, within both the five military services and the broader interagency legal offices, who combine the needed qualities. The uniformed judge advocate general corps attorneys who serve as deployed staff judge advocates and in the Pentagon, combatant commander, fleet, Fleet Marine Force and Coast Guard headquarters, and district offices are unique in that they combine expertise in the relevant law and legal methods with a keen understanding of and appreciation for the services' missions and modes of operations. In the coming decades it will largely fall to them to represent the interests of the seagoing services and officers in the various forums where the evolving maritime legal regime will be shaped and to provide those services and officers with the expert advice they will need to carry out their operations in accordance with an increasingly complex body of law. Godspeed.

Glossary

A

abrogation The destruction or annulment of a law by an act of legislative power, by constitutional authority, or by usage; the act of a party, whether lawful or not, in giving notice that it considers itself no longer bound by a treaty.

abstention Primarily relevant in international law in reference to votes on the UN Security Council. By abstaining, a member does not signify objection to the approval of what is being proposed. Therefore, abstentions do not constitute a bar to the adoption of a resolution requiring unanimity of the permanent members (i.e., votes on nonprocedural matters).

abuse of rights Doctrine asserting that a state is in breach of international law if it exercises a right in such a way as to prejudice another state in exercising a right it enjoys. See, e.g., 1982 UN Convention on the Law of the Sea, art. 300.

accession The act whereby a state accepts the opportunity or offer of becoming a party to a treaty already signed by other states although not necessarily yet in force. The state acceding to the treaty did not take part in its negotiation. Not infrequently, a treaty may provide that accession may be made only to a party of the treaty.

act of aggression Generally, the use of force by one state against another state that is not justified by the right of individual or collective self-defense or any other legally recognized exceptions (i.e., force approved by the UN itself). In Resolution 3314, the UN General Assembly defined "act of aggression" as: "the use of armed force by a State against the sovereignty, territorial integrity or political independence of another State, or in any other manner inconsistent with the Charter." See the UN Charter, Chapter VII.

adjudication The giving or pronouncing of a judgment or decree; also, the judgment given.

admissible Finding by a tribunal that has jurisdiction that the claim presented meets the preliminary qualifications (e.g., standing/nationality, timeliness, exhaustion of local remedies) necessary for adjudication.

agent A diplomatic agent is a person employed by a sovereign to manage the affairs of his or her state at the seat of a foreign government.

air defense identification zone Airspace of defined dimensions within which the ready identification, location, and control of airborne vehicles are required. Also called ADIZ.

ambassador Traditional title given to a diplomatic agent of the highest class in interstate relations; a public officer, clothed with high diplomatic powers, commissioned to transact the international business of one government with another.

amendment A modification or alteration to a law or treaty. For default rules, see Vienna Convention on the Law of Treaties, art. 39.

APPS The U.S. Act to Prevent Pollution by Ships, which implements the MARPOL Convention in the United States.

arbitration The process by which parties to a dispute submit their differences to the judgment of an impartial third person or group selected by mutual consent; a method of settlement of disputes between states in which the disputed matter is submitted to selected parties whose decision is substituted for the judgment of a court.

archipelagic state A state constituted wholly by one or more archipelagos; it may include other islands.

Area, the The deep seabed region beyond the jurisdiction of any state.

armed conflict All cases of declared war or of any other armed conflict that may arise between two or more states, even if the state of war is not recognized by one of them; a hostile military engagement between nations that may or may not constitute a state of war.

asylum The right of asylum asserts that the fact that every state exercises territorial supremacy over all persons on its territory, whether they are its subjects or aliens, excludes the exercise of power of foreign states over their nationals in the territory of another state. Thus, a foreign state is, provisionally, at least, an asylum for every individual who, being prosecuted at home, crosses its frontier.

authority Governmental powers conferred on an agency or selected officials by domestic statute or through delegation by higher authority.

B

baseline Constructed line dividing a state's internal waters for adjacent maritime uses.

belligerent A state engaged in an international armed conflict, whether or not a formal declaration of war has been declared. May also refer to individuals engaged in such belligerencies. In the United States, Congress has distinguished between "privileged" belligerents and "unprivileged" belligerents. See 10 U.S.C. § 948a.

blockade Measures to obstruct or cut off commerce; blocking by men-of-war of the approach to the enemy coast, or part of it, for the purpose of preventing ingress and egress of vessels or aircraft of all nations. Traditionally, naval blockades were regarded as an act of war.

boarding agreement An agreement between a flag state and another state authorizing the second state to board vessels of the flag state subject to the conditions and terms of the agreement. Colloquially referred to as "bilats" because of the bilateral nature of most such agreements.

C

casus belli An act or proceeding of a provocative nature on the part of one state that, in the opinion of the offended state, justifies it in making or declaring war.

cession (From Latin *cessio*: "to yield") Denotes any transfer of sovereignty over territory by one state to another.

chapeau (French: "hat") An introductory provision. Conditions set out in a chapeau must be satisfied in conjunction with those that follow the chapeau (i.e., the chapeau controls the enumeration that follows). See, e.g., WTO Panel Report on U.S. Import Prohibitions of Certain Shrimp and Shrimp Products, ¶¶ 7.28 & 7.29, WTO Doc. No. WT/DS58/AB/R, 37 I.L.M. 832 (1998).

chargé d'affaires (French: "person in charge of affairs") The title of a diplomatic representative who does not have the title or dignity of minister but may be charged with those functions and offices.

***Charming Betsy* canon** The canon of statutory construction announced in Murray v. The Schooner *Charming Betsy*, 6 U.S. 64, 2 Cranch 64 (1804), admonishing that an act of Congress ought never to be construed to violate the law of nations if any other possible construction remains.

citizenship The status of a person who owes allegiance to a country and is entitled to enjoy that country's full civil rights. In strictness, "citizenship" is a term of municipal law rather than international law; it connotes membership in a political community with republican forms of government but is often used to describe nationals even of monarchical states.

collective self-defense See **self-defense**.

COLREGS International Regulations for Preventing Collisions at Sea (1972); also called the International Rules of the Road.

combatant A person taking an active/direct part in armed conflict; also called a belligerent. Combatants are all members of an armed force, with the exception of medical and religious personnel. Combatants are under a responsive command, wear distinctive insignia, carry arms openly, and follow international humanitarian law. Combatants enjoy privileged status during an armed conflict in that they are, inter alia, immune from prosecution for their (lawful) hostile acts and entitled to POW protections.

comity (From Latin *comitas*: "courteousness" or *comitas gentium*: "the courteousness of nations") Refers to the effect one state gives to the legislative, executive, and judicial acts of another state. It is more than mere courtesy but less than a legal obligation. Comity is to be distinguished from international law, because international law is a binding obligation and comity is not.

Common Article 3 Article in common to all four 1949 Geneva conventions that provides rules governing conduct during cases of "armed conflict not of an international character occurring in the territory of one of the . . . Parties."

complementarity Principle embodied in treaty provisions providing that a tribunal will be a last resort, and will hear a case only if domestic authorities are unable or unwilling to prosecute. See, e.g., Rome Statute for the ICC, art. 17: "the Court shall determine that a case in inadmissible where: (a) The case is being investigated or prosecuted by a State which has jurisdiction over it, unless the State is unwilling or unable to genuinely to carry out the investigation or prosecution."

compromis Ad hoc agreement among states to refer a dispute to an international tribunal for resolution.

compromissory clause Clause in an agreement or treaty prescribing compulsory dispute settlement means and forum.

conciliation The process of settling a dispute by referring it to a commission of persons whose task it is to elucidate the facts and to make a report containing proposals for a settlement, but not having the binding character of a judgment; the process by which an impartial third party makes an independent investigation and suggests a solution to a dispute.

conference A meeting of the representative of different states to discuss international problems or determine general policy.

congressional-executive international agreement International agreement (IA) promulgated pursuant to legislation. Congressional-executive IAs do not go through the Article II advice and consent process, but are still "treaties" for the purposes of the Vienna Convention on the Law of Treaties. NAFTA is a congressional-executive IA.

constitutive doctrine Doctrine relating to the recognition of states, asserting that the legal existence of a state or government is dependent on recognition by other states; an entity is a state only if it has been recognized as such.

consul An officer appointed by a sovereign state to watch over its subject and commercial interests in a foreign country.

consular convention An agreement or treaty between two countries establishing the rights and duties of their respective consuls. See the Vienna Convention on Consular Relations, 596 U.N.T.S. 261 (1963).

contentious jurisdiction The power of a court to hear a matter that involves a dispute between two or more parties.

contiguous zone Maritime zone adjacent to the territorial sea that may not extend beyond twenty-four nautical miles from the baseline. Within the contiguous zone the coastal state may exercise the control necessary to prevent and punish infringement of its customs, fiscal, immigration, and sanitary laws and regulations within its territory or territorial sea. In all other respects the contiguous zone is an area subject to high-seas freedom of navigation, overflight, and related freedoms.

convention Legally binding agreement between states sponsored by an international organization; a pact or agreement between states in the nature of a treaty.

corporation Any organization or association formed for commercial, charitable, or other purposes under the private laws of the state. For the purposes of international law, a corporation has the nationality of the state under whose law the corporation is organized.

countermeasures Unilateral, nonjudicial self-help remedies. See Draft Articles on State Responsibility for Internationally Wrongful Acts, art. 56.

crimes against humanity A category of legal offenses created at the Nuremberg trials to encompass genocide and other acts committed by the political and military leaders of the Third Reich (Nazi Germany). Now largely codified in the Rome Statute of the ICC, art. 7.

custom/customary international law A long-established tradition or usage becomes customary law if it is (a) consistently and regularly observed and (b) recognized by those states observing it as a practice that they must follow. That is, customary international law is evidenced by consistent state practice followed out of a sense of legal obligation.

D

de facto (Latin: "by fact") Actually; existing as a matter of fact. De facto (implied) recognition of statehood is treating an entity as a state without formally recognizing it as such (note the effect under the constitutive doctrine). Cf. **de jure**.

de jure (Latin: "by law") Legal, rightful, legitimate; existing as a matter of law. De jure (express) recognition of statehood is formal recognition of an entity as a state, thereby providing an essential element under the constitutive theory. Cf. **de facto**.

delimitation (boundary) Description of the alignment of a boundary in a treaty or other written source, or by means of a line marked on a map.

démarche A course of action; a diplomatic move, countermove, or maneuver; any formal or informal representation or statement of views to a public official.

demilitarized zone A defined area in which the stationing or concentrating of military forces, or the retention or establishment of military installations of any description, is prohibited.

de minimis non curat lex (Latin: "the law does not concern itself with trifles") Often shortened to *de minimis*, this principle addresses a fact or thing so insignificant that a court may overlook it in deciding an issue or case.

derogation Contracting out of or suspending one or more provisions of a treaty under the terms of that treaty or by separate agreement (typically in time or war or other public emergency threatening the life of the nation).

diplomatic authorization Authority for overflight or landing obtained at government-to-government level through diplomatic channels.

diplomatic immunity The general exemption of diplomatic ministers from the operation of local law. See Vienna Convention on Diplomatic Relations (codifying the law of diplomatic relations); Restatement (Third) of Foreign Relations § 464.

diplomatic protection Principle of international law asserting that a state is entitled to protect its subjects who are injured by acts contrary to international law committed by another state and from whom they have been unable to obtain satisfaction through ordinary channels.

distress A high-level threat to the ship or aircraft that may be caused by an external condition or an internal condition, such as fire or flooding. Sometimes limited to risks threatening life, not merely cargo. Cf. **force majeure**.

DoD Dictionary Department of Defense *Dictionary of Military and Associated Terms* (Joint Publication 1-02) sets forth standard U.S. military and associated terminology to encompass the joint activity of the armed forces of the United States. These military and associated terms, together with their definitions, constitute approved DoD terminology for general use by all DoD components.

domicile   The place where a person has his or her true, fixed, and permanent home and principal establishment, and to which he or she has the intention of returning when absent from it.

dualism   Theory according to which international and domestic legal systems are separate and distinct. Therefore, international law is applied in a state's domestic courts only to the extent that the state incorporates it as domestic law. Cf. **monism**.

E

embargo   A proclamation or order, usually issued in time of war or threatened hostilities, prohibiting the departure of ships or goods from the ports of the issuing state.

embassy   The residence or office of an ambassador; the functions, business, or position of an ambassador.

envoy   A public minister of the second class whose rank is next after an ambassador.

erga omnes   Obligations *erga omnes* are obligations of a state toward the international community as a whole. All states have standing to seek redress for violations of international obligations *erga omnes* because they are offensive to the entire international community.

espionage   The act of obtaining, delivering, transmitting, communicating, or receiving information about a nation's defenses with an intent, or reason to believe, that the information may be used to the injury of that nation or to the advantage of a foreign nation. Espionage is a violation of Title 18 U.S.C. §§ 792–98; and Art. 106, Uniform Code of Military Justice.

ex aequo et bono   (Latin: "out of equity or fairness") The ICJ has the power, subject to the consent of the parties to a contentious case, to render a decision not on the basis of the sources listed in art. 38 of the ICJ Statute but *ex aequo et bono*.

ex ante   (Latin: "from before") Based on assumption and prediction, on how things appeared beforehand rather than in hindsight; subjective; prospective. Cf. **ex post**.

exclusive economic zone   The area, not to extend beyond 200 miles, adjacent to the territorial sea (which generally extends 12 miles in international law, making the EEZ 188 miles wide), in which a coastal state enjoys sovereign rights over both living and nonliving resources of the seabed, subsoil, and superjacent waters; other economic activities; and, additionally, has jurisdiction over certain other activities.

executive agreement   See **congressional-executive international agreement** and **sole-executive international agreement**.

ex gratia   (Latin: "out of grace") Gratuitous; done out of goodwill rather than out of obligation.

exhaustion (of local remedies)   Rule of customary international law requiring that local remedies be exhausted prior to instituting international proceedings.

ex injuria jus non oritur   Principle declaring that a right does not arise from a wrong. See Military & Paramilitary Activities (Nicaragua v. U.S.) 1986 I.C.J. 14 (June 27).

ex post   (Latin: "from after") An ex post facto law is any law that creates and punishes as a criminal offense an act that was not a criminal offense when committed. Cf. **ex ante**.

expropriation   The compulsory divestment of ownership of private property for public purposes; a taking of privately owned tangible property by the government, either with or without compensation.

extradition   The act or process by which one sovereign state, in compliance with a formal demand, surrenders to another sovereign state for formal prosecution a criminal who has sought or taken refuge within the territory of the first state; the act of delivering up a fugitive criminal by one state to another. See also **rendition**.

F

flag state The state where a ship is registered.

force majeure A superior force that threatens the ship; generally one external to the ship, such as an approaching hurricane; a doctrine of international law that confers limited legal immunity on vessels that are forced to seek refuge or repairs within the jurisdiction of another state as a result of uncontrollable external forces or conditions. Cf. **distress**.

Foreign Sovereign Immunities Act U.S. statute granting federal courts subject matter jurisdiction over certain claims against foreign states. The FSIA says that foreign states are immune from jurisdiction in the United States, subject to a few exceptions. The burden is on the plaintiff to show that the case falls within one of the exceptions.

frontier Term often used interchangeably with "boundary," though perhaps containing less exact significance. "Frontier" connotes a zone with width or depth as well as length.

fundamental change of circumstances With regard to a treaty, a fundamental change from conditions existing at the time the treaty was concluded, and which was not foreseen by the parties to it, that provides a ground for terminating or withdrawing from the treaty in a limited number of circumstances. Also called *rebus sic stantibus*. See Vienna Convention on the Law of Treaties, art. 62.

G

General Agreement on Tariffs and Trade (1994) Part of the WTO family of agreements. GATT seeks to promote international trade and development, end protectionism and discrimination in trade, abolish import quotas, and reduce and eventually eliminate tariffs. Important provisions include the "national treatment obligation" and "most favored nation" treatment. Must be read together with GATT 1947.

Geneva conventions The four widely ratified conventions on the law of armed conflict completed in 1949 (not to be confused with the four conventions on the law of the sea concluded in Geneva in 1958).

genocide Acts of killing and similar offenses committed with the intent to destroy, in whole or in part, a national, ethnic, racial, or religious group.

good offices The offer and voluntary effort of one nation to act as intermediary in a dispute between two or more other nations.

guerrilla A member of a body of armed persons not regularly or organically connected with an army.

guerrilla warfare Military and paramilitary operations conducted in enemy-held or hostile territory by irregular, predominantly indigenous forces.

H

Hague law Reference to the Hague conventions and regulations on the law of armed conflict.

high seas, freedom of the Includes, inter alia, the freedom of navigation and fishing, subject to a requirement that states give due regard to the interests of other states to engage in high-seas freedoms. 1982 UN Convention on the Law of the Sea, art. 87.

hors de combat (French: "outside the fight") A person incapable of combat because he or she is in the power of an adverse party, clearly expresses an intention to surrender, or has been rendered unconscious or is otherwise incapacitated by wound or sickness and is therefore incapable of self-defense, who abstains from hostile acts and does not attempt to escape.

hostile act An attack or other use of force against a nation, its forces, or other designated persons or property. See **rules of engagement**.

hostile intent The threat of imminent use of force against a nation, its forces, or other designated persons or property. See **rules of engagement**.

hostilities A state of open war; actual fighting.

hostis humani generis An enemy of all humankind. Piracy, as an international crime, renders its perpetrators *hostis humani generis*.

humanitarian intervention Armed intrusion into a state, without its consent, to prevent or alleviate widespread or severe human rights violations.

human rights law A body of international law (both customary and codified in conventions) that protects individuals against abuses by states and their officials. Human rights law is applicable during peace and armed conflict (may be subject to derogation in emergencies).

I

idealism An international relations theory positing that international politics is shaped by persuasive ideas and collective values.

immunity Exemption from legal process. International law distinguishes immunity from prescriptions and immunity from enforcement of those prescriptions.

innocent passage, right of The right of the vessels of one state to navigate peacefully through the territorial sea of another state. See U.S. Senate understanding no. 2.

instruments of national power All of the means available to a government in its pursuit of national objectives: diplomatic, economic, informational, and military.

intelligence The product resulting from the collection, processing, integration, evaluation, analysis, and interpretation of available information concerning foreign nations, hostile or potentially hostile forces or elements, or areas of actual or potential operations. The term is also applied to the activity that results in the product and to the organizations engaged in such activity.

International Committee of the Red Cross International NGO that is assigned responsibility under the Geneva conventions to monitor compliance with international humanitarian law (the law of armed conflict).

International Court of Justice International tribunal headquartered at The Hague, Netherlands, established by art. 7 of the UN Charter in 1946. Only states may be parties to disputes before the ICJ, and because it is not a court of court of compulsory jurisdiction, states must consent to have the ICJ adjudicate their respective disputes.

international humanitarian law See *jus in bello*.

international law The body of legal rules that apply between and among sovereign states and such other entities as have been granted international personality. Based on the twin precepts of sovereignty and consent.

International Law Commission A body of legal scholars who codify customary international law and encourage progressive development of international law.

international organizations Organizations created by convention or treaty whose members are states (e.g., United Nations, World Trade Organization).

J

judge advocate An officer of the Judge Advocate General's Corps of the Army, Air Force, Marine Corps, Navy, and Coast Guard who is trained to provide legal advice and participate in military court-martial proceedings.

jurisdiction, territorial The competence of a state to exercise jurisdiction over persons and events within its territory. See **jurisdiction to prescribe**.

jurisdiction to adjudicate Power of a state to subject persons or things to the processes of its courts or administrative tribunals, whether in civil or criminal proceedings, and whether the state is a party to the adjudication or not; competence of a court to issue a binding judgment.

jurisdiction to enforce Competence of a state to induce or compel compliance with its laws. See The S.S. *Lotus* (France v. Turkey) 1927 P.C.I.J. (ser. A) No. 10 (holding that "a State . . . may not exercise its power in any form in the territory of another State").

jurisdiction to prescribe   Competence of a state to make laws applicable to certain controversies.

jurisdiction, universal   One of the four types of extraterritorial prescriptive jurisdiction. The principle of universality provides for jurisdiction over crimes committed by aliens outside the territory on the sole basis of the presence of the alien within the territory of the state assuming jurisdiction. Universal crimes are not self-executing; each state must define the crime in its laws. See, e.g., 18 U.S.C. § 1651 ("Whoever, on the high seas, commits the crime of piracy as defined by the law of nations, and is afterwards brought into or found in the United States, shall be imprisoned for life").

jus ad bellum   Law governing whether use of force is permissible; the right to resort to war. Cf. *jus in bello.*

jus cogens   See **peremptory norms**.

jus gentium   Originally, *jus gentium* was the body of law governing the status of foreigners in ancient Rome and their relations with Roman citizens. From the time of Grotius onward, *jus gentium* refers to the customary law of nations.

jus in bello   Law governing the conduct of warfare (sometimes referred to as "international humanitarian law" or "the law of armed conflict"). Cf. *jus ad bellum.*

jus sanguinis   (Latin: "the law of blood") The determination of citizenship based on the citizenship of parents; the law of descent, according to which being the descendent of a national is the basis for nationality. Cf. *jus soli.*

jus soli   (Latin: "the law of the soil") The determination of citizenship based on place of birth, in which being born in the territory of a state is the basis for nationality. Cf. *jus sanguinis.*

just war doctrine   A branch of international law and political theory that defines when wars can be justly started (*jus ad bellum*) and how they can be justly fought (*jus in bello*).

L

lacunae   Term that connotes, in relation to international law, gaps in international law due to the absence of express rules governing a case or situation.

law, customary   See **customary international law**.

law, domestic   The internal laws of states that regulate the conduct of individuals and other legal entities within the states' jurisdiction. Also called municipal law.

lawful permanent resident (LPR)   Any person not a citizen of the United States who is residing in the United States under legally recognized and lawfully recorded permanent residence as an immigrant (as evidenced by the so-called green card).

law of war   That part of international law that regulates the conduct of armed hostilities. Also called the law of armed conflict.

legal positivism   The theory holding that international law is based on the express or implied consent of sovereign states. Its underlying principle is that in any legal system, whether a given norm is legally valid, and hence whether it forms part of the law of that system, depends on its sources, not its merits.

legal realism   A theory championed by such jurists as Oliver Wendell Holmes Jr. that critiques classical legal thought. Legal realism is not concerned with what the law "ought to be." It simply seeks to describe what the law is.

lex ferenda **(or** *de lege ferenda*)   What the law ought to be; norms in the process of ripening into law. Cf. *lex lata.*

lex lata **(or** *de lege lata*)   The law as it exists. Cf. *lex ferenda.*

lex patriae   The law of nationality or, in the case of vessels, the law of the flag.

lex posteriori derogat lex anteriori   Principle holding that when there is a conflict between statutes, treaties, etc., the last in time controls.

lex scripta   (Latin: "written law") Law authorized or created by statute rather than by custom or usage.

liberalism   An international relations theory positing that the spread of democracy, global economic ties, and international organizations strengthens peace.

littoral state   A state adjacent to a shore.

LOAC   The law of armed conflict. Body of law governing actions during international and noninternational armed conflict.

locus delicti   The place of the offense.

M

maritime interception operations (MIO)   Operations designed to monitor, query, and board merchant vessels in international waters to enforce sanctions against other nations such as those in support of UN Security Council resolutions or to prevent the transport of restricted goods.

Maritime Operational Threat Response (MOTR) Plan   The presidentially approved plan to achieve a coordinated U.S. government response to threats against the United States and its interests in the maritime domain. The MOTR Plan contains operational coordination requirements to ensure quick and decisive action to counter maritime threats. It replaces the former PD-27 coordination process for maritime threats.

MARPOL Convention   International Convention for the Prevention of Pollution of the Sea by Vessels (1973), as amended.

material breach   Breach of a bilateral treaty by one of the parties that gives the other party a ground for terminating the treaty or suspending its operation in whole or in part. See Vienna Convention on the Law of Treaties, art. 60.

military necessity   A principle of international humanitarian law addressing targeting criteria (i.e., is the target a military objective, is it necessary to destroy the target?).

MLE   Maritime law enforcement.

MLE Manual   U.S. Coast Guard *Maritime Law Enforcement Manual*, COMDTINST M16247.1 (series).

modus vivendi   A temporary or provisional agreement, usually intended to be replaced by one of a more permanent and detailed character.

monism   Theory asserting that international and domestic legal orders are but component parts of a single universal legal order in which international law is supreme and must be applied in both international and domestic legal systems when applicable (i.e., all international law is self-executing). Cf. **dualism**.

Montevideo Convention on the Rights and Duties of States (1933)   Convention providing the (generally regarded) standard definition of a state. A state: has a defined territory, a permanent population, is under control of its own government, and engages in (or has the capacity to engage in) formal relations with other states.

most favored nation clause/treatment (MFN)   A nondiscrimination principle: a state is obligated to treat a state, its nationals, and its goods no less favorably than any other state, nationals, or goods. Modernly referred to as normal trade relations (NTR). Cf. **national treatment obligation**.

MOTR   Maritime Operational Threat Response. The U.S. network of integrated national-level maritime command centers designed to achieve coordinated, unified, timely, and effective planning and maritime command and control.

N

national   A person enjoying the nationality of a given state as determined by the internal laws of the applicable state; however, other states have no obligation to recognize nationality in the absence of a genuine link.

nationality   Term denoting the legal connection between an individual and a state.

nationality principle   One of the four bases of extraterritorial prescriptive jurisdiction. The nationality principle provides that, for the most part, it is for each state to establish the standards for conferring nationality. Generally, individuals obtain nationality by birth (*jus soli* [place of birth] and/or *jus sanguinis* [parents]) or by naturalization. Vessels have the nationality of their flag state. See 1982 UN Convention on the Law of the Sea, art. 91.

nationalization   The taking over of a privately held business by a government.

national treatment obligation   A nondiscrimination principle: a state is obligated to treat the nationals and goods of another state as the state treats its own nationals and goods (with respect to content). Cf. **most favored nation clause/treatment**.

naturalization   Reception of an alien into the citizenship of a state through a formal act on the application of the individual concerned.

natural law   Theory asserting that the rules of international law are drawn from the moral law of nature, which has its roots in human reason and which can therefore be discerned without any knowledge of positive law. Cf. **positivist school of international law**.

ne bis in idem   The principle that no one shall be liable to be tried or punished again in criminal proceedings for an offense for which he or she has already been finally acquitted or convicted in accordance with the law by another state. See the ICC Statute, art. 20.

neutral   A state not taking an active part in hostilities when others are at war. Neutral states are those that, consistent with international law, either have proclaimed neutrality or have otherwise assumed neutral status with respect to an ongoing conflict.

neutrality   Attitude of impartiality during periods of war adopted by third states toward a belligerent and subsequently recognized by the belligerent, which creates rights and duties between the impartial states and the belligerent.

noncombatant   A person connected with an armed force for purposes other than fighting, such as medical or religious personnel, prisoners of war, and the wounded. According to the law of armed conflict, noncombatants are not valid military targets; similarly, they are not permitted to take direct part in hostilities (doing so causes them to lose their protected status and renders them subject to criminal prosecution).

nongovernmental organizations (NGOs)   Groups or entities that interact with states, multinational corporations (MNCs), other NGOs, and international organizations (IOs). Unlike IOs, which are created by treaties and consequently have their origins in international law, NGOs originate in the domestic arena.

non liquet   Juristic doctrine asserting that an international tribunal should decline to decide a case when the rules are not available for its determination because of lacunae in international law.

norm   A model or standard accepted by society or other large groups and against which society judges something or something; shared expectations about what behavior is considered proper; expectations held by participants about normal relations among states.

notes   Any type of written diplomatic communication between states.

nullem crimen sin lege; nulla poena sine lege   (Latin: "no crime without law; no punishment without law") Principle denoting that no one should be subject to prosecution for a crime unless pursuant to a previous law establishing that crime.

O

opinio juris sive necessitates   Phrase connoting an element in the formation of customary international law, expressed in art. 38(1)(b) of the ICJ Statute as "a general practice accepted as law." *Opinio juris* describes a behavior that is required by law as opposed to behaviors that are motivated by other concerns such as comity.

opposability   The application of a principle of law vis-à-vis an argument to the contrary by a party to a dispute (i.e., legal arguments for both sides of a dispute).

P

pacific settlement of disputes   Obligation of UN member states to seek the peaceful settlement of disputes under the UN Charter, chapter VI.

pacta sunt servanda   Doctrine asserting that agreements must be honored in good faith. See Vienna Convention on the Law of Treaties, art. 26 (providing that "every treaty in force is binding upon the parties and must be performed by them in good faith").

passive personality principle   One of the four bases of extraterritorial prescriptive jurisdiction. This jurisdiction is based on the nationality of the victim.

peace enforcement   Application of military force, or the threat of its use, normally pursuant to international authorization, to compel compliance with resolutions or sanctions designed to maintain or restore peace and order.

peaceful use/peaceful purpose   Uses or purposes consistent with the UN Charter, including the inherent right of self-defense. See Senate understanding no. 1.

peacekeeping   An operation involving military personnel, but without enforcement power, undertaken by the UN to help maintain or restore international peace and security in areas of conflict.

peace making   An action to bring hostile parties to agreement, essentially through such peaceful means as those foreseen in Chapter VI of the Charter of the United Nations.

peremptory norm   "Norm accepted and recognized by the international community of States as a whole as a norm from which no derogation is permitted" (*jus cogens*). See Vienna Convention on the Law of Treaties, art. 53.

Permanent Court of International Justice   The first World Court, established pursuant to art. 14 of the Covenant of the League of Nations. The PCIJ opened in 1922 and closed in 1946, and was succeeded by the International Court of Justice.

persistent objector rule   Rule asserting that even if a general or regional norm of customary international law has been shown to exist, a state that persistently objected to it when it was developing is not bound by that norm.

persona non grata   (Latin: "unacceptable person") The process by which an ambassador or other diplomatic agent who is personally unacceptable to the receiving government is removed.

piracy   An illegal act of violence, depredation (e.g., plundering, robbing, or pillaging), or detention in or over international waters committed for private ends by the crew or passengers of a private ship or aircraft against another ship or aircraft or against persons or property on board such ship or aircraft.

plebiscite   The vote of the entire population of a country or area expressing choice for or against a proposed law; an expression of choice as to sovereignty.

positivist school of international law   School that seeks to describe the existing rules with reference to formal, rather than moral, criteria. Positivist theory asserts that international law is no more and no less than the rules to which states have consented. Cf. **natural law**.

Posse Comitatus Act   The Posse Comitatus Act (18 U.S.C. § 1385) prohibits search, seizure, or arrest by U.S. military personnel. Amended in 1981 to permit increased Department of Defense support of drug interdiction and other law enforcement activities.

pratique   License given to a ship to enter port on assurance from the captain sufficient to convince the authorities that it is free from contagious disease. The Quebec signal flag signals "my vessel is healthy and I request free pratique."

preemption, federal   U.S. constitutional law principle asserting that federal law will preempt contrary state law if: (a) there is *express preemption* (by the Constitution, a statute or agency regulation, treaty, executive international agreement, or federal common law), or (b) there is *implied* *preemption* (when federal law "occupies the field," or when state law conflicts with federal law because it would be impossible to comply with both state law and federal law, or when state law frustrates the objects and purpose of the federal law).

prisoner of war　A combatant meeting the test in art. 4 of the Third Geneva Convention who falls into the power of an adverse party.

private international law　In the United States: international law applicable to private transactions such as contracts for international sales of goods and bills of lading. In Europe: the branch of domestic law that deals with cases having a foreign element; rules that govern the choice of law in private matters when those questions arise in an international context.

prize　Property (generally ships, but also munitions and other cargo) captured at sea during war. The law of prize refers to the domestic and international rules governing the capture of enemy property during war.

procès-verbal　A detailed official record of diplomatic, deliberative, or legal proceedings.

progressive development　The preparation of draft conventions on subjects that have not yet been regulated by international law or in regard to which the law has not yet been sufficiently developed in the practice of states. ILC Statute, art. 15.

proliferation　The transfer of weapons of mass destruction, related materials, technology, and expertise from suppliers to hostile state or nonstate actors.

Proliferation Security Initiative　Multilateral effort launched in 2003 that aims to stop trafficking of weapons of mass destruction (WMD), their delivery systems, and related materials to and from states and nonstate actors of proliferation concern. Operations are conducted in accordance with the PSI Statement of Interdiction Principles.

proportionality　A principle of international humanitarian law addressing whether the military response is proportionate to the threat posed by the opposition. Involves considerations of weapon choice, incidental injury, and collateral damage. Cf. **military necessity**.

protective principle　One of the four bases of extraterritorial prescriptive jurisdiction. This principle provides that a state has jurisdiction to prescribe laws to define, prevent, and punish certain conduct outside its territory by persons not its nationals that is directed against the security of the state or against a limited class of other state interests.

protest　A solemn declaration by a merchant vessel master made on oath attesting that circumstances beyond his or her control have, or may have, given rise to loss or damage to the ship or its cargo, or may have caused him to take action (such as leaving an unsafe port) that may render the owners liable to legal action by another party. Protests must be noted no later than twenty-four hours after arrival.

protocol　Term usually denoting a treaty amending, or supplemental to, another treaty.

public international law　Law addressing the relations between states. Public international law defines the rights and obligations of states, as opposed to those of private actors.

publicist　An expert in international law. Art. 38(1) of the ICJ Statute provides that "the teachings of the most highly qualified publicists of the various nations [are a] subsidiary means for the determination of rules of [international] law." Such writings are material, not formal, sources of international law, and serve to furnish evidence of state practice and evaluate whether an alleged rule has risen to customary international law status.

public vessel　A vessel that is owned or demise chartered and operated by the government and is not engaged in commercial service. See 46 U.S.C. § 2101(24). Includes but is not limited to warships.

Q

quarantine　Legal measures imposed on arriving vessels, aircraft, or travelers to separate and restrict the movement of persons who may have been exposed to a communicable disease to see if they become ill. In some usages, the Lima signal flag indicates a vessel is under quarantine. See also **pratique**.

R

rapporteur   Person appointed by a committee of an international conference or an organ of an international organization to present the discussions and conclusions on an issue in the form of a report.

ratification   Domestically, the process whereby a state puts itself in a position to indicate its acceptance of the obligations contained in a treaty. See U.S. Constitution, art. II. Internationally, the term used to describe the final confirmation given by the parties to an international treaty concluded by their representatives; it is commonly used to include the exchange of the documents embodying that confirmation.

ratione materiae   Rule addressing official immunity that says immunity exists only for official acts; therefore, on leaving office, the official has no immunity for personal acts committed while he/she held office.

ratione personae   Rule addressing official immunity that says immunity is more-or-less absolute while the official remains in office.

realism   The international relations theory claiming that world politics is driven by competitive self-interest.

rebus sic stantibus   (Latin: "at this point of affairs") The doctrine denoting that treaties may cease to be binding on the parties through a fundamental change of circumstances.

recognition of governments   The acknowledgment by the government of one state of that of another state. It may be de facto or de jure (i.e., recognition can be implied or express).

recognition of states   The acknowledgment by the government of an existing state of the international personality of a new state (i.e., recognition that the new state possesses the essential elements of statehood). Recognition of states can be express or implied. Refer to **constitutive doctrine**.

refugee   A person who, owing to a well-founded fear of being persecuted for reasons of race, religion, nationality, membership of a particular social group, or political opinion, is outside the country of his or her nationality and is unable or, owing to such fear, unwilling to avail himself or herself of the protection of that country. See the Convention relating to the Status of Refugees.

regime   A system of norms, laws, rules, regulations, and decision-making processes that converge and apply to a particular issue, place, or activity.

rendition   The return of a fugitive, by the authorities of the capturing state, to the state from which he/she fled.

reparation   See Draft Articles on State Responsibility for Internationally Wrongful Acts, art. 34 ("Full reparation for the injury caused by the internationally wrongful act shall take the form of restitution, compensation and satisfaction").

reprisal   A type of countermeasure or self-help remedy (not involving the use of force), otherwise illegal, taken by one state in response to another state's internationally unlawful act, with the intent of compelling the latter to consent to a satisfactory settlement of a difference created by its own international delinquency. Cf. **retorsion**.

res communis   (Latin: "a thing common to all") An area or resource enjoyed by everyone and not subject to appropriation or exclusive acquisition; property owned by all, in common.

reservation   A unilateral statement, however phrased or named, made by a state when signing, ratifying, accepting, approving, or acceding to a treaty, whereby it purports to exclude or to modify the legal effect of certain provisions of the treaty in their application to that state. See Vienna Convention on the Law of Treaties, art. 2(1)(d).

res judicata   Doctrine asserting that once a matter is judicially determined, it may not be litigated again by the same parties or parties in the same interest.

res nullius See *terra nullius*.

restitution The fundamental principle governing the duty to make a reparation for an internationally wrongful act (*restitutio in integrum*). Reparation must, as far as possible, wipe out all the consequences of the illegal act and reestablish the situation that would, in all probability, have existed if that act had not been committed.

retorsion The taking of legal (but unfriendly) nonforceful countermeasures in response to another state's discourteous but not illegal act (e.g., severing diplomatic relations, economic sanctions, or terminating MFN status). "Retorsion" is the technical term for retaliation for discourteous, unkind, or inequitable acts with acts of the same or similar kind.

rules of engagement (ROE) Directives issued by competent military authority that delineate the circumstances and limitations under which U.S. forces will initiate and/or continue combat engagement with other forces encountered.

S

SALCON International Convention on Salvage (1988).

sanctions Measures taken in support of law by the general authority. Sanctions can be punitive or preventive. See, e.g., UN Charter, arts. 41 & 42 (providing for the application of sanctions by the Security Council against a state guilty of a threat to the peace, breach of the peace, or act of aggression).

satisfaction Term used to describe any form of redress that is available under international law to make good a wrong done by one state to another.

secession A type of state succession whereby the old state remains and one or more new states emerge; the establishment of one or more new states on territory formerly part of a predecessor state without bringing about the complete disappearance thereof.

self-defense Under customary international law, self-defense is permitted only when the "necessity of that self-defense is instant, overwhelming, and leaving no choice of means, and no moment for deliberation . . . [and] the act, justified by the necessity of self-defense must be limited by that necessity." The *Caroline* Incident (1841). A right of individual or collective self-defense in response to an armed attack against a member of the UN is recognized in art. 51 of the UN Charter. It is unclear to what extent art. 51 supersedes customary international law rules.

self-help measures Measures (forcible or nonforcible) taken by a state in response to unfriendly and illegal acts by another state; a state's extrajudicial action to remedy another state's violation of international law. If the initial act is unfriendly and the response is not contrary to international law, the response is called "retorsion"; if the initial act is illegal and the response would otherwise be contrary to international law, the response is called "reprisal."

servitude A restriction on the exercise of sovereignty over territory; a binding obligation of a state to permit a specific use to be made of all or part of its territory by another state.

ship See **vessel** (the two terms convey the same meaning).

soft law Generally, international norms that, while not enforceable, might carry normative force; e.g., UNCED Declaration of Principles, UNFAO Code of Conduct for Responsible Fisheries.

SOLAS Convention International Convention for the Safety of Life at Sea (1974), as amended.

sole-executive international agreement An international agreement (IA) promulgated pursuant to the constitutional authority of the president. Sole-executive IAs do not go through the Article II process (the House and Senate have no role, but the IA may still require implementing legislation), but are still "treaties" for the purposes of the Vienna Convention on the Law of Treaties.

sovereign The supreme repository of power in a political state. A sovereign state is a political entity comprising a territory and a government that possesses and exercises exclusive power over that territory. Sovereign states are the principal subjects of international law.

sovereign immunity   There are two competing concepts in the doctrine of sovereign immunity. According to the classical/absolute theory, a sovereign cannot, without its consent, be made a respondent in the courts of another sovereign. According to the newer restrictive theory, adhered to by the majority of states, the immunity of the sovereign is recognized with regard to sovereign or public acts of a state, but not with respect to private or commercial acts.

sovereignty   "The whole body of rights and attributes that a state possesses in its territory, to the exclusion of all other states" (ICJ in *Corfu Channel* case); the exclusive right to exercise governmental power. Sovereignty includes an internal dimension that defines the relationship of the state to the persons, objects, and activities within its territory, and an external dimension that defines its foreign relations.

standing   The determination of whether a specific party is the proper party to bring a matter to a tribunal for adjudication.

state   For the generally accepted criteria for determining statehood, see the Montevideo Convention on the Rights and Duties of States.

state responsibility   The responsibility of a state under international law for its internationally wrongful acts. Such responsibility arises when an act or omission of a state constitutes a breach of an international obligation incumbent on the state.

status-of-forces agreement (SOFA)   An agreement that defines the legal position of a visiting military force deployed in the territory of a friendly state. Agreements delineating the status of visiting military forces may be bilateral or multilateral. Provisions pertaining to the status of visiting forces may be set forth in a separate agreement, or they may form a part of a more comprehensive agreement. These provisions describe how the authorities of a visiting force may control members of that force and the amenability of the force or its members to the local law or to the authority of local officials.

STCW Convention   International Convention on Standards of Training, Certification and Watchkeeping for Seafarers, 1978.

SUA Convention   Convention for the Suppression of Unlawful Acts against the Safety of Maritime Navigation (1988), as amended. The SUA Convention is supplemented by the Protocol for the Suppression of Unlawful Acts against the Safety of Fixed Platforms located on the Continental Shelf.

subsidiarity   The principle that matters ought to be handled by the smallest, lowest, or least centralized authority capable of addressing that matter effectively.

succession   The branch of international law addressing the legal consequences of a change of sovereignty over a territory; the replacement of one state by another in the responsibility for the international relations of the territory. Succession occurs through transfer, absorption, merger, decolonization, secession, or dissolution. A change in government does not give rise to a succession question because internal governmental changes do not alter a state's international obligations.

supranational organization   A particular form of international organization, distinguishable from traditional international organizations by a number of factors, including that the decisions of these organizations are generally binding on the member governments, the organization has the power to enforce its decisions, and unilateral withdrawal is usually not possible.

T

tariffs   Duties/taxes collected on imports.

terra nullius   Unoccupied or unowned territory; land that is not claimed by any existing state. *Terra nullius* was a legal term of art employed in connection with occupation as one of the accepted legal methods of acquiring sovereignty over territory.

territorial sea The belt of water immediately adjacent to a state's landmass and subject to its sovereignty. In international law, the territorial sea may extend up to twelve nautical miles from the coastline.

territory The area of land over which a sovereign exercises jurisdiction.

terrorism The unlawful use of violence or threat of violence to instill fear and coerce governments or societies. Terrorism is often motivated by religious, political, or other ideological beliefs and committed in the pursuit of goals that are usually political.

thalweg (German: "road through a valley") The middle of the deepest part of the channel of a river or stream; the main channel of a river.

transit passage A right of all ships and aircraft to navigate a strait used for international navigation for the sole purpose of continuous and expeditious transit.

travaux préparatoires The legislative history (preparatory work) of a treaty, used as a means of interpretation. See Vienna Convention on the Law of Treaties, art. 32.

treaty An agreement between two or more independent states.

treaty, multilateral (Latin: "many-sided") An agreement among a number of sovereign states.

treaty, non-self-executing A treaty that requires states parties to enact enabling municipal legislation before it becomes effective domestically. The provisions of a non-self-executing treaty, in contrast to those of a self-executing treaty, require a formal or specific act of incorporation by state authorities before becoming part of the law of the land and enforceable in municipal courts.

treaty, self-executing Doctrine in dualist states dictating whether international treaties apply in domestic law systems without implementing domestic legislation.

treaty, validity of The grounds for invalidating a treaty are described in the Vienna Convention on the Law of Treaties. A treaty is voidable for manifest lack of capacity (arts. 46 & 47), error (art. 48), fraud (art. 49), or corruption (art. 50). A treaty is void for coercion (arts. 51 & 52) or if it conflicts with a peremptory norm (arts. 53 & 64).

trusteeship, international A system by which countries whose inhabitants are not sufficiently advanced for self-government are administered by other countries responsible to the United Nations. See the UN Charter, ch. XII.

U

UAV Unmanned aerial vehicle.

UMV Unmanned marine vehicle (in some applications, unmanned military vehicle). The term includes unmanned underwater vehicles (UUVs) and unmanned surface vehicles (USVs).

universality principle See **jurisdiction, universal**.

uti possidetis (Latin: "as you possess, so may you continue to possess") This principle, applied in the decolonial context, provides that states emerging from decolonization shall presumptively inherit the colonial administrative boundaries that they held at the time of independence.

V

VBSS Vessel board, search, and seizure operations.

vessel Although not defined in the LOS Convention, under U.S. law "vessel" refers to every description of watercraft used or capable of being used as a means of transportation on the water. Some maritime conventions, such as COLREGS, include more specific definitions.

veto (Latin: "I forbid") The nonapproval of an act or a resolution in the UN Security Council by the decisive negative vote of one of its permanent members. Article 27 of the UN Charter, concerning voting of Security Council, requires unanimity (or abstention) of all permanent members on nonprocedural matters.

Vienna Convention on the Law of Treaties International convention containing, inter alia, provisions for the resolution of ambiguities in treaties, termination of treaties, and suspension of treaty rights and obligations. The United States is not a party to this convention but accepts the majority of its provisions as a codification of customary international law.

visa An official endorsement made on a passport, denoting that the passport has been examined and its bearer may enter the country that issued the endorsement; a travel document, usually a stamp and validation on a page of the passport, allowing entry into or exit from a country.

W

war See **armed conflict**.

war crimes Grave violations of the law of armed conflict, which governs the conduct of warfare. See Rome Statute of the ICC, art. 8; ICTY Statute, art. 2, 18 U.S.C. § 2441.

warship A ship belonging to the armed forces of a state and bearing the external marks distinguishing such ships of its nationality, under the command of an officer duly commissioned by the government of the state and whose name appears in the appropriate service list or its equivalent, and manned by a crew that is under the discipline of regular armed forces (see 1982 Convention on the Law of the Sea, art. 29); a vessel designed for the conduct of naval warfare.

weapons of mass destruction Chemical, biological, radiological, or nuclear weapons capable of a high order of destruction or of causing mass casualties; excludes the means of transporting or propelling the weapon where such means is a separable and divisible part from the weapon.

Charter of the United Nations (1945)

CHAPTER I. PURPOSES AND PRINCIPLES

Article 1

The Purposes of the United Nations are:

1. To maintain international peace and security, and to that end: to take effective collective measures for the prevention and removal of threats to the peace, and for the suppression of acts of aggression or other breaches of the peace, and to bring about by peaceful means, and in conformity with the principles of justice and international law, adjustment or settlement of international disputes or situations which might lead to a breach of the peace;
2. To develop friendly relations among nations based on respect for the principle of equal rights and self-determination of peoples, and to take other appropriate measures to strengthen universal peace;
3. To achieve international cooperation in solving international problems of an economic, social, cultural, or humanitarian character, and in promoting and encouraging respect for human rights and for fundamental freedoms for all without distinction as to race, sex, language, or religion; and
4. To be a center for harmonizing the actions of nations in the attainment of these common ends.

Article 2

The Organization and its Members, in pursuit of the Purposes stated in Article 1, shall act in accordance with the following Principles.

1. The Organization is based on the principle of the sovereign equality of all its Members.
2. All Members, in order to ensure to all of them the rights and benefits resulting from membership, shall fulfill in good faith the obligations assumed by them in accordance with the present Charter.
3. All Members shall settle their international disputes by peaceful means in such a manner that international peace and security, and justice, are not endangered.
4. All Members shall refrain in their international relations from the threat or use of force against the territorial integrity or political independence of any state, or in any other manner inconsistent with the Purposes of the United Nations.
5. All Members shall give the United Nations every assistance in any action it takes in accordance with the present Charter, and shall refrain from giving assistance to any state against which the United Nations is taking preventive or enforcement action.
6. The Organization shall ensure that states which are not Members of the United Nations act in accordance with these Principles so far as may be necessary for the maintenance of international peace and security.
7. Nothing contained in the present Charter shall authorize the United Nations to intervene in matters which are essentially within the domestic jurisdiction of any state or shall require the Members to submit such matters to settlement under the present Charter; but this principle shall not prejudice the application of enforcement measures under Chapter VII.

CHAPTER II. MEMBERSHIP

Article 3

The original Members of the United Nations shall be the states which, having participated in the United Nations Conference on International Organization at San Francisco, or having previously signed the Declaration by United Nations of January 1, 1942, sign the present Charter and ratify it in accordance with Article 110.

Article 4

1. Membership in the United Nations is open to all other peace-loving states which accept the obligations contained in the present Charter and, in the judgment of the Organization, are able and willing to carry out these obligations.
2. The admission of any such state to membership in the United Nations will be effected by a decision of the General Assembly upon the recommendation of the Security Council.

Article 5

A member of the United Nations against which preventive or enforcement action has been taken by the Security Council may be suspended from the exercise of the rights and privileges of membership by the General Assembly upon the recommendation of the Security Council. The exercise of these rights and privileges may be restored by the Security Council.

Article 6

A Member of the United Nations which has persistently violated the Principles contained in the present Charter may be expelled from the Organization by the General Assembly upon the recommendation of the Security Council.

CHAPTER III. ORGANS

Article 7

1. There are established as the principal organs of the United Nations: a General Assembly, a Security Council, an Economic and Social Council, a Trusteeship Council, an International Court of Justice, and a Secretariat.
2. Such subsidiary organs as may be found necessary may be established in accordance with the present Charter.

Article 8

The United Nations shall place no restrictions on the eligibility of men and women to participate in any capacity and under conditions of equality in its principal and subsidiary organs.

CHAPTER IV. THE GENERAL ASSEMBLY

Composition

Article 9

1. The General Assembly shall consist of all the Members of the United Nations.
2. Each member shall have not more than five representatives in the General Assembly.

Functions and Powers

Article 10

The General Assembly may discuss any questions or any matters within the scope of the present Charter or relating to the powers and functions of any organs provided for in the present Charter, and, except as provided in Article 12, may make recommendations to the Members of the United Nations or to the Security Council or to both on any such questions or matters.

Article 11

1. The General Assembly may consider the general principles of cooperation in the maintenance of international peace and security, including the principles governing disarmament and the regulation of armaments, and may make recommendations with regard to such principles to the Members or to the Security Council or to both.
2. The General Assembly may discuss any questions relating to the maintenance of international peace and security brought before it by any Member of the United Nations, or by the Security Council, or by a state which is not a Member of the United Nations in accordance with Article 35, paragraph 2, and, except as provided in Article 12, may make recommendations with regard to any such questions to the state or states concerned or to the Security Council or to both. Any such question on which action is necessary shall be referred to the Security Council by the General Assembly either before or after discussion.
3. The General Assembly may call the attention of the Security Council to situations which are likely to endanger international peace and security.
4. The powers of the General Assembly set forth in this Article shall not limit the general scope of Article 10.

Article 12

1. While the Security Council is exercising in respect of any dispute or situation the functions assigned to it in the present Charter, the General Assembly shall not make any recommendation with regard to that dispute or situation unless the Security Council so requests.
2. The Secretary-General, with the consent of the Security Council, shall notify the General Assembly at each session of any matters relative to the maintenance of international peace and security which are being dealt with by the Security Council and shall similarly notify the General Assembly, or the Members of the United Nations if the General Assembly is not in session, immediately the Security Council ceases to deal with such matters.

Article 13

1. The General Assembly shall initiate studies and make recommendations for the purpose of:
   a. promoting international cooperation in the political field and encouraging the progressive development of international law and its codification;
   b. promoting international cooperation in the economic, social, cultural, educational, and health fields, and assisting in the realization of human rights and fundamental freedoms for all without distinction as to race, sex, language, or religion.
2. The further responsibilities, functions, and powers of the General Assembly with respect to matters mentioned in paragraph 1(b) above are set forth in Chapters IX and X.

Article 14

Subject to the provisions of Article 12, the General Assembly may recommend measures for the peaceful adjustment of any situation, regardless of origin, which it deems likely to impair the general welfare or friendly relations among nations, including situations resulting from a violation of the provisions of the present Charter setting forth the Purposes and Principles of the United Nations.

Article 15

1. The General Assembly shall receive and consider annual and special reports from the Security Council; these reports shall include an account of the measures that the Security Council has decided upon or taken to maintain international peace and security.
2. The General Assembly shall receive and consider reports from the other organs of the United Nations.

Article 16

The General Assembly shall perform such functions with respect to the international trusteeship system as are assigned to it under Chapters XII and XIII, including the approval of the trusteeship agreements for areas not designated as strategic.

Article 17

1. The General Assembly shall consider and approve the budget of the Organization.
2. The expenses of the Organization shall be borne by the Members as apportioned by the General Assembly.
3. The General Assembly shall consider and approve any financial and budgetary arrangements with specialized agencies referred to in Article 57 and shall examine the administrative budgets of such specialized agencies with a view to making recommendations to the agencies concerned.

Voting

Article 18

1. Each member of the General Assembly shall have one vote.
2. Decisions of the General Assembly on important questions shall be made by a two-thirds majority of the members present and voting. These questions shall include: recommendations with respect to the maintenance of international peace and security, the election of the non-permanent members of the Security Council, the election of the members of the Economic and Social Council, the election of members of the Trusteeship Council in accordance with paragraph 1(c) of Article 86, the admission of new Members to the United Nations, the suspension of the rights and privileges of membership, the expulsion of Members, questions relating to the operation of the trusteeship system, and budgetary questions.
3. Decisions on other questions, including the determination of additional categories of questions to be decided by a two-thirds majority, shall be made by a majority of the members present and voting.

Article 19

A Member of the United Nations which is in arrears in the payment of its financial contributions to the Organization shall have no vote in the General Assembly if the amount of its arrears equals or exceeds the amount of the contributions due from it for the preceding two full years. The General Assembly may, nevertheless, permit such a Member to vote if it is satisfied that the failure to pay is due to conditions beyond the control of the Member.

Procedure

Article 20

The General Assembly shall meet in regular annual sessions and in such special sessions as occasion may require. Special sessions shall be convoked by the Secretary-General at the request of the Security Council or of a majority of the Members of the United Nations.

Article 21

The General Assembly shall adopt its own rules of procedure. It shall elect its President for each session.

Article 22

The General Assembly may establish such subsidiary organs as it deems necessary for the performance of its functions.

CHAPTER V. THE SECURITY COUNCIL

Article 23

1. The Security Council shall consist of fifteen Members of the United Nations. The Republic of China, France, the Union of Soviet Socialist Republics, the United Kingdom of Great Britain and Northern Ireland, and the United States of America shall be permanent members of the Security Council. The General Assembly shall elect ten other Members of the United Nations to be non-permanent members of the Security Council, due regard being specially paid, in the first instance to the contribution of Members of the United Nations to the maintenance of international peace and security and to the other purposes of the Organization, and also to equitable geographical distribution.
2. The non-permanent members of the Security Council shall be elected for a term of two years. In the first election of the non-permanent members after the increase of the membership of the Security Council from eleven to fifteen, two of the four additional members shall be chosen for a term of one year. A retiring member shall not be eligible for immediate re-election.
3. Each member of the Security Council shall have one representative.

Functions and Powers

Article 24

1. In order to ensure prompt and effective action by the United Nations, its Members confer on the Security Council primary responsibility for the maintenance of international peace and security, and agree that in carrying out its duties under this responsibility the Security Council acts on their behalf.
2. In discharging these duties the Security Council shall act in accordance with the Purposes and Principles of the United Nations. The specific powers granted to the Security Council for the discharge of these duties are laid down in Chapters VI, VII, VIII, and XII.
3. The Security Council shall submit annual and, when necessary, special reports to the General Assembly for its consideration.

Article 25

The Members of the United Nations agree to accept and carry out the decisions of the Security Council in accordance with the present Charter.

Article 26

In order to promote the establishment and maintenance of international peace and security with the least diversion for armaments of the world's human and economic resources, the Security Council shall be responsible for formulating, with the assistance of the Military Staff Committee referred to in Article 47, plans to be submitted to the Members of the United Nations for the establishment of a system for the regulation of armaments.

Voting

Article 27

1. Each member of the Security Council shall have one vote.
2. Decisions of the Security Council on procedural matters shall be made by an affirmative vote of nine members.
3. Decisions of the Security Council on all other matters shall be made by an affirmative vote of nine members including the concurring votes of the permanent members; provided that, in decisions under Chapter VI, and under paragraph 3 of Article 52, a party to a dispute shall abstain from voting.

Procedure

Article 28

1. The Security Council shall be so organized as to be able to function continuously. Each member of the Security Council shall for this purpose be represented at all times at the seat of the Organization.
2. The Security Council shall hold periodic meetings at which each of its members may, if it so desires, be represented by a member of the government or by some other specially designated representative.
3. The Security Council may hold meetings at such places other than the seat of the Organization as in its judgment will best facilitate its work.

Article 29

The Security Council may establish such subsidiary organs as it deems necessary for the performance of its functions.

Article 30

The Security Council shall adopt its own rules of procedure, including the method of selecting its President.

Article 31

Any Member of the United Nations which is not a member of the Security Council may participate, without vote, in the discussion of any question brought before the Security Council whenever the latter considers that the interests of that Member are specially affected.

Article 32

Any Member of the United Nations which is not a member of the Security Council or any state which is not a Member of the United Nations, if it is a party to a dispute under consideration by the Security Council, shall be invited to participate, without vote, in the discussion relating to the dispute. The Security Council shall lay down such conditions as it deems just for the participation of a state which is not a Member of the United Nations.

CHAPTER VI. PACIFIC SETTLEMENT OF DISPUTES

Article 33

1. The parties to any dispute, the continuance of which is likely to endanger the maintenance of international peace and security, shall, first of all, seek a solution by negotiation, enquiry, mediation, conciliation, arbitration, judicial settlement, resort to regional agencies or arrangements, or other peaceful means of their own choice.
2. The Security Council shall, when it deems necessary, call upon the parties to settle their dispute by such means.

Article 34

The Security Council may investigate any dispute, or any situation which might lead to international friction or give rise to a dispute, in order to determine whether the continuance of the dispute or situation is likely to endanger the maintenance of international peace and security.

Article 35

1. Any Member of the United Nations may bring any dispute, or any situation of the nature referred to in Article 34, to the attention of the Security Council or of the General Assembly.
2. A state which is not a Member of the United Nations may bring to the attention of the Security Council or of the General Assembly any dispute to which it is a party if it accepts in advance, for the purposes of the dispute, the obligations of pacific settlement provided in the present Charter.

3. The proceedings of the General Assembly in respect of matters brought to its attention under this Article will be subject to the provisions of Articles 11 and 12.

Article 36

1. The Security Council may, at any stage of a dispute of the nature referred to in Article 33 or of a situation of like nature, recommend appropriate procedures or methods of adjustment.
2. The Security Council should take into consideration any procedures for the settlement of the dispute which have already been adopted by the parties.
3. In making recommendations under this Article the Security Council should also take into consideration that legal disputes should as a general rule be referred by the parties to the International Court of Justice in accordance with the provisions of the Statute of the Court.

Article 37

1. Should the parties to a dispute of the nature referred to in Article 33 fail to settle it by the means indicated in that Article, they shall refer it to the Security Council.
2. If the Security Council deems that the continuance of the dispute is in fact likely to endanger the maintenance of international peace and security, it shall decide whether to take action under Article 36 or to recommend such terms of settlement as it may consider appropriate.

Article 38

Without prejudice to the provisions of Articles 33 to 37, the Security Council may, if all the parties to any dispute so request, make recommendations to the parties with a view to a pacific settlement of the dispute.

CHAPTER VII. ACTION WITH RESPECT TO THREATS TO THE PEACE, BREACHES OF THE PEACE, AND ACTS OF AGGRESSION

Article 39

The Security Council shall determine the existence of any threat to the peace, breach of the peace, or act of aggression and shall make recommendations, or decide what measures shall be taken in accordance with Articles 41 and 42, to maintain or restore international peace and security.

Article 40

In order to prevent an aggravation of the situation, the Security Council may, before making the recommendations or deciding upon the measures provided for in Article 39, call upon the parties concerned to comply with such provisional measures as it deems necessary or desirable. Such provisional measures shall be without prejudice to the rights, claims, or position of the parties concerned. The Security Council shall duly take account of failure to comply with such provisional measures.

Article 41

The Security Council may decide what measures not involving the use of armed force are to be employed to give effect to its decisions, and it may call upon the Members of the United Nations to apply such measures. These may include complete or partial interruption of economic relations and of rail, sea, air, postal, telegraphic, radio, and other means of communication, and the severance of diplomatic relations.

Article 42

Should the Security Council consider that measures provided for in Article 41 would be inadequate or have proved to be inadequate, it may take such action by air, sea, or land forces as may be necessary to maintain or restore international peace and security. Such action may include demonstrations, blockade, and other operations by air, sea, or land forces of Members of the United Nations.

Article 43

1. All Members of the United Nations, in order to contribute to the maintenance of international peace and security, undertake to make available to the Security Council, on its call and in accordance with a special agreement or agreements, armed forces, assistance, and facilities, including rights of passage, necessary for the purpose of maintaining international peace and security.
2. Such agreement or agreements shall govern the numbers and types of forces, their degree of readiness and general location, and the nature of the facilities and assistance to be provided.
3. The agreement or agreements shall be negotiated as soon as possible on the initiative of the Security Council. They shall be concluded between the Security Council and Members or between the Security Council and groups of Members and shall be subject to ratification by the signatory states in accordance with their respective constitutional processes.

Article 44

When the Security Council has decided to use force it shall, before calling upon a Member not represented on it to provide armed forces in fulfillment of the obligations assumed under Article 43, invite that Member, if the Member so desires, to participate in the decisions of the Security Council concerning the employment of contingents of that Member's armed forces.

Article 45

In order to enable the United Nations to take urgent military measures Members shall hold immediately available national air-force contingents for combined international enforcement action. The strength and degree of readiness of these contingents and plans for their combined action shall be determined, within the limits laid down in the special agreement or agreements referred to in Article 43, by the Security Council with the assistance of the Military Staff Committee.

Article 46

Plans for the application of armed force shall be made by the Security Council with the assistance of the Military Staff Committee.

Article 47

1. There shall be established a Military Staff Committee to advise and assist the Security Council on all questions relating to the Security Council's military requirements for the maintenance of international peace and security, the employment and command of forces placed at its disposal, the regulation of armaments, and possible disarmament.
2. The Military Staff Committee shall consist of the Chiefs of Staff of the permanent members of the Security Council or their representatives. Any Member of the United Nations not permanently represented on the Committee shall be invited by the Committee to be associated with it when the efficient discharge of the Committee's responsibilities requires the participation of that Member in its work.
3. The Military Staff Committee shall be responsible under the Security Council for the strategic direction of any armed forces placed at the disposal of the Security Council. Questions relating to the command of such forces shall be worked out subsequently.
4. The Military Staff Committee, with the authorization of the Security Council and after consultation with appropriate regional agencies, may establish regional subcommittees.

Article 48

1. The action required to carry out the decisions of the Security Council for the maintenance of international peace and security shall be taken by all the Members of the United Nations or by some of them, as the Security Council may determine.
2. Such decisions shall be carried out by the Members of the United Nations directly and through their action in the appropriate international agencies of which they are members.

Article 49

The Members of the United Nations shall join in affording mutual assistance in carrying out the measures decided upon by the Security Council.

Article 50

If preventive or enforcement measures against any state are taken by the Security Council, any other state, whether a Member of the United Nations or not, which finds itself confronted with special economic problems arising from the carrying out of those measures shall have the right to consult the Security Council with regard to a solution of those problems.

Article 51

Nothing in the present Charter shall impair the inherent right of individual or collective self-defense if an armed attack occurs against a Member of the United Nations, until the Security Council has taken measures necessary to maintain international peace and security. Measures taken by Members in the exercise of this right of self-defense shall be immediately reported to the Security Council and shall not in any way affect the authority and responsibility of the Security Council under the present Charter to take at any time such action as it deems necessary in order to maintain or restore international peace and security.

CHAPTER VIII. REGIONAL ARRANGEMENTS

Article 52

1. Nothing in the present Charter precludes the existence of regional arrangements or agencies for dealing with such matters relating to the maintenance of international peace and security as are appropriate for regional action, provided that such arrangements or agencies and their activities are consistent with the Purposes and Principles of the United Nations.
2. The Members of the United Nations entering into such arrangements or constituting such agencies shall make every effort to achieve pacific settlement of local disputes through such regional arrangements or by such regional agencies before referring them to the Security Council.
3. The Security Council shall encourage the development of pacific settlement of local disputes through such regional arrangements or by such regional agencies either on the initiative of the states concerned or by reference from the Security Council.
4. This Article in no way impairs the application of Articles 34 and 35.

Article 53

1. The Security Council shall, where appropriate, utilize such regional arrangements or agencies for enforcement action under its authority. But no enforcement action shall be taken under regional arrangements or by regional agencies without the authorization of the Security Council, with the exception of measures against any enemy state, as defined in paragraph 2 of this Article, provided for pursuant to Article 107 or in regional arrangements directed against renewal of aggressive policy on the part of any such state, until such time as the Organization may, on request of the Governments concerned, be charged with the responsibility for preventing further aggression by such a state.
2. The term enemy state as used in paragraph 1 of this Article applies to any state which during the Second World War has been an enemy of any signatory of the present Charter.

Article 54

The Security Council shall at all times be kept fully informed of activities undertaken or in contemplation under regional arrangements or by regional agencies for the maintenance of international peace and security.

CHAPTER IX. INTERNATIONAL ECONOMIC AND SOCIAL CO-OPERATION

Article 55

With a view to the creation of conditions of stability and well-being which are necessary for peaceful and friendly relations among nations based on respect for the principle of equal rights and self-determination of peoples, the United Nations shall promote:

   a. higher standards of living, full employment, and conditions of economic and social progress and development;
   b. solutions of international economic, social, health, and related problems; and international cultural and educational co-operation; and
   c. universal respect for, and observance of, human rights and fundamental freedoms for all without distinction as to race, sex, language, or religion.

Article 56

All Members pledge themselves to take joint and separate action in co-operation with the Organization for the achievement of the purposes set forth in Article 55.

Article 57

1. The various specialized agencies, established by intergovernmental agreement and having wide international responsibilities, as defined in their basic instruments, in economic, social, cultural, educational, health, and related fields, shall be brought into relationship with the United Nations in accordance with the provisions of Article 63.
2. Such agencies thus brought into relationship with the United Nations are hereinafter referred to as specialized agencies.

Article 58

The Organization shall make recommendations for the coordination of the policies and activities of the specialized agencies.

Article 59

The Organization shall, where appropriate, initiate negotiations among the states concerned for the creation of any new specialized agencies required for the accomplishment of the purposes set forth in Article 55.

Article 60

Responsibility for the discharge of the functions of the Organization set forth in this Chapter shall be vested in the General Assembly and, under the authority of the General Assembly, in the Economic and Social Council, which shall have for this purpose the powers set forth in Chapter X.

CHAPTER X. THE ECONOMIC AND SOCIAL COUNCIL

[Omitted]

CHAPTER XI. DECLARATION REGARDING NON-SELF-GOVERNING TERRITORIES

[Omitted]

CHAPTER XII. INTERNATIONAL TRUSTEESHIP SYSTEM

[Omitted]

CHAPTER XIII. THE TRUSTEESHIP COUNCIL

[Omitted]

CHAPTER XIV. THE INTERNATIONAL COURT OF JUSTICE

Article 92

The International Court of Justice shall be the principal judicial organ of the United Nations. It shall function in accordance with the annexed Statute which is based upon the Statute of the Permanent Court of International Justice and forms an integral part of the present Charter.

Article 93

1. All Members of the United Nations are ipso facto parties to the Statute of the International Court of Justice.
2. A state which is not a Member of the United Nations may become a party to the Statute of the International Court of Justice on conditions to be determined in each case by the General Assembly upon the recommendation of the Security Council.

Article 94

1. Each Member of the United Nations undertakes to comply with the decision of the International Court of Justice in any case to which it is a party.
2. If any party to a case fails to perform the obligations incumbent upon it under a judgment rendered by the Court, the other party may have recourse to the Security Council, which may, if it deems necessary, make recommendations or decide upon measures to be taken to give effect to the judgment.

Article 95

Nothing in the present Charter shall prevent Members of the United Nations from entrusting the solution of their differences to other tribunals by virtue of agreements already in existence or which may be concluded in the future.

Article 96

1. The General Assembly or the Security Council may request the International Court of Justice to give an advisory opinion on any legal question.
2. Other organs of the United Nations and specialized agencies, which may at any time be so authorized by the General Assembly, may also request advisory opinions of the Court on legal questions arising within the scope of their activities.

CHAPTER XV. THE SECRETARIAT

Article 97

The Secretariat shall comprise a Secretary-General and such staff as the Organization may require. The Secretary-General shall be appointed by the General Assembly upon the recommendation of the Security Council. He shall be the chief administrative officer of the Organization.

Article 98

The Secretary-General shall act in that capacity in all meetings of the General Assembly, of the Security Council, of the Economic and Social Council, and of the Trusteeship Council, and shall perform such other functions as are entrusted to him by these organs. The Secretary-General shall make an annual report to the General Assembly on the work of the Organization.

Article 99

The Secretary-General may bring to the attention of the Security Council any matter which in his opinion may threaten the maintenance of international peace and security.

Article 100

1. In the performance of their duties the Secretary-General and the staff shall not seek or receive instructions from any government or from any other authority external to the Organization. They

shall refrain from any action which might reflect on their position as international officials responsible only to the Organization.

2. Each Member of the United Nations undertakes to respect the exclusively international character of the responsibilities of the Secretary-General and the staff and not to seek to influence them in the discharge of their responsibilities.

Article 101

1. The staff shall be appointed by the Secretary-General under regulations established by the General Assembly.

2. Appropriate staffs shall be permanently assigned to the Economic and Social Council, the Trusteeship Council, and, as required, to other organs of the United Nations. These staffs shall form a part of the Secretariat.

3. The paramount consideration in the employment of the staff and in the determination of the conditions of service shall be the necessity of securing the highest standards of efficiency, competence, and integrity. Due regard shall be paid to the importance of recruiting the staff on as wide a geographical basis as possible.

CHAPTER XVI. MISCELLANEOUS PROVISIONS

Article 102

1. Every treaty and every international agreement entered into by any Member of the United Nations after the present Charter comes into force shall as soon as possible be registered with the Secretariat and published by it.

2. No party to any such treaty or international agreement which has not been registered in accordance with the provisions of paragraph I of this Article may invoke that treaty or agreement before any organ of the United Nations.

Article 103

In the event of a conflict between the obligations of the Members of the United Nations under the present Charter and their obligations under any other international agreement, their obligations under the present Charter shall prevail.

Article 104

The Organization shall enjoy in the territory of each of its Members such legal capacity as may be necessary for the exercise of its functions and the fulfillment of its purposes.

Article 105

1. The Organization shall enjoy in the territory of each of its Members such privileges and immunities as are necessary for the fulfillment of its purposes.

2. Representatives of the Members of the United Nations and officials of the Organization shall similarly enjoy such privileges and immunities as are necessary for the independent exercise of their functions in connection with the Organization.

3. The General Assembly may make recommendations with a view to determining the details of the application of paragraphs 1 and 2 of this Article or may propose conventions to the Members of the United Nations for this purpose.

CHAPTER XVII. TRANSITIONAL SECURITY ARRANGEMENTS

[Omitted]

CHAPTER XVIII. AMENDMENTS

Article 108

Amendments to the present Charter shall come into force for all Members of the United Nations when they have been adopted by a vote of two-thirds of the members of the General Assembly and ratified in accordance with their respective constitutional processes by two-thirds of the Members of the United Nations, including all the permanent members of the Security Council.

Article 109

1. A General Conference of the Members of the United Nations for the purpose of reviewing the present Charter may be held at a date and place to be fixed by a two-thirds vote of the members of the General Assembly and by a vote of any nine members of the Security Council. Each Member of the United Nations shall have one vote in the conference.
2. Any alteration of the present Charter recommended by a two-thirds vote of the conference shall take effect when ratified in accordance with their respective constitutional processes by two-thirds of the Members of the United Nations including all the permanent members of the Security Council.
3. If such a conference has not been held before the tenth annual session of the General Assembly following the coming into force of the present Charter, the proposal to call such a conference shall be placed on the agenda of that session of the General Assembly, and the conference shall be held if so decided by a majority vote of the members of the General Assembly and by a vote of any seven members of the Security Council.

CHAPTER XIX. RATIFICATION AND SIGNATURE

[Omitted]

APPENDIX C

United Nations Convention on the Law of the Sea (1982)

PART I. INTRODUCTION

Article 1. Use of terms and scope

1. For the purposes of this Convention:
    (1) "Area" means the sea-bed and ocean floor and subsoil thereof, beyond the limits of national jurisdiction;
    (2) "Authority" means the International Sea-Bed Authority;
    (3) "activities in the Area" means all activities of exploration for, and exploitation of, the resources of the Area;
    (4) "pollution of the marine environment" means the introduction by man, directly or indirectly, of substances or energy into the marine environment, including estuaries, which results or is likely to result in such deleterious effects as harm to living resources and marine life, hazards to human health, hindrance to marine activities, including fishing and other legitimate uses of the sea, impairment of quality for use of sea water and reduction of amenities;
    (5) (a) "dumping" means:
        (i) any deliberate disposal of wastes or other matter from vessels, aircraft, platforms or other man-made structures at sea;
        (ii) any deliberate disposal of vessels, aircraft, platforms or other man-made structures at sea;
    (b) "dumping" does not include:
        (i) the disposal of wastes or other matter incidental to, or derived from the normal operations of vessels, aircraft, platforms or other man-made structures at sea and their equipment, other than wastes or other matter transported by or to vessels, aircraft, platforms or other man-made structures at sea, operating for the purpose of disposal of such matter or derived from the treatment of such wastes or other matter on such vessels, aircraft, platforms or structures;
        (ii) placement of matter for a purpose other than the mere disposal thereof, provided that such placement is not contrary to the aims of this Convention.
2. (1) "States Parties" means States which have consented to be bound by this Convention and for which this Convention is in force.
    (2) This Convention applies *mutatis mutandis* to the entities referred to in Article 305, paragraph 1(b), (c), (d), (e) and (f), which become Parties to this Convention in accordance with the conditions relevant to each, and to that extent "States Parties" refers to those entities.

PART II. TERRITORIAL SEA AND CONTIGUOUS ZONE

Section 1. General Provisions

Article 2. Legal status of the territorial sea, of the air space over the territorial sea and of its bed and subsoil

1. The sovereignty of a coastal State extends, beyond its land territory and internal waters and, in the case of an archipelagic State, its archipelagic waters, to an adjacent belt of sea, described as the territorial sea.

2. This sovereignty extends to the airspace over the territorial sea as well as to its bed and subsoil.

3. The sovereignty over the territorial sea is exercised subject to this Convention and to other rules of international law.

Section 2. Limits of the Territorial Sea

Article 3. Breadth of the territorial sea

Every State has the right to establish the breadth of its territorial sea up to a limit not exceeding 12 nautical miles, measured from baselines determined in accordance with this Convention.

Article 4. Outer limit of the territorial sea

The outer limit of the territorial sea is the line every point of which is at a distance from the nearest point of the baseline equal to the breadth of the territorial sea.

Article 5. Normal baseline

Except where otherwise provided in this Convention, the normal baseline for measuring the breadth of the territorial sea is the low-water line along the coast as marked on large-scale charts officially recognized by the coastal State.

Article 6. Reefs

In the case of islands situated on atolls or of islands having fringing reefs, the baseline for measuring the breadth of the territorial sea is the seaward low-water line of the reef, as shown by the appropriate symbol on charts officially recognized by the coastal State.

Article 7. Straight baselines

1. In localities where the coastline is deeply indented and cut into, or if there is a fringe of islands along the coast in its immediate vicinity, the method of straight baselines joining appropriate points may be employed in drawing the baseline from which the breadth of the territorial sea is measured.

2. Where because of the presence of a delta and other natural conditions the coastline is highly unstable, the appropriate points may be selected along the furthest seaward extent of the low-water line and, notwithstanding subsequent regression of the low-water line, the straight baselines shall remain effective until changed by the coastal State in accordance with this Convention.

3. The drawing of straight baselines must not depart to any appreciable extent from the general direction of the coast, and the sea areas lying within the lines must be sufficiently closely linked to the land domain to be subject to the regime of internal waters.

4. Straight baselines shall not be drawn to and from low-tide elevations, unless lighthouses or similar installations which are permanently above sea level have been built on them or except in instances where the drawing of baselines to and from such elevations has received general international recognition.

5. Where the method of straight baselines is applicable under paragraph 1, account may be taken, in determining particular baselines, of economic interests peculiar to the region concerned, the reality and the importance of which are clearly evidenced by long usage.

6. The system of straight baselines may not be applied by a State in such a manner as to cut off the territorial sea of another State from the high seas or an exclusive economic zone.

Article 8. Internal waters

1. Except as provided in Part IV, waters on the landward side of the baseline of the territorial sea form part of the internal waters of the State.

2. Where the establishment of a straight baseline in accordance with the method set forth in article 7 has the effect of enclosing as internal water areas which had not previously been considered as such, a right of innocent passage as provided in this Convention shall exist in those waters.

Article 9. Mouths of rivers
If a river flows directly into the sea, the baseline shall be a straight line across the mouth of the river between points on the low-water line of its banks.

Article 10. Bays
1. This article relates only to bays the coasts of which belong to a single State.
2. For the purposes of this Convention, a bay is a well-marked indentation whose penetration is in such proportion to the width of its mouth as to contain land-locked waters and constitute more than a mere curvature of the coast. An indentation shall not, however, be regarded as a bay unless its area is as large as, or larger than, that of the semi-circle whose diameter is a line drawn across the mouth of that indentation.
3. For the purpose of measurement, the area of an indentation is that lying between the low-water mark around the shore of the indentation and a line joining the low-water mark of its natural entrance points. Where, because of the presence of islands, an indentation has more than one mouth, the semi-circle shall be drawn on a line as long as the sum total of the lengths of the lines across the different mouths. Islands within an indentation shall be included as if they were part of the water area of the indentation.
4. If the distance between the low-water marks of the natural entrance points of a bay does not exceed 24 nautical miles, a closing line may be drawn between these two low-water marks, and the waters enclosed thereby shall be considered as internal waters.
5. Where the distance between the low-water marks of the natural entrance points of a bay exceeds 24 nautical miles, a straight baseline of 24 nautical miles shall be drawn within the bay in such a manner as to enclose the maximum area of water that is possible with a line of that length.
6. The foregoing provisions do not apply to so-called "historic" bays, or in any case where the system of straight baselines provided for in article 7 is applied.

Article 11. Ports
For the purpose of delimiting the territorial sea, the outermost permanent harbor works which form an integral part of the harbor system are regarded as forming part of the coast. Off-shore installations and artificial islands shall not be considered as permanent harbor works.

Article 12. Roadsteads
Roadsteads which are normally used for the loading, unloading and anchoring of ships, and which would otherwise be situated wholly or partly outside the outer limit of the territorial sea, are included in the territorial sea.

Article 13. Low-tide elevations
1. A low-tide elevation is a naturally formed area of land which is surrounded by and above water at low tide but submerged at high tide. Where a low-tide elevation is situated wholly or partly at a distance not exceeding the breadth of the territorial sea from the mainland or an island, the low-water line on that elevation may be used as the baseline for measuring the breadth of the territorial sea.
2. Where a low-tide elevation is wholly situated at a distance exceeding the breadth of the territorial sea from the mainland or an island, it has no territorial sea of its own.

Article 14. Combination of methods for determining baselines
The coastal State may determine baselines in turn by any of the methods provided for in the foregoing articles to suit different conditions.

Article 15. Delimitation of the territorial sea between States with opposite or adjacent coasts
Where the coasts of two States are opposite or adjacent to each other, neither of the two States is entitled, failing agreement between them to the contrary, to extend its territorial sea beyond the

median line every point of which is equidistant from the nearest points on the baselines from which the breadth of the territorial seas of each of the two States is measured. The above provision does not apply, however, where it is necessary by reason of historic title or other special circumstances to delimit the territorial seas of the two States in a way which is at variance therewith.

Article 16. Charts and lists of geographical co-ordinates

1. The baselines for measuring the breadth of the territorial sea determined in accordance with articles 7, 9 and 10, or the limits derived therefrom, and the lines of delimitation drawn in accordance with articles 12 and 15 shall be shown on charts of a scale or scales adequate for ascertaining their position. Alternatively, a list of geographical co-ordinates of points, specifying the geodetic datum, may be substituted.
2. The coastal State shall give due publicity to such charts or lists of geographical co-ordinates and shall deposit a copy of each such chart or list with the Secretary-General of the United Nations.

Section 3. Innocent Passage in the Territorial Sea

Subsection A. Rules Applicable to All Ships

Article 17. Right of innocent passage

Subject to this Convention, ships of all States, whether coastal or land-locked, enjoy the right of innocent passage through the territorial sea.

Article 18. Meaning of passage

1. Passage means navigation through the territorial sea for the purpose of:
    (a) traversing that sea without entering internal waters or calling at a roadstead or port facility outside internal waters; or
    (b) proceeding to or from internal waters or a call at such roadstead or port facility.
2. Passage shall be continuous and expeditious. However, passage includes stopping and anchoring, but only in so far as the same are incidental to ordinary navigation or are rendered necessary by *force majeure* or distress or for the purpose of rendering assistance to persons, ships or aircraft in danger or distress.

Article 19. Meaning of innocent passage

1. Passage is innocent so long as it is not prejudicial to the peace, good order or security of the coastal State. Such passage shall take place in conformity with this Convention and with other rules of international law.
2. Passage of a foreign ship shall be considered to be prejudicial to the peace, good order or security of the coastal State if in the territorial sea it engages in any of the following activities:
    (a) any threat or use of force against the sovereignty, territorial integrity or political independence of the coastal State, or in any other manner in violation of the principles of international law embodied in the Charter of the United Nations;
    (b) any exercise or practice with weapons of any kind;
    (c) any act aimed at collecting information to the prejudice of the defense or security of the coastal State;
    (d) any act of propaganda aimed at affecting the defense or security of the coastal State;
    (e) the launching, landing or taking on board of any aircraft;
    (f) the launching, landing or taking on board of any military device;
    (g) the loading or unloading of any commodity, currency or person contrary to the customs, fiscal, immigration or sanitary laws and regulations of the coastal State;
    (h) any act of willful and serious pollution contrary to this Convention;
    (i) any fishing activities;
    (j) the carrying out of research or survey activities;

(k) any act aimed at interfering with any systems of communication or any other facilities or installations of the coastal State;

(l) any other activity not having a direct bearing on passage.

Article 20. Submarines and other underwater vehicles

In the territorial sea, submarines and other underwater vehicles are required to navigate on the surface and to show their flag.

Article 21. Laws and regulations of the coastal State relating to innocent passage

1. The coastal State may adopt laws and regulations, in conformity with the provisions of this Convention and other rules of international law, relating to innocent passage through the territorial sea, in respect of all or any of the following:

   (a) the safety of navigation and the regulation of maritime traffic;

   (b) the protection of navigational aids and facilities and other facilities or installations;

   (c) the protection of cables and pipelines;

   (d) the conservation of the living resources of the sea;

   (e) the prevention of infringement of the fisheries laws and regulations of the coastal State;

   (f) the preservation of the environment of the coastal State and the prevention, reduction and control of pollution thereof;

   (g) marine scientific research and hydrographic surveys;

   (h) the prevention of infringement of the customs, fiscal, immigration or sanitary laws and regulations of the coastal State.

2. Such laws and regulations shall not apply to the design, construction, manning or equipment of foreign ships unless they are giving effect to generally accepted international rules or standards.

3. The coastal State shall give due publicity to all such laws and regulations.

4. Foreign ships exercising the right of innocent passage through the territorial sea shall comply with all such laws and regulations and all generally accepted international regulations relating to the prevention of collisions at sea.

Article 22. Sea lanes and traffic separation schemes in the territorial sea

1. The coastal State may, where necessary having regard to the safety of navigation, require foreign ships exercising the right of innocent passage through its territorial sea to use such sea lanes and traffic separation schemes as it may designate or prescribe for the regulation of the passage of ships.

2. In particular, tankers, nuclear-powered ships and ships carrying nuclear or other inherently dangerous or noxious substances or materials may be required to confine their passage to such sea lanes.

3. In the designation of sea lanes and the prescription of traffic separation schemes under this article, the coastal State shall take into account:

   (a) the recommendations of the competent international organization;

   (b) any channels customarily used for international navigation;

   (c) the special characteristics of particular ships and channels; and

   (d) the density of traffic.

4. The coastal State shall clearly indicate such sea lanes and traffic separation schemes on charts to which due publicity shall be given.

Article 23. Foreign nuclear-powered ships and ships carrying nuclear or other inherently dangerous or noxious substances

Foreign nuclear-powered ships and ships carrying nuclear or other inherently dangerous or noxious substances shall, when exercising the right of innocent passage through the territorial sea, carry documents and observe special precautionary measures established for such ships by international agreements.

Article 24. Duties of the coastal State

1. The coastal State shall not hamper the innocent passage of foreign ships through the territorial sea except in accordance with this Convention. In particular, in the application of this Convention or of any laws or regulations adopted in conformity with this Convention, the coastal State shall not:
    (a) impose requirements on foreign ships which have the practical effect of denying or impairing the right of innocent passage; or
    (b) discriminate in form or in fact against the ships of any State or against ships carrying cargoes to, from or on behalf of any State.
2. The coastal State shall give appropriate publicity to any danger to navigation, of which it has knowledge, within its territorial sea.

Article 25. Rights of protection of the coastal State

1. The coastal State may take the necessary steps in its territorial sea to prevent passage which is not innocent.
2. In the case of ships proceeding to internal waters or a call at a port facility outside internal waters, the coastal State also has the right to take the necessary steps to prevent any breach of the conditions to which admission of those ships to internal waters or such a call is subject.
3. The coastal State may, without discrimination in form or in fact among foreign ships, suspend temporarily in specified areas of its territorial sea the innocent passage of foreign ships if such suspension is essential for the protection of its security, including weapons exercises. Such suspension shall take effect only after having been duly published.

Article 26. Charges which may be levied upon foreign ships

1. No charge may be levied upon foreign ships by reason only of their passage through the territorial sea.
2. Charges may be levied upon a foreign ship passing through the territorial sea as payment only for specific services rendered to the ship. These charges shall be levied without discrimination.

Subsection B. Rules Applicable to Merchant Ships and Government Ships Operated for Commercial Purposes

Article 27. Criminal jurisdiction on board a foreign ship

1. The criminal jurisdiction of the coastal State should not be exercised on board a foreign ship passing through the territorial sea to arrest any person or to conduct any investigation in connection with any crime committed on board the ship during its passage, save only in the following cases:
    (a) if the consequences of the crime extend to the coastal State;
    (b) if the crime is of a kind to disturb the peace of the country or the good order of the territorial sea;
    (c) if the assistance of the local authorities has been requested by the master of the ship or by a diplomatic agent or consular officer of the flag State; or
    (d) if such measures are necessary for the suppression of illicit traffic in narcotic drugs or psychotropic substances.
2. The above provisions do not affect the right of the coastal State to take any steps authorized by its laws for the purpose of an arrest or investigation on board a foreign ship passing through the territorial sea after leaving internal waters.
3. In the cases provided for in paragraphs 1 and 2, the coastal State shall, if the master so requests, notify a diplomatic agent or consular officer of the flag State before taking any steps, and shall facilitate contact between such agent or officer and the ship's crew. In cases of emergency this notification may be communicated while the measures are being taken.

4. In considering whether or in what manner an arrest should be made, the local authorities shall have due regard to the interests of navigation.
5. Except as provided in Part XII or with respect to violations of laws and regulations adopted in accordance with Part V, the coastal State may not take any steps on board a foreign ship passing through the territorial sea to arrest any person or to conduct any investigation in connection with any crime committed before the ship entered the territorial sea, if the ship, proceeding from a foreign port, is only passing through the territorial sea without entering internal waters.

Article 28. Civil jurisdiction in relation to foreign ships

1. The coastal State should not stop or divert a foreign ship passing through the territorial sea for the purpose of exercising civil jurisdiction in relation to a person on board the ship.
2. The coastal State may not levy execution against or arrest the ship for the purpose of any civil proceedings, save only in respect of obligations or liabilities assumed or incurred by the ship itself in the course or for the purpose of its voyage through the waters of the coastal State.
3. Paragraph 2 is without prejudice to the right of the coastal State, in accordance with its laws, to levy execution against or to arrest, for the purpose of any civil proceedings, a foreign ship lying in the territorial sea, or passing through the territorial sea after leaving internal waters.

Subsection C. Rules Applicable to Warships and Other Government Ships Operated for Non-commercial Purposes

Article 29. Definition of warships

For the purpose of this Convention, "warship" means a ship belonging to the armed forces of a State bearing the external marks distinguishing such ships of its nationality, under the command of an officer duly commissioned by the government of the State and whose name appears in the appropriate service list or its equivalent, and manned by a crew which is under regular armed forces discipline.

Article 30. Non-compliance by warships with the laws and regulations of the coastal State

If any warship does not comply with the laws and regulations of the coastal State concerning passage through the territorial sea and disregards any request for compliance therewith which is made to it, the coastal State may require it to leave the territorial sea immediately.

Article 31. Responsibility of the flag State for damage caused by a warship or other government ship operated for non-commercial purposes

The flag State shall bear international responsibility for any loss or damage to the coastal State resulting from the non-compliance by a warship or other government ship operated for non-commercial purposes with the laws and regulations of the coastal State concerning passage through the territorial sea or with the provisions of this Convention or other rules of international law.

Article 32. Immunities of warships and other government ships operated for non-commercial purposes

With such exceptions as are contained in subsection A and in articles 30 and 31, nothing in this Convention affects the immunities of warships and other government ships operated for non-commercial purposes.

Section 4. Contiguous Zone

Article 33. Contiguous zone

1. In a zone contiguous to its territorial sea, described as the contiguous zone, the coastal State may exercise the control necessary to:
    (a) prevent infringement of its customs, fiscal, immigration or sanitary laws and regulations within its territory or territorial sea;
    (b) punish infringement of the above laws and regulations committed within its territory or territorial sea.

2. The contiguous zone may not extend beyond 24 nautical miles from the baselines from which the breadth of the territorial sea is measured.

PART III. STRAITS USED FOR INTERNATIONAL NAVIGATION

Section 1. General Provisions

Article 34. Legal status of waters forming straits used for international navigation

1. The regime of passage through straits used for international navigation established in this Part shall not in other respects affect the legal status of the waters forming such straits or the exercise by the States bordering the straits of their sovereignty or jurisdiction over such waters and their air space, bed and subsoil.
2. The sovereignty or jurisdiction of the States bordering the straits is exercised subject to this Part and to other rules of international law.

Article 35. Scope of this Part

Nothing in this Part affects:

   (a) any areas of internal waters within a strait, except where the establishment of a straight baseline in accordance with the method set forth in article 7 has the effect of enclosing as internal waters areas which had not previously been considered as such;
   (b) the legal status of the waters beyond the territorial seas of States bordering straits as exclusive economic zones or high seas; or
   (c) the legal regime in straits in which passage is regulated in whole or in part by long-standing international conventions in force specifically relating to such straits.

Article 36. High seas routes or routes through exclusive economic zones through straits used for international navigation

This Part does not apply to a strait used for international navigation if there exists through the strait a route through the high seas or through an exclusive economic zone of similar convenience with respect to navigational and hydrographical characteristics; in such routes, the other relevant Parts of this Convention, including the provisions regarding the freedoms of navigation and overflight, apply.

Section 2. Transit Passage

Article 37. Scope of this section

This section applies to straits which are used for international navigation between one part of the high seas or an exclusive economic zone and another part of the high seas or an exclusive economic zone.

Article 38. Right of transit passage

1. In straits referred to in article 37, all ships and aircraft enjoy the right of transit passage, which shall not be impeded; except that, if the strait is formed by an island of a State bordering the strait and its mainland, transit passage shall not apply if there exists seawards of the island a route through the high seas or through an exclusive economic zone of similar convenience with respect to navigational and hydrographical characteristics.
2. Transit passage means the exercise in accordance with this Part of the freedom of navigation and overflight solely for the purpose of continuous and expeditious transit of the strait between one part of the high seas or an exclusive economic zone and another part of the high seas or an exclusive economic zone. However, the requirement of continuous and expeditious transit does not preclude passage through the strait for the purpose of entering, leaving or returning from a State bordering the strait, subject to the conditions of entry to that State.
3. Any activity which is not an exercise of the right of transit passage through a strait remains subject to the other applicable provisions of this Convention.

Article 39. Duties of ships and aircraft during transit passage

1. Ships and aircraft, while exercising the right of transit passage, shall:
   (a) proceed without delay through or over the strait;
   (b) refrain from any threat or use of force against the sovereignty, territorial integrity or political independence of States bordering the strait, or in any other manner in violation of the principles of international law embodied in the Charter of the United Nations;
   (c) refrain from any activities other than those incident to their normal modes of continuous and expeditious transit unless rendered necessary by *force majeure* or by distress;
   (d) comply with other relevant provisions of this Part.
2. Ships in transit passage shall:
   (a) comply with generally accepted international regulations, procedures and practices for safety at sea, including the International Regulations for Preventing Collisions at Sea;
   (b) comply with generally accepted international regulations, procedures and practices for the prevention, reduction and control of pollution from ships.
3. Aircraft in transit passage shall:
   (a) observe the Rules of the Air established by the International Civil Aviation Organization as they apply to civil aircraft; state aircraft will normally comply with such safety measures and will at all times operate with due regard for the safety of navigation;
   (b) at all times monitor the radio frequency assigned by the competent internationally designated air traffic control authority or the appropriate international distress radio frequency.

Article 40. Research and survey activities

During transit passage, foreign ships, including marine scientific research and hydrographic survey ships, may not carry out any research or survey activities without the prior authorization of the States bordering straits.

Article 41. Sea lanes and traffic separation schemes in straits used for international navigation

1. In conformity with this Part, States bordering straits may designate sea lanes and prescribe traffic separation schemes for navigation in straits where necessary to promote the safe passage of ships.
2. Such States may, when circumstances require, and after giving due publicity thereto, substitute other sea lanes or traffic separation schemes for any sea lanes or traffic separation schemes previously designated or prescribed by them.
3. Such sea lanes and traffic separation schemes shall conform to generally accepted international regulations.
4. Before designating or substituting sea lanes or prescribing or substituting traffic separation schemes, States bordering straits shall refer proposals to the competent international organization with a view to their adoption. The organization may adopt only such sea lanes and traffic separation schemes as may be agreed with the States bordering the straits, after which the States may designate, prescribe or substitute them.
5. In respect of a strait where sea lanes or traffic separation schemes through the waters of two or more States bordering the straits are being proposed, the States concerned shall co-operate in formulating proposals in consultation with the competent international organization.
6. States bordering straits shall clearly indicate all sea lanes and traffic separation schemes designated or prescribed by them on charts to which due publicity shall be given.
7. Ships in transit passage shall respect applicable sea lanes and traffic separation schemes established in accordance with this article.

Article 42. Laws and regulations of States bordering straits relating to transit passage

1. Subject to the provisions of this section, States bordering straits may adopt laws and regulations relating to transit passage through straits, in respect of all or any of the following:

(a) the safety of navigation and the regulation of maritime traffic, as provided in article 41;

(b) the prevention, reduction and control of pollution, by giving effect to applicable international regulations regarding the discharge of oil, oily wastes and other noxious substances in the strait;

(c) with respect to fishing vessels, the prevention of fishing, including the stowage of fishing gear;

(d) the loading or unloading of any commodity, currency or person in contravention of the customs, fiscal, immigration or sanitary laws and regulations of States bordering straits.

2. Such laws and regulations shall not discriminate in form or in fact among foreign ships or in their application have the practical effect of denying, hampering or impairing the right of transit passage as defined in this section.

3. States bordering straits shall give due publicity to all such laws and regulations.

4. Foreign ships exercising the right of transit passage shall comply with such laws and regulations.

5. The flag State of a ship or the State of registry of an aircraft entitled to sovereign immunity which acts in a manner contrary to such laws and regulations or other provisions of this Part shall bear international responsibility for any loss or damage which results to States bordering straits.

Article 43. Navigational and safety aids and other improvements and the prevention, reduction and control of pollution

User States and States bordering a strait should by agreement co-operate:

(a) in the establishment and maintenance in a strait of necessary navigational and safety aids or other improvements in aid of international navigation; and

(b) for the prevention, reduction and control of pollution from ships.

Article 44. Duties of States bordering straits

States bordering straits shall not hamper transit passage and shall give appropriate publicity to any danger to navigation or overflight within or over the strait of which they have knowledge. There shall be no suspension of transit passage.

Section 3. Innocent Passage

Article 45. Innocent passage

1. The regime of innocent passage, in accordance with Part II, section 3, shall apply in straits used for international navigation:

(a) excluded from the application of the regime of transit passage under article 38, paragraph 1; or

(b) between a part of the high seas or an exclusive economic zone and the territorial sea of a foreign State.

2. There shall be no suspension of innocent passage through such straits.

PART IV. ARCHIPELAGIC STATES

Article 46. Use of terms

For the purposes of this Convention:

(a) "archipelagic State" means a State constituted wholly by one or more archipelagos and may include other islands;

(b) "archipelago" means a group of islands, including parts of islands, interconnecting waters and other natural features which are so closely interrelated that such islands, waters and other natural features form an intrinsic geographical, economic and political entity, or which historically have been regarded as such.

Article 47. Archipelagic baselines

1. An archipelagic State may draw straight archipelagic baselines joining the outermost points of the outermost islands and drying reefs of the archipelago provided that within such baselines are included the main islands and an area in which the ratio of the area of the water to the area of the land, including atolls, is between 1 to 1 and 9 to 1.

2. The length of such baselines shall not exceed 100 nautical miles, except that up to 3 percent of the total number of baselines enclosing any archipelago may exceed that length, up to a maximum length of 125 nautical miles.

3. The drawing of such baselines shall not depart to any appreciable extent from the general configuration of the archipelago.

4. Such baselines shall not be drawn to and from low-tide elevations, unless lighthouses or similar installations which are permanently above sea level have been built on them or where a low-tide elevation is situated wholly or partly at a distance not exceeding the breadth of the territorial sea from the nearest island.

5. The system of such baselines shall not be applied by an archipelagic State in such a manner as to cut off from the high seas or the exclusive economic zone the territorial sea of another State.

6. If a part of the archipelagic waters of an archipelagic State lies between two parts of an immediately adjacent neighboring State, existing rights and all other legitimate interests which the latter State has traditionally exercised in such waters and all rights stipulated by agreement between those States shall continue and be respected.

7. For the purpose of computing the ratio of water to land under paragraph 1, land areas may include waters lying within the fringing reefs of islands and atolls, including that part of a steep-sided oceanic plateau which is enclosed or nearly enclosed by a chain of limestone islands and drying reefs lying on the perimeter of the plateau.

8. The baselines drawn in accordance with this article shall be shown on charts of a scale or scales adequate for ascertaining their position. Alternatively, lists of geographical co-ordinates of points, specifying the geodetic datum, may be substituted.

9. The archipelagic State shall give due publicity to such charts or lists of geographical co-ordinates and shall deposit a copy of each such chart or list with the Secretary-General of the United Nations.

Article 48. *Measurement of the breadth of the territorial sea, the contiguous zone, the exclusive economic zone and the continental shelf*

The breadth of the territorial sea, the contiguous zone, the exclusive economic zone and the continental shelf shall be measured from archipelagic baselines drawn in accordance with article 47.

Article 49. *Legal status of archipelagic waters, of the air space over archipelagic waters and of their bed and subsoil*

1. The sovereignty of an archipelagic State extends to the waters enclosed by the archipelagic baselines drawn in accordance with article 47, described as archipelagic waters, regardless of their depth or distance from the coast.

2. This sovereignty extends to the air space over the archipelagic waters, as well as to their bed and subsoil, and the resources contained therein.

3. This sovereignty is exercised subject to this Part.

4. The regime of archipelagic sea lanes passage established in this Part shall not in other respects affect the status of the archipelagic waters, including the sea lanes, or the exercise by the archipelagic State of its sovereignty over such waters and their air space, bed and subsoil, and the resources contained therein.

Article 50. *Delimitation of the internal waters*

Within its archipelagic waters, the archipelagic State may draw closing lines for the delimitation of internal waters, in accordance with articles 9, 10 and 11.

Article 51. *Existing agreements, traditional fishing rights and existing submarine cables*

1. Without prejudice to article 49, an archipelagic State shall respect existing agreements with other States and shall recognize traditional fishing rights and other legitimate activities of the imme-

diately adjacent neighboring States in certain areas falling within archipelagic waters. The terms and conditions for the exercise of such rights and activities, including the nature, the extent and the areas to which they apply, shall, at the request of any of the States concerned, be regulated by bilateral agreements between them. Such rights shall not be transferred to or shared with third States or their nationals.

2. An archipelagic State shall respect existing submarine cables laid by other States and passing through its waters without making a landfall. An archipelagic State shall permit the maintenance and replacement of such cables upon receiving due notice of their location and the intention to repair or replace them.

Article 52. Right of innocent passage

1. Subject to article 53 and without prejudice to article 50, ships of all States enjoy the right of innocent passage through archipelagic waters, in accordance with Part II, section 3.
2. The archipelagic State may, without discrimination in form or in fact among foreign ships, suspend temporarily in specified areas of its archipelagic waters the innocent passage of foreign ships if such suspension is essential for the protection of its security. Such suspension shall take effect only after having been duly published.

Article 53. Right of archipelagic sea lanes passage

1. An archipelagic State may designate sea lanes and air routes thereabove, suitable for the continuous and expeditious passage of foreign ships and aircraft through or over its archipelagic waters and the adjacent territorial sea.
2. All ships and aircraft enjoy the right of archipelagic sea lanes passage in such sea lanes and air routes.
3. Archipelagic sea lanes passage means the exercise in accordance with this Convention of the rights of navigation and overflight in the normal mode solely for the purpose of continuous, expeditious and unobstructed transit between one part of the high seas or an exclusive economic zone and another part of the high seas or an exclusive economic zone.
4. Such sea lanes and air routes shall traverse the archipelagic waters and the adjacent territorial sea and shall include all normal passage routes used as routes for international navigation or overflight through or over archipelagic waters and, within such routes, so far as ships are concerned, all normal navigational channels, provided that duplication of routes of similar convenience between the same entry and exit points shall not be necessary.
5. Such sea lanes and air routes shall be defined by a series of continuous axis lines from the entry points of passage routes to the exit points. Ships and aircraft in archipelagic sea lanes passage shall not deviate more than 25 nautical miles to either side of such axis lines during passage, provided that such ships and aircraft shall not navigate closer to the coasts than 10 percent of the distance between the nearest points on islands bordering the sea lane.
6. An archipelagic State which designates sea lanes under this article may also prescribe traffic separation schemes for the safe passage of ships through narrow channels in such sea lanes.
7. An archipelagic State may, when circumstances require, after giving due publicity thereto, substitute other sea lanes or traffic separation schemes for any sea lanes or traffic separation schemes previously designated or prescribed by it.
8. Such sea lanes and traffic separation schemes shall conform to generally accepted international regulations.
9. In designating or substituting sea lanes or prescribing or substituting traffic separation schemes, an archipelagic State shall refer proposals to the competent international organization with a view to their adoption. The organization may adopt only such sea lanes and traffic separation schemes as may be agreed with the archipelagic State, after which the archipelagic State may designate, prescribe or substitute them.

10. The archipelagic State shall clearly indicate the axis of the sea lanes and the traffic separation schemes designated or prescribed by it on charts to which due publicity shall be given.

11. Ships in archipelagic sea lanes passage shall respect applicable sea lanes and traffic separation schemes established in accordance with this article.

12. If an archipelagic State does not designate sea lanes or air routes, the right of archipelagic sea lanes passage may be exercised through the routes normally used for international navigation.

Article 54. Duties of ships and aircraft during their passage, research and survey activities, duties of the archipelagic State and laws and regulations of the archipelagic State relating to archipelagic sea lanes passage

Articles 39, 40, 42 and 44 apply mutatis mutandis to archipelagic sea lanes passage.

PART V. EXCLUSIVE ECONOMIC ZONE

Article 55. Specific legal regime of the exclusive economic zone

The exclusive economic zone is an area beyond and adjacent to the territorial sea, subject to the specific legal regime established in this Part, under which the rights and jurisdiction of the coastal State and the rights and freedoms of other States are governed by the relevant provisions of this Convention.

Article 56. Rights, jurisdiction and duties of the coastal State in the exclusive economic zone

1. In the exclusive economic zone, the coastal State has:
   (a) sovereign rights for the purpose of exploring and exploiting, conserving and managing the natural resources, whether living or non-living, of the waters superjacent to the sea-bed and of the sea-bed and its subsoil, and with regard to other activities for the economic exploitation and exploration of the zone, such as the production of energy from the water, currents and winds;
   (b) jurisdiction as provided for in the relevant provisions of this Convention with regard to:
      (i) the establishment and use of artificial islands, installations and structures;
      (ii) marine scientific research;
      (iii) the protection and preservation of the marine environment;
   (c) other rights and duties provided for in this Convention.

2. In exercising its rights and performing its duties under this Convention in the exclusive economic zone, the coastal State shall have due regard to the rights and duties of other States and shall act in a manner compatible with the provisions of this Convention.

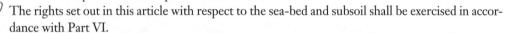3. The rights set out in this article with respect to the sea-bed and subsoil shall be exercised in accordance with Part VI.

Article 57. Breadth of the exclusive economic zone

The exclusive economic zone shall not extend beyond 200 nautical miles from the baselines from which the breadth of the territorial sea is measured.

Article 58. Rights and duties of other States in the exclusive economic zone

1. In the exclusive economic zone, all States, whether coastal or land-locked, enjoy, subject to the relevant provisions of this Convention, the freedoms referred to in article 87 of navigation and overflight and of the laying of submarine cables and pipelines, and other internationally lawful uses of the sea related to these freedoms, such as those associated with the operation of ships, aircraft and submarine cables and pipelines, and compatible with the other provisions of this Convention.

2. Articles 88 to 115 and other pertinent rules of international law apply to the exclusive economic zone in so far as they are not incompatible with this Part.

3. In exercising their rights and performing their duties under this Convention in the exclusive economic zone, States shall have due regard to the rights and duties of the coastal State and shall comply with the laws and regulations adopted by the coastal State in accordance with the provisions

of this Convention and other rules of international law in so far as they are not incompatible with this Part.

Article 59. Basis for the resolution of conflicts regarding the attribution of rights and jurisdiction in the exclusive economic zone

In cases where this Convention does not attribute rights or jurisdiction to the coastal State or to other States within the exclusive economic zone, and a conflict arises between the interests of the coastal State and any other State or States, the conflict should be resolved on the basis of equity and in the light of all the relevant circumstances, taking into account the respective importance of the interests involved to the parties as well as to the international community as a whole.

Article 60. Artificial islands, installations and structures in the exclusive economic zone

1. In the exclusive economic zone, the coastal State shall have the exclusive right to construct and to authorize and regulate the construction, operation and use of:
   (a) artificial islands;
   (b) installations and structures for the purposes provided for in article 56 and other economic purposes;
   (c) installations and structures which may interfere with the exercise of the rights of the coastal State in the zone.
2. The coastal State shall have exclusive jurisdiction over such artificial islands, installations and structures, including jurisdiction with regard to customs, fiscal, health, safety and immigration laws and regulations.
3. Due notice must be given of the construction of such artificial islands, installations or structures, and permanent means for giving warning of their presence must be maintained. Any installations or structures which are abandoned or disused shall be removed to ensure safety of navigation, taking into account any generally accepted international standards established in this regard by the competent international organization. Such removal shall also have due regard to fishing, the protection of the marine environment and the rights and duties of other States. Appropriate publicity shall be given to the depth, position and dimensions of any installations or structures not entirely removed.
4. The coastal State may, where necessary, establish reasonable safety zones around such artificial islands, installations and structures in which it may take appropriate measures to ensure the safety both of navigation and of the artificial islands, installations and structures.
5. The breadth of the safety zones shall be determined by the coastal State, taking into account applicable international standards. Such zones shall be designed to ensure that they are reasonably related to the nature and function of the artificial islands, installations or structures, and shall not exceed a distance of 500 meters around them, measured from each point of their outer edge, except as authorized by generally accepted international standards or as recommended by the competent international organization. Due notice shall be given of the extent of safety zones.
6. All ships must respect these safety zones and shall comply with generally accepted international standards regarding navigation in the vicinity of artificial islands, installations, structures and safety zones.
7. Artificial islands, installations and structures and the safety zones around them may not be established where interference may be caused to the use of recognized sea lanes essential to international navigation.
8. Artificial islands, installations and structures do not possess the status of islands. They have no territorial sea of their own, and their presence does not affect the delimitation of the territorial sea, the exclusive economic zone or the continental shelf.

Article 61. Conservation of the living resources

1. The coastal State shall determine the allowable catch of the living resources in its exclusive economic zone.

2. The coastal State, taking into account the best scientific evidence available to it, shall ensure through proper conservation and management measures that the maintenance of the living resources in the exclusive economic zone is not endangered by over-exploitation. As appropriate, the coastal State and competent international organizations, whether subregional, regional or global, shall co-operate to this end.

3. Such measures shall also be designed to maintain or restore populations of harvested species at levels which can produce the maximum sustainable yield, as qualified by relevant environmental and economic factors, including the economic needs of coastal fishing communities and the special requirements of developing States, and taking into account fishing patterns, the interdependence of stocks and any generally recommended international minimum standards, whether subregional, regional or global.

4. In taking such measures the coastal State shall take into consideration the effects on species associated with or dependent upon harvested species with a view to maintaining or restoring populations of such associated or dependent species above levels at which their reproduction may become seriously threatened.

5. Available scientific information, catch and fishing effort statistics, and other data relevant to the conservation of fish stocks shall be contributed and exchanged on a regular basis through competent international organizations, whether subregional, regional or global, where appropriate and with participation by all States concerned, including States whose nationals are allowed to fish in the exclusive economic zone.

Article 62. Utilization of the living resources

1. The coastal State shall promote the objective of optimum utilization of the living resources in the exclusive economic zone without prejudice to article 61.

2. The coastal State shall determine its capacity to harvest the living resources of the exclusive economic zone. Where the coastal State does not have the capacity to harvest the entire allowable catch, it shall, through agreements or other arrangements and pursuant to the terms, conditions, laws and regulations referred to in paragraph 4, give other States access to the surplus of the allowable catch, having particular regard to the provisions of articles 69 and 70, especially in relation to the developing States mentioned therein.

3. In giving access to other States to its exclusive economic zone under this article, the coastal State shall take into account all relevant factors, including, *inter alia*, the significance of the living resources of the area to the economy of the coastal State concerned and its other national interests, the provisions of articles 69 and 70, the requirements of developing States in the subregion or region in harvesting part of the surplus, and the need to minimize economic dislocation in States whose nationals have habitually fished in the zone or which have made substantial efforts in research and identification of stocks.

4. Nationals of other States fishing in the exclusive economic zone shall comply with the conservation measures and with the other terms and conditions established in the laws and regulations of the coastal State. These laws and regulations shall be consistent with this Convention and may relate, *inter alia*, to the following:

    (a) licensing of fishermen, fishing vessels and equipment, including payment of fees and other forms of remuneration, which, in the case of developing coastal States, may consist of adequate compensation in the field of financing, equipment and technology relating to the fishing industry;

(b) determining the species which may be caught, and fixing quotas of catch, whether in relation to particular stocks or groups of stocks or catch per vessel over a period of time or to the catch by nationals of any State during a specified period;

(c) regulating seasons and areas of fishing, the types, sizes and amount of gear, and the types, sizes and number of fishing vessels that may be used;

(d) fixing the age and size of fish and other species that may be caught;

(e) specifying information required of fishing vessels, including catch and effort statistics and vessel position reports;

(f) requiring, under the authorization and control of the coastal State, the conduct of specified fisheries research programs and regulating the conduct of such research, including the sampling of catches, disposition of samples and reporting of associated scientific data;

(g) the placing of observers or trainees on board such vessels by the coastal State;

(h) the landing of all or any part of the catch by such vessels in the ports of the coastal State;

(i) terms and conditions relating to joint ventures or other co-operative arrangements;

(j) requirements for the training of personnel and the transfer of fisheries technology, including enhancement of the coastal State's capability of undertaking fisheries research;

(k) enforcement procedures.

5. Coastal States shall give due notice of conservation and management laws and regulations.

Article 63. Stocks occurring within the exclusive economic zones of two or more coastal States or both within the exclusive economic zone and in an area beyond and adjacent to it

1. Where the same stock or stocks of associated species occur within the exclusive economic zones of two or more coastal States, these States shall seek, either directly or through appropriate subregional or regional organizations, to agree upon the measures necessary to co-ordinate and ensure the conservation and development of such stocks without prejudice to the other provisions of this Part.

2. Where the same stock or stocks of associated species occur both within the exclusive economic zone and in an area beyond and adjacent to the zone, the coastal State and the States fishing for such stocks in the adjacent area shall seek, either directly or through appropriate subregional or regional organizations, to agree upon the measures necessary for the conservation of these stocks in the adjacent area.

Article 64. Highly migratory species

1. The coastal State and other States whose nationals fish in the region for the highly migratory species listed in Annex I shall co-operate directly or through appropriate international organizations with a view to ensuring conservation and promoting the objective of optimum utilization of such species throughout the region, both within and beyond the exclusive economic zone. In regions for which no appropriate international organization exists, the coastal State and other States whose nationals harvest these species in the region shall co-operate to establish such an organization and participate in its work.

2. The provisions of paragraph 1 apply in addition to the other provisions of this Part.

Article 65. Marine mammals

Nothing in this Part restricts the right of a coastal State or the competence of an international organization, as appropriate, to prohibit, limit or regulate the exploitation of marine mammals more strictly than provided for in this Part. States shall co-operate with a view to the conservation of marine mammals and in the case of cetaceans shall in particular work through the appropriate international organizations for their conservation, management and study.

Article 66. Anadromous stocks

1. States in whose rivers anadromous stocks originate shall have the primary interest in and responsibility for such stocks.

2. The State of origin of anadromous stocks shall ensure their conservation by the establishment of appropriate regulatory measures for fishing in all waters landward of the outer limits of its exclusive economic zone and for fishing provided for in paragraph 3(b). The State of origin may, after consultations with the other States referred to in paragraphs 3 and 4 fishing these stocks, establish total allowable catches for stocks originating in its rivers.

3. (a) Fisheries for anadromous stocks shall be conducted only in waters landward of the outer limits of exclusive economic zones, except in cases where this provision would result in economic dislocation for a State other than the State of origin. With respect to such fishing beyond the outer limits of the exclusive economic zone, States concerned shall maintain consultations with a view to achieving agreement on terms and conditions of such fishing giving due regard to the conservation requirements and the needs of the State of origin in respect of these stocks.

   (b) The State of origin shall co-operate in minimizing economic dislocation in such other States fishing these stocks, taking into account the normal catch and the mode of operations of such States, and all the areas in which such fishing has occurred.

   (c) States referred to in subparagraph (b), participating by agreement with the State of origin in measures to renew anadromous stocks, particularly by expenditures for that purpose, shall be given special consideration by the State of origin in the harvesting of stocks originating in its rivers.

   (d) Enforcement of regulations regarding anadromous stocks beyond the exclusive economic zone shall be by agreement between the State of origin and the other States concerned.

4. In cases where anadromous stocks migrate into or through the waters landward of the outer limits of the exclusive economic zone of a State other than the State of origin, such State shall co-operate with the State of origin with regard to the conservation and management of such stocks.

5. The State of origin of anadromous stocks and other States fishing these stocks shall make arrangements for the implementation of the provisions of this article, where appropriate, through regional organizations.

Article 67. Catadromous species

1. A coastal State in whose waters catadromous species spend the greater part of their life cycle shall have responsibility for the management of these species and shall ensure the ingress and egress of migrating fish.

2. Harvesting of catadromous species shall be conducted only in waters landward of the outer limits of exclusive economic zones. When conducted in exclusive economic zones, harvesting shall be subject to this article and the other provisions of this Convention concerning fishing in these zones.

3. In cases where catadromous fish migrate through the exclusive economic zone of another State, whether as juvenile or maturing fish, the management, including harvesting, of such fish shall be regulated by agreement between the State mentioned in paragraph 1 and the other State concerned. Such agreement shall ensure the rational management of the species and take into account the responsibilities of the State mentioned in paragraph 1 for the maintenance of these species.

Article 68. Sedentary species

This Part does not apply to sedentary species as defined in article 77, paragraph 4.

Article 69. Right of land-locked States

1. Land-locked States shall have the right to participate, on an equitable basis, in the exploitation of an appropriate part of the surplus of the living resources of the exclusive economic zones of coastal

States of the same subregion or region, taking into account the relevant economic and geographical circumstances of all the States concerned and in conformity with the provisions of this article and of articles 61 and 62.

2. The terms and modalities of such participation shall be established by the States concerned through bilateral, subregional or regional agreements taking into account, *inter alia*:
   (a) the need to avoid effects detrimental to fishing communities or fishing industries of the coastal State;
   (b) the extent to which the land-locked State, in accordance with the provisions of this article, is participating or is entitled to participate under existing bilateral, subregional or regional agreements in the exploitation of living resources of the exclusive economic zones of other coastal States;
   (c) the extent to which other land-locked States and geographically disadvantaged States are participating in the exploitation of the living resources of the exclusive economic zone of the coastal State and the consequent need to avoid a particular burden for any single coastal State or a part of it;
   (d) the nutritional needs of the populations of the respective States.

3. When the harvesting capacity of a coastal State approaches a point which would enable it to harvest the entire allowable catch of the living resources in its exclusive economic zone, the coastal State and other States concerned shall co-operate in the establishment of equitable arrangements on a bilateral, subregional or regional basis to allow for participation of developing land-locked States of the same subregion or region in the exploitation of the living resources of the exclusive economic zones of coastal States of the subregion or region, as may be appropriate in the circumstances and on terms satisfactory to all parties. In the implementation of this provision the factors mentioned in paragraph 2 shall also be taken into account.

4. Developed land-locked States shall, under the provisions of this article, be entitled to participate in the exploitation of living resources only in the exclusive economic zones of developed coastal States of the same subregion or region having regard to the extent to which the coastal State, in giving access to other States to the living resources of its exclusive economic zone, has taken into account the need to minimize detrimental effects on fishing communities and economic dislocation in States whose nationals have habitually fished in the zone.

5. The above provisions are without prejudice to arrangements agreed upon in subregions or regions where the coastal States may grant to land-locked States of the same subregion or region equal or preferential rights for the exploitation of the living resources in the exclusive economic zones.

Article 70. Right of geographically disadvantaged States

1. Geographically disadvantaged States shall have the right to participate, on an equitable basis, in the exploitation of an appropriate part of the surplus of the living resources of the exclusive economic zones of coastal States of the same subregion or region, taking into account the relevant economic and geographical circumstances of all the States concerned and in conformity with the provisions of this article and of articles 61 and 62.

2. For the purposes of this Part, "geographically disadvantaged States" means coastal States, including States bordering enclosed or semi-enclosed seas, whose geographical situation makes them dependent upon the exploitation of the living resources of the exclusive economic zones of other States in the subregion or region for adequate supplies of fish for the nutritional purposes of their populations or parts thereof, and coastal States which can claim no exclusive economic zones of their own.

3. The terms and modalities of such participation shall be established by the States concerned through bilateral, subregional or regional agreements taking into account, *inter alia*:

(a) the need to avoid effects detrimental to fishing communities or fishing industries of the coastal State;

(b) the extent to which the geographically disadvantaged State, in accordance with the provisions of this article, is participating or is entitled to participate under existing bilateral, subregional or regional agreements in the exploitation of living resources of the exclusive economic zones of other coastal States;

(c) the extent to which other geographically disadvantaged States and land-locked States are participating in the exploitation of the living resources of the exclusive economic zone of the coastal State and the consequent need to avoid a particular burden for any single coastal State or a part of it;

(d) the nutritional needs of the populations of the respective States.

4. When the harvesting capacity of a coastal State approaches a point which would enable it to harvest the entire allowable catch of the living resources in its exclusive economic zone, the coastal State and other States concerned shall co-operate in the establishment of equitable arrangements on a bilateral, subregional or regional basis to allow for participation of developing geographically disadvantaged States of the same subregion or region in the exploitation of the living resources of the exclusive economic zones of coastal States of the subregion or region, as may be appropriate in the circumstances and on terms satisfactory to all parties. In the implementation of this provision the factors mentioned in paragraph 3 shall also be taken into account.

5. Developed geographically disadvantaged States shall, under the provisions of this article, be entitled to participate in the exploitation of living resources only in the exclusive economic zones of developed coastal States of the same subregion or region having regard to the extent to which the coastal State, in giving access to other States to the living resources of its exclusive economic zone, has taken into account the need to minimize detrimental effects on fishing communities and economic dislocation in States whose nationals have habitually fished in the zone.

6. The above provisions are without prejudice to arrangements agreed upon in subregions or regions where the coastal States may grant to geographically disadvantaged States of the same subregion or region equal or preferential rights for the exploitation of the living resources in the exclusive economic zones.

Article 71. Non-applicability of articles 69 and 70

The provisions of articles 69 and 70 do not apply in the case of a coastal State whose economy is overwhelmingly dependent on the exploitation of the living resources of its exclusive economic zone.

Article 72. Restrictions on transfer of rights

1. Rights provided under articles 69 and 70 to exploit living resources shall not be directly or indirectly transferred to third States or their nationals by lease or license, by establishing joint ventures, or in any other manner which has the effect of such transfer unless otherwise agreed by the States concerned.

2. The foregoing provision does not preclude the States concerned from obtaining technical or financial assistance from third States or international organizations in order to facilitate the exercise of the rights pursuant to articles 69 and 70, provided that it does not have the effect referred to in paragraph 1.

Article 73. Enforcement of laws and regulations of the coastal State

1. The coastal State may, in the exercise of its sovereign rights to explore, exploit, conserve and manage the living resources in the exclusive economic zone, take such measures, including boarding, inspection, arrest and judicial proceedings, as may be necessary to ensure compliance with the laws and regulations adopted by it in conformity with this Convention.

2. Arrested vessels and their crews shall be promptly released upon the posting of reasonable bond or other security.

3. Coastal State penalties for violations of fisheries laws and regulations in the exclusive economic zone may not include imprisonment, in the absence of agreements to the contrary by the States concerned, or any other form of corporal punishment.

4. In cases of arrest or detention of foreign vessels the coastal State shall promptly notify the flag State, through appropriate channels, of the action taken and of any penalties subsequently imposed.

Article 74. Delimitation of the exclusive economic zone between States with opposite or adjacent coasts

1. The delimitation of the exclusive economic zone between States with opposite or adjacent coasts shall be effected by agreement on the basis of international law, as referred to in Article 38 of the Statute of the International Court of Justice, in order to achieve an equitable solution.

2. If no agreement can be reached within a reasonable period of time, the States concerned shall resort to the procedures provided for in Part XV.

3. Pending agreement as provided for in paragraph 1, the States concerned, in a spirit of understanding and co-operation, shall make every effort to enter into provisional arrangements of a practical nature and, during this transitional period, not to jeopardize or hamper the reaching of the final agreement. Such arrangements shall be without prejudice to the final delimitation.

4. Where there is an agreement in force between the States concerned, questions relating to the delimitation of the exclusive economic zone shall be determined in accordance with the provisions of that agreement.

Article 75. Charts and lists of geographical co-ordinates

1. Subject to this Part, the outer limit lines of the exclusive economic zone and the lines of delimitation drawn in accordance with article 74 shall be shown on charts of a scale or scales adequate for ascertaining their position. Where appropriate, lists of geographical co-ordinates of points, specifying the geodetic datum, may be substituted for such outer limit lines or lines of delimitation.

2. The coastal State shall give due publicity to such charts or lists of geographical co-ordinates and shall deposit a copy of each such chart or list with the Secretary-General of the United Nations.

PART VI. CONTINENTAL SHELF

Article 76. Definition of the continental shelf

1. The continental shelf of a coastal State comprises the sea-bed and subsoil of the submarine areas that extend beyond its territorial sea throughout the natural prolongation of its land territory to the outer edge of the continental margin, or to a distance of 200 nautical miles from the baselines from which the breadth of the territorial sea is measured where the outer edge of the continental margin does not extend up to that distance.

2. The continental shelf of a coastal State shall not extend beyond the limits provided for in paragraphs 4 to 6.

3. The continental margin comprises the submerged prolongation of the land mass of the coastal State, and consists of the sea-bed and subsoil of the shelf, the slope and the rise. It does not include the deep ocean floor with its oceanic ridges or the subsoil thereof.

4. (a) For the purposes of this Convention, the coastal State shall establish the outer edge of the continental margin wherever the margin extends beyond 200 nautical miles from the baselines from which the breadth of the territorial sea is measured, by either:

    (i) a line delineated in accordance with paragraph 7 by reference to the outermost fixed points at each of which the thickness of sedimentary rocks is at least 1 percent of the shortest distance from such point to the foot of the continental slope; or

(ii) a line delineated in accordance with paragraph 7 by reference to fixed points not more than 60 nautical miles from the foot of the continental slope.

(b) In the absence of evidence to the contrary, the foot of the continental slope shall be determined as the point of maximum change in the gradient at its base.

5. The fixed points comprising the line of the outer limits of the continental shelf on the sea-bed, drawn in accordance with paragraph 4 (a)(i) and (ii), either shall not exceed 350 nautical miles from the baselines from which the breadth of the territorial sea is measured or shall not exceed 100 nautical miles from the 2,500 meter isobath, which is a line connecting the depth of 2,500 meters.

6. Notwithstanding the provisions of paragraph 5, on submarine ridges, the outer limit of the continental shelf shall not exceed 350 nautical miles from the baselines from which the breadth of the territorial sea is measured. This paragraph does not apply to submarine elevations that are natural components of the continental margin, such as its plateau, rises, caps, banks and spurs.

7. The coastal State shall delineate the outer limits of its continental shelf, where that shelf extends beyond 200 nautical miles from the baselines from which the breadth of the territorial sea is measured, by straight lines not exceeding 60 nautical miles in length, connecting fixed points, defined by co-ordinates of latitude and longitude.

8. Information on the limits of the continental shelf beyond 200 nautical miles from the baselines from which the breadth of the territorial sea is measured shall be submitted by the coastal State to the Commission on the Limits of the Continental Shelf set up under Annex II on the basis of equitable geographical representation. The Commission shall make recommendations to coastal States on matters related to the establishment of the outer limits of their continental shelf. The limits of the shelf established by a coastal State on the basis of these recommendations shall be final and binding.

9. The coastal State shall deposit with the Secretary-General of the United Nations charts and relevant information, including geodetic data, permanently describing the outer limits of its continental shelf. The Secretary-General shall give due publicity thereto.

10. The provisions of this article are without prejudice to the question of delimitation of the continental shelf between States with opposite or adjacent coasts.

Article 77. Rights of the coastal State over the continental shelf

1. The coastal State exercises over the continental shelf sovereign rights for the purpose of exploring it and exploiting its natural resources.

2. The rights referred to in paragraph 1 are exclusive in the sense that if the coastal State does not explore the continental shelf or exploit its natural resources, no one may undertake these activities without the express consent of the coastal State.

3. The rights of the coastal State over the continental shelf do not depend on occupation, effective or notional, or on any express proclamation.

4. The natural resources referred to in this Part consist of the mineral and other non-living resources of the sea-bed and subsoil together with living organisms belonging to sedentary species, that is to say, organisms which, at the harvestable stage, either are immobile on or under the sea-bed or are unable to move except in constant physical contact with the sea-bed or the subsoil.

Article 78. Legal status of the superjacent waters and air space and the rights and freedoms of other States

1. The rights of the coastal State over the continental shelf do not affect the legal status of the superjacent waters or of the air space above those waters.

2. The exercise of the rights of the coastal State over the continental shelf must not infringe or result in any unjustifiable interference with navigation and other rights and freedoms of other States as provided for in this Convention.

Article 79. Submarine cables and pipelines on the continental shelf

1. All States are entitled to lay submarine cables and pipelines on the continental shelf, in accordance with the provisions of this article.
2. Subject to its right to take reasonable measures for the exploration of the continental shelf, the exploitation of its natural resources, and the prevention, reduction and control of pollution from pipelines, the coastal State may not impede the laying or maintenance of such cables or pipelines.
3. The delineation of the course for the laying of such pipelines on the continental shelf is subject to the consent of the coastal State.
4. Nothing in this Part affects the right of the coastal State to establish conditions for cables or pipelines entering its territory or territorial sea, or its jurisdiction over cables and pipelines constructed or used in connection with the exploration of its continental shelf or exploitation of its resources or the operations of artificial islands, installations and structures under its jurisdiction.
5. When laying submarine cables or pipelines, States shall have due regard to cables or pipelines already in position. In particular, possibilities of repairing existing cables or pipelines shall not be prejudiced.

Article 80. Artificial islands, installations and structures on the continental shelf

Article 60 applies *mutatis mutandis* to artificial islands, installations and structures on the continental shelf.

Article 81. Drilling on the continental shelf

The coastal State shall have the exclusive right to authorize and regulate drilling on the continental shelf for all purposes.

Article 82. Payments and contributions with respect to the exploitation of the continental shelf beyond 200 nautical miles

1. The coastal State shall make payments or contributions in kind in respect of the exploitation of the non-living resources of the continental shelf beyond 200 nautical miles from the baselines from which the breadth of the territorial sea is measured.
2. The payments and contributions shall be made annually with respect to all production at a site after the first five years of production at that site. For the sixth year, the rate of payment or contribution shall be 1 percent of the value or volume of production at the site. The rate shall increase by 1 percent for each subsequent year until the twelfth year and shall remain at 7 percent thereafter. Production does not include resources used in connection with exploitation.
3. A developing State which is a net importer of a mineral resource produced from its continental shelf is exempt from making such payments or contributions in respect of that mineral resource.
4. The payments or contributions shall be made through the Authority, which shall distribute them to States Parties to this Convention, on the basis of equitable sharing criteria, taking into account the interests and needs of developing States, particularly the least developed and the land-locked among them.

Article 83. Delimitation of the continental shelf between States with opposite or adjacent coasts

1. The delimitation of the continental shelf between States with opposite or adjacent coasts shall be effected by agreement on the basis of international law, as referred to in Article 38 of the Statute of the International Court of Justice, in order to achieve an equitable solution.
2. If no agreement can be reached within a reasonable period of time, the States concerned shall resort to the procedures provided for in Part XV.
3. Pending agreement as provided for in paragraph 1, the States concerned, in a spirit of understanding and co-operation, shall make every effort to enter into provisional arrangements of a practical nature and, during this transitional period, not to jeopardize or hamper the reaching of the final agreement. Such arrangements shall be without prejudice to the final delimitation.

4. Where there is an agreement in force between the States concerned, questions relating to the delimitation of the continental shelf shall be determined in accordance with the provisions of that agreement.

Article 84. Charts and lists of geographical co-ordinates

1. Subject to this Part, the outer limit lines of the continental shelf and the lines of delimitation drawn in accordance with article 83 shall be shown on charts of a scale or scales adequate for ascertaining their position. Where appropriate, lists of geographical co-ordinates of points, specifying the geodetic datum, may be substituted for such outer limit lines or lines of delimitation.
2. The coastal State shall give due publicity to such charts or lists of geographical co-ordinates and shall deposit a copy of each such chart or list with the Secretary-General of the United Nations and, in the case of those showing the outer limit lines of the continental shelf, with the Secretary-General of the Authority.

Article 85. Tunneling

This Part does not prejudice the right of the coastal State to exploit the subsoil by means of tunneling, irrespective of the depth of water above the subsoil.

PART VII. HIGH SEAS

Section 1. General Provisions

Article 86. Application of the provisions of this Part

The provisions of this Part apply to all parts of the sea that are not included in the exclusive economic zone, in the territorial sea or in the internal waters of a State, or in the archipelagic waters of an archipelagic State. This article does not entail any abridgement of the freedoms enjoyed by all States in the exclusive economic zone in accordance with article 58.

Article 87. Freedom of the high seas

1. The high seas are open to all States, whether coastal or land-locked. Freedom of the high seas is exercised under the conditions laid down by this Convention and by other rules of international law. It comprises, *inter alia*, both for coastal and land-locked States:
   (a) freedom of navigation;
   (b) freedom of overflight;
   (c) freedom to lay submarine cables and pipelines, subject to Part VI;
   (d) freedom to construct artificial islands and other installations permitted under international law, subject to Part VI;
   (e) freedom of fishing, subject to the conditions laid down in section 2;
   (f) freedom of scientific research, subject to Parts VI and XIII.
2. These freedoms shall be exercised by all States with due regard for the interests of other States in their exercise of the freedom of the high seas, and also with due regard for the rights under this Convention with respect to activities in the Area.

Article 88. Reservation of the high seas for peaceful purposes

The high seas shall be reserved for peaceful purposes.

Article 89. Invalidity of claims of sovereignty over the high seas

No State may validly purport to subject any part of the high seas to its sovereignty.

Article 90. Right of navigation

Every State, whether coastal or land-locked, has the right to sail ships flying its flag on the high seas.

Article 91. Nationality of ships

1. Every State shall fix the conditions for the grant of its nationality to ships, for the registration of ships in its territory, and for the right to fly its flag. Ships have the nationality of the State whose flag they are entitled to fly. There must exist a genuine link between the State and the ship.

2. Every State shall issue to ships to which it has granted the right to fly its flag documents to that effect.

Article 92. Status of ships

1. Ships shall sail under the flag of one State only and, save in exceptional cases expressly provided for in international treaties or in this Convention, shall be subject to its exclusive jurisdiction on the high seas. A ship may not change its flag during a voyage or while in a port of call, save in the case of a real transfer of ownership or change of registry.

2. A ship which sails under the flags of two or more States, using them according to convenience, may not claim any of the nationalities in question with respect to any other State, and may be assimilated to a ship without nationality.

Article 93. Ships flying the flag of the United Nations, its specialized agencies and the International Atomic Energy Agency

The preceding articles do not prejudice the question of ships employed on the official service of the United Nations, its specialized agencies or the International Atomic Energy Agency, flying the flag of the organization.

Article 94. Duties of the flag State

1. Every State shall effectively exercise its jurisdiction and control in administrative, technical and social matters over ships flying its flag.

2. In particular every State shall:

    (a) maintain a register of ships containing the names and particulars of ships flying its flag, except those which are excluded from generally accepted international regulations on account of their small size; and

    (b) assume jurisdiction under its internal law over each ship flying its flag and its master, officers and crew in respect of administrative, technical and social matters concerning the ship.

3. Every State shall take such measures for ships flying its flag as are necessary to ensure safety at sea with regard, *inter alia*, to:

    (a) the construction, equipment and seaworthiness of ships;

    (b) the manning of ships, labor conditions and the training of crews, taking into account the applicable international instruments;

    (c) the use of signals, the maintenance of communications and the prevention of collisions.

4. Such measures shall include those necessary to ensure:

    (a) that each ship, before registration and thereafter at appropriate intervals, is surveyed by a qualified surveyor of ships, and has on board such charts, nautical publications and navigational equipment and instruments as are appropriate for the safe navigation of the ship;

    (b) that each ship is in the charge of a master and officers who possess appropriate qualifications, in particular in seamanship, navigation, communications and marine engineering, and that the crew is appropriate in qualification and numbers for the type, size, machinery and equipment of the ship;

    (c) that the master, officers and, to the extent appropriate, the crew are fully conversant with and required to observe the applicable international regulations concerning the safety of life at sea, the prevention of collisions, the prevention, reduction and control of marine pollution, and the maintenance of communications by radio.

5. In taking the measures called for in paragraphs 3 and 4 each State is required to conform to generally accepted international regulations, procedures and practices and to take any steps which may be necessary to secure their observance.
6. A State which has clear grounds to believe that proper jurisdiction and control with respect to a ship have not been exercised may report the facts to the flag State. Upon receiving such a report, the flag State shall investigate the matter and, if appropriate, take any action necessary to remedy the situation.
7. Each State shall cause an inquiry to be held by or before a suitably qualified person or persons into every marine casualty or incident of navigation on the high seas involving a ship flying its flag and causing loss of life or serious injury to nationals of another State or serious damage to ships or installations of another State or to the marine environment. The flag State and the other State shall co-operate in the conduct of any inquiry held by that other State into any such marine casualty or incident of navigation.

Article 95. Immunity of warships on the high seas
Warships on the high seas have complete immunity from the jurisdiction of any State other than the flag State.

Article 96. Immunity of ships used only on government non-commercial service
Ships owned or operated by a State and used only on government non-commercial service shall, on the high seas, have complete immunity from the jurisdiction of any State other than the flag State.

Article 97. Penal jurisdiction in matters of collision or any other incident of navigation
1. In the event of a collision or any other incident of navigation concerning a ship on the high seas, involving the penal or disciplinary responsibility of the master or of any other person in the service of the ship, no penal or disciplinary proceedings may be instituted against such person except before the judicial or administrative authorities either of the flag State or of the State of which such person is a national.
2. In disciplinary matters, the State which has issued a master's certificate or a certificate of competence or license shall alone be competent, after due legal process, to pronounce the withdrawal of such certificates, even if the holder is not a national of the State which issued them.
3. No arrest or detention of the ship, even as a measure of investigation, shall be ordered by any authorities other than those of the flag State.

Article 98. Duty to render assistance
1. Every State shall require the master of a ship flying its flag, in so far as he can do so without serious danger to the ship, the crew or the passengers:
   (a) to render assistance to any person found at sea in danger of being lost;
   (b) to proceed with all possible speed to the rescue of persons in distress, if informed of their need of assistance, in so far as such action may reasonably be expected of him;
   (c) after a collision, to render assistance to the other ship, its crew and its passengers and, where possible, to inform the other ship of the name of his own ship, its port of registry and the nearest port at which it will call.
2. Every coastal State shall promote the establishment, operation and maintenance of an adequate and effective search and rescue service regarding safety on and over the sea and, where circumstances so require, by way of mutual regional arrangements co-operate with neighboring States for this purpose.

Article 99. Prohibition of the transport of slaves
Every State shall take effective measures to prevent and punish the transport of slaves in ships authorized to fly its flag and to prevent the unlawful use of its flag for that purpose. Any slave taking refuge on board any ship, whatever its flag, shall *ipso facto* be free.

Article 100. Duty to co-operate in the repression of piracy

All States shall co-operate to the fullest possible extent in the repression of piracy on the high seas or in any other place outside the jurisdiction of any State.

Article 101. Definition of piracy

Piracy consists of any of the following acts:

    (a) any illegal acts of violence or detention, or any act of depredation, committed for private ends by the crew or the passengers of a private ship or a private aircraft, and directed:

        (i) on the high seas, against another ship or aircraft, or against persons or property on board such ship or aircraft;

        (ii) against a ship, aircraft, persons or property in a place outside the jurisdiction of any State;

    (b) any act of voluntary participation in the operation of a ship or of an aircraft with knowledge of facts making it a pirate ship or aircraft;

    (c) any act of inciting or of intentionally facilitating an act described in subparagraph (a) or (b).

Article 102. Piracy by a warship, government ship or government aircraft whose crew has mutinied

The acts of piracy, as defined in article 101, committed by a warship, government ship or government aircraft whose crew has mutinied and taken control of the ship or aircraft are assimilated to acts committed by a private ship or aircraft.

Article 103. Definition of a pirate ship or aircraft

A ship or aircraft is considered a pirate ship or aircraft if it is intended by the persons in dominant control to be used for the purpose of committing one of the acts referred to in article 101. The same applies if the ship or aircraft has been used to commit any such act, so long as it remains under the control of the persons guilty of that act.

Article 104. Retention or loss of the nationality of a pirate ship or aircraft

A ship or aircraft may retain its nationality although it has become a pirate ship or aircraft. The retention or loss of nationality is determined by the law of the State from which such nationality was derived.

Article 105. Seizure of a pirate ship or aircraft

On the high seas, or in any other place outside the jurisdiction of any State, every State may seize a pirate ship or aircraft, or a ship or aircraft taken by piracy and under the control of pirates, and arrest the persons and seize the property on board. The courts of the State which carried out the seizure may decide upon the penalties to be imposed, and may also determine the action to be taken with regard to the ships, aircraft or property, subject to the rights of third parties acting in good faith.

Article 106. Liability for seizure without adequate grounds

Where the seizure of a ship or aircraft on suspicion of piracy has been effected without adequate grounds, the State making the seizure shall be liable to the State the nationality of which is possessed by the ship or aircraft for any loss or damage caused by the seizure.

Article 107. Ships and aircraft which are entitled to seize on account of piracy

A seizure on account of piracy may be carried out only by warships or military aircraft, or other ships or aircraft clearly marked and identifiable as being on government service and authorized to that effect.

Article 108. Illicit traffic in narcotic drugs or psychotropic substances

1. All States shall co-operate in the suppression of illicit traffic in narcotic drugs and psychotropic substances engaged in by ships on the high seas contrary to international conventions.

2. Any State which has reasonable grounds for believing that a ship flying its flag is engaged in illicit traffic in narcotic drugs or psychotropic substances may request the co-operation of other States to suppress such traffic.

Article 109. *Unauthorized broadcasting from the high seas*

1. All States shall co-operate in the suppression of unauthorized broadcasting from the high seas.
2. For the purposes of this Convention, "unauthorized broadcasting" means the transmission of sound radio or television broadcasts from a ship or installation on the high seas intended for reception by the general public contrary to international regulations, but excluding the transmission of distress calls.
3. Any person engaged in unauthorized broadcasting may be prosecuted before the court of:
   (a) the flag State of the ship;
   (b) the State of registry of the installation;
   (c) the State of which the person is a national;
   (d) any State where the transmissions can be received; or
   (e) any State where authorized radio communication is suffering interference.
4. On the high seas, a State having jurisdiction in accordance with paragraph 3 may, in conformity with article 110, arrest any person or ship engaged in unauthorized broadcasting and seize the broadcasting apparatus.

Article 110. *Right of visit*

1. Except where acts of interference derive from powers conferred by treaty, a warship which encounters on the high seas a foreign ship, other than a ship entitled to complete immunity in accordance with articles 95 and 96, is not justified in boarding it unless there is reasonable ground for suspecting that:
   (a) the ship is engaged in piracy;
   (b) the ship is engaged in the slave trade;
   (c) the ship is engaged in unauthorized broadcasting and the flag State of the warship has jurisdiction under article 109;
   (d) the ship is without nationality; or
   (e) though flying a foreign flag or refusing to show its flag, the ship is, in reality, of the same nationality as the warship.
2. In the cases provided for in paragraph 1, the warship may proceed to verify the ship's right to fly its flag. To this end, it may send a boat under the command of an officer to the suspected ship. If suspicion remains after the documents have been checked, it may proceed to a further examination on board the ship, which must be carried out with all possible consideration.
3. If the suspicions prove to be unfounded, and provided that the ship boarded has not committed any act justifying them, it shall be compensated for any loss or damage that may have been sustained.
4. These provisions apply *mutatis mutandis* to military aircraft.
5. These provisions also apply to any other duly authorized ships or aircraft clearly marked and identifiable as being on government service.

Article 111. *Right of hot pursuit*

1. The hot pursuit of a foreign ship may be undertaken when the competent authorities of the coastal State have good reason to believe that the ship has violated the laws and regulations of that State. Such pursuit must be commenced when the foreign ship or one of its boats is within the internal waters, the archipelagic waters, the territorial sea or the contiguous zone of the pursuing State, and may only be continued outside the territorial sea or the contiguous zone if the pursuit has not been interrupted. It is not necessary that, at the time when the foreign ship within the territorial

sea or the contiguous zone receives the order to stop, the ship giving the order should likewise be within the territorial sea or the contiguous zone. If the foreign ship is within a contiguous zone, as defined in article 33, the pursuit may only be undertaken if there has been a violation of the rights for the protection of which the zone was established.

2. The right of hot pursuit shall apply *mutatis mutandis* to violations in the exclusive economic zone or on the continental shelf, including safety zones around continental shelf installations, of the laws and regulations of the coastal State applicable in accordance with this Convention to the exclusive economic zone or the continental shelf, including such safety zones.

3. The right of hot pursuit ceases as soon as the ship pursued enters the territorial sea of its own State or of a third State.

4. Hot pursuit is not deemed to have begun unless the pursuing ship has satisfied itself by such practicable means as may be available that the ship pursued or one of its boats or other craft working as a team and using the ship pursued as a mother ship is within the limits of the territorial sea, or, as the case may be, within the contiguous zone or the exclusive economic zone or above the continental shelf. The pursuit may only be commenced after a visual or auditory signal to stop has been given at a distance which enables it to be seen or heard by the foreign ship.

5. The right of hot pursuit may be exercised only by warships or military aircraft, or other ships or aircraft clearly marked and identifiable as being on government service and authorized to that effect.

6. Where hot pursuit is effected by an aircraft:
   (a) the provisions of paragraphs 1 to 4 shall apply *mutatis mutandis*;
   (b) the aircraft giving the order to stop must itself actively pursue the ship until a ship or another aircraft of the coastal State, summoned by the aircraft, arrives to take over the pursuit, unless the aircraft is itself able to arrest the ship. It does not suffice to justify an arrest outside the territorial sea that the ship was merely sighted by the aircraft as an offender or suspected offender, if it was not both ordered to stop and pursued by the aircraft itself or other aircraft or ships which continue the pursuit without interruption.

7. The release of a ship arrested within the jurisdiction of a State and escorted to a port of that State for the purposes of an inquiry before the competent authorities may not be claimed solely on the ground that the ship, in the course of its voyage, was escorted across a portion of the exclusive economic zone or the high seas, if the circumstances rendered this necessary.

8. Where a ship has been stopped or arrested outside the territorial sea in circumstances which do not justify the exercise of the right of hot pursuit, it shall be compensated for any loss or damage that may have been thereby sustained.

Article 112. Right to lay submarine cables and pipelines
1. All States are entitled to lay submarine cables and pipelines on the bed of the high seas beyond the continental shelf.
2. Article 79, paragraph 5, applies to such cables and pipelines.

Article 113. Breaking or injury of a submarine cable or pipeline
Every State shall adopt the laws and regulations necessary to provide that the breaking or injury by a ship flying its flag or by a person subject to its jurisdiction of a submarine cable beneath the high seas done willfully or through culpable negligence, in such a manner as to be liable to interrupt or obstruct telegraphic or telephonic communications, and similarly the breaking or injury of a submarine pipeline or high-voltage power cable, shall be a punishable offense. This provision shall apply also to conduct calculated or likely to result in such breaking or injury. However, it shall not apply to any break or injury caused by persons who acted merely with the legitimate object of saving their lives or their ships, after having taken all necessary precautions to avoid such break or injury.

Article 114. Breaking or injury by owners of a submarine cable or pipeline of another submarine cable or pipeline

Every State shall adopt the laws and regulations necessary to provide that, if persons subject to its jurisdiction who are the owners of a submarine cable or pipeline beneath the high seas, in laying or repairing that cable or pipeline, cause a break in or injury to another cable or pipeline, they shall bear the cost of the repairs.

Article 115. Indemnity for loss incurred in avoiding injury to a submarine cable or pipeline

Every State shall adopt the laws and regulations necessary to ensure that the owners of ships who can prove that they have sacrificed an anchor, a net or any other fishing gear, in order to avoid injuring a submarine cable or pipeline, shall be indemnified by the owner of the cable or pipeline, provided that the owner of the ship has taken all reasonable precautionary measures beforehand.

Section 2. Conservation and Management of the Living Resources of the High Seas

Article 116. Right to fish on the high seas

All States have the right for their nationals to engage in fishing on the high seas subject to:
   (a) their treaty obligations;
   (b) the rights and duties as well as the interests of coastal States provided for, *inter alia*, in article 63, paragraph 2, and articles 64 to 67; and
   (c) the provisions of this section.

Article 117. Duty of States to adopt with respect to their nationals measures for the conservation of the living resources of the high seas

All States have the duty to take, or to co-operate with other States in taking, such measures for their respective nationals as may be necessary for the conservation of the living resources of the high seas.

Article 118. Co-operation of States in the conservation and management of living resources

States shall co-operate with each other in the conservation and management of living resources in the areas of the high seas. States whose nationals exploit identical living resources, or different living resources in the same area, shall enter into negotiations with a view to taking the measures necessary for the conservation of the living resources concerned. They shall, as appropriate, co-operate to establish subregional or regional fisheries organizations to this end.

Article 119. Conservation of the living resources of the high seas

1. In determining the allowable catch and establishing other conservation measures for the living resources in the high seas, States shall:
   (a) take measures which are designed, on the best scientific evidence available to the States concerned, to maintain or restore populations of harvested species at levels which can produce the maximum sustainable yield, as qualified by relevant environmental and economic factors, including the special requirements of developing States, and taking into account fishing patterns, the interdependence of stocks and any generally recommended international minimum standards, whether subregional, regional or global;
   (b) take into consideration the effects on species associated with or dependent upon harvested species with a view to maintaining or restoring populations of such associated or dependent species above levels at which their reproduction may become seriously threatened.
2. Available scientific information, catch and fishing effort statistics and other data relevant to the conservation of fish stocks shall be contributed and exchanged on a regular basis through competent international organizations, whether subregional, regional or global, where appropriate and with participation by all States concerned.
3. States concerned shall ensure that conservation measures and their implementation do not discriminate in form or in fact against the fishermen of any State.

Article 120. Marine mammals
Article 65 also applies to the conservation and management of marine mammals in the high seas.

PART VIII. REGIME OF ISLANDS
Article 121. Regime of islands
1. An island is a naturally formed area of land, surrounded by water, which is above water at high tide.
2. Except as provided for in paragraph 3, the territorial sea, the contiguous zone, the exclusive economic zone, and the continental shelf of an island are determined in accordance with the provisions of this Convention applicable to other land territory.
3. Rocks which cannot sustain human habitation or economic life of their own shall have no exclusive economic zone or continental shelf.

PART IX. ENCLOSED OR SEMI-ENCLOSED SEAS
Article 122. Definition
For the purposes of this Convention, "enclosed or semi-enclosed sea" means a gulf, basin or sea surrounded by two or more States and connected to another sea or the ocean by a narrow outlet or consisting entirely or primarily of the territorial seas and exclusive economic zones of two or more coastal States.

Article 123. Co-operation of States bordering enclosed or semi-enclosed seas
States bordering an enclosed or semi-enclosed sea should co-operate with each other in the exercise of their rights and in the performance of their duties under this Convention. To this end they shall endeavor, directly or through an appropriate regional organization:
- (a) to co-ordinate the management, conservation, exploration and exploitation of the living resources of the sea;
- (b) to co-ordinate the implementation of their rights and duties with respect to the protection and preservation of the marine environment;
- (c) to co-ordinate their scientific research policies and undertake where appropriate joint programs of scientific research in the area;
- (d) to invite, as appropriate, other interested States or international organizations to co-operate with them in furtherance of the provisions of this article.

PART X. RIGHT OF ACCESS OF LAND-LOCKED STATES TO AND FROM THE SEA AND FREEDOM OF TRANSIT
Article 124. Use of terms
1. For the purposes of this Convention:
   - (a) "land-locked State" means a State which has no sea-coast;
   - (b) "transit State" means a State, with or without a sea-coast, situated between a land-locked State and the sea, through whose territory traffic in transit passes;
   - (c) "traffic in transit" means transit of persons, baggage, goods and means of transport across the territory of one or more transit States, when the passage across such territory, with or without trans-shipment, warehousing, breaking bulk, or change in the mode of transport, is only a portion of a complete journey which begins or terminates within the territory of the land-locked State;
   - (d) "means of transport" means:
     - (i) railway rolling stock, sea, lake and river craft and road vehicles;
     - (ii) where local conditions so require, porters and pack animals.
2. Land-locked States and transit States may, by agreement between them, include as means of transport pipelines and gas lines and means of transport other than those included in paragraph 1.

Article 125. Right of access to and from the sea and freedom of transit

1. Land-locked States shall have the right of access to and from the sea for the purpose of exercising the rights provided for in this Convention including those relating to the freedom of the high seas and the common heritage of mankind. To this end, land-locked States shall enjoy freedom of transit through the territory of transit States by all means of transport.
2. The terms and modalities for exercising freedom of transit shall be agreed between the land-locked States and transit States concerned through bilateral, subregional or regional agreements.
3. Transit States, in the exercise of their full sovereignty over their territory, shall have the right to take all measures necessary to ensure that the rights and facilities provided for in this Part for land-locked States shall in no way infringe their legitimate interests.

Article 126. Exclusion of application of the most-favored-nation clause

The provisions of this Convention, as well as special agreements relating to the exercise of the right of access to and from the sea, establishing rights and facilities on account of the special geographical position of land-locked States, are excluded from the application of the most-favored-nation clause.

Article 127. Customs duties, taxes and other charges

1. Traffic in transit shall not be subject to any customs duties, taxes or other charges except charges levied for specific services rendered in connection with such traffic.
2. Means of transport in transit and other facilities provided for and used by land-locked States shall not be subject to taxes or charges higher than those levied for the use of means of transport of the transit State.

Article 128. Free zones and other customs facilities

For the convenience of traffic in transit, free zones or other customs facilities may be provided at the ports of entry and exit in the transit States, by agreement between those States and the land-locked States.

Article 129. Co-operation in the construction and improvement of means of transport

Where there are no means of transport in transit States to give effect to the freedom of transit or where the existing means, including the port installations and equipment, are inadequate in any respect, the transit States and land-locked States concerned may co-operate in constructing or improving them.

Article 130. Measures to avoid or eliminate delays or other difficulties of a technical nature in traffic in transit

1. Transit States shall take all appropriate measures to avoid delays or other difficulties of a technical nature in traffic in transit.
2. Should such delays or difficulties occur, the competent authorities of the transit States and land-locked States concerned shall co-operate towards their expeditious elimination.

Article 131. Equal treatment in maritime ports

Ships flying the flag of land-locked States shall enjoy treatment equal to that accorded to other foreign ships in maritime ports.

Article 132. Grant of greater transit facilities

This Convention does not entail in any way the withdrawal of transit facilities which are greater than those provided for in this Convention and which are agreed between States Parties to this Convention or granted by a State Party. This Convention also does not preclude such grant of greater facilities in the future.

PART XI. THE AREA

Cautionary note: This Part must be read in conjunction with the Part XI Implementation Agreement.*

Section 1. General Provisions

Article 133. *Use of terms*

For the purposes of this Part:

(a) "resources" means all solid, liquid or gaseous mineral resources *in situ* in the Area at or beneath the sea-bed, including polymetallic nodules;

(b) resources, when recovered from the Area, are referred to as "minerals."

Article 134. *Scope of this Part*

1. This Part applies to the Area.

2. Activities in the Area shall be governed by the provisions of this Part.

3. The requirements concerning deposit of, and publicity to be given to, the charts or lists of geographical co-ordinates showing the limits referred to in article 1, paragraph 1(1), are set forth in Part VI.

4. Nothing in this article affects the establishment of the outer limits of the continental shelf in accordance with Part VI or the validity of agreements relating to delimitation between States with opposite or adjacent coasts.

Article 135. *Legal status of the superjacent waters and air space*

Neither this Part nor any rights granted or exercised pursuant thereto shall affect the legal status of the waters superjacent to the Area or that of the air space above those waters.

Section 2. Principles Governing the Area

Article 136. *Common heritage of mankind*

The Area and its resources are the common heritage of mankind.

Article 137. *Legal status of the Area and its resources*

1. No State shall claim or exercise sovereignty or sovereign rights over any part of the Area or its resources, nor shall any State or natural or juridical person appropriate any part thereof. No such claim or exercise of sovereignty or sovereign rights nor such appropriation shall be recognized.

2. All rights in the resources of the Area are vested in mankind as a whole, on whose behalf the Authority shall act. These resources are not subject to alienation. The minerals recovered from the Area, however, may only be alienated in accordance with this Part and the rules, regulations, and procedures of the Authority.

3. No State or natural or juridical person shall claim, acquire, or exercise rights with respect to the minerals recovered from the Area except in accordance with this Part. Otherwise, no such claim, acquisition or exercise of such rights shall be recognized.

Article 138. *General conduct of States in relation to the Area*

The general conduct of States in relation to the Area shall be in accordance with the provisions of this Part, the principles embodied in the Charter of the United Nations and other rules of international law in the interests of maintaining peace and security and promoting international co-operation and mutual understanding.

---

* Agreement, done at New York on 28 July 1994, relating to the Implementation of Part XI of the United Nations Convention on the Law of the Sea of 10 December 1982. A consolidated text that incorporates the revisions to Part XI made by the 1994 Implementation Agreement is available in International Seabed Authority, The Law of the Sea: Compendium of Basic Documents (2001) and is reproduced in Documentary Annex II of United Nations Convention on the Law of the Sea 1982: A Commentary, vol. VI, at 877–921 (Myron H. Nordquist et al. eds., 2002).

Article 139. Responsibility to ensure compliance and liability for damage

1. States Parties shall have the responsibility to ensure that activities in the Area, whether carried out by States Parties, or state enterprises or natural or juridical persons which possess the nationality of States Parties or are effectively controlled by them or their nationals, shall be carried out in conformity with this Part. The same responsibility applies to international organizations for activities in the Area carried out by such organizations.

2. Without prejudice to the rules of international law and Annex III, article 22, damage caused by the failure of a State Party or international organization to carry out its responsibilities under this Part shall entail liability; States Parties or international organizations acting together shall bear joint and several liability. A State Party shall not however be liable for damage caused by any failure to comply with this Part by a person whom it has sponsored under article 153, paragraph 2(b), if the State Party has taken all necessary and appropriate measures to secure effective compliance under article 153, paragraph 4, and Annex III, article 4, paragraph 4.

3. States Parties that are members of international organizations shall take appropriate measures to ensure the implementation of this article with respect to such organizations.

Article 140. Benefit of mankind

1. Activities in the Area shall, as specifically provided for in this Part, be carried out for the benefit of mankind as a whole, irrespective of the geographical location of States, whether coastal or land-locked, and taking into particular consideration the interests and needs of developing States and of peoples who have not attained full independence or other self-governing status recognized by the United Nations in accordance with General Assembly resolution 1514(XV) and other relevant General Assembly resolutions.

2. The Authority shall provide for the equitable sharing of financial and other economic benefits derived from activities in the area through any appropriate mechanism, on a non-discriminatory basis, in accordance with article 160, paragraph 2(f)(i).

Article 141. Use of the Area exclusively for peaceful purposes

The Area shall be open to use exclusively for peaceful purposes by all States, whether coastal or land-locked, without discrimination and without prejudice to the other provisions of this Part.

Article 142. Rights and legitimate interests of coastal States

1. Activities in the Area, with respect to resource deposits in the Area which lie across limits of national jurisdiction, shall be conducted with due regard to the rights and legitimate interests of any coastal State across whose jurisdiction such deposits lie.

2. Consultations, including a system of prior notification, shall be maintained with the State concerned, with a view to avoiding infringement of such rights and interests. In cases where activities in the Area may result in the exploitation of resources lying within national jurisdiction, the prior consent of the coastal State concerned shall be required.

3. Neither this Part nor any rights granted or exercised pursuant thereto shall affect the rights of coastal States to take such measures consistent with the relevant provisions of Part XII as may be necessary to prevent, mitigate or eliminate grave and imminent danger to their coastline, or related interests from pollution or threat thereof or from other hazardous occurrences resulting from or caused by any activities in the Area.

Article 143. Marine scientific research

1. Marine scientific research in the Area shall be carried out exclusively for peaceful purposes and for the benefit of mankind as a whole, in accordance with Part XIII.

2. The Authority may carry out marine scientific research concerning the Area and its resources, and may enter into contracts for that purpose. The Authority shall promote and encourage the

conduct of marine scientific research in the Area, and shall co-ordinate and disseminate the results of such research and analysis when available.

3. States Parties may carry out marine scientific research in the Area. States Parties shall promote international co-operation in marine scientific research in the Area by:
   (a) participating in international programs and encouraging co-operation in marine scientific research by personnel of different countries and of the Authority;
   (b) ensuring that programs are developed through the Authority or other international organizations as appropriate for the benefit of developing States and technologically less developed States with view to:
      (i)   strengthening their research capabilities;
      (ii) training their personnel and the personnel of the Authority in the techniques and applications of research;
      (iii) fostering the employment of their qualified personnel in research in the Area;
   (c) effectively disseminating the results of research and analysis when available, through the Authority or other international channels when appropriate.

Article 144. Transfer of technology

1. The Authority shall take measures in accordance with this Convention:
   (a) to acquire technology and scientific knowledge relating to activities in the Area; and
   (b) to promote and encourage the transfer to developing States of such technology and scientific knowledge so that all States Parties benefit therefrom.
2. To this end the Authority and States Parties shall co-operate in promoting the transfer of technology and scientific knowledge relating to activities in the Area so that the Enterprise and all States Parties may benefit therefrom. In particular they shall initiate and promote:
   (a) programs for the transfer of technology to the Enterprise and to developing States with regard to activities in the Area, including, *inter alia*, facilitating the access of the Enterprise and of developing States to the relevant technology, under fair and reasonable terms and conditions;
   (b) measures directed towards the advancement of the technology of the Enterprise and the domestic technology of developing States, particularly by providing opportunities to personnel from the Enterprise and from developing States for training in marine science and technology and for their full participation in activities in the Area.

Article 145. Protection of the marine environment

Necessary measures shall be taken in accordance with this Convention with respect to activities in the Area to ensure effective protection for the marine environment from harmful effects which may arise from such activities. To this end the Authority shall adopt appropriate rules, regulations and procedures for *inter alia*:
   (a) the prevention, reduction and control of pollution and other hazards to the marine environment, including the coastline, and of interference with the ecological balance of the marine environment, particular attention being paid to the need for protection from harmful effects of such activities as drilling, dredging, excavation, disposal of waste, construction and operation or maintenance of installations, pipelines and other devices related to such activities;
   (b) the protection and conservation of the natural resources of the Area and the prevention of damage to the flora and fauna of the marine environment.

Article 146. Protection of human life

With respect to activities in the Area, necessary measures shall be taken to ensure effective protection of human life. To this end the Authority shall adopt appropriate rules, regulations and procedures to supplement existing international law as embodied in relevant treaties.

Article 147. Accommodation of activities in the Area and in the marine environment
1. Activities in the Area shall be carried out with reasonable regard for other activities in the marine environment.
2. Installations used for carrying out activities in the Area shall be subject to the following conditions:
   (a) such installations shall be erected, emplaced and removed solely in accordance with this Part and subject to the rules, regulations and procedures of the Authority. Due notice must be given of the erection, emplacement and removal of such installations, and permanent means for giving warning of their presence must be maintained;
   (b) such installations may not be established where interference may be caused to the use of recognized sea lanes essential to international navigation or in areas of intense fishing activity;
   (c) safety zones shall be established around such installations with appropriate markings to ensure the safety of both navigation and installations. The configuration and location of such safety zones shall not be such as to form a belt impeding the lawful access of shipping to particular maritime zones or navigation along international sea lanes;
   (d) such installations shall be used exclusively for peaceful purposes;
   (e) such installations do not possess the status of islands. They have no territorial sea of their own, and their presence does not affect the delimitation of the territorial sea, the exclusive economic zone or the continental shelf.
3. Other activities in the marine environment shall be conducted with reasonable regard for activities in the Area.

Article 148. Participation of developing States in activities in the Area
The effective participation of developing States in activities in the Area shall be promoted as specifically provided for in this Part, having due regard to their special interests and needs, and in particular to the special need of the land-locked and geographically disadvantaged among them to overcome obstacles arising from their disadvantaged location, including remoteness from the Area and difficulty of access to and from it.

Article 149. Archaeological and historical objects
All objects of an archaeological and historical nature found in the Area shall be preserved or disposed of for the benefit of mankind as a whole, particular regard being paid to the preferential rights of the State or country of origin, or the State of cultural origin, or the State of historical and archaeological origin.

Section 3. Development of Resources of the Area
[Omitted]

Section 4. The Authority
[Omitted]

Section 5. Settlement of Disputes and Advisory Opinions
[Omitted]

PART XII. PROTECTION AND PRESERVATION OF THE MARINE ENVIRONMENT
Section 1. General Provisions

Article 192. General obligations
States have the obligation to protect and preserve the marine environment.

Article 193. Sovereign right of States to exploit their natural resources
States have the sovereign right to exploit their natural resources pursuant to their environmental policies and in accordance with their duty to protect and preserve the marine environment.

Article 194. Measures to prevent, reduce and control pollution of the marine environment

1. States shall take, individually or jointly as appropriate, all measures consistent with this Convention that are necessary to prevent, reduce and control pollution of the marine environment from any source, using for this purpose the best practicable means at their disposal and in accordance with their capabilities, and they shall endeavor to harmonize their policies in this connection.

2. States shall take all measures necessary to ensure that activities under their jurisdiction or control are so conducted as not to cause damage by pollution to other States and their environment, and that pollution arising from incidents or activities under their jurisdiction or control does not spread beyond the areas where they exercise sovereign rights in accordance with this Convention.

3. The measures taken pursuant to this Part shall deal with all sources of pollution of the marine environment. These measures shall include, *inter alia*, those designed to minimize to the fullest possible extent:

   (a) the release of toxic, harmful or noxious substances, especially those which are persistent, from land-based sources, from or through the atmosphere or by dumping;

   (b) pollution from vessels, in particular measures for preventing accidents and dealing with emergencies, ensuring the safety of operations at sea, preventing intentional and unintentional discharges and regulating the design, construction, equipment, operation and manning of vessels;

   (c) pollution from installations and devices used in exploration or exploitation of the natural resources of the sea-bed and subsoil, in particular measures for preventing accidents and dealing with emergencies, ensuring the safety of operations at sea and regulating the design, construction, equipment, operation and manning of such installations or devices;

   (d) pollution from other installations and devices operating in the marine environment, in particular measures for preventing accidents and dealing with emergencies, ensuring the safety of operations at sea, and regulating the design, construction, equipment, operation and manning of such installations or devices.

4. In taking measures to prevent, reduce or control pollution of the marine environment, States shall refrain from unjustifiable interference with activities carried out by other States in the exercise of their rights and in pursuance of their duties in conformity with this Convention.

5. The measures taken in accordance with this Part shall include those necessary to protect and preserve rare or fragile ecosystems as well as the habitat of depleted, threatened or endangered species and other forms of marine life.

Article 195. Duty not to transfer damage or hazards or transform one type of pollution into another

In taking measures to prevent, reduce and control pollution of the marine environment, States shall act so as not to transfer, directly or indirectly, damage or hazards from one area to another or transform one type of pollution into another.

Article 196. Use of technologies or introduction of alien or new species

1. States shall take all measures necessary to prevent, reduce and control pollution of the marine environment resulting from the use of technologies under their jurisdiction or control, or the intentional or accidental introduction of species, alien or new, to a particular part of the marine environment, which may cause significant and harmful changes thereto.

2. This article does not affect the application of this Convention regarding the prevention, reduction and control of pollution of the marine environment.

Section 2. Global and Regional Co-operation

Article 197. Co-operation on a global or regional basis

States shall co-operate on a global basis and, as appropriate, on a regional basis, directly or through competent international organizations, in formulating and elaborating international rules, standards, and recommended practices and procedures consistent with this Convention, for the protection and preservation of the marine environment, taking into account characteristic regional features.

Article 198. Notification of imminent or actual damage

When a State becomes aware of cases in which the marine environment is in imminent danger of being damaged or has been damaged by pollution, it shall immediately notify other States it deems likely to be affected by such damage, as well as the competent international organizations.

Article 199. Contingency plans against pollution

In the cases referred to in article 198, States in the area affected, in accordance with their capabilities, and the competent international organizations shall co-operate, to the extent possible, in eliminating the effects of pollution and preventing or minimizing the damage. To this end, States shall jointly develop and promote contingency plans for responding to pollution incidents in the marine environment.

Article 200. Studies, research programs and exchange of information and data

States shall co-operate, directly or through competent international organizations, for the purpose of promoting studies, undertaking programs of scientific research and encouraging the exchange of information and data acquired about pollution of the marine environment. They shall endeavor to participate actively in regional and global programs to acquire knowledge for the assessment of the nature and extent of pollution, exposure to it, and its pathways, risks and remedies.

Article 201. Scientific criteria for regulations

In the light of the information and data acquired pursuant to article 200, States shall co-operate, directly or through competent international organizations, in establishing appropriate scientific criteria for the formulation and elaboration of rules, standards and recommended practices and procedures for the prevention, reduction and control of pollution of the marine environment.

Section 3. Technical Assistance

Article 202. Scientific and technical assistance to developing States

States shall, directly or through competent international organizations:

(a) promote programs of scientific, educational, technical and other assistance to developing States for the protection and preservation of the marine environment and the prevention, reduction and control of marine pollution. Such assistance shall include, *inter alia*:

(i)   training of their scientific and technical personnel;

(ii) facilitating their participation in relevant international programs;

(iii) supplying them with necessary equipment and facilities;

(iv) enhancing their capacity to manufacture such equipment;

(v) advice on and developing facilities for research, monitoring, educational and other programs;

(b) provide appropriate assistance, especially to developing States, for the minimization of the effects of major incidents which may cause serious pollution of the marine environment;

(c) provide appropriate assistance, especially to developing States, concerning the preparation of environmental assessments.

Article 203. Preferential treatment for developing States

Developing States shall, for the purposes of prevention, reduction and control of pollution of the marine environment or minimization of its effects, be granted preference by international organizations in:

(a) the allocation of appropriate funds and technical assistance; and

(b) the utilization of their specialized services.

Section 4. Monitoring and Environmental Assessment

Article 204. Monitoring of the risks or effects of pollution

1. States shall, consistent with the rights of other States, endeavor, as far as practicable, directly or through the competent international organizations, to observe, measure, evaluate and analyze, by recognized scientific methods, the risks or effects of pollution of the marine environment.
2. In particular, States shall keep under surveillance the effects of any activities which they permit or in which they engage in order to determine whether these activities are likely to pollute the marine environment.

Article 205. Publication of reports

States shall publish reports of the results obtained pursuant to article 204 or provide such reports at appropriate intervals to the competent international organizations, which should make them available to all States.

Article 206. Assessment of potential effects of activities

When States have reasonable grounds for believing that planned activities under their jurisdiction or control may cause substantial pollution of or significant and harmful changes to the marine environment, they shall, as far as practicable, assess the potential effects of such activities on the marine environment and shall communicate reports of the results of such assessments in the manner provided in article 205.

Section 5. International Rules and National Legislation to Prevent, Reduce and Control Pollution of the Marine Environment

Article 207. Pollution from land-based sources

1. States shall adopt laws and regulations to prevent, reduce and control pollution of the marine environment from land-based sources, including rivers, estuaries, pipelines and outfall structures, taking into account internationally agreed rules, standards and recommended practices and procedures.
2. States shall take other measures as may be necessary to prevent, reduce and control such pollution.
3. States shall endeavor to harmonize their policies in this connection at the appropriate regional level.
4. States, acting especially through competent international organizations or diplomatic conference, shall endeavor to establish global and regional rules, standards and recommended practices and procedures to prevent, reduce and control pollution of the marine environment from land-based sources, taking into account characteristic regional features, the economic capacity of developing States, and their need for economic development. Such rules, standards and recommended practices and procedures shall be re-examined from time to time as necessary.
5. Laws, regulations, measures, rules, standards and recommended practices and procedures referred to in paragraphs 1, 2 and 4 shall include those designed to minimize, to the fullest extent possible, the release of toxic, harmful or noxious substances, especially those which are persistent, into the marine environment.

Article 208. Pollution from sea-bed activities subject to national jurisdiction

1. Coastal States shall adopt laws and regulations to prevent, reduce and control pollution of the marine environment arising from or in connection with sea-bed activities subject to their jurisdiction and from artificial islands, installations and structures under their jurisdiction, pursuant to articles 60 and 80.
2. States shall take other measures as may be necessary to prevent, reduce and control such pollution.
3. Such laws, regulations and measures shall be no less effective than international rules, standards and recommended practices and procedures.

4. States shall endeavor to harmonize their policies in this connection at the appropriate regional level.

5. States, acting especially through competent international organizations or diplomatic conference, shall establish global and regional rules, standards and recommended practices and procedures to prevent, reduce and control pollution of the marine environment referred to in paragraph 1. Such rules, standards and recommended practices and procedures shall be re-examined from time to time as necessary.

Article 209. Pollution from activities in the Area

1. International rules, regulations and procedures shall be established in accordance with Part XI to prevent, reduce and control pollution of the marine environment from activities in the Area. Such rules, regulations and procedures shall be re-examined from time to time as necessary.

2. Subject to the relevant provisions of this section, States shall adopt laws and regulations to prevent, reduce and control pollution of the marine environment from activities in the Area undertaken by vessels, installations, structures and other devices flying their flag or of their registry or operating under their authority, as the case may be. The requirements of such laws and regulations shall be no less effective than the international rules, regulations and procedures referred to in paragraph 1.

Article 210. Pollution by dumping

1. States shall adopt laws and regulations to prevent, reduce and control pollution of the marine environment by dumping.

2. States shall take other measures as may be necessary to prevent, reduce and control such pollution.

3. Such laws, regulations and measures shall ensure that dumping is not carried out without the permission of the competent authorities of States.

4. States, acting especially through competent international organizations or diplomatic conference, shall endeavor to establish global and regional rules, standards and recommended practices and procedures to prevent, reduce and control such pollution. Such rules, standards and recommended practices and procedures shall be re-examined from time to time as necessary.

5. Dumping within the territorial sea and the exclusive economic zone or onto the continental shelf shall not be carried out without the express prior approval of the coastal State, which has the right to permit, regulate and control such dumping after due consideration of the matter with other States which by reason of their geographical situation may be adversely affected thereby.

6. National laws, regulations and measures shall be no less effective in preventing, reducing and controlling such pollution than the global rules and standards.

Article 211. Pollution from vessels

1. States, acting through the competent international organization or general diplomatic conference, shall establish international rules and standards to prevent, reduce and control pollution of the marine environment from vessels and promote the adoption, in the same manner, wherever appropriate, of routeing systems designed to minimize the threat of accidents which might cause pollution of the marine environment, including the coastline, and pollution damage to the related interests of coastal States. Such rules and standards shall, in the same manner, be re-examined from time to time as necessary.

2. States shall adopt laws and regulations for the prevention, reduction and control of pollution of the marine environment from vessels flying their flag or of their registry. Such laws and regulations shall at least have the same effect as that of generally accepted international rules and standards established through the competent international organization or general diplomatic conference.

3. States which establish particular requirements for the prevention, reduction and control of pollution of the marine environment as a condition for the entry of foreign vessels into their ports or internal waters or for a call at their off-shore terminals shall give due publicity to such requirements

and shall communicate them to the competent international organization. Whenever such requirements are established in identical form by two or more coastal States in an endeavor to harmonize policy, the communication shall indicate which States are participating in such co-operative
arrangements. Every State shall require the master of a vessel flying its flag or of its registry, when
navigating within the territorial sea of a State participating in such co-operative arrangements, to
furnish, upon the request of that State, information as to whether it is proceeding to a State of
the same region participating in such co-operative arrangements and, if so, to indicate whether it
complies with the port entry requirements of that State. This article is without prejudice to the
continued exercise by a vessel of its right of innocent passage or to the application of article 25,
paragraph 2.

4. Coastal States may, in the exercise of their sovereignty within their territorial sea, adopt laws
   and regulations for the prevention, reduction and control of marine pollution from foreign vessels, including vessels exercising the right of innocent passage. Such laws and regulations shall, in
   accordance with Part II, section 3, not hamper innocent passage of foreign vessels.

5. Coastal States, for the purpose of enforcement as provided for in section 6, may in respect of their
   exclusive economic zones adopt laws and regulations for the prevention, reduction and control of
   pollution from vessels conforming to and giving effect to generally accepted international rules
   and standards established through the competent international organization or general diplomatic
   conference.

6. (a) Where the international rules and standards referred to in paragraph 1 are inadequate to meet
       special circumstances and coastal States have reasonable grounds for believing that a particular,
       clearly defined area of their respective exclusive economic zones is an area where the adoption
       of special mandatory measures for the prevention of pollution from vessels is required for rec-
       ognized technical reasons in relation to its oceanographical and ecological conditions, as well
       as its utilization or the protection of its resources and the particular character of its traffic, the
       coastal States, after appropriate consultations through the competent international organiza-
       tion with any other States concerned, may, for that area, direct a communication to that orga-
       nization, submitting scientific and technical evidence in support and information on necessary
       reception facilities. Within 12 months after receiving such a communication, the organization
       shall determine whether the conditions in that area correspond to the requirements set out
       above. If the organization so determines, the coastal States may, for that area, adopt laws and
       regulations for the prevention, reduction and control of pollution from vessels implementing
       such international rules and standards or navigational practices as are made applicable, through
       the organization, for special areas. These laws and regulations shall not become applicable to
       foreign vessels until 15 months after the submission of the communication to the organization.

   (b) The coastal States shall publish the limits of any such particular, clearly defined area.

   (c) If the coastal States intend to adopt additional laws and regulations for the same area for the
       prevention, reduction and control of pollution from vessels, they shall, when submitting the
       aforesaid communication, at the same time notify the organization thereof. Such additional
       laws and regulations may relate to discharges or navigational practices but shall not require
       foreign vessels to observe design, construction, manning or equipment standards other than
       generally accepted international rules and standards; they shall become applicable to foreign
       vessels 15 months after the submission of the communication to the organization, provided
       that the organization agrees within 12 months after the submission of the communication.

7. The international rules and standards referred to in this article should include *inter alia* those relating to prompt notification to coastal States, whose coastline or related interests may be affected by
   incidents, including maritime casualties, which involve discharges or probability of discharges.

Article 212. Pollution from or through the atmosphere

1. States shall adopt laws and regulations to prevent, reduce and control pollution of the marine environment from or through the atmosphere, applicable to the air space under their sovereignty and to vessels flying their flag or vessels or aircraft of their registry, taking into account internationally agreed rules, standards and recommended practices and procedures and the safety of air navigation.
2. States shall take other measures as may be necessary to prevent, reduce and control such pollution.
3. States, acting especially through competent international organizations or diplomatic conference, shall endeavor to establish global and regional rules, standards and recommended practices and procedures to prevent, reduce and control such pollution.

Section 6. Enforcement

Article 213. Enforcement with respect to pollution from land-based sources

States shall enforce their laws and regulations adopted in accordance with article 207 and shall adopt laws and regulations and take other measures necessary to implement applicable international rules and standards established through competent international organizations or diplomatic conference to prevent, reduce and control pollution of the marine environment from land-based sources.

Article 214. Enforcement with respect to pollution from sea-bed activities

States shall enforce their laws and regulations adopted in accordance with article 208 and shall adopt laws and regulations and take other measures necessary to implement applicable international rules and standards established through competent international organizations or diplomatic conference to prevent, reduce and control pollution of the marine environment arising from or in connection with sea-bed activities subject to their jurisdiction and from artificial islands, installations and structures under their jurisdiction, pursuant to articles 60 and 80.

Article 215. Enforcement with respect to pollution from activities in the Area

Enforcement of international rules, regulations and procedures established in accordance with Part XI to prevent, reduce and control pollution of the marine environment from activities in the Area shall be governed by that Part.

Article 216. Enforcement with respect to pollution by dumping

1. Laws and regulations adopted in accordance with this Convention and applicable international rules and standards established through competent international organizations or diplomatic conference for the prevention, reduction and control of pollution of the marine environment by dumping shall be enforced:
    (a) by the coastal State with regard to dumping within its territorial sea or its exclusive economic zone or onto its continental shelf;
    (b) by the flag State with regard to vessels flying its flag or vessels or aircraft of its registry;
    (c) by any State with regard to acts of loading of wastes or other matter occurring within its territory or at its off-shore terminals.
2. No State shall be obliged by virtue of this article to institute proceedings when another State has already instituted proceedings in accordance with this article.

Article 217. Enforcement by flag States

1. States shall ensure compliance by vessels flying their flag or of their registry with applicable international rules and standards, established through the competent international organization or general diplomatic conference, and with their laws and regulations adopted in accordance with this Convention for the prevention, reduction and control of pollution of the marine environment from vessels and shall accordingly adopt laws and regulations and take other measures necessary for their implementation. Flag States shall provide for the effective enforcement of such rules, standards, laws and regulations, irrespective of where a violation occurs.

2. States shall, in particular, take appropriate measures in order to ensure that vessels flying their flag or of their registry are prohibited from sailing, until they can proceed to sea in compliance with the requirements of the international rules and standards referred to in paragraph 1, including requirements in respect of design, construction, equipment and manning of vessels.

3. States shall ensure that vessels flying their flag or of their registry carry on board certificates required by and issued pursuant to international rules and standards referred to in paragraph 1. States shall ensure that vessels flying their flag are periodically inspected in order to verify that such certificates are in conformity with the actual condition of the vessels. These certificates shall be accepted by other States as evidence of the condition of the vessels and shall be regarded as having the same force as certificates issued by them, unless there are clear grounds for believing that the condition of the vessel does not correspond substantially with the particulars of the certificates.

4. If a vessel commits a violation of rules and standards established through the competent international organization or general diplomatic conference, the flag State, without prejudice to articles 218, 220 and 228, shall provide for immediate investigation and where appropriate institute proceedings in respect of the alleged violation irrespective of where the violation occurred or where the pollution caused by such violation has occurred or has been spotted.

5. Flag States conducting an investigation of the violation may request the assistance of any other State whose co-operation could be useful in clarifying the circumstances of the case. States shall endeavor to meet appropriate requests of flag States.

6. States shall, at the written request of any State, investigate any violation alleged to have been committed by vessels flying their flag. If satisfied that sufficient evidence is available to enable proceedings to be brought in respect of the alleged violation, flag States shall without delay institute such proceedings in accordance with their laws.

7. Flag States shall promptly inform the requesting State and the competent international organization of the action taken and its outcome. Such information shall be available to all States.

8. Penalties provided for by the laws and regulations of States for vessels flying their flag shall be adequate in severity to discourage violations wherever they occur.

Article 218. Enforcement by port States

1. When a vessel is voluntarily within a port or at an off-shore terminal of a State, that State may undertake investigations and, where the evidence so warrants, institute proceedings in respect of any discharge from that vessel outside the internal waters, territorial sea, or exclusive economic zone of that State in violation of applicable international rules and standards established through the competent international organization or general diplomatic conference.

2. No proceedings pursuant to paragraph 1 shall be instituted in respect of a discharge violation in the internal waters, territorial sea or exclusive economic zone of another State unless requested by that State, the flag State or a State damaged or threatened by the discharge violation, or unless the violation has caused or is likely to cause pollution in the internal waters, territorial sea or exclusive economic zone of the State instituting the proceedings.

3. When a vessel is voluntarily within a port or at an off-shore terminal of a State, that State shall, as far as practicable, comply with requests from any State for investigation of a discharge violation referred in paragraph 1, believed to have occurred in, caused or threatened damage to the internal waters, territorial sea or exclusive economic zone of the requesting State. It shall likewise, as far as practicable, comply with requests from the flag State for investigation of such a violation, irrespective of where the violation occurred.

4. The records of the investigation carried out by a port State pursuant to this article shall be transmitted upon request to the flag State or to the coastal State. Any proceedings instituted by the port State on the basis of such an investigation may, subject to section 7, be suspended at the request of the coastal State when the violation has occurred within its internal waters, territorial sea or

exclusive economic zone. The evidence and records of the case, together with any bond or other financial security posted with the authorities of the port State, shall in that event be transmitted to the coastal State. Such transmittal shall preclude the continuation of proceedings in the port State.

Article 219. Measures relating to seaworthiness of vessels to avoid pollution

Subject to section 7, States which, upon request or on their own initiative, have ascertained that a vessel within one of their ports or at one of their off-shore terminals is in violation of applicable international rules and standards relating to seaworthiness of vessels and thereby threatens damage to the marine environment shall, as far as practicable, take administrative measures to prevent the vessel from sailing. Such States may permit the vessel to proceed only to the nearest appropriate repair yard and, upon removal of the causes of the violation, shall permit the vessel to continue immediately.

Article 220. Enforcement by coastal States

1. When a vessel is voluntarily within a port or at an off-shore terminal of a State, that State may, subject to section 7, institute proceedings in respect of any violation of its laws and regulations adopted in accordance with this Convention or applicable international rules and standards for the prevention, reduction and control of pollution from vessels when the violation has occurred within the territorial sea or the exclusive economic zone of that State.

2. Where there are clear grounds for believing that a vessel navigating in the territorial sea of a State has, during its passage therein, violated laws and regulations of that State adopted in accordance with this Convention or applicable international rules and standards for the prevention, reduction and control of pollution from vessels, that State, without prejudice to the application of the relevant provisions of Part II, section 3, may undertake physical inspection of the vessel relating to the violation and may, where the evidence so warrants, institute proceedings, including detention of the vessel, in accordance with its laws, subject to the provisions of section 7.

3. Where there are clear grounds for believing that a vessel navigating in the exclusive economic zone or the territorial sea of a State has, in the exclusive economic zone, committed a violation of applicable international rules and standards for the prevention, reduction and control of pollution from vessels or laws and regulations of that State conforming and giving effect to such rules and standards, that State may require the vessel to give information regarding its identity and port of registry, its last and its next port of call and other relevant information required to establish whether a violation has occurred.

4. States shall adopt laws and regulations and take other measures so that vessels flying their flag comply with requests for information pursuant to paragraph 3.

5. Where there are clear grounds for believing that a vessel navigating in the exclusive economic zone or the territorial sea of a State has, in the exclusive economic zone, committed a violation referred to in paragraph 3 resulting in a substantial discharge causing or threatening significant pollution of the marine environment, that State may undertake physical inspection of the vessel for matters relating to the violation if the vessel has refused to give information or if the information supplied by the vessel is manifestly at variance with the evident factual situation and if the circumstances of the case justify such inspection.

6. Where there is clear objective evidence that a vessel navigating in the exclusive economic zone or the territorial sea of a State has, in the exclusive economic zone, committed a violation referred to in paragraph 3 resulting in a discharge causing major damage or threat of major damage to the coastline or related interests of the coastal State, or to any resources of its territorial sea or exclusive economic zone, that State may, subject to section 7, provided that the evidence so warrants, institute proceedings, including detention of the vessel, in accordance with its laws.

7. Notwithstanding the provisions of paragraph 6, whenever appropriate procedures have been established, either through the competent international organization or as otherwise agreed,

whereby compliance with requirements for bonding or other appropriate financial security has been assured, the coastal State if bound by such procedures shall allow the vessel to proceed.

8. The provisions of paragraphs 3, 4, 5, 6 and 7 also apply in respect of national laws and regulations adopted pursuant to article 211, paragraph 6.

Article 221. *Measures to avoid pollution arising from maritime casualties*

1. Nothing in this Part shall prejudice the right of States, pursuant to international law, both customary and conventional, to take and enforce measures beyond the territorial sea proportionate to the actual or threatened damage to protect their coastline or related interests, including fishing, from pollution or threat of pollution following upon a maritime casualty or acts relating to such a casualty, which may reasonably be expected to result in major harmful consequences.

2. For the purposes of this article, "maritime casualty" means a collision of vessels, stranding or other incident of navigation, or other occurrence on board a vessel or external to it resulting in material damage or imminent threat of material damage to a vessel or cargo.

Article 222. *Enforcement with respect to pollution from or through the atmosphere*

States shall enforce, within the air space under their sovereignty or with regard to vessels flying their flag or vessels or aircraft of their registry, their laws and regulations adopted in accordance with article 212, paragraph 1, and with other provisions of this Convention and shall adopt laws and regulations and take other measures necessary to implement applicable international rules and standards established through competent international organizations or diplomatic conference to prevent, reduce and control pollution of the marine environment from or through the atmosphere, in conformity with all relevant international rules and standards concerning the safety of air navigation.

Section 7. Safeguards

Article 223. *Measures to facilitate proceedings*

In proceedings instituted pursuant to this Part, States shall take measures to facilitate the hearing of witnesses and the admission of evidence submitted by authorities of another State, or by the competent international organization, and shall facilitate the attendance at such proceedings of official representatives of the competent international organization, the flag State, and any State affected by pollution arising out of any violation. The official representatives attending such proceedings shall have such rights and duties as may be provided under national laws and regulations or international law.

Article 224. *Exercise of powers of enforcement*

The powers of enforcement against foreign vessels under this Part may only be exercised by officials or by warships, military aircraft or other ships or aircraft clearly marked and identifiable as being on government service and authorized to that effect.

Article 225. *Duty to avoid adverse consequences in the exercise of the powers of enforcement*

In the exercise under this Convention of their powers of enforcement against foreign vessels, States shall not endanger the safety of navigation or otherwise create any hazard to a vessel, or bring it to an unsafe port or anchorage, or expose the marine environment to an unreasonable risk.

Article 226. *Investigation of foreign vessels*

1. (a) States shall not delay a foreign vessel longer than is essential for purposes of the investigations provided for in articles 216, 218 and 220. Any physical inspection of a foreign vessel shall be limited to an examination of such certificates, records or other documents as the vessel is required to carry by generally accepted international rules and standards or of any similar documents which it is carrying; further physical inspection of the vessel may be undertaken only after such an examination and only when:

   (i) there are clear grounds for believing that the condition of the vessel or its equipment does not correspond substantially with the particulars of those documents;

    (ii) the contents of such documents are not sufficient to confirm or verify a suspected violation; or

    (iii) the vessel is not carrying valid certificates and records.

  (b) If the investigation indicates a violation of applicable laws and regulations or international rules and standards for the protection and preservation of the marine environment, release shall be made promptly subject to reasonable procedures such as bonding or other appropriate financial security.

  (c) Without prejudice to applicable international rules and standards relating to the seaworthiness of vessels, the release of a vessel may, whenever it would present an unreasonable threat of damage to the marine environment, be refused or made conditional upon proceeding to the nearest appropriate repair yard. Where release has been refused or made conditional, the flag State of the vessel must be promptly notified, and may seek release of the vessel in accordance with Part XV.

2. States shall co-operate to develop procedures for the avoidance of unnecessary physical inspection of vessels at sea.

Article 227. Non-discrimination with respect to foreign vessels

In exercising their rights and performing their duties under this Part, States shall not discriminate in form or in fact against vessels of any other State.

Article 228. Suspension and restrictions on institution of proceedings

1. Proceedings to impose penalties in respect of any violation of applicable laws and regulations or international rules and standards relating to the prevention, reduction and control of pollution from vessels committed by a foreign vessel beyond the territorial sea of the State instituting proceedings shall be suspended upon the taking of proceedings to impose penalties in respect of corresponding charges by the flag State within six months of the date on which proceedings were first instituted, unless those proceedings relate to a case of major damage to the coastal State or the flag State in question has repeatedly disregarded its obligations to enforce effectively the applicable international rules and standards in respect of violations committed by its vessels. The flag State shall in due course make available to the State previously instituting proceedings a full dossier of the case and the records of the proceedings, whenever the flag State has requested the suspension of proceedings in accordance with this article. When proceedings instituted by the flag State have been brought to a conclusion, the suspended proceedings shall be terminated. Upon payment of costs incurred in respect of such proceedings, any bond posted or other financial security provided in connection with the suspended proceedings shall be released by the coastal State.

2. Proceedings to impose penalties on foreign vessels shall not be instituted after the expiry of three years from the date on which the violation was committed, and shall not be taken by any State in the event of proceedings having been instituted by another State subject to the provisions set out in paragraph 1.

3. The provisions of this article are without prejudice to the right of the flag State to take any measures, including proceedings to impose penalties, according to its laws irrespective of prior proceedings by another State.

Article 229. Institution of civil proceedings

Nothing in this Convention affects the institution of civil proceedings in respect of any claim for loss or damage resulting from pollution of the marine environment.

Article 230. Monetary penalties and the observance of recognized rights of the accused

1. Monetary penalties only may be imposed with respect to violations of national laws and regulations or applicable international rules and standards for the prevention, reduction and control of pollution of the marine environment, committed by foreign vessels beyond the territorial sea.

2. Monetary penalties only may be imposed with respect to violations of national laws and regulations or applicable international rules and standards for the prevention, reduction and control of pollution of the marine environment, committed by foreign vessels in the territorial sea, except in the case of a willful and serious act of pollution in the territorial sea.

3. In the conduct of proceedings in respect of such violations committed by a foreign vessel which may result in the imposition of penalties, recognized rights of the accused shall be observed.

Article 231. Notification to the flag State and other States concerned

States shall promptly notify the flag State and any other State concerned of any measures taken pursuant to section 6 against foreign vessels, and shall submit to the flag State all official reports concerning such measures. However, with respect to violations committed in the territorial sea, the foregoing obligations of the coastal State apply only to such measures as are taken in proceedings. The diplomatic agent or consular officers and where possible the maritime authority of the flag State, shall be immediately informed of any such measures taken pursuant to section 6 against foreign vessels.

Article 232. Liability of States arising from enforcement measures

States shall be liable for damage or loss attributable to them arising from measures taken pursuant to section 6 when such measures are unlawful or exceed those reasonably required in the light of available information. States shall provide for recourse in their courts for actions in respect of such damage or loss.

Article 233. Safeguards with respect to straits used for international navigation

Nothing in sections 5, 6 and 7 affects the legal regime of straits used for international navigation. However, if a foreign ship other than those referred to in section 10 has committed a violation of the laws and regulations referred to in article 42, paragraph 1(a) and (b), causing or threatening major damage to the marine environment of the straits, the States bordering the straits may take appropriate enforcement measures and if so shall respect *mutatis mutandis* the provisions of this section.

Section 8. Ice-Covered Areas

Article 234. Ice-covered areas

Coastal States have the right to adopt and enforce non-discriminatory laws and regulations for the prevention, reduction and control of marine pollution from vessels in ice-covered areas within the limits of the exclusive economic zone, where particularly severe climatic conditions and the presence of ice covering such areas for most of the year create obstructions or exceptional hazards to navigation, and pollution of the marine environment could cause major harm to or irreversible disturbance of the ecological balance. Such laws and regulations shall have due regard to navigation and the protection and preservation of the marine environment based on the best available scientific evidence.

Section 9. Responsibility and Liability

Article 235. Responsibility and liability

1. States are responsible for the fulfillment of their international obligations concerning the protection and preservation of the marine environment. They shall be liable in accordance with international law.

2. States shall ensure that recourse is available in accordance with their legal systems for prompt and adequate compensation or other relief in respect of damage caused by pollution of the marine environment by natural or juridical persons under their jurisdiction.

3. With the objective of assuring prompt and adequate compensation in respect of all damage caused by pollution of the marine environment, States shall co-operate in the implementation of existing international law and the further development of international law relating to responsibility and liability for assessment of and compensation for damage and the settlement of related disputes,

as well as, where appropriate, development of criteria and procedures for payment of adequate compensation, such as compulsory insurance or compensation funds.

Section 10. Sovereign Immunity

Article 236. Sovereign immunity

The provisions of this Convention regarding the protection and preservation of the marine environment do not apply to any warship, naval auxiliary, other vessels or aircraft owned or operated by a State and used, for the time being, only on government non-commercial service. However, each State shall ensure, by the adoption of appropriate measures not impairing operations or operational capabilities of such vessels or aircraft owned or operated by it, that such vessels or aircraft act in a manner consistent, so far as is reasonable and practicable, with this Convention.

Section 11. Obligations under Other Conventions on the Protection and Preservation of the Marine Environment

Article 237. Obligations under other conventions on the protection and preservation of the marine environment

1. The provisions of this Part are without prejudice to the specific obligations assumed by States under special conventions and agreements concluded previously which relate to the protection and preservation of the marine environment and to agreements which may be concluded in furtherance of the general principles set forth in this Convention.
2. Specific obligations assumed by States under special conventions, with respect to the protection and preservation of the marine environment, should be carried out in a manner consistent with the general principles and objectives of this Convention.

PART XIII. MARINE SCIENTIFIC RESEARCH

Section 1. General Provisions

Article 238. Right to conduct marine scientific research

All States, irrespective of their geographical location, and competent international organizations have the right to conduct marine scientific research subject to the rights and duties of other States as provided for in this Convention.

Article 239. Promotion of marine scientific research

States and competent international organizations shall promote and facilitate the development and conduct of marine scientific research in accordance with this Convention.

Article 240. General principles for the conduct of marine scientific research

In the conduct of marine scientific research the following principles shall apply:

(a) marine scientific research shall be conducted exclusively for peaceful purposes;
(b) marine scientific research shall be conducted with appropriate scientific methods and means compatible with this Convention;
(c) marine scientific research shall not unjustifiably interfere with other legitimate uses of the sea compatible with this Convention and shall be duly respected in the course of such uses;
(d) marine scientific research shall be conducted in compliance with all relevant regulations adopted in conformity with this Convention including those for the protection and preservation of the marine environment.

Article 241. Non-recognition of marine scientific research activities as the legal basis for claims

Marine scientific research activities shall not constitute the legal basis for any claim to any part of the marine environment or its resources.

Section 2. International Co-operation

Article 242. *Promotion of international co-operation*

1. States and competent international organizations shall, in accordance with the principle of respect for sovereignty and jurisdiction and on the basis of mutual benefit, promote international co-operation in marine scientific research for peaceful purposes.

2. In this context, without prejudice to the rights and duties of States under this Convention, a State, in the application of this Part, shall provide, as appropriate, other States with a reasonable opportunity to obtain from it, or with its co-operation, information necessary to prevent and control damage to the health and safety of persons and to the marine environment.

Article 243. *Creation of favorable conditions*

States and competent international organizations shall co-operate, through the conclusion of bilateral and multilateral agreements, to create favorable conditions for the conduct of marine scientific research in the marine environment and to integrate the efforts of scientists in studying the essence of phenomena and processes occurring in the marine environment and the interrelations between them.

Article 244. *Publication and dissemination of information and knowledge*

1. States and competent international organizations shall, in accordance with this Convention, make available by publication and dissemination through appropriate channels information on proposed major programs and their objectives as well as knowledge resulting from marine scientific research.

2. For this purpose, States, both individually and in co-operation with other States and with competent international organizations, shall actively promote the flow of scientific data and information and the transfer of knowledge resulting from marine scientific research, especially to developing States, as well as the strengthening of the autonomous marine scientific research capabilities of developing States through, *inter alia*, programs to provide adequate education and training of their technical and scientific personnel.

Section 3. Conduct and Promotion of Marine Scientific Research

Article 245. *Marine scientific research in the territorial sea*

Coastal States, in the exercise of their sovereignty, have the exclusive right to regulate, authorize and conduct marine scientific research in their territorial sea. Marine scientific research therein shall be conducted only with the express consent of and under the conditions set forth by the coastal State.

Article 246. *Marine scientific research in the exclusive economic zone and on the continental shelf*

1. Coastal States, in the exercise of their jurisdiction, have the right to regulate, authorize and conduct marine scientific research in their exclusive economic zone and on their continental shelf in accordance with the relevant provisions of this Convention.

2. Marine scientific research in the exclusive economic zone and on the continental shelf shall be conducted with the consent of the coastal State.

3. Coastal States shall, in normal circumstances, grant their consent for marine scientific research projects by other States or competent international organizations in their exclusive economic zone or on their continental shelf to be carried out in accordance with this Convention exclusively for peaceful purposes and in order to increase scientific knowledge of the marine environment for the benefit of all mankind. To this end, coastal States shall establish rules and procedures ensuring that such consent will not be delayed or denied unreasonably.

4. For the purposes of applying paragraph 3, normal circumstances may exist in spite of the absence of diplomatic relations between the coastal State and the researching State.

5. Coastal States may however in their discretion withhold their consent to the conduct of a marine scientific research project of another State or competent international organization in the exclusive economic zone or on the continental shelf of the coastal State if that project:

    (a) is of direct significance for the exploration and exploitation of natural resources, whether living or non-living;

    (b) involves drilling into the continental shelf, the use of explosives or the introduction of harmful substances into the marine environment;

    (c) involves the construction, operation or use of artificial islands, installations and structures referred to in articles 60 and 80;

    (d) contains information communicated pursuant to article 248 regarding the nature and objectives of the project which is inaccurate or if the researching State or competent international organization has outstanding obligations to the coastal State from a prior research project.

6. Notwithstanding the provisions of paragraph 5, coastal States may not exercise their discretion to withhold consent under subparagraph (a) of that paragraph in respect of marine scientific research projects to be undertaken in accordance with the provisions of this Part on the continental shelf, beyond 200 nautical miles from the baselines from which the breadth of the territorial sea is measured, outside those specific areas which coastal States may at any time publicly designate as areas in which exploitation or detailed exploratory operations focused on those areas are occurring or will occur within a reasonable period of time. Coastal States shall give reasonable notice of the designation of such areas, as well as any modifications thereto, but shall not be obliged to give details of the operations therein.

7. The provisions of paragraph 6 are without prejudice to the rights of coastal States over the continental shelf as established in article 77.

8. Marine scientific research activities referred to in this article shall not unjustifiably interfere with activities undertaken by coastal States in the exercise of their sovereign rights and jurisdiction provided for in this Convention.

Article 247. Marine scientific research projects undertaken by or under the auspices of international organizations

A coastal State which is a member of or has a bilateral agreement with an international organization, and in whose exclusive economic zone or on whose continental shelf that organization wants to carry out a marine scientific research project, directly or under its auspices, shall be deemed to have authorized the project to be carried out in conformity with the agreed specifications if that State approved the detailed project when the decision was made by the organization for the undertaking of the project, or is willing to participate in it, and has not expressed any objection within four months of notification of the project by the organization to the coastal State.

Article 248. Duty to provide information to the coastal State

States and competent international organizations which intend to undertake marine scientific research in the exclusive economic zone or on the continental shelf of a coastal State shall, not less than six months in advance of the expected starting date of the marine scientific research project, provide that State with a full description of:

   (a) the nature and objectives of the project;

   (b) the method and means to be used, including name, tonnage, type and class of vessels and a description of scientific equipment;

   (c) the precise geographical areas in which the project is to be conducted;

   (d) the expected date of first appearance and final departure of the research vessels, or deployment of the equipment and its removal, as appropriate;

   (e) the name of the sponsoring institution, its director and the person in charge of the project; and

(f) the extent to which it is considered that the coastal State should be able to participate or to be represented in the project.

Article 249. Duty to comply with certain conditions

1. States and competent international organizations when undertaking marine scientific research in the exclusive economic zone or on the continental shelf of a coastal State shall comply with the following conditions:
    (a) ensure the right of the coastal State, if it so desires, to participate or be represented in the marine scientific research project, especially on board research vessels and other craft or scientific research installations, when practicable, without payment of any remuneration to the scientists of the coastal State and without obligation to contribute towards the costs of the project;
    (b) provide the coastal State, at its request, with preliminary reports, as soon as practicable, and with the final results and conclusions after the completion of the research;
    (c) undertake to provide access for the coastal State, at its request, to all data and samples derived from the marine scientific research project and likewise to furnish it with data which may be copied and samples which may be divided without detriment to their scientific value;
    (d) if requested, provide the coastal State with an assessment of such data, samples and research results or provide assistance in their assessment or interpretation;
    (e) ensure, subject to paragraph 2, that the research results are made internationally available through appropriate national or international channels, as soon as practicable;
    (f) inform the coastal State immediately of any major change in the research program;
    (g) unless otherwise agreed, remove the scientific research installations or equipment once the research is completed.
2. This article is without prejudice to the conditions established by the laws and regulations of the coastal State for the exercise of its discretion to grant or withhold consent pursuant to article 246, paragraph 5, including requiring prior agreement for making internationally available the research results of a project of direct significance for the exploration and exploitation of natural resources.

Article 250. Communications concerning marine scientific research projects

Communications concerning the marine scientific research projects shall be made through appropriate official channels, unless otherwise agreed.

Article 251. General criteria and guidelines

States shall seek to promote through competent international organizations the establishment of general criteria and guidelines to assist States in ascertaining the nature and implications of marine scientific research.

Article 252. Implied consent

States or competent international organizations may proceed with a marine scientific research project six months after the date upon which the information required pursuant to article 248 was provided to the coastal State unless within four months of the receipt of the communication containing such information the coastal State has informed the State or organization conducting the research that:
    (a) it has withheld its consent under the provisions of article 246; or
    (b) the information given by that State or competent international organization regarding the nature or objectives of the project does not conform to the manifestly evident facts; or
    (c) it requires supplementary information relevant to conditions and the information provided for under articles 248 and 249; or
    (d) outstanding obligations exist with respect to a previous marine scientific research project carried out by that State or organization, with regard to conditions established in article 249.

Article 253. Suspension or cessation of marine scientific research activities

1. A coastal State shall have the right to require the suspension of any marine scientific research activities in progress within its exclusive economic zone or on its continental shelf if:
   (a) the research activities are not being conducted in accordance with the information communicated as provided under article 248 upon which the consent of the coastal State was based; or
   (b) the State or competent international organization conducting the research activities fails to comply with the provisions of article 249 concerning the rights of the coastal State with respect to the marine scientific research project.
2. A coastal State shall have the right to require the cessation of any marine scientific research activities in case of any non-compliance with the provisions of article 248 which amounts to a major change in the research project or the research activities.
3. A coastal State may also require cessation of marine scientific research activities if any of the situations contemplated in paragraph 1 are not rectified within a reasonable period of time.
4. Following notification by the coastal State of its decision to order suspension or cessation, States or competent international organizations authorized to conduct marine scientific research activities shall terminate the research activities that are the subject of such a notification.
5. An order of suspension under paragraph 1 shall be lifted by the coastal State and the marine scientific research activities allowed to continue once the researching State or competent international organization has complied with the conditions required under articles 248 and 249.

Article 254. Rights of neighboring land-locked and geographically disadvantaged States

1. States and competent international organizations which have submitted to a coastal State a project to undertake marine scientific research referred to in article 246, paragraph 3, shall give notice to the neighboring land-locked and geographically disadvantaged States of the proposed research project, and shall notify the coastal State thereof.
2. After the consent has been given for the proposed marine scientific research project by the coastal State concerned, in accordance with article 246 and other relevant provisions of this Convention, States and competent international organizations undertaking such a project shall provide to the neighboring land-locked and geographically disadvantaged States, at their request and when appropriate, relevant information as specified in article 248 and article 249, paragraph 1(f).
3. The neighboring land-locked and geographically disadvantaged States referred to above shall, at their request, be given the opportunity to participate, whenever feasible, in the proposed marine scientific research project through qualified experts appointed by them and not objected to by the conformity with the provisions of this Convention, between the coastal State concerned and the State or competent international organizations conducting the marine scientific research.
4. States and competent international organizations referred to in paragraph 1 shall provide to the above-mentioned land-locked and geographically disadvantaged States, at their request, the information and assistance specified in article 249, paragraph 1(d), subject to the provisions of article 249, paragraph 2.

Article 255. Measures to facilitate marine scientific research and assist research vessels

States shall endeavor to adopt reasonable rules, regulations and procedures to promote and facilitate marine scientific research conducted in accordance with this Convention beyond their territorial sea and, as appropriate, to facilitate, subject to the provisions of their laws and regulations, access to their harbors and promote assistance for marine scientific research vessels which comply with the relevant provisions of this Part.

Article 256. Marine scientific research in the Area

All States, irrespective of their geographical location, and competent international organizations have the right, in conformity with the provisions of Part XI, to conduct marine scientific research in the Area.

Article 257. Marine scientific research in the water column beyond the exclusive economic zone

All States, irrespective of their geographical location, and competent international organizations have the right, in conformity with this Convention, to conduct marine scientific research in the water column beyond the limits of the exclusive economic zone.

Section 4. Scientific Research Installations or Equipment in the Marine Environment

Article 258. Deployment and use

The deployment and use of any type of scientific research installations or equipment in any area of the marine environment shall be subject to the same conditions as are prescribed in this Convention for the conduct of marine scientific research in any such area.

Article 259. Legal status

The installations or equipment referred to in this section do not possess the status of islands. They have no territorial sea of their own, and their presence does not affect the delimitation of the territorial sea, the exclusive economic zone or the continental shelf.

Article 260. Safety zones

Safety zones of a reasonable breadth not exceeding a distance of 500 meters may be created around scientific research installations in accordance with the relevant provisions of this Convention. All States shall ensure that such safety zones are respected by their vessels.

Article 261. Non-interference with shipping routes

The deployment and use of any type of scientific research installations or equipment shall not constitute an obstacle to established international shipping routes.

Article 262. Identification markings and warning signals

Installations or equipment referred to in this section shall bear identification markings indicating the State of registry or the international organization to which they belong and shall have adequate internationally agreed warning signals to ensure safety at sea and the safety of air navigation, taking into account rules and standards established by competent international organizations.

Section 5. Responsibility and Liability

Article 263. Responsibility and liability

1. States and competent international organizations shall be responsible for ensuring that marine scientific research, whether undertaken by them or on their behalf, is conducted in accordance with this Convention.
2. States and competent international organizations shall be responsible and liable for the measures they take in contravention of this Convention in respect of marine scientific research conducted by other States, their natural or juridical persons, or by competent international organizations, and shall provide compensation for damage resulting from such measures.
3. States and competent international organizations shall be responsible and liable pursuant to article 235 for damage caused by pollution of the marine environment arising out of marine scientific research undertaken by them or on their behalf.

Section 6. Settlement of Disputes and Interim Measures

Article 264. Settlement of disputes

Disputes concerning the interpretation or application of the provisions of this Convention with regard to marine scientific research shall be settled in accordance with Part XV, sections 2 and 3.

Article 265. Interim measures

Pending settlement of a dispute in accordance with Part XV, sections 2 and 3, the State or competent international organization authorized to conduct a marine scientific research project shall not allow research activities to commence or continue without the express consent of the coastal State concerned.

PART XIV. DEVELOPMENT AND TRANSFER OF MARINE TECHNOLOGY
[Omitted]

PART XV. SETTLEMENT OF DISPUTES
Section 1. General Provisions
Article 279. Obligation to settle disputes by peaceful means
States Parties shall settle any dispute between them concerning the interpretation or application of this Convention by peaceful means in accordance with Article 2, paragraph 3, of the Charter of the United Nations and, to this end, shall seek a solution by the means indicated in Article 33, paragraph 1, of the Charter.

Article 280. Settlement of disputes by any peaceful means chosen by the parties
Nothing in this Part impairs the right of any States Parties to agree at any time to settle a dispute between them concerning the interpretation or application of this Convention by any peaceful means of their own choice.

Article 281. Procedure where no settlement has been reached by the parties
1. If the States Parties which are parties to a dispute concerning the interpretation or application of this Convention have agreed to seek settlement of the dispute by a peaceful means of their own choice, the procedures provided for in this Part apply only where no settlement has been reached by recourse to such means and the agreement between the parties does not exclude any further procedure.
2. If the parties have also agreed on a time-limit, paragraph 1 applies only upon the expiration of that time-limit.

Article 282. Obligations under general, regional or bilateral agreements
If the States Parties which are parties to a dispute concerning the interpretation or application of this Convention have agreed through a general, regional or bilateral agreement or otherwise, that such dispute shall, at the request of any party to the dispute, be submitted to a procedure that entails a binding decision, that procedure shall apply in lieu of the procedures provided for in this Part, unless the parties to the dispute otherwise agree.

Article 283. Obligation to exchange views
1. When a dispute arises between States Parties concerning the interpretation or application of this Convention, the parties to the dispute shall proceed expeditiously to an exchange of views regarding its settlement by negotiation or other peaceful means.
2. The parties shall also proceed expeditiously to an exchange of views where a procedure for the settlement of such a dispute has been terminated without a settlement or where a settlement has been reached and the circumstances require consultation regarding the manner of implementing the settlement.

Article 284. Conciliation
1. A State Party which is a party to a dispute concerning the interpretation or application of this Convention may invite the other party or parties to submit the dispute to conciliation in accordance with the procedure under Annex V, section 1, or another conciliation procedure.
2. If the invitation is accepted and if the parties agree upon the conciliation procedure to be applied, any party may submit the dispute to that procedure.

3. If the invitation is not accepted or the parties do not agree upon the procedure, the conciliation proceedings shall be deemed to be terminated.

4. Unless the parties otherwise agree, when a dispute has been submitted to conciliation, the proceedings may be terminated only in accordance with the agreed conciliation procedure.

Article 285. *Application of this section to disputes submitted pursuant to Part XI*

This section applies to any dispute which pursuant to Part XI, section 5, is to be settled in accordance with procedures provided for in this Part. If an entity other than a State Party is a party to such a dispute, this section applies *mutatis mutandis*.

Section 2. Compulsory Procedures Entailing Binding Decisions

Article 286. *Application of procedures under this section*

Subject to section 3, any dispute concerning the interpretation or application of this Convention shall, where no settlement has been reached by recourse to section 1, be submitted at the request of any party to the dispute to the court or tribunal having jurisdiction under this section.

Article 287. *Choice of procedure*

1. When signing, ratifying or acceding to this Convention or at any time thereafter, a State shall be free to choose, by means of a written declaration, one or more of the following means for the settlement of disputes concerning the interpretation or application of this Convention:
   (a) the International Tribunal for the Law of the Sea established in accordance with Annex VI;
   (b) the International Court of Justice;
   (c) an arbitral tribunal constituted in accordance with Annex VII;
   (d) a special arbitral tribunal constituted in accordance with Annex VIII for one or more of the categories of disputes specified therein.

2. A declaration made under paragraph 1 shall not affect or be affected by the obligation of a State Party to accept the jurisdiction of the Sea-Bed Disputes Chamber of the International Tribunal for the Law of the Sea to the extent and in the manner provided for in Part XI, section 5.

3. A State Party, which is a party to a dispute not covered by a declaration in force, shall be deemed to have accepted arbitration in accordance with Annex VII.

4. If the parties to a dispute have accepted the same procedure for the settlement of the dispute, it may be submitted only to that procedure, unless the parties otherwise agree.

5. If the parties to a dispute have not accepted the same procedure for the settlement of the dispute, it may be submitted only to arbitration in accordance with Annex VII, unless the parties otherwise agree.

6. A declaration made under paragraph 1 shall remain in force until three months after notice of revocation has been deposited with the Secretary-General of the United Nations.

7. A new declaration, a notice of revocation, or the expiry of a declaration does not in any way affect proceedings pending before a court or tribunal having jurisdiction under this article, unless the parties otherwise agree.

8. Declarations and notices referred to in this article shall be deposited with the Secretary-General of the United Nations, who shall transmit copies thereof to the States Parties.

Article 288. *Jurisdiction*

1. A court or tribunal referred to in article 287 shall have jurisdiction over any dispute concerning the interpretation or application of this Convention which is submitted to it in accordance with this Part.

2. A court or tribunal referred to in article 287 shall also have jurisdiction over any dispute concerning the interpretation or application of an international agreement related to the purposes of this Convention, which is submitted to it in accordance with the agreement.

3. The Sea-Bed Disputes Chamber of the International Tribunal for the Law of the Sea established in accordance with Annex VI, and any other chamber or arbitral tribunal referred to in Part XI, section 5, shall have jurisdiction in any matter which is submitted to it in accordance therewith.

4. In the event of a dispute as to whether a court or tribunal has jurisdiction, the matter shall be settled by decision of that court or tribunal.

Article 289. *Experts*

In any dispute involving scientific or technical matters, a court or tribunal exercising jurisdiction under this section may, at the request of a party or *proprio motu*, select in consultation with the parties no fewer than two scientific or technical experts chosen preferably from the relevant list prepared in accordance with Annex VIII, article 2, to sit with the court or tribunal but without the right to vote.

Article 290. *Provisional measures*

1. If a dispute has been duly submitted to a court or tribunal which considers that *prima facie* it has jurisdiction under this Part or Part XI, section 5, the court or tribunal may prescribe any provisional measures which it considers appropriate under the circumstances to preserve the respective rights of the parties to the dispute or to prevent serious harm to the marine environment, pending the final decision.

2. Provisional measures may be modified or revoked as soon as the circumstances justifying them have changed or ceased to exist.

3. Provisional measures may be prescribed, modified or revoked under this article only at the request of a party to the dispute and after the parties have been given an opportunity to be heard.

4. The court or tribunal shall forthwith give notice to the parties to the dispute, and to such other States Parties as it considers appropriate, of the prescription, modification or revocation of provisional measures.

5. Pending the constitution of an arbitral tribunal to which a dispute is being submitted under this section, any court or tribunal agreed upon by the parties or, failing such agreement within two weeks from the date of the request for provisional measures, the International Tribunal for the Law of the Sea or, with respect to activities in the Area, the Sea-Bed Disputes Chamber, may prescribe, modify or revoke provisional measures in accordance with this article if it considers that *prima facie* the tribunal which is to be constituted would have jurisdiction and that the urgency of the situation so requires. Once constituted, the tribunal to which the dispute has been submitted may modify, revoke, or affirm those provisional measures, acting in conformity with paragraphs 1 to 4.

6. The parties to the dispute shall comply promptly with any provisional measures prescribed under this article.

Article 291. *Access*

1. All the dispute settlement procedures specified in this Part shall be open to States Parties.

2. The dispute settlement procedures specified in this Part shall be open to entities other than States Parties only as specifically provided for in this Convention.

Article 292. *Prompt release of vessels and crews*

1. Where the authorities of a State Party have detained a vessel flying the flag of another State Party and it is alleged that the detaining State has not complied with the provisions of this Convention for the prompt release of the vessel or its crew upon the posting of a reasonable bond or other financial security, the question of release from detention may be submitted to any court or tribunal agreed upon by the parties or, failing such agreement within 10 days from the time of detention, to a court or tribunal accepted by the detaining State under article 287 or to the International Tribunal for the Law of the Sea, unless the parties otherwise agree.

2. The application for release may be made only by or on behalf of the flag State of the vessel.

3. The court or tribunal shall deal without delay with the application for release and shall deal only with the question of release, without prejudice to the merits of any case before the appropriate domestic forum against the vessel, its owner, or its crew. The authorities of the detaining State remain competent to release the vessel or its crew at any time.

4. Upon the posting of the bond or other financial security determined by the court or tribunal, the authorities of the detaining State shall comply promptly with the decision of the court or tribunal concerning the release of the vessel or its crew.

Article 293. Applicable law

1. A court or tribunal having jurisdiction under this section shall apply this Convention and other rules of international law not incompatible with this Convention.

2. Paragraph 1 does not prejudice the power of the court or tribunal having jurisdiction under this section to decide a case *ex aequo et bono*, if the parties so agree.

Article 294. Preliminary proceedings

1. A court or tribunal provided for in article 287 to which an application is made in respect of a dispute referred to in article 297 shall determine at the request of a party, or may determine *proprio motu*, whether the claim constitutes an abuse of legal process or whether *prima facie* it is well founded. If the court or tribunal determines that the claim constitutes an abuse of legal process or is *prima facie* unfounded, it shall take no further action in the case.

2. Upon receipt of the application, the court or tribunal shall immediately notify the other party or parties of the application, and shall fix a reasonable time-limit within which they may request it to make a determination in accordance with paragraph 1.

3. Nothing in this article affects the right of any party to a dispute to make preliminary objections in accordance with the applicable rules of procedure.

Article 295. Exhaustion of local remedies

Any dispute between States Parties concerning the interpretation or application of this Convention may be submitted to the procedures provided for in this section only after local remedies have been exhausted where this is required by international law.

Article 296. Finality and binding force of decisions

1. Any decision rendered by a court or tribunal having jurisdiction under this section shall be final and shall be complied with by all the parties to the dispute.

2. Any such decision shall have no binding force except between the parties and in respect of that particular dispute.

Section 3. Limitations and Exceptions to Applicability of Section 2

Article 297. Limitations on applicability of section 2

1. Disputes concerning the interpretation or application of this Convention with regard to the exercise by a coastal State of its sovereign rights or jurisdiction provided for in this Convention shall be subject to the procedures provided for in section 2 in the following cases:

    (a) when it is alleged that a coastal State has acted in contravention of the provisions of this Convention in regard to the freedom and rights of navigation, overflight, or the laying of submarine cables and pipelines, or in regard to other internationally lawful uses of the sea specified in article 58;

    (b) when it is alleged that a State in exercising the aforementioned freedoms, rights, or uses has acted in contravention of this Convention or of laws or regulations adopted by the coastal State in conformity with this Convention and other rules of international law not incompatible with this Convention; or

(c) when it is alleged that a coastal State has acted in contravention of specified international rules and standards for the protection and preservation of the marine environment which are applicable to the coastal State and which have been established by this Convention or through a competent international organization or diplomatic conference in accordance with this Convention.

2. (a) Disputes concerning the interpretation or application of the provisions of this Convention with regard to marine scientific research shall be settled in accordance with section 2, except that the coastal State shall not be obliged to accept the submission to such settlement of any dispute arising out of:

   (i) the exercise by the coastal State of a right or discretion in accordance with article 246; or

   (ii) a decision by the coastal State to order suspension or cessation of a research project in accordance with article 253.

   (b) A dispute arising from an allegation by the researching State that with respect to a specific project the coastal State is not exercising its rights under articles 246 and 253 in a manner compatible with this Convention shall be submitted, at the request of either party, to conciliation under Annex V, section 2, provided that the conciliation commission shall not call in question the exercise by the coastal State of its discretion to designate specific areas as referred to in article 246, paragraph 6, or of its discretion to withhold consent in accordance with article 246, paragraph 5.

3. (a) Disputes concerning the interpretation or application of the provisions of this Convention with regard to fisheries shall be settled in accordance with section 2, except that the coastal State shall not be obliged to accept the submission to such settlement of any dispute relating to its sovereign rights with respect to the living resources in the exclusive economic zone or their exercise, including its discretionary powers for determining the allowable catch, its harvesting capacity, the allocations of surpluses to other States and the terms and conditions established in its conservation and management laws and regulations.

   (b) Where no settlement has been reached by recourse to section 1 of this Part, a dispute shall be submitted to conciliation under Annex V, section 2, at the request of any party to the dispute, when it is alleged that:

   (i) a coastal State has manifestly failed to comply with its obligations to ensure through proper conservation and management measures that the maintenance of the living resources in the exclusive economic zone is not seriously endangered;

   (ii) a coastal State has arbitrarily refused to determine, at the request of another State, the allowable catch and its capacity to harvest living resources with respect to stocks which that other State is interested in fishing; or

   (iii) a coastal State has arbitrarily refused to allocate to any State, under articles 62, 69 and 70 and under the terms and conditions established by the coastal State consistent with this Convention, the whole or part of the surplus it has declared to exist.

   (c) In no case shall the conciliation commission substitute its discretion for that of the coastal State.

   (d) The report of the conciliation commission shall be communicated to the appropriate international organizations.

   (e) In negotiating agreements pursuant to articles 69 and 70, States Parties, unless they otherwise agree, shall include a clause on measures which they shall take in order to minimize the possibility of a disagreement concerning the interpretation or application of the agreement, and on how they should proceed if a disagreement nevertheless arises.

Article 298. Optional exceptions to applicability of section 2

1. When signing, ratifying or acceding to this Convention or at any time thereafter, a State may, without prejudice to the obligations arising under section 1, declare in writing that it does not accept any one or more of the procedures provided for in section 2 with respect to one or more of the following categories of disputes:

   (a) (i) disputes concerning the interpretation or application of articles 15, 74 and 83 relating to sea boundary delimitations, or those involving historic bays or titles, provided that a State having made such a declaration shall, when such a dispute arises subsequent to the entry into force of this Convention and where no agreement within a reasonable period of time is reached in negotiations between the parties, at the request of any party to the dispute, accept submission of the matter to conciliation under Annex V, section 2; and provided further that any dispute that necessarily involves the concurrent consideration of any unsettled dispute concerning sovereignty or other rights over continental or insular land territory shall be excluded from such submission;

   (ii) after the conciliation commission has presented its report, which shall state the reasons on which it is based, the parties shall negotiate an agreement on the basis of that report; if these negotiations do not result in an agreement, the parties shall, by mutual consent, submit the question to one of the procedures provided for in section 2, unless the parties otherwise agree;

   (iii) this subparagraph does not apply to any sea boundary dispute finally settled by an arrangement between the parties, or to any such dispute which is to be settled in accordance with a bilateral or multilateral agreement binding upon those parties;

   (b) disputes concerning military activities, including military activities by government vessels and aircraft engaged in non-commercial service, and disputes concerning law enforcement activities in regard to the exercise of sovereign rights or jurisdiction excluded from the jurisdiction of a court or tribunal under article 297, paragraph 2 or 3;

   (c) disputes in respect of which the Security Council of the United Nations is exercising the functions assigned to it by the Charter of the United Nations, unless the Security Council decides to remove the matter from its agenda or calls upon the parties to settle it by the means provided for in this Convention.

2. A State Party which has made a declaration under paragraph 1 may at any time withdraw it, or agree to submit a dispute excluded by such declaration to any procedure specified in this Convention.

3. A State Party which has made a declaration under paragraph 1 shall not be entitled to submit any dispute falling within the excepted category of disputes to any procedure in this Convention as against another State Party, without the consent of that party.

4. If one of the States Parties has made a declaration under paragraph 1 (a), any other State Party may submit any dispute falling within an excepted category against the declarant party to the procedure specified in such declaration.

5. A new declaration, or the withdrawal of a declaration, does not in any way affect proceedings pending before a court or tribunal in accordance with this article, unless the parties otherwise agree.

6. Declarations and notices of withdrawal of declarations under this article shall be deposited with the Secretary-General of the United Nations, who shall transmit copies thereof to the States Parties.

Article 299. Right of the parties to agree upon a procedure

1. A dispute excluded under article 297 or excepted by a declaration made under article 298 from the dispute settlement procedures provided for in section 2 may be submitted to such procedures only by agreement of the parties to the dispute.

2. Nothing in this section impairs the right of the parties to the dispute to agree to some other procedure for the settlement of such dispute or to reach an amicable settlement.

PART XVI. GENERAL PROVISIONS

Article 300. *Good faith and abuse of rights*

States Parties shall fulfill in good faith the obligations assumed under this Convention and shall exercise the rights, jurisdiction and freedoms recognized in this Convention in a manner which would not constitute an abuse of right.

Article 301. *Peaceful uses of the seas*

In exercising their rights and performing their duties under this Convention, States Parties shall refrain from any threat or use of force against the territorial integrity or political independence of any State, or in any other manner inconsistent with the principles of international law embodied in the Charter of the United Nations.

Article 302. *Disclosure of information*

Without prejudice to the right of a State Party to resort to the procedures for the settlement of disputes provided for in this Convention, nothing in this Convention shall be deemed to require a State Party, in the fulfillment of its obligations under this Convention, to supply information the disclosure of which is contrary to the essential interests of its security.

Article 303. *Archaeological and historical objects found at sea*

1. States have the duty to protect objects of an archaeological and historical nature found at sea and shall co-operate for this purpose.
2. In order to control traffic in such objects, the coastal State may, in applying article 33, presume that their removal from the sea-bed in the zone referred to in that article without its approval would result in an infringement within its territory or territorial sea of the laws and regulations referred to in that article.
3. Nothing in this article affects the rights of identifiable owners, the law of salvage or other rules of admiralty, or laws and practices with respect to cultural exchanges.
4. This article is without prejudice to other international agreements and rules of international law regarding the protection of objects of an archaeological and historical nature.

Article 304. *Responsibility and liability for damage*

The provisions of this Convention regarding responsibility and liability for damage are without prejudice to the application of existing rules and the development of further rules regarding responsibility and liability under international law.

PART XVII. FINAL PROVISIONS

Article 305. *Signature*

1. This Convention shall be open for signature by:
    (a) All States;
    (b) Namibia, represented by the United Nations Council for Namibia;
    (c) all self-governing associated States which have chosen that status in an act of self-determination supervised and approved by the United Nations in accordance with General Assembly resolution 1514(XV) and which have competence over the matters governed by this Convention, including the competence to enter into treaties in respect of those matters;
    (d) all self-governing associated States which, in accordance with their respective instruments of association, have competence over the matters governed by this Convention, including the competence to enter into treaties in respect of those matters;

(e) all territories which enjoy full internal self-government, recognized as such by the United Nations, but have not attained full independence in accordance with General Assembly resolution 1514(XV) and which have competence over the matters governed by this Convention, including the competence to enter into treaties respect of those matters;

(f) international organizations, in accordance with Annex IX.

2. This Convention shall remain open for signature until 9 December 1984 at the Ministry of Foreign Affairs of Jamaica and also, from 1 July 1983 until 9 December 1984, at United Nations Headquarters in New York.

Article 306. Ratification and formal confirmation

This Convention is subject to ratification by states and the other entities referred to in article 305, paragraph 1(b), (c), (d) and (e), and to formal confirmation, in accordance with Annex IX, by the entities referred to in article 305, paragraph 1(f). The instruments of ratification and of formal confirmation shall be deposited with the Secretary-General of the United Nations.

Article 307. Accession

This Convention shall remain open for accession by States and the other entities referred to in article 305. Accession by the entities referred to in article 305, paragraph 1(f), shall be in accordance with Annex IX. The instruments of accession shall be deposited with the Secretary-General of the United Nations.

Article 308. Entry into force

1. This Convention shall enter into force 12 months after the date of deposit of the sixtieth instrument of ratification or accession.

2. For each State ratifying or acceding to this Convention after the deposit of the sixtieth instrument of ratification or accession, the Convention shall enter into force on the thirtieth day following the deposit of its instrument of ratification or accession, subject to paragraph 1.

3. The Assembly of the Authority shall meet on the date of entry into force of this Convention and shall elect the Council of the Authority. The first Council shall be constituted in a manner consistent with the purpose of article 161 if the provisions of that article cannot be strictly applied.

4. The rules, regulations and procedures drafted by the Preparatory Commission shall apply provisionally pending their formal adoption by the Authority in accordance with Part XI.

5. The Authority and its organs shall act in accordance with resolution II of the Third United Nations Conference on the Law of the Sea relating to preparatory investment and with decisions of the Preparatory Commission taken pursuant to that resolution.

Article 309. Reservations and exceptions

No reservations or exceptions may be made to this Convention unless expressly permitted by other articles of this Convention.

Article 310. Declarations and statements

Article 309 does not preclude a State, when signing, ratifying or acceding to this Convention, from making declarations or statements, however phrased or named, with a view, *inter alia*, to the harmonization of its laws and regulations, provided that such declarations or statements do not purport to exclude or to modify the legal effect of the provisions of this Convention in their application to that State.

Article 311. Relation to other conventions and international agreements

1. This Convention shall prevail, as between States Parties, over the Geneva Conventions on the Law of the Sea of 29 April 1958.

2. This Convention shall not alter the rights and obligations of States Parties which arise from other agreements compatible with this Convention and which do not affect the enjoyment by other States Parties of their rights or the performance of their obligations under this Convention.

3. Two or more States Parties may conclude agreements modifying or suspending the operation of provisions of this Convention, applicable solely to the relations between them, provided that such agreements do not relate to a provision derogation from which is incompatible with the effective execution of the object and purpose of this Convention, and provided further that such agreements shall not affect the application of the basic principles embodied herein, and that the provisions of such agreements do not affect the enjoyment by other States Parties of their rights or the performance of their obligations under this Convention.

4. States Parties intending to conclude an agreement referred to in paragraph 3 shall notify the other States Parties through the depositary of this Convention of their intention to conclude the agreement and of the modification or suspension for which it provides.

5. This article does not affect international agreements expressly permitted or preserved by other articles of this Convention.

6. States Parties agree that there shall be no amendments to the basic principle relating to the common heritage of mankind set forth in article 136 and that they shall not be party to any agreement in derogation thereof.

Article 312. Amendment

1. After the expiry of a period of 10 years from the date of entry into force of this Convention, a State Party may, by written communication addressed to the Secretary-General of the United Nations, propose specific amendments to this Convention, other than those relating to activities in the Area, and request the convening of a conference to consider such proposed amendments. The Secretary-General shall circulate such communication to all States Parties. If, within 12 months from the date of the circulation of the communication, not less than one-half of the States Parties reply favorably to the request, the Secretary-General shall convene the conference.

2. The decision-making procedure applicable at the amendment conference shall be the same as that applicable at the Third United Nations Conference on the Law of the Sea unless otherwise decided by the conference. The conference should make every effort to reach agreement on any amendments by way of consensus and there should be no voting on them until all efforts at consensus have been exhausted.

Article 313. Amendment by simplified procedure

1. A State Party may, by written communication addressed to the Secretary-General of the United Nations, propose an amendment to this Convention, other than an amendment relating to activities in the Area, to be adopted by the simplified procedure set forth in this article without convening a conference. The Secretary-General shall circulate the communication to all States Parties.

2. If, within a period of 12 months from the date of the circulation of the communication, a State Party objects to the proposed amendment or to the proposal for its adoption by the simplified procedure, the amendment shall be considered rejected. The Secretary-General shall immediately notify all States Parties accordingly.

3. If, 12 months from the date of the circulation of the communication, no State Party has objected to the proposed amendment or to the proposal for its adoption by the simplified procedure, the proposed amendment shall be considered adopted. The Secretary-General shall notify all States Parties that the proposed amendment has been adopted.

Article 314. Amendments to the provisions of this Convention relating exclusively to activities in the Area

1. A State Party may, by written communication addressed to the Secretary-General of the Authority, propose an amendment to the provisions of this Convention relating exclusively to activities in the Area, including Annex VI, section 4. The Secretary-General shall circulate such communication to all States Parties. The proposed amendment shall be subject to approval by the Assembly

following its approval by the Council. Representatives of States Parties in those organs shall have full powers to consider and approve the proposed amendment. The proposed amendment as approved by the Council and the Assembly shall be considered adopted.

2. Before approving any amendment under paragraph 1, the Council and the Assembly shall ensure that it does not prejudice the system of exploration for and exploitation of the resources of the Area, pending the Review Conference in accordance with article 155.

Article 315. Signature, ratification of, accession to and authentic texts of amendments

1. Once adopted, amendments to this Convention shall be open for signature by States Parties for 12 months from the date of adoption, at United Nations Headquarters in New York, unless otherwise provided in the amendment itself.

2. Articles 306, 307 and 320 apply to all amendments to this Convention.

Article 316. Entry into force of amendments

1. Amendments to this Convention, other than those referred to in paragraph 5, shall enter into force for the States Parties ratifying or acceding to them on the thirtieth day following the deposit of instruments of ratification or accession by two-thirds of the States Parties or by 60 States Parties, whichever is greater. Such amendments shall not affect the enjoyment by other States Parties of their rights or the performance of their obligations under this Convention.

2. An amendment may provide that a larger number of ratifications or accessions shall be required for its entry into force than are required by this article.

3. For each State Party ratifying or acceding to an amendment referred to in paragraph 1 after the deposit of the required number of instruments of ratification or accession, the amendment shall enter into force on the thirtieth day following the deposit of its instrument of ratification or accession.

4. A State which becomes a Party to this Convention after the entry into force of an amendment in accordance with paragraph 1 shall, failing an expression of a different intention by that State:
   (a) be considered as a Party to this Convention as so amended; and
   (b) be considered as a Party to the unamended Convention in relation to any State Party not bound by the amendment.

5. Any amendment relating exclusively to activities in the Area and any amendment to Annex VI shall enter into force for all States Parties one year following the deposit of instruments of ratification or accession by three-fourths of the States Parties.

6. A State which becomes a Party to this Convention after the entry into force of amendments in accordance with paragraph 5 shall be considered as a Party to this Convention as so amended.

Article 317. Denunciation

1. A State Party may, by written notification addressed to the Secretary-General of the United Nations, denounce this Convention and may indicate its reasons. Failure to indicate reasons shall not affect the validity of the denunciation. The denunciation shall take effect one year after the date of receipt of the notification, unless the notification specifies a later date.

2. A State shall not be discharged by reason of the denunciation from the financial and contractual obligations which accrued while it was a Party to this Convention, nor shall the denunciation affect any right, obligation, or legal situation of that State created through the execution of this Convention prior to its termination for that State.

3. The denunciation shall not in any way affect the duty of any State Party to fulfill any obligation embodied in this Convention to which it would be subject under international law independently of this Convention.

Article 318. Status of Annexes

The Annexes form an integral part of this Convention and, unless expressly provided otherwise, a reference to this Convention or to one of its Parts includes a reference to the Annexes relating thereto.

Article 319. Depositary

1. The Secretary-General of the United Nations shall be the depositary of this Convention and amendments thereto.

2. In addition to his functions as depositary, the Secretary-General shall:
   (a) report to all States Parties, the Authority, and competent international organizations on issues of a general nature that have arisen with respect to this Convention;
   (b) notify the Authority of ratifications and formal confirmations of and accessions to this Convention and amendments thereto, as well as of denunciations of this Convention;
   (c) notify States Parties of agreements in accordance with article 311, paragraph 4;
   (d) circulate amendments adopted in accordance with this Convention to States Parties for ratification or accession;
   (e) convene necessary meetings of States Parties in accordance with this Convention.

3. (a) The Secretary-General shall also transmit to the observers referred to in article 156:
   (i) reports referred to in paragraph 2(a);
   (ii) notifications referred to in paragraph 2(b) and (c); and
   (iii) texts of amendments referred to in paragraph 2(d), for their information.
   (b) The Secretary-General shall also invite those observers to participate as observers at meetings of States Parties referred to in paragraph 2(e).

Article 320. Authentic texts

The original of this Convention, of which the Arabic, Chinese, English, French, Russian and Spanish texts are equally authentic, shall, subject to article 305, paragraph 2, be deposited with the Secretary-General of the United Nations.

IN WITNESS WHEREOF, the undersigned Plenipotentiaries, being duly authorized thereto, have signed this Convention.

DONE AT MONTEGO BAY, this tenth day of December, one thousand nine hundred and eighty-two.

Note: the Convention entered into force 16 November 1994.

United States Senate Committee on Foreign Relations Draft Declarations, Understandings, and Conditions, 2007

The Senate Committee of Foreign Relations held hearings on the question whether the United States should accede to the 1982 UN Convention on the Law of the Sea and the 1994 Part XI Implementation Agreement in 2004, 2007, and 2012. In 2004 and 2007 the committee recommended accession, subject to a number of proposed understandings and declarations (the accession question was not brought to a committee vote in 2012). See S. Exec. Rpt. 108-10 (Mar. 11, 2004) and S. Exec. Rpt. 110-09 (Dec. 18, 2007). The following draft declarations and understandings, taken from the 2007 committee report, should be read in conjunction with statements by President Clinton and Secretary of State Warren Christopher in the letters and Department of State Commentary transmitting the Convention to the Senate for advice and consent. See S. Treaty Doc. 103-39, at iii–xi and pp. 1–97.

SECTION 1. SENATE ADVICE AND CONSENT SUBJECT TO DECLARATIONS AND UNDERSTANDINGS

The Senate advises and consents to the accession to the United Nations Convention on the Law of the Sea, with annexes, adopted on December 10, 1982 (hereafter in this resolution referred to as the "Convention"), and to the ratification of the Agreement Relating to the Implementation of Part XI of the United Nations Convention on the Law of the Sea, with annex, adopted on July 28, 1994 (hereafter in this resolution referred to as the "Agreement") (T. Doc. 103-39), subject to the declarations of section 2, to be made under articles 287 and 298 of the Convention, the declarations and understandings of section 3, to be made under article 310 of the Convention, and the conditions of section 4.

SECTION 2. DECLARATIONS UNDER ARTICLES 287 AND 298

The advice and consent of the Senate under section 1 is subject to the following declarations:
1. The Government of the United States of America declares, in accordance with article 287(1), that it chooses the following means for the settlement of disputes concerning the interpretation or application of the Convention:
   A. a special arbitral tribunal constituted in accordance with Annex VIII for the settlement of disputes concerning the interpretation or application of the articles of the Convention relating to (1) fisheries, (2) protection and preservation of the marine environment, (3) marine scientific research, and (4) navigation, including pollution from vessels and by dumping; and
   B. an arbitral tribunal constituted in accordance with Annex VII for the settlement of disputes not covered by the declaration in subparagraph (A).
2. The Government of the United States of America declares, in accordance with article 298(1), that it does not accept any of the procedures provided for in section 2 of Part XV (including, inter alia, the Seabed Disputes Chamber procedure referred to in article 287(2)) with respect to the categories of disputes set forth in subparagraphs (a), (b), and (c) of article 298(1). The United States further declares that its consent to accession to the Convention is conditioned upon the understanding that, under article 298(1)(b), each State Party has the exclusive right to determine whether its activities are or were "military activities" and that such determinations are not subject to review.

SECTION 3. OTHER DECLARATIONS AND UNDERSTANDINGS UNDER ARTICLE 310

The advice and consent of the Senate under section 1 is subject to the following declarations and understandings:

1. The United States understands that nothing in the Convention, including any provisions referring to "peaceful uses" or "peaceful purposes," impairs the inherent right of individual or collective self-defense or rights during armed conflict.

2. The United States understands, with respect to the right of innocent passage under the Convention, that—

   A. all ships, including warships, regardless of, for example, cargo, armament, means of propulsion, flag, origin, destination, or purpose, enjoy the right of innocent passage;

   B. article 19(2) contains an exhaustive list of activities that render passage non-innocent;

   C. any determination of non-innocence of passage by a ship must be made on the basis of acts it commits while in the territorial sea, and not on the basis of, for example, cargo, armament, means of propulsion, flag, origin, destination, or purpose; and

   D. the Convention does not authorize a coastal State to condition the exercise of the right of innocent passage by any ships, including warships, on the giving of prior notification to or the receipt of prior permission from the coastal State.

3. The United States understands, concerning Parts III and IV of the Convention, that—

   A. all ships and aircraft, including warships and military aircraft, regardless of, for example, cargo, armament, means of propulsion, flag, origin, destination, or purpose, are entitled to transit passage and archipelagic sea lanes passage in their "normal mode";

   B. "normal mode" includes, inter alia—

      i. submerged transit of submarines;

      ii. overflight by military aircraft, including in military formation;

      iii. activities necessary for the security of surface warships, such as formation steaming and other force protection measures;

      iv. underway replenishment; and

      v. the launching and recovery of aircraft;

   C. the words "strait" and "straits" are not limited by geographic names or categories and include all waters not subject to Part IV that separate one part of the high seas or exclusive economic zone from another part of the high seas or exclusive economic zone or other areas referred to in article 45;

   D. the term "used for international navigation" includes all straits capable of being used for international navigation; and

   E. the right of archipelagic sea lanes passage is not dependent upon the designation by archipelagic States of specific sea lanes and/or air routes and, in the absence of such designation or if there has been only a partial designation, may be exercised through all routes normally used for international navigation.

4. The United States understands, with respect to the exclusive economic zone, that—

   A. all States enjoy high seas freedoms of navigation and overflight and all other internationally lawful uses of the sea related to these freedoms, including, inter alia, military activities, such as anchoring, launching, and landing of aircraft and other military devices, launching and recovering water-borne craft, operating military devices, intelligence collection, surveillance and reconnaissance activities, exercises, operations, and conducting military surveys; and

   B. coastal State actions pertaining to these freedoms and uses must be in accordance with the Convention.

5. The United States understands that "marine scientific research" does not include, inter alia—

   A. prospecting and exploration of natural resources;

B. hydrographic surveys;

C. military activities, including military surveys;

D. environmental monitoring and assessment pursuant to section 4 of Part XII; or

E. activities related to submerged wrecks or objects of an archaeological and historical nature.

6. The United States understands that any declaration or statement purporting to limit navigation, overflight, or other rights and freedoms of all States in ways not permitted by the Convention contravenes the Convention. Lack of a response by the United States to a particular declaration or statement made under the Convention shall not be interpreted as tacit acceptance by the United States of that declaration or statement.

7. The United States understands that nothing in the Convention limits the ability of a State to prohibit or restrict imports of goods into its territory in order to, inter alia, promote or require compliance with environmental and conservation laws, norms, and objectives.

8. The United States understands that articles 220, 228, and 230 apply only to pollution from vessels (as referred to in article 211) and not, for example, to pollution from dumping.

9. The United States understands, with respect to articles 220 and 226, that the "clear grounds" requirement set forth in those articles is equivalent to the "reasonable suspicion" standard under United States law.

10. The United States understands, with respect to article 228(2), that—

A. the "proceedings" referred to in that paragraph are the same as those referred to in article 228(1), namely those proceedings in respect of any violation of applicable laws and regulations or international rules and standards relating to the prevention, reduction and control of pollution from vessels committed by a foreign vessel beyond the territorial sea of the State instituting proceedings; and

B. fraudulent concealment from an officer of the United States of information concerning such pollution would extend the three-year period in which such proceedings may be instituted.

11. The United States understands, with respect to article 230, that—

A. it applies only to natural persons aboard the foreign vessels at the time of the act of pollution;

B. the references to "monetary penalties only" exclude only imprisonment and corporal punishment;

C. the requirement that an act of pollution be "willful" in order to impose non-monetary penalties would not constrain the imposition of such penalties for pollution caused by gross negligence;

D. in determining what constitutes a "serious" act of pollution, a State may consider, as appropriate, the cumulative or aggregate impact on the marine environment of repeated acts of pollution over time; and

E. among the factors relevant to the determination whether an act of pollution is "serious," a significant factor is non-compliance with a generally accepted international rule or standard.

12. The United States understands that sections 6 and 7 of Part XII do not limit the authority of a State to impose penalties, monetary or non-monetary, for, inter alia—

A. non-pollution offenses, such as false statements, obstruction of justice, and obstruction of government or judicial proceedings, wherever they occur; or

B. any violation of national laws and regulations or applicable international rules and standards for the prevention, reduction, and control of pollution of the marine environment that occurs while a foreign vessel is in any of its ports, rivers, harbors, or offshore terminals.

13. The United States understands that the Convention recognizes and does not constrain the longstanding sovereign right of a State to impose and enforce conditions for the entry of foreign vessels into its ports, rivers, harbors, or offshore terminals, such as a requirement that ships exchange ballast water beyond 200 nautical miles from shore or a requirement that tank vessels carrying oil be constructed with double hulls.

14. The United States understands, with respect to article 21(2), that measures applying to the "design, construction, equipment or manning" do not include, inter alia, measures such as traffic separation schemes, ship routing measures, speed limits, quantitative restrictions on discharge of substances, restrictions on the discharge and/or uptake of ballast water, reporting requirements, and record-keeping requirements.

15. The United States understands that the Convention supports a coastal State's exercise of its domestic authority to regulate discharges into the marine environment resulting from industrial operations on board a foreign vessel.

16. The United States understands that the Convention supports a coastal State's exercise of its domestic authority to regulate the introduction into the marine environment of alien or new species.

17. The United States understands that, with respect to articles 61 and 62, a coastal State has the exclusive right to determine the allowable catch of the living resources in its exclusive economic zone, whether it has the capacity to harvest the entire allowable catch, whether any surplus exists for allocation to other States, and to establish the terms and conditions under which access may be granted. The United States further understands that such determinations are, by virtue of article 297(3)(a), not subject to binding dispute resolution under the Convention.

18. The United States understands that article 65 of the Convention lent direct support to the establishment of the moratorium on commercial whaling, supports the creation of sanctuaries and other conservation measures, and requires States to cooperate not only with respect to large whales, but with respect to all cetaceans.

19. The United States understands that, with respect to article 33, the term "sanitary laws and regulations" includes laws and regulations to protect human health from, inter alia, pathogens being introduced into the territorial sea.

20. The United States understands that decisions of the Council pursuant to procedures other than those set forth in article 161(8)(d) will involve administrative, institutional, or procedural matters and will not result in substantive obligations on the United States.

21. The United States understands that decisions of the Assembly under article 160(2)(e) to assess the contributions of members are to be taken pursuant to section 3(7) of the Annex to the Agreement and that the United States will, pursuant to section 9(3) of the Annex to the Agreement, be guaranteed a seat on the Finance Committee established by section 9(1) of the Annex to the Agreement, so long as the Authority supports itself through assessed contributions.

22. The United States declares, pursuant to article 39 of Annex VI, that decisions of the Seabed Disputes Chamber shall be enforceable in the territory of the United States only in accordance with procedures established by implementing legislation and that such decisions shall be subject to such legal and factual review as is constitutionally required and without precedential effect in any court of the United States.

23. The United States—
    A. understands that article 161(8)(f) applies to the Council's approval of amendments to section 4 of Annex VI;
    B. declares that, under that article, it intends to accept only a procedure that requires consensus for the adoption of amendments to section 4 of Annex VI; and
    C. in the case of an amendment to section 4 of Annex VI that is adopted contrary to this understanding, that is, by a procedure other than consensus, will consider itself bound by such an amendment only if it subsequently ratifies such amendment pursuant to the advice and consent of the Senate.

24. The United States declares that, with the exception of articles 177–183, article 13 of Annex IV, and article 10 of Annex VI, the provisions of the Convention and the Agreement, including amendments thereto and rules, regulations, and procedures thereunder, are not self-executing.

SECTION 4. CONDITIONS

a. IN GENERAL.—The advice and consent of the Senate under section 1 is subject to the following conditions:

1. Not later than 15 days after the receipt by the Secretary of State of a written communication from the Secretary-General of the United Nations or the Secretary-General of the Authority transmitting a proposal to amend the Convention pursuant to article 312, 313, or 314, the President shall submit to the Committee on Foreign Relations of the Senate a copy of the proposed amendment.

2. Prior to the convening of a Conference to consider amendments to the Convention proposed to be adopted pursuant to article 312 of the Convention, the President shall consult with the Committee on Foreign Relations of the Senate on the amendments to be considered at the Conference. The President shall also consult with the Committee on Foreign Relations of the Senate on any amendment proposed to be adopted pursuant to article 313 of the Convention.

3. Not later than 15 days prior to any meeting—
   A. of the Council of the International Seabed Authority to consider an amendment to the Convention proposed to be adopted pursuant to article 314 of the Convention; or
   B. of any other body under the Convention to consider an amendment that would enter into force pursuant to article 316(5) of the Convention; the President shall consult with the Committee on Foreign Relations of the Senate on the amendment and on whether the United States should object to its adoption.

4. All amendments to the Convention, other than amendments under article 316(5) of a technical or administrative nature, shall be submitted by the President to the Senate for its advice and consent.

5. The United States declares that it shall take all necessary steps under the Convention to ensure that amendments under article 316(5) are adopted in conformity with the treaty clause in Article II, section 2 of the United States Constitution.

b. INCLUSION OF CERTAIN CONDITIONS IN INSTRUMENT OF RATIFICATION.—Conditions 4 and 5 shall be included in the United States instrument of ratification to the Convention.

Index

acronyms, ix–xiii
adjudication, 352–54
admiralty law (private maritime law), 17, 38
African piracy and counterpiracy operations, xvi, 288–89n116, 288–90, 293
aggression and nonaggression norm, 5, 5n16, 311–12
air defense identification zone (ADIZ), 122
air pollution, xvi, 208, 209
aircraft: assistance entry, 107; distress claims and refuge, 84–85; drug transport with, 267; flight information regions (FIRs), 123; innocent passage right, 112, 122; nationality concept, 17; status of, 199–201; transit passage right, 112n78
airspace: air navigation over coastal waters, 121–23; distress claims and refuge, 84–85; freedom of overflight, 42, 78, 101, 128, 154–55, 423; legal boundaries, 49; Open Skies Treaty (OST), 123; outerspace, beginning of, 122, 122n142; over internal waters, 81
Alaska, United States v., 74–75
alien species, 436
aliens, 17
Anglo-Norwegian Fisheries case, 44, 64, 66
Antarctica, 219–20, 222–23
Antelope (Spain), 9–10
arbitration, 10, 351–52, 351n19, 362–63
archaeological and historical objects, 121, 459
archipelagic waters and states: baseline determination, 73, 73n55, 75–76, 118, 410–11; definition of, 75, 75n75, 118, 410; innocent passage, 76, 118–19, 412; internal waters and, 80, 80n2; LOS Convention provisions, 410–13; navigation in, 118–19; rights and obligations in, 101; sea lanes and traffic separation schemes, 118–19, 412–13
Arctic Ocean: climate change and access to, xvi; environmental protection for, 219–22; navigation of, 40; resource exploitation in, xvi; shipping in, 117, 117n105
Area: boundaries of, 140; definition of, 139, 149; LOS Convention provisions, 432–35; pollution from activities in, 439; resources in, 140, 149
assistance, duty to render, 168, 242, 425
Austin, John, 7
Australia, 125, 137n101

ballast water, 41, 208, 209
baselines: definition and concept of, 64; determination of, 51, 64, 66; excessive maritime claims, 78–79; legal boundaries and, 49; legal tests for establishing, 66–75, 66n7; LOS Convention provisions, 402–4; normal method for establishing, 66–71, 402; publicizing claims, 67n15, 75, 75n72, 76, 404; sources of controversies, 65–66; straight method for establishing, 66, 71–73, 402
bays: baseline determination, 65, 65n2, 403; historic, 65, 65n2, 73–75, 74–75n69, 74n60; juridical, 65, 68–69, 68n23
belligerent right to visit, 285, 302, 308–9, 309n255, 309n257
Bentham, Jeremy, 3, 3n8
Blackstone, William, 3n8
blockades, 274, 285–86, 285n89, 303–5, 303n212, 304n218, 305n226, 307n242
boarding agreements, bilateral and multilateral, 228–29, 257–59, 322–23
Bretton Woods Conference, 4
Brittin, Burdick H., xv, 1
broadcasting from high sea, unauthorized, 31–32, 161, 166, 166n90, 228, 228n5, 261

cables and pipelines, 128, 145, 148, 171–72, 171n125, 411–12, 413, 428–29, 456
canals: laws and treaties governing use, 87–88, 87nn49–50; opening of to trade, 4; trade and shipping through, 40
cannon-shot territorial sea claims, 43, 43n11
chapeau, 104–5, 105n21
charts: baseline claims, 67, 67n15, 75, 75n72; large-scale, 67, 67n15
China: counterpiracy operations, xvi; East China Sea Air Defense Identification Zone, 122n148; naval and paranaval fleet buildup, xv; paranavy vessels, 178, 178n23–24; South China Sea sovereignty claims, 51; UN Security Council role, 14–15
Clausewitz, Carl, 7n32
climate change, xvi, 50
Coast Guard, U.S.: captain of the port (COTP), authority of, 86; law enforcement authority, 229–32, 273–74, 283n77, 285n85, 329–32; migrant interdiction and enforcement, 245; missions of, 230n15; Port State Control

Initiative, 99n122; security, safety, and steward-ship commitment, 227, 230n15

Cold War, xv, 5, 15, 85

collisions: collisions and casualties, investigation of, 170–71; COLREGS Convention, 108, 108n40; prevention regulations, 3–4

Combined Maritime Forces (CMF), 289–90, 289n119

comity, 20–21, 20n104

Commander's Handbook on the Law of Naval Operations, 63, 272, 300n195

Commission on the Limits of the Continental Shelf (CLCS), 52–53

communities, sea-based, 40–41, 41nn4–6

competent international organization (CIO), 13–14

compulsory jurisdiction, 341, 351, 353, 353n26, 353n31

Congress, U.S.: legislative powers of, 13n62; Senate advice and consent on LOS Convention, 56–57, 56n62; Senate Committee on Foreign Relations draft declarations, 56, 274, 465–69; treaty and agreements negotiation and ratification process, 25–26, 26n138

Constitution, 6

Constitution, U.S., necessary and proper clause, 13, 13n62

constructive presence doctrine, 263, 266–67

contiguous zone: boundaries and breadth of, 49, 55, 121, 121n139; definition of, 119nn127–128; rights and obligations in, 101, 119–21; rules applicable to, 407–8

continental shelf: artificial islands and offshore structures and installations, 144, 144nn33–34, 422; boundaries and boundary delimitation, 49, 77–78, 140, 141–43, 141n11, 142n12, 422–23; claims to, 46, 140; convention on, 45, 46, 57n67, 140–41; EEZ regime and, 137–38, 141–42, 145–46; environment protection and preservation, 143; legal regime and definition, 46, 139, 140, 141–43; LOS Convention provisions, 420–23; marine resources management, 143–44, 225; rights and obligations in, 141–45; safety zone regulations, 144, 144–45n38; scientific research in, 131–35, 143–44; US continental shelf, 137–38, 146–47

Continental Shelf cases: Libya v. Malta, 20, 60; North Sea case, 21, 60, 129

contraband, 307–8, 323–24, 323n97

Convention for the Suppression of Unlawful Acts against the Safety of Maritime Navigation (SUA Convention)., 135, 233, 237, 257, 269, 295–96, 300, 328, 365

Convention on Fishing and Conservation of the Living Resources of the High Seas, 44n15, 45, 125, 354

Convention on Search and Rescue, 84n27

Convention on the Continental Shelf, 45, 46, 57n67, 140–41

Convention on the High Seas, 45, 58, 148, 261

Convention on the International Regulations for Preventing Collisions at Sea (COLREGS Convention), 108, 108n40

Convention on the Territorial Sea and Contiguous Zone, 45, 46, 55, 80, 83, 119

conventional international law. *See* treaties (conventional international law)

Corfu Channel case, 44, 80, 103, 108, 108–9n48, 203

corporations: international law and, 17–18; state-owned enterprises (SOEs), 17–18, 17n89; transnational corporations (TNCs), 17, 18

countermeasures (self-help remedies), 340–43, 341n58, 341n60, 343n83

country, use of term, 11n47

courts, international: decisions as basis for rules of international law, 27–28, 27nn144–145; domestic law and, 33–34, 34nn177–179, 34–35nn180–182; hierarchical relationships, 27–28; role and influence of, 10. *See also* International Court of Justice (ICJ)

crime/criminal activity: choice-of-law rules and, 38, 38n204; duty to cooperate in suppression of, 228–29; international crimes, 16, 16n81; maritime crimes, 236–52; transnational criminal activities, 228–29; universality principle, 32, 233–35; vessels engaged in universal crimes, 160–61

customary international law, 58–59; definition and concept of, 19–22; domestic law relationship to, 57–59, 59n76; history of, 43–45; LOS Convention relationship to, 57, 59–61; *opinio juris*, 20–21, 25, 63, 84; persistent objector rule, 10; protection of interests through, 19–22, 60–61; treaties relationship to, 19, 25, 25nn133–134, 60

customs: enforcement of laws and regulations, 42; regulation of in contiguous zone, 119–20, 121n139

Dallas, 9–10

damage and remedies: countermeasures (self-help remedies), 340–43, 341n58, 341n60, 343n83; defenses to responsibility, 339, 346; harassment through frivolous complaints, 360; pollution and environmental damage, responsibilites and liabilities for, 223–24, 446–47; private claims of damage, 335–37; remedies in state responsibility cases, 340, 346–47; responsibilities and liabilities, concepts of, 335; responsibilities and liabilities of states, 337–40, 344–47

dangers in territorial sea, duty of state to warn about, 108, 108–9n48

derogation during armed conflicts, 301–3

disasters and natural hazards, 41

disputes and dispute resolution: adjudication, 352–54; arbitration, 10, 351–52, 351n19, 362–63; binding decisions, 357–60; courts and arbitral tribunals, 362–65; Geneva conventions resolution provisions, 354; harassment through frivolous complaints, 360; international dispute, concept of, 350, 350n13; LOS Convention provisions, 354–65, 453–59; private claims of damage, 348–49; prompt release actions, 361–62; provisional measures, 360–61; resolution methods and means, 2, 348; resolution of disputes between states, 348, 350–54; settlement of, 453–59; treaties that address, 365–66

distress and force majeure: assistance entry, 106–7, 106n29; duty to assist, 168, 242, 425; on the high seas, 168–69, 168n101, 168n104, 169n107; in internal waters, 82–87, 83nn23–25, 84nn27–28, 85n34

domestic law, U.S.: court decisions and, 27, 27n144; customary international law relationship to, 57–59, 59n76; extraterritorial application of, 235–36; international law and, 6–7, 33–38, 367–68; law of nations and, 3n8; piracy statutes, 294, 294n147; self-defense by nonstate actors, 332–34; sources of, 19; territorial sea regime, 111, 111n67, 111n69

drugs and drug smuggling: aircraft use for, 267; counterdrug operations, 227, 231, 271; enforcement of laws related to, 42, 235–36; laws, acts, and treaties related to, 55, 237–41; LOS Convention provisions, 239–40, 426–27; mother ships and contact boats, 266–67; noncompliant vessels, 267–68; stateless vessels, 189, 192–93; suppression of activity, 160–61, 233–35, 237–41; threat from, 236, 237

embargoes, 285–86, 285n89

enclosed/semi-enclosed seas: definition of, 172–73; innocent passage, 73; LOS Convention provisions, 430; rights and obligations in, 172–73

Enduring Freedom, Operation, xvi

England. See Great Britain/United Kingdom

environment, marine: alien species, 436; continental shelf and protection and preservation of, 143; crimes related to, 227, 236, 251–52; EEZ and protection and preservation of, 131, 131n53, 207–8, 210, 220–21, 251; green mandate for protection of, xvi; law of armed conflict and protection of, 224; LOS Convention provisions, 49n34, 435–47; polar regions

and ice-covered areas, 219–23, 446; protection and preservation of, 41–42, 50–51, 228; protests to protect, 155, 155nn25–26; public vessels and protection of, 223; responsibilities and liabilities, 446–47; responsibilities and liabilities for damage to, 223–24; state obligations to protect, 205–19; stress on US coastline and coastal waters, 41–42; treaties that protect, 236–37; vulnerable ecosystems, protection for, 219. See also pollution

environmental law, 202

excessive maritime claims, 78

exclusion zones and military activities, 281–82, 281n65

exclusive economic zone (EEZ): archipelagic state baseline claims, 76; artificial islands and offshore structures and installations, 126, 135–36, 135–36nn83–85, 414; boundaries and breadth of, 49, 55, 60, 125–26, 137–38, 145; boundary delimitation, 77–78; continental shelf regime and, 137–38, 141–42, 145–46; economic benefits of, 125; enforcement of laws and regulations, 419; environment protection and preservation, 131, 131n53, 207–8, 210, 220–21, 251; geographically disadvantaged states, 418–19; historical development of, 124–25, 124n2; islands and claims to, 70–71, 70–71n40, 71nn42–43; land-locked states, rights of, 417–18; living marine resources management, 129–31, 130n36, 130n39, 225, 415–16; LOS Convention provisions, 413–20; military activities in, 136–37, 136n93, 138, 276–77; rights, duties, and jurisdiction in, 126–29, 127n16, 127–128nn20–22, 128n24; rights and obligations in, 101; scientific research in, 131–35, 132n56, 133n63, 133nn66–67, 134n70, 134nn73–74, 138, 138nn104–105, 277; US EEZ, 137–38

extradition agreements and procedures, 4

fishing operations: decline and collapse of fisheries, xvi, 47, 203, 225n185, 252–53; disputes related to, 357–58, 359–60; drift-net activity, 236–37, 252; EEZ rights and regulations, 129–31, 130n39; harvest levels, 41; illegal, unregulated, and unreported (IUU) fishing, 236–37; protests against, 155, 155nn25–26; regulations and acts to control, 44n15, 47, 47nn24–25, 51, 51n38; sustainability of, 41, 225–26, 251–52

flight information regions (FIRs), 123

Food and Agriculture Organization (FAO), 30, 53–54, 225–26, 225n185, 228, 252

force, threat or use of: armed force at sea, 310–21; hot pursuit and, 265; international law sources, 322–23; law enforcement use of force, 310,

321–32, 327n115; law of armed conflict, 224, 318–19; nonaggression norm, 5, 5n16, 311–12; opposition to, 17; rules governing, 2; rules of engagement, 319–21; Security Council authorization for use of force, 316–18; self-defense, right of, 285, 312–17, 319n67, 321n77, 322, 331–32; self-defense by nonstate actors, 310, 332–34; sovereignty and protection from, 5; UN guidance documents, 328–29, 334

France: collision-prevention regulations, early, 3–4; EEZ rights, 125; international law contributions from, 3; UN Security Council role, 14

friendship, commerce, and navigation (FCN) treaties, 82, 84, 91, 96, 97, 99

Geneva conventions, 44–45, 354

geographically disadvantaged states. See landlocked and geographically disadvantaged states (LLGDS)

Germany, 3, 15

Girrier, Robert, 1

global governance, 12n56

glossary, 369–85

Great Britain/United Kingdom: collision-prevention regulations, early, 3–4; international law contributions from, 3; UN Security Council role, 14

Greece, international law contributions from, 3

greenhouse gas emissions, xvi, 208, 209

Greenpeace, 18, 18n92, 155

Greenwich meridian, adoption as global reference, 4

Grotius (de Groot), Hugo, 3, 40, 43, 43n9, 272, 288

Hamilton, Alexander, 229–30, 306n234

heave-to law and noncompliant vessels, 267–68

high seas: assistance to distressed persons, vessels, and aircraft, 168–69, 168n101, 168n104, 169n107; boundaries of, 49; collisions and casualties, investigation of, 170–71; conservation zones, 44, 44n15; definition of, 119n127, 151–52; flag state obligations, 155–59, 159n56; jurisdiction and control over vessels, 160–68, 161n63; living marine resources management, 172, 225, 228, 429–30; LOS Convention provisions, 423–30; principles of laws that govern, 151, 151n2, 152–55; protests on, 155, 155nn25–26; rights and obligations in, 101; search-and-rescue activities, 169–70; submarine cables and pipelines, 171–72, 171n125

High Seas Fishing Convention, 46

high-level principles, 21–22

historical and archaeological objects, 121, 459

Holland, 43, 43nn9–10

Homeland Security, U.S. Department of, xv–xvi, 283

hot pursuit, right of, 127, 161, 263–66, 264nn247–248, 265nn250–252, 427–28

hovering vessels, 44, 104n19, 119, 121, 121n141, 260

Huber, Max, 5

human rights and human rights law, 17, 268–70

human trafficking. See slavery, slave trading, and human trafficking

humanitarian intervention, 317–18, 317n50

ice-covered areas and polar regions, 219–23, 446

I'm Alone incident, 323–24, 323n97, 324n99, 329

India, xvi, 15

Indian Ocean, counterpiracy operations in, xvi

individuals: citizenship and nationality concept, 15–16, 16n74, 16nn78–80; self-determination right, 17; as subject of international law, 15–17

innocent passage: aircraft and, 112; archipelagic waters, 76, 118–19, 412; definition and concept of, 404–5; enclosed/semi-enclosed seas, 73; environment protection and preservation and, 210; internal waters, 81, 83, 84, 86, 95, 402; straits, 44, 47, 112, 112n78, 114n85, 410; submarines, 22, 47, 112, 405; suspension of right, 23–24, 47, 112, 114n85, 406; territorial sea, 47, 102–6, 104n19, 105–6nn23–24, 105n27, 109–10, 109–10nn59–61, 404–7, 440; warships, 47, 110, 110n61

Institute of International Law, 44

intelligence activities, 274–77, 276n30, 276n33

interest-based theories, 5–6, 6nn19–20

interference and noninterference norm, 5, 5n16

internal waters, 80–87; coastal state laws, 81–82, 81n12; distress and force majeure claims, 82–87, 83nn23–25, 84nn27–28, 85n34; foreign vessels in, 80–81; innocent passage, 81, 83, 84, 86, 95, 402; navigation and overflight in, 81

International Civil Aviation Organization (ICAO), 30, 123

International Commission for Northwest Atlantic Fisheries (ICNAF), 47, 47n24

International Convention for the Prevention of Pollution of the Sea (MARPOL Convention), 98, 99, 131, 175, 185, 197, 203–4, 208–10, 219, 221, 251n164, 252, 365

International Court of Justice (ICJ): adjudication, 352–54; consent to jurisdiction of, 10, 10n46; decisions as basis for rules of international law, 27–28, 27nn144–145, 44; jurisdiction of, 352–54; rulings by, 9; statute of, 19, 19n94; subjects of international law, 13

International Covenant on Civil and Political Rights (ICCPR), 16, 245, 269, 269n281, 323

International Covenant on Economic, Social, and Cultural Rights (ICESCR), 16, 16n84
international law: adoption of by states, 7; application of, 61, 367–68; attitudes toward and opinions about, 7–8, 7n32, 8nn34–35; compliance with, requirement for, 1; definition and scope of, 2, 4, 61; disregard for, consequences of, 1; domestic law and, 6–7, 33–38, 367–68; historical background, 2–4; importance of knowledge of, 1, 367–68; international relations relationship to, 4; interstate and intrastate relations and, 5n12; limitations of, 4; norms compared to laws, 18–19; organizations created to enhance, 4; peace-war approach to, 272, 283; reciprocity and, 7; sources of, 18–30, 19n95, 44, 61, 62–63, 367–68; study of, 2; subjects and objects of, 10–18; theories related to, 4–5, 5n12, 6–10, 8–9nn39–40; validity of, 2; violations of, obligation to report, 1. *See also* customary international law; treaties (conventional international law)
International Law Association, 44
International Law Commission (ILC), xv, 44–45, 163–64
International Maritime Organization (IMO)/ Inter-governmental Maritime Consultative Organization (IMCO): counterpiracy recommendations, 288; establishment of, 53, 53n45; Greenpeace status in, 18; mission and purpose of, 14, 53; place of refuge, establishment of, 87, 87n42; sea lane and traffic separation scheme recommendations, 108, 108n45; standards, directives, and guidelines from, 30, 53, 228; WMD counterproliferation measures, 300
international relations: international law relationship to, 4; organizations created to enhance, 4; principles of, 5; sovereignty of states and, 5; theories related to, 4–6
International Seabed Authority (ISA), 52, 150, 150n82
International Tribunal for the Law of the Sea (ITLOS), 10, 10n46, 52, 363–65, 363n93
Iranian nuclear weapons program, xv, 287, 297, 298, 299n181
Iraq: invasion of Kuwait by, 15; offshore oil structures, destruction of, 224; Operation Iraqi Freedom, xvi; Security Council resolutions against, 286; Strait of Hormuz sovereignty claims, 51; terrorism operations, 194
islands: artificial, 71; artificial in EEZ, 126, 135–36, 135–36nn84–85, 414; artificial islands in EEZ, 126, 135–36, 135–36nn83–85, 414; artificial on continental shelf, 144, 144nn33–34, 422; baseline controversies, 65–66; baseline determination, 70–71, 70–71n40, 71nn42–43,

72–73; definition of, 70, 70n33, 430; LOS Convention provisions, 430
Italy, international law contributions from, 3

Japan: counterpiracy operations, xvi; SOFA between US and, 91–92, 92n80; transit passage right in island channels, 113n81
Jessup, Philip, 4, 4n10, 6
Jones, John Paul, 1, 367
Judge Advocate General, Navy: International Law Division, xv; sources of international law evidence, 63
judge advocate, staff: access to and legal advice from, 1–2, 368; international law questions and evidence, 61–63
jurisdiction: analysis and determination of, 33; bases of, 31–32, 31nn168–169, 32nn171–175; boundaries of, 49; civil jurisdiction in relation to foreign ship, 407; compulsory jurisdiction, 341, 351, 353, 353n26, 353n31; creeping jurisdictions, 51; criminal jurisdiction on board foreign ship, 406–7; definition and concept of, 30–31, 30n160, 30n162, 31n164–165; effects of treaties on, 32–33, 32n175; enforcement jurisdiction, 2, 232–33, 252–60; ICJ jurisdiction, 352–54; prescriptive jurisdiction, 2, 232–36; territorial jurisdiction, 233; universal jurisdiction, 32, 233–35, 292

Kennan, George, 8
Kissing, Henry, 8n34
Koh, Harold, 6
Kosovo, 9, 9n42
Kuwait, 15

landlocked and geographically disadvantaged states (LLGDS): continental shelf claim limits, 46; EEZ rights, 417–18; LOS Convention provisions, 430–31; right of access of, 92, 430–31
law: advice about, 1–2, 368; basis and sources for, 368; general principles of, 26, 26n142; norms compared to laws, 18–19
law enforcement/maritime law enforcement (MLE), 227; authority for, 229–32; boarding agreements, bilateral and multilateral, 228–29, 257–59, 322–23; Coast Guard role in, 227, 229–32, 230n15, 283n77, 285n85, 329–32; constructive presence doctrine, 263, 266–67; definition and concept of, 227, 227n2; extradition agreements and procedures, 4; flag state jurisdiction, 253, 254–56; focus of, 2; force used during, 310, 321–32, 327n115; hot pursuit, right of, 127, 161, 263–66, 264nn247–248, 265nn250–252, 427–28; jurisdiction to enforce, 252–60; maritime security through, 271–72,

283; military activities and, 271–72, 273–74, 283; mutual legal assistance treaties (MLATs), 229; Posse Comitatus Act, 231–32, 273–74, 277–78n39, 283; prescriptive jurisdiction, 232–36; pursuit and entry provisions, 260; security, safety, and stewardship protection, 227, 228; ship-rider agreements, 229; tactics, techniques, and procedures publications, 231; US enforcement, 42

law of armed conflict (LOAC)/law of war, 282, 283, 293n144, 303, 311, 318–19, 318n54, 320

law of nations: definition and concept of, 3n8; expansion of, 3–4; usage of term, 11n47. *See also* international law

law of naval warfare: applicability of, 272; basis and sources for, 45, 272, 300–301, 300n195; clarification and revision of, 50; definition and concept of, 39; EEZ rights and duties, 127; military activities, 272; peaceful uses of seas and, 153, 153n9; ships compared to vessels and, 174

law of the sea: adaptation and revision of, 51; application of, 61–63; definition and concept of, 39; excessive maritime claims, 78; history of, 42–51; importance of knowledge of, 39–42; international organizations and, 51–54; ships compared to vessels and, 174; sources of, 44, 50–51, 61, 236–37; spatial approach, 64; zonal approach, 64

League of Nations: creation of, 4; international law, role in development of, 44; role in global relations, 4; structure of, 13, 13n63

legal positivism, 6

legal realism, 6

legitimacy, 6

Libya, 14–15

living marine resources: alien species, 436; conservation and management in EEZ, 129–31, 225; conservation and management of, 251–52, 415–16; conservation and management on high seas, 172, 225, 228, 429–30; marine mammals, xvi, 130, 130n36, 138n104, 208, 217n131, 225, 226, 235n51, 416, 430; sedentary species, 146, 146n52; sustainability of, 225–26

LOS Convention. *See* United Nations Convention on the Law of the Sea (LOS Convention, 1982)

Lotus case, 8–9nn39–40, 20, 44, 60, 157n44, 188

Mahan, Alfred Thayer, 40

Marianna Flora case, 162–63

marine mammals, xvi, 130, 130n36, 138n104, 208, 217n131, 225, 226, 235n51, 416, 430

maritime boundary delimitation, 64, 76–78, 77n94, 77nn88–90, 78n94, 422–23

Maritime Counter-drug and Alien Migrant Interdiction Operations Manual, 231, 231n16, 245

Maritime Drug Law Enforcement Act (MDLEA), 189–90, 192, 193, 198, 241, 257, 258–59, 269

Maritime Interception Operations, 231, 284–85, 308–9, 329–30

maritime interception operations (MIO), 284–87, 285nn83–85

Maritime Law Enforcement Manual, 30n159, 231, 231n16, 245, 285, 320, 329–30

maritime security: Code of Conduct for Private Security Providers, 333–34; counter-x era, 271; EEZ activities, 136–37, 136n93, 138; implementation of measures after September 11th attack, xv–xvi; intelligence activities, 274–77; law enforcement approach to, 271–72, 283; military approach to, 271–72, 282–87, 283n75; operational zones, 279–82, 279nn52–53; US security framework, 42

MARPOL Convention (International Convention for the Prevention of Pollution of the Sea), 98, 99, 131, 175, 185, 197, 203–4, 208–10, 219, 221, 251n164, 252, 365

Marshall, John, 9–10, 57–58

McFadden, Schooner Exchange *v.*, 82, 84, 93

merchant vessels, neutral, 166, 306–7, 306n239, 309

migrants, migrant smuggling, and immigration: assistance to distressed persons, vessels, and aircraft, 168n104, 169, 169n107, 170, 242; enforcement of laws related to, 42, 227, 245; human trafficking and migrant smuggling, 245; irregular immigration, 242, 245, 245–51; laws and treaties related to, 241–42, 246–51; reasons for migration, 242; regular immigration procedures, 242; regulation of in contiguous zone, 119–20

military activities: covert activities, 278; definition and concept of, 272–74; in EEZ, 136–37, 136n93, 138, 276–77; intelligence activities, 274–77, 276n30, 276n33; interception operations, 284–87, 285nn83–85; law enforcement activities and, 271–72, 273–74, 283; maritime operational zones, 274, 279–82; maritime security through, 271–72, 282–87, 283n75; peacetime naval operations, 282–300; special operations, 274, 277–78, 277–78n39; unmanned military vehicles, 278–79

mother ships and contact boats, 323n97

Murray v. Schooner Charming Betsy, 37, 37–38n202, 59, 236, 236n56

mutual legal assistance treaties (MLATs), 229

nation, use of term, 11n47

NATO: counterpiracy operations, xvi; Open Skies Treaty (OST), 123; Yugoslavian operations, 15

natural law, 6, 8–10
natural resources. *See* resources, marine
naval doctrine, 272, 272n5
Naval War College, U.S., international law department, 1, 62–63
navigation: DOD freedom of navigation program, 78–79, 78n99; excessive maritime claims, 78; freedom of navigation, 42, 44, 78, 101, 128–29, 154–55, 423; indelible navigability, 71, 71n44; internal waters, 81
Navy, U.S.: law enforcement activities, 273–74; number of ships in, xv; six-hundred-ship-Navy plan, xv
Navy Regulations, 1, 19
neutrality, 154, 274, 281–82, 285n89, 301, 301n200, 303n211, 305–7, 306n229, 306n234, 306n239, 307n242
Neutrality Act (1794), 5n16
New World Order, 5, 15
Noble Eagle, Operation, xvi
nonaggression norm, 5, 5n16, 311–12
noncompliant vessels, 267–68, 284, 329–32
Nongovernmental Organizations (NGOs), 18, 18n90, 18nn92–93
norms: *erga omnes* obligations, 21; laws compared to, 18–19; peremptory norms, 21, 21n107
North Korea: missile sales by, 287; nuclear weapons program in, xv, 287, 297, 299n181; *Pueblo* incident, 276, 276n31, 321
Northwest Atlantic Fisheries Organization (NAFO), 47n24
Nottebohm's case, 16, 129, 156n34, 180–81
nuclear weapons: counterproliferation operations, 285; Iranian program, xv, 287, 297, 298, 299n181; non-proliferation treaty, 297–98; North Korean program, xv, 287, 297, 299n181. *See also* weapons of mass destruction (WMD)
nuclear-powered ships, 23n123, 47, 89, 94n96, 103, 106, 108, 110, 112, 404–5

oceans and seas: coverage of planet by, 124; free access to all, 4; legal boundaries, 49; ocean enclosure movement, 44; operational zones, 279–82, 279nn52–53; particularly sensitive sea areas (PSSAs), 219, 220–21; peaceful uses of, 47n26, 152–53, 152n7, 153n9, 271, 282, 459
Open Skies Treaty (OST), 123
organizations, international: competent international organization (CIO), 13–14; creation of to enhance international relations and law, 4; documents and instruments as basis for rules of international law, 29–30, 29nn155–156; law of the sea and, 51–54; structure of, 13–14, 13n63; subjects of international law, 12–15

Pakistan, xvi, 297
Paquete Habana decision, 29, 35–36, 36n191, 58–59, 368
particularly sensitive sea areas (PSSAs), 219, 220–21
Peace of Westphalia, 3, 3n9
peaceful uses of seas, 47n26, 152–53, 152n7, 153n9, 271, 282, 459
peacetime law of the sea, 39, 50, 169, 174, 176–77, 177n21, 269, 272, 282, 300–301
Permanent Court of International Justice (PCIJ), 9, 9n42, 352. *See also* International Court of Justice (ICJ)
pipelines and cables, 128, 145, 148, 171–72, 171n125, 411–12, 413, 428–29, 456
piracy: African coast operations, xvi, 288–89n116, 288–90, 293; counterpiracy operations, xvi, 227, 271, 288–94; definition of, 290, 290n123; EEZ rights and duties, 127; history of, 288; Indian Ocean operations, xvi; laws of, development of, 290–92; LOS Convention provisions, 291–92, 426, 427; prevalence of, 288; privateering compared to, 307, 307n242; ransom piracy, 288–89, 288–89n116; Security Council resolutions against, 293; stateless vessels, 188, 191; suppression of activity, 160–61; threat from, 40, 288–89, 292–93; universal jurisdiction, 32, 234, 292; US law statutes, 294, 294n147
polar regions and ice-covered areas, 219–23, 446
pollution: air pollution, xvi, 208, 209; atmospheric sources, 41, 205, 207, 218–19; dumping and discharge of waste, 41, 215–17, 252, 439; greenhouse gas emissions, xvi, 208, 209; land-based sources, 217; laws and regulations to control, development of, 203–5; laws and regulations to control, enforcement of, 441–44; LOS Convention provisions, 436; MARPOL Convention, 98, 99, 131, 175, 185, 197, 203–4, 208–10, 219, 221, 252, 365; MARPOL Convention (International Convention for the Prevention of Pollution of the Sea), 251n164; monitoring risks or effects of, 438–41; prevention and control of, 53, 203–19, 251, 251n164, 252, 436, 437; public vessel responsibilities, 223; responsibilites and liabilities, 223–24, 446–47; safeguards, 444–46; seabed activities as source, 217–18; state obligation to prevent, reduce, and control, 205–19; vessels as source of, 208–15, 439–40, 443
ports: access to by foreign vessels, 88–92, 89nn57–61; baseline accommodations, 69, 403; conditions on entry, 95–97, 95nn103–104, 96n106; crew and passenger requirements, 93, 93n90; definition and concept of, 88; environment protection and preservation, 213–15; laws and treaties governing use, 87–100; quarantine

conditions, 94–95; regulation and control of vessels in, 97–100, 99n120, 99n122, 100n129; status of foreign ships in, 92–95, 93–94nn93–96
Portugal, 43, 43nn9–10
posivist legal theory, 9, 9n40
Posse Comitatus Act, 231–32, 273–74, 277–78n39, 283
postal and mail procedures and agencies, 4
Prestige (Bahamas), 33
privateering, 307, 307n242, 307n244
Proliferation Security Initiative (PSI), 258, 296, 298–300, 299n181, 299n185
publications and writings: basis for rules of international law, 28–29, 28n150, 62–63; *Commander's Handbook on the Law of Naval Operations*, 63, 272, 300n195; *Maritime Counter-drug and Alien Migrant Interdiction Operations Manual*, 231, 231n16, 245; *Maritime Law Enforcement Manual*, 30n159, 231, 231n16, 245, 285, 320, 329–30; military manuals, 30, 30n159, 231
Pueblo incident, 276, 276n31, 321

quarantine conditions, 120n129

ransom piracy, 288–89, 288–89n116
Red Crusader incident, 324–26, 325n104
refugees and asylum seekers, 17, 94, 94n98, 249–51
Regional Seas Programmes, 54
resources, marine: conservation and management of, 225–26; continental shelf rights and regulations, 143–44, 225; crimes related to, 227, 236, 251–52; deep seabed and the Area, 55–56, 143–44, 147–48, 149, 150; exploration and exploitation of, xvi, 40, 46; rights of states, 435; stewardship ethic, 202; sustainability of, 225–26; treaties that protect, 236–37. *See also* living marine resources
Richardson, Elliott, xv
rivers: baselines at mouth of, 68, 403; laws and treaties governing use, 88
roadsteads, 69, 75, 403
Rome and Roman Empire, 3, 3n9, 43, 288
rule of law, respect for, 1, 6
rules of engagement, 319–21
Russia: EEZ rights, 125; naval fleet buildup, xv; UN Security Council role, 14–15

Safety of Life at Sea (SOLAS) Convention, 92, 99, 107, 108, 131, 170, 182, 185, 197, 209, 210, 221
Saiga case, 51, 51n39, 126, 128–29, 326–27, 326n108, 328, 346
salvage operations, 168–69, 168n100
sanitary laws and regulations, 4, 119–20, 120n129, 204, 204n20

Schooner Charming Betsy, *Murray v.*, 37, 37–38n202, 59, 236, 236n56
Schooner Exchange v. McFadden case, 82, 84, 93
scientific research, marine: conduct and promotion of, 448–52; continental shelf rights and regulations, 131–35, 143–44; cooperation in, 448; disputes concerning, 452–53; EEZ rights and regulations, 131–35, 132n56, 133n63, 133nn66–67, 134n70, 134nn73–74, 138, 138nn104–105, 277; installations or equipment, 452; LOS Convention provisions, 49n34, 447–53; responsibilites and liabilities, 452
sea lanes and traffic separation schemes: archipelagic waters, 118–19, 412–13; COLREGS rule on, 108, 108n40; IMO recommendations on, 108, 108n45; straits, 409; territorial sea, 108, 405
Sea Shepherd Conservation Society (SSCS), 155, 155nn25–26
seabed: authority with regulatory powers over, 52, 150, 150n82; beneath territorial sea, 139; deep seabed mining, 55–56; definition and characteristics of, 139, 139n1, 147, 149; drilling and mining activities, 55–56, 143–44, 147–48, 217–18; historical development of, 147–49; legal regime, 139, 148–49; marine resources management, 55–56, 143–44, 147–48, 149, 150; pollution from exploration and exploitation activities, 217–18; US position on deep seabed and resources, 150. *See also* Area
search and rescue: on the high seas, 169–70; phases of, 84n27; territorial sea and assitance entry, 107, 107n33
self-defense, right of, 285, 312–17, 319n67, 321n77, 322, 331–32
self-defense by nonstate actors, 310, 332–34
self-determination right, 17
self-help remedies (countermeasures), 340–43, 341n58, 341n60, 343n83
slavery, slave trading, and human trafficking: assistance to distressed persons, vessels, and aircraft, 242; definition and concept of human trafficking, 244–45; laws and treaties related to, 4, 241–42, 243–45, 243n94; LOS Convention provisions, 425, 427; migrant smuggling and human trafficking, 245; peremptory norm to prohibit, 21; suppression of activity, 160–61, 161n63, 228; Supreme Court ruling on, 9–10; threat from, 236, 242
soft law, 18–19, 50–51, 225–26
SOLAS (Safety of Life at Sea) Convention, 92, 99, 107, 108, 131, 170, 182, 185, 197, 209, 210, 221
Somalia, 288–89n116, 288–90, 293
sonar use, xvi
Southern Bluefin Tuna case, 365–66, 365n104

sovereign immunity: state responsibility and, 38, 336, 336n8, 446–47; of warships, 93, 93n93, 159, 179–80, 223, 336–37, 347

sovereignty: basis for, 9; boundaries of, 49; claims of and competing claimants, 51; definition and concept of, 2, 42–43, 42n8; international relations and, 5; protection of, 5; territory as element of, 65, 65n5; writings about, 5

Soviet Union, xv, 5, 11, 15

spacecraft and satellites, international law and, 17, 17n87

Spain: international law contributions from, 3; sovereignty claims, 43, 43n10

special operations, 274, 277–78, 277–78n39

stateless vessels, 17

state-owned enterprises (SOEs), 17–18, 17n89

states: consent of and validity of international law, 2; criminal activity, duty to cooperate in suppression of, 228–29; definition and concept of, 2, 11; flag state jurisdiction, 253, 254–56; flag state obligations, 155–59, 159n56, 180–86, 184nn63–65; interest-based theories and, 5–6, 6nn19–20; international law and, 10, 11–12; internationally wrongful acts, responsibility for, 2; protection of citizens, obligation of, 271; responsibilities and liabilities, 337–40, 344–47; rights and obligations of, 11–12, 11–12n52; sovereign immunity and state responsibility, 38, 336, 336n8, 446–47; usage of term, 11n47. *See also* sovereignty

status-of-forces agreements (SOFAs), 82, 91–92, 92n80

Stavridis, James, 1

Story, Joseph, 9–10, 86, 162–63

stowaways, 93, 93n91

straits: definition of, 112–13, 113n80; expansion of territorial sea and, 112, 112n74; innocent passage, 44, 47, 112, 112n78, 114n85, 410; laws and treaties governing use, 87–88; LOS Convention provisions, 408–10; rights and obligations in, 112–17; sea lanes and traffic separation schemes, 409; transit passage right, 112–17, 112n78, 113–14nn81–83, 114nn87–88, 115n91, 408–10; US transit passage, 117

SUA Convention (Convention for the Suppression of Unlawful Acts against the Safety of Maritime Navigation)., 135, 233, 237, 257, 269, 295–96, 300, 328, 365

submarine cables, 128, 148, 171–72, 171n125, 411–12, 413, 428–29, 456

submarines and innocent passage, 22, 47, 112, 405

telegraph procedures and agencies, 4

territorial sea: assistance entry, 106–7, 106n29, 107n33; boundaries and breadth of, 45, 45n20,
46, 49, 55, 64, 101–2, 101n2, 111, 112, 402; boundary delimitation, 64, 77; claims to, 43, 43nn9–12; dangers in, duty of state to warn about, 108, 108–9n48; definition and concept of, 101–2, 101n1; excessive maritime claims, 78; innocent passage, 47, 102–6, 104n19, 105–6nn23–24, 105n27, 109–10, 109–10nn59–61, 404–7, 440; jurisdiction over vessels, 109–10nn59–61, 109–11, 110n65, 111n67; LOS Convention provisions, 401–8; noninnocent passage, 105, 105n23, 108–9; overlap zones, 64, 78; protective rights of state, 108–9, 406; rights and obligations in, 101, 101–11; sea lanes and traffic separation schemes, 108, 405; seabed beneath, 139; straits and expansion of, 112, 112n74; US territorial sea regime, 111, 111n67, 111n69

terrorism: counterterrorism conventions and operations, 271, 287, 294–96, 295n151; Global War on Terror, 5; Security Council resolutions against, 295–96; suppression of activity, 233–35; threat from, 40, 294–96

Thames Formula, 155

tides: low-tide elevation, 62, 65, 67, 70, 71, 73, 76, 403; low-water line, 67, 67nn13–14

timekeeping: Greenwich meridian, adoption as global reference, 4; time zones, 4

trade and trade activities: General Agreement on Tariffs and Trade (GATT), 54, 54n47, 89n58, 90, 365; scope of, 40

traffic separation schemes. *See* sea lanes and traffic separation schemes

Trail Smelter case, 203

transit passage, 408–10

transnational law and legal process, 6–7, 6n26

treaties (conventional international law): applicability of, 60, 61–62; conflicts between rules and treaties, 24–25; customary international law relationship to, 19, 25, 25nn133–134, 60; definition and concept of, 22; dispute settlement provisions, 365–66; formation and termination of, 23–24, 23nn118–119; interpretation of, 24–25, 24n125, 24nn127–128, 61–62, 61–62n88; nonparties status, 22; parties obligations under, 22, 60; self-executing, 23n119, 57–58nn67–69, 57–59, 58n71, 58n73; suspension of, 23–24, 23n123, 301–3, 302n201; unwritten treaties, 22; US negotiation and ratification process, 25–26, 25n137, 26n138; validity of international law and, 2

Treaty on the Non-proliferation of Nuclear Weapons (NPT), 297–98

United Kingdom. *See* Great Britain/United Kingdom

United Nations: charter of, 5, 12, 14, 22, 282, 387–99; establishment of, 4, 14; force use, guidance on, 328–29, 334; General Assembly resolutions, 29–30, 29nn155–156, 234; law of the sea and, 52, 52n42; membership of, 11, 14; organization of, 14, 14n65; peacekeeping operations, 13n61, 285–86, 286n90; role in global relations, 4; Security Council and Security Council resolutions, 14–15, 14n71, 285–87, 286nn90–91, 293, 295–96; Security Council authorization for use of force, 316–18; as subject of international law, 13

United Nations Conference on the Law of the Sea (UNCLOS I, 1958), 44–45, 46–47, 55, 55n49, 125, 164

United Nations Conference on the Law of the Sea (UNCLOS II, 1960), 45–46

United Nations Conference on the Law of the Sea (UNCLOS III, 1973-1982), xv, 47–48, 47n26

United Nations Conference on Trade and Development (UNCTAD), 54

United Nations Convention on the Law of the Sea (LOS Convention, 1982): adoption of, 48; application of, 39, 49–50; conflicts between rules and treaties, 24–25; customary international law relationship to, 57, 59–61; drafting of, xv, 47–48, 47n26, 48nn28–29; implementation of, 50–51, 50–51nn37–39; jurisdictional provisions, 32n175; number of states parties, xvi, 57; parties to, 39, 49; ratification of, 49; text of, 49, 401–62; US as nonparty to, xvi, 39, 55–57, 60–61, 368; zonal approach of provisions, 49, 49n34

United Nations Educational, Scientific, and Cultural Organization (UNESCO), 54

United States (US): coastline and coastal waters of, 41–42; collision-prevention regulations, early, 3–4; EEZ rights, 125; intelligence community, 275; international agreements and treaties, 25–26, 25n137, 26n138; international law role and effect in, 35–37, 35nn186–187, 36n191, 36n198, 36nn195–196, 37–38nn199–202, 38n204; law of the sea conventions and, xvi, 39, 55–59, 60–61; maritime boundary delimitation, 77–78, 77n94, 78n94; national interests, national identity, and values of, 6; nonparty status, LOS Convention, xvi, 39, 55–57, 60–61, 368; UN Security Council role, 14

Universal Declaration of Human Rights (UDHR, 1948), 16, 269

universality principle, 32, 233–35

unmanned aerial vehicles (UAVs), xvi, 199–201, 200n160, 278–79

unmanned marine vehicles (UMVs), xvi, 194–99, 278–79

vessels: belligerent right to visit, 285, 302, 308–9, 309n255, 309n257; boarding noncompliant vessels, 267–68, 284, 329–32; boarding of, 257–61; definition of and ships compared to, 174–76, 174n1, 175nn6–7; foreign vessels, rights of, 4; jurisdiction and control over, 160–68, 161n63, 184–86, 184nn63–65; nationality concept, 17, 156–57, 156n38, 180–84; normal mode of transit, 115–16, 115n93; nuclear-powered ships, 23n123, 47, 89, 94n96, 103, 106, 108, 110, 112, 404–5; place of refuge, establishment of, 87, 87n42; pollution from, 208–15, 439–40, 443; public vessels, 176–80; registration of, 155–58, 156nn30–31, 181–84; salvage operations, 168–69, 168n100; stateless and assimilation to statelessness, 17, 160, 186–94, 191n110, 257; visit, board, search, and seizure (VBSS), 274, 274n20, 284–85, 308–9, 309n255; visit and board, right to, 161–67, 162n69, 163n79, 256–57, 260–63, 261nn228–230, 263n236. See also warships

Vienna Convention on the Law of Treaties, 10

Vienna Convention on the Law of Treaties (VCLT), 21, 21nn106–107, 22, 24, 24nn127–128

visit, board, search, and seizure (VBSS), 274, 274n20, 284–85, 308–9, 309n255

war crimes, 16, 16n81

warfare: legitimacy and, 6; overlaps between peacetime operations and, 301; principles of, 6. See also law of naval warfare

warning shots, 268, 281, 322n85, 325, 327, 330–31, 331n134

warning zones, 280–81

warships: access to ports by, 89, 89nn59–60, 91–92; belligerent right to visit, 285, 302, 308–9, 309n255, 309n257; definition of, 177–78, 177n21; EEZ rights and duties, 127; environmental protection regulations and, 223; innocent passage, 47, 110, 110n61; law enforcement activities, 273–74; normal mode of transit, 115–16; rights and obligations of, 176–77; rules applicable to, 407; Security Council resolution enforcement, 286–87; sovereign immunity of, 94, 93n93, 159, 179–80, 223, 336–37, 347; status in ports, 93–94, 93–94nn93–96

waste: dumping and discharge of, 41, 215–17, 252, 439; restrictions on emissions, xvi; vessels as source of, 208

weapons of mass destruction (WMD): counterproliferation interdiction, 285; counterproliferation operations, 287, 296–300; interdiction of, 298–300; Security Council resolutions against, 287, 296, 297–98; threat from, 297–98, 299n181. See also nuclear weapons

whaling and antiwhaling activities, 18, 222, 226
Wildenhus' case, 97–98
Wilsonian school of international relations, 8–9, 8–9n39
World Court, 44, 352. *See also* International Court of Justice (ICJ)

world government, 12, 12n56
World Trade Organization (WTO) and General Agreement on Tariffs and Trade (GATT), 54, 54n47, 89n58, 90, 365

Yugoslavia, 11, 15, 27nn144–145, 286, 354

About the Author

CRAIG H. ALLEN is the Judson Falknor Professor of Law at the University of Washington, where he teaches maritime and international law. He is a retired Coast Guard officer and cutterman who formerly held the Charles Stockton Chair in International Law at the U.S. Naval War College and served as a Distinguished Visiting Professor of Maritime Studies at the U.S. Coast Guard Academy and a Visiting Professor at Yale Law School. He is the author of *Farwell's Rules of the Nautical Road* (8th. Naval Institute Press, 2005) and *Maritime Counterproliferation Operations and the Rule of Law* (Praeger, 2007) and serves on the Board of Editors for the *Journal of Navigation* and *Ocean Development and International Law*.

The Naval Institute Press is the book-publishing arm of the U.S. Naval Institute, a private, nonprofit, membership society for sea service professionals and others who share an interest in naval and maritime affairs. Established in 1873 at the U.S. Naval Academy in Annapolis, Maryland, where its offices remain today, the Naval Institute has members worldwide.

Members of the Naval Institute support the education programs of the society and receive the influential monthly magazine *Proceedings* or the colorful bimonthly magazine *Naval History* and discounts on fine nautical prints and on ship and aircraft photos. They also have access to the transcripts of the Institute's Oral History Program and get discounted admission to any of the Institute-sponsored seminars offered around the country.

The Naval Institute's book-publishing program, begun in 1898 with basic guides to naval practices, has broadened its scope to include books of more general interest. Now the Naval Institute Press publishes about seventy titles each year, ranging from how-to books on boating and navigation to battle histories, biographies, ship and aircraft guides, and novels. Institute members receive significant discounts on the Press's more than eight hundred books in print.

Full-time students are eligible for special half-price membership rates. Life memberships are also available.

For a free catalog describing Naval Institute Press books currently available, and for further information about joining the U.S. Naval Institute, please write to:

Member Services
U.S. Naval Institute
291 Wood Road
Annapolis, MD 21402-5034
Telephone: (800) 233-8764
Fax: (410) 571-1703
Web address: www.usni.org

avaricious - adj. having or showing extreme greed for wealth or material gain

comity - n. an association of nations for their mutual benefit